Morphological Perspectives

Morphological Perspectives
Papers in Honour of Greville G. Corbett

Edited by Matthew Baerman,
Oliver Bond and Andrew Hippisley

EDINBURGH
University Press

Edinburgh University Press is one of the leading university presses in the UK. We publish academic books and journals in our selected subject areas across the humanities and social sciences, combining cutting-edge scholarship with high editorial and production values to produce academic works of lasting importance. For more information visit our website: edinburghuniversitypress.com

© editorial matter and organisation Matthew Baerman, Oliver Bond and Andrew Hippisley, 2019, 2021
© the chapters their several authors, 2019, 2021

First published in hardback by Edinburgh University Press 2019

Edinburgh University Press Ltd
The Tun – Holyrood Road, 12(2f) Jackson's Entry, Edinburgh EH8 8PJ

Typeset in 11/13pt Times New Roman by
Servis Filmsetting Ltd, Stockport, Cheshire

A CIP record for this book is available from the British Library

ISBN 978 1 4744 4600 6 (hardback)
ISBN 978 1 4744 4601 3 (paperback)
ISBN 978 1 4744 4602 0 (webready PDF)
ISBN 978 1 4744 4603 7 (epub)

The right of Matthew Baerman, Oliver Bond and Andrew Hippisley to be identified as the editors of this work has been asserted in accordance with the Copyright, Designs and Patents Act 1988, and the Copyright and Related Rights Regulations 2003 (SI No. 2498).

Contents

Abbreviations and Glosses	xii
List of Contributors	xviii

1 Taking the Morphological Perspective — 1
Matthew Baerman, Oliver Bond and Andrew Hippisley
   1.1 Introduction — 1
   1.2 A Paradigmatic Perspective — 2
      1.2.1 Mismatches in Paradigms — 2
      1.2.2 Compositional Inconsistency in Paradigms — 4
      1.2.3 Conditions on Paradigms — 5
   1.3 A Defaults Perspective — 5
      1.3.1 Inflection Classes — 6
      1.3.2 Syncretism — 9
      1.3.3 Gender Assignment — 11
      1.3.4 The Morphology–Syntax Interface — 12
   1.4 A Canonical Perspective — 13
      1.4.1 Features — 13
      1.4.2 Agreement — 15
      1.4.3 Canonical Typology — 19
   1.5 Outline of the Book — 21
      1.5.1 Form–Feature Mapping — 21
      1.5.2 Words and Paradigms — 22
      1.5.3 Syntactic Dependencies — 22

Part I Form–Feature Mapping

2 Canonical Compounds   31
   Andrew Spencer
   2.1 Introduction   31
   2.2 The Bisetto–Scalise Typology   33
   2.3 Canonical Criteria for Compounds   35
   2.4 Lexical Integrity   37
   2.5 Recursion in Compounds   41
   2.6 Compound-Like Constructions and Non-canonical Compounds   45
   2.7 Conclusions   58

3 How (Non-)canonical Is Italian Morphology?   65
   Anna M. Thornton
   3.1 Canonical Inflection   65
      3.1.1 Preamble   65
      3.1.2 Corbett's View of Canonical Inflection   66
   3.2 Italian Inflection: Features and Values   69
   3.3 Deviations across the Cells of a Lexeme   70
      3.3.1 Alternations and Suppletion   70
      3.3.2 Syncretism and Uninflectability   71
      3.3.3 Affixal Inconsistency   73
      3.3.4 Periphrasis   76
      3.3.5 Featural Inconsistency   78
   3.4 Deviations across Lexemes   79
      3.4.1 Homonymy   79
      3.4.2 Inflectional Classes, Heteroclisis and Deponency   79
      3.4.3 Affixal Inconsistency and Antiperiphrasis   88
      3.4.4 Featural Inconsistency   89
   3.5 Conclusions   92

4 Waiting for the Word: Distributed Deponency and the Semantic Interpretation of Number in the Nen Verb   100
   Nicholas Evans
   4.1 Introduction   100
   4.2 The Nen Language: Background   102
      4.2.1 Extramorphological Unification of Verbs with Pronouns, TAM Particles and Adverbs   103
      4.2.2 Unification within the Verbal Word   104
      4.2.3 A Bit More on Verbal Word Structure   106
   4.3 Morphemes, Morphomes and In-between   108
      4.3.1 Definition   108
      4.3.2 Prefix Series and TAM   108

		4.3.3 Verbal Arguments: The Basic System (SG vs DU vs PL)	110
	4.4	Elaborations Bringing in a Plural vs Greater Plural Contras	111
		4.4.1 Greater Plurals in Positional Constructions	112
		4.4.2 Greater Plurals with 'come/go'	112
		4.4.3 Greater Plurals with 'be'	113
		4.4.4 Greater Plurals with Middle Verbs	113
		4.4.5 Greater Plurals with Future Imperatives	114
		4.4.6 Greater Plural Objects with Transitive Verbs	115
	4.5	Summary of Nen Strategies for Composing Four-Way Number System	116

5 Feature Duality — 124
Matthew Baerman

5.1	Flavours of Inflection	124
5.2	Number in the Hualapai Verb	125
5.3	The Morphology of Hualapai Verbs	127
5.4	Reconciling Meaning and Form	131
5.5	Semi-autonomous Morphology	135

6 Canonical Syncretism and Chomsky's S — 138
Mark Aronoff

6.1	Introduction	138
	6.1.1 Canonical Non-canonicity	138
	6.1.2 Canonical Syncretism and Morphomes	139
6.2	Chomsky's Morpheme S	140
	6.2.1 S in Syntactic Structures	140
	6.2.2 Affix Hopping and the English Verb	141
	6.2.3 Is S a Morpheme?	143
6.3	Minimalism: Less Is More	144
6.4	Conclusion	145

7 Canonical Tough Cases — 148
Johanna Nichols

7.1	Introduction	148
7.2	Extensions	149
7.3	Other Stem-Forming Morphology	150
7.4	Auto-gender	154
7.5	Auto-person	156
7.6	Auto-valence	157
7.7	Toggles	158
7.8	Registration	158
7.9	Conclusions	162

Part II Words and Paradigms

8 Paradigm Uniformity and the French Gender System — 171
    Olivier Bonami and Gilles Boyé
    8.1 Introduction — 171
    8.2 Empirical Evidence — 173
        8.2.1 Gender in the Stable Lexicon — 174
        8.2.2 Gender in Lexeme Formation — 176
        8.2.3 Interim Conclusion — 183
    8.3 The Shape of French Nominal Paradigms — 184
        8.3.1 Common Gender and Gender Specificity — 184
        8.3.2 Gender-Iconic Pairs and Paradigm Uniformity — 185
        8.3.3 Variable Content Paradigms, Uniform Form Paradigms — 188
    8.4 Conclusion — 189

9 Case Loss in Pronominal Systems: Evidence from Bulgarian — 193
    Alexander Krasovitsky
    9.1 Dialectal Variation in Case Marking on Personal Pronouns in Bulgarian — 193
    9.2 The Data — 194
    9.3 Cross-Dialectal Variation — 195
    9.4 Directions of Change — 197
    9.5 Patterns of Synchronic Variation: Quantitative Data — 199
    9.6 Conclusions — 202

10 Measuring the Complexity of the Stem Alternation Patterns of Spanish Verbs — 205
    Enrique L. Palancar
    10.1 Introduction — 205
    10.2 Basics of Spanish Verbal Inflection: Inflectional Classes — 208
        10.2.1 The Paradigm of Regular Verbs of Class I — 208
        10.2.2 The Paradigm of Regular Verbs of Class II — 209
    10.3 Inflectional Deviations: Stem Classes and Stem Alternation Patterns — 213
        10.3.1 Stem Alternation Pattern 1 — 214
        10.3.2 Stem Alternation Pattern 2 — 214
        10.3.3 Stem Alternation Pattern 3 — 215
        10.3.4 Stem Alternation Pattern 4 — 215
        10.3.5 Stem Alternation Pattern 5 — 217
        10.3.6 A Typology of Deviations Involving Stem Alternation Patterns — 217
    10.4 Calculating the Inflectional Complexity of Spanish Verbs — 220
        10.4.1 Measuring the Deviation of P1 and P2 — 223

	10.4.2 Measuring the Deviation of P3–P5	224
10.5	Reducing the Inflectional Complexity of Spanish Verbs	226
10.6	Concluding Remarks	227

11 Verb Root Ellipsis   233
Bernard Comrie and Raoul Zamponi

11.1	Introduction	233
11.2	Zero Verb Roots and Zero Allomorphs of Verb Roots	234
11.3	Verb Ellipsis	244
11.4	Verb Root Ellipsis	249
	11.4.1 Inuktitut	249
	11.4.2 Kwaza	251
	11.4.3 Akabea and Other Great Andamanese Languages	253
	11.4.4 Jingulu	258
11.5	Verb Root Ellipsis and Phonological Words	262
11.6	Comparisons	267
	11.6.1 Functional and Semantic Parallels	267
	11.6.2 Formal Parallels	270
11.7	Conclusions	272

12 Bound but Still Independent: Quotative and Verificative in Archi   281
Marina Chumakina

12.1	Introduction	281
12.2	Archi Inflectional System at a Glance	281
12.3	Archi Quotative	284
	12.3.1 Archi Quotative: Introduction	284
	12.3.2 Syntactic Properties of the Quotative	289
	12.3.3 Inflectional Properties of the Quotative	290
	12.3.4 Quotative: Conclusion	293
12.4	Archi Verificative	293
	12.4.1 Archi Verificative: Origin	294
	12.4.2 Verificative: Inflectional Possibilities and Syntax	296
	12.4.3 Verificative: Conclusion	297
12.5	Conclusion	297

Part III Syntactic Dependencies

13 To Agree or Not to Agree? A Typology of Sporadic Agreement   303
Sebastian Fedden

13.1	Introduction	303
13.2	The Sample	305
13.3	Predictors of Sporadic Agreement	306
	13.3.1 Phonotactic Predictors	306

		13.3.2	Phonological Predictors	308
		13.3.3	Morphological Predictors	308
		13.3.4	Semantic Predictors	311
		13.3.5	Etymological Predictors	315
	13.4	Borderline Cases		316
		13.4.1	Phonology Obscuring Morphology: Like-Segment Coalescence in Hausa Adjectives	316
		13.4.2	Optional Agreement: Modifiers in Ngan'gityemerri	317
		13.4.3	Different Word Class: Modal Auxiliaries in English	317
		13.4.4	Word Class Continua: Cardinal Numerals in Russian and Italian	318
	13.5	Frequency		319
	13.6	Conclusions		319
14	Where Are Gender Values and How Do I Get to Them? *Oliver Bond*			327
	14.1	Introduction		327
	14.2	Sex-Based Gender in Kulina		331
		14.2.1	Distribution of Sex-Based Gender Values	331
		14.2.2	Nouns with Variable Sex-Based Gender Agreements	334
		14.2.3	Sex-Based Referential Agreement with Pronominal Controllers	336
		14.2.4	Agreement with Possessor Phrases	337
		14.2.5	Constraints on Agreement in Transitive Predicates	340
		14.2.6	Summary of Sex-Based Gender in Kulina	346
	14.3	Class-Based Gender in Kulina		347
		14.3.1	Distribution of Class-Based Gender Values	348
		14.3.2	Targets of Class-Based Gender	349
		14.3.3	Conditions on Class-Based Agreement	350
		14.3.4	Controllers of Class-Based Gender Agreement	353
		14.3.5	Summary of Class-Based Gender in Kulina	359
	14.4	Discussion		359
		14.4.1	Modelling Non-syntactic Agreement	360
		14.4.2	Where Are Gender Values?	362
		14.4.3	How Do I Get to Them?	363
15	Focus as a Morphosyntactic and Morphosemantic Feature *Irina Nikolaeva*			370
	15.1	The Focus Feature		370
	15.2	The Focus Marker		372
	15.3	Multiple Representation of Focus		377
	15.4	Focus Spreading		381
	15.5	The Status of the Focus Feature in Tundra Nenets		385

| 16 | When Agreement and Binding Go Their Separate Ways: Generic Second Person Pronoun in Russian | 390 |

Maria Polinsky

- 16.1 Introduction — 390
- 16.2 Structural Properties of Sentences with Arbitrary 2SG — 392
  - 16.2.1 The Pattern — 392
  - 16.2.2 2SG-ARB vs 3PL — 393
  - 16.2.3 2SG-ARB vs 2SG-ADDR: Distributional Differences — 395
- 16.3 Interpretive Properties of Sentences with Arbitrary 2SG — 404
  - 16.3.1 2SG-ARB Sentences vs 2SG-ADDR Sentences: Differences in Interpretation — 404
  - 16.3.2 Null vs Overt *ty* in 2SG-ARB Sentences: Differences in Interpretation — 407
- 16.4 Putting It All Together — 407
- 16.5 Conclusions — 410

| 17 | *Rara* and Theory Testing in Typology: The Natural Evolution of Non-canonical Agreement | 414 |

Erich Round

- 17.1 Generalisation, Theory and *Rara* — 414
- 17.2 Non-canonical Outcomes of Natural Historical Changes — 417
- 17.3 Tangkic — 419
- 17.4 Clausal Morphosyntax in Tangkic — 422
  - 17.4.1 Overview — 422
  - 17.4.2 Subordinate Clauses with No SCCM — 422
  - 17.4.3 Main Clauses in Lardil and Kayardild — 423
  - 17.4.4 Main Clauses in Yukulta — 424
- 17.5 SCCM and Its Evolution — 427
  - 17.5.1 SCCM in Australian Languages — 427
  - 17.5.2 SCCM in Yukulta — 427
  - 17.5.3 SCCM in a Plausible Ancestral State — 430
  - 17.5.4 SCCM in Kayardild — 433
  - 17.5.5 SCCM in Lardil — 435
  - 17.5.6 Whence Kayardild's Syntax? — 436
- 17.6 Shifts in the Systems of Agreement — 437
- 17.7 Typology with and without Diachrony — 438
- 17.8 The Scientific Response to *Rara*: Examine Diachrony — 440

Language Index — 447
Author Index — 450
Subject Index — 457

Abbreviations and Glosses

>	acting upon (subject upon object)
1	first person
2	second person
2|3	second or third person
3	third person
A	actor, or agent-like argument of a transitive verb
ABL	ablative
ABS	absolutive
ACC	accusative
ACT	active; actuality mood
ADJ	adjunct
ADMON	admonitive
AGAIN	'again' adverbial
ALL	allative
AN	action nominal
ANIM	animate
AOR	aorist
AS	associated person
ASF	adjective suffix
ASPL	associative plural
ASS	associative
ATTR	attributive
AUG	augmentative
AUX	auxiliary
AVRS	aversive
AW	away
AWAY	'away' directional
B.IPFV	basic imperfective

BACK	'back' directional
BEN	benefactive
CAUS	causative
CL	classifier
COLL	collative case
COM	comitative
COMP	complementisation
COND	conditional converb
CONT	contact localisation
COP	copula
CORE	A, S, or O non-focus argument
CTG	contingent
CVB	converb
DAT	dative
DEB	debitive
DEC(L)	declarative
DEF	definite (article)
DEIC	deictic (noun)
DEM	demonstrative
DET	determiner
DIST	distal
DISTPST	distant past
DON	donative case
DOWN	'downwards' directional
DP	determiner phrase
DU	dual
DUB	dubitative
DUR	durative
EMPH	emphatic
EPEN	epenthetic
ERG	ergative
EVID	evidential
EXCL	exclusive
F	feminine
F.IMP	future imperative
F_CL	F-class
FIN	finalis
FM	formative
FOC	focus
FUT	future
G	general gender
GEN	genitive
HAB	habitual

HEST	hesternal (yesterday)
HITHER	'hither' directional
HORT	hortative
HPST	hodiernal past
I	gender I
IFUT	immediate future
II	gender II
III	gender III
IMM	immediate
IMMPST	immediate past
IMP	imperative
IMPF	imperfect
IN	'in' locational
INCH	inchoative
INCL	inclusive
IND	indicative
INDEF	indefinite
INF	infinitive
INFR	inferential
ING	ingressive
INP	involved mode of past tense
INS	instrumental
INT	interrogative
INV	inverse
INvO	object of inverse construction
IO	indirect object
IPFV	imperfective
IRR	irrealis
ITER	iterative
IV	gender IV
K	*ka*-gender
LAT	lative
LBASE	ellipted base
LOC	locative
LOGOPH	logophoric pronoun
LP	linking particle
LROOT	ellipted root
M	masculine
M_CL	M-classifier
MC	main clause
MED	medial verb
MID	middle
MIN	minimal

MIX	mixed (gender)
MON	monitory
MU	multal
MWE	multiword expression
N	neuter
N1	neuter 1
N2	neuter 2
NAR	narrative
ND	non-dual
NEARFUT	near future
NEARPST	near past
NEG	negative
NFOC	narrow focus
NFRST	non-firsthand evidential
nM	non-masculine
NMLS	nominaliser
NOM	nominative
NP	noun phrase
NPREH	non-prehodiernal, any time from during the night last night on into the future
nPST	non-past
NSG	non-singular
NTrMC	non-transitive main clause
NTrS	non-transitive subject
NTrSC	non-transitive subordinate clause
NVC	nominalised verbal clause
O, OBJ	object
OBL	oblique
P	patient-like argument of a transitive verb
PAR	participial
PART	partitive
PASS	passive
PDO	Principle of Derivational Opacity
PF	perfect
PFV	perfective
PIC	Principle of Islandhood for Compounds
PIT	Principle of Inflectional Transparency
PL	plural
PL△	greater plural
PN	proper name
POL	polite
POSS	possessive
POT	potential

PR	pronominal
PREP	prepositional (case)
PRET	preterite
PREV	preverb
PROC	procrastinative
PROG	progressive
PROL	prolative
PROX	proximal, proximate
PRS	present
PST	past
PST.EVID	past evidential
PTCP	participle
PTM	phrase terminal maker
Q	question
QUOT	quotative
R	recipient
REFL	reflexive
REL	relative
REMPST, RPST	remote past
REP	reputative
RR	reflexive/reciprocal
S, SBJ	subject, single argument of an intransitive verb
SBJV	subjunctive
SC	subordinate clause
SCCM	subordinate clause complementisation marking
SEQ	sequential
SF	stem formative
SG	singular
SIM	simultaneous converb
SIMUL	simultaneous
SOL	solidarity
SP	somatic prefix
SPAT	spatial
SS	same subject
STAT	stative
SUP	'super' (on) localisation
SW	switch-reference
T	termination
TAM	tense-aspect-mood
TC	temporal-causal
THV	thematic vowel
TNS	tense

TOC	toward command (deictic prefix indicating motion toward speaker, used on imperatives)
TODPST	today's past
TOP	topic
TOW	towards
TR	transitive
TRMC	transitive main clause
TrO	transitive object
TV	radical-thematic vowel
U	undergoer
UNM	unmarked tense
UNP	uninvolved mode of non-past tense
UP	uninvolved mode of 'before today' past tense, 'upwards' directional
VC	voice
VENT	ventive
VERIF	verificative
VOL	volitive
WATER	'into water' directional
X > Y	subject/agent X acting on object/patient Y, or possessor X of possessum Y
XABL	ablative comparative morphomic category
XDAT	dative comparative morphomic category
XERGLOC	ergative–locative comparative morphomic category
XGEN	genitive comparative morphomic category
XLOC	locative comparative morphomic category
XNOMZ	nominalisation comparative morphomic category
XOBL	oblique comparative morphomic category
XPROP	proprietive/comparative morphomic category
XPST	past comparative morphomic category
Y/N	polarity question

List of Contributors

Aronoff, Mark, Professor, Department of Linguistics, Stonybrook University.

Baerman, Matthew, Principal Research Fellow, Surrey Morphology Group, University of Surrey.

Bonami, Olivier, Professor, Laboratoire de Linguistique Formelle, Université Paris Diderot.

Bond, Oliver, Senior Lecturer, Surrey Morphology Group, University of Surrey.

Boyé, Gilles, Maître de conférences, Département Sciences du Langage, Université Bordeaux Montaigne.

Chumakina, Marina, Research Fellow, Surrey Morphology Group, University of Surrey.

Comrie, Bernard, Professor, Department of Linguistics, University of California at Santa Barbara.

Evans, Nicholas, Professor, Department of Linguistics, Australian National University.

Fedden, Sebastian, Professor, Institut de linguistique et phonétique générales et appliquées, Université Sorbonne Nouvelle, Paris 3.

Hippisley, Andrew, Professor and Dean, Fairmount College of Liberal Arts and Sciences, Wichita State University.

Krasovitsky, Alexander, Faculty Lector in Russian, Faculty of Medieval and Modern Languages, University of Oxford.

Nichols, Johanna, Professor Emerita, Department of Slavic Languages and Literatures, University of California at Berkeley.

Nikolaeva, Irina, Professor, Department of Linguistics, School of Oriental and African Studies, University of London.

Palancar, Enrique L., Researcher, National Centre for Scientific Research (CNRS).

Polinsky, Maria, Professor, Department of Linguistics, University of Maryland at College Park.

Round, Erich, Senior Research Fellow, School of Languages and Cultures, University of Queensland.

Spencer, Andrew, Emeritus Professor, Department of Language and Linguistics, University of Essex.

Thornton, Anna M., Professor, Dipartimento di Scienze Umane, Università degli Studi dell'Aquila.

Zamponi, Raoul, Macerata, Italy.

1

Taking the Morphological Perspective

Matthew Baerman, Oliver Bond and Andrew Hippisley

1.1 Introduction

In a field still dominated by syntactic perspectives, it is sometimes easy to overlook the words that are the building blocks of language. A *morphological* perspective on language takes words as the starting point for investigating linguistic structure: their form, their internal structure, their paradigmatic extensions, and their role in expressing and manipulating syntactic configurations. With a team of authors who run the typological gamut of languages, this book tackles questions in contemporary morphology from multiple perspectives, examining both the canonical and the non-canonical. By taking seriously the autonomy of morphology, and letting loose a full battery of analytical techniques, the chapters in this volume celebrate the pioneering work of Greville G. Corbett, whose illustrious career is marked by an endless search for answers, with stunning insights along the way.

Corbett is one of the world's most influential typologists, responsible for leading the field into new and exciting territory. He has done this by tackling the most difficult and challenging of questions in morphology, a component of language so idiosyncratic and language specific that it might seem scarcely amenable to typological generalisations.

His work on morphosyntactic features has become defining in the field, and no discussion of gender or number would be complete without reference to his ground-breaking work, which has succeeded in making sense of these complex and cross-linguistically varied features. At the level of morphological expression, he has contributed significantly to a defaults-based approach to locate whatever generalisations there may be, and has elaborated a taxonomy of paradigmatic deviations that has provided a framework for understanding how morphological structure can break through the confines of other established linguistic structures. His forays into unexplored typological realms have led to the development of a careful and rigorous framework, Canonical Typology, which has been instrumental in clarifying our understanding of a wide range of linguistic phenomena.

Here we highlight some of the major themes of Corbett's work that have informed his morphological perspective on language, and influenced the ideas and outlook of each and every contributor to this volume: the autonomous principles of morphology revealed by mismatches in form and meaning (§1.2), the role of defaults in accounting for complex morphological phenomena (§1.3) and the insight that can be gained by decomposing linguistic patterns into fine-grained variables (§1.4).

1.2 A Paradigmatic Perspective

A running theme throughout Corbett's work has been the autonomy of morphology, manifested most obviously through morphological mismatches, where elements of form behave in ways which appear to be independent of the meaning they (are supposed to) instantiate. If we take the evidence of these mismatches seriously, they describe the outlines of a purely morphological system of considerable scope and complexity, much more than the mere interface of syntax and phonology that it is sometimes understood to be.

1.2.1 Mismatches in Paradigms

The notion of paradigmatic mismatches can be defined in terms of canonical inflection (see in particular Corbett 2007a, 2015). The idea behind this is that an inflected word form expresses both lexical and grammatical meaning, and that in each case there is a one-to-one mapping between meaning and form. The consequences of this are mapped out in Table 1.1. In practical terms this means that the canonical inflected word will consist of a stem (the lexical material) and an affix or affixes (the grammatical material). Each lexeme will have a single invariant stem which is different from the stems of other lexemes. Affixes will be distinct from each other within the paradigm of a lexeme, but identical across the paradigms of different lexemes.

Word forms that deviate from the canonical situation either fail to make the distinctions in meaning that otherwise seem to underlie the system (the upper right or lower left cells in Table 1.1), or encode distinctions which are irrelevant or at cross-purposes to that system (the upper left or lower right cells). It is important to bear in mind that deviations from canonical inflection should not be regarded as aberrant or uncommon, merely that the conceptual and descriptive tools we avail ourselves of presuppose that things are set up in this way. In fact, most if not all inflectional systems show some kind of deviation from this schema.

The upper right-hand corner of Table 1.1 falls outside of a typology of inflectional mismatches, since homonymy exists entirely at the lexical level. The inflectional equivalent, however – syncretism – has been a key theoretical concern since at least the days of Hjelmslev (1935–7) and Jakobson ([1936] 1971). Syncretism refers to instances where inflected words fail to formally differentiate values which appear otherwise to be relevant in the grammar, either in inflection, or in other morphosyntactic processes. This is often taken as indicative of underlying properties of the

Table 1.1 Deviations in form established by comparison across cells and lexemes (adapted from Corbett 2015)

	Canonical situation		Types of deviation	
	Cells	Lexemes	Cells	Lexemes
1. Lexical material (≈ shape of stem)	Same	Different	Stem alternations Suppletion	Homonymy
2. Inflectional material (≈ shape of affix)	Different	Same	Syncretism Uninflectability	Inflection classes Heteroclisis Deponency

feature system, both in terms of feature structure (e.g. where dual and plural number are expressed by a single 'non-singular' form in some contexts, but not others) and in terms of so-called markedness relationships (the tendency of values of one feature to be neutralised in the context of more marked values of another feature; see Haspelmath 2006 for a critical review of the notion), as in German or Russian, where gender values are not distinguished in the plural (see §1.3.2). As such, this view of syncretism is opposed to one in which the patterns of identity lie outside the feature system, i.e. as the result of regular sound change. Baerman et al. (2005) explore syncretism across a large and heterogeneous set of languages and find clear examples of both types, demonstrating the autonomy of morphology while at the same time acknowledging its dependence, however conditional, on a coherent system of features. And while most would probably reject the idea that a morphological formative that spans not just different values, but different word classes, warrants being seen as the same entity (e.g. the ending -s that marks third person singular present in *she cooks* but plural in *three cooks*), sometimes the temptation is too great, as pointed out by Aronoff (this volume).

The other type of deviation – encoding too many distinctions – represents a more diverse range of phenomena. (After all, there are more ways to be different than there are to be the same.) On the lexical side, it means that stems or roots take up at least part of the task of realising morphosyntactic distinctions, creating rich morphological subsystems of their own (see Palancar, this volume). In one sense this could be understood as just a detail of morphological realisation, amenable to a model in which inflectional material includes not just easily segmental affixes, but also floating features or otherwise abstract exponents that induce stem alternations; in some cases there is evidence of a class of hybrid entities, stem augments, which are part lexical and part affixal (Nichols, this volume). The existence of stem alternations has important ramifications on how we understand inflectional paradigms. Firstly, stem alternations often occur alongside purely affixal inflection, creating a situation of multiple exponence (Baerman and Corbett 2012) or distributed exponence (Carroll 2016; Evans, this volume), with all the attendant challenges to morphological description. Secondly, the morphological manipulation of lexical material may be so extreme as to cross over the line into suppletion, where by all appearances two or more lexemes have been joined into a single paradigm. Corbett (2007a) shows both the internal diversity of the phenomenon, and that many deeply held assumptions about its nature and distribution (in particular, the role of semantic and frequency-based constraints) are not empirically supported.

On the grammatical side, the encoding of too many distinctions is manifested in the proliferation of lexically peculiar inflectional exponence. The clearest instance of this is seen in inflection class distinctions (Corbett 2009), where morphological realisation of inflectional features is different across different (sets of) lexical items – most canonically where this is completely arbitrary, unaffiliated with any other semantic, morphological or phonological properties. In this sense inflection class represents a purely *morphological* feature (Corbett and Baerman 2006) whose role is restricted to the distribution of morphological forms, unrelated to their meaning or function. Deponency, at least in its original guise, involves lexemes whose morphology is perfectly normal but has been derailed from its usual function (Corbett 2007b). For example, the Latin verb *mīrātur* 'admires' looks like a passive verb that ought to mean something like 'is admired', given the prevailing morphological regularities in the system, but instead behaves like an ordinary active transitive.

1.2.2 Compositional Inconsistency in Paradigms

One of the guiding notions behind our conception of how paradigms are composed is that they should be internally consistent. The identification of the morphological components of a word form depends on this assumption, with morphemes, formatives and position classes as a result; morphological zeros are a poignant reminder of thwarted expectations, either morphosyntactic (in the case of zero affixes) or lexical (in the case of zero roots; Comrie and Zamponi, this volume). Compositional inconsistency can take many forms, but perhaps the most extreme example is the use of periphrastic constructions in a paradigm otherwise characterised by synthetic inflected forms (Corbett 2012b). It is precisely the expectation of paradigmatic consistency which encourages the identification of a multiword expression – which might otherwise be understood as syntactically constructed – as an inflected form.

Equally, morphosyntactic features lend themselves to being understood as cross-classifying, leading to the expectation that every form in a paradigm is somehow responsible for declaring where it stands in relation to every single feature expressed anywhere in the paradigm. This leads to a continual tension between analyses which maintain featural consistency and thereby tolerate what might be seen as frivolous syncretism (do all past tense verbs in English syncretise the 3SG value found in the present?), and those which allow different feature systems to operate in different parts of the paradigm (the English past tense simply does not care about the 3SG). While such configurations may lead to a reframing of the system of features, a more catastrophic instance of inconsistency occurs in cases of defectiveness (Baerman and Corbett 2010), where the very expectation that there be a form at all is not met, leaving a gap in the paradigm. That said, the expectation that all lexemes belonging to the same part of speech should have the same paradigm shape is itself open to dispute, as discussed by Bonami and Boyé (this volume).

1.2.3 Conditions on Paradigms

The typology of mismatches sketched above assumes, quite intentionally, a static and mechanical mapping between morphosyntax and morphology, since the aim is a consistent characterisation of the deviations between a baseline model of inflection and the actual paradigms we encounter in languages. But a more nuanced approach to inflectional description will recognise that morphological realisation is mediated by further *conditions* that skew the mapping (Corbett 2006; Baerman et al. 2017). Various properties of the inflecting lexeme – phonological, morphological, semantic – influence the expression of morphosyntactic features, so that an inflectional rule when fully analysed may come to resemble a decision tree more than a simple mapping relationship. Consequently, there is no general consensus as to where exactly such conditions fit in the architecture of inflectional rules: are they an integral component, or just an annotation?

The tension between rules and conditions becomes particularly apparent when both appear to draw upon what are arguably inflectional features. For example, in a pattern repeated across a number of unrelated languages, the realisation of gender and number is conditioned by values of person (Chumakina et al. 2007; Baerman and Corbett 2013). Thus, in Tucano (a Tucanoan language of Columbia), there is no explicit person agreement on the verb, only gender and number agreement (West and Welch 2004). But only third person subjects actually distinguish these features, while first and second person subjects share a single form with the neuter. The end effect is a limited system of person marking as manifested through conditions on gender and number agreement: animate subjects take the semantically appropriate gender and number form if third person, but the neuter form if first and second person. Bond (this volume), explores further dimensions of this question in Kulina, a language of Peru, which has the further wrinkle that there are only two genders, masculine and feminine, with feminine serving as the default.

1.3 A Defaults Perspective

Compared with syntax and phonology, the world of morphology can be a daunting one. In this realm of ambiguity, irregularity and exception, often the result of historical change, it can be challenging to locate the system that both holds this world together and interfaces with syntax, phonology and semantics. Round (this volume) offers an extreme example of how historical developments in Kayardild have led to a typologically unusual personal agreement system, an instance of a linguistic 'rarum'. Forcing morphological phenomena into the highly systematic realm of syntax, the approach taken by Distributed Morphology, for example, often turns out to be overly optimistic or overly artificial; most languages resist, though some do not. For instance, Chumakina (this volume) presents two exponents in Archi with highly syntactic behaviour, i.e. they appear to have their own argument structure, like lexemes. One avenue into this partially systematic world is to take a *defaults* perspective on morphology. This is an avenue that has been well travelled by Corbett and others, and has led to insights on generalisations about inflection classes, the nature of morphological irregularity, the role of syncretism in morphological organisation, gender assignment, and morphology's interface with syntax. Corbett's journey began when he met Gerald Gazdar in 1988 who demonstrated a defaults-based lexical knowledge representation language. Together with Norman Fraser, Corbett put this language to use on Russian nominal morphology, yielding a 'new perspective' on familiar data (Corbett and Fraser 1993: 113). These are the foundations on which the theory of Network Morphology was built.[1]

1.3.1 Inflection Classes

Inflection classes (see §1.2.1) are a means of regulating inflectional allomorphy. Some Latin noun inflection classes are given in Table 1.2, where the dative singular inflectional endings are highlighted.

Such a strategy has the disadvantage of concealing sameness in order to emphasise distinction. Thus, while most of the classes shown here have distinct exponents of the dative singular (*-ae* (*aquae* 'water'), *-ō* (*servō* 'slave'), *-i* (*iūdic-i* 'judge') and *-ī* (*reī* 'thing')), for two classes the dative singular is in fact the same: both classes 3 and 4 use *-i*: *iūdici* and *frūctui*. At least for this particular set of features there is no distinction between classes 3 and 4. On closer inspection a class 3/4 distinction disappears for other feature sets. Both use the same exponent for genitive plural (*-um*), dative plural (*-ibus*), and ablative plural (*-ibus*). Other instances of inter-class sharing also take place; for example, classes 1 and 2 have the same dative plural forms: *-īs*. To

Table 1.2 Nominal inflection classes in Latin

	1	2	3	4	5
	aqua 'water'	servus 'slave'	iūdecs 'judge'	frūctus 'fruit'	rēs 'thing'
			SINGULAR		
NOMINATIVE	aqua	servus	iūdecs	frūctus	rēs
GENITIVE	aquae	servī	iūdicis	frūctūs	reī
DATIVE	aqu**ae**	serv**ō**	iūdic**i**	frūct**ui**	re**ī**
ACCUSATIVE	aquam	servum	iūdicem	frūctum	rem
ABLATIVE	aquā	servō	iūdice	frūctū	rē
			PLURAL		
NOMINATIVE	aquae	servī	iūdicēs	frūctūs	rēs
GENITIVE	aquārum	servōrum	iūdicum	frūctuum	rērum
DATIVE	aquīs	servīs	iūdicibus	frūctibus	rēbus
ACCUSATIVE	aquās	servōs	iūdicēs	frūctūs	rēs
ABLATIVE	aquīs	servīs	iūdicibus	frūctibus	rēbus

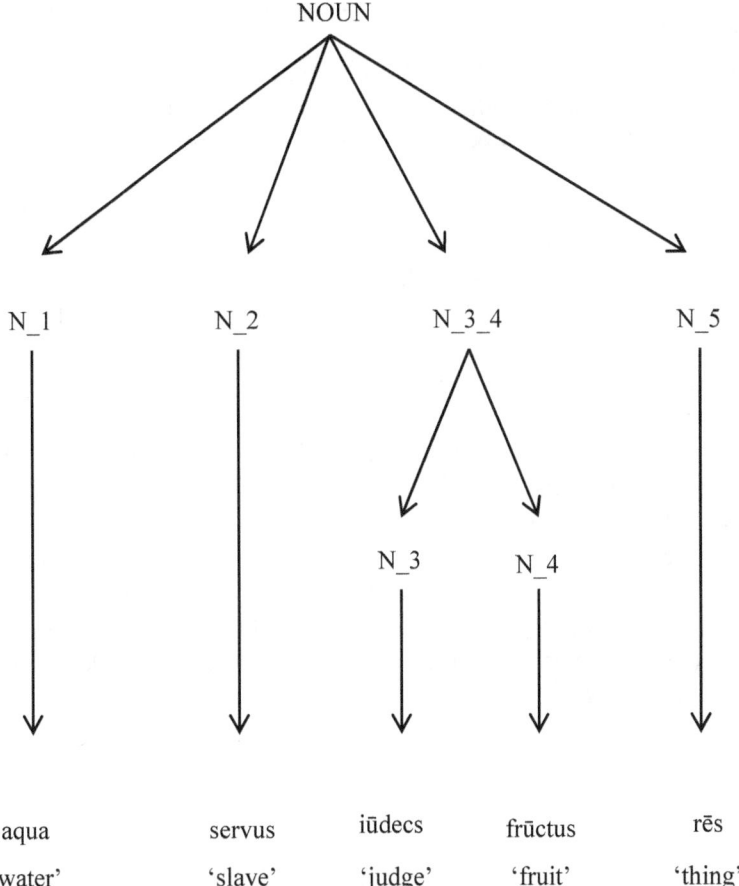

Figure 1.1 Latin inflection classes as a hierarchy

capture sharing and distinction, the information registered in inflection classes can be reorganised into a network of nodes that are linked by inheritance. The Latin data in Table 1.2 can be represented by the inheritance hierarchy in Figure 1.1.

The five classes in Figure 1.1 are viewed as nodes that inherit from a single source NOUN. While there are distinctions between the classes, all share properties that can be stated as inheritable facts placed at the root node: the part of speech in question is noun, specifically they are count nouns, and their primitive semantics is 'thing' in the sense of Jackendoff (1975), for example. The sharing of exponents by classes 3 and 4 is captured by holding this information at the abstraction node N_3_4 that provides a source of inheritance for classes 3 and 4. A node abstracting common information from the neuter (class IV) and masculine (class I) nodes in Russian was used in the Russian noun class analysis in Corbett and Fraser (1993). Distinction and sameness was nicely summarised as: 'Looking down from the top, Russian has three noun declensional classes ... looking up from the bottom it has four ...' (Corbett and Fraser 1993: 129). Such a network analysis 'dissolves' the notion of inflection class (1993: 127).

Another exponent that is shared by different classes is *-(i)bus* for the dative plural: classes 3, 4 and 5. Rather than creating an abstraction node just for this exponent and just for these classes, we might want to think more in terms of probability: there is a three in five chance that the inflection class uses *-(i)bus* for its dative plural, or it is *generally* the case that a Latin noun inflectional class has *-(i)bus* for its dative plural. By interpreting inheritance between nodes as inheritance by default, such a generalisation can be expressed by situating this fact at the root node NOUN. Classes 3, 4 and 5 inherit it; classes 1 and 2 override it with their class-specific alternative. Using default inheritance, Corbett and Fraser captured the fact that generally the nominative plural for a Russian noun is in *-i*, among other generalisations.

Inheritance by default also recasts irregularity as semi-regularity. The Latin for 'coin' *nummus* behaves like a typical class 2 noun except that its genitive plural is *nummum* instead of the expected *nummōrum*. Rather than thinking of the noun as irregular, Network Morphology treats it as *semi-regular* by situating it in the inheritance path of the class 1 node, and simply overriding the realisation of the genitive plural. A regular lexical entry is given in (1), which can be compared with the irregular (2). A network organisation of nodes connected via default inheritance minimises the differences.

(1) Servus
     class ← N_2
     stem = *serv*
     gloss = slave
(2) Nummus
     class ← N_2
     stem = *numm*
     gloss = coin
     {CASE: GEN, NUMBER: PLURAL} = /stem + *um*/

As shown in Corbett and Fraser for Russian and subsequent work for other languages, a defaults inheritance approach to irregularity correlates number of overrides with *degree* of regularity, thus getting at the nature of the item's irregularity.

In fact, (2) misses a generalisation because it introduces redundancy into the system. A defaults-based network aims to reduce or even eliminate redundancy altogether. The alternative *-um* exponent that *nummus* chooses to use is not exclusive to *nummus*: it appears elsewhere in the network, namely as a fact situated at N_3_4. Through default orthogonal multiple inheritance, a node can plug into the network through multiple nodes. The more redundant-free representation of *nummus* is given in (3) reducing further its irregularity by viewing it as a case of mild heteroclisis.

(3) Nummus
　　　class ← N_2 [primary source of inheritance]
　　　stem = *numm*
　　　gloss = coin
　　　{CASE: GEN, NUMBER: PLURAL} ← N_3_4 [secondary source of inheritance]

1.3.2 Syncretism

While inflection classes regulate choices of exponents, Latin, as with many languages, is characterised by a lack of any choice in some instances. In class 2, the dative singular and the ablative singular share the same exponent -$\bar{o}$. It is as if there is no exponent for the dative; instead it has to 'borrow' from the ablative (or, of course, the other way around). A defaults-based network representation of inflectional classes captures exponent sharing in the spirit of reducing redundancy, and in this way offers an account of syncretism (see §1.2.1). Instead of stating the exponent twice, an intra-node referral is made in the node representing N_2.

(4) 　N_2
　　　class ← NOUN
　　　{CASE: DAT, NUMBER: SING} ← {CASE: ABL, NUMBER: SING}
　　　CASE: ABL, NUMBER: SING} = /stem + o/

DATR, the lexical knowledge representation language that Corbett and Fraser adopted, expresses the situation in (4) as in (5).[2]

(5) 　N_2:
　　　◇ == NOUN
　　　<sg dat> == "<sg abl>"
　　　<sg abl> == "<stem>" o
　　　. . .

The ellipsis indicates that there are a lot more facts that are registered at N_2, i.e. all the other case and number combinations.

Being able to point to different parts of the network for already available information allows for a natural account of directional syncretism, where the pointing expresses a rule of referral (Zwicky 1985; Stump 1993; 2001: 212–41). Of course, there should be some observable motivation for positing a particular directionality. Arguing for the dative pointing to the ablative, rather than the other way around, could be based on the fact that in the singular the dative shares an exponent with the genitive (class 1), the ablative (class 2) and the genitive (class 5), whereas the ablative has its own exponent for all classes except for class 2. A stronger argument for the link between dative and ablative can be made by looking at the situation in the plural. In all classes the dative and ablative exponents are shared. While the actual exponents themselves differ to some extent across the classes, the relationship is common to all. Generalised syncretisms are naturally captured as facts stated at a higher node, in this instance the highest node NOUN, as in (6).

Table 1.3 Paradigm of the Slovene noun *človek* 'person' (Priestly 1993: 401)

	SINGULAR	DUAL	PLURAL
NOMINATIVE	človek	človeka	ljudje
ACCUSATIVE	človeka	človeka	ljudi
GENITIVE	človeka	ljudi	ljudi
DATIVE	človeku	človekoma	ljudem
INSTRUMENTAL	človekom	človekoma	ljudmi
LOCATIVE	človeku	ljudeh	ljudeh

(6) NOUN:
    <pl dat> == "<pl abl>"
    ...

The target of the syncretism is represented in quotes, meaning 'whatever exponent you find for the plural ablative, use that'. The systematic nature of the animate genitive–accusative syncretism in Russian has been captured in this way, from Corbett and Fraser (1993) onwards.

A now famous case for the necessity of a rule of referral in some circumstances was made by Corbett based on data from Slovene (i.e. Corbett and Fraser 1997; Baerman et al. 2005: 176). In nouns, the genitive and locative dual are always identical to the genitive and locative plural, from which one might conclude that it would be impossible to isolate any directionality. However, the paradigm of the noun 'person', illustrated in Table 1.3, provides evidence in the form of suppletion: for most of the paradigm, singular and dual share a stem (*človek-*) opposed to a plural stem (*ljud-*). But in the genitive and locative, this otherwise plural stem is also found in the dual, suggesting that it can only be described by a rule referring the dual genitive to the plural genitive, and the dual locative to the plural locative. Moreover, this directionality is in fact generalisable for Slovene demonstrative pronouns and adjectives (Priestly 1993: 410, 411).

A rule of referral is not always the optimal analysis of a syncretism. A better analysis can be feature neutralisation. For instance, Lower Sorbian adjectives such as *dobry* 'good' clearly distinguish three genders in the singular, yet masculine, feminine and neuter adjectives in the nominative case share the same exponent in the plural, as shown in Table 1.4. It is less intuitive to use rules of referral to account for this, than to simply think of the gender feature being neutralised in plural contexts. As the syncretism occurs in all cases, not just the nominative, neutralisation is the favoured analysis.[3]

Neutralisation of gender distinctions is formally captured in DATR, by ordering the attributes in a path that denotes the feature values of a word form (see §1.2.2, allowing a different feature system to operate in a different part of the paradigm). Neutralisation of gender in the plural is captured by the ordered attribute paths in (7), where number precedes case, and both precede gender.

Table 1.4 Paradigm of the Lower Sorbian adjective *dobry* 'good' (Starosta 1999: 35)

	SINGULAR			DUAL	PLURAL
	MASCULINE	FEMININE	NEUTER		
NOMINATIVE	dobry	dobra	dobre	dobrej	dobre
ACCUSATIVE	dobry	dobru	dobre	dobrej	dobre
GENITIVE	dobrego	dobreje	dobrego	dobreju	dobrych
DATIVE	dobremu	dobrej	dobremu	dobryma	dobrym
INSTRUMENTAL	dobrym	dobreju	dobrym	dobryma	dobrymi
LOCATIVE	dobrem	dobrej	dobrem	dobryma	dobrych

(7) <pl nom> == "<stem>" e
<pl gen> == "<stem>" ych
etc.

An attribute path representing a morphosyntactic feature set implies any extension of itself by one or more attributes. For example, <pl nom> implies <pl nom fem>. This implication captures observed cases of feature underspecification. In fact, this implication holds by default. It means we can also take a neutralisation approach where there is syncretism between the masculine and neuter case forms in the singular in Table 1.4. This is first captured by the generalisation in (8).

(8) <sg gen> == "<stem>" ego
<sg dat> == "<stem>" emu
etc.

Where there is no syncretism, the implied value is overridden by a more specific path, of the type in (9).

(9) <sg gen fem> == "<stem>" eje
<sg dat fem> == "<stem>" ej
etc.

Neutralisation syncretism formally modelled as 'longest path wins', i.e. Pāṇini style default inference, originates in Corbett and Fraser's (1993) account of Russian, with additional detail in Baerman et al. (2005: ch. 5), and in other subsequent work.[4] Contexts for such neutralisation have been thoroughly investigated from a crosslinguistic perspective and are reported in Baerman et al. (2002), and discussed in Brown et al. (2009) and Brown and Hippisley (2012: 165–6).

1.3.3 Gender Assignment

The inflection class nodes in Figure 1.1 inherit shareable information, hold class-specific information and serve as a source of inheritance for lexical entries. Nouns in Latin have gender: masculine, feminine and neuter. Each of the classes in Figure 1.1 is strongly associated with a gender, for example class 1 with feminine nouns and class 2 with masculine. To capture class-based gender, we could add the fact <gender> == masc to N_1. A similar situation holds for Russian, and in the DATR analysis in Corbett and Fraser (1993) gender assignment is captured as inheritance of the feature from the inflection class nodes. Thus, default inheritance is used to express Corbett's longstanding claim that in Russian (as in many languages) inflection classes assign gender (Corbett 1982, 1988; 1991: 36–43). The often-advanced alternative, gender as the determiner of inflection class, leads to a much less economical analysis. Since there are more inflection classes than gender, every noun that could not be categorised according to the biological sex of its referent would have to be lexically specified for both gender and inflection class. In Corbett's analysis you just need to specify inflection class. However, the Latin noun *agricola* 'farmer' is a little odd as it declines like a regular class 1 noun but controls masculine rather than feminine agreement. Some nouns in Russian are exceptional in the same way. Corbett has claimed that languages can have a predominantly formal system of gender assignment but all gender systems have a semantic core albeit with complex interactions. For example, in Bininj Gun-wok, a language of the Gunwinyguan family spoken in central Arnhem Land in Australia's Northern Territory, assignment is essentially animacy-based with highly complex interactions with other features and conditions (Evans et al. 2002). Semantic assignment, i.e. male means masculine, always take precedence (see Bond, this volume, on gender assignment for Kulina nouns). In Corbett (1991: 36–7) this is captured by rule ordering and diagrammed as a flow chart. In Corbett and Fraser (1993) the same claim is captured declaratively, using defaults: by default, the gender value inherited from the class is the one used in syntax; this is overridden by a semantic value assigned due to biological sex.

This of course underscores the importance of defaults for capturing the general situation while allowing for exceptions, and the advantage of a declarative over a procedural approach. It also results in two types of gender feature evaluation: class-based formal gender, and one based on semantics. They normally coincide; or by default they coincide. But in cases like *agricola*, they can be at odds. In Corbett and Fraser (1993) and all subsequent Network Morphology analyses, a formal distinction is made between the machinery of morphology and syntax by labelling each path that states a morphological fact with the attribute mor. So the accusative singular for class 1 is expressed as <mor sg acc> == "<stem>" am. For *agricola* the gender inheritable from class 1 is therefore <mor gender> == fem; but the gender used for syntax is <syn gender> == masc. The default that the two attribute paths have the same value is neatly expressed as <syn gender> == <mor gender>. Because it is a default, for sex-differentiable nouns like *agricola*, the evaluation of <syn gender> can be made elsewhere, i.e. based on semantic sex. These ideas are further developed in Fraser and Corbett (1995, 1997) and Corbett and Fraser (2000).

1.3.4 The Morphology–Syntax Interface

The gender values inherited from the morphological hierarchy and the gender values that syntax cares about (expressed in DATR as <mor gender> vs <syn gender>), are equivalent by default, yet their autonomous status in the formal architecture captures the important insight that this is not always the case. Morphology is a semi-autonomous system that can be at work on purely organisational problems that have little or nothing to do with syntax (the notion of purely morphological features introduced in §1.2.1). Morphology often serves syntax, but not always in a direct way.

By way of example, consider the non-syntactic roles of gender values in Russian, which guide the choice of derivational operations in Russian evaluative morphology (Hippisley 1996), and derivational operations in possessive adjective formation (Corbett 1987; Hippisley 1996). It can be classified as a 'pure' morphological feature (Corbett and Baerman 2006; Corbett 2012a). Stem indexes, theme vowels and stress indexes in Russian (Brown et al. 1996) are other examples of features that seem to have little purpose beyond morphology, and all are represented as extensions of the path <mor>. Separating the morphological world from the syntactic world provides for the possibility of other disconnects besides gender based on semantics and gender based on inflection class. For example, deponency in Latin, where verb forms that resemble passives in morphological terms have a syntactically active interpretation (see §1.2.1), constitutes a classic mismatch between the two worlds. Such a mismatch is captured naturally by <mor> paths, as exemplified by (10), based on Hippisley (2010) and Brown and Hippisley (2012: ch. 5).

(10) DEPONENT:
 ◇ == VERB
 <mor active> == "<mor passive>"

A defaults approach thus provides for the notion of autonomous morphology and the various mismatches that result from juxtaposing it with syntax to be formalised in a simple and intuitively satisfying way.

1.4 A Canonical Perspective

One of the key areas where Corbett's work has had considerable impact is the way in which linguists look beyond the surface, and beyond the most frequently attested patterns, to consider not only what we are familiar with, but also what could be.

1.4.1 Features

If words are the basic building blocks of syntax, then feature values are the atoms of morphology. Features provide the means to explain properties shared across lexical items and capture paradigmatic relations between word forms as well as syntactic relationships between constituents.

In much of Corbett's work features have taken centre stage. Two of his monographs discuss specific features in extensive detail, namely *Gender* (Corbett 1991) and *Number* (Corbett 2000). A third, *Features* (Corbett 2012a), provides a broad perspective on what a well-developed theory of features must contend with. In these works, and many others, the diversity of linguistic systems and the principles giving rise to the morphological expression of feature values are systematically dissected, allowing many important insights that can only be revealed in this way (Corbett 1981, 1999, 2010a; see also papers in Kibort and Corbett 2010).

While various analyses of feature structures have been proposed, the most widely accepted variety function as an attribute with two or more mutually exclusive values, which may or may not exhibit internal structure (Corbett 2012a). The values of a given feature differ across languages. In languages with case, values can range from just two, to close to twenty, with the exact number dependent on how they are counted (Comrie and Polinsky 1998; Iggesen 2005, 2013). The emergence or loss of values of a feature may have profound effects on how the morphological system operates, as argued by Krasovitsky (this volume) with respect to the loss of case values in Bulgarian dialects.

In gender systems, a similar amount of variation is observed in the number of possible feature values attested (Corbett 2005, 2013a), but determining the number of values a feature has is not always straightforward, especially since values may be non-autonomous, or indirectly observable (Chumakina et al. 2007; Corbett 2008; Baerman and Corbett 2013). In languages which appear to have more than one gender feature, the principles for determining the number of values in a system are even more complex (Fedden and Corbett 2017).

Features can also be typologised on the basis of the modules of grammar in which they are operational. Morphosyntactic features are those that are relevant for both morphology (in the formation of word forms) and syntax (through operations such as government and agreement). This apparently finite set of features comprises person, number, gender and case, and less commonly definiteness and respect (Corbett 2006). The most canonical features are morphosyntactic, since these have the widest possible distribution across word forms and have the greatest potential for orthogonality (Corbett 2013b), but other types of feature are found as well.

Meaningful features that typically do not participate in morphosyntactic processes, such as tense and aspect, are morphosemantic. They are relevant to morphology and to semantics, but not syntax. Others are strictly morphological, such as inflection class (§1.2.1, §1.3.4).

Some features, such as number, can be either morphosyntactic or morphosemantic, depending on their distribution in a language. This gives rise to a wide range of possible morphological number systems (Corbett 2000; and see both Baerman and Evans, this volume, for some particularly challenging data). Features that are usually morphosemantic do occasionally come to participate in syntax. Such is the case with nominal tense. Nikolaeva (this volume) examines evidence that suggests that focus belongs to the set of features that are typically morphosemantic, yet occasionally morphosyntactic.

Another important property of features concerns the internal structure of their values. For instance, values can be hierarchically arranged to make sense of the contrasts most regularly observed in number systems (see Corbett 2000). Hierarchical relationships between values can also be observed when they are undergoing a neutralisation process. This is illustrated here with discussion of data from Jingulu, a non-Pama-Nyungun language described by Pensalfini (2003) and discussed in Corbett (2012a: 22–5). Jingulu has four genders (masculine, feminine, vegetable and neuter), demonstrable through agreement. However, in some circumstances, the genders are 'superclassed' such that masculine and feminine controllers pattern together to take masculine agreements, while vegetable and neuter controllers pattern together to take neuter agreements. For instance, a noun in the vegetable gender can take a demonstrative that agrees with its vegetable value (11a), or its superclass value, i.e. neuter (11b). This is a facultative feature, in that an alternation is available.

(11)   Jingulu (Corbett 2012a: 23)
    a. ngimaniki   barndumi   b. ngininiki   barndumi
       this.VEG   lower.back(VEG)   this.N   lower.back(VEG)
       'this lower back'   'this lower back'

Additional evidence demonstrates that masculine is the ultimate default for agreement, such that both vegetable and neuter nouns can also take masculine agreements, while feminine nouns can only take feminine or masculine.[5] This structure is represented in Figure 1.2.

The view that not all feature values have equal status pervades Corbett's oeuvre. The possibility of an asymmetry is central to accounts of defaults (§1.2), non-autonomous feature values, and the ways in which mismatches are resolved through agreement.

1.4.2 Agreement

Agreement is typically thought of as a syntactic relation, operational within a well-defined set of domains. Corbett's (1983, 2003a, 2003b, 2006) work on agreement sets out the core concepts central to describing agreement relations (controller, target, domain), the features that participate in agreement (the 'phi' features, case, plus

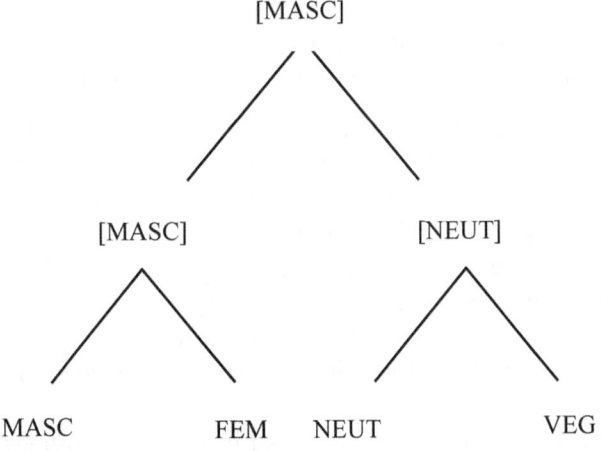

Figure 1.2 Gender superclassing in Jingulu (Corbett 2012a: 24)

some more marginal morphosyntactic features) and conditions on agreement. His perspective on the issue provides a working method for examining agreement relations on empirical grounds, in order to better understand deviations from what is formalised in theoretical models of syntax. These themes are carried forward in many of the contributions to this volume. For instance, Fedden (this volume) surveys the properties of aberrant targets – those that do not agree, while others of the same class do. Bond (this volume), examines the role of features in a system of agreement that permits controllers that do not function as arguments of the clause. Polinsky (this volume) examines the Russian generic pronoun *ty* as a target for syntactic agreement mismatch with controller due to the semantic considerations of binding.

One area where Corbett's work on agreement has been most influential is in highlighting the distinction between syntactic and semantic agreement. Consider the British English examples in (12) based on Corbett (1979), especially the key data point in (12c). In these examples a contrast is observed between syntactic agreement in number between the subject and the predicate, as in (12a,b), and semantic agreement between a formally singular but semantically 'plural' controller, as in (12c). The opposite pattern is not grammatical, as shown in (12d).

(12) a. The committee has decided.
 b. The committees have decided.
 c. The committee have decided.
 d. *The committees has decided.

While predicates can behave in this way, within the nominal domain of British English, semantic agreement is not permitted, as shown in (13).

(13) a. This committee
 b. *These committee

Observation of this kind led to the formulation of a hierarchy with predictive power, known as the Agreement Hierarchy, shown in (14).

(14) The Agreement Hierarchy (Corbett 1979)
 attributive > predicate > relative pronoun > personal pronoun

The Agreement Hierarchy connects together a series of related implicational statements about the agreement domains in which semantic agreement is permitted. It claims that if semantic agreement is possible with a given (type of) target ranked on the hierarchy, it will also be possible with the targets to the right.

The leftmost agreement targets on the hierarchy – those in the 'attributive position' – are the most syntactically conservative. They are more resistant to permitting semantic agreement than targets in other domains. Personal pronouns, at the right edge, are the most susceptible to interference from the semantic properties of their antecedent.

The reach of the Agreement Hierarchy can be also seen with syntactically complex controllers such as French *ton phénomène de fille* 'your amazing daughter' (lit. 'your phenomenon of a daughter'). Here there is a misalignment between the syntactic and semantic heads. The first noun (masculine *phénomène* 'phenomenon') is the syntactic head of the nominal. The semantic head, the element governing the selectional restrictions, is the second component (feminine *fille* 'daughter'). The fact that the second component in structures of this kind has some (semantic) head properties gives rise to agreement mismatches, as shown by the French examples in (15) and (16).

(15) French (Hulk and Tellier 1999: 183)
[**Ton** phénomène de fille] est
your.M.SG phenomenon(M) of daughter(F).SG COP.3SG
bien distrait-e.
quite absent-minded-F.SG
'That amazing daughter of yours is quite absent-minded.'

In (15), the syntactic head of the subject is inanimate and masculine, yet the entire phrase makes reference to a person, and the semantic head is *fille* 'daughter'. This mismatch has an impact on the syntax. The attributive modifier *ton* 'your', which is masculine singular, agrees with the syntactic head; agreeing with the semantic head is not acceptable (cf. *ta (F)). The predicate on the other hand agrees with the gender value of *fille* 'daughter'; agreement with the syntactic head is unacceptable (cf. *distrait (M)). The Agreement Hierarchy in (14) predicts that since semantic agreement is observed with predicate targets, it should also be possible with relative pronouns and personal pronouns. Agreement is understood in its broadest sense here, i.e. that it ranges from NP-internal agreement to antecedent–anaphor relations (Corbett 2006: 21–3).

(16) French (Corbett 2016)
Ton phénomène de fille, avec **laquelle**
your.M.SG phenomenon(M) of daughter(F) with REL.F.SG
je viens de parl-er ... **Elle** ...
1SG come.1SG of speak-INF ... 3SG.F ...
'That amazing daughter of yours, with whom I have just been speaking ...
She ...'

In (16), the relative pronoun agrees with the semantic head, as does the personal pronoun (the masculine forms *lequel and *il are not acceptable). Thus, we find a pattern of syntactic agreement in attributive position, and semantic agreement elsewhere, a pattern fully in accord with the Agreement Hierarchy.[6]

The hierarchy monotonically predicts that if any language exhibits semantic agreement between an attributive modifier and its head, then semantic agreement will also be observed on predicates. It provides an empirically justified set of constraints on the domains in which morphosyntactic and 'semantic' features are operational.

Another area where semantic agreement is operational is in gender resolution. Resolution rules come into play when the gender specification of a syntactically complex controller needs to be computed. For instance, in Slovene, when the subject of a predicate comprises two conjoined noun phrases with heads belonging to different genders, as in (17), the gender clash is resolved by resorting to masculine agreement on the predicate. Number, on the other hand, is computed, such that when two singular noun phrases are coordinated, agreement is dual, not singular.

(17) Slovene (Corbett 2006: 238)
Oče   in   mati   sta   me   obiska-l-a
father(M)[SG] and mother(F)[SG] AUX.3DU 1SG.ACC visit-PST-M.DU
'(My) father and mother visited me.'

If agreement with the gender and number of the subject were purely syntactic, we would expect agreement with the closest conjunct of the coordinated subject.

When there is no gender clash, resolution is as we might expect; if both co-ordinands have masculine gender, the predicate is masculine. Similarly, when both co-ordinands are feminine, the predicate bears feminine agreement. However, when the two conjoined noun phrases are both neuter, a somewhat unexpected situation arises. Conjoined neuter noun phrases control masculine agreement, as in (18). Number, on the other hand, is computed, resulting in plural agreement.

(18) Slovene (Priestly 1993: 433, discussed in Corbett 2006: 242)
Dv-e   telet-i   in   en-o   žrebe   so   bi-l-i   zunaj
two-N calf(N)-DU and one-N.SG foal.N[SG] AUX.3PL be-PST-M.PL outside
'Two calves and a foal were outside.'

So why does Slovene behave in this way? Building on his earlier work (Corbett 1991, 2003c), and that of Weschler and Zlatić (2003), Corbett (2006) argues that in languages like Slovene, where assignment to a particular gender may be semantic or formal in nature (cf. languages where gender assignment is purely semantic), formal resolution rules can be 'piggy-backed' on semantic resolution rules. For Slovene, he proposes the resolution rules in (19) (Corbett 2006: 261).

(19) a. If all conjuncts refer to female humans, agreement is feminine.
     b. If all conjuncts refer to humans, whether all male or mixed sexes, agreement is masculine.

In his proposal, the formal resolution rules in (19) that apply to non-humans, including the neuter animates, result from the appropriation of semantic rules into the formal domain. One appealing aspect of this account is that it provides a coherent approach to all types of gender resolution, because even those systems which appear to be highly constrained by formal features have semantics at the core of their resolution rules. Since gender resolution is partly motivated by semantics, even in a system like Slovene, gender resolution adheres to the Agreement Hierarchy in (14); the larger the agreement domain, the more likely that gender resolution rules apply.

1.4.3 Canonical Typology

Corbett's typological approach to dissecting the complexities of morphological systems ultimately led to the birth of a new approach to defining linguistic phenomena: Canonical Typology (Corbett 2003a, 2003b, 2005, 2006, 2007a, 2009, among others). The primary objective of this enterprise is to be able to calibrate the differences between the 'clearest, best' instances of a linguistic phenomenon, together with those that share some, but not all the properties of the 'indisputable' cases.

In Canonical Typology fine-grained parameters of typological variation are distinguished as independent variables with two or more ordered values. One of these values is considered 'canonical' while the others are non-canonical. For instance, consider the criterion in (20), from Corbett's (2006: 19–23) discussion of the canonical domains for agreement, in which a local domain for agreement is considered canonical.

(20) local domain > non-local domain

This criterion captures the observation that the smaller the structural distance between the controller and the target, the more likely that syntactic agreement, rather than semantic agreement, will be operational. Together, a series of criteria provide a framework for comparing attested instances of a phenomenon against a hypothetical and idealised benchmark. This is known as the canon.

Canonical Typology was first developed as a means to systematically analyse morphosyntactic and morphological phenomena, such as agreement and inflection (Corbett 2003a, 2003b, 2005, 2006, 2009, 2015), as well as derivation (Corbett 2010b) and compounding (Spencer, this volume), but has been widely applied within and beyond these initial domains (see papers in Brown et al. 2013 and Fedden et al. 2018, as well as references in Bond 2018).

Within the framework, canonical inflection is determined by a series of properties that identify canonical paradigmatic relationships (see §1.2.1). Here, we will consider just three criteria identified at various points by Corbett (2005, 2007a, 2007b, 2009). Based on criteria discussed in these works, the following set of clines can be distilled (see Bond 2018 for detailed discussion). The canonical property for each criterion is on the left, whereas the non-canonical property is on the right.

(21) A canonical inflectional paradigm is:
      Criterion 1: Exhaustive > Non-exhaustive
      Criterion 2: Complete > Incomplete
      Criterion 3: Unambiguous > Ambiguous

In an exhaustive paradigm, every logically compatible combination of values of the morphosyntactic features relevant for a given item defines a cell in its paradigm. For instance, consider a paradigm in which the relevant features are number (singular, plural) and gender (masculine, feminine, neuter). If these feature values are maximally orthogonal, this results in a 2 x 3 matrix with a maximal set of six cells as in the logically exhaustive paradigm in Table 1.5. In a non-exhaustive paradigm, certain logically possible distinctions are not made, and lexical splits are observed (Corbett 2015). This is the case in the non-exhaustive paradigm in Table 1.6.

Table 1.5 Exhaustive paradigm

	SG	PL
M	1	4
F	2	5
N	3	6

Table 1.6 Non-exhaustive paradigm

	SG	PL
M	1	
F	2	4
N	3	

The exhaustivity of a lexeme's paradigm can be determined only by comparing paradigms of different lexical items with the same syntactic distribution.

The properties of the paradigm with respect to completeness are interpretable with respect to the number of cells defined (i.e. with respect to the exhaustivity of a paradigm). Assuming that for some lexical items it is possible to define six cells, a paradigm which has a form associated with each of its cells is complete, as in Table 1.7. An incomplete paradigm is defective, as in Table 1.8.

Table 1.7 Complete paradigm

x1	SG	PL
M	✓	✓
F	✓	✓
N	✓	✓

Table 1.8 Incomplete paradigm

	SG	PL
M	✓	✓
F	✓	
N	✓	✓

In an unambiguous paradigm, each cell contains a distinct form, as in Table 1.9. A paradigm without a distinct form in each of its cells is ambiguous because some cells share a form, resulting in syncretism or a morphomic pattern, as in Table 1.10.

Table 1.9 Unambiguous paradigm

	SG	PL
M	A	D
F	B	E
N	C	F

Table 1.10 Ambiguous paradigm

	SG	PL
M	A	D
F	B	A
N	C	B

Not only do these parameters allow us to explicitly calibrate the ways in which the paradigms of individual lexemes deviate from the canon, they provide an opportunity to explore the ways in which parameters cluster together. Thornton (this volume) provides a nice case study of how these considerations play out in the inflectional morphology of a single language, Italian.

The multivariate nature of the canonical approach to cross-linguistic research is echoed in works of many other scholars (Haspelmath 2007; Hyman 2009; Bickel 2010, 2011). As in Canonical Typology, they advocate making observations on a large number of empirically motivated variables to gauge the similarities and differences between linguistic structures (within or across languages).[7]

1.5 Outline of the Book

For much of linguistic theory the role of the word is simply that of a repository of lexical semantics and a vehicle for syntactic operations. In a *canonical* linguistic system that would be all we would need to say about morphology. In practice though, it does not work this way: morphology has a structure and logic of its own, often enough running counter to what would seem to be the requirements of an optimal system. This book places morphology at the centre of its research agenda, both as an independent component of language and as a starting point for explorations into all aspects of language. The book sets out three main morphological perspectives: the mapping of form to feature, the organisation of word forms into paradigms, and marking syntactic dependencies. Each of these perspectives pinpoints various serious challenges that morphology throws down for linguistic description.

1.5.1 Form–Feature Mapping

Corbett (2009) defines canonical inflection in terms of the tension between inflectional and lexical material within word forms: inflectional material is different across the cells of a paradigm, but the same across lexemes, while lexical material is the same across the cells of a paradigm but different across lexemes. Canonical inflection is thus a one-to-one mapping between morphosyntactic feature values and morphological formatives which is consistent across the lexicon. Of course, this idealised configuration is rarely, if ever, found in natural language, and it is the deviations which are the stuff of morphological theory: without them, morphology would just be a notational variant of syntax. The resulting mismatches between linguistic features and their morphological expression is the topic of this part. **Spencer** takes one of the clearest cases – the juxtaposition of multiple independent words into a compound word with a single meaning – and subjects it to an analysis in terms of Canonical Typology, tracing the different threads of what turns out to be a complex and diverse phenomenon. **Thornton** follows the same approach within the domain of the inflectional morphology of Italian, classifying different varieties of non-canonical inflectional phenomena and locating them within the larger context of inflectional typology. The Papuan language described by **Evans** displays what he calls *distributed deponency*, where morphological formatives already in use in the system are repurposed in novel combinations to express additional functions. **Baerman** attempts to reconcile the parallel but disjointed semantic and morphological paradigms in a Yuman language, whose morphological formatives approach meaning without being fully deterministic. **Aronoff** offers a cautionary tale about the seductive appeal of elegant but deceptive abstractions in the interpretation of morphological patterns. Finally, **Nichols** pushes the limits of a canonical approach to inflection through a series of phenomena that seem to fall in-between the cracks, defying characterisation along any known parameters.

1.5.2 Words and Paradigms

Inflectional morphology furnishes the set of word forms that belong to a lexeme's paradigm. This process entails a number of system-level 'constants', and each one of these is shown to be wobbly in the chapters in Part II. First the set of cells that partition the feature space that morphology fills is expected to be constant across lexemes. If the partition is due to a distinction in gender features for some lexemes, then a gender-based shape should characterise the paradigms of all lexemes. **Bonami and Boyé**'s study of French common gender nouns is presented as evidence that paradigm uniformity is not a given. Non-uniformity of paradigms is perhaps more expected across dialects as a result of variation in the historical trajectories of paradigmatic reorganisation. As an example of this **Krasovitsky** presents the loss of case features in Bulgarian, with the various dialects showing its greater or lesser preservation in personal pronoun paradigms where person and number features appear to exert different degrees of influence on the outcome. Looking within the paradigm itself, there are certain expectations about the structure of the word forms that fill the cells. The stem stays constant; what is added to it varies. This notion is turned on its head in **Palancar**'s account of morphomic stems in Spanish verbs where such multi-stem behaviour is shown to heavily impact the complexity of the morphological system. Our expectations of possible systems are further challenged by **Comrie and Zamponi**. They discuss the case of verb root ellipsis in Inuktitut, Kwaza and Great Andamanese whereby the verb root is elided if retrievable by the discourse, but the exponents of morphological features remain. This context-based behaviour is contrasted with zero roots, a lexically specified phenomenon. While verb root ellipsis shows that boundedness of affixes cannot always be assumed, **Chumakina**'s examination of quotative and verficative markers in Archi shows that morphological exponents can have a syntactic independence, namely they can contain argument structure requirements that are normally associated with lexemes.

1.5.3 Syntactic Dependencies

The role of morphology in marking dependencies in syntax is far from straightforward. This problem underlies the development of the notion of canonical agreement (Corbett 2006), an archetype from which possible properties and behaviour of controllers, targets, domains, features and conditions involved in an agreement relation can be calibrated. The most interesting – and ultimately informative – examples of agreement are non-canonical in nature. They reveal something about the limits of language and how systems come to be, while providing compelling evidence for the ways in which morphology and syntax interface. In **Fedden**'s survey of 'sporadic agreement', he proposes a typology of defective agreement targets – those items within a class of words that are expected to agree, but don't – demonstrating that they belong to inflection classes that are shaped, but not defined, by a range of non-arbitrary factors. **Bond** discusses the role of non-syntactic conditions on agreement in Kulina, a language with two orthogonal gender systems. He argues that gender features and their values must be accessible to syntax not only via lexical entries or the content paradigm of word forms, but through their information structure descriptions too. **Nikolaeva** considers the nature of features involved in morphosyntactic processes in Tundra Nenets, proposing that a language may simultaneously exhibit a (run of the mill) morphosemantic focus feature, as well as a morphosyntactic one that participates in a syntactic operation that exhibits some properties of grammatical agreement. **Polinsky** provides evidence from Russian to support the view that the features relevant for binding may be either synchronised with or dissociated from the sets of values operational in agreement domains. **Round** argues that in typology, *rara* provide valuable test-cases for theoretical hypotheses, using the diachronic development of a non-canonical agreement pattern in the Australian language Kayardild to demonstrate that theory-building needs a historical perspective to succeed.

Acknowledgement

We are grateful to Tim Feist for helpful comments on a draft of this paper, and to Penny Everson, Lisa Mack and Gihyun Gal for help in the production of the volume.

Notes

1. For a monograph treatment of Network Morphology, see Brown and Hippisley (2012).
2. For a detailed description of DATR, see Evans and Gazdar (1996); Corbett and Fraser (1993).
3. The form of the masculine singular and dual forms is conditioned, such that modifiers of animate accusative masculine non-plural nouns use the genitive rather than the accusative form. Starosta (1999) also gives *dobrych* as an alternative animate accusative plural, although Stone (1993: 630) states that animacy is not relevant in the plural except in highly restricted contexts.
4. For a discussion of Pāṇini style inference in the history of linguistic analysis, see Gisborne and Hippisley (2017).
5. Corbett (2012a: 24) argues that superclassing is different from syncretism since a speaker always has a choice available that is not restricted by syntactic domain.
6. Hulk and Tellier (1999) discuss data from French, Italian and Spanish, and the French and Spanish constructions are analysed further in Casillas Martínez (2003).
7. See Forker (2014) for an explicit comparison of multivariate typology and Canonical Typology.

References

Baerman, Matthew, Dunstan Brown and Greville G. Corbett (2002), *Surrey Syncretisms Database*, Guildford: University of Surrey, doi: 10.15126/SMG.10/1.

Baerman, Matthew, Dunstan Brown and Greville G. Corbett (2005), *The Syntax–Morphology Interface: A Study of Syncretism*, Cambridge: Cambridge University Press.
Baerman, Matthew, Dunstan Brown and Greville G. Corbett (2017), *Morphological Complexity*, Cambridge: Cambridge University Press.
Baerman, Matthew and Greville G. Corbett (2010), 'Defectiveness: typology and diachrony', in Matthew Baerman, Dunstan Brown and Greville G. Corbett (eds), *Defective Paradigms: Missing Forms and What They Tell Us*, Oxford: Oxford University Press, pp. 1–18.
Baerman, Matthew and Greville G. Corbett (2012), 'Stem alternations and multiple exponence', *Word Structure*, 5 (1), pp. 52–68.
Baerman, Matthew and Greville G. Corbett (2013), 'Person by other means', in Dik Bakker and Martin Haspelmath (eds), *Languages across Boundaries: Studies in Memory of Anna Siewierska*, Berlin: De Gruyter Mouton, pp. 13–26.
Bickel, Balthasar (2010), 'Capturing particulars and universals in clause linkages: A multivariate analysis', in Isabelle Bril (ed.), *Clause-Hierarchy and Clause-Linking: The Syntax and Pragmatics Interface*, Amsterdam: John Benjamins, pp. 51–102.
Bickel, Balthasar (2011), 'Multivariate typology and field linguistics: A case study on detransitivization in Kiranti (Sino-Tibetan)', in Peter K. Austin, Oliver Bond, David Nathan and Lutz Marten (eds), *Proceedings of Conference on Language Documentation and Linguistic Theory 3*, London: SOAS, pp. 3–13.
Bond, Oliver (2018), 'Canonical Typology', in Jenny Audring and Francesca Masini (eds), *The Oxford Handbook of Morphological Theory*, Oxford: Oxford University Press.
Brown, Dunstan, Marina Chumakina and Greville G. Corbett (eds) (2013), *Canonical Morphology and Syntax*, Oxford: Oxford University Press.
Brown, Dunstan, Greville G. Corbett, Norman Fraser, Andrew Hippisley and Alan Timberlake (1996), 'Russian noun stress and Network Morphology', *Linguistics*, 34, pp. 53–107.
Brown, Dunstan and Andrew Hippisley (2012), *Network Morphology: A Defaults-Based Theory of Word Structure*, Cambridge: Cambridge University Press.
Brown, Dunstan, Carol Tiberius, Marian Chumakina, Greville G. Corbett and Alexander Krasovitsky (2009), 'Databases designed for investigating specific phenomena', in Martin Everaert, Simon Musgrave and Alexis Dimitriadis (eds), *The Use of Databases in Cross-Linguistics Studies*, Berlin and New York: Mouton de Gruyter, pp. 117–54.
Carroll, Matthew J. (2016), *The Ngkolmpu Language with Special Reference to Distributed Exponence*, PhD dissertation, Australian National University.
Casillas Martínez, Luis D. (2003), 'Gender mismatches in Spanish and French N1/A de N2 affective constructions: Index agreement vs morphosyntactic concord', in Jong Bok Kim and Stephen Weschler (eds), *Proceeding of the 9th International Conference on Head-Driven Phrase Structure Grammar*, Stanford, CA: CSLI Publications, pp. 1–17.
Chumakina, Marina, Anna Kibort and Greville G. Corbett (2007), 'Determining a language's feature inventory: Person in Archi', in Peter K. Austin and Andrew Simpson (eds), *Endangered Languages*, special issue of *Linguistische Berichte*, 14, Hamburg: Helmut Buske, pp. 143–72.
Comrie, Bernard and Maria Polinsky (1998), 'The Great Dagestanian Case Hoax', in Anna Siewierska and Jae Jung Song (eds), *Case, Typology and Grammar: In Honor of Barry J. Blake*, Amsterdam: John Benjamins, pp. 95–114.
Corbett, Greville G. (1979), 'The Agreement Hierarchy', *Journal of Linguistics*, 15 (2), pp. 203–24.
Corbett, Greville G. (1981), 'Syntactic features', *Journal of Linguistics*, 17 (1), pp. 55–76.
Corbett, Greville G. (1982), 'Gender in Russian: An account of gender specification and its relationship to declension', *Russian Linguistics*, 6, pp. 197–232.

Corbett, Greville G. (1983), *Hierarchies, Targets and Controllers: Agreement Patterns in Slavic*, London: Croom Helm.
Corbett, Greville G. (1987), 'The morphology/syntax interface: Evidence from possessive adjectives in Slavonic', *Language*, 63, pp. 299–345.
Corbett, Greville G. (1988), 'Gender in Slavonic from the standpoint of a general typology of gender systems', *Slavonic and East European Review*, 66, pp. 1–20.
Corbett, Greville G. (1991), *Gender*, Cambridge: Cambridge University Press.
Corbett, Greville G. (1999), 'The place of agreement features in a specification of possible agreement systems', *Folia Linguistica*, 33 (1–2), pp. 211–24.
Corbett, Greville G. (2000), *Number*, Cambridge: Cambridge University Press.
Corbett, Greville G. (2003a), 'Agreement: Canonical instances and the extent of the phenomenon', in Geert Booij, Janet DeCesaris, Angela Ralli and Sergio Scalise (eds), *Topics in Morphology: Selected Papers from the Third Mediterranean Morphology Meeting (Barcelona, September 20–22, 2001)*, Barcelona: Universitat Pompeu Fabra, pp. 109–28.
Corbett, Greville G. (2003b), 'Agreement: The range of the phenomenon and the principles of the Surrey Database of Agreement', in Dunstan Brown, Greville G. Corbett and Carole Tiberius (eds), *Agreement: A Typological Perspective*, special issue of *Transactions of the Philological Society*, 101 (2), pp. 155–202.
Corbett, Greville G. (2003c), 'Types of typology, illustrated from gender systems', in Frans Plank (ed.), *Noun Phrase Structure in the Languages of Europe*, Empirical Approaches to Language Typology EUROTYP 20-7, Berlin: Mouton de Gruyter, pp. 155–202.
Corbett, Greville G. (2005), 'The canonical approach in typology', in Zygmunt Frajzyngier, Adam Hodges and David S. Rood (eds), *Linguistic Diversity and Language Theories*, Studies in Language Companion Series, 72, Amsterdam: John Benjamins, pp. 25–49.
Corbett, Greville G. (2006), *Agreement*, Cambridge: Cambridge University Press.
Corbett Greville G. (2007a), 'Canonical typology, suppletion and possible words', *Language*, 83 (1), pp. 8–42.
Corbett Greville G. (2007b), 'Deponency, syncretism and what lies between', in Matthew Baerman, Greville G. Corbett, Dunstan Brown and Andrew Hippisley (eds), *Deponency and Morphological Mismatches*, Proceedings of the British Academy, 145, London: British Academy and Oxford University Press, pp. 21–43.
Corbett, Greville G. (2008), 'Determining morphosyntactic feature values: The case of case', in Greville G. Corbett and Michael Noonan (eds), *Case and Grammatical Relations: Papers in Honour of Bernard Comrie*, Oxford: Oxford University Press, pp. 1–34.
Corbett, Greville G. (2009), 'Canonical inflectional classes', in Fabio Montermini, Gilles Boyé and Jesse Tseng (eds), *Selected Proceedings of the 6th Décembrettes: Morphology in Bordeaux*, Somerville, MA: Cascadilla Proceedings Project, pp. 1–11.
Corbett, Greville G. (2010a), 'Features: Essential notions', in Anna Kibort and Greville G. Corbett (eds), *Features: Perspective on a Key Notion in Linguistics*, Oxford: Oxford University Press, pp. 17–36.
Corbett, Greville G. (2010b), 'Canonical derivational morphology', *Word Structure*, 3, pp. 141–55.
Corbett, Greville G. (2012a), *Features*, Cambridge: Cambridge University Press.
Corbett Greville G. (2012b), 'Periphrasis and possible lexemes', in Marina Chumakina and Greville G. Corbett (eds), *Periphrasis: The Role of Syntax and Morphology in Paradigms*, Proceedings of the British Academy, 180, Oxford: Oxford University Press and British Academy, pp. 169–89.
Corbett, Greville G. (2013a), 'Number of genders', in Matthew S. Dryer and Martin Haspelmath (eds), *The World Atlas of Language Structures Online*, Leipzig: Max Planck

Institute for Evolutionary Anthropology, <http://wals.info/chapter/30> (last accessed 4 May 2018).

Corbett, Greville G. (2013b), 'Canonical morphosyntactic features', in Dunstan Brown, Marina Chumakina and Greville G. Corbett (eds), *Canonical Morphology and Syntax*, Oxford: Oxford University Press, pp. 48–65.

Corbett, Greville G. (2015), 'Morphosyntactic complexity: A typology of lexical splits', *Language*, 91 (1), pp. 145–93.

Corbett, Greville G. (2016), 'Heads – a canonical approach', presented at the Workshop on Prominent Internal Possessors, SOAS, University of London, 23 September 2016.

Corbett, Greville G. and Matthew Baerman (2006), 'Prolegomena to a typology of morphological features', *Morphology*, 16, pp. 231–46.

Corbett, Greville G. and Norman M. Fraser (1993), 'Network Morphology: A DATR account of Russian nominal inflection', *Journal of Linguistics*, 29, pp. 113–42.

Corbett, Greville G. and Norman M. Fraser (1997), 'Vyčislitel'naja lingvistika i tipologija [Computational linguistics meets typology]', *Vestnik Moskovskogo Universiteta. Serija 9. Filologija*, pp. 122–40.

Corbett, Greville G. and Norman Fraser (2000), 'Default genders', in Barbara Unterbeck, Matti Rissanen, Terttu Nevalainen and Mirja Saari (eds), *Gender in Grammar and Cognition*, Berlin: Mouton de Gruyter, pp. 55–97. [Reprinted 2002 in the Mouton Jubilee Collection *Mouton Classics: From Syntax to Cognition: From Phonology to Text*, vol. 1, pp. 297–339.]

Evans, Nicholas, Dunstan Brown and Greville G. Corbett (2002), 'The semantics of gender in Mayali: Partially parallel systems and formal implementation', *Language*, 78 (1), pp. 111–55.

Evans, Roger and Gerald Gazdar (1996), 'DATR: A language for lexical knowledge representation', *Computational Linguistics*, 22 (2), pp. 167–216.

Fedden, Sebastian, Jenny Audring and Greville G. Corbett (eds) (2018) *Non-canonical Gender Systems*, Oxford: Oxford University Press.

Fedden, Sebastian and Greville G. Corbett (2017), 'Gender and calssifiers in concurrent systems: Refining the typology of nominal classification', *Glossa: A Journal of General Linguistics*, 2(1), 34, pp. 1–47.

Forker, Diana (2014), 'A canonical approach to the argument/adjunct distinction', *Linguistic Discovery*, 12 (2), pp. 27–40.

Fraser, Norman and Greville G. Corbett (1995), 'Gender, animacy and declensional class assignment: A unified account for Russian', in Geert Booij and Jaap van Marle (eds), *Yearbook of Morphology 1994*, Dordrecht: Kluwer, pp. 123–50.

Fraser, Norman and Greville G. Corbett (1997), 'Defaults in Arapesh', *Lingua*, 103, pp. 25–57.

Gisborne, Nikolas and Andrew Hippisley (2017), 'Defaults in linguistics', in Nikolas Gisborne and Andrew Hippisley (eds), *Defaults in Morphological Theory*, Oxford: Oxford University Press, pp. 1–17.

Haspelmath, Martin (2006), 'Against markedness (and what to replace it with)', *Journal of Linguistics*, 42 (1), pp. 25–70.

Haspelmath, Martin (2007), 'Pre-established categories don't exist: Consequences for language description and typology', *Linguistic Typology*, 11 (1), pp. 119–32.

Hippisley, Andrew (1996), 'Russian expressive derivation: A Network Morphology account', *Slavonic and East European Review*, 74 (2), pp. 201–22.

Hippisley, Andrew (2010), 'Paradigmatic realignment and morphological change: Diachronic deponency in Network Morphology', in Franz Rainer, Wolfgang U. Dressler, Dieter Kastovsky and Hans Christian Luschützky (eds), *Variation and Change in Morphology*, Amsterdam: John Benjamins, pp. 107–27.

Hjelmslev, Louis (1935–7), *La catégorie des cas: étude de grammaire générale*, Acta Jutlandica, 7 (1), Aarhus: Universitetsforlaget.

Hulk, Aafke and Christine Tellier (1999), 'Conflictual agreement in Romance nominals', in Jean-Marc Authier, Barbara E. Bullock and Lisa A. Reed (eds), *Formal Perspectives on Romance Linguistics*, Amsterdam: John Benjamins, pp. 179–95.

Hyman, Larry M. (2009), 'How (not) to do phonological typology: The case of pitch-accent', in Michael J. Kenstowicz (ed.), *Data and Theory: Papers in Phonology in Celebration of Charles W. Kisseberth*, special issue of *Language Sciences*, 31 (2–3), pp. 213–38.

Iggesen, Oliver A. (2013), 'Number of cases', in Matthew S. Dryer and Martin Haspelmath (eds), *The World Atlas of Language Structures Online*, Leipzig: Max Planck Institute for Evolutionary Anthropology, <http://wals.info/chapter/49> (last accessed 4 May 2018).

Jackendoff, Ray (1975), 'Morphological and semantic regularities in the lexicon', *Language*, 51 (3), pp. 639–71.

Jakobson, Roman O. [1936] (1971), 'Beitrag zur allgemeinen Kasuslehre: Gesamtbedeutung der russischen Kasus', reprinted in *Selected Writings*, vol. II: *Word and Language*, The Hague: Mouton, pp. 23–71. [Originally published in *Travaux du Cercle Linguistique de Prague*, VI, pp. 240–99.]

Kibort, Anna and Greville G. Corbett (2010), *Features: Perspective on a Key Notion in Linguistics*, Oxford: Oxford University Press.

Pensalfini, Robert J. (2003), *A Grammar of Jingulu: An Aboriginal Language of the Northern Territory*, Pacific Linguistics, 536, Canberra: Pacific Linguistics.

Priestly, T. M. S. (1993), 'Slovene', in Bernard Comrie and Greville G. Corbett (eds), *The Slavonic Languages*, London and New York: Routledge, pp. 388–454.

Starosta, Manfred (1999), *Dolnoserbsko-nimski słownik* [Lower Sorbian–German dictionary], Bautzen: Domowina.

Stone, Gerald (1993), 'Sorbian', in Bernard Comrie and Greville G. Corbett (eds), *The Slavonic Languages*, London and New York: Routledge, pp. 593–685.

Stump, Gregory T. (1993), 'On rules of referral', *Language*, 69 (3), pp. 449–79.

Stump, Gregory T. (2001), *Inflectional Morphology: A Theory of Paradigm Structure*, Cambridge: Cambridge University Press.

Wechsler, Stephen and Larisa Zlatić (2003), *The Many Faces of Agreement*, Stanford, CA: CSLI Publications.

West, Birdie and Betty Welch (2004), *Gramática pedagógica del tucano*, Bogotá: Fundación para el Desarrollo de los Pueblos Marginados.

Zwicky, Arnold (1985), 'How to describe inflection', in M. Niepokuj, M. van Clay, V. Nikiforidou and D. Feder (eds), *Proceedings of the Eleventh Annual Meeting of the Berkeley Linguistics Society*, Berkeley, CA: Berkeley Linguistics Society, pp. 372–86.

PART I
FORM–FEATURE MAPPING

2

Canonical Compounds

Andrew Spencer

2.1 Introduction

A compound is a paradoxical type of expression. On the one hand it is built out of (at least) two distinct lexemes, and is therefore a multiword expression (MWE). Canonically, therefore, a compound should be a syntactic phrase. However, a compound is also a single word with respect to syntactic structure. It is thus both two words and one word simultaneously, an impossible word. In this paper I propose to resolve this paradox by arguing that a canonical compound is an expression type that is at once a non-canonical word and a non-canonical MWE or phrase. By casting the typological question in a canonical mode I hope to avoid two pitfalls which commonly threaten typological research. The first is the seduction of what is frequent, familiar or, in some sense, prototypical. We do not have to select a prototypical compound (for a single language or universally) and try to measure actual compounds against this prototype (Brown and Chumakina 2013; Corbett 2006, 2007). The second pitfall is the urge to define sets of necessary and sufficient conditions for compoundhood. Compounds, like much else in the linguistic universe, are the result of a descriptive categorisation, but they are (probably) not natural kinds in the way that some linguistic phenomena may be natural kinds. It is quite possible, for instance, that notions such as 'syllable', 'quantifier', 'agent', 'property', 'event' or even 'word' correspond to sets of mental, cognitive states which exist independently of our descriptions of them, but it is probably a mistake to think that there are compounds 'out there' and that it is our task to describe them.[1]

The Canonical Typology approach is particularly well suited to the exploration of descriptive categories such as 'compound'. By adopting a set of more-or-less uncontroversial criteria based purely on a logical/conceptual analysis of the descriptive space we can arrive at an 'ideal' characterisation from which real-world examples will diverge in various ways. In some cases, the divergent exemplars will actually be closer in some respects to the canon for some other category, making it possible to conduct comparative typology against the background of well-defined and agreed criteria.

Bond (2013, 2018; see also Brown and Chumakina 2013) distinguishes two strategies in the conduct of Canonical Typology. In the first, 'exploratory' Canonical Typology, the researcher takes a phenomenon which recurs in (the grammars of) the languages of the world and establishes a set of criteria which will define a canonical instance of that phenomenon. This typology is defined against a base, i.e. a set of exemplars of the phenomenon in languages of various types. Bond's work on negation is a good example of this strategy (Bond 2013), since it explores what is presumably a universal linguistic category, in a sense, a linguistic natural kind. Corbett's (2006) essay on agreement is another clear example of the exploratory type. Bond's characterisation is useful outside the confines of Canonical Typology – classical typology typically takes an established dataset (say, a set of word order patterns, or a set of causative constructions) and seeks to uncover cross-linguistic generalisations emerging from that dataset. I shall refer to this general strategy as the dataset strategy, or dataset-based typology.

The other type of approach to Canonical Typology is what Bond calls 'retrospective'. The typical study of this kind will take some reasonably well-established (though perhaps controversial) category of a kind which seems to fall between two descriptive stools, so to speak, being intermediate between two, usually less controversial, categories. Examples of this strategy include Spencer and Luís's (2013) study of the canonical clitic, which proposes that canonical clitics are at once non-canonical function words and non-canonical affixes, and Brown et al.'s (2012) study of periphrasis, which treats canonical (inflectional) periphrastic constructions as phrases (canonically syntactic MWEs) which fill cells in a lexeme's morphological paradigm (canonically occupied by single inflected word forms). For typological research of this kind it is not actually necessary to have a definitive database of clitics or periphrases; indeed, such a search would often be counter-productive and just lead to conceptual confusion and discord amongst researchers. Nor is it even necessary that the researcher be committed to the existence of such things. Rather, the research aims to identify the kinds of properties that we would wish to associate with any construction that we could felicitously label 'clitic', 'periphrase' or whatever.

I take as my starting point the assumption that compounds fall into such a troublesome intermediate category. While it is easy to identify a body of phenomena cross-linguistically which are conventionally described as compounds, there are numerous instances in both the descriptive and the theoretical literature where the attribution of compoundhood to a construction is at best controversial and at worst completely misleading. Much of the problem arises because of the difficulty of characterising the intermediate cases, a problem which is far less acute with negation, agreement, or even suppletion (Corbett 2007).

I begin with a brief summary of a typology of compounding proposed by Bisetto and Scalise (2005) and Scalise and Bisetto (2009). Although their analyses are interesting and valuable, it is difficult to incorporate most of them into a Canonical

Typology analysis. The reason is that Bisetto and Scalise are effectively trying to establish a 'base' for compounding; indeed, construction of a database of compounds is an important aspect of their project. However, this begs the important question of what counts as a compound. For instance, the typology of Bisetto and Scalise distinguishes endocentric from exocentric compounding, but it is far from clear that these form a natural constructional class.[2] Likewise, the datasets they rely on do not seem able to make a clear distinction between examples of productive, semantically compositional compounding and unproductive, non-compositional lexicalised compounds. This is important because lexicalisation is one of the prototypical properties of compounding, but it is not a canonical property, and arguably a typology of compounding should abstract away from frozen or lexicalised types.

In §2.3, I propose (with little comment) a set of canonical criteria for compounds and also for words and phrases. One of the compound criteria is that of 'being a word', which leads me in §2.4 to propose a descriptive refinement to the notion of lexical integrity, splitting the concept into lexical integrity proper and lexical opacity, which guarantees that syntax cannot have access to the internal parts of words for modification, agreement, government, and other syntactic dependencies that are not expressed as surface discontinuities or 'displacements'.

In §2.5 I turn to an important 'phrase-based' property of compounds, recursion. I argue that a weak notion of recursion, the capacity of a compound to contain another compound, is a logical consequence of the proposed criteria.

Finally, in §2.6 I survey, selectively, a collection of phenomena that bear a family resemblance to compounding but which can, and should, be distinguished using the proposed canonical criteria.

I conclude with a summary of the argument and comments about possible further research in the general domain. I suggest that the set of criteria developed in a Canonical Typology account can be deployed as sets of fine-grained categories, which could form the basis for a multifactor analysis of descriptive categories such as 'compound', and which could then inform empirical studies and database development.

2.2 The Bisetto–Scalise Typology

In this section I briefly consider those aspects of the model proposed by Bisetto and Scalise (2005), and especially the revised model of Scalise and Bisetto (2009), which are most relevant to the canonical approach adopted here (see also Guevara and Scalise 2009). I shall refer to this model as the Morbo model (after the name of the project which gave rise to it).[3]

As is customary in the literature the Morbo model distinguishes headed (endocentric) from non-headed (exocentric) compounds. As is also customary, it limits discussion of compounding to constructions defined over the three main open lexical categories of noun, verb and adjective, and excluding adpositions (a closed lexical category). This means that there are nine logically possible types of each of the two main classes of compound (headed/non-headed), listed in (1).

(1)   a. N N, V N, A N
      b. N V, V V, A V
      c. N A, V A, A A

Given these basic templates we can ask what kinds of grammatical and semantic relations hold between the components. This is the basis of the Morbo typological model. In that model a distinction is drawn between subordinative compounding and attributive/appositional compounding. Subordinative compounds are of the type *train driver* (endocentric) and *windmill* or Italian *lavapiatti* 'dishwasher' (lit. 'washes dishes') (exocentric). Attributive compounds express a relation of attributive modification between the non-head and a noun. Scalise and Bisetto (2009) cite *high school* and *blue-eyed* as endocentric compounds and *redskin* as an exocentric compound. They cite *snail mail, sword fish, mushroom cloud* as appositive compounds, noting that there are no equivalent exocentric cases.

Although Scalise and Bisetto make a number of important observations in their typological survey (and in related work associated with the Bologna-based typological project), there are a number of reasons why we cannot use the Morbo scheme as a complete basis for a Canonical Typology (see also Spencer 2011: 493–4 for additional discussion of the Morbo model's semantic criteria).

The first, relatively minor, point is that the Morbo model provides comparatively little coverage for most of the compound types which involve verbs, including verb-headed compounds. This means, in particular, that (as far as I can tell) the published literature arising from the MorboComp project contains no systematic discussion of noun incorporation (though presumably, canonical noun incorporation would be an instance of the endocentric subordinative compound type, akin to English synthetic compounds such as *train driver*).

The second problem with the Morbo typology lies with the interpretation given by the project authors to the crucial grammatical relations between the components of compounds. Of necessity their classification scheme is broad-brushed, but the nature of the dataset itself raises problems. One such difficulty arises because the examples they discuss in detail tend to be lexicalised compounds of the kind *blackbird*. This is described by Scalise and Bisetto (2009) as an attributive N-headed compound with adjectival modifier. This seems reasonable enough until we note that the component *black* in *blackbird* actually has virtually no lexical or grammatical properties other than its phonology (Spencer 2011, 2013). In particular, there are no linguistic tests that would identify *black* as an adjective in *blackbird*. Moreover, *black* cannot mean 'black': 'X is a blackbird' does not entail 'X is a black bird'. Classifying *black-* as an adjective with attributive modifier function is more of an exercise in etymology than in synchronic typology. In other words, *black* is a kind of cranberry morph (though one whose etymology is somewhat more transparent than *cran-*).

The third reason why I cannot use the Morbo typology 'as is' relates to my earlier comments about the ontological status of compounds. The Morbo typology effectively takes compounds as a given and then proposes a number of (possibly universal) properties that they exhibit. In other words, the model adopts the dataset strategy. However, the concept of 'compounding' is an abstract relational concept defined over sets of linguistic representations. It is therefore more like concepts such as 'subject' or 'head'. The retrospective Canonical Typology approach allows us to ask questions about the nature of compounding even in the absence of an agreed cross-linguistic dataset of compounds. Instead, we ask the subtler question of what it means for a linguistic description to assign the label of 'compound' to a concrete set of construction types in a language. Among other things, this allows the typologist to consider the relationships between compounds and a wider set of non-compounding constructions than is possible in the Morbo model.

For these reasons I will be selective in drawing on the insights of the Morbo typology, and instead will attempt a typology based on first principles, in keeping with the methodology of Canonical Typology. The typology takes as its point of departure the idea that a compound is a word which itself consists of two (potentially independent) lexemes. The canonical compound thus has some properties of a canonical word but also some properties of a canonical phrase.

2.3 Canonical Criteria for Compounds

In this section I enumerate a set of canonical criteria for compounds, together with relevant criteria for words and phrases. I present here the basic criteria, to be supplemented by other criteria in later sections.

Canonical criteria for compounds:

(C1) A compound is a single syntactic word (zero-level syntactic terminal).
(C2) A compound is a MWE, formed from two independently occurring (canonical) lexemes (hence, neither component realises a feature, as would be the case for affixed forms).
(C3) The components of a compound bear a grammatical relation to each other, canonical (and hence, productive) for the word classes of those lexemes, either:
 (a) subordinative (predicate–argument, modifier–head, depending on the semantics of the components), or
 (b) coordinative.
(C4) The compounding relation is expressed solely by juxtaposition (and not, for instance, by any phrasal relationship or any morphologically expressed relationship).
(C5) A compound is (a) productively formed, and (b) semantically compositional.[4]

These criteria effectively limit (canonical) compounds to being formed from the categories of noun, verb and adjective. (Adpositional compounds are possible, but they can only be semantically canonical for a very restricted set of, mainly spatial, semantic relations.)

We now need to supplement these criteria with criteria for phrasehood and wordhood, specifically, syntactic wordhood.

Canonical criteria for (syntactic, inflected) words:

(W1) A word form (inflected, or the sole word form of an uninflectable word) realises exactly one syntactic word.
(W2) An inflected word expresses a single lexical (lexemic) concept.

There are, of course, a number of other canonical criteria we could adduce. These would include phonological criteria (a canonical word is a single phonological or prosodic word, while a canonical compound is two or more prosodic words), but I leave those considerations aside here.

Canonical criteria for (syntactic) phrases:

(P1) A phrase is a MWE, consisting of two independent word forms.
(P2) The word forms of a phrase are syntactic terminals.
(P3) The word forms of a phrase bear a standard grammatical relation to each other.
(P4) The grammatical relation between the components of a phrase is expressed by the standard morphosyntactic means for the language (i.e. canonical agreement, government, . . .).
(P5) Where a phrase type can appear in more than one syntactic environment, that phrase type is realised uniformly throughout its distribution.

In P1, 'independent word form' means that the word form is an inflected form, for an inflectable lexeme. In any case the word form cannot be a bare bound form (e.g. a 'combining base' or such like). The force of P5 is that, where a phrase type can appear in more than one syntactic environment there will be no syntactic restrictions on what form it may take in those environments. This criterion will become important when we consider the non-canonical distribution of adjective phrases in English, French and other languages. In general, an adjective phrase can take a post-head complement, such as a PP, a comparative phrase or even a clause: *proud of her daughter*, *more proud than he should be/than us*, *proud to be here*. However, such phrase types are excluded in prenominal position, in violation of criterion P5.

The criteria for compounds are compatible with some of the word/phrase criteria but not with others. This is summarised in (2).

(2) a. Compatible criteria (where ~ means 'is compatible with')
     C1 ~ W1
     C2 ~ P1
     C3 ~ P3
    b. Incompatible criteria (where ≁ means 'is incompatible with')
     C2, C3 ≁ W2
     C1 ≁ P2
     C4 ≁ P4

The criteria C1 ~ W1 are compatible in that they require both compounds and words to be realised as single syntactic terminals, so that the compound *dog biscuit* is a single N, [$_N$[$_N$dog][$_N$biscuit]], just like *dog*, [$_N$dog], and *biscuit*, [$_N$biscuit].

The criteria C2 ~ P1 require both a compound and a phrase to be realised by (at least) two distinct lexemes. Thus, the particle verb *write (the paper) up* is non-canonical, because it seems to form a two-word phrase but it realises a single lexeme, and the compound (?) noun *write-up*, likewise, realises a single lexeme, not two. Rather more canonical would be pairs such as (*a*) *dog biscuit* (compound) and (*a*) *dog's biscuit* (phrase). (See also the discussion of separable prefixes in Hungarian in §2.4.)

Criteria C3 ~ P3 should be self-explanatory: a compound such as *swearword* is non-canonical because a verb (*swear*) cannot on its own legitimately serve as a noun's attributive modifier, just as a phrase such as *by and large* is non-canonical. Thus, an expression that would be non-canonical as a compound on criterion C3 would equally be non-canonical as a phrase by criterion P3.

Criterion C3 requires the components of a compound to bear some kind of recognisable grammatical relation, and criterion C2 requires those components to be distinct lexemes. This means that any inflected form of the compound will violate the requirement W2 that a word form realise exactly one lexeme. For instance, *dog biscuits* is the plural of *dog biscuit*, and *dog* is a (special kind of) attributive modifier of *biscuits*, and it therefore expresses two lexical concepts, not one.

Criterion P2, together with criterion P1, requires a phrase to be realised as two syntactic terminals, while C1 requires a compound to be realised by a single syntactic terminal. Thus, (*a*) *dog's biscuit* is a less canonical compound than *dog biscuit* because *dog's* and *biscuit* are distinct syntactic terminals, while *dog biscuit* is syntactically just N. Conversely, (*a*) *dog's biscuit* is a more canonical phrase than *dog biscuit*.

Finally, C4 will be incompatible with P4 in any language that has function words and/or inflections. Thus, while it is difficult to distinguish an AN compound from a two-word phrase, [$_{NP}$[$_{AP}$A]N] in English (*blackbird* vs *black bird*, ignoring possible prosodic differences), it is possible to distinguish a N N compound from, say, a possessive phrase because possessive phrases are expressed by the [$_{NP}$NP's N] construction ((*a*) *dog's biscuit*) or by an *of*-phrase: [$_{NP}$N [$_{PP}$ of [$_{NP}$N]]] (*the biscuit of a dog*).

2.4 Lexical Integrity

Words consist of units (stems, affixes) which cannot be split up by other words. This is the property of lexical integrity. Canonical compounds are at once words and multiword expressions. We must therefore ask how they behave with respect to lexical integrity. I argue that the crucial property turns out to be that compounds are single syntactic words, C1, and that this overrides the phrase criterion P2. This means that compounds must respect lexical integrity to be canonical.

The phenomenon of lexical integrity actually encompasses two conceptually distinct properties. The first, which I shall call 'lexical integrity proper' or just 'lexical integrity', requires that a single (inflected) word form be expressed uniformly as a single syntactic word (leaf, terminal). Violations of lexical integrity are seen in the phenomenon of the 'separable preverb' familiar from Dutch, German, Hungarian and other languages. Thus, the Hungarian preverb *meg* in *megoldani* 'to solve' seems to be a prefixal part of the verb root, in that it is preserved in all inflected forms and also in derived words such as *megoldhatatlen* 'unsolvable'. However, in well-defined morphosyntactic contexts the preverb is separated from its verb base.

(3) Hungarian (Ackerman and LeSourd 1997)
    Ön   nem   oldott   azt   a   problémát   meg
    s/he NEG   solve.PST   this.ACC   the   problem.ACC   MEG
    'S/he didn't solve this problem'

When an apparent single word violates lexical integrity in this way and thus behaves more like a phrase than a word, we can say that it exhibits phrasal transparency.

Another symptom of lexical integrity is resistance to contextually induced elision. Syntactic phrases permit a coordinated modifier to modify a single head: [*the younger, but not all of the older*] *children*. This is not possible with frequently cited, prototypical, instances of compounds: *blackbirds and bluebirds* ≠> **black- and bluebirds*. Similarly, while it is common for a single modifier to modify a coordinated head, as in *good* [*boys and girls*], this is not found with prototypical compounds: *blackberries and blackcurrants* ≠> **black* [*berries and currants*] (on the required reading). However, as Kenesei (2007: 274) points out, this principle is often violated by compounds.

(4)   a. book- and newspaper-stands
      b. book-[binders and sellers]

Now, the point of Kenesei's article is to show that similar violations of lexical integrity are not especially uncommon with affixed word forms, as in *pre- and post-war (economy)* or German *trink- und ess-bar* 'drinkable and edible' (lit. '[drink- and eat-] able'). However, such behaviour is non-canonical for affixed words, by word criterion W1. Likewise, it is non-canonical for compounds, to the extent that compounds are single syntactic words. Phrasal transparency (i.e. violation of lexical integrity) makes a compound look more like a phrase and reduces our confidence in the validity of the descriptor 'compound'.

The complementary property to lexical integrity is what I shall call lexical opacity. By this I mean that the constitutive components of a morphologically complex word are not visible to external syntactic principles. Lexical opacity is a hallmark of derivational morphology, in that, canonically, derived lexemes respect the Principle of Derivational Opacity, PDO, (5).

(5) Principle of Derivational Opacity (PDO)
Given a word W bearing a canonical 'derived from' lexical relationship to a base lexeme B. Then no morphosyntactic principle is permitted to access any morphosyntactic property of B alone.

This principle is descriptive in the sense that it expresses a fact about the architecture of the grammar that should emerge from more general architectural principles.

Inflected word forms are like derived lexemes in respecting lexical integrity. However, unlike derived words, inflected word forms respect a Principle of Inflectional Transparency, PIT, the contrary of lexical opacity, (6).

(6) Principle of Inflection Transparency (PIT)
Given a word form ω of some lexeme £ realising some feature set {F}. Then any morphosyntactic principle π that accesses ω will equally access every other word form of £, ω', provided only that π does not refer to feature values realised by ω' that conflict with any member of {F}.

For example, verb-subject agreement will apply (say) to all tense forms of a given verb lexeme, provided that no tense form specifically excludes agreement. The Principle of Inflectional Transparency does not seem to follow automatically from the canonical word criteria W1, W2 so we must add a further criterion for canonical words, criterion W6.[5]

(W6) A canonical word respects the PIT.

Perceived in terms of traditional morphemics, the PIT would say that affixing a tense morpheme to a verb root does not prevent subject–verb agreement from treating the resulting stem form as a verb stem and hence the target of agreement. However, by the Principle of Derivational Opacity, when a verb is affixed by a subject nominalising morpheme (say, the -er of *driver*) it loses its verbal morphosyntax, and cannot, for instance, be inflected for tense. In a morpheme-based model, as is well known, this is a puzzling difference in behaviour.

In an inferential-realisational model of inflection the Principle of Inflectional Transparency is an automatic consequence of the way that inflectional realisation is defined. However, in the standard inferential-realisational models it is hard to see what it is in the model that entails the Principle of Derivational Opacity. In large part this is the topic of Spencer (2013) so I refer the reader to that discussion.

Let us refer to the properties of lexical integrity and lexical opacity jointly as the property of lexical islandhood (or just islandhood). Compared with derivation, a characterisation of lexical islandhood in compounds can make more direct reference to the actual components of the compound (a derived lexeme may be derived by some non-affixal process, *sing ~ song*). This allows us to state the Principle of Islandhood for Compounds, PIC, (7).

(7) Principle of Islandhood for Compounds (PIC)
Given a multiword expression $\mathcal{E}$ consisting of two word forms, W_1, W_2, realising

respectively lexemes £$_1$, £$_2$, such that W$_2$ is the head of $\mathcal{E}$, and $\mathcal{E}$ is a single syntactic word (i.e. a compound). Then no syntactic principle can apply to the non-head W$_1$ uniquely.

'Syntactic principle' is intended to include principles that might be expected to induce transparency at the lexical level, (8a,b), and those that might be expected to induce transparency at the phrasal level, (8c).

(8) a. *[boring book] exhibition
    b. *[whose book?] exhibition
    c. * [books which have been published in the last year] exhibition

Now, in part, the content of the PIC will follow from compound criterion C1, i.e. the fact that compounds are words. However, since compounds are also MWEs we would expect all of their components, including the non-head, to be accessible to syntactic principles, in the same way that the words making up canonical phrases are accessible to syntax. However, it is only the head of a compound that is accessible. We therefore need to add C6 to the list of compound criteria.

(C6) A canonical compound respects the PIC.

The head of a canonical compound respects the PIT, and behaves in this respect like a non-compounded word. However, it seems that we do not need to stipulate this. A compound is a MWE, but it is headed, just like a canonical phrase. Therefore, the head of a compound should canonically inflect just as though it were the head of a homologous phrase.

The PDO, (5), and the PIC, (7), are clearly reflexes of the same islandhood phenomenon applied to word-sized units, though it is not clear how to generalise the two principles to a single overarching principle. One possibility might be to assume that compounds, like (canonically) derived words, are distinct lexemes from their bases, and especially from their heads. However, this seems implausible given that the compound, unlike a derived lexeme, canonically inherits most of its properties from its head. In addition, we should note that the literature almost always distinguishes a class of exocentric compounds. I have argued that these are best regarded as non-canonical compound-like MWEs. However, exocentric compounds share with their canonical endocentric cousins the property of respecting the islandhood principles.[6] Since exocentric compounds tend overwhelmingly to be lexicalised expressions and not productively formed (hence their non-canonicity) we might be tempted to associate islandhood with lexicalisation, but this would then leave unexplained the fact that the PDO and PIC canonically apply to fully productive derivation and compounding. I therefore leave the unification of principles (5) and (7) to future research.

In sum, compounds are like derived lexemes in that their non-heads are lexical/phrasal islands (respecting the PIC). By contrast, the head of a compound, like inflected word forms generally, is lexically transparent (respects the PIT), though both compounds and inflected word forms canonically respect lexical integrity.

2.5 Recursion in Compounds

In §2.3 I raised the possibility that one canonical property of compounds might be that of recursion. The notion of recursion is sometimes misunderstood, especially when compared with formal notions (such as 'recursive function', Fitch 2010; Widmer et al. 2017), so I will leave the concept unformalised. There are two senses in which we can describe compounds as recursive, a strong sense and a weak sense. In the strong sense recursion is defined over elements of the same lexical category. In this sense a category, N, is recursive if it can dominate an element of category N. In the weaker sense of recursion, a compound will be recursive provided that it can admit a compound, of any category, as a proper subpart of itself. Thus, if we have a language with, say, productive noun incorporation and also productive compounding of an adjective by a head noun (e.g. one of the Chukotko-Kamchatkan languages, such as Chukchi, Spencer 1995), then a verb which incorporates a noun compounded with an adjective, say, [*large=whale*], to give, say, [*large=whale*] *kill* ('kill a large whale/ large whales') will exhibit weak (though not strong) recursion.[7]

I will take it that the crucial notion for a typology of compounding is weak recursion. A compound is a word, but a word can itself be a compound, so we expect to see compounds inside canonical compounds. Now, this reasoning rests on the standard assumption that compounds are a subspecies of multiword expression and that therefore their constituents are words. However, there is an important sense in which this is misleading, depending on exactly what we mean by 'word'. One important property of a compound is that it can serve as a syntactic word. This means that its head must be able to inflect (in an inflecting language) and more generally that the compound should show the same kind of syntactic distribution as its head. Indeed, that is one of the key definitions of the concept 'head (of a compound)'. However, in claiming that compounds canonically exhibit (weak) recursion, we encounter a conceptual problem. Since the canonical compound is also a single syntactic word, neither component is itself a syntactic word *sensu stricto*. This is particularly true of the non-head element, because this does not even have the same distribution as a syntactic word in general, an entailment of the PIC introduced in §2.4. One instance of this can be seen from English synthetic compounding, as in *train driver*: the incorporated noun, *train*, which functions as the direct object of the base verb of the compound is in a syntactically non-canonical position for direct objects (preverbal). More generally, given the PIC, a non-head cannot inflect and therefore by definition cannot have the same distribution as a (possibly homophonous) syntactic (inflected) word form.

A convenient way of conceptualising the problem is to consider the case of languages in which the head and/or non-head are marked in such a way as to distinguish them from corresponding inflected word forms appearing as lexical terminals. One way in which this can happen is where we have a linking element joining the two components of the compound. In some languages such a linker is clearly part of the first component and not simply an intervening morph. This is true of linkers in

Germanic, which are mainly derived historically from inflectional suffixes, but which have lost their inflectional properties (Kürschner and Szczepaniak 2013). German compounds with a linker ('Fugenelement') are not canonical (they violate compound criterion C4), but they have a non-head component which is a stem form, not an inflected word form and which is hence not a potential syntactic word. Therefore, the compound has the (canonical) property of being a multiword expression distinct from a syntactic phrase. Examples of such compounds, as illustrated in (9), are very common, though compounds formed on the same nouns without a linker are also common, often with no obvious difference in structure or semantics, sometimes differentiating distinct meanings of homophonous or polysemous words, as in (9b, 10b). In some cases either possibility is found, so that, for instance, alongside *Kalb-s-leber* 'calf's liver' (*Kalb* 'calf', *Leber* 'liver'), with Fugenelement -*s*-, we see the (less common) form *Kalb-leber*.[8]

(9)   German compounds with a linker
   a. *Buch* 'book'
      Bücher-regal
      book-shelf
      'book shelf'
   b. *Land* 'land, countryside; German political region'
      Land-es-bank
      land-ES-bank
      'regional bank (of a Land)'

(10)   German compounds without a linker
   a. *Buch* 'book'
      Buch-messe
      book-fair
      'book fair'
   b. *Land* 'land, countryside; German political region'
      Land-haus
      land-house
      'country house'
   c. *Schule* 'school'
      Schul-haus
      school-house
      'schoolhouse'

The stem form *Bücher* is formally identical to the plural of this lexeme but there does not seem to be any clear semantic relation between the use of the singular stem form and the plural stem form. A book fair does not just involve one book, for instance. *Land* is ambiguous between 'land = country as opposed to town' and a technical term referring to one of 16 semi-autonomous geopolitical entities within the Bundesrepublik. In the first meaning it forms compounds without the

Fugenelement -es- and in the second meaning its compounds have the Fugenelement. The example *Schulhaus* is interesting in that the citation form of the noun 'school' is *Schule*, /ʃuːlə/, but the final schwa is elided in the compound, giving rise to a bound stem form, /ʃuːl/.

Given these preliminaries we can ask whether German nouns based on a (possibly bound) stem form with linking element show recursion. The answer is that they do.[9]

(11) a. *Tag* 'day'
 b. *Ausflug* 'excursion'
 c. *Ziel* 'goal, target, destination'
 d. *Ort* 'place'
(12) a. *Tag* 'day'
 b. *Tagesausflug* 'day trip'
 c. *Tagesausflugsziel* [[Tagesausflugs]ziel] 'day trip destination'
 d. *Tagesausflugsort* [[Tagesausflugs]ort] 'day trip place'

The only element of a headed compound which canonically inflects as though it were an independent, simplex syntactic word is the compound's head itself. From this we can conclude that canonical headed compounds consist of an inflecting head lexeme and a non-inflecting stem or combining form. This is obscured in languages such as English: the form of the non-head in a compound such as *dog food* looks much like the singular form (especially when the compound is written as separate words), but this is misleading. In particular, there is no possibility in English of contrasting singular with plural forms in such compounds. If we wished to stress that Smith owned one dog while Jones owned more than one dog, we would not be able to refer to Jones as a **dogs owner*, as opposed to Smith, the *dog owner*. Thus, *dog* in *dog owner* is a stem form, not an inflected word form.

From this reasoning it follows that compounds consist of concatenated lexemes, or more specifically, of Lexemic Indices which uniquely identify lexemes. Thus, if £$_{29}$ is the LI of the lexeme DOG and £$_{57}$ is the LI of the lexeme FOOD then the representation for the compound should be as in Figure 2.1.

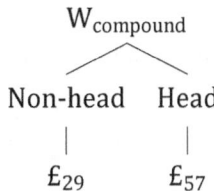

Figure 2.1 Concatenated compound

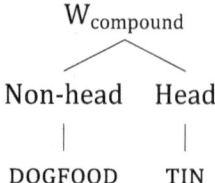

Figure 2.2 Recursive compound

This raises the question of how to represent recursive compounds in English, for instance, *dog food tin* (Figure 2.2).

The clue comes from German recursive compounds with linker, such as *Tag-es=Ausflug-s=Ziel* 'day trip destination'. Here, the non-head is itself a compound noun, *Tagesausflug*, but when that compound appears as the non-head modifying the head *Ziel* 'destination' its own head, *Ausflug* 'trip', appears in the combining form, *ausflug-s*. Presumably, the same structure can be proposed for English compounds, so that the *food* of *dogfood* in *dogfood tin* is effectively a bound form, as shown in Figure 2.3.

Since FOOD heads an expression which functions as the non-head of a compound the rules of compounding will determine the form of the FOOD lexeme, in this case the compound combining form /fuːd/. In German, the rule is slightly more complex, but essentially the same: the head AUSFLUG of the compound TAGESAUSFLUG assumes the appropriate combining form when that compound is incorporated as the non-head of a compound, as in TAGESAUSFLUGSZIEL. In both languages we have to assume that what is compounded is not a set of forms directly, but rather a set of lexemes, here represented as their Lexemic Indices. Thus, compounds are not so much multiword expressions as multilexeme expressions.

Consideration of a canonically phrasal property, recursion, thus leads to the conclusion that the canonical non-head in N N compounds (and presumably all compounds) has to be a non-inflected stem form. This conclusion is compatible with the

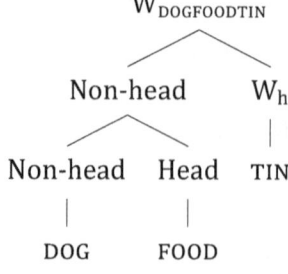

Figure 2.3 Bound compound

Principle of Islandhood for Compounds, (7). Indeed, one possible avenue of research would be to replace criterion C6 with criterion C7.

(C7) In a canonical compound the non-head is the bare (default) stem form.

Together with criterion C4, criterion C7 will make the Fugenelement non-canonical, even if it is treated as a stem-extender of the non-head.

2.6 Compound-Like Constructions and Non-canonical Compounds

The canonical compound is a non-canonical word which is also a non-canonical MWE. Being a MWE (specifically a two-lexeme construction) the construction has to be characterised by a grammatical relation between the two components, either some kind of dependency or coordination. Being a single word, the construction cannot (canonically!) express that dependency by normal morphosyntactic principles. In particular, the dependency cannot be expressed by inflections (by criteria C4, C6, or equally by criterion C7).

In this section I review a number of multiword construction types which resemble compounds in various ways, but which lack certain criterial properties. I consider in turn constructions headed by nouns then verbs. (Constructions headed by adjectives, including compounds, are not so common, and I have little to say about them at this point.) In some cases the constructions I describe are (usually) not labelled as compounds in traditional descriptions or in theoretical discussion, but in other cases we are dealing with controversial constructions which are sometimes viewed as compounds and which are therefore potential candidates for inclusion in a dataset-based typology. In some cases, we will see a construction which is labelled 'compound' (or 'syntactic compound') but which is then analysed as something other than a (true) compound by some authors, for instance, the Japanese 'syntactic' verb-verb compounds and the English 'composite nominals' discussed at the end of this section. The noun-headed constructions are those in which some word or phrase serves as an attributive modifier to the noun. The canonical modifier in languages which distinguish that category is the adjective. Compounding of an adjective into a noun head is not very common and in some of the languages that permit it (e.g. German, Spencer 2011), it is not fully productive or compositional. Note that in English, A N compounds such as *blackbird* are completely non-productive, despite this example being cited regularly in handbooks (an instance of the 'Venus effect'). In Chukchi, on the other hand, 'adjective incorporation' is not only fully productive, it is obligatory in a number of morphosyntactic and discourse contexts. It is fairly easy to distinguish words from phrases in Chukchi because words are the domain of (fully productive) dominant-recessive vowel harmony and because nouns, verbs and adjectives all have circumfixal inflected forms and those circumfixes regularly flank incorporated stems (Spencer 1995). Chukchi A N compounds thus fulfil the criteria for canonical compounding. The standard syntactic AdjP-N constructions are found in Chukchi, of course, and the incorporated construction then has a special discourse function – an adjective is normally incorporated when it is not focused. In addition, adjectives modifying nouns in one of the two comitative cases (marked by circumfixes) obligatorily incorporate.

A (non-canonical) situation is found in a number of languages with an adjective category, in which certain types of adjective appear to form a more closely knit construction than normal and in which some of the syntactic potential of the adjective is lost. English demonstrates this: prenominal adjectives can take at most degree modifiers, to their left, and do not permit complements (to their right) of any kind: *a very proud (*of her daughter) woman*; *somewhat difficult (*to reconcile with the facts) decisions*; *a more successful (*than her brother) girl*. Sadler and Arnold (1994), discussing comparable constructions in French, speak of 'small constructions', midway between the word category and the phrase category (X^1 or X^2; cf. also the notion of 'W^+' in Japanese, Kageyama 2001). The point is that genuine compounds are expected to be unequivocally word/X^0 categories, so the small constructions have to be seen as intermediate between canonical compounds and canonical phrases (or perhaps as highly non-canonical instances of each or either category).

Verbs can also be used to modify nouns, though the canonical way to do this is through some kind of relative clause construction, for instance by transposing the verb into a participial form. Examples of a bare verb stem modifying a noun in a compound (such as *swearword*) are rather rare in English (see the list in Huddleston and Pullum 2002: 1650).[10]

In children's speech we find examples of compound agent nominals such as *drive man* preceding the acquisition of *-er* nominalisation (Clark 1998; Clark and Hecht 1982) but comparable examples are found in Asian languages such as Chinese: *màidiǎn* $[V + N]_N$ 'sell + point', 'selling point' (Ceccagno and Basciano 2007: 481). However, compounding in many of the languages that permit such constructions is formally rather similar to lexicalised syntax, so it is not clear how canonical such expression types are as compounds.

The prototypical function of the noun-headed compound is to permit the head noun to be attributively modified by another nominal expression, what Nikolaeva and Spencer (2013) call 'modification-by-noun'. There are several morphosyntactic devices for achieving this cross-linguistically, all of which can become grammaticalised to give construction types close to compounding. Before I survey these I will clarify an important distinction between two distinct ways in which nouns can modify other nouns.

In a simple instance of noun-noun compounding, such as *dog food*, a contextually specified relation ℜ is predicated of two common noun denotations, in effect 'the concept of dog' and 'the concept of food'. The head *food* can then be specified or determined, to denote some particular instance of dog food. However, the non-head remains non-determined and therefore non-referential. The term *dog food* does not refer to any particular dog. At best it might refer to the generic kind ('doghood'), but even this is too specific. In, say, *dog walker* the entity taken for walks is not a generic dog: *dog* is entirely non-referential and has a 'non-anchoring' role (Koptjevskaja-Tamm 2004). The compounds contrast with genuine possessive constructions such as *a/the dog's food*. Here we see a relation ℜ between the concept food, and the referent of the term *a/the dog*, say *Fido*.

The pure noun concept is expressed canonically by a bare noun (stem), compound criteria C4, C6, C7, while a referential expression such as *a/the dog* has to be expressed by a NP/DP in English. The boundaries between possessive phrases and compounds can get blurred, however. First, there is a formal blurring in languages with very little morphosyntax, or where morphosyntactic constructions defined over NPs are co-opted to realise compounding. Second, the semantic distinction can get blurred when the possessor phrase is not a canonical referring expression but instead refers to a kind or a generic entity. For instance, the expression *food for a dog* is ambiguous between a specific and a generic interpretation of *dog*. The same ambiguity is seen in compounds based on possessive phrases in English such as *children's literature* or *child's portion* (as opposed to *child seat*).

I now turn to a brief survey of a number of common devices used to express modification-by-noun (phrase) and their implications for the notion of canonical compounding.

The modifying noun (phrase) can be marked by an adposition such as English *of*. When lexicalised such expressions can give the appearance of compounds (*point of view*, *man o' war*, or, with other prepositions, *case in point*, *minister-without-portfolio*). However, in languages where such constructions abound, such as French, there is little reason to try to include them in a typology of canonical compounding as such, except as highly non-canonical outliers.

Nouns can be modified by case-marked nouns, whether genitive case or other cases such as locatives, as in the Finnish examples in (13).

(13) Finnish (Karlsson 1987)
    a. mere-n   =ranta
       see-GEN   =shore
       'sea shore'
    b. praha-ssa   =käymättömyys   =kompleksi
       Prague-INESSIVE =not.having.been =complex
       'complex about not having been to Prague'

One construction that is very close to compounds is the construct of Semitic (and a few other) languages (Creissels 2009). In the typical construct a dependency between a head noun and a modifier noun is expressed by placing the dependent noun in a special form, the construct form (construct state). Schematically, the equivalent of *bookshop* would be *shop.CF book*, where *shop.CF* is the construct form of *shop*. The construct form is typically some specially marked morphophonological form. In some of the Semitic languages and in the Western Nilotic language DhoLuo, for instance, this construct form is morphophonologically distinct from all the standard inflected noun forms (Tucker 1994: 189–224), and in particular it is not a case form.[11]

The segmental alternations are illustrated in (14), where we see that essentially the voicing of the final consonant switches, along with other more complex alternations in some cases (c = /ʧ/, dh = /ð/, th = /θ/).

(14) DhoLuo construct (Tucker 1994)
    welo 'visitor'   *wend dala* 'visitors to the village'
    kitab 'book'   *kitap kwano* 'an arithmetic book'
    bidhi 'spear'   *bith rec* 'a fish spear'
    kidi 'stone'   *kit got* 'a stone from the hill'
    sigana 'story' *sigand apwoyo* 'the story of the hare'
    wer 'song'   *wend Luo* 'a Luo song'
    ot 'house'   *od winyo* 'a bird's nest'
    udi 'houses'   *ut winyi* 'birds' nests'

The construct state is closely related to a number of other compound-like constructions. One of these is the Persian ezāfe, in which a formative *e*, 'EZ', unites a noun head with any modifier, including a noun: N_{head}-e $N_{dependent}$. In (15) we see simple instances of the Persian ezāfe construction linking two nouns in a manner reminiscent of a compound, while in (16) we see a typical possessor construction. In (17) we see the ezāfe construction functioning to signal that the head noun is modified by a straightforward attributive adjective (Lambton 1963: 9, 20, 129; for further uses of the Persian ezāfe, see Lambton 1963: 128–30).

(15) Persian (Lambton 1963)
    bag-e   manzel
    garden-EZ house
    'the garden of the house'

(16) ketâb-e   an   mard
    book-EZ   that   man
    'that man's book'

(17) mard-e   xub
    man-EZ   good
    'the good man'

Although there are lexicalised cases of ezāfe, this is a productive construction, just like productive compounding or the construct state. The corresponding construction in Kurdish has an interesting variant, in which the ezāfe marker (historically a relative or demonstrative pronoun) agrees in number and gender with the non-head noun to which it attaches: N_{head}[GENDER.NUMBER]-EZ.AGR $N_{dependent}$. A similar construction is found in Hausa (Creissels 2009).

A further construction type in which the head rather than the dependent noun is marked involves possessor agreement morphology on the head noun: *forest$_i$ tree-AGR$_i$* (lit. 'forest, its-tree'). In Turkish the possessor agreement construction is traditionally called izafet (etymologically derived from the Arabic term *iḍāfah* and cognate with the Persian term *ezāfe*). It has the same range of uses as, say, a genitive construction in other languages, i.e. it denotes some kind of relation, often contextually specified and not necessarily 'possessive' in any sense, between the head and the dependent. In a number of languages with possessor agreement morphosyntax the possessor is not marked for case itself, but in others it can be marked with a genitive or similar case (e.g. dative case in Hungarian). In Turkish both case-less and genitive case-marked dependent nouns are found, giving rise to the so-called indefinite izafet (case-less dependent) and the definite izafet (genitive case-marked dependent), illustrated in (18).

(18) Turkish (Lewis 1967: 43)
    a. çoban   kızı
       shepherd girl.3POSS
       'the shepherd-girl'
    b. çoban-ın   kızı
       shepherd-GEN girl.3POSS
       'the shepherd's daughter'

In (18b) we see the definite izafet, essentially a relation between two noun phrases, while in (18a) we see the indefinite izafet, in which the non-head is essentially a non-referential noun modifying the head noun, just as in endocentric (Germanic) N N compounds (Spencer 1991: 314–19). This parallel with noun-noun compounding is such that Göksel and Kerslake (2005: 103), in a chapter on 'Noun Compounds', describe the indefinite izafet (what they call the '-(s)I compound') as 'by far the most common type of compounding in Turkish', more common that the 'bare noun' compounds, i.e. appositional or right-headed noun-noun compounds such as *çelik kapı* 'steel door', *Alman mimar* 'German architect'. (They refer to the definite izafet as the 'genitive-possessive construction', Göksel and Kerslake 2005: 182–5.)

In a definite izafet construction the head noun and the possessor N(P) can be directly pre-modified by an adjective or determiner, as in (19).

(19) a. bu   ordu-nun   subaylar-ı
       this army-GEN officers-3POSS
       'the officers of this army'
    b. bu   ordu-nun   bu   subaylar-ı
       this army-GEN these officers-3POSS
       'these officers of this army'

The head noun of an indefinite izafet can be modified, though the modifier has to appear to the left of the izafet construction as a whole, as shown in (20).

(20) bu   ordu   subaylar-ı
    this army officers-3POSS
    'these army officers'

In contrast to the definite izafet, the dependent (possessor) noun in the indefinite construction cannot be modified in any way at all, with one exception. It is possible to form left-branching recursive indefinite izafets, as in (21).

(21) [[Türk dil-i] dergi-si]
      Türk dil-i   dergi-si
      Turk language-3POSS   journal-3POSS
      'Turkish language journal' (lit. 'journal of the Turkish language')

Notice that constructions such as (21) differ from, say, English compound nouns in that in the Turkish examples it is impossible to impose any bracketing other than [[Turkish language] journal]. Right-branching modification with indefinite izafets, is, however, possible when we stack bare noun modifiers to the left of a head, as in (22).

(22) [Türk [dil kurum-u]]
      Türk   dil kurum-u
      Turk language society-3POSS
      'Turkish language society' (lit. '[language society] of the Turk')

This corresponds to the right-branching constituent structure [Turkish [language society]]. The failure of modification can be attributed to the fact that the components of the compound are not syntactic terminals and hence violate the criterion for canonical phrasehood, P2. Conversely, they respect the compound criterion C6.

There is a clear structural parallel between the construct of, say, DhoLuo and the indefinite izafet, but there is an important difference. The morphology that expresses the 'construct state' of a head noun in Turkish is possessor agreement, whose default interpretation is that of a possessive determiner. In particular, nouns can be inflected for possession by all three persons and both numbers: *oda* 'room': *oda-m*, 'my room', *oda-n* 'your(SG) room', *oda-sı* 'his/her/its room', *oda-mız* 'our room', *oda-nız* 'your(PL) room', *oda-ları* 'their room'. In the indefinite izafet construction, therefore, this possessive meaning has been co-opted for realising a compounding structure. However, the original possessive morphology is still 'visible', so to speak. A noun such as *oda* cannot inflect more than once for possessor agreement. What happens, then, when an indefinite izafet is itself possessed? In fact, the possessor agreement marker which signals the izafet is then replaced by the genuine possessor suffix. Thus, from the indefinite izafet seen in (23a) we have (23b), not (23c).

(23) a. yatak   oda-sı
         bed   room-3POSS
         'bedroom'
      b. yatak   oda-m
         bed   room-1SG.POSS
         'my bedroom'
      c. * yatak oda-sı-m

Here we see that it is not possible to have two possessive markers in a row, so the innermost is truncated. (This means, of course, that (23a) is actually ambiguous, having the additional meaning 'his/her/its bedroom'.) There are a handful of expressions (which Lewis refers to as 'frozen izafets') which are lexicalised to the extent that the possessor marker is no longer perceived as such, with the result that the whole word can take a further possessor marking, as exemplified in (24).

(24)   a.   bin-baş-ı
            thousand-head-3POSS
            'major (in army)'
      b.   bin-baş-ı-sı
            thousand-head-POSS-POSS
            'his major'

Moreover, (24a) is pluralised by the addition of *-lar-* to the whole expression, to give (25), while (23a) is pluralised by affixation of *-lar-* directly to the noun root to give (26).

(25)   binbaş-ı-lar 'majors'

(26)   yatak oda-lar-ı 'bedrooms'

These observations suggest that the possessor agreement marker of the indefinite izafet retains some of its syntactic properties, specifically its ability to identify an attribute noun by agreement. Otherwise, we would not be able to account for the difference in behaviour between regular indefinite izafets such as 'bedroom', (23a), and the truly lexicalised varieties such as 'major', (24). This vestigial morphosyntactic structure makes the indefinite izafet less than canonical as a compound.[12] All the construct, ezāfe, izafet and related constructions violate the compound criterion C4, of course.

Adpositions corresponding to *of* frequently give rise to similarly compound-like structures such as French *nom de plume* 'alias' (lit. 'name of pen'). In English, compounds based on the *'s* possessive marker are lexicalised. However, it is possible to find languages in which genuine compounds seem to be based on genitive-marked constructions. One of the compounding types of Latvian, for instance, is like this (Kalnača and Lokmane 2016): *Latviešu valoda* 'Latvian language' (lit. 'language of Latvians').[13] To the extent that such compounds are productive and compositional they respect the compound criteria C2–5, while violating criterion C4. To the extent that they respect islandhood they respect criterion C1. They can be thought of as the dependent marking equivalent of constructs or the Turkish indefinite izafet.

There are a fair number of other instances of constructions which violate one or other of the compound criteria by showing phrasal properties and which are sometimes described as compounds (or at least 'syntactic compounds') and sometimes described as some other construction that is not, however, a fully-fledged phrase. A case in point is the English 'composite nominal' construction identified by the authors of *The Cambridge Grammar of the English Language* (*CGEL*: Huddleston and Pullum 2002: 448–51). English N N compounds generally respect compound criterion C1, and hence respect lexical integrity. However, it is quite common to encounter examples such as (27) in which a non-head position is realised by a coordinated phrase, (28), in which a dependent noun takes scope over a coordinated head, and (29), in which an adjective intervenes between the dependent noun and the head. (In (29b), note, the dependent is itself a N N compound.)

(27) a. [Oxford and Cambridge] colleges
 b. [pension or tax] regulations
 c. [noun but not adjective] phrases

(28) London [schools or colleges]

(29) a. London financial markets
 b. [nerve cell] metabolic rates
 c. home electrical goods

CGEL notes that the distinctive syntactic shape of the composite nominals is essentially that of AdjP + N, and hence that these are syntactic constructions (phrases) and not morphological ones (true compounds). However, the parallel with attributive adjective phrases is not perfect. For instance, the position of the non-head attribute is fixed in pre-modifier position and it cannot be extracted or repositioned in any way. Relational adjectives are generally disallowed as predicates, but occasionally they can be found, (30).

(30) financial or administrative regulations ⇒
 They treat these regulations as financial or administrative

This is completely excluded with the composite nominals, (31).

(31) finance or administration law ⇏
 *They treat this law as finance or administration [in the relevant interpretation]

Similarly, the well-known restrictions against inflected noun dependents inside compounds also apply to the composite nominals, (32).

(32) a. *incomes calculations
 b. *taxes calculations
 c. *incomes or taxes calculations

As we have seen, adjective phrases in pre-modifier position have a very restricted structure in English and a number of other languages (Sadler and Arnold 1994). Adjective phrases which are extended to their right have to be postposed to a postmodifier position, as illustrated in (33).

(33) a. * any [extended with a clause] phrase
 b. any phrase [extended with a clause]

This option is not open to composite nominals. For instance, compare (34a,b) and (34c). (Further ungrammatical examples can be seen in (35).)

(34) a. * any [preposition consisting of two syllables] phrase
     b. * any phrase [preposition consisting of two syllables]
     c. any preposition phrase

(35) a. * these [home for newly-weds] electrical goods
     b. * these electrical goods [home for newly-weds]

Moreover, the kind of adjective that can intervene between a modifying dependent noun and the head of the compound seems limited to denominal or relational adjectives. Compare (36) with (29).

(36) a. London finance markets
     b. nerve cell metabolism rates

Other types of adjective are not possible between the noun dependent and the head.

(37) a. * London (financial) buoyant markets
     b. * nerve cell (metabolic) elevated rates

Thus, the composite nominals fail to meet most of the criteria for phrasehood in English, while violating C1.[14] Whatever solution the grammar writer proposes for handling such phenomena, the typologist interested in exploring the notion of 'compound noun' cross-linguistically will probably have to accept that the composite nominals are a species of compound, but that they exhibit a noticeable degree of non-canonicity. An exhaustive typology would then detail the deviation from the canonical compounding criteria as well as the deviation from canonical phrase structure and word structure criteria.

I turn now to verb-headed compounds. The parade example here is the frequently discussed case of noun incorporation (NI), prototypically, indeed, canonically, the compounding of a direct object noun stem into the stem of a transitive verb.[15] There are several issues that arise with the characterisation of NI, though some of the most hotly debated are, perhaps, the result of theory-internal considerations rather than genuine analytic, descriptive, or conceptual problems of interest to language typology. This is particularly true of the issue of whether NI is 'really' a lexical phenomenon (Mithun 1984, 1986; Rosen 1989) or 'really' a syntactic one (Baker 1988; Sadock 1980, 1986). The simple answer to that question is that in a lexicalist framework such as LFG or HPSG, NI is by definition lexical, while in a syntactico-centric framework such as Minimalism it is equally by definition syntactic.[16]

Within the Canonical Typology framework the question revolves around to what extent a construction respects canonical criteria for wordhood as opposed to phrasehood. For the purposes of the typology I have to assume some kind of lexicalist model, in the sense that I need to be able to define a level of wordhood distinct from the level of the phrase, and such a distinction is not reproducible in Minimalist syntax. Given this, it is not obvious to what extent we can say that NI (or any other kind of compound formation) 'happens in the syntax' or 'happens in the morphology'. The pertinent questions are 'to what extent does the compound respect word criteria (such as lexical integrity/opacity) and to what extent does it respect phrase criteria?'

A canonical instance of NI as compounding will therefore show the morphological properties of a single word form. In this respect the NI of Chukchi is canonical, in contrast to the kinds of construction that Miner (1986) refers to as 'noun stripping' in Zuni, and which are found throughout the Oceanic languages, as well as in Turkish, Hungarian and other languages. An instructive instance of this kind of loose concatenation is provided by German examples such as *rad-fahren* 'to ride (*fahren*) the/a bicycle (*Rad*)' (generically, a non-specific bicycle). A compound such as German *radfahren* is particularly non-canonical because the 'stripped' noun, *Rad*, behaves like a separable prefix or particle in finite clauses.

(38) German
    a. Ich will heute Rad fahren
       I want today bicycle ride
       'I want to go cycling today.'
    b. Ich fahre gern Rad
       I ride willingly bicycle
       'I like to cycle.'

In (38a) we see what seems to be a typical compound form,[17] but in (38b) the 'incorporated' noun appears at the right periphery of the clause.

Another instance of morphologically non-canonical NI is seen in English. Synthetic compounds, in which a noun stem realises a verb's direct object, can be found not only with subject nominalisations of the kind *train driver*, but also with the *-ing* form of verbs, whether realising a nominalisation (*horse-riding is dangerous*), or an adjective (*the horse-riding warriors of the Golden Horde*). What is not usually noted in the literature is that even a present participle realising the progressive aspect permits this incorporation: *Harriet was horse-riding all yesterday*; *Harriet has been horse-riding all afternoon*. However, the construction does not achieve the status of genuine NI because it is excluded with other forms of the verb, especially finite forms, (39).

(39)   a. to-infinitive: *Harriet likes to horse-ride (cf. Harriet likes horse-riding)
       b. imperative: *Horse-ride with us tomorrow!
         (cf. Come horse-riding with us tomorrow!)
       c. perfect participle: *Harriet has already horse-ridden today
         (cf. Harriet has been horse-riding)
       d. base form: *Harriet will horse-ride tomorrow; *Harriet can horse-ride very well
       e. any tensed form: *Harriet horse-rides every day; *Harriet horse-rode yesterday

Compounds are canonically opaque, being words, but NI often gives rise to violations of opacity. The most familiar such violation is seen when a modifier external to the NI complex is able to modify the incorporated noun. Examples from the Eskimo languages such as West Greenlandic are sometimes cited in illustration of this. Van Geenhoven (1998: 17–21) provides a list of instances in which adjectives, numerals, wh-words, nouns, and even relative clauses can modify the incorporated noun (or better, the noun that takes the derivational verbal postbase affix).[18] In the canonical framework such constructions are not unexpected, but they are not canonical as compounds (or as anything, in fact).

Adjectives do not (canonically!) modify verbs, so we would only expect to see AV compounds with verbs which take an adjectival complement, such as English *seem, become,* . . . In English such compounds appear marginally possible with *seem*: *a happy seeming child*, but not with other verbs: **a frustrated becoming/getting child*.

The nearest equivalent to adjectival modification of a head verb is modification by an adverb(ial). In languages with productive NI it is often perfectly possible to incorporate adverbial modifiers, as illustrated for Chukchi in Spencer (1995).[19] Chukchi permits incorporation of verb stems by verbs, in which the incorporated verb functions as a kind of gerundive modifier to the head verb. In addition, formatives with phasic meanings *begin/finish* seem to incorporate verb stems. However, descriptions of Chukotkan generally treat such formatives as aspectual affixes rather than incorporating verb heads, although the formatives themselves can be used as verb stems in their own right (Dunn 1999: 257). Grammaticalisation of lexical elements with rather general meanings such as these is extremely common, of course, and is one of the main sources of derivational morphology. However, this often gives rise to lexicalisation rather than grammaticalisation, in which the morphologised element does not become a member of a more-or-less abstract feature system, rather it becomes a highly idiosyncratic marker of usually unpredictable meaning (Gerdts 1998). In this respect, the erstwhile verb stems are reminiscent of the polyfunctional adverbial/prepositional elements which become lexical prefixes to verbs in many languages, including Indo-European languages such as Germanic, Slavic and Indo-Aryan.

There are, however, languages in which verb heads appear to form compounds with verb stems. A case in point is the verb-verb compounding process found in Japanese and described by Kageyama in a number of publications (Kageyama 1989, 1999, 2009; see also the *Compound Verb Lexicon* website, which also includes a useful introduction to the phenomena[20]). Kageyama distinguishes two types of VV compound. The lexical compounds exhibit lexical integrity and lexical opacity, as befits words. Although such compounds are abundant (the *Compound Verb Lexicon* lists some 2,700 of them), they are not formed productively and they are not (necessarily) compositional. Kageyama (2009) cites the examples in (40), his 'Type A'.

(40) Japanese 'Type A' lexical compounds (Kageyama 2009: 521)
   a. kaki-komu
      write-insert
      'to write in'
   b. tobi-agaru
      jump-rise
      'to jump up'
   c. nomi-aruku
      drink-walk
      'go around drinking'

The lexical compounds are contrasted with the syntactic compounds, 'Type B'. These are similar to the lexical compounds in that they are formed from two verbs, the first of which is generally in a bound stem form. The head verb is restricted, however, to one of about 30 verbs, with mainly phasic or aspectual meaning (the *Compound Verb Lexicon* lists meanings such as inception, continuation, completion, incompletion, retrial, habitual as well as reciprocal, potential and excessive action). Kageyama (2009: 522) also lists examples based on stative predicates with adjective-like meanings, *-tai* and *-asui*. Examples are shown in (41).

(41) Japanese 'Type B' syntactic compounds (Kageyama 2009: 521)
   a. *kaki-hazimeru* 'begin to write'
   b. *tabe-oeru* 'finish eating'
   c. *syaberi-tuzukeru* 'continue speaking'
   d. *ugoki-dasu* 'begin to move'
   e. *tasuke-au* 'help each other'
   f. *tobe-sokoneru* 'miss eating'
   g. *tabe-kakeru* 'be about to eat'
   h. *tabe-sugiru* 'overeat'
   i. *iki-tai* 'eager to go'
   j. *yomi-asui* 'easy to read'

The syntactic V V compounds are productive and compositional, and thus come closer to the canonical ideal than do the semantically idiosyncratic, non-productive lexical compounds. However, the syntactic compounds also have properties that make them non-canonical as words, namely they exhibit lexical and phrasal transparency (Kageyama 1989: 79–81). Inbound anaphora with the VP anaphoric element *soo* combined with the verb stem *si-* from SURU 'do', is possible with syntactic compounds, (42), but not with lexical compounds, (43).

(42) soo   si-hazimeru/tuzukeru/tai
     so   do-begin/continue/be.eager
     'begin/continue/eager to (be) so'
     Cf. *soo mo* [*si-hazimeru*] 'begin to do so too', with *mo* 'too, also'

(43) tobi-agaru ≠ *soo si-ageru
 jump-rise   so do-rise
 'jump up'

Japanese also has a multiword honorific construction in which the *-i* form of the verb stem is prefixed with the honorific *o-* formative and suffixed with *-ni*, while the tense-mood-polarity inflections are placed on the light verb NARU. Thus, corresponding to *tabeta* '... ate [plain]' we would have *o-tabe-ni natta* '(someone of higher status) ate'. Such honorification is possible with syntactic compounds (44a), but not with lexical compounds (44b) (Kageyama 1989: 81–3).

(44) a. kaki-hazimeru ⇒ o-kaki-ni   nari   hazimeru
     write-begin   O-write-NI   NARU   begin
     'begin to write'
  b. osi-taosu   ⇒ *o-osi-ni   nari   taosu
     push-down   O-push-NI   NARU   down
     'push down'

The *soo si-* anaphoric construction and the honorification construction when applied to the syntactic compounds constitute violations of the compounding criterion C1, but respect the phrase criterion P2.

Finally, Kageyama (1989: 83–4) notes that it is possible to compound the passive form of a dependent verb in a syntactic V V compound (45a), while this is impossible with a lexical compound (45b).

(45) a. yomi-hazimeru ⇒ yom-are-hazimeru
     read-begin   read-PASS-begin
     'begin to read'   'begin to be written'
  b. kaki-komu   ⇒ *kak-are-komu
     write-insert   write-PASS-insert
     'write in'

Application of a fully productive morphological process such as Japanese passive formation to the non-head of a compound represents a clear violation of lexical opacity and hence of compound criterion C1.

Finally, I briefly mention one further construction type that seems to be related to verb-headed compounds, the serial verb construction (SVC), well known from the languages of Asia, Papua New Guinea, West Africa and elsewhere. Haspelmath (2016: 292) characterises a SVC as 'a monoclausal construction consisting of multiple independent verbs with no element linking them and with no predicate–argument relation between the verbs'. He cites the examples in (46)–(48).

(46) Dagaare (Gur group) (Haspelmath 2016)
  ò   dà   sɛ́   lá   nénè   ɔ́ɔ́
  3SG PST roast FOC meat   eat
  'He roasted meat and ate it.'

(47) Cantonese (Haspelmath 2016)
   keoi⁵ haam³-sap¹-zo   go   zam²tau⁴
   she   cry-wet-PFV   CLF   pillow
   'She made her pillow wet by crying.'

(48) Nêlêma (Haspelmath 2016)
   i   fuk   ulep   daxi   ni   fwaa-mwa
   3SG   fly   cross.threshold   up.away   in   hole-house
   'It flies into the house.'

The SVC behaves as though it were a single clause, for instance with respect to polarity specification (negation), often with respect to tense-aspect-mood specification, and also with respect to valency, in the sense that we usually see 'subject sharing' and often see 'object sharing' across the SVC. The SVC is also said to express a 'single event', though pinning down just what that means is somewhat controversial (Foley 2010; see also Haspelmath 2016: 306).

Certain types of SVC construction are reminiscent of a copulative or coordinative compound with other categories, in that in some languages the components of the SVC are typically juxtaposed, as though forming a compound verb, as seen in the Cantonese example, (47). However, this is neither a typical nor a canonical property of SVCs, and so I will assume that compound verbs but not SVCs respect compound criterion C4. On the other hand, we might find it difficult to distinguish copulative or coordinative verb-verb compounds from SVCs (canonical or otherwise). I leave this matter open.[21]

2.7 Conclusions

Compounds are canonically MWEs which function as single words with respect to syntax. They thus respect the principles that make the internal structure of words invisible to syntactic processes, lexical integrity and lexical opacity. By virtue of lexical integrity parts of compounds cannot be displaced or elided. By lexical opacity parts of compounds cannot be externally modified, nor can they govern externally represented dependents. At the same time a canonical compound consists of at least two forms each realising a distinct lexeme. The relationship between the two lexemes must be one mandated by general syntactic and semantic principles. This means that canonical compounds (like canonical phrases) are built on the principle of dependency, which requires that exactly one of the members be the head. Hence, for this reason alone, exocentric compounds have to be regarded as non-canonical. In some cases, canonical compounding gives rise to a construction expressing a grammatical dependency which is comparable to that realised by a syntactic phrase formed from the same lexemes, as when an attributive adjective is compounded with a head noun or a noun is incorporated as the direct object of a verb head. In other cases, the relation may not appear fully canonical, as in the case of modification-by-noun. It is not canonical for a noun to serve as the attributive modifier of another noun, whether in a compound or in a syntactic phrase, but in both cases, by default, the modification is mediated by a contextually defined relation, so that the internal grammatical relations inside the compound again mirror those of a phrase.

An important canonical property of phrases which compounds inherit is that of recursion, here understood in the weakest sense, namely that compounds are canonically permitted inside compounds. This is most clearly seen with noun-headed compounds. In practice, other factors may render even weak recursion uncommon in certain types of compounds (perhaps, for instance, in the case of V V compounds), just as in the case of certain types of NP (Widmer et al. 2017).

The canonical characterisation of compounds raises a number of questions for future research. I have given short shrift to exocentric compounding, but it might be interesting to establish just exactly how far exocentric compounds deviate from canonicity (assuming that sufficient agreement could be reached on what expressions in a given language can justifiably be labelled as compounds in the first place). I have likewise made only passing mention of copulative or coordinative compounds (Olsen 2001), even though there is much to say about them, and interesting questions might arise concerning their canonical properties. It would be important to have a statement of canonical coordination for the major lexical classes and their phrasal projections, and to compare these with coordinative or copulative compounds. In this connection it would be useful to see a canonical definition of serial verb constructions and their relationship to compounds and to phrase coordinate constructions (Li, 2018).

A number of questions surrounding compounds can perhaps best be answered by developing canonical criteria for related constructions. These would include canonical attributive modification of nouns and canonical modification-by-noun (as explored by Nikolaeva and Spencer 2013), canonical NP structure generally, and canonical modification of verb heads.

Finally, I have left open the question of lexical transparency and compoundhood: why is it that the non-head of a compound behaves on a par with the base lexeme of a derived lexeme in remaining opaque to syntactic processes such as attributive modification? It is clearly an important word-like characteristic of compounds and I have reflected this stipulatively by saying that a canonical compound respects lexical opacity. No doubt a more thoroughgoing comparison between derivation and compounding on the one hand in contrast to phrase formation on the other would throw light on the question.

One lesson to be drawn from the Canonical Typology exercise applied to compounding is the more general point elaborated on in detail in Spencer (2013) in the context of lexical relatedness, namely that traditional linguistic categorisation frequently needs to be replaced by a taxonomy defined over more fine-grained categories. The canonical criteria of Canonical Typology naturally provide such categories. One direction for typology research would therefore be to replace typologies based on coarse-grained categories with multifactor typologies based on the canonical criteria. Thus, put crudely, we might deploy a Canonical Typology-motivated categorisation to define sets of compound types along the lines 'compounds which violate C1, ..., C_i, ...', 'compounds which respect P1, ..., P_j, ...', and so forth. For instance, we could in this fashion include Finnish case-marked N N compounds, English composite nominals, Japanese syntactic V V compounds and other such controversial types without being obliged to lump them together as just 'compounds' for all our descriptive purposes. This strategy would also permit us to include non-canonical types such as exocentric compounds, or non-productive, non-compositional types such as English A N compounds, without distorting the taxonomy.

Such a strategy is, of course, highly sensitive to the quality of the descriptions available. It is surely premature to undertake such a project given our current datasets (one of the lessons, as I see it, of the Morbo project). However, a (suitably refined) set of criteria for compoundhood should be able to serve as the basis for the construction of appropriate model-driven datasets by guiding the research community to ask more sophisticated questions about individual languages and about cross-linguistic comparisons. In that way, we might see developed a third Canonical Typology strategy, under which a retrospective typology motivates the construction of datasets, i.e. a base, suitable for developing a multifactor exploratory typology.

In sum, the canonical approach to the characterisation of one specific and somewhat paradoxical subtype of word, the compound, is a promising way of cutting through some of the conceptual confusion and disagreement which surrounds this notion. Nonetheless, our brief survey of compounding has revealed that there remain a good many interesting questions in our quest for a characterisation of the possible word.

Acknowledgements

I am grateful to the editors and an anonymous referee for comments on an earlier draft of this paper.

Notes

1. It is also possible that this is not true of some or all of those notions mentioned, of course. An important challenge in linguistics is to find ways of making such ontological questions empirical rather than the subject of theory-internal 'just-so' stories.
2. See Bauer (2016) for discussion of exocentric compounds.
3. The MorboComp project description can be found at <http://morbocomp.sslmit.unibo.it> (last accessed 12 February 2017). See also Guevara et al. (n.d.).
4. Note that these are arguably just canonical properties of linguistic expressions generally. I include them because, for many observers, lexicalisation and non-compositionality are prototypical properties of compounds. They are not, however, canonical.
5. It would appear that criterion W6 ought to follow from more general criteria, perhaps governing the canonical definitions of 'lexeme' and 'word form', but I have been unable to find a satisfactory formulation.
6. Exocentric compounds do not respect the PIT, however, precisely because they are not headed. This is one of the reflexes of their non-canonicity as compounds.
7. Widmer et al. (2017) deploy an intermediate sense of recursion. For them, recursion has to be possible on the left branch of right-headed compounds, so that [*student film*] *club*]] 'a club for showing student films' (e.g. in a Film and Theatre Studies Department) would instantiate recursion, but [*student* [*film club*]] 'a film club for students' would not. I leave

it open whether Widmer et al.'s stronger definition is appropriate as a canonical criterion, and restrict myself to consideration of the weakest type. Huddleston and Pullum (2002: 450–1) explicitly argue against recursion in compounds (or in morphology generally), and claim that putative recursion in English compounds is only found with their 'composite nominals', which they take to be ordinary syntactically formed phrases (see §2.6). Clearly, however, examples such as Chukchi noun incorporation show that recursion in the weakest sense adopted here is, indeed, possible in morphology. This weakens the case for treating expressions such as *student film club* as syntactic phrases and not as genuine compounds.

8. For a summary of German compounding, see Der Große Duden (2006: 720–6).
9. The examples in (11) are taken from <https://www.bergwelten.com/h/holledauerhuette>, <http://www.schwarzwaldbahn-erlebnispfad.de/index.php?id=324> and <https://de.wikipedia.org/wiki/Alpthal> (all last accessed 14 March 2018). I have just given examples of uniformly left-branching compounds but right or mixed branching is also possible, as in English, for instance [[Bund-es]=[bildung-s=ministerium]] 'Federal Education Ministry' (Der Große Duden 2006: 725).
10. Care is needed here because so many verbs in English can be converted into nouns. Scalise and Bisetto (2009: 53) cite *playground* as an instance of a V N compound, for example, but it is more plausible to assume that *play* is a noun here (to the extent that it makes any sense to ask what the category is of a morphosyntactically inert component).
11. There are sometimes also tonal differences and/or shift in vowel type between lax/tense articulations. These are not indicated in the standard orthography.
12. Lewis (1967: 50–2) notes that Ottoman bureaucratic Turkish imported and coined a large number of compounds modelled on or borrowed directly from the Persian ezāfe construction. The dependency relations of the Persian idiom are exactly the opposite of those of Turkish, of course. Most of these Persian ezāfes have been incorporated as lexicalised units and are generally written as a single word. They are therefore a kind of non-canonical lexicalised compound.
13. See also Koptjevskaja-Tamm (2004) for discussion of the 'compounding' function of Lithuanian genitives with non-anchoring, i.e. non-referential functions.
14. And in any case, as Kenesei (2007) stresses, it is an overstatement to say that morphological constructions resist the kind of elision seen in (30). Not only can we find conjoined prefixes, as in *pre- and post-war*, we also find that a single affix can scope over coordinated bases. In English this is rather restricted (*fox- or dog-like* might be an instance, if *-like* is considered a suffix and not the head of a compound), but in other languages it is attested in both inflection and derivation, and is often referred to under the heading of 'suspended affixation'. Kenesei (2007: 270) cites German *trink- und ess-bar* 'drinkable and edible' (lit. '[drink- and eat-]able') and Hungarian *ajtó- és ablak-talan* 'door- and window-less' (whose English translation equivalent sounds acceptable, too).
15. It would be interesting to see a study specifically of NI conducted within the Canonical Typology framework.
16. Baker (1988) proposed that some NI was syntactic and some lexical but this was couched in the now defunct framework of Government-Binding theory, which permitted both possibilities. In Minimalism there is, in effect, no morphology and no lexicon of an appropriate kind over which to define the notion 'lexical compound'.
17. Indeed, it used to be written *radfahren*, as one word beginning with lower case 'r', like a verb, not the noun 'Rad'.
18. Van Geenhoven (1998: 147–59) provides a lexical, i.e. a non-syntactic, analysis of these constructions.

19. This blatantly counter-exemplifies the 'head-movement' analysis of Baker (1988), of course.
20. Available at <http://vvlexicon.ninjal.ac.jp/en/> (last accessed 12 September 2018).
21. For a characterisation of SVSs in terms of Canonical Typology see Li (2018).

References

Ackerman, Farrel and Philip LeSourd (1997), 'Toward a lexical representation of phrasal predicates', in Alex Alsina, Joan Bresnan and Peter Sells (eds), *Complex Predicates*, Stanford, CA: CSLI Publications, pp. 67–106.
Baker, Mark C. (1988), *Incorporation: A Theory of Grammatical Function Changing*, Chicago: University of Chicago Press.
Bauer, Laurie 2016, 'Re-evaluating exocentricity in word-formation', in Daniel Siddiqi and Heidi Harley (eds), *Morphological Metatheory*, Amsterdam: John Benjamins, pp. 461–77.
Bisetto, Antonietta and Sergio Scalise (2005), 'The classification of compounds', *Lingue e Linguaggio*, 4, pp. 319–32.
Bond, Oliver (2013), 'A base for canonical negation', in Dunstan P. Brown, Marina Chumakina and Greville G. Corbett (eds), *Canonical Morphology and Syntax*, Oxford: Oxford University Press, pp. 20–47.
Bond, Oliver (2018), 'Canonical Typology', in Jenny Audring and Francesca Masini (eds), *The Oxford Handbook of Morphological Theory*, Oxford: Oxford University Press.
Brown, Dunstan P. and Marina Chumakina (2013), 'What there might be and what there is: An introduction to Canonical Typology', in Dunstan P. Brown, Marina Chumakina and Greville G. Corbett (eds), *Canonical Morphology and Syntax*, Oxford: Oxford University Press, pp. 1–19.
Brown, Dunstan P., Marina Chumakina, Greville G. Corbett, Gergana D. Popova and Andrew Spencer (2012), 'Defining "periphrasis": Key notions', *Morphology*, 22, pp. 233–75.
Ceccagno, Antonella and Basilio Basciano (2007), 'Compound headedness in Chinese: An analysis of neologisms', *Morphology*, 17, pp. 207–31.
Clark, Eve V. (1998), 'Morphology in language acquisition', in Andrew Spencer and Arnold Zwicky (eds), *The Handbook of Morphology*, Oxford: Blackwell, pp. 374–89.
Clark, Eve V. and Barbara Frant Hecht (1982), 'Learning to coin agent and instrument nouns', *Cognition*, 12, pp. 1–24.
Corbett, Greville G. (2006), *Agreement*, Cambridge: Cambridge University Press.
Corbett, Greville G. (2007), 'Canonical typology, suppletion, and possible words', *Language*, 83 (1), pp. 8–42.
Creissels, Denis (2009), 'Construct forms of nouns in African languages', in Peter K. Austin, Oliver Bond, Monica Charette, David Nathan and Peter Sells (eds), *Proceedings of Conference on Language Documentation and Linguistic Theory 2*, London: SOAS, pp. 73–82.
Der große Duden (2006), *Die Grammatik. Band 4*, Mannheim, Leipzig, Vienna and Zürich: Bibliographisches Institut and F. A. Brockhaus.
Dunn, Michael. J. (1999), *A Grammar of Chukchi*, PhD thesis, Australian National University.
Fitch, W. Tecumseh (2010), 'Three meanings of "recursion": Key distinctions for biolinguistics', in Richard K. Larson, Vivianne Déprez and Hiroko Yamakido (eds), *The Evolution of Human Language*, Cambridge: Cambridge University Press, pp. 73–91.
Foley, William A. (2010), 'Events and serial verb constructions', in Mengistu Amberber,

Brett Baker and Mark Harvey (eds), *Complex Predicates: Cross-Linguistic Perspectives on Event Structure*, Cambridge: Cambridge University Press, pp. 79–109.

Gerdts, Donna. B. (1998), 'Incorporation', in Andrew Spencer and Arnold Zwicky (eds), *Handbook of Morphology*, Oxford: Blackwell, pp. 84–100.

Göksel, Aslı and Celia Kerslake (2005), *Turkish: A Comprehensive Grammar*, London: Routledge.

Guevara, Emiliano and Sergio Scalise (2009), 'Searching for universals in compounding', in Sergio Scalise, Elisabetta Magni and Antonietta Bisetto (eds), *Universals of Language Today*, Dordrecht: Springer, pp. 101–28.

Guevara, Emiliano, Sergio Scalise, Antonietta Bisetto and Chiara Melloni (n.d.), 'MORBO/COMP: A multilingual database of compound words', <lingvr.univr.it/live/people/Chiara/guevara-etal_morbocomp_Downloadable.pdf> (last accessed 12 February 2017).

Haspelmath, Martin (2016), 'The serial verb construction: Comparative concept and crosslinguistic generalizations', *Language and Linguistics*, 17 (3), pp. 291–319.

Huddleston, Rodney and Geoffrey K. Pullum (2002), *The Cambridge Grammar of the English Language*, Cambridge: Cambridge University Press.

Kageyama, Taro (1989), 'The place of morphology in the grammar: Verb-verb compounds in Japanese', in Geert Booij and Jaap van Marle (eds), *Yearbook of Morphology 2*, Dordrecht: Kluwer, pp. 73–94.

Kageyama, Taro (1999), 'Word formation', in Natsuko Tsujimura (ed.), *Handbook of Japanese Linguistics*, Oxford: Blackwell, pp. 297–325.

Kageyama, Taro (2001), 'Word plus: The intersection of words and phrases', in Jeroen van der Weijer and Tetsuo Nishihara (eds), *Issues in Japanese Phonology and Morphology*, Berlin: Mouton de Gruyter, pp. 245–76.

Kageyama, Taro (2009), 'Isolate: Japanese', in Rochelle Lieber and Pavol Štekauer (eds), *The Oxford Handbook of Compounding*, Oxford: Oxford University Press, pp. 512–26.

Kalnača, Aandra and Ilze Lokmane (2016), 'Compound genitives in Latvian', in Lívia Körtvélyessy, Pavol Štekauer and Salvador Valera (eds), *Word-Formation across Languages*, Cambridge: Cambridge Scholars Press, pp. 169–96.

Karlsson, Fred (1987), *Finnish Grammar*, 2nd edn, Helsinki: Werner Söderström Osakeyhtiö.

Kenesei, Istvan (2007), 'Semiwords and affixoids: The territory between word and affix', *Acta Linguistica Hungarica*, 54, pp. 263–93.

Koptjevskaja-Tamm, Maria (2004), '"Maria's ring of gold": Adnominal possession and nonanchoring relations in the European languages', in Ji-Yung Kim, Yuri Lander and Barbara H. Partee (eds), *Possessives and Beyond: Semantics and Syntax*, Amherst, MA: GLSA Publications, pp. 155–81.

Kürschner, Sebastian and Renata Szczepaniak (2013), 'Linking elements—origin, change, and functionalization', *Morphology*, 23, pp. 1–6.

Lambton, Ann K. S. (1963), *Persian Grammar*, Cambridge: Cambridge University Press.

Lewis, Geoffrey L. (1967), *Turkish Grammar*, Oxford: Clarendon Press.

Li, Tianyu (2018), The Serial Verb Construction. Unpublished PhD thesis, University of Essex.

Miner, Kenneth (1986), 'Noun stripping and loose incorporation in Zuni', *International Journal of American Linguistics*, 52, pp. 242–54.

Mithun, Marianne (1984), 'The evolution of noun incorporation', *Language*, 60 (4), pp. 847–93.

Mithun, Marianne (1986), 'On the nature of noun incorporation', *Language*, 62 (1), pp. 32–7.

Nikolaeva, Irina and Andrew Spencer (2013), 'Canonical Typology and the Possession-Modification Scale', in Dunstan P. Brown, Marina Chumakina and Greville G. Corbett (eds), *Canonical Morphology and Syntax*, Oxford: Oxford University Press, pp. 207–38.

Olsen, Susan (2001), 'Copulative compounds: A closer look at the interface between syntax and morphology', in Geert Booij and Jaap van Marle (eds), *Yearbook of Morphology 2000*, Dordrecht: Kluwer, pp. 279–320.

Rosen, Sara (1989), 'Two types of noun incorporation: A lexical analysis', *Language*, 64, pp. 294–317.

Sadler, Louisa and Doug Arnold (1994), 'Prenominal adjectives and the phrasal/lexical distinction', *Journal of Linguistics*, 30, pp. 187–226.

Sadock, Jerrold M. (1980), 'Noun incorporation in Greenlandic', *Language*, 56, pp. 300–19.

Sadock, Jerrold M. (1986), 'Some notes on noun incorporation', *Language*, 62, pp. 19–32.

Scalise, Sergio and Antonietta Bisetto (2009), 'The classification of compounds', in Rochelle Lieber and Pavol Štekauer (eds), *The Oxford Handbook of Compounding*, Oxford: Oxford University Press, pp. 34–53.

Spencer, Andrew (1991), *Morphological Theory: An Introduction to Word Structure in Generative Grammar*, Oxford: Blackwell.

Spencer, Andrew (1995), 'Incorporation in Chukchi', *Language*, 71, pp. 439–89.

Spencer, Andrew (2011), 'What's in a compound?' Review article on Lieber and Štekauer (eds), 2009. "The Oxford Handbook of Compounding"', *Journal of Linguistics*, 47, pp. 481–507.

Spencer, Andrew (2013), *Lexical Relatedness: A Paradigm-Based Model*, Oxford: Oxford University Press.

Spencer, Andrew and Ana R. Luís (2013), 'The canonical clitic', in Dunstan P. Brown, Marina Chumakina and Greville G. Corbett (eds), *Canonical Morphology and Syntax*, Oxford: Oxford University Press, pp. 123–50.

Tucker, A. N. (1994), *A Grammar of Kenya Luo (Dholuo)*, Cologne: Rüdiger Köppe.

van Geenhoven, Veerle (1998), *Semantic Incorporation and Indefinite Descriptions*, Stanford, CA: CSLI Publications.

Widmer, Manuel, Sandra Auderset, Johanna Nichols, Paul Widmer and Balthasar Bickel (2017), 'NP recursion over time: Evidence from Indo-European', *Language*, 93, pp. 799–826.

3

How (Non-)canonical Is Italian Morphology?

Anna M. Thornton

3.1 Canonical Inflection

3.1.1 Preamble

This paper attempts to give an overview of the inflectional morphology of Italian adopting the point of view of Canonical Typology. Most of the material is relatively well known (although new analyses are proposed for certain verb forms in §3.3.3.3.1, and new interpretations for other phenomena are discussed in §3.3.3.2 and §3.3.4.2.3). What is at least partly original is the perspective adopted: I look at well-known phenomena from a well-described language with the aim of assessing their degree of canonicity. The results should ideally be compared with those obtained for other languages by applying the same method. It is my hope that this paper will stimulate other scholars to provide these comparable data. Another contribution of the paper lies in an attempt to apply mathematical measures to assess the canonicity of certain phenomena. Last but not least, this is a piece of Corbettian philology, in that it draws attention to how each phenomenon is defined in Corbett's work, and to how certain definitions have changed in diachrony (the canonical approach to the description of inflection has been adopted by Corbett since 2005, and major refinements have been proposed in Corbett 2015).

The paper is organised as follows: after a presentation of Corbett's view of canonical inflection in §3.1.2, §3.2 gives an overview of Italian inflection. §3.3 describes deviations across the cells of single lexemes (alternations and suppletion; syncretism and uninflectability; fused exponence; periphrasis; featural inconsistency). §3.4 describes deviations across lexemes (homonymy; inflectional classes, heteroclisis and deponency; a possible case of antiperiphrasis; defectiveness); this section concludes by discussing possible alternative analyses of certain adjectival paradigms, that can be seen either as cases of syncretism or as cases of featural inconsistency. §3.5 offers some concluding remarks.[1]

3.1.2 Corbett's View of Canonical Inflection

Greville G. Corbett has worked on a definition of canonical inflection since at least 2005 (see at least Corbett 2005, 2007a, 2007b), and offers a refinement of his definition in Corbett (2015). The properties of a fully canonical inflectional paradigm, in Corbett's work, are presented by means of tables that illustrate the requirements for the composition/structure of inflectional forms (a concept that will be clarified below), and the lexical material and inflectional material appearing in the inflected forms occupying each cell, at two levels: across cells of a single lexeme (where composition/structure and lexical material are canonically the same in all cells, and inflectional material is canonically different in each cell), and across lexemes (where, obviously, lexical material is canonically different, while composition/structure of each cell and inflectional material in each cell with a given morphosyntactic specification are canonically the same). When these requirements are met, the outcome is a different form in each cell of each lexeme. Corbett (2015: 151) observes that '[t]he same result can be achieved by recasting the requirements as properties of the system', and attributes this approach to Thornton (then unpublished; see Thornton forthcoming) and Stump (2012).[2] Indeed, both Thornton and Stump openly acknowledge that listing 'properties of the system' is a 'paraphrase' of Corbett's work (Stump 2012: 255); in my case, I must confess that recasting the requirements for canonical paradigms in terms of global 'properties of the system', rather than separate specifications for composition/structure, lexical material and inflectional material, was done mostly to save space in the presentation; I felt confident with this move because Corbett himself pursued this line in early presentations, and occasionally also in more recent work:

> We might [expect] that for any given lexeme, every cell of its paradigm will be filled by the inflectional system (**completeness**), each form will be defined (**distinctiveness**), the stem will be predictable, and the inflections will be predictable. (Corbett 2005: 33; emphasis mine; see also Figure 5 in Corbett 2005: 34)
>
> [I]f a given language has four cases and three numbers in its nominal system, the paradigm of a noun should have twelve cells. (This is equivalent to Spencer's notion of **exhaustivity** [. . .]). (Corbett 2007a: 9; emphasis mine)

So, a space-saving way of presenting the requirements for canonical inflection is the one in Table 3.1 (adapted from Thornton forthcoming), where the properties of canonical paradigms are listed in the first column and succinctly explained in the second, while in the third column traditional or recently proposed names for phenomena that violate each property are given.[3]

Another apparent advantage of the style of presentation adopted in Table 3.1 and by Stump (2012) is that it provides labels, often consisting of a single word, for each canonical property. On the other hand, as Corbett has often warned us, labels run the risk of obscuring similarities between phenomena listed under different labels, and differences between phenomena ranged under the same label; besides, there is the risk of overlooking phenomena for which there is no label (cf. Corbett 2007b: 21).

Table 3.1 Properties of canonical inflection

Property of a canonical paradigm	Definition	Violations
Complete	Every cell contains a form	Defectiveness
Distinctive	Every cell contains a different form	Syncretism Uninflectability
Predictable	(a) The form of the stem is predictable	Stem allomorphy Suppletion
	(b) The form of the inflection is predictable	Inflectional classes Heteroclisis Deponency
Synthetic	Every cell contains a single word-form	Periphrasis
Uniform	All paradigms in a given part of speech have the same structure and the same number of cells	Overdifferentiation

An illustration of how a label has at first obscured distinctions to be made, within the history of the application of the canonical approach to inflectional morphology, concerns the label 'Composition/structure'. Corbett (2007a: 9) employs this label without defining it. The label occurs first in his Table 1 and is clarified only by means of an example a few lines later: if a cell of a given lexeme hosts a form composed of a stem and a prefix, 'for the lexeme to have a canonical paradigm, every other cell must be the "same" in this regard' (Corbett 2007a: 10). Further tokens of the label in the same paper, however, show that something more than just 'uniformity of exponence' (to use Stump's paraphrase) is hidden behind it. Commenting on the inflection of the present tense of 'go' in some Romanian dialects, which alternate synthetic forms in 1PL and 2PL and periphrastic forms in the remaining cells, Corbett (2007a: 31) states that 'this means that the composition/structure of cells is not the same throughout the paradigm of this lexeme': this shows that at this stage the periphrastic realisation of certain cells, i.e. the absence of uniformity in the means of exponence employed, is conceived of as a difference in 'composition/structure' of the cells within a paradigm (rather than as a violation of a separate requirement of 'synthetic realisation', as proposed for instance in Table 3.1). A few lines below, however, a completely different phenomenon is ranged under the violations of (uniformity of) 'composition/structure': in Kolami, the numerals 'two', 'three' and 'four' have three different forms (for agreement with 'male human', 'female human' and 'other'), while all other agreement targets have only two forms (for 'male human' and 'other'). Corbett (2007a: 31) comments: 'the composition of the paradigm is not the same across lexemes (some have an additional cell)' – so here a completely different phenomenon from that captured by the distinction between synthetic vs periphrastic realisation is still ranged under a difference in 'composition/structure'.

In subsequent papers, 'paraphrases' of the label 'composition/structure' are offered: 'means of exponence' in Corbett (2007b: 24), 'morphotactics' in Corbett (2009: 2). Both these paraphrases imply that differences in the morphemic make-up of a form, or in synthetic vs periphrastic realisation, are violations of 'composition/ structure', while a difference in the number and/or kinds of feature values expressed (like in the Kolami case) does not seem to belong here (contrary to what is said in Corbett 2007a: 31).

The puzzle is solved in Corbett (2015), where the factor 'composition/structure' is split into two distinct ones, called 'composition' and 'feature signature'.[4] 'Composition' is reserved to refer to the 'structural pattern' of exponence:

> Exponence (within a lexeme, and across lexemes) 'should' be according to the same structural pattern, for instance, if the first-person singular is constructed from a stem and a suffix, it would not be canonical for the second-person singular to consist of prefix plus stem. (Corbett 2015: 153)

Another paraphrase makes it clear that to be canonical in composition inflected forms should be 'built in the same way' (Corbett 2015: 153). 'Feature signature', instead, deals with the 'morphosyntactic requirements' realised by inflected forms:

> The feature signature can be thought of as an abstract feature specification: we may say, for instance, that cells in a given paradigm realize a selection from a fixed set of values belonging to a fixed set of features. The feature specifications of the individual cells vary, of course, but within the possibilities defined by the features and their values (the feature signature). (Corbett 2015: 154–5)

A distinction between these two levels is certainly welcome. After its institution, Corbett (2015) can offer a more articulate typology of the possible deviations from canonicity in inflectional paradigms. I recapitulate Corbett's factors, canonicity values, and labels for the different deviations in Tables 3.2 and 3.3 (based on Tables 4, 5, 7, 8, 9 and 10 in Corbett 2015).

The list of deviations in Tables 3.2 and 3.3 probably does not exhaust the possible types of non-canonical behaviour that inflectional paradigms may show. For example, Thornton (2011, 2012a, 2012b, forthcoming) has defined and investigated a further non-canonical phenomenon in inflectional paradigms, overabundance, i.e.

Table 3.2 Deviations from canonicity established by comparison across the cells of a lexeme

Factor	Canonical behaviour	Types of deviation
Lexical material (≈ shape of stem)	Same	Alternations Suppletion
Inflectional material (≈ shape of affix)	Different	Syncretism Uninflectability
Composition (≈ means of exponence)	Same	Affixal inconsistency, e.g. fused exponence, periphrasis
Feature signature (≈ morphosyntactic requirement)	Same	Featural inconsistency

Table 3.3 Deviations from canonicity established by comparison across lexemes

Factor	Canonical behaviour	Types of deviation
Lexical material (≈ shape of stem)	Different	Homonymy
Inflectional material (≈ shape of affix)	Same	Inflectional classes Heteroclisis Deponency
Composition (≈ means of exponence)	Same	Affixal inconsistency Antiperiphrasis
Feature signature (≈ morphosyntactic requirement)	Same	Featural inconsistency, e.g. defectiveness, overdifferentiation

the situation in which two (or more) inflectional forms are available to realise the same cell in an inflectional paradigm. This phenomenon does not fit easily in Tables 3.2 and 3.3. It should ideally appear in both tables, because overabundance can be detected both by comparing cells within a single lexeme (e.g. Italian SEPPELLIRE 'bury' is overabundant in its PST.PTCP cell, not in any other cell) and by comparing cells with the same morphosyntactic specification across lexemes (e.g. Italian 'bury' is overabundant in its PST.PTCP cell, while most other Italian verbs are not overabundant in this cell). Besides, for overabundance to occur, the two or more forms that realise the same morphosyntactic specification must differ from each other in one of the ways listed in Tables 3.2 and 3.3, for example by exhibiting different stems, by belonging to different inflectional classes, by having synthetic exponence in one case and periphrastic exponence in the other, and so on (see Thornton forthcoming for a more detailed list of the different possibilities). Thornton (2012a: 252) observes that overabundance 'adds a dimension' to the two dimensions represented in Tables 3.2 and 3.3, and documents the fact that mention of the phenomenon appeared in some of Corbett's conference presentations of canonical inflection but was not included in his published papers. In this paper, I will not address overabundance, which I have extensively described in previous publications. I will adopt the typology of deviations from canonical inflection illustrated in Tables 3.2 and 3.3, and investigate which ones are attested in contemporary Italian.

3.2 Italian Inflection: Features and Values

Corbett often observes that for assessing the degree to which a given inflectional paradigm is canonical one must have preliminarily defined the features used by the language in question and their values ('the syntactic part of morphosyntax', Corbett 2007a: 9). In this section I give a brief description of Italian inflection (for more detailed presentations, see Iacobini and Thornton 2016; Vincent 1988).

Inflecting parts of speech in Italian are nouns, articles, adjectives, pronouns and verbs. Nouns have inherent GENDER (with two possible values: MASCULINE and FEMININE) and inflect for NUMBER (with two possible values: SINGULAR and PLURAL). Articles (and some other determiners, like demonstratives) and adjectives agree in GENDER and NUMBER with a head noun within a NP; possessives agree in gender and number with the possessed noun, and in person and number with the possessor; 3SG and some 3PL pronouns agree in GENDER and NUMBER with an antecedent NP; PST.PTCP in periphrastic verb forms built with the auxiliary ESSERE 'be' agree in GENDER and NUMBER with the subject NP; PST.PTCP in periphrastic verb forms built with the auxiliary AVERE 'have' agree in GENDER and NUMBER with a clitic DO (obligatorily with third person clitics, and optionally with first and second person ones). Articles are subject to shape conditions depending mostly on the phonological identity of the initial segment(s) of the following word; similar or identical shape conditions affect the prenominal distal demonstrative QUELLO 'that', the prenominal adjective BELLO 'beautiful' and the word SANTO 'Saint' when followed by a proper name. Pronouns inflect for PERSON, NUMBER and CASE; most third person pronouns also inflect for GENDER. There are two series of pronouns, stressed and clitic ones. Stressed pronouns distinguish two case values: SUBJECT vs NON-SUBJECT; there are no clitic subject pronouns, and clitic pronouns distinguish two case values, ACCUSATIVE and DATIVE; some clitic forms appear to express also various other functions, corresponding to case values like GENITIVE (*ne*), and various locative cases (*ci, ne*). The status of an ANIMACY or HUMANNESS distinction in third person pronouns is controversial (see Cappellaro 2017 for useful data on diachronic variation). Finite verb forms agree with their subjects in PERSON and NUMBER, and inflect for TENSE, ASPECT, MOOD (with verbal tenses often combining these three features) and VOICE; participles in periphrastic verb forms agree in GENDER and NUMBER as detailed above.

In §3.3 and §3.4 I will present an overview of the properties of Italian inflectional forms and paradigms, from the point of view of canonical inflection, presenting a catalogue of non-canonical phenomena encountered in Italian. I will not deal with articles and pronouns, not because their paradigms, small as they are, do not present interesting material, but rather because they offer such a wealth of material that they deserve a separate treatment. I will dwell more on nouns and adjectives than on verbs, to keep the descriptive part shorter (since nominal and adjectival paradigms have at most 4 cells, while verbs have at least 50 synthetic and 44 (if intransitive) or 88 (if transitive) periphrastic forms in the active conjugation, and at least 186 periphrastic forms in the passive[5]). Phenomena from verb paradigms will be generally sketched, for the sake of completeness; verbal forms will be discussed in detail only when I believe that an original analysis can be offered (as in §3.3.3.1).

3.3 Deviations across the Cells of a Lexeme

3.3.1 Alternations and Suppletion

Nouns have a two-cell paradigm, distinguishing SG vs PL NUMBER; cases in which the two cells host different stems exist, but are limited. There are three cases of weak suppletion: *uom-o/uomin-i* 'man', *di-o/de-i* 'god', *bu-e/buo-i* 'ox'. Systematic alternations fall into several categories. Nouns ending in /jo/ (orthographic <io>)

'should' have a plural in /ji/, but this sequence is reduced to /i/ (Camilli 1965: 93), e.g. *operaio/operai* 'workman', *dubbio/dubbi* 'doubt'; however, TEMPIO has *templi* as its most frequently used plural, alongside *tempi* (<tempi> is the orthographic representation of both /tempi/ 'temples', SG /tempjo/, and /tɛmpi/ 'times', SG /tɛmpo/, and Serianni 1988: III, §104 maintains that a wish for distinguishing the two forms explains the maintenance of the weakly suppletive plural *templi*). Another alternation is that between stem final /k/ or /g/ in the SG and /tʃ/ or /dʒ/ in the PL (e.g. SG /aˈmiko/ vs PL /aˈmitʃi/ 'friend', SG /kiˈrurgo/ vs PL /kiˈrurdʒi/ 'surgeon'): this is not systematic, as there are nouns that keep the velar consonants in both forms (e.g. SG /ombeˈliko/, PL /ombeˈliki/ 'navel'; SG /alˈbɛrgo/, PL /alˈbɛrgi/ 'hotel').

This alternation takes place also in adjectives; adjectives in *-ico* display it only if *-ico* is a derivational suffix (so, for example, not in FICO 'cool', PL /ˈfiki/; CARICO 'charged', PL /ˈkariki/). The adjective AMPIO 'ample' has a weakly suppletive stem *ampl-* which is used more frequently than the default stem in superlatives (*amplissimo* is much more frequent than *ampissimo*), and rarely even in positive forms (M.SG *amplio*, M.PL *ampli*).

Italian verb paradigms exhibit a wealth of alternations and several cases of suppletion, which have been very well described; see Pirrelli and Battista (2000) for extensive data and an analysis in terms of morphology by itself, and Iacobini and Thornton (2016: 198–201) for a quick overview.

3.3.2 Syncretism and Uninflectability

Syncretism and uninflectability have different status and different incidence in the three main parts of speech considered here.

There are no fully uninflectable verbs in Italian;[6] systematic syncretisms in verbal paradigms are the following (exemplified with forms of AMARE 'love' and/or DORMIRE 'sleep'):[7]

- 1/2/3.SG.PRS.SBJV *ami, dorma*
- 1PL.PRS.IND/SBJV *amiamo, dormiamo*
- 2PL.PST.IND/IMPF.SBJV *amaste, dormiste*
- 2PL.PRS.IND/IMP *amate, dormite*
- 3SG.PRS.IND/2SG.IMP *ama* in 1st conjugation
- 2SG.PRS.IND/1/2/3.SG.PRS.SBJV *ami* in 1st conjugation
- 2SG.PRS.IND/2SG.IMP *dormi* in non-1st conjugation.

A further case, 1/3SG.PST.IPFV *amava, dormiva*, was reduced around the end of the nineteenth century, and now 1SG.PST.IPFV is *amavo, dormivo* (by analogy with 1SG.PRS.IND *am-o, dorm-o*).

In Italian noun paradigms, syncretism and uninflectability cannot be distinguished: since the paradigm has two cells, syncretism between the SG and the PL form results in uninflectability of the lexeme. Uninflectable nouns (traditionally called *invariabili* 'invariable' in Italian dictionaries and grammars) are well attested in Italian, and their number is growing. D'Achille and Thornton (2003) show that in their corpus of Italian texts covering all stages of the language this class had 2.4 per cent of tokens and 2.7 per cent of types in the thirteenth century, and grew to 8.6 per cent of tokens and 9.5 per cent of types in the period 1969–2000.[8] At the time of writing (January 2017) I heard *i sisma* 'the earthquakes' and *le motoslitta* 'the snowmobiles' (lit. *moto-* 'motor' + *slitta* 'sleigh') on national TV news; in my competence, these plural forms would be *sismi* and *motoslitte*, but masculine nouns in inflectional class 4 like SISMA, and some compounds with neoclassical elements, like MOTOSLITTA, have been undergoing inflection class shift, towards the invariable class, for some time, as documented in D'Achille and Thornton (2003) and D'Achille (2005).[9]

Invariable adjectives also exist in Italian: in the Italian Basic Vocabulary, they form 1.9 per cent of the adjectival lemmata (of 1,129 adjectives; cf. Thornton et al. 1997: 74; Fedden, this volume). They are mostly monosyllabic adjectives, and loanwords (often both), such as BLU, CHIC, HALAL.[10] Turning to syncretism, Italian adjectival paradigms pose an analytical issue. Table 3.4 (adapted from Iacobini and Thornton 2016) shows inflectional classes of Italian adjectives. Recall that attributive adjectives agree in gender and number with a head noun, and predicative adjectives agree with a subject NP. Adjectives in class 1 have four different forms that overtly express all the possible combinations of agreement features (indeed, they are used by Corbett 2006: 9 as an example of canonical agreement). In all other classes, there appear to be cases of syncretism (up to complete syncretism, that results in uninflectability, in class 5). The question is whether we should treat the neutralisation of the gender opposition in class 2 and in the SG of class 3 as syncretism or as an instance of another non-canonical phenomenon, featural inconsistency across lexemes. This issue will be discussed in §3.4.4. The homonymy of M.SG and F.PL in Class 4 seems completely accidental, and a genuine case of syncretism; class 4 can be analysed as a case of heteroclisis, with M forms inflecting according to class 2 and F forms according to class 1; F forms in class 3 also behave like class 1 F forms.

If we assume that the homonymies in classes 2 and 3 are instances of syncretism, the data in the rightmost column in Table 3.4 (from *BDVDB*, a database of the Italian Basic Vocabulary; Thornton et al. 1997: 74) show that over a third of Italian adjectives have syncretism in their paradigm.

Table 3.4 Inflectional classes and endings of Italian adjectives

Class	M.SG	F.SG	M.PL	F.PL	Examples	% BDVDB
1	-o	-a	-i	-e	NUOVO 'new'	65.3
2	-e	-e	-i	-i	FORTE 'strong'	31.7
3	-a	-a	-i	-e	IDIOTA 'idiot'	0.9
4	-e	-a	-i	-e	SORNIONE 'sly'	0.1
5	–	–	–	–	PARI 'even'	1.9
					BLU 'blue'	
					CHIC 'chic'	

3.3.3 Affixal Inconsistency

3.3.3.1 Fused exponence

Before discussing whether Italian inflectional morphology presents cases of fused exponence, it is necessary to define this notion, which does not appear to be used in a completely consistent way in different sources. Matthews (1997: 140) defines fusion as '[a]ny process by which units, etc. that are separate at one level of representation are realized by a form in which there is no corresponding boundary'. This is a reasonable definition, which would include, for example, any unsegmentable form realising a cell of an inflectional paradigm that carries several morphosyntactic feature values, like the Italian verb forms analysed in §§3.3.3.1.1–3.3.3.1.5. In practice, however, Matthews (1997; see also Matthews 1991: 180) seems to restrict the usage of 'fusion' and 'fused marking' to cases in which a sandhi process obscures the boundary between two (or more) formatives, in a way that is synchronically or diachronically demonstrable: his example in the 1997 dictionary entry is English *fly-er*, which in some varieties is realised as [flaː] because '[ʌɪ] and [ə] are fused to a single long vowel [...]. The morphological units *fly* and *-er* may then be said to have fused exponents' (Matthews 1997: 140). Corbett's usage of the term 'fused exponence' does not seem to include the strict requirement that actual fusion of phonological material present at some level of representation has taken place. Corbett presents fused exponence as a situation in which 'the morphosyntactic distinctions are realized but not according [to] the pattern of the remaining paradigm' (2007b: 25), and 'it is not possible to distinguish stem and affix' (2007a: 14), as in English *worse*. I will adopt this less restrictive definition here.

In Italian nouns and adjectives there do not seem to be cases of genuine fused exponence – unless one wants to count cases that have already been considered as instances of uninflectability.

In verbs, instead, there are a number of potential cases. All of them are amenable to analyses that avoid recognising fused exponence, but they do so at the cost of invoking a considerable amount of zero exponents, even lexical ones. Let us review the cases. The four forms I will consider are listed in (1); other forms that must be considered to understand the analytical possibilities are listed in (2); a further candidate form is discussed in §3.3.3.1.5.

(1) Italian (personal knowledge): fused exponence?
   a. fu 'be.3SG.PST.PFV.IND'
   b. ha /a/ 'have.3SG.PRS.IND'
   c. è /ɛ/ 'be.3SG.PRS.IND'
   d. ho /ɔ/ 'have.1SG.PRS.IND'

(2) Italian (personal knowledge): forms for comparison
   a. fui 'be.1SG.PST.PFV.IND', furono 'be.3PL.PST.PFV.IND'
   b. amai 'love.1SG.PST.PFV.IND', amarono 'love.3PL.PST.PFV.IND'
   c. amò/temé/vide/sentì 'love/fear/see/hear.3SG.PST.PFV.IND'

d. ama 'love.3SG.PRS. IND' (1st conjugation verb)
e. vede /'vede/ 'see.3SG.PRS.IND' (non-1st conjugation verb)
f. sa, dà, sta, va, fa 'know/give/stay/go/do.3SG.PRS.IND'
g. so /sɔ/, do /sɔ/, sto /stɔ/, vo /vɔ/, fo /fɔ/ 'know/give/stay/go/do.1SG.PRS.IND'

3.3.3.1.1 *Fu* 'be.3SG.PST.PFV.IND' *Fu* can be analysed either as a bare (morphomic) stem, with a zero morph in place of an expected 3SG.PST.PFV ending (the expected form would be *fue*, a form that is attested in Old Italian but has gone out of usage), or as a fusional form, in which it is not possible to recognise a stem and an ending. Both analyses have pros and cons. A stem *fu-* can certainly be posited for the PST.PFV: compare *fu-i, fu-rono* in (2a) and *fu-mmo* 'be.1PL.PST.PFV.IND'. A zero ending (accompanied by stress on the final syllable), parallel to the one that would have to be posited for *fu* in this analysis, can be posited for forms such as *temè, sentì*, which appear to use the default stem (or a stem segmentally homophonous to it) accompanied by stress on the last syllable (of course *fu*, being monosyllabic, is stressed on its last (and only) syllable, although Italian spelling does not note this stress).[11] A difficulty arises, however, in considering *vide* 'see.PST.PFV.IND.3SG', which is clearly segmentable in stem (S5 in Pirrelli and Battista's 2000 system for distinguishing morphomic stems in Italian verbs) and ending (*vid-e*, cf. *vid-i* 'see.PST.PFV.IND-1SG'[12]), and *amò* ('love.PST.PFV.IND.3SG', taken as representative of thousands of regular 1st conjugation verbs), which is more naturally analysed as *am-ò*, with a default root and an ending which only appears in 1st conjugation 3SG.PST.PFV.IND forms. Traditional Italian grammars state that the verb 'be' has its own conjugation, and does not belong to any of the traditionally recognised conjugations (different forms seem to belong to different conjugations, at least if we look at the thematic vowels; for example, *er-a-vamo* 'be-THV-PST.IPFV.1PL' points to the 1st conjugation, where the THV is /a/ (it parallels *am-a-vamo* 'love-THV-PST.IPFV.1PL' rather than *ved-e-vamo* 'see-THV-PST.IPFV.1PL'), *ess-e-re* to the 2nd conjugation, where the THV is /e/ (it parallels *legg-e-re* 'read-THV-INF' rather than *am-a-re* 'love-THV-INF'), etc. So it is not clear what forms should be given more weight when trying to find an analysis for *fu* which has some parallel in the system. One could say that *fu* has a zero 3SG ending accompanied by stress, or a suprasegmental morph expressing 3SG, like *temè, sentì* (employing a different morphomic stem, however), or that it lacks a 3SG ending, as opposed to *amò, vide*. Depending on which factor is given more weight, we will analyse *fu* as fusional or as just displaying a zero ending.

This whole discussion gives a flavour of the problems involved, and probably helps to see why an inferential-realisational theory of morphology has advantages over a lexical one, since it does not compel us to take a stance on these segmentation issues.

However, the very concept of fusion as non-canonical behaviour presupposes that neat segmentability in stem and ending is the canonical behaviour. Therefore, to assess whether a specific form is an instance of fusion, we must carefully review the possibilities of segmentation. We will proceed to do so for the other candidates for fusion in §§3.3.3.1.2–3.3.3.1.4.

3.3.3.1.2 *Ha* 'have.3SG.PRS.IND' In *ha* 'have.3SG.PRS.IND', <h> is a purely orthographic element, which does not correspond to any phonological element. The form is /a/, i.e. it is a monophonemic form. This form coincides with the 3SG ending of 1st conjugation verbs (cf. (2b)). The verb 'have', like 'be', does not fully belong to any of the traditionally recognised conjugations, and inasmuch as it can be ascribed to one, this would be the 2nd conjugation and not the 1st (it displays the thematic vowel -*e*- in many forms, such as *av-e-re* 'have-THV-INF', *av-e-vamo* 'have-THV-PST.IPFV.1PL'). A few other verbs have monosyllabic 3SG.PRS.IND forms ending in -*a*, where a lexical stem can be segmented (2d), and all except 'go' (which is otherwise famous for the amount of suppletion in its paradigm) are heteroclitic to various degrees. If we analyse the forms in (2d) as *s-a* 'know-3SG' etc., we could analyse *ha* /a/ in a parallel way, as *Ø-a* 'have-3SG'. This analysis implies that 'have' has heteroclitic inflection ('3SG.PRS.IND' inflects according to the 1st conjugation, other forms according to the 2nd conjugation), and posits a rather uncommon instance of a zero lexical morph.

An alternative would be to analyse *ha* /a/ as a fusional form, in which it is not possible to distinguish lexical and inflectional material. Again, neither analysis avoids recognising some degree of non-canonicity, be it fusion or heteroclisis and zero lexical stems.

3.3.3.1.3 *È* 'be.3SG.PRS.IND' The analysis of *è* /ɛ/ has some points in common with the one just presented for *ha*. It is possible to analyse *è* /ɛ/ as a fusion of lexical and inflectional material, as this form is monophonemic. This analysis seems corroborated by the observation that /ɛ/ is not homophonous to any 3SG ending: 3SG endings used in PRS.IND forms are -*a* /a/ (in 1st conjugation verbs) or -*e* /e/ (elsewhere). So at first sight an analysis of *è* /ɛ/ as a case of fusion seems a possibility worth considering.

However, another analysis is possible. To understand it, it is necessary to bear in mind that standard Italian has seven vowels /i e ɛ a ɔ o u/ in stressed syllables, but the contrast between open-mid and closed-mid vowels is lost in unstressed syllables, where only the five vowels /i e a o u/ appear (open-mid vowels raise to closed-mid). 3SG.PRS.IND endings are unstressed, so the non-1st conjugation ending surfaces as /e/. But we could assume that it is underlyingly /ɛ/, and it is realised as [e] only because it is unstressed. If we accept this hypothesis, we could analyse *è* /ɛ/ in the same way as *ha*: *Ø-ɛ* 'be-3SG'. Since this word form is monosyllabic, its only vowel carries word stress, and emerges as [ɛ]. This analysis is a possible alternative to recognising *è* /ɛ/ as a case of fusion. The cost is very high: *è* /ɛ/ would be the **only** form in the whole language that allows the speakers to recognise that the underlying form of the 3SG ending in non-1st conjugation verbs is /ɛ/ rather than /e/. On the other hand, *è* /ɛ/ is the most frequent verb form in both spoken and written Italian,[13] so maybe its relevance for constructing an underlying representation should not be discounted. This representation would still need to posit a zero lexical morph, though. There is non-canonicity either way: the choice is between fusion and a zero lexical morph.

At this point, it must also be observed that the two lexical zero morphs that would have to be posited to maintain an analysis of *ha* and *è* that dispenses with fusion belong to different inflectional classes: Ø 'have' belongs to the 1st conjugation, since it takes the 3SG ending /a/, while Ø 'be' belongs to the non-1st conjugation, since it takes the 3SG ending /ɛ/.

3.3.3.1.4 *Ho* **'have.1SG.PRS.IND'** The analysis of *ho* /ɔ/ is parallel to that of *è* and *ha*. We can assume that the (default) 1SG ending is /ɔ/, which emerges as [o] when it is unstressed. In this case, there are several monosyllabic (therefore, stressed) and easily segmentable 1SG forms that display an ending /ɔ/ after an otherwise attested lexical stem ((2g), to be compared with (2f)).

We can have parallel analyses for *s-ɔ* 'know-1SG', etc., and *Ø-ɔ* 'have-1SG', at the only cost of positing a zero lexical morph. The number of forms allowing speakers to construct /ɔ/ as the underlying representation of the 1SG ending is higher than in the case of /ɛ/ '3SG'; *so*, *sto* and *do* are in the top frequency ranks (while *vo* and *fo* are diatopically and diaphasically conditioned, as shown in Thornton 2011, 2013).

3.3.3.1.5 *Può* **'can/may.3SG.PRS.IND'** Another form that deserves consideration in the present context is *può* /pwɔ/ 'can/may.3SG.PRS.IND'. The verb POTERE 'can/may' has a very irregular conjugation, but it definitely belongs to the non-1st conjugation, where the expected '3SG.PRS.IND' ending is *-e*.[14]

Synchronically, the best option seems to analyse *può* as a bare stem – compare *puoi* /ˈpwɔi/ 'can/may.2SG.PRS.IND', where a 2SG ending *-i* is clearly segmentable. The situation is then parallel to that of *fu* (see §3.3.3.1.1): one can posit a zero ending, or fusion of lexical and inflectional material, or a realisation rule that does not have to choose between these options, depending on theoretical preferences.[15]

3.3.3.1.6 Conclusion on fused exponence Cases of fusion of lexical and inflectional material are either rare or non-existing in Italian verb paradigms. To avoid positing fused exponence, however, we have to posit zero morphs, both grammatical and lexical, and heteroclisis, and allow for some abstraction in constructing phonological underlying representations. But these alternatives equally result in lack of canonicity. Heteroclisis is a deviation from canonicity as much as fusion (see Table 3.3 and §3.4.2.2). Zero morphs are certainly non-canonical, both as stems and as affixes. This is not stated explicitly in Corbett's numerous discussions of canonicity, probably because he adheres to an inferential-realisational model of morphology, that dispenses with zero morphs. But the absence of a signifier is defined as non-canonical in several cases. For example, criterion 2 for Canonical Agreement (Corbett 2006: 11) considers overt expression of agreement features as more canonical than covert expression; a zero morph does not express any (lexical or grammatical) content overtly, and must therefore be considered non-canonical.

3.3.3.2 Periphrasis

Verb paradigms make abundant use of periphrastic realisations: there are 44 active periphrastic forms for intransitive verbs and 88 for transitive verbs, and all the passive forms are periphrastic. These will not be discussed here in the interest of brevity.

Adjectives make use of periphrastic realisation for comparatives and relative superlatives, for example *grande / più grande / il più grande* 'big / bigger (lit. "more big") / the biggest (lit. "the more big")'.[16]

Nouns do not seem to make use of periphrasis. But, as always, there are issues to be discussed, that depend on the analysis one subscribes to.

I assume that the only inflectional feature in Italian nouns is NUMBER, with two values SG and PL; this gives us a paradigm with two cells. There is no periphrasis involved in the realisation of SG vs PL forms.

However, some authors (such as Di Domenico 1997, and the Italian reference dictionary *GRADIT* 1999) assume that at least a subset of nouns, those denoting humans or animals that are significant for humans or have very salient sex-differentiating features, also inflect for GENDER. This would give us a four-cell paradigm for these nouns, with M.SG, M.PL, F.SG and F.PL forms – like adjectives of class 1. Some nouns denoting humans and other animates are indeed apparently amenable to such an analysis (which, however, has been rejected, convincingly in my view, by Matthews 1991: 44–9; see also Iacobini and Thornton 2016: 194), as shown in (3).

(3)   a. il ragazzo / i ragazzi / la ragazza / le ragazze
         'the.M.SG boy / the.M.PL boys / the.F.SG girl / the.F.PL girls'
    b. il gatto / i gatti / la gatta / le gatte
         'the.M.SG cat / the.M.PL cats / the.F.SG she-cat / the.F.PL she-cats'

If we accept that nouns denoting humans inflect for gender,[17] some of the forms realising the feminine can be analysed as periphrastic (sometimes in a relation of overabundance with non-periphrastic forms). The lexeme used to create periphrastic denominations is *donna* 'woman'. Examples are given in Table 3.5.

Note, however, that the analysis does not carry over completely to nouns denoting animals. Some of these behave as shown in (3) for 'cat'; but in other cases, even if a sequence of words is used to designate an individual of a given sex, gender is unaffected, as shown in (4).

(4)   a. la volpe
        l-a   volp-e
        DEF-F.SG fox(F)-SG
        'the fox (sex unspecified)'
    b. la volpe maschio
        l-a   volp-e   maschi-o
        DEF-F.SG fox(F)-SG male(M)-SG
        'the male fox'

Table 3.5 Some putatively periphrastic forms in noun inflection

Gloss	M.SG form	F.SG form(s)
'lawyer'	avvocato	avvocata, avvocatessa, avvocato donna
'policeman/policewoman'	poliziotto	donna poliziotto, poliziotta

c. la volpe femmina
l-a   volp-e   femmin-a
DEF-F.SG fox(F)-SG female(F)-SG
'the female fox'

Data like those in (4) clearly show that a syntactic construction is used to refer to an individual of a specific sex, but morphosyntactic gender remains unaffected: to refer to a male fox, Italian uses a feminine noun that controls feminine agreement on the article, and is modified by a noun meaning 'male'. This is not inflection for gender, and therefore it is not an instance of periphrasis in noun paradigms.

3.3.4 Featural Inconsistency

Italian does not seem to present cases of featural inconsistency within paradigms of nouns and adjectives, while there are such cases in verbs.

Synthetic finite forms agree with their subject in person and number, not in gender (5a); periphrastic forms have a more complex agreement rule: the auxiliary agrees with the subject NP in person and number; the past participle appears in the (default) M.SG form when the auxiliary is 'have', and there is no clitic object (5b); when the auxiliary is 'have' and there is a clitic object, the past participle agrees in gender and number with the object, obligatorily if it is third person (5c) and optionally if it is first or second person (5d); when the auxiliary is 'be', the past participle agrees in gender and number with the subject NP (with obligatory semantic agreement based on the sex of the referent if the subject is first or second person) (5e,f).

(5) a. Maria parla / Paolo parla
       'Mary speaks / Paul speaks.'
    b. Maria ha parlato / Paolo ha parlato
       'Mary has spoken / Paul has spoken.'
    c. Maria / Paolo   la / l'   ha   vist-a / *vist-o
       Mary / Paul   3SG.F.ACC / 3SG.ACC[F]   have.PRS.IND.3SG   see.PST.PTCP-F.SG/*-M.SG
       'Mary / Paul has seen her / it.F.'
    d. Paolo ti   ha   vista / visto
       Paul   2SG.ACC   have.PRS.IND.3SG   see.PST.PTCP.F.SG/M.SG
       'Paul has seen you [female addressee].'
    e. Maria è   partit-a /   Paolo è   partit-o
       Mary be.PRS.IND.3SG leave.PST.PTCP-F.SG /   Paul be.PRS.IND.3SG leave.PST.PTCP-M.SG
       'Mary has left / Paul has left.'
    f. Sono   partit-a / *partit-o
       be.PRS.IND.1SG   leave.PST.PTCP-F.SG/M.SG
       'I (female speaker) have left.'

Therefore, agreement rules for verbs are not consistent throughout the paradigm; they change depending on the synthetic or periphrastic realisation of the verb form; different controllers operate according to the clitic vs free realisation of an object NP; there is agreement for different features according to the nature of the auxiliary.

Corbett (2015: 146) comments on a similar situation in the Russian verb saying that 'there is a deep split in the paradigm [. . .] in the features to which the two segments are sensitive'.

3.4 Deviations across Lexemes

3.4.1 Homonymy

A thorough discussion of homonymy would take far more space than is available for the present contribution. I refer to Chiari (2013) for useful considerations and data on Italian. It would be interesting to be able to compare the relative incidence of homonymy in Italian and in other languages. According to Chiari (2013: 14), about 2.6 per cent of the entries in *GRADIT* (an Italian reference dictionary with ~250K lemmata) are homographic, while about 0.5 per cent of the entries in the *OED* are. In general, the percentage of homographs (the only kind of homonyms for which it is relatively easy to collect data) decreases as the size of the reference dictionary increases, and the more low-frequency lexemes are added to the corpus. In the Italian Basic Vocabulary (~7,000 lemmata) homographs are 14.3 per cent. In the *NVDB* (an updated Basic Vocabulary of Italian, Chiari and De Mauro forthcoming), there are 301 homographic nouns, 83 homographic verbs and 28 homographic adjectives.[18] Whether the relative proportion of homographs in different parts of speech is parallel in other languages is an interesting question for further research.

The data presented so far concern so-called absolute homographs, i.e. different lexemes belonging to the same part of speech and homographic in all their inflected forms (e.g. It. CALCIO^1 'soccer' and CALCIO^2 'calcium'; IMPORTARE^1 'matter' and IMPORTARE^2 'import'). The percentage of so-called textual homographs, i.e. homographic word forms that can belong to any part of speech (e.g. It. *faccia* 'face' and 'make. SG.PRS.SBJV') is much higher, about 50 per cent of tokens in an Italian corpus (Chiari 2013: 6); again, comparison with other languages would be interesting.

3.4.2 Inflectional classes, heteroclisis and deponency

3.4.2.1 Inflectional classes

Italian has inflectional classes in nouns (Dressler and Thornton 1996; D'Achille and Thornton 2003), verbs (Dressler et al. 2003; Napoli and Vogel 1990) and adjectives (see §3.2). In this section I will discuss only nominal inflectional classes. I assume that the classes are the ones proposed by D'Achille and Thornton (2003) and shown in Table 3.6.

I will evaluate these classes against the criteria for canonical inflectional classes

Table 3.6 Italian inflectional classes for nouns

Class	Endings (SG/PL)	Examples	Gender	Percentage of nouns in the class	Notes and exceptions[a]
1	-o/-i	libro/libri 'book'	M	37.7	mano/mani 'hand' F
2	-a/-e	casa/case 'house'	F	34.4	
3	-e/-i	fiore/fiori 'flower' siepe/siepi 'hedge' cantante/cantanti 'singer'	M F M/F	20.8	44.4% M 43.4% F 12% M/F
4	-a/-i	poeta/poeti 'poet'	M	1.3	ala/ali 'wing' F, arma/armi 'weapon' F
5	-o/-a	uovo/uova 'egg'	SG.M, PL.F	0.3	
6	invariable	re 'king' brindisi 'toast' caffè 'coffee' gru 'crane' città 'city' crisi 'crisis' foto 'snapshot' ...	M F	5.4	48.6% M 51.4% F

[a] Percentages have been calculated on the ~4,500 nouns contained in the Italian Basic Vocabulary, using the *BDVDB* database (Thornton et al. 1997).

discussed by Corbett (2009) and Palancar (2012). Corbett proposed nine criteria stemming from two principles, and Palancar added a tenth criterion, as detailed in Table 3.7.

Palancar (2012) proposes a method for comparing the degree of canonicity of different inflectional classes: he assigns a score of 1 to situations in which a given class behaves as maximally canonical according to a certain criterion, and 0 when it behaves as non-canonical; besides, he assigns 0.5 in cases in which the behaviour lies somewhere in-between maximal and minimal canonicity (see Palancar 2012: 821 for discussion of this practical choice, which implies that all criteria are given equal weight in shaping the canon, and that no attempt is made at fine-tuning the degree of partial non-canonicity). In Palancar's system, given the ten criteria, any class could have a score lying between 0 (completely non-canonical) and 10 (fully canonical), and a higher score means a higher degree of canonicity. In this paper, I will reverse the sense of the marking, following a suggestion by Corbett (personal communication) that the maximally canonical case should be represented by 0, and progressively higher scores should signal progressive distance from the canonical ideal. In this reversed system, a higher score means higher non-canonicity, and a score of 0 would

Table 3.7 Principles and criteria for canonical inflectional classes

Principle I – Distinctiveness
Canonical inflectional classes are fully comparable and are distinguished as clearly as possible

Criterion 1
In the canonical situation, forms differ as consistently as possible *across* inflectional classes, cell by cell

Criterion 2
Canonical inflectional classes realise the same morphosyntactic or morphosemantic distinctions (they are of the same structure)

Criterion 3
Within a canonical inflectional class each member behaves identically

Criterion 4
Within a canonical inflectional class each paradigm cell is of equal status

Principle II – Independence
The distribution of lexical items over canonical inflectional classes is synchronically unmotivated

Criterion 5
The larger the number of members of an inflectional class (up to an equal 'share' of the available items), the more canonical that class

Criterion 6
In the canonical situation, the distribution of lexical items over inflectional classes is not phonologically motivated

Criterion 7
In the canonical situation, the distribution of lexical items over inflectional classes is not syntactically motivated

Criterion 8
In the canonical situation, the distribution of lexical items over inflectional classes is not motivated by part of speech

Criterion 9
In the canonical situation, the distribution of lexical items over inflectional classes is not motivated by pragmatics (including information structure)

Criterion 10 (Palancar 2012)
In the canonical situation, the distribution of lexical items over inflectional classes is not semantically motivated

be attained by the canonical ideal (which, as repeatedly observed by Corbett, might be rare or even non-existent).

Assigning scores is not an easy task, for two sorts of reasons: first, the exact interpretation of specific criteria may be debatable; second, data on the behaviour of a given class with respect to a specific criterion might be unavailable. The following

Table 3.8 Degree of canonicity of Italian inflectional classes

Criterion	Class 1	Class 2	Class 3	Class 4	Class 5	Class 6	Canonical ideal
1	1	0.5	0.5	1	0.5	0	0
2	0	0	0	0	0	0	0
3	0.5	0	0.5	0.5	0	0	0
4	?	?	?	?	?	?	0
5	1	1	0.5	1	1	1	0
6	0	0	0	0	0	1	0
7	0	0	0	0	0	0	0
8	0	0	0	0	1	0	0
9	0	0	0	0	0	0	0
10	0	0	0	0	1	0	0
Total	2.5	1.5	1.5	2.5	3.5	2	0

application of the criteria to Italian nominal inflectional classes is to be understood as a preliminary attempt, based on currently available data: further work might allow the scores to be refined, on the basis of more accurate case studies of specific classes, which must be left for further research. Table 3.8 presents the scores for the six Italian nominal inflection classes, where 0 means canonical behaviour, 0.5 some degree non-canonicity and 1 fully non-canonical behaviour.

I will briefly comment on the reasons for particular scores.[19] Criterion 1 poses a question of interpretation: should we compare each cell with all other cells in all other classes, or compare each cell only with cells with the same morphosyntactic feature specification in other classes? The two options would yield different results in several cases; choosing the first option would result in assigning a score of 1 (maximal non-canonicity) to all the classes. I assumed that the intended interpretation is the second one, since the criterion states that in the canonical case forms differ 'cell by cell'. On this basis, classes 2, 3 and 5 get a score of 0.5 because only one of their endings is homophonous to the ending in the same cell in another class: class 2 SG = class 4 SG (-*a*), class 3 PL = classes 1 and 4 PL (-*i*), class 5 SG = class 1 SG (-*o*), while class 2 PL (-*e*) and class 5 PL (-*a*) are not homophonous with the plural ending in any other class, and class 3 SG (-*e*) is not homophonous with the singular in any other class. Classes 1 and 4 get a score of 1 because none of their endings is unique to the class. I gave a 0 score to class 6, which technically has no ending. One could disagree with this decision, however, by considering the fact that class 6, besides hosting nouns ending in consonants, stressed vowels and /u/, also hosts invariable nouns ending in /a/, /e/, /i/ and /o/ (such as SOSIA 'lookalike', SPECIE 'species', CRISI 'crisis', AUTO 'car'), i.e. in segments that are homophonous to endings in other classes; however, since these segments are not technically endings, I did not count their existence as making this class less different from the other ones.

The classes do not differ with respect to criterion 2.[20]

Criterion 3 sets aside class 1, and less strongly classes 3 and 4, in that these are the only classes which exhibit alternations or suppletion. Corbett (2009: 4) explicitly notes that canonicity according to criterion 3 'implies that there are no stem differences, alternants or other subclasses'. Alternations in classes 1 and 3 were described in §3.3.1; in class 4, the palatal/velar alternation appears only in the noun BELGA 'Belgian (M)', with SG /bɛlga/ and PL /bɛldʒi/ (Dressler 1985: 169). The question remains of how to weight these cases: there are more alternations in class 1 than in classes 3 (where only *bue/buoi* alternates) and 4, but also in class 1 the suppletive alternations are few and the palatal/velar alternation is receding (Dressler and Thornton 1996). To differentiate between the different cases, I was tempted to give a score of 1 to class 1 and 0.5 to classes 3 and 4 for criterion 3; however, this would depart from Palancar's practical choice of not giving different weights to different amounts of non-canonicity, so I gave a score of 0.5 to all the classes containing alternations, in consideration of the fact that alternations are few, very well defined, and partly recessive.

Criterion 4 concerns the status of each cell in the paradigm. Corbett (2009: 5) observes that 'in the canonical situation [...] the form for each cell predicts all the others within a class'. In Italian nouns, the situation is far from canonical. To assess exactly how far requires a preliminary decision, i.e. whether nouns of class 6 ending in one of the vowels that are exploited as endings in the other classes should be included in the comparison, or not. If we include them, no form in any class can be seen as reliably predicting the other form in its paradigm, as shown in Table 3.9, where predictions concerning class 6 are shaded.

If we disregard class 6 nouns ending in the vowels /a e i o/, because these vowels are part of the stem and not inflectional endings in this class, and only consider the predictions concerning inflectional endings, we see that not all forms (as represented by their ending) fare equally. SG *-e*, PL *-e* and PL *-a* are good predictors, in that they predict unambiguously the form of the inflectional ending that appears in the other number value for the same lexeme; SG *-o*, SG *-a* and especially PL *-i*, instead, fail to predict unambiguously the ending of the form with the opposite number value in the same paradigm, because they appear in more than one class. One would be tempted to give a score of 0.5 to classes that exhibit one ending that unambiguously predicts the other one, and a score of 1 to classes in which neither ending unambiguously predicts the other one. However, class 6 would still need to be evaluated, and since it contains not only nouns ending in consonants, stressed vowels and /u/, whose form allows to predict uninflectability, but also nouns ending in /a o e i/, whose form could be interpreted as an inflectional ending of some other class, we cannot assign a score that makes this class canonical. The choice is between either taking full account of these nouns, and assigning a score of 1 to class 6 – but then, if these nouns count for scoring class 6, they should count also as possible predictions in all the other cases,

Table 3.9 Predictions from one form to the other in Italian noun paradigms

Number value and ending	Possible correspondences in the other number value
SG -o	PL -i (class 1)
	PL -a (class 5)
	PL -o (class 6)
SG -a	PL -e (class 2)
	PL -i (class 4)
	PL -a (class 6)
SG -e	PL -i (class 3)
	PL -e (class 6)
PL -i	SG -o (class 1)
	SG -e (class 3)
	SG -a (class 4)
	SG -i (class 6)
PL -e	SG -a (class 2)
	SG -e (class 6)
PL -a	SG -o (class 5)
	SG -a (class 6)

and all classes should receive a score of 1; or, we could give a score of 0.5 to class 6, because some of its members (the ones that are uninflectable for purely phonological reasons) allow predictions of the form with the other number value, but others (those ending in /a e i o/) do not. But this would mean assigning a score of 0.5 for different reasons to class 6 and to classes 2, 3 and 5. Altogether, this exercise in applying criterion 4 to Italian nominal inflectional classes illustrates the difficulty of working with the simple scoring system devised by Palancar, which does not seem to allow to capture satisfactorily the differences among the inflectional classes of Italian nouns. In Table 3.8 I have refrained from assigning a score for this criterion altogether.

The application of criterion 5 poses another question. This criterion states that 'the larger the number of members of an inflectional class (**up to** an equal "share" of the available items) the more canonical that class' (emphasis mine). Palancar (2012) interprets this criterion as if it meant 'the more, the better', and considers fully canonical conjugation I of Tilapa Otomi, which comprises 62.5 per cent of the verbs in the language, while the 'equal share' would be 33.3 per cent, since there are three conjugation classes in the language. But I think that this interpretation runs counter to the spirit of criterion 5, which is that all lexical items in the language should distribute in a balanced way among the different classes. Having considerably more members than the equal share in a class necessarily implies that some other class will have less than an equal share of members, making the overall system less canonical.[21] In the inflectional classes for Italian nouns, an equal share would be 16.6 per cent; as can be seen from the percentages of nouns in each class in the Italian Basic Vocabulary given in Table 3.6, no single class has an equal share of members: classes 1, 2 and 3 have more than an equal share, and classes 4, 5 and 6 have far less than an equal share.[22] Somewhat arbitrarily, I gave a score of 0.5 to class 3, which comes closer to the equal share (it has 20.8 per cent of nouns), while classes 1 and 2 have more than twice the equal share of nouns each, and all other classes have very few members. These scores are extremely tentative: one should bear in mind that counts on a list of nouns larger than the one used could give different results.[23]

Moving on to criterion 6 (lack of phonological motivation for class membership), if we assume that the phonology of the stem, minus the vocalic endings, should be evaluated,[24] we have considerable evidence for lack of phonological motivation, since stems of similar or identical shape can appear in several classes, as shown for some arbitrarily chosen strings in Table 3.10 (only singular forms, which constitute citation forms, are shown).

It is quite clear that classes 1, 2 and 3 do not exhibit phonological restrictions on the stem shape of their members; for the other classes, more needs to be said. Class 4 hosts many learned borrowings from Greek, and a good number of these end in -*Vma* (e.g. PROBLEMA, CLIMA, CARCINOMA 'problem, climate, malignant tumour'); it is possible that PIGIAMA 'pyjamas' (< English PYJAMAS) was attracted to this class rather than to class 6 like other masculine loanwords ending in -*a* because of its phonological shape (trisyllabic and ending in -*Vma*) that makes it look like a Greek loanword – but LAMA 'Tibetan monk' and 'Andean mammal' is in class 6. Also, a great number of class 4 nouns are denominal agent nouns containing the suffix -*ista*, but I would argue that this suffix counts as just one member of the class, and there are stems ending in *ist*- in the other classes too (VISTO 'visa', LISTA 'list', CISTE and CISTI 'cyst'). So it seems to me that there is no strong case for phonological motivation in the membership of class 4.

Class 5 contains very few nouns (fewer than 30, see Acquaviva 2008; Thornton 2010–11), and these nouns exhibit a limited range of segments preceding the vocalic ending: of the 24 nouns considered by Thornton (2010–11) on the basis of Acquaviva's

Table 3.10 Examples of different stem shapes in Italian inflectional classes for nouns

Class 1	Class 2	Class 3	Class 4	Class 5	Class 6
cub-o	tub-a	nub-e	scrib-a		baluba, club
diviet-o	diet-a	ariet-e	poet-a		yeti, jet
rinnov-o	prov-a	bov-e		uov-o	Volvo, Vov
am-o	lam-a	fam-e	pigiam-a		lama, tram

(2008) survey, 5 have stems ending in /l/, 4 in /j/, 3 in /ʎ/, 3 in /r/, 2 each in /t/, /d/, /s/, and 1 each in /tʃ/, /v/, /n/. Only 10 of the 23 consonants of Italian appear stem-finally in this class, and there is a clear prevalence of sonorants and coronal obstruents. Still, these segments commonly appear in stem-final position in most other classes (exemplifying with just /l/: PALO, BALLO, PALA, PALLA, MALE, CALLE, CRAL 'pole, ball (dance), shovel, ball, evil, Venetian street, name of a club (acronym)'), so the presence of these stem-final segments does not constitute phonological motivation to go into class 5 (although one might wonder whether it is (part of the) motivation to remain in this class, which is constantly losing members).

The only class for which there is clear phonological motivation is class 6, which hosts all nouns ending in consonants and stressed vowels; besides, this class also hosts masculine nouns in -a and feminine nouns in -o (D'Achille and Thornton 2008), which display a 'contradiction' between their final vowel and the gender normally associated with that vowel when it is an inflectional ending. This is a kind of complex motivation, involving gender and phonology. One may wonder whether this factor, since it involves evaluation of a noun's gender, should be counted as syntactic motivation for assignment to class 6, in which case, this class should receive a score of 1 also for criterion 7. In general, however, purely syntactic motivation for inflectional class assignment on the basis of gender cannot be maintained for Italian, since there are two genders and six inflectional classes, and each gender maps to several classes.[25]

Criterion 8 sets aside as non-canonical class 5, which has no parallel in adjectival inflection, while all other classes do (compare Tables 3.4 and 3.6).[26] No class seems to be non-canonical with respect to criterion 9 (pragmatic motivation; Corbett 2009: 7 observes that '[s]uch motivation would be clearly non-canonical, and it may well be that there are no examples'). A strong case has been made by Acquaviva (2008) for the semantic motivation (criterion 10) of membership in class 5: he maintains that nouns in this class denote 'weakly differentiated entities'. The problem is that not all the entities that Acquaviva considers weakly differentiated are denoted by nouns belonging to this class. For example, among symmetrical body parts, arms, lips and eyebrows are denoted by nouns in class 5, while legs, hands and eyes are not; within units of measure, miles are denoted by a noun in class 5, but kilometres and metres are not. So, again, this semantic factor maybe helps to explain why certain nouns stay in this class, but not why they are assigned to it. Indeed, the class is unproductive and has not received new members for centuries, while it has lost many members (e.g. CASTELLO 'castle' and ANELLO 'ring' used to belong to class 5, but now belong to class 1). Anyway, I tentatively assigned a score of 1 to class 5 for criterion 10, because semantic elements common to several members of the class are more clearly visible than in any other class.

At this point, it appears that all Italian nominal inflection classes have some degree of non-canonicity, and class 5 is the least canonical one. To draw more far-reaching conclusions it would be necessary to compare the results obtained for the inflectional classes of Italian nouns with those obtained for inflectional classes of nouns in other languages by applying the same method – a task that exceeds the boundaries of this paper and must be left for further research.

This section has also shown the difficulty of devising and applying mathematical measures to establish levels of canonicity. Several cases have been difficult to decide; criterion 5 has been interpreted differently here and by Palancar (2012), and even the scoring system has been changed with respect to Palancar's original proposal. There have been so far very few attempts at operationalising canonicity criteria,[27] and the fact that even two studies that depart from exactly the same premises, and address the same domain (inflectional classes), such as Palancar's and the present one, do not agree completely on all points is problematic. I think that the operationalisation of canonicity measures is in urgent need of further research within the Canonical Typology approach.

3.4.2.2 Heteroclisis

Cases of heteroclisis exist in Italian in the inflection of all three major parts of speech, and have been briefly mentioned already. In verbs, there is heteroclisis in most of the verb paradigms discussed in §3.3.3.1; in nouns, Thornton (2010–11: 423) proposed to analyse ALA 'wing' and ARMA 'weapon', the only feminine nouns in class 4 according to D'Achille and Thornton (2003), as heteroclitic, with SG in class 2 and PL in class 3 (which is also diachronically the case); for adjectives, it was suggested in §3.3.2 that the class represented as inflection class 4 in Table 3.4 could also be analysed as heteroclitic, with M forms inflecting according to class 2 and F forms according to class 1.

3.4.2.3 Deponency

Cases of extended deponency have not been investigated for Italian. I will only briefly mention two areas in which possible candidates appear.

In nouns, several SG endings are homophonous with PL endings of other inflectional classes, for example class 2 SG = class 5 PL -*a*, class 3 SG = class 2 PL -*e*. Given that five classes must express two number values each by means of only four vowels, a certain amount of homophony is unavoidable, and treating these homophonies between endings with different number specifications as cases of extended deponency does not seem very enlightening.

In verbs, there is a more interesting case. Certain verbs (commonly called *verbi procomplementari*) have obligatory clitic pronouns which do not refer to any argument, such as *aver=ci* 'have' (lit. 'have=LOC'), in a context such as *c'ho 20 anni* 'I am 20 years old' (lit. 'LOC=have.1SG.PRS 20 years'). The literature on the topic is abundant and I cannot possibly do justice to it here (see at least Russi 2008). I only wish to point to a possible case that could be analysed from the point of view of extended deponency. Evans (2007: 294) also observes that it may be profitable to widen the definition of extended deponency beyond cases that involve strictly bound morphology, to include phenomena like the Italian verbs + clitics mentioned here.

3.4.3 *Affixal Inconsistency and Antiperiphrasis*

3.4.3.1 Affixal inconsistency

Affixal consistency is defined by Corbett (2015: 154) as the situation in which 'the number and position of the affixes that we find in one cell should be matched in all other cells of the lexeme's paradigm'. Italian nouns and adjectives seem to be quite consistent (barring invariable ones). An exception has been pointed out by Ricca (2003): deverbal adjectives derived by means of the suffixes -*TORE*(M)/-*TRICE*(F) are an exception to the cumulative exponence of GENDER and NUMBER values in Italian adjectives (see §3.3.2 above), in that they cumulate the expression of GENDER with the derivational suffix, and express only NUMBER in the inflectional ending (like nouns), as in *uno sguardo rivelatore* 'a revealing look', where *rivela-tor-e* can be glossed, following Ricca (2003: 195), as 'reveal-(V→A):M-SG'.

Italian verb forms certainly lend themselves to be scrutinised to assess their affixal consistency, or lack thereof; a flavour of the kind of analyses involved has been given in §3.3.3.1.

3.4.3.2 Antiperiphrasis

Antiperiphrasis can only occur if there is periphrasis somewhere else in the system. As shown in §3.3.3.2, Italian has periphrasis in verbs and adjectives. As far as I can see, there are no candidate cases for antiperiphrasis in Italian verb paradigms, while there are possible candidates for antiperiphrasis in adjectives.

While Italian has replaced the Latin synthetic comparative with a periphrastic one, a few adjectives that continue Latin synthetic comparatives are in usage in Italian. They are shown in (6).

(6) Italian synthetic comparatives?
    a. MIGLIORE 'better', PEGGIORE 'worse', MAGGIORE 'bigger, older',
       MINORE 'smaller, younger'
    b. SUPERIORE 'higher', INFERIORE 'lower', ESTERIORE 'external', ULTERIORE 'further',
       INTERIORE 'interior', ANTERIORE 'anterior, front', POSTERIORE 'back, later'

Adjectives in (6b) are not related to any positive degree adjectives, and cannot be analysed as comparatives (often they have no inherently comparative meaning, as noted by Serianni 1988: V, §83); the ones in (6a), instead, are usually presented as synthetic comparatives corresponding to the adjectives BUONO 'good', CATTIVO 'bad', GRANDE 'big', PICCOLO 'small'. This analysis is not without problems, however. Periphrastic comparatives and relative superlatives for these adjectives are well attested. Santilli (2014) analysed all the tokens of PIÙ BUONO and MIGLIORE in *la Repubblica* 1985–2000 (a corpus of written Italian containing about 330M tokens, i.e. 16 years of issues of the daily newspaper *la Repubblica*) and concluded that contexts in which both types modify the same head noun are very rare. He also found contexts in which the two types have a clear semantic difference, for example *giudice più buono* 'kinder judge [more prone to acquit the defendant]' vs *giudice migliore* 'better / the best judge [more experienced]'. From this research, it appears that PIÙ BUONO is mainly used in the semantic field of food, roughly in the sense of 'tastier', or with reference to kindness; for example, *lo scolaro più buono* is the pupil who behaves better, while *lo scolaro migliore* is the one who has the best intellectual achievement. So, it appears that MIGLIORE, and possibly the other so-called synthetic comparatives, for which we lack corpus-based studies, are far along the way of becoming independent adjectives, like the ones in (6b).

Besides, these adjectives serve as input for lexeme-formation, which is at least very non-canonical for inflected forms (albeit realising inherent inflection in Booij's 1996 sense). Some derivatives based on these putative comparatives are listed in (7).

(7) Italian derivatives based on putative synthetic comparatives
MIGLIORARE 'make/become better', PEGGIORARE 'worsen, make worse', MAGGIORARE 'to raise (spec. prices)', MAGGIORATA 'woman, spec. actress, with an oversize bust', MINORATO 'affected with mental disability'

3.4.4 Featural Inconsistency

Corbett's examples of featural inconsistency across lexemes are defectiveness and overdifferentiation.

3.4.4.1 Defectiveness

Verb paradigms have some well-known cases of defectiveness; for example, several verbs are used only in third person forms, and in a subset of tenses (e.g. OSTARE 'prevent', PRUDERE 'itch'), while several others lack a PST.PTCP (e.g. COMPETERE 'compete', SPLENDERE 'shine'). Grammars and dictionaries offer extensive descriptions of these cases (cf. Serianni 1988: XI, §§96–122).

Defectiveness in noun paradigms is also mostly run of the mill. Grammars mention it as *pluralia tantum*:

- nouns that denote twofold objects, such as PANTALONI 'trousers', OCCHIALI 'glasses' – but the singular can be used to denote a single pair, i.e. *un pantalone* 'a pair of trousers', so these nouns are at best plural-dominant nouns, not really *pluralia tantum*
- various other nouns, such as SPEZIE 'spices', STOVIGLIE 'crockery' and VETTOVAGLIE 'victuals', most of which are at best plural-dominant, except VIVERI 'food, victuals' which appears to be a genuine *plurale tantum*
- nouns for festivities and celebrations, such as IDI 'ides', NOZZE 'wedding', ESEQUIE 'funeral service' and a few more, which are indeed *pluralia tantum*.

Grammars also mention several kinds of supposedly singular-only nouns (Serianni 1988: III, §152), for most of which there is a semantic factor at work (e.g. nouns denoting single entities, like EQUATORE 'equator', and mass nouns); in many cases, again, these nouns are at best singular-dominant, not really defective, as plural forms can be used in appropriate contexts.

3.4.4.2 Overdifferentiation

Overdifferentiation 'is shown by a lexeme which, in comparison with others, has additional cells' (Corbett 2007b: 28). There do not appear to be cases of overdifferentiation in Italian morphology. Thornton (2010–11: 438–55) has discussed the case of double plurals like *bracci/braccia* 'arms', concluding that they do not represent a case of overdifferentiation, since no further value of the feature NUMBER (not even a 'minor number value' as defined by Corbett 2000: 97–101) is expressed by the *-a* plurals. The forms ending in *-a*, therefore, cannot be analysed as occupying an additional cell: they are plural forms, in a relation of overabundance with the forms ending in *-i*.

3.4.4.3 The case of adjectives: featural inconsistency or syncretism?

In §3.3.2 the question was raised whether the difference in the paradigms of Italian adjectives belonging to the inflectional classes 1 (i.e. *rosso* M.SG / *rossi* M.PL / *rossa* F.SG / *rosse* F.PL 'red'), 2 (i.e. *verde* M/F.SG / *verdi* M/F.PL 'green') and 5 (i.e. *blu* M/F.SG/PL 'blue') should be analysed by positing syncretism between the two gender values in class 2, and syncretism of both gender and number values, leading to uninflectability, in class 5. An alternative option is to treat adjectives belonging to these three classes as instances of featural inconsistency.

The problem has been clearly stated by Corbett:

> Of course, one can stipulate that featural requirements are always identical through a paradigm [. . .] and that there is massive systematic syncretism; indeed, in some models one would be forced into that position. (Corbett 2015: 157)

In the Canonical Typology literature both positions have been taken for similar examples. Corbett favours the featural inconsistency analysis: he contrasts the Macedonian adjectives in Table 3.11, here distinguished as types I and II, which differ in a way similar to Italian adjectives of class 1 and 2, by expressing vs neutralising a gender contrast in the singular.

Corbett (2015: 157) states that 'the two types have different feature signatures'.

Bond (2018) entertains different solutions in different parts of the paper. He contrasts the Spanish adjectives *ALTO* 'tall' and *INTELIGENTE* 'intelligent', whose paradigms he presents as shown in Table 3.12.

Table 3.11 Macedonian (based on Corbett 2015: 157)

| | SG | | | PL | GLOSS |
	M	F	N		
I	nov	nova	novo	novi	'new'
II		kasmetlija		kasmetlii	'lucky'

Table 3.12 Spanish adjectives (Bond 2018: 413–41)

	ALTO 'tall'	
	SG	PL
M	alto	altos
F	alta	altas

A paradigm with forms distinguished by two intersecting features.

	INTELIGENTE 'intelligent'	
	SG	PL
	inteligente	inteligentes

A paradigm with forms distinguished by a single feature.

This presentation assumes an analysis in terms of featural inconsistency rather than syncretism. However, later in the same paper, Bond decomposes the definition of a canonical paradigm in terms of three separate criteria: exhaustiveness (there is a cell for every possible feature combination, within a given part of speech), completeness (all cells are filled by a form) and non-ambiguity (each cell contains a form that is different from all the forms contained in the other cells of the same paradigm). According to these criteria, 'Spanish adjectives that have distinct forms within each of the four cells defined by the matrix (i.e. *alto* "tall") necessarily have canonical exhaustive, complete, unambiguous paradigms' (Bond 2018: 417), while adjectives like Spanish INTELIGENTE 'intelligent' can be analysed as exhaustive and complete, but containing ambiguous forms. Bond defends this analysis; he maintains that the status of a paradigm with respect to the properties of completeness and non-ambiguity can only be assessed with respect to the number of cells defined for the paradigm by the criterion of exhaustiveness, and observes:

> The crucial observation for assessing whether a paradigm is exhaustive or non-exhaustive is not whether there is a distinct form in every logically possible cell of the paradigm, but rather whether there is evidence for this combination of feature-values being distinguished somewhere in the language. (Bond 2018: 419)

Therefore, for example, Russian adjectives (which distinguish M, F and N in the SG but not in the PL) are analysed as having non-exhaustive paradigms, 'because we find no evidence anywhere in the language for a distinction in gender for plural forms, either in terms of the morphological form of Russian plural adjectives or in agreement with those forms' (Bond 2018: 419). On the other hand, since in Spanish and Italian there is abundant evidence for a distinction of gender in both numbers, and indeed most adjectives belong to the inflectional classes that have distinct forms for the different combinations of feature values, cases like Italian class 2 adjectives and Spanish adjectives like INTELIGENTE 'intelligent' should be analysed as syncretic (i.e. ambiguous) paradigms, not as paradigms with a different feature signature from Italian class 1 adjectives and Spanish adjectives like ALTO 'tall'.

3.5 Conclusions

The exercise in Canonical Typology conducted on Italian inflection has shown that most non-canonical phenomena are attested in Italian: Tables 3.13 and 3.14 recapitulate our findings.

However, often it has proven difficult to decide exactly which non-canonical phenomenon is represented by a certain situation (e.g. zero morphs vs fusion in the verb forms discussed in §3.3.3.1, or syncretism vs difference in feature signature for certain classes of adjectives, discussed in §3.3.2 and §3.4.4.3). This is consistent with the observation that canonicity criteria converge on identifying certain instances as non-canonical (cf. Corbett 2007a: 35). The present study shows that this convergence occurs not only among criteria used to define the Canonical Typology of a specific non-canonical phenomenon (e.g. suppletion), but also among the criteria of canonicity used for assessing an entire system of inflection.

Table 3.13 Deviations from canonicity established by comparison across the cells of a lexeme in Italian nouns, adjectives and verbs

	Types of deviation	Nouns	Adjectives	Verbs
Lexical material (≈ shape of stem)	Alternations	✓	✓	✓
	Suppletion	✓	✓	✓
Inflectional material (≈ shape of affix)	Syncretism	✓	✓	✓
	Uninflectability	(undistinguishable)	✓	?
Composition (≈ means of exponence)	Affixal inconsistency: fused exponence	* (= uninflectability?)	* (= uninflectability?)	✓
	Affixal inconsistency: periphrasis	?	✓	✓
Feature signature (≈ morphosyntactic requirement)	Featural inconsistency	*	*	✓

Table 3.14 Deviations from canonicity established by comparison across lexemes in Italian nouns, adjectives and verbs

	Types of deviation	Nouns	Adjectives	Verbs
Lexical material (≈ shape of stem)	Homonymy	✓	✓	✓
Inflectional material (≈ shape of affix)	Inflectional classes	✓	✓	✓
	Heteroclisis	✓	✓	✓
	Deponency	*? (= syncretism?)	*? (= syncretism?)	?
Composition (≈ means of exponence)	Affixal inconsistency	*	✓	✓
	Antiperiphrasis	*	?	*
Feature signature (≈ morphosyntactic requirement)	Featural inconsistency: defectiveness	✓	*	✓
	Featural inconsistency: overdifferentiation	*	Debatable: syncretism or featural inconsistency?	✓

This study also shows that it is often difficult to operationalise specific canonicity criteria. An attempt to operationalise the criteria for canonical inflectional classes, along the lines proposed by Palancar (2012), has not been entirely successful. The research on how to operationalise canonicity criteria, in order to allow comparison between the degree of canonicity of parallel phenomena in different languages, or of different instances of a phenomenon in a single language (e.g. different inflectional classes, or degree of syncretism in different parts of speech) is certainly an area in which further research would be very welcome.

Acknowledgements

I thank Matthew Baerman, Oliver Bond, Chiara Cappellaro, Paolo D'Achille and Sebastian Fedden for reading a first draft of this paper and making several helpful suggestions, and Greville Corbett for discussion on various points, and for never asking where I was going to publish the paper I was working on. Part of the research was carried out during a stay at the Surrey Morphology Group in February and March

2017; I am grateful to the Faculty of Arts and Social Sciences, University of Surrey, for granting me a Visiting Professorship in the School of English and Languages that allowed me to spend time in that stimulating environment.

Notes

1. Representations will be in the standard Italian orthography, or in IPA broad transcription only when necessary for illustrating a specific point. Lexemes are represented in italic small capitals, inflectional forms in italics. Glossing follows the Leipzig Glossing Rules.
2. The same approach is taken by Bond (2018). Corbett (2009: 1) quotes the formulation 'uniformity and distinctiveness of paradigms' from Wurzel (1989: 63).
3. Stump's (2012: 255–6) list of properties and definitions is the following: 'a) Properties of a canonical inflectional paradigm: **Exhaustivity**: every compatible combination of the relevant morphosyntactic properties defines a cell; **Completeness**: every cell has a realization; **Unambiguousness**: all realizations are distinct; **Freedom from stem alternation**: every realization is based on the same stem; **Morphotactic uniformity**: the same morphotactic pattern (i.e. stem + suffix) is used in every realization, b) Properties of a canonical system of paradigms (for some syntactic category): **Parallelism**: all individual paradigms realize the same morphosyntactic property sets and all are canonical; **Distinctness**: distinct paradigms are based on distinct stems and therefore have distinct realizations; **Uniformity of exponence**: across paradigms, the same morphosyntactic property set is expressed by the same exponence.'
4. One could say that 'composition' deals with the *signifiant* of inflected forms, and 'feature signature' with their *signifié*; or, composition deals with their autonomous morphology and feature signature with their morphosyntax and morphosemantics.
5. The number of forms depends on what is included in the paradigm; I only counted two forms in the active imperative (2SG, 2PL) and one (2SG) in the passive imperative and I did not count the so-called present participle, since, according to Haspelmath (1996: 61), it is 'clearly derivational'; the PST.PTCP was counted only once, in the active conjugation, somewhat arbitrarily. Passive periphrastic forms exhibiting same person/number but different gender (e.g. *sono amato* 'I (male speaker) am loved', *sono amata* 'I (female speaker) am loved') were counted twice, as were active forms such as *ho amato* 'I have loved' and *ho amata* 'id.', the latter used when it governs a feminine clitic object (see §3.3.4).
6. Although the case of *ecco* should be mentioned in this connection; *ecco* (< Latin **eccum* < *ecce hunc* '≈here this') is usually classified as a peculiar kind of adverb by Italian dictionaries and grammars, but exhibits several properties in common with verbs: it can be a predicate, it hosts clitics (*ecco=lo! ecco*=M.SG.OBJ 'Here it/he is!') and can be prefixed by *ri-* 'again', which is otherwise used only with verbs. Gaeta (2013: 46–50) reviews the literature and points out that some scholars consider *ecco* a defective verb. But *ecco* has a single form, so if it is a verb, it appears to be not just defective but uninflectable. The issue is complicated by the fact that it is not clear which verbal morphosyntactic properties *ecco* would express.
7. Glosses of the verb forms mostly reproduce the traditional labels used in Italian grammaticography; IMPF.SBJV is a particularly unsatisfactory gloss, but a discussion on how to represent the values expressed by these forms would take us too much afar, and is orthogonal to the issues that concern us here.
8. An extremely small corpus – 5,000 noun tokens were analysed. But no data on larger corpora are available, to the best of my knowledge.
9. The inflectional classes of Italian nouns are described in §3.4.2.1.

10. If one looks beyond the basic vocabulary, however, other kinds of invariable adjectives exist, such as verb + noun compounds, or *anti* + N adjectives (e.g. *salvabanche* 'lit. *salva* "save" + *banche* "banks"', *antibomba* 'lit. *anti-* "against" + *bomba* "bomb"').
11. Unless, to account for these forms, one posits a 'suprasegmental morph' which has the effect of assigning stress to the final syllable, as proposed by Thornton (1999: 494–5).
12. The gloss given for *vidi* renders only partially the intricacy of the exponence of feature values in this form and comparable ones; we have cases of what Matthews (1991) calls 'extended exponence', in that values such as PST.PFV are signalled both by the stem (S5 *vid-*) and by the ending *-i*, which is not a default 1SG ending, but only occurs in certain tenses.
13. Thanks to Miriam Voghera for allowing me to consult unpublished data elaborated from the LIP corpus of spoken Italian (De Mauro et al. 1993).
14. This ending does appear in the form *puote* 'can/may.3SG.PRS.IND', segmentable as *puot-e*, a form that has been in an overabundance relation with *può* from the thirteenth to the eighteenth centuries; from the nineteenth century *puote*, which was always the less frequent cell mate, has been confined to poetry, and in the twentieth century it has disappeared from active usage.
15. Some scholars might even want to exploit the parallel between the final *-ò* /ɔ/ appearing in *può* and that appearing in *amò* 'love.3SG.PST.PFV.IND' and all 1st conjugation 3SG.PST.PFV.IND. I will not go down this path.
16. I will not address the issue of the inflectional status of these forms, which is not recognised by all authors (see Corbett 2007a: 15 n.14 for similar remarks).
17. For a proposal along these lines applied to French, see Bonami and Boyé (2015, this volume).
18. Thanks to Isabella Chiari for these data.
19. Scores which are open to debate appear in cells with a grey background.
20. The question could be raised whether the presence of lexemes belonging to different genders in classes 3 and 6 (and to a lesser extent in classes 1 and 4) and the gender switch between SG and PL in class 5 should be treated as a factor of non-canonicity (thereby making class 2 the only really canonical one according to criterion 2). I decided not to do so, because, whatever the gender of the single lexeme or form, all forms in all classes realise the same two morphosyntactic features, GENDER (inherent, fixed) and NUMBER (inherent, selected). It should also be observed that the different classes behave in a parallel way with respect to mass nouns, which either are not pluralised or receive a unit or type reading if used in the plural: nouns such as VINO, BIRRA, LATTE, MAGMA, WHISKY 'wine, beer, milk, magma, whisky', in classes 1, 2, 3, 4, 6 respectively, behave in parallel ways in this respect (no relevant example is available from class 5).
21. Thanks to Grev Corbett for discussing this point with me.
22. In discussing criterion 5, Corbett (2009: 6) observes that 'if a class had a small number of members, this could allow listing of the forms for each item'. With regard to Italian nouns, this move could be defended for class 5, but certainly not for class 6, which is a productive class, continually gaining members; it is debatable whether the move should be applied to class 4, which gains members almost exclusively through the output of lexeme formation rules.
23. Let us also bear in mind, however, that for the vast majority of the world's languages our generalisations are based on far smaller datasets than the one being used for Italian in the present context. Thanks to Sebastian Fedden for discussing this point with me.
24. This is the natural option according to Corbett (2009: 6 n.8).
25. For the complex relation between gender, inflectional class and phonology in Italian nominal inflection, see Thornton (2001, 2003).

26. Dressler and Thornton (1996: 14) observe that this 'is motivated by the fact that adjectives must agree with nouns, i.e. they have no inherent gender, and therefore they cannot show different gender in Sg. and Pl. and are thus excluded from the class where each number shows a different gender'. One could wonder whether all nominal inflection classes should be deemed non-canonical because they are not used in verb inflection. Literally, criterion 8 would require this; see Palancar (2012: 823 and n.60) for discussion. I did not apply criterion 8 so strictly, because I find it more important to differentiate between classes that have parallels in the inflection of adjectives (and to a lesser extent, also articles and third person pronouns) and class 5, which is truly confined to nouns.
27. An attempt in the domain of agreement in Russian is found in Brown et al. (2009). The method used in this study is not comparable with the one used here and by Palancar (2012) because of the difference in the criteria of canonicity in the domains of agreement and inflectional classes.

References

Acquaviva, Paolo (2008), *Lexical Plurals: A Morphosemantic Approach*, Oxford: Oxford University Press.

Bonami, Olivier and Gilles Boyé (2015), 'Gender in French: Inflection or flexibility', paper presented at the workshop 'The Structure of Forms, the Form of Structure', Paris, January 2015, <http://www.llf.cnrs.fr/sites/llf.cnrs.fr/files/biblio//tonton-pres.pdf> (last accessed 19 February 2017).

Bond, Oliver (2018), 'Canonical Typology', in Jenny Audring and Francesca Masini (eds), *The Oxford Handbook of Morphological Theory*, Oxford: Oxford University Press, pp. 409–31.

Booij, Geert (1996), 'Inherent versus contextual inflection and the split morphology hypothesis', in Geert Booij and Jaap van Marle (eds), *Yearbook of Morphology 1995*, Dordrecht: Kluwer, pp. 1–16.

Brown, Dunstan, Carole Tiberius, Marina Chumakina, Greville Corbett and Alexander Krasovitsky (2009), 'Databases designed for investigating specific phenomena', in Martin Everaert, Simon Musgrave and Alexis Dimitriadis (eds), *The Use of Databases in Cross-Linguistic Studies*, Berlin and Boston: Mouton de Gruyter, pp. 117–54.

Camilli, Amerindo (1965), *Pronuncia e grafia dell'italiano*, 3rd rev. edn, ed. Piero Fiorelli, Florence: Sansoni.

Cappellaro, Chiara (2017), 'The semantic specialization of third person pronoun "esso" as [-human] in standard Italian', *Revue Romane*, 52 (2), pp. 113–36.

Chiari, Isabella (2013), 'Basic vocabulary and absolute homonyms', paper presented at Corpus Linguistics 2013, Lancaster University.

Chiari, Isabella and Tullio De Mauro (forthcoming), *Il nuovo vocabolario di base della lingua Italiana*, Rome: Sapienza Università Editrice.

Corbett, Greville G. (2000), *Number*, Cambridge: Cambridge University Press.

Corbett, Greville G. (2005), 'The canonical approach in typology', in Zygmunt Frajzyngier, Adam Hodges and David S. Rood (eds), *Linguistic Diversity and Language Theories*, Studies in Language Companion Series, 72, Amsterdam and Philadelphia: John Benjamins, pp. 25–49.

Corbett, Greville G. (2006), *Agreement*, Cambridge: Cambridge University Press.

Corbett, Greville G. (2007a), 'Canonical typology, suppletion, and possible words', *Language*, 83 (1), pp. 8–42.

Corbett, Greville G. (2007b), 'Deponency, syncretism and what lies between', in Matthew Baerman, Greville G. Corbett, Dunstan Brown and Andrew Hippisley (eds), *Deponency*

and Morphological Mismatches, Proceedings of the British Academy, 145, London: British Academy and Oxford University Press, pp. 21–43.
Corbett, Greville G. (2009), 'Canonical inflectional classes', in Fabio Montermini, Gilles Boyé and Jesse Tseng (eds), *Selected Proceedings of the 6th Décembrettes: Morphology in Bordeaux*, Somerville, MA: Cascadilla Proceedings Project, pp. 1–11.
Corbett, Greville G. (2015), 'Morphosyntactic complexity: A typology of lexical splits', *Language*, 91 (1), pp. 145–93.
D'Achille, Paolo (2005 [but 2007]), 'L'invariabilità dei nomi nell'italiano contemporaneo', *Studi di Grammatica Italiana*, 24, , pp. 189–209.
D'Achille, Paolo and Anna M. Thornton (2003), 'La flessione del nome dall'italiano antico all'italiano contemporaneo', in Nicoletta Maraschio and Teresa Poggi Salani (eds), *Italia linguistica anno Mille – Italia linguistica anno Duemila. Atti del XXXIV Congresso della Società di Linguistica Italiana*, Rome: Bulzoni, pp. 211–30.
D'Achille, Paolo and Anna M. Thornton (2008), 'I nomi femminili in -o', in Emanuela Cresti (ed.), *Prospettive nello studio del lessico italiano. Atti del IX Congresso Internazionale della SILFI*, Florence: Firenze University Press, pp. 473–81.
De Mauro, Tullio, Federico Mancini, Massimo Vedovelli and Miriam Voghera (1993), *Lessico di frequenza dell'italiano parlato*, Milan: Etas.
Di Domenico, Elisa (1997), *Per una teoria del genere grammaticale*, Padua: Unipress.
Dressler, Wolfgang U. (1985), *Morphonology: The Dynamics of Derivation*, Ann Arbor, MI: Karoma.
Dressler, Wolfgang U., Marianne Kilani-Schoch, Rossella Spina and Anna M. Thornton (2003), 'Le classi di coniugazione in italiano e francese', in Mathée Giacomo-Marcellesi and Alvaro Rocchetti (eds), *Il verbo italiano. Studi diacronici, sincronici, contrastivi, didattici. Atti del XXXV Congresso della Società di Linguistica Italiana, Parigi, 20–22 settembre 2002*, Rome: Bulzoni, pp. 397–416.
Dressler, Wolfgang U. and Anna M. Thornton (1996), 'Italian nominal inflection', *Wiener linguistische Gazette*, 57–9, pp. 1–26.
Evans, Nicholas (2007), 'Pseudo-argument affixes in Iwaidja and Ilgar: A case of deponent subject and object agreement', in Matthew Baerman, Greville G. Corbett, Dunstan Brown and Andrew Hippisley (eds), *Deponency and Morphological Mismatches*, Proceedings of the British Academy, 145, London: British Academy and Oxford University Press, pp. 271–96.
Gaeta, Livio (2013), '*Ecco, ecco, l'ho trovata*: La tenace persistenza di un'impalcatura cognitiva primaria', in Sabine De Knop, Fabio Mollica and Julia Kuhn (eds), *Konstruktionsgrammatik in den romanischen Sprachen*, Frankfurt am Main: Lang, pp. 45–74.
GRADIT (*Grande Dizionario Italiano dell'Uso*) (1999), ideato e diretto da Tullio De Mauro, Turin: UTET.
Haspelmath, Martin (1996), 'Word-class changing inflection and morphological theory', in Geert Booij and Jaap van Marle (eds), *Yearbook of Morphology 1995*, Dordrecht: Kluwer, pp. 43–66.
Iacobini, Claudio and Anna M. Thornton (2016), 'Morfologia e formazione delle parole', in Sergio Lubello (ed.), *Manuale di linguistica italiana*, Berlin and Boston: De Gruyter, pp. 190–221.
Matthews, P. H. (1991), *Morphology*, 2nd edn, Cambridge: Cambridge University Press.
Matthews, P. H. (1997), *The Concise Oxford Dictionary of Linguistics*, Oxford and New York: Oxford University Press.
Napoli, Donna Jo and Irene Vogel (1990), 'The conjugations of Italian', *Italica*, 67 (4), pp. 479–502.

Palancar, Enrique (2012), 'The conjugations classes of Tilapa Otomi: An approach from Canonical Typology', *Linguistics*, 50, pp. 782–832.

Pirrelli, Vito and Marco Battista (2000), 'The paradigmatic dimension of stem allomorphy in Italian verb inflection', *Rivista di Linguistica*, 12, pp. 307–80.

Ricca, Davide (2003), 'Cumulazione tra flessione e derivazione: un problema per una morfologia modulare', in Antonietta Bisetto, Claudio Iacobini and Anna M. Thornton (eds), *Scritti di morfologia in onore di Sergio Scalise in occasione del suo 60° compleanno*, Cesena: Caissa Italia, pp. 189–202.

Russi, Cinzia (2008), *Italian Clitics: An Empirical Study*, Berlin and New York: Mouton de Gruyter.

Santilli, Enzo (2014), *Italian Comparatives: A Case of Overabundance?*, bachelor's thesis, Università dell'Aquila, <https://www.academia.edu/9307153/Italian_Comparatives_a_Case_of_Overabundance> (last accessed 16 March 2017).

Serianni, Luca (in cooperation with Alberto Castelvecchi) (1988), *Grammatica italiana. Italiano comune e lingua letteraria*, Turin: UTET.

Stump, Gregory T. (2012), 'The formal and functional architecture of inflectional morphology', in Angela Ralli, Geert Booij, Sergio Scalise and Athanasios Karasimos (eds), *On-line Proceedings of the Eighth Mediterranean Morphology Meeting (MMM8)*, pp. 255–71.

Thornton, Anna M. (1999), 'Diagrammaticità, uniformità di codifica e morfomicità nella flessione verbale italiana', in Paola Benincà, Alberto M. Mioni and Laura Vanelli (eds), *Fonologia e morfologia dell'italiano e dei dialetti d'Italia*, Rome: Bulzoni, pp. 483–502.

Thornton, Anna M. (2001), 'Some reflections on gender and inflectional class assignment in Italian', in Chris Schaner-Wolles, John R. Rennison and Friedrich Neubarth (eds), *Naturally! Linguistic Studies in Honour of Wolfgang Ulrich Dressler Presented on the Occasion of his 60th Birthday*, Turin: Rosenberg and Sellier, pp. 479–87.

Thornton, Anna M. (2003), 'La rappresentazione dell'informazione morfologica nelle entrate lessicali', in Antonietta Bisetto, Claudio Iacobini and Anna M. Thornton (eds), *Scritti di morfologia in onore di Sergio Scalise in occasione del suo 60° compleanno*, Cesena: Caissa Italia, pp. 203–21.

Thornton, Anna M. (2010–11 [but 2013]), 'La non canonicità del tipo it. *braccio* // *braccia* / *bracci*: sovrabbondanza, difettività o iperdifferenziazione?', *Studi di grammatica italiana*, 29–30, pp. 419–77.

Thornton, Anna M. (2011), 'Overabundance (multiple forms realizing the same cell): A non-canonical phenomenon in Italian verb morphology', in Martin Maiden, John Charles Smith, Maria Goldbach and Marc-Olivier Hinzelin (eds), *Morphological Autonomy: Perspectives from Romance Inflectional Morphology*, Oxford: Oxford University Press, pp. 358–81.

Thornton, Anna M. (2012a), 'Overabundance in Italian verb morphology and its interactions with other non-canonical phenomena', in Thomas Stolz, Hitomi Otsuka, Aina Urdze and Johan van der Auwera (eds), *Irregularity in Morphology (and Beyond)*, Berlin: Akademie, pp. 251–69.

Thornton, Anna M. (2012b), 'La sovrabbondanza nei paradigmi verbali dell'italiano contemporaneo', in Patricia Bianchi, Nicola De Blasi, Chiara De Caprio and Francesco Montuori (eds), *La variazione nell'italiano e nella sua storia, Varietà e varianti linguistiche e testuali*, Atti dell'XI Congresso SILFI (Napoli, 5–7 ottobre 2010), Florence: Franco Cesati Editore, pp. 445–56.

Thornton, Anna M. (2013), 'Compagni di cella in una gabbia dorata: sull'uso di *vo* vs *vado* nell'italiano contemporaneo', in Cesáreo Calvo Rigual and Emili Casanova (eds), *Actes du XXVIe Congrès International de Linguistique et de Philologie Romanes (València, 6–11 de septembre de 2010)*, Berlin: Walter de Gruyter, pp. 1190–201.

Thornton, Anna M. (forthcoming), 'Overabundance: A Canonical Typology', in Franz Rainer, Francesco Gardani, Hans Christian Luschützky and Wolfgang U. Dressler (eds), *Competition in Inflection and Wordformation*, Dordrecht: Springer.

Thornton, Anna M., Claudio Iacobini and Cristina Burani (1997), *BDVDB: Una base di dati per il vocabolario di base della lingua italiana*, 2nd edn, Rome: Bulzoni.

Vincent, Nigel (1988), 'Italian', in Martin Harris and Nigel Vincent (eds), *The Romance Languages*, New York: Oxford University Press, pp. 279–313.

Wurzel, Wolfgang U. (1989), *Inflectional Morphology and Naturalness*, Dordrecht: Kluwer.

4

Waiting for the Word: Distributed Deponency and the Semantic Interpretation of Number in the Nen Verb

Nicholas Evans

> In attempting to define the notion 'possible human language', linguists must be able to define what is a possible word. Part of that enterprise is establishing the possible phenomena within inflectional morphology. (Corbett 2007: 21)

4.1 Introduction

A key question in exploring what is a possible word, across the languages of the world, is the issue of how it is composed internally from smaller units. In the canonical case, words will follow a principle of compositionality:

> Given the lexical semantics of a lexical item and a specification of its feature values, the meaning of the whole is fully predictable. (Corbett 2013: 56)

But there are many flies in this canonical ointment. Though there certainly are many languages close to the canonical one-form one-meaning agglutinative type (e.g. as exemplified by Swahili, Turkish or Warlpiri), the need to take varied classes of exception into account has led many theories of morphology to take the fully inflected word as the primary unit of analysis (cf. Anderson 2015). In this analytic shift, the key units are no longer classic 'morphemes' but paradigms (resisting simple factorial decomposition) or morphomes (in the form of phonological strings without straightforward semantic or inflectional values), accompanied by representational methods which allow for the gradual building up of word semantics in complex ways that can capture templatic ordering, discontinuous dependencies, and multiple, cumulative and distributed exponence.

For the typologist, however, this still leaves us asking what kinds of deviation from morphological compositionality are actually found in the world's languages. Only when we answer this can we develop a satisfying typology of these forms of non-canonical behaviour.

Generalised deponency – in which 'morphological forms ... give the "wrong signal" about their function' (Baerman et al. 2007: x) – is one particularly intriguing type of deviation from the compositional canon. The traditional use of the term 'deponent' is to refer 'to an anomaly in the inflection of verbs, throughout or in part of a paradigm' (Matthews 2007: 297), with the etymology of the metalinguistic term deponent, based on the notion of 'putting down', that they 'laid aside' (Matthews 2007: 297) their usual role. Classically, this would refer to a Latin verb like *sequor* 'I am following' putting aside its expected behaviour as a passive, as signalled by the *-r* suffix shared with true passives such as *caedor* 'I am being killed' (vs *caedo* 'I kill'). Work generalising the notion of deponency as a way of exploring 'misleading morphology', as represented by the chapters in Baerman et al. (2007), has shown how fruitful a notion deponency is as a way of systematising different ways that morphology can depart from the compositional canon. In particular, both Baerman et al. (2007) and Corbett (2007) set out typologies of various types of deviation, fitting in a number of subtypes of deponency in which the 'wrong signal' principle holds just within the morphological paradigm, rather than between the morphology of a word and its syntactic behaviour, as with the Latin example just mentioned.

My concern in this paper is to set out one type of 'extreme which has no name' (cf. Corbett 2007: 31), which is clearly morphological deponency but does not fit into the typology established so far.[1] I shall term this 'distributed deponency' because the mismatches only become evident once two or more subparadigms of a verbal word are combined (e.g. prefix and suffix; prefix, root and suffix). Typically, the deponencies result from a process of maximising morphomic combinatoriality, even where this creates combinations which appear at first sight to be semantically contradictory or impossible given the meanings of the constituents, or else by putting together morphemes in ways that would not normally be permitted by the morphotactic structure of the word they occur in. Heuristically I will define 'distributed deponency' as 'deponency which results from the non-compositional combination of inflectional material from different stem or affix positions, each with a clear basic meaning or function that is suppressed in the context of particular combinations'.

The present paper will illustrate the phenomenon with evidence from the four-valued system of verbal number agreement in the Papuan language Nen.[2] Nen, like its fellow languages of the Yam family, is spoken in Southern New Guinea, an area in which complex systems of verbal number agreement are common (Evans et al. 2017).[3] Yam family languages are characterised by complex systems of distributed exponence, by which 'morphosyntactic feature values can only be determined after unification of multiple structural positions' (Carroll 2017: 1). The norm is for them to distinguish three number values in verbal agreement – singular, dual and plural – with the distinction available for any core argument codable by verbal agreement (subject, object and indirect object). However, Nen has innovated a fourth 'greater plural' number value (Corbett 2000: 30–5), confined to absolutive arguments in declaratives, and subjects in imperatives. This development is seemingly recent, given the lack of constructional congeners in other Yam languages. What is interesting for the purposes of this paper is the wide variety of morphological mechanisms that have been recruited to yield the fourth number, according to the verb type involved. Intuitively, the developments we will discuss appear to have been guided by two diachronic principles:

(i) Greater-plural morphological target. The innovative form always adds the largest-cardinality number value over the top of the pre-existing number set, even if a knock-on effect is that the formally 'expected' plural now is pushed down to something more like a paucal value since it is opposed to a new value of higher cardinality. Innovative forms never come in and create paucals under the existing plural.

(ii) Opportunistic recombination of existing forms. None of the innovative forms recruit new morphological material by grammaticalisation. Instead, new semantic values are created by innovative recombination of existing morphological material, often by bringing in combinations that would appear to be ruled out either on the basis of the semantics of the individual components, or by the standard positional templates of the construction type.

The combined effect of (i) and (ii) is to amplify the system's semantic expressivity by adding a fourth inflectional number value, available for all relevant verbal subclasses. But this comes at the expense of moving away from a system in which morphological elements are always directly interpretable semantically. As such, Nen is an intriguing example of rapid paradigmaticisation leading to the creation of distributed deponency.

4.2 The Nen Language: Background

Nen is a language of the Nambu branch of the Yam family, a Papuan family counting around 15 languages in Southern New Guinea, just north of the Torres Strait, in the Morehead District of Western Province, Papua New Guinea and in Merauke District, Papua province, Indonesia. See Evans (2012a) and Evans et al. (2017) for overall surveys of the region, Evans (2012b, 2014, 2015a, 2015b) and Evans and Miller (2016) on various aspects of Nen grammar and phonology, and Siegel (2014) on the morphology of aspect in the closely related language Nama, which includes discussion of how the three-valued system of verbal agreement works in that language.

Regarding its basic typological traits, Nen and its relatives have the following characteristics:

(i) ergative/absolutive case morphology
(ii) split-S verbal agreement, whereby there is a closed set of verbs (mostly statives) which code subject agreement by the identical prefixes used for objects (henceforth 'U-prefixes') and a much larger set of 'middle' verbs which code subject agreement by the same prefixes used for transitive subjects (henceforth 'A-suffixes'). Case-marking is not affected by this split: subjects of both types take the absolutive, as behoves an intransitive subject. Middle verbs are characterised semantically by dynamicity rather than agentivity, since alongside

agentive verbs like *owabs* 'talk' there are dynamic but non-agentive verbs like *uwis* 'fall'

(iii) SOV word order in general, though subject to considerable pragmatic flexibility, and with the exception of 'experiencer object' constructions (like 'hunger-ERG does me') which are OSV

(iv) widespread use of nominalised clauses for a range of purposes, such as adverbial clauses of purpose or circumstance, with the nominalised verb generally inflected for case; unlike in typical Trans New Guinea languages there is no verb serialisation

(v) morphologically complex verbs, with a rich TAM system

(vi) like other languages of Southern New Guinea, inflectional categories are (1) constructed – incrementing subcategories across sites (i.e. combining prefix and suffix series to give TAM values), and (2) distributed, i.e. integrating material from various affix positions and free pronouns to give full person/number/TAM specification, including choices (such as prefix grade) that cannot themselves be assigned any semantic significance (examples below). A further characteristic that becomes relevant as deponency extends its reach are that parts of the system become non-monotonic: provisional semantic values for inflectional categories may be overridden as morphological information is assembled for the whole word.

In the remainder of this section, we elaborate on these characteristics, with particular reference to the verbal morphology, so as to give the reader enough background to follow the discussion of number in subsequent sections. In §4.2.1 I show how unificational procedures are not just found within the verb, but also involve external elements like pronouns, TAM particles and time adverbs. In §4.2.2 I illustrate some of the main features of unification within the verbal word, and in §4.2.3 I illustrate the main verb-structure templates, since the different methods of forming greater plurals are largely conditioned by differences in verbal template.

4.2.1 Extramorphological Unification of Verbs with Pronouns, TAM Particles and Adverbs

Verbal affixes, free pronouns and preverbal TAM particles/adverbs are complementary in the information they contain, and need to be unified before full semantic specification is achieved. Compare the isolated words in (1), each semantically underspecified in some way, with the mini-clauses in (2a–f), in which unification across the various sites has in each case eliminated any ambiguity in TAM or person.

(1) a. *yäm* [be:IPFV:NPREH:2|3PL] 'you (PL)/they (PL) are, were (earlier today), will be'
 b. *bm* [2.ABS (any number)] 'you'
 c. *bä* [3.ABS (any number] 'he, she, they, him, her, them'
 d. *nowabte* [talk:IPFV:NPREH:2|3SG] 'you (SG) talk/talked (earlier today), will talk, (s)he talks, talked (earlier today), will talk';

e. *nowabtat* [talk:IPFV:NPREH:2|3PL] 'you (> 2) talk/talked (earlier today), will talk, they (> 2) talk, talked (earlier today), will talk'
f. *kae* 'yesterday, tomorrow; ± 1 day'

(2) a. bä yä-m
 3ABS 2|3NSG-be:ND
 'They (more than two) are.'
 b. bm yä-m
 2ABS 2|3NSG-be:ND
 'You (more than two) are.'
 c. bm tba n-owab-t-e
 2ABS IMM M:α-talk-B.IPFV:ND-2|3SGA
 'You (SG) talked just now.'
 d. bm bä n-owab-t-e
 2ABS FUT M:α-talk-B.IPFV:ND-2|3SGA
 'You (SG) will talk.'
 e. bä bä n-owab-t-e
 3ABS FUT M:α-talk-B.IPFV:ND-2|3SGA
 '(S)he will talk.'
 f. bä kae (bä) n-owab-t-e
 3ABS ±1day FUT M:α-talk-B.IPFV:ND-2|3SGA
 '(S)he will talk tomorrow.'

Note that whereas in (1) I give word-level glosses of inflectional values, in (2) I have shown more of the internal structure of the word using traditional 'morphemic' glosses, though in some cases ambiguities need to be preserved (e.g. 2|3, 'second or third person') and in others no semantic value can be assigned until information at more than one site is combined. For example, the U-prefixes, including the middle prefix [glossed M], can belong to any one of three series, glossed α, β and γ; these cannot be assigned meanings of their own but combine with the TAM suffixes to give a precise TAM value (§4.3.2; Evans 2015b).

4.2.2 Unification within the Verbal Word

As mentioned above, transitive verbs generally index their objects by prefix ('U-prefixes') and their subjects by suffix ('A-suffixes'); in ditransitive verbs it is the indirect object which is indexed by prefix. A closed class of monovalent verbs index their sole argument by U-prefixes, and a larger class ('middle verbs') index their sole argument by A-suffix. Both U- and A-affixes include TAM information which needs to be unified across these sites before the semantics is clear. For example, the '(basic declarative) imperfective' suffix can combine with the α-series of U-prefixes to give 'non-prehodiernal' (any time after yesterday, i.e. today past, present or future, then selected by preverbal particle), and with the β-series to give 'yesterday past'.

(3) a. tba   y-aka-ta-n   b. kae   t-aka-ta-n
       IMM   3SGU:α-see-B.IPFV:ND-1SGA   ±1.day 3SGU:β-see-B.IPFV:ND-1SGA
       'I saw him just now.'   'I saw him yesterday.'

For some A + U combinations, information 'leaks' so that the A-suffix also has information about U, or the U-prefix has information about A. I term these 'interactive' affixes.[4] Since the behaviour of the interactive suffixes is complex, I confine myself here to illustrating the interactive suffix -ng, which indicates that a second or third person singular subject is acting on a dual object (any person); it is confined to imperfective aspect. First consider how the non-singular object values are built up in (4a–c), which have a first singular subject: the dual value of the object's number in (4b) is composed by combining the non-singular value of the U-prefix with the dual value of the thematic.

(4) a. **ye-ze-na-n**   b. **ye-zer-Ø-n**
       2|3NSGU:α-cook-B.IPFV:ND-1SGA   2|3NSGU:α-cook-B.IPFV:ND-1SGA
       'I cook them (more than two).'   'I cook them (two).'
    c. **ye-ze-n-e**   d. **ye-zer-Ø-ng**
       2|3NSGU:α-cook-B.IPFV:ND-2|3SGA   2|3NSGU:α-cook- B.IPFV:DU-2|3SGA>DUU
       'You/(s)he cooks them (more than two).'   'You/(s)he cooks them (two).'

Now contrast the dual in (4b) with that in (4d), which also build up object number, but employ the interactive suffix -ng. This suffix indicates both that the subject is second or third person singular, **and** that the object is dual. In fact, we have an occurrence of dual exponence here as well, since the 'zero' thematic already marks the verb as dual and imperfective – it is opposed to the non-dual imperfective form -ta, as in (2d–f) and (3a,b).

In general, then, the system of U-prefixes + A-suffixes forms a 'circumfixal paradigm' where prefixes plus suffixes need to be integrated to give specified features for the person and number of actor and undergoer, as well as for TAM. A system that would reflect this distributed-morphology view better would gloss (4d), for example, as (5a), where ye\. . ./ng is a circumfix with the specified values, or would adopt an even more clearly paradigm-based model which does not delineate root boundaries, as in (5b).

(5) a. ye\zer/ng
       2|3NSGS>2|3DUO:NPREH.IPFV\cook
    b. yezerng
       cook:2|3NSGS>2|3DUO:NPREH.IPFV

According to my expository purpose I will move between the types of gloss used in (4d) and (5b), and when it is useful I will place a gloss of the (5b) type in brackets after a segmented word.

Table 4.1 Morphological structure for ambifixing verbs

Inflectional prefixes				Stem		Suffix	
						Thematic	Desinence
U (pers/num) + TAM	(Directional)	(Future imperative)	(Diathetic prefix)*	Root		Aspect + num^du	A (pers/num) + TAM

*A limited number of double occurrences and arguably one triple occurrence are possible in this slot.[5] Effectively there is a valence-increasing prefix *(w)a-*, which can function as either a causative or an applicative, and a valence-decreasing prefix *a-*, which can function as an autobenefactive, decausative, reflexive or reciprocal. Both *(w)a-* and *a-* have a number of allomorphs, sensitive to the following vowel, which are not discussed here.

4.2.3 A Bit More on Verbal Word Structure

Nen verb structure is best understood by beginning with the maximal case – 'transitive ambifixing verbs' with full prefixing and suffixing possibilities – and then looking at various restrictions producing subsets of this structure. Table 4.1 illustrates the structure of ambifixing verbs, and (6) gives an example with a relatively elaborated word.

(6) yä-ng-wa-yab-ta-n
 3NSGU:α-AW-BEN-show-B.IPFV:ND-1SGA
 'I showed them to them (e.g. the coconuts).'

Middle verbs (Table 4.2) are also ambifixing, but are more restricted in what can occupy the initial prefix slot. Instead of the range of person/number sensitive U-prefixes, there is just a single prefix form, invariant for person and number, which takes the variants *n-* (α-series), *k-* (β-series) or *g-* (γ-series). The one exception to this is the special greater-plural construction to be discussed in §4.4.3, which uses coding that looks like a transitive verb. Some middle verbs are derived from transitives by diathetic prefix (e.g. *awakaes* 'see each other/self' from *wakaes* 'see'), as illustrated in (7a), while others like *owans* 'set off' are intrinsic middles not derived from any other verb, as illustrated in (7b); see §4.3.2 for further discussion.

(7) a. n-ng-owan-t-e (nngowante)
 M:α-AW-set.off-B.IPFV:ND-2|3SGA set.off:AW:NPREH.IPFV:2|3SGS
 'You/(s)he are/is setting off.'

Table 4.2 Morphological structure for middle verbs

Inflectional prefixes				Stem	Suffix	
					Thematic	Desinence
M + TAM	(Directional)	(Future imperative)	(Diathetic prefix)*	Root	Aspect + num^du	A(pers/num) + TAM

b. k-a-wakae-we-ng!   (kawakaeweng)
   M:β-RR-look.at-IPFV.IMP:DU-2NSGA:IMP   look.at:RR:2DUS:IPFV.IMP
   'You two look at yourselves/each other!'

The template for prefixing verbs is shown in Table 4.3. Inflectional prefixes on prefixing verbs resemble the situation with ambifixing verbs (though the use of diathetic prefixes is heavily restricted), but suffixes are limited or non-existent: they never show the person values of any argument, though the 'stative' suffix, found with positionals, encodes a dual vs non-dual contrast. Prefixing verbs are also much more limited aspectually, essentially drawing only on the imperfective series, and the use of suffixation to encode TAM is highly restricted. A further important difference is that prefixing verbs lack infinitives, whereas ambifixing verbs have them – forming them by suffixing -s to the verb stem (including any diathetic prefixes).

Of the 50 or so prefixing verbs, the vast majority are positionals, which alone among Nen verbs take a special 'stative' suffix (8a). But there are a few other prefixing verbs, most importantly the verb 'be' (non-dual root *m*, dual root *ren*, (2a,b)) and its derivatives 'come' (8b) and 'go', formed by prefixing the appropriate directional (e.g. *n*- 'toward' to give 'come').

Table 4.3 Morphological template for prefixing verbs

Inflectional prefixes				Stem	Suffix	
					Thematic	Desinence
U (pers/num) + TAM	(Directional)	(Future imperative)	(Diathetic prefix)*	Root	STAT + num^du	TAM

(8) a. mnɡ̄   y-trom-ngr
       house(ABS)   3SGU:α-be.erected-STAT:ND
    'A house is standing.'
    b. ybe   dgae-ngama   yna   mer   wimb   y-n-m
       INDEF where-ABL   DEM   good   smell(ABS) 3SGU:α-TOW-be:ND
    'There's a good smell coming from somewhere.'

4.3 Morphemes, Morphomes and In-between

4.3.1 Definition

Nen verbs – as well as other parts of speech – offer many examples of very tidily behaved 'morphemes', in the classic sense of a minimal part of a word exhibiting a clear correspondence of meaning to form, as well as a clearly defined combinatorics (including specified position within the word). To take two well-behaved citizens, each with the form /n/, we can cite the 'towards' directional prefix *n-* (8b), and the 1SGA desinence *-n* (6). Once their word-position is allowed for, these forms are not only precise and exclusive in what they mean – neither can express anything else than 'towards' and '1SGA' respectively – but they are the only formal means of expressing these meanings. They therefore exhibit a perfect one-to-one correspondence between form and meaning, of the type assumed in classic 'item and arrangement' models of morphology during the American structuralist era.

On the other hand, there are many other morphological units for which the relationship to semantics is much more tortuous, or absent altogether, and which are better considered as 'purely morphological functions' (Aronoff 1994: 25) or as '*morphomic categories* ... which figure in the systematic organisation of a language's morphology but which are not isomorphic with any morphosyntactic, semantic, or phonological categories' (Round's 2013: 33 exegesis of Aronoff 1994; emphasis mine). We illustrate the usefulness of the 'morphome' concept in the following section by considering the functioning of the three U-prefix series.

4.3.2 Prefix Series and TAM

As we have already seen, the U-prefix slot, in all types of verb, provides information about the person/number of the 'undergoer' (subject of prefixing verbs, object or indirect objects) or, with middle verbs, it simply acts as a placeholder without giving argumental information. In addition to this information, however, it also provides information about TAM, in conjunction with the verbal suffixes, through three form-series arbitrarily labelled α, β and γ. For example, the 1SG U-prefix takes the form *w-* in the α-series, *q-* (/k͡p/) in the β-series, and *ḡ-* (/g͡b/) in the γ-series, while the 3SG U-prefix takes the form *y-* in the α-series, *t-* in the β-series, and *d-* in the γ-series. In general, α-prefixes begin with sonants, β-prefixes with voiceless stops at the same or a related place of articulation, and γ-prefixes are simply the voiced equivalents of the β-prefixes. A sample triplet is given in (9).

(9) a. wakatat   <w-(w)akae-ta-t
    see:3plS>1sGO:IPFV.NPREH   1sGU:α-see-B.IPFV:ND-3NSGA
    'They see me.'
  b. qakatat   <q-(w)akae-ta-t
    see:3PLS>1sGO:IPFV.HEST.PST   1sGU:β-see-B.IPFV:ND-3NSGA
    'They saw me (yesterday).'
  c. ḡakatawt   <ḡ-(w)akae-taw-t
    see:3PLS>1sGO:IPFV.RP   1sGU:γ-see-R.IPFV:ND-3NSGA
    'They saw me (long ago).'

The full semantics of all prefix + suffix combinations is shown in Table 4.4.

The three series of undergoer prefixes are difficult to characterise by precise semantic glosses. For example, for imperatives the β-series is associated with the present ('do it now!') and the α-series for commands to perform an action further away in time ('do it later!'), while for imperfective declaratives the α-series is associated with the present and the β-series with the yesterday past. Likewise, the γ series leads back to remote past in the imperfective, but forward to the future in the perfective. Although some glimpse of semantic commonality for the γ-series might be salvaged ('remote' past and future, as well as irrealis), there are other times which may be even more remote (preterite and primordial) which take the α-series.

Table 4.4 Combinations of prefix and suffix series and their meanings

Aspect category	Prefix series			Suffix
	α	β	γ	
Imperfective	Future imperative	Immediate imperative	Mediated imperative	Imperative
	Present, future or today past (non-prehodiernal past)	Yesterday past (hesternal past); definite future prediction		Basic
			Remote past	Past
Neutral	Primordial		Hope	Primordial
	Preterite			Preterite
	Customary/habitual past		Unrealised action	Irrealis
Perfective		Immediate imperative		Imperative
			Perfective future	Future
	Accomplished past action	Unexpected past action		Past

Instead of coming up with highly contorted semantic characterisations for the three series, it seems better to regard them as abstract morphomes which combine with TAM suffixes to produce a semantically specified circumfixal series.

Our discussion in this section has touched on two extremes. At one end of the spectrum are what one might call 'trusties' – classic 'morphemes' in an item-arrangement model, with a stable triplet of form::meaning::combinatorics, e.g. *-n* '1sGA'. At the other extreme are canonical morphomes, such as the three prefixal series just mentioned, which have no identifiable semantic value but combined with other morphomes during the process of morphological composition, and it is only when the whole word is assembled that they contribute to the cashing out of a semantic value, such as 'present imperative', 'yesterday past imperfective', and so forth. We could call these morphomes 'jokers'.

If all of a language's morphology sat at one or the other of these extremes, the concept of deponency would not be needed. Morphemes, in their classic definition, have a clear meaning – there is nothing 'misleading' about their semantics. On the other hand, morphomes (at least canonical ones) have given up any claim to semantics, so there is no basic meaning for them to mislead with.

Between these poles, however, lies another case.[6] We can call these entities 'double-agents': they look like 'trusties' most of the time, but in particular combinations they switch their value. In other words, their behaviour is occasionally non-monotonic – there is a default semantic interpretation, found in most contexts, but there are also cases where this is overwritten once other elements are present in the word. This is the stuff of deponency, and will be particularly relevant to our discussion of number in Nen. To show how it works, we first examine the 'basic' three-way number system in §4.4.3, where the semantics works in a relatively straightforward manner, before passing, in §4.4.4, to the many ways in which groups of morphemes produce number values that do not fall out from the values of their parts.

4.3.3 Verbal Arguments: The Basic System (SG VS DU VS PL)

Number, as expressed by verbal agreement, basically has a three-valued number system – singular, dual and plural. This is obtained by crossing a singular vs non-singular distinction in agreement indexing (e.g. *n-* '2sGU' vs *yä-* '2NSGU', *-n* '1sGA' vs *-m* '1NSGA') with a dual vs non-dual system in its thematics or (suppletive) roots, e.g. √*m* 'be:ND' vs √*ren* 'be:DU' or *-t(a)* 'IPFV:ND' vs *-Ø-* 'B.IPFV:DU' or *-e* 'IPFV. IMP:DU'.

Table 4.5 illustrates this system for the actor arguments of the verb *waprs* 'make'. Note that we are holding undergoer constant at 3sG, and actor at second person; *bm* is second person in all numbers in the absolutive, but in the ergative is singular only, with *bmbem* used for non-singular. These forms do not make any distinction between paucals and greater plurals.

There are three criteria for considering this three-valued number system to be basic.

First, the basic values are in principle codable by inflection at a regular site, or

Table 4.5 Crossing of SG vs NSG and dual vs non-dual morphology to give basic three-way contrast[a]

	'make it!' (IMP)	'made it (just now)'
Thematic or root	-ta- 'IPFV:ND' vs -e- 'IPFV:IMP:DU'	-ta- 'IPFV:ND' vs -ø- 'B.IPFV:DU'
Affix	-ø 2SGA:IMP -ng 2NSGA:IMP	-e 2|3SGA -t 2|3NSGA
2SG	bm taprta 'you (SG) make it!'	bm yaprte 'you (sg) made it'
2DU	bmbem tapreng 'you (DU) make it!'	bmbem yaprt 'you (DU) made it'
2PL	bmbem taprtang 'you (PL) make it!'	bmbem yaprtat 'you (PL) made it'

[a] Note that for the sake of conciseness recent past translations are offered for the right-hand column, but present or future translations are also possible.

combination of two regular sites in the case of the thematic plus prefix/desinence combination.

Second the basic values are equally available for both arguments that can be verbally indexed: subject, and object or indirect object, or to cast this in terms of the affix types, the arguments indexed by both actor and undergoer morphology.

Third, a consistent coding strategy is available across all verb classes and all types of argument.

Once we pass to the fourth number value, to be discussed in the next section, we will see that, according to the construction type, one or more of these criteria are violated: the means for encoding the fourth number are cobbled together from a number of methods. These are inconsistent in terms of their site, restricted to one verbal argument (absolutive, except for future imperatives), and particular to the verb class involved.

4.4 Elaborations Bringing in a Plural vs Greater Plural Contrast

We now examine the range of very disparate methods that Nen has developed for encoding a four-way number contrast. A note on the semantics of the two largest categories: according to the verb class, speakers sometimes characterise this as a contrast between paucal (three or four) vs plural contrast, and sometimes as a plural vs greater plural ('many like a rugby team', 'the majority', etc.).

Since, as mentioned above, it is always the largest cardinality which is expressed by the special, marked method and the second-largest cardinality which aligns formally with the basic construction, I will use the terms 'plural' and 'greater plural' to describe the semantic contrast in each case, glossing the latter as PL△ (where the symbol suggests 'upwardly boosted plural'), and leaving for further investigation the precise question of where the cardinality cut-off lies in each case and what determines it.

4.4.1 Greater Plurals in Positional Constructions

Positionals are stative verbs encoding posture (e.g. sit, stand, lie) or position (e.g. 'be up high', 'be low', 'be in a tree fork'). Person/number information is shown by prefix in the same way as with prefixing verbs like 'be'. About 45 positional verbs have been recorded so far. They are morphologically distinctive in being the only verbs to take a 'stative' suffix which is a portmanteau for number, as well as having other distinctive morphosyntactic characteristics discussed in Evans (2014). Since the 'stative' suffix is obligatory, and hence semantically uninformative, it will be glossed when giving morpheme-by-morpheme glosses but not in whole-word glosses.

Positional verbs are unique in constructing the extra number contrast by forming the greater plural out of the *singular prefix* plus the *dual suffix*, as shown in Table 4.6.

Sentence examples illustrating this are given in (10a–d).

(10) a. mnḡ   y-trom-ngr   [ytromngr]
        house 3SGU:α-be.erected-STAT:ND   be.erected:3SGS:NPREH
        'A house is standing.'
     b. mnḡ   yä-trom-aran   [yätromaran]
        house 3NSGU:α-be.erected-STAT:DU   be.erected:3DUS:NPREH
        'Two houses are standing.'
     c. mnḡ   yä-trom-ngr   [yätromngr]
        house 3NSGU:α -be.erected-STAT:ND   be.erected:3PLS:NPREH
        'Three or a few house(s) are standing.' (paucal)
     d. mnḡ   y-trom-aran   [ytromaran]
        house 3SGU:α-be.erected-STAT:DU   be.erected:3PL⚠S:NPREH
        'All the/many houses are standing.' (greater/exhaustive plural)[7]

4.4.2 Greater Plurals with 'come/go'

Normally 'come' and 'go' are formed by prefixing the 'towards' and 'away' forms to the root for 'be' (thus 'come' is 'be hither'). However, for 'come' and 'go' (i.e. not for 'be') there is a suppletive root √ewelmän used for greater plurals. This takes

Table 4.6 Four-way number contrast with positionals

Number	Pronominal prefix	Stative suffix (non-remote)	Stative suffix (remote past)
Singular	SG	-ngr	-ngron
Dual	NSG	-aran	-aron
Plural	NSG	-ngr	-ngron
Greater plural	SG	-aran	-aron

singular undergoer prefixes (11g,h); note that if the subject is universally quantified by *gbres* it is placed in the oblique case rather than the expected absolutive, as with *tbe* in (11g).

(11) a. ynd   w-ng-m
          1ABS   1SGU:α-AW-be:ND
          'I am going.'

      b. bä   y-ng-m
          3ABS   3SGU:α-AW-be:ND
          '(S)he is going.'

      c. ynd   yn-ng-ren
          1ABS   1NSGU:α-AW-be:DU
          'We two are going.'

      d. bä   yä-ng-ren
          3ABS   3NSGU:α-AW-be:DU
          'They (two) are going.'

      e. ynd   yn-ng-m
          1ABS   1NSGU:α-AW-be:ND
          'We (few) are going.'

      f. bä   yä-ng-m
          3ABS   3NSGU:α-AW-be:ND
          'They (a few) are going.'

      g. tbe   gbres   w-ng-ewelmän
          1NSG.OBL all   1SGU:α-AW-be:PL△
          'We are all going.'

      h. bä   y-ng-ewelmän
          3ABS   3SGU:α-AW-be:PL△
          'They (many) are going.'

This is the only verb that has a special suppletive form for greater plural.

4.4.3 Greater Plurals with 'be'

The prefixing verb 'be' in Nen has a number-suppletive root: non-dual √m is used for singulars, and for any number larger than two, while √ren is used for duals. Combining this with our regular undergoer prefixes, in the third person, gives: *ym* '(s)he is', *yären* 'they two are', *yäm* 'they (more than two) are'. There are of course other forms for first and second person, and other tense values, which are not given here.

Just in the third person, the prefix *ng-*, which otherwise means 'away', can be combined with the third singular prefix and the non-dual root to give a greater plural meaning. As a result, the word form *yngm* is ambiguous between a third singular 'away' reading – '(s)he goes' – and a third person greater plural 'be' meaning: 'they (many) are'. I shall call this use of *ng-* 'multal', and we shall see below that it is also found with the objects of transitive verbs. Its occurrence is mutually exclusive with a prefix encoding direction: **ynngm* [3SG-TOW-MU-be:ND] or **yngnm* [3SG-MU-TOW-be:ND] cannot mean 'they (many) come' and **yngngm* cannot mean 'they (many) go' – these are expressed by the suppletive root *ewelmän* as we saw in the previous section.[8] An example of the greater plural use is provided in (12).

(12) tendewere   är-bende   yétqén   gbres   y-ng-m
      old.time   person-PL.GEN   name(ABS)   all   3SGU:α-MU-be:DU
      'They are all old people's names.'

4.4.4 Greater Plurals with Middle Verbs

With middle verbs, the undergoer prefix is normally invariant for person/number,[9] while the actor suffix shows the person/number of the subject; compare the *n-* in *nowabtan* 'I talk', *nowabtam* 'we (more than two) talk', *nowabte* '(s)he/you (SG) talk(s)', *nowabtat* 'you (PL)/they (PL) talk', etc.

However, just with greater plurals, the locus of number marking is reversed: now it is the actor suffix that is invariant (using the 3SG form), while the prefix gives the person/number of the subject.[10] Thus from the middle verb *aebyängs* 'to fly' we get (13).[11]

(13) a. amni   n-aebn-d-e   (naebnde)
       bird   M:α-fly-B.IPFV:ND-2|3SGA   fly:2|3SGS:IPFV:NPREH
       'A bird is flying.'
   b. amni   n-aebyäng-Ø-t   (naebyängt)
       bird   M:α-fly-B.IPFV:DU-2|3NSGA fly:2|3DUS:IPFV:NPREH
       'Two birds are flying.'
   c. amni   n-aebn-da-t   (naebndat)
       bird   M:α-fly-B.IPFV:ND-2|3NSGA fly:2|3PLS:IPFV:NPREH
       'Some birds are flying.'
   d. amni   yaw-aebn-d-e   (yawaebnde)
       bird   2|3NSGU:α-fly-B.IPFV:ND-2|3SGA fly:2|3PL△S:IPFV:NPREH
       'Many birds are flying.'

Note that, morphologically, large plurals of this class, as exemplified by (13d), are formally identical to ambifixing transitive verbs: if we just had the verb, its form would suggest the parsing 'it is flying them'.

4.4.5 Greater Plurals with Future Imperatives

So far all examples of greater plurals have involved intransitive subjects – of positionals, 'come' and 'go', 'be', and monovalent middle verbs like 'fly'. However, just in the case of a special type of imperative, namely the future imperative, the four-way number contrast is extended to transitive subjects as well.

Regular imperatives in Nen are confined to the giving of commands to do something here and now. They are expressed by combining the β-prefix series with the imperative suffix (cf. Table 4.4), and this imperative suffix (combined with the thematic) is confined to the basic three-valued number system.

Future imperatives are more complex, both semantically and morphologically. These give a command for a state of affairs to be brought about or hold at some point in the future. Whereas regular imperatives select β-series U-prefixes, future imperatives select α-series prefixes, and in addition deploy the future imperative prefix just before the root, as shown in (14).

(14) a. k-n-m!   (knm)
       M:β-TOW-be:ND be:towards:2SGS:IMP
       'Come (SG) (now)!'
   b. n-n-a-m   poa!   (nnam)
       M:α-TOW-FUT.IMP-be:ND later be:towards:2SGS:F.IMP
       'Come (SG) (later)!'

Table 4.7 Imperative forms for *owabs* 'talk' in the regular and future imperatives

Reg. imp.	SG	DU	PL	
2 (bm)	kowabta	kowabeng	kowabtang	
Fut. imp.	SG	DU	PL	PL△
2 (bm)	nangowabta	nandowabe	nandowabta	nandowabtang
3 (bä)	nangowabta	nandowabe	nandowabta	nandowabtang

Morphologically, future imperatives of ambifixing verbs differ from all other inflected forms in having a regular method for encoding the number of their subjects through prefixation, contrasting singular (*ng-*) vs non-singular (*nd-*). The presence of this prefix 'frees up', as it were, the singular vs non-singular imperative suffix, which contrasts Ø vs -*ng* in present imperatives, so that -*ng* can be used specifically in future imperatives to code greater plurals, while regular plurals are expressed through the combination of the future imperative plural prefix *nd-* and the lack of an overt desinence, which would express singular in present imperatives. Note the different values of -*ng* in the regular and future imperatives in Table 4.7.

Note also that the thematic -*e* keeps its value of dual (imperfective) imperative in both constructions, and thematic -*ta* keeps its value of non-dual (imperfective) imperative.

An example of the greater plural use of this verb is given in (15), with the further twist that the future imperative subject prefix is left-reduplicated – a possibility only available with future imperatives – to give the meaning 'keep doing X over and over, in the future'.

(15) Megaphone announcement by village headman:
Bm   n-nd-a-nd-owab-ta-ng!
2ABS   M:α-ITER-F.IMP-2NSGa.F.IMP-talk-ND.IPFV-2|3PL△A.F.IMP
(nndandowabtang)
talk:ITER:2|3PL△:S:F.IMP
'All of you keep on talking (to the linguist) over and over again!' (so he learns the language)

4.4.6 Greater Plural Objects with Transitive Verbs

To get greater plurals for the objects of transitive verbs, yet another strategy is used. This involves three elements: the singular form of the undergoer prefix, the multal prefix *ng-* (already encountered with 'be' in §4.4.3), and the choice of the imperfective aspect. Since the 'imperfective' vs 'perfective' contrast in Nen is essentially one of durative vs momentaneous action (see Siegel 2014 on the similar system in Nama), it is certainly not unexpected to get greater plural readings through the choice of the imperfective.

This construction is illustrated with the following quadruplet of sentences, (16). Note that these were given as a paradigmatic series and all but the greater plural were given using the perfective past form, whereas the greater plural used the imperfective.

(16) a. ynd   ämbs   dalmadalma mnḡ   krug-an   y-mse-nd-n
        1SG.ERG one   ladder(ABS) house side-LOC 3SGU:α-lean-PST.PFV:ND-1SGA
        'I leaned one ladder against the side of the house.'
    b. ynd   sombes dalmadalma mnḡ   krug-an   yä-ms-a-n
        1SG.ERG two   ladder(ABS) house side-LOC 3NSGU:α-lean-PST.PFV:DU-1SGA
        'I leaned two ladders against the side of the house.'
    c. ynd   nambis dalmadalma mnḡ   krug-an   yä-mse-nd-n
        1SG.ERG three   ladder(ABS) house side-LOC 3NSGU:α-lean-PST.PFV:ND-1SGA
        'I leaned three ladders against the side of the house.'
    d. ynd   terber dalmadalma mnḡ   krug-an   y-ng-ms-ta-n
        1SG.ERG many   ladder(ABS) house side-LOC 3SGU:α-MU-lean-B.IPFV:ND-1SG
        'I leaned many ladders against the side of the house.'

4.5 Summary of Nen Strategies for Composing Four-Way Number System

As the preceding discussion will have made clear, a diverse range of strategies are used to compose greater plural values. These are summarised in Table 4.8.

A natural first line of attack, confronted with any individual construction, is to try and rationalise the grounds for extending the component number meanings to a greater plural reading, when co-occurring in a particular combination. For example, it might be argued that singulars often have an affinity with universal quantification (as in English statements like *The kangaroo is a hopping animal*). Or, to cite a second pattern, the peculiar patterning of the positional data (Table 4.6) might be accounted for by positing two cross-cutting values: an 'outer' vs 'inner' value for *y-* vs *yä-* (where 'outer' is singular and greater plural, 'inner' is dual and plural) and an 'odd' vs 'even' value for *-ngr* vs *-aran*, as in (17).[12]

Table 4.8 Construction types composing plural vs greater plural contrast

Construction type	Formation	Composition of greater plural (and ordinary plural where unexpected)
Positional verbs (§4.4.1)	SGU + DU stative suffix > plural	SG + DU > PL△
'come/go' (§4.4.2)	SGU (in appropriate person) + suppletive plural stem	SG + √Suppl > PL△
'be' (§4.4.3)	SGU + multal (with 'be')	SG + multal > PL△
Middle verbs (§4.4.4)	SGU (replacing invariant M, and with 2SG = 3SG syncretism) + RR + 3SGA	3SG + NSG > PL△
Subjects of future imperatives (§4.4.5)	NSGA:F.IMP + SG.IMP > pl NSGA:F.IMP + PL.IMP > PL+	PL + SG > PL PL + PL > PL△
Objects of transitive verbs (§4.4.6)	SGU + multal + imperfective aspect	SG + multal + imperfective > PL△

(17) outer y-   odd   -ngr   singular
      inner yä- even -aran dual
      inner yä- odd   -ngr   plural
      outer y-   even -aran greater plurals

Or again, one might motivate a semantic extension, in the case of prefixal *ng-*, from an original 'away, along' meaning, to greater iterated plural in the case of actions carried out, with a singular object, one at a time along a trajectory, e.g. planting many yams out one at a time along a row.

Each of these attempted rationalisations has a modicum of plausibility – as is desirable, if we are to see each development in a particular subsystem as motivated rather than arbitrary, and to ground each semantic extension in a 'bridging context' (Evans and Wilkins 2000) which allows for a pragmatic extension of meaning in a particular context, then conventionalised to the point where context is no longer needed to induce the reading. However, such proposals founder on two problems: first, even though they can be motivated in some way, they cannot be made totally compositional, in the sense of precisely deriving the cardinality of the whole verbal word from that of its inflectional parts; and second, if these methods for building up number are taken to be convincing, why is a single method not used throughout?

For example, why is the greater plural of 'be' not formed in the same way as the positionals, by combining the singular prefix with the dual root (so that the unattested *y-ren, for example, would be the form for 'they (many) are', instead of *y-ng-m* (§4.4.3))? And why do middle verbs not combine the dual thematic with the singular suffix, for example saying *n-aebyäng-Ø-e* [M:α-fly-IPFV:DU-3SGA] for 'they (many) are flying' instead of the actually attested *yawaebnde* (§4.4.4)? If the ingenious analyses of semantic extensions mentioned above were really convincing, they should carry across all verbal classes, instead of us finding the bewildering variety of methods actually employed. A more realistic view, then, is that while individual compositions may have originally been motivated, the synchronic Nen system simply assembles morphomes in different ways, in different verb classes, to produce a result which allows all monovalent verbs, and the subjects of future imperatives, to encode a greater plural category once all word elements have been parsed together. In other words, it is best to see the structures as arbitrary evolutionary 'patches' opportunistically seizing unexploited combinations of morphomic material to create new gestalts with a unique but non-compositional morphological profile.

But this then raises another problem: if the relevant elements only mean something when assembled together into a paradigm, then is it not invalid to ever assign them a fixed gloss, or treat them as morphological elements whose meaning is clear enough for it to be 'misleading' (as the term 'deponency' implies) when used in another way?[13] However, overall there are many points in the system where semantic values can be straightforwardly assigned. Table 4.9 summarises the data presented in this paper from two angles: the 'atomic vs unificational' column contrasts number values that are always encoded at a single site with those which are only given after

Table 4.9 Unification and compositionality in Nen number values

	Atomic vs unificational + direct (i.e. single site) – unified (composed from multiple sites)	Monotonicity + composed monotonically by non-conflicting values – non-monotonic in the sense that some morpheme values are 'overwritten' in construction
SG	+	+
DU	+	+
PL	– (+)[a]	+ (– in future imperative only)
PL🅐	–	– (+ in future imperative only)

[a] Most of the time, basic plurals do not have dedicated exponents, being composed by the combination of non-singular and non-dual as illustrated in §4.3. However, there are just a few TAM values for which a distinct plural form exists, for example the preterite: cf. *inğanzt* 'you two/they two saw it' (dual preterite *-anz-* plus 2|3 dual preterite *-t*) vs *ingowend* 'you PL./they PL. saw it' (non-dual preterite *(o)we* plus 2|3 plural preterite *-nd*). In other words, third person dual and plural are usually syncretised, but kept apart for just a few TAM values.

unification across sites, while the 'monotonicity' column asks: for a given 'final' number value (i.e. a number value obtained in a fully inflected word), will it always have been composed monotonically, or is some overwriting needed for the number of one or more constituent morphemes?

Looking at Table 4.9, three tendencies are present, though none is without exception:

(i) The splitting of the plural category into plural and greater plural is generally achieved by using special methods to form the greater plural. The sole exception is future imperatives, where it is the standard plurals which have an unusual/non-compositional feature combination, employing the singular desinence in combination with the non-singular future imperative prefix.

(ii) Greater plurals generally involve combining a singular with some other value, but there is considerable variation in what this can be:[14]
SG + SG (middles, first person[15])
SG + DU (positionals)
SG + NSG   (middles, second and third person)
SG + suppletive stem (come/go)
SG + multal (< away) + imperfective aspect (object number).
Moreover, in the future imperative it is formed from a non-singular:
NSG + NSG (different sites, i.e. future imperative prefix + regular imperative suffix).

(iii) In the one construction where it is the plural which employs a seemingly contradictory set of values (namely the future imperative), it too involves a combination of SG + NSG: non-singular in the future imperative prefix slot, and singular in the regular imperative suffix.

There is one more way to look at the number data presented in this paper, which is to return to our informal three-way categorisation into 'trusties', 'jokers' and 'double-agents', and ask: examining the exponents of each of the number categories, are there any that never have their basic cardinality overwritten? Or, using the vocabulary of deponency, are there any number values which are never deponent?

The answer is no, at least at the level of the overall system: singulars regularly combine with other material to form greater plurals, duals combine with singular prefixes in positional verbs to form greater plurals, and plurals can end up as regular plural or greater plural depending on the combination.[16] (Greater plurals are always composed and thus never directly expressed by a single morphological element, so the question is irrelevant for them.) All of these, then, are 'double-agents'. The only 'trusties' among the verbal number morphology are the 'non-singular' – which never combines with something else to produce a singular.[17] At the same time, unlike in the prefix system where the three prefix series cannot be assigned clear TAM semantics, there are no 'jokers' – all number marking morphology has at least a basic number meaning.

Corbett (2007: 41) notes that the more deponency interacts with other phenomena, the more it leads to 'a higher order of exceptionality. Such extremes of inflection are of interest not only to morphologists and typologists but also to psycholinguists.' In the case of Nen, deponency interacts with the general pattern of distributed exponence already entrenched in languages of the Yam family to allow the encoding of a semantic number value – greater plurals – across all eligible verb types, without the need for any new formal material to be grammaticalised.

But the system of distributed deponency in Nen also gives us a valuable insight into a further potentiality of language. Hockett (1963) famously employed the term 'double articulation' to describe the fact that the basic form-units of language (phonemes in a spoken language) do not generally have a direct semantic value: *p* vs *b* have different values in *pack* vs *back* and *pin* vs *bin*. Freeing elements of form from determinate meaning would have been a major evolutionary step in allowing languages to make infinite use of finite means, since no semantic obstacles hobble the efficiency with which the basic phonological building blocks can be combined. But why stop at double articulation? It is helpful to see some of the morphological elements we find in Nen, like morphomes more generally as we look across languages, as examples of 'triple articulation': phonemes, without specific meaning, are assembled into phoneme strings or morphomes, again without specific meaning, and it is only when a number of morphomes are combined together that we obtain a specified inflectional meaning. How far languages can push this principle – building complex morphologies in which all strings of phonemes, all morphomes, i.e. lack semantic specification altogether – remains a vital but still unanswered question.[18]

Acknowledgements

It is an honour and a pleasure to dedicate this paper to Grev Corbett, who has been a friend and a mentor to me over many decades. Without his unfailing ability to see through the jungle of morphological complexity to the hidden order within, my understanding of many languages I have worked on would have remained stunted. As a typologist I have been deeply influenced by his ability to dimensionalise problems and imagine unexplored regions of the design space in a crisp and challenging way. His trademark combination of warmth, courtesy, subtlety and astuteness, duly leavened with a whacky humour, has touched many.

I thank Jeff Siegel, Christian Döhler, Matt Carroll, Wayan Arka and Eri Kashima for discussions of how number works in other languages of Southern New Guinea, Susan Ford for assistance with preparing the manuscript, and the following organisations for financial support of my work on Nen: the Australian Research Council (Grants: Languages of Southern New Guinea and The Wellsprings of Linguistic Diversity), the Volkswagen Foundation (DoBES project 'Nen and Tonda'), the Alexander von Humboldt Foundation (Anneliese Maier Forschungspreis), the Australian National University (Professorial Setup Grant) and the ARC Centre of Excellence for the Dynamics of Language (CoEDL). Most importantly, I think the entire population of Bimadbn village for their hospitality and friendship, and especially Jimmy Nébni, Michael Binzawa, Yosang Amto and Goe Dibod. In terms of the ideas presented here, I would like to thank audiences who attended earlier presentations of this material in the Department of Linguistics, Universität zu Köln, at CoEDL, ANU, and at the workshop 'The Morphological Eye: The Surrey Morphology Group Turns 25', and the editors of the present volume plus Erich Round and two anonymous referees.

Notes

1. It is natural to ask whether the phenomena described here can in fact be accommodated within existing typologies. Baerman (in Baerman et al. 2007: 14–16) discusses three types of deponency that might appear plausible candidates, but none covers what I discuss here. Polarity involves a mirror-image mismatch (not appropriate here because there is not a precise 'swap over'); heteroclisis refers to the mixing of different inflection classes within a single paradigm, such that 'in place of . . . missing forms, the expected forms of another inflection class are found' (not appropriate because for the case we will discuss the 'greater plural' is not directly encoded in any inflectional class, so there are no 'expected forms'); and syncretism is found where 'a particular exponent retains its normal function under deponency alongside the irregular function' – not appropriate because the deponent combinations discussed here do not in general have formally comparable 'normal' functions.
2. There are other languages in the Yam family where some verbal number is better analysed as pluractionality (e.g. Lee 2014), but in Nen it is clearly a case of verbal agreement tracking argument number.
3. Cf. Carroll (2017) and Döhler (2016) on the related languages Ngkolmpu and Komnzo, which have comparably complex systems of 'distributed exponence', though they lack four-valued systems of number agreement of the type discussed here.
4. An anonymous referee asks why I do not simply call these portmanteau affixes. They are indeed portmanteaux, since they encode information about more than one semantic value, but they are by no means unique in this and many other Nen affixes are also portmanteaux; for example, the suffix -*ta* in (3a,b) is a portmanteau encoding information both about aspect (imperfective) and number (dual). For this reason, I retain the term

'interactive', to stress the fact that these affixes, alone among the argument-indexing affixes of Nen, give information about more than one argument in the same affixal slot.
5. An example of triple occurrence, though with some semantic specialisation as one progresses through the steps, is the following quadruplet: *aebyängs* 'to fly (v.i.)', *waebyängs* 'to fly (v.t.), cause to fly', *awaebyängs* 'swat flies off oneself, i.e. cause to fly from oneself, wait around' (i.e. detransitive of causative, with autobenefactive meaning), *wawaebyängs* 'wait for someone' (i.e. benefactive of *awaebyängs*).
6. It seems plausible that distributed deponency is one of the pathways leading from a canonical agglutinative organisation to a full-blown fusional one, with many non-monotonic extensions of this type – each extension motivated to a greater or lesser degree, but cumulatively making the semantics of system elements less and less compositional and favouring an ever more paradigm-based view of the verbal word.
7. Both 'all' and 'many' have been given as translations for this type of construction. Note that in Tok Pisin *ol* (< English 'all') is simply a plural marker, and while Tok Pisin is not a lingua franca in the area it does exert some influence in contexts of multilingual communication. Note also that the quantifier *gbres* can mean both 'all' and 'many'; see Evans (2017).
8. The word form *ynngm* is, however, acceptable with another morphological parsing, namely *yn-ng-m* [1NSGU:α-AW-be:ND] 'we go'.
9. Orthogonal to present concerns, it varies according to TAM, with *n-* replaced by *k-* in, for example, the yesterday past or the imperative (*kowabte* '(s)he talked (yesterday)', *kowabta!* 'talk!') and *g-* in, for example, the remote past or the perfective future (*gowabtawn* 'I talked (last year)', *gowabngn* 'I will talk').
10. There is one further twist for which I still lack full data. It looks like the number agreement of the prefix in the greater plural middle construction depends on whether the subject is a regular greater plural (with an absolutive subject) or an exhaustive plural (formed with the oblique pronoun + *gbres* 'all'). In the former case, the number of the subject is registered on the prefix, as illustrated in (12d), while in the latter case both the prefix and the suffix take singular number, for example *Tbe gbres Mär-ngama w-n-awang̱-t-e* [1NSG.OBL all Mär-ABL 1SGU-TOW-return-B.IPFV:ND-2|3SGA] 'we are all returning from Mär' or *Ybe gbres te y-ng-aowa-nd-a* [3NSG.OBJ all already 3SGU-set.off-PST.PFV:ND-3SGA] 'they have already all set off'.
11. To keep things simple, I am treating strings like *yaw-* (or its vowel-harmonised variants *yew-* and *yiw-*) as undecomposable non-singular prefixes. However, a deeper segmentation is possible, into *y-* plus *aw-* (or even further into 3SG *y-* plus RR *a-* plus transitiviser *w-*); compare the layered infinitive derivations in *armbs* 'ascend', *warmbs* 'cause to ascend', *awarmbs* 'cause each other/self to ascend'. Further grist for this analysis comes from the fact that the sequence *yaw-* can be interrupted by directional prefixes, for example *yngawarmbte* 'they (many) ascend' (*yaw-* interrupted by 'away' *ng-*) and *ynewesne* 'they (many) descend' (*yew-* interrupted by *n-* 'towards'). Despite the atomistic appeal of this analysis, I do not adopt it here because the semantics of plurality does not fall out compositionally from the combination of transitiviser plus reflexive/reciprocal. Rather, it seems better to regard this as a further example of morphomic behaviour, where morphological units of a particular phonological and positional character only take on a semantic value once the whole word has been assembled.
12. I thank Bob Dixon (personal communication) for suggesting this analysis.
13. Needless to say, glossing should not be confused with the full panoply of methods for representing inflectional meanings in morphology. Phonological strings that always have the same meaning can readily be handled, in theories like Network Morphology, by having a one-to-one association of form and meaning in the rule that introduces them.

However, glossing remains so central to the practice of describing little-known languages that I believe it is worth discussing appropriate practice here rather than simply dismissing it as a theoretically uninteresting issue.
14. The possibility of motivating this extension through singular universal statements (of the type *The kangaroo is a hopping marsupial*) has already been mentioned. Another possible bridging context that would explain why singulars get greater plural readings is the counting of bunches, for example of bananas or braces of coconuts, where the object is simultaneously singular (as a bunch) and plural (in terms of the entities it contains – bananas or coconuts).
15. See note 6 above.
16. An anonymous reviewer suggests that the SG-DU contrast may derive from an earlier SG-PL one, i.e. that the dual morphology was originally plural (i.e. non-singular), as part of a two-valued system (SG vs NON-SG), and that the plural in a subsequent three-valued system was, like the large plural discussed here, cobbled together from an available system, compressing the semantic value of the old 'simple non-singular' it was built upon down to a dual. This suggestion has some merit; for example, it could motivate the entanglement of dual marking with the aspectual system by seeing it as an erstwhile pluractional system from which the pluractional as opposed to number function got lost once the number value was compressed down to dual. A full evaluation of this interesting hypothesis must await more detailed reconstruction of the semantics of the relevant morphology across the Yam family.
17. If we just looked at ambifixing verbs, we could add the dual, since the only time that the dual behaves non-monotonically is with positionals.
18. Another related notion, put forward by Bickel (following Hockett 1987), is that of 'eidemic resonance': 'parts of words resonate with each other and can therefore be extracted as meaningful formatives or morphemes . . . [B]ut in addition the forms of a paradigm often resonate with each other through alliteration, rhyme or other paronomasia without entailing any general and consistent semantics or morpheme extractability. Rather, the resonances serve to structure paradigms, compartmentalize the lexicon, and provide psycholinguistic processing cues' (Bickel and Nichols 2007: 209).

References

Anderson, Stephen R. (2015), 'The morpheme: Its nature and use', in Matthew Baerman (ed.), *The Oxford Handbook of Inflection*, Oxford: Oxford University Press, pp. 11–33.

Aronoff, Mark (1994), *Morphology by Itself: Stems and Inflectional Classes*, Cambridge, MA: MIT Press.

Baerman, Matthew, Greville G. Corbett, Dunstan Brown and Andrew Hippisley (eds) (2007), *Deponency and Morphological Mismatches*, Proceedings of the British Academy, 145, London: British Academy and Oxford University Press.

Bickel, Balthasar and Johanna Nichols (2007), 'Inflectional morphology', in Timothy Shopen (ed.), *Linguistic Typology and Language Description. Vol. III: Grammatical Categories and the Lexicon*, 2nd edn, pp. 169–240.

Carroll, Matt (2017), 'The Ngkolmpu Language, with Special Reference to Distributed Exponence', unpublished PhD thesis, Australian National University.

Corbett, Greville G. (2000), *Number*, Cambridge: Cambridge University Press.

Corbett, Greville G. (2007), 'Deponency, syncretism, and what lies between', in Matthew Baerman, Greville G. Corbett, Dunstan Brown and Andrew Hippisley (eds), *Deponency and Morphological Mismatches*, Proceedings of the British Academy, 145, London: British Academy and Oxford University Press, pp. 21–43.

Corbett, Greville G. (2013), 'Canonical morphosyntactic features', in Dunstan Brown, Marina

Chumakina and Greville G. Corbett (eds), *Canonical Morphology and Syntax*, Oxford: Oxford University Press, pp. 48–65.

Döhler, Christian (2016), 'A Grammar of Komnzo', unpublished PhD thesis, Australian National University.

Evans, Nicholas (2012a), 'Even more diverse than we thought: The multiplicity of Trans-Fly languages', in Nicholas Evans and Marian Klamer (eds), *Melanesian Languages on the Edge of Asia: Challenges for the 21st Century*, Language Documentation and Conservation Special Publication No. 5, Honolulu: University of Hawai'i Press, pp. 109–49.

Evans, Nicholas (2012b), 'Nen assentives and the problem of dyadic parallelisms', in Andrea C. Schalley (ed.), *Practical Theories and Empirical Practice: Facets of a Complex Interaction*, Amsterdam: John Benjamins, pp. 159–83.

Evans, Nicholas (2014), 'Positional verbs in Nen', *Oceanic Linguistics*, 53 (2), pp. 225–55.

Evans, Nicholas (2015a), '26 Valency in Nen', in Andrej Malchukov and Bernard Comrie (eds), *Valency Classes in the World's Languages*, Berlin: Mouton de Gruyter, pp. 1069–116.

Evans, Nicholas (2015b), 'Inflection in Nen', in Matthew Baerman (ed.), *The Oxford Handbook of Inflection*, Oxford: Oxford University Press, pp. 543–75.

Evans, Nicholas (2017), 'Quantification in Nen', in Edward L. Keenan and Denis Paperno (eds), *Handbook of Quantifiers in Natural Language: Vol. 2*, Dordrecht: Springer, pp. 571–607.

Evans, Nicholas, Wayan Arka, Matthew Carroll, Yun Jung Choi, Christian Döhler, Volker Gast, Eri Kashima, Emil Mittag, Bruno Olsson, Kyla Quinn, Dineke Schokkin, Philip Tama, Charlotte van Tongeren and Jeff Siegel (2017), 'The languages of Southern New Guinea', in Bill Palmer (ed.), *The Languages and Linguistics of New Guinea: A Comprehensive Guide*, Berlin: Walter de Gruyter, pp. 641–774.

Evans, Nicholas and Julia Colleen Miller (2016), 'Nen', *Journal of the International Phonetic Association*, 46 (3), pp. 331–49.

Evans, Nicholas and David Wilkins (2000), 'In the mind's ear: The semantic extensions of perception verbs in Australian languages', *Language*, 76 (3), pp. 546–92.

Hockett, Charles F. (1963), 'The problem of universals in language', in Joseph H. Greenberg (ed.), *Universals of Language*, Cambridge, MA: MIT Press, pp. 1–29.

Hockett, Charles F. (1987), *Refurbishing Our Foundations*, Amsterdam: John Benjamins.

Lee, Jenny S. (2014), 'Root allomorphy in Ranmo (Papuan)', handout from the 50th Meeting of the Chicago Linguistics Society.

Matthews, P. H. (2007), 'How safe are our analyses?', in Matthew Baerman, Greville G. Corbett, Dunstan Brown and Andrew Hippisley (eds), *Deponency and Morphological Mismatches*, Proceedings of the British Academy, 145, London: British Academy and Oxford University Press, pp. 297–315.

Round, Erich (2013), *Kayardild Morphology and Syntax*, Oxford: Oxford University Press.

Siegel, Jeff (2014), 'The morphology of tense and aspect in Nama, a Papuan language of Southern New Guinea', *Open Linguistics*, 1 (1), pp. 211–31.

5

Feature Duality

Matthew Baerman

5.1 Flavours of Inflection

Inflectional paradigms come in two possible flavours: either the forms line up with the featural system whose values they express, or they do not. For example, the formatives in Table 5.1 from Chamorro (an Oceanic language of Guam) can be readily characterised in terms of aspect-mood distinctions: *ha-* is the realis 3SG prefix, *u-* the irrealis prefix, and reduplication marks the incompletive. Contrast this with the three tense-aspect paradigms from Gulmancema, a Gur language of Burkina Faso. There is a suffix *-di* which is found with each verb, but it cannot readily be characterised in featural terms, because it can in fact be used for any feature: with a verb like 'pass' it is used for the imperfective, with a verb like 'love' it is used for the perfective, and with a verb like 'hear' it is used for the aorist and perfective. In this case a description of the possible forms in the paradigm (unsuffixed, or with suffix *-di*) is separate from the feature values behind it.

What I would like to look at here is a set of paradigms that falls in between these two extremes, where the distribution of forms appears to **approximate** the feature system they express. That is, there is neither complete correspondence (as in Chamorro) or complete divergence (as in Gulmancema). This is either a challenge to morphological theory, which cannot readily accommodate this, as far as I know, or it

Table 5.1 Different flavours of inflectional paradigm

Chamorro (Stolz 2015: 487)		Gulmancema (Naba 1994: 358–9, 361)			
	'transfer(3SG)'		'pass'	'love'	'hear'
CPL	ha-loffan	AOR	cié	bua	gbà-dì
ICPL	ha-lo~loffan	IPFV	cié-dí	buà	gbà
IRR	u-loffan	PFV	ciê	bua-dì	gba-dì

demonstrates that my interpretation of the facts is wrong, in which case this may be a useful exercise in clarifying what is or is not a possible morphological analysis. The example involves number marking on the verb in Hualapai, a Yuman language spoken in Arizona. Verbs distinguish four forms which, I will argue, can be understood as representing four degrees of number, ranging from low (singular) to high (greater plural). The morphological paradigm in turn follows an incremental principle where the addition of a morphological marker corresponds to an increase in the number value. However, the terms by which this morphological system is constructed do not correspond to the values of the morphosemantic system. In effect, the morphological system approximates the morphosemantic system without quite matching it. In §5.2 I present the structure of the verbal paradigm and argue for my particular interpretation of it in terms of morphosemantic number. In §5.3 I present the morphological paradigm and argue for an interpretation in terms of incremental quantity. In §5.4 I attempt to relate the two, arguing for what this might mean for morphological theory. All the data here is taken from the reference grammar by Watahomigie et al. (1982, revised version from 2001), or their dictionary (2003).

5.2 Number in the Hualapai Verb

Hualapai verbs mark number, as illustrated in (1). The practical orthography used in the reference grammar is retained here.[1] For reasons that are made clear below, the relevant parts of the verb form are neither segmented nor glossed here.

(1) a. Josie-ch i' ɖabil-k-wi
J-NOM wood burn-SS-AUX
'Josie is burning the wood.'
b. Josie-ch Jorigine-m i' ɖabilj-k-wi
J-NOM J-COM wood burn-SS-AUX
'Josie and Jorigine are burning the wood.'
c. Josie-ch gwejalay nyuwi ɖaɖbi:l-k-wi
J-NOM trash burn-SS-AUX
'Josie is burning lots of trash.'[2]
d. Ba:jach gwejalay nyuwi ɖaɖbi:lj-k-wi
people-NOM trash burn-SS-AUX
'People are burning lots of trash.'
(Watahomigie et al. 2001: 247–8)

In their presentation of this system, Watahomigie et al. (2001) characterise it in terms of subject and object number. However, there are also intransitive verbs that make a comparable distinction, expressed with the same morphology (discussed in greater detail in §5.3), where in place of *object plurality* they speak of *distributives*, for example *div'ik* 'one person kneels down once' ~ *div'i:j'k* 'one person kneels down many times' (Watahomigie et al. 2003: 62). I suggest that the two can be conflated under a single rubric of event number, with different interpretations depending on argument structure.

On the face of it then, we have two number features in Hualapai, subject number and event number, which raises the question of how comparable the notion of number even is across these two so semantically disparate domains. However, I will argue that there is little reason for positing two features here, and that all the values can more insightfully be subsumed under the rubric of a single feature.

Round and Corbett (2017) and Corbett et al. (2017) lay out in some detail the criteria for positing distinct features in a paradigm, chief among which is the ability to cross-classify. This is precisely where a two-feature analysis of Hualapai would fall apart. The four-cell paradigm represented by (1) can be broken down as in (2), with further illustrations in (3). Note in particular that a combination of a singular value and a plural value is possible, but which feature these values would be linked to depends on the verb (compare 'burn' and 'beat up' in (3c)).[3]

(2) a. both subject and event (object) are singular
 b. the subject is paucal ('two' or 'a few') and the event (object) is singular
 c. depending on the verb or verb class, either the subject or the event (object) is plural, and the other one is singular: see 'burn' vs 'beat up' in (4c)
 d. both subject and event (object) are plural

(3) a. dabil   'one burns one'   dagwan   'one beats up someone'
 b. dabilj   'two/a few burn one'   dadgwanj   'two/a few beat up someone'
 c. dadbi:l 'one burns many'   dadgwan   'many beat up someone'
 d. dadbi:lj 'many burn many'   dadgwanj   'many beat up many'
 (Watahomigie et al. 2001)

If the values for the two candidate features are laid out along the two axes of a grid, it is apparent that they are characterised more by mutual exclusivity than the ability to cross-classify. Table 5.2 represents the two paradigm types illustrated in (3), with ticks denoting those combinations of values that are represented by a distinct form. There is no consistent cross-classification across both types: there is no column or row which is consistently filled. What this means is that a given value for one feature largely implies the value for the other feature; the only instance of combinatorability comes with singular events, which are compatible either with singular

Table 5.2 Attempted two-feature analysis of number values in Hualapai

		EVENT NUMBER	
		SG	PL
SUBJECT NUMBER	SG	✓	(✓) 'burn' type only
	PC	✓	
	PL	(✓) 'beat up' type only	✓

or with paucal subjects. Representing this system as the intersection of two features seems more confusing than helpful.

However, construed along a single dimension, matters are more straightforward, because they can be understood in terms of relative quantity. Taking just the values in (2) and stripping them of their putative featural associations, we arrive at the quantificational hierarchy in (4a), going from less to more, for which I suggest the labels in (4b); the term 'greater plural' is taken from Corbett (2000: 30); see also Evans (this volume).

(4) a. {singular, singular} < {paucal, singular} < {plural, singular} < {plural, plural}
    b. singular < paucal < plural < greater plural

But with subject and event number conflated into a single feature, the question still remains as to what sort of feature this is. Given the role ascribed to event number, it cannot be an agreement feature. For that matter, *greater plural* is a feature value associated with morphosyntactic number as marked on nominals, but it does not feature in agreement systems, as far as I know. Langdon (1992), who looks only at subject number, proposes that number marking in Hualapai originates on the verb; in effect, that number is a morphosyntactic feature proper to the verb, and that nominal arguments may, optionally, agree with the verb. I will not explore the syntactic ramifications of this proposal, but retain here the notion that this is some kind of verbal feature. Equally, the route to a semantic interpretation of these values in terms of subjects, objects and events is not a trivial matter, but I will take that as an independent question for another occasion. For the present purposes it is enough to establish the repertoire of values, because it is the way these map onto the morphological forms which is the main point.

5.3 The Morphology of Hualapai Verbs

The morphological realisation of these values follows a principle which is in some sense iconic, in that the incremental addition of morphological markers aligns with the increase in quantity. However, the qualification 'in some sense' is the crux, because the morphosemantic values cannot be directly derived from the morphological values by simple computation. If we take the content paradigm and the form paradigm as representing two feature systems, the relationship between similar or even identical values across them represents a possible instance of feature duality.

To make the issues clearer it will help to divide the bulk of the verbs described by Watahomigie et al. (2001) into three classes. Two morphological markers are common to all three classes: (i) a suffix -*j*, and (ii) lengthening of the stem. Both of these are also found as plural markers on nouns (Watahomigie et al. 2001: 159–62), for example *sal* ~ *sal-j* 'hand(s)' and *hnal* ~ *hna:l* 'gourd(s)', or combined in *yumbul* ~ *yumbu:l-j* 'forehead(s)'. (Note that, unlike verbs, nouns mark only singular and plural.) The classes differ in the repertoire of other devices they employ, and also in part in the meanings ascribed to the forms.

The first class of verbs employs no other markers, and falls into different

Table 5.3 Suffixing/lengthening verbs

Singular	Paucal	Plural	Greater plural	
gilgyo	gilgyo-j	gilgyo:	gilgyo:-j	'tie something large'
hwal	hwa:l	hwa:l-j		'dig'
yom	yo:m-j			'go out and get X'
mad	mad-j			'win'

subclasses depending on how they are combined and distributed within the paradigm, as illustrated in Table 5.3. The subclass represented by 'tie something large' represents the maximal system, with all four cells distinguished. Lengthening produces two stems, one used for the lesser values (singular and paucal), and one for the greater quantities (plural and greater plural). The suffix -j adds an increment of quantity to the respective plain and lengthened stem, turning singular into paucal and plural into greater plural.[4] The next two subclasses also employ a lengthened stem, in this case used for **all** the non-singular values. With subclass represented by 'dig', the addition of -j still adds an increment of quantity, turning a paucal into something more than a paucal, namely plural and greater plural. With the subclass represented by 'go out and get X', lengthening and suffixation go hand-in-hand, resulting in a simple singular ~ non-singular distinction. Verbs such as 'win' are like the preceding subclass, but lack a length alternation. Thus, even though the subclasses display different configurations of their paradigms, morphologically they all follow a consistent principle, where the incremental addition of morphological markers corresponds to the addition of quantity within the system of number values.

The second class of verbs has a prefixed ɖ- or j- in the plural and greater plural forms. The nature of these prefixes is somewhat unclear. This is connected with the stem structure of the verbs that belong to this class, all of which bear one of various causative prefixes, as with *yahan* 'fix.SG', from *han* 'be fixed.SG'.[5] The number marking prefixes come between the causative prefix and the root, thus *yijhan* 'fix. PL'. (The prefix vowel – both for the causative prefixes and for the number marking prefixes – apparently varies freely between /i/ and /a/, judging from the comments in Watahomigie et al. 2001, and no significance should be ascribed to it. The forms as given here reflect what is given in the source.) The choice of number marking prefix is determined by the causative prefix, which leads to a certain ambiguity in most cases, because (i) by far the most common causative prefixes are ɖ- and j-, and (ii) causative ɖ- selects the number marker ɖ-, and causative j- selects the number marker j-, thus *ɖiboq ~ ɖiɖbo:q* 'spill something (SG~PL)', or *jithul ~ jijthu:l* 'wash (SG~PL)'. This led Redden (1966) and Watahomigie et al. (1982) to treat this as reduplication, though Watahomigie et al. (2001) opt instead to treat it as number marking prefixation which is accidental homophonous with the causative. For the present purposes these differing analyses are of no consequence, because they simply mean the presence or absence of an additional allomorph of the number marker (reduplication), alongside ɖ- and j-.

Table 5.4 Distribution of suffix with prefixing (or reduplicating) verbs

Singular	Paucal	Plural	Greater plural	
ɖalap	ɖalap-j	ɖaɖlap	ɖaɖlap-j	'flatten'
jigwan	jigwan-j	jijgwan	jijgwan-j	'kill'

As in the first class, this second class employs suffixation of -*j* and, for some verbs, lengthening as well. The distribution of -*j* follows the same principles as with 'tie something large' in Table 5.3. This is as illustrated in Table 5.4. The number marking prefix (or reduplication) creates two stems, each of which then serves as a host for -*j* suffixation: added to the singular form it yields the paucal, and added to the plural form it yields the greater plural. Again, this system follows a straightforward incremental principle: prefixation (or reduplication) creates a stem denoting greater quantity, and suffixation adds an incremental quantity to each of the resulting stems.

For those verbs that employ lengthening, its distribution can be described in much the same terms as with the three subclasses of the first class. Thus, in Table 5.5, the plural and greater plural forms are lengthened, as with 'tie something large' in Table 5.3. In Table 5.6, all the non-singular forms are lengthened, as with 'dig' in Table 5.3. And in Table 5.7, lengthening is concomitant with suffixation, as with 'go out and get X' in Table 5.3. (There are no examples with the prefix *ɖ-* of this last type.)

A further difference between this second class and the first one is in the meaning of the plural form, i.e. whether it refers to plurality of the subject or of the object/ event. With the first class, it indicates a plural subject with a singular object or event, for example *le:lk* 'many people tear something' (Watahomigie et al. 2003: 148). This class is split, however, as already seen in (3): a minority of verbs behaves like the first

Table 5.5 Prefixing verbs with lengthening in the plural and greater plural

Singular	Paucal	Plural	Greater plural	
ɖiboq	ɖiboq-j	ɖiɖbo:q	ɖiɖbo:q-j	'spill something'
jithul	jithul-j	jijthu:l	jijthu:l-j	'wash'

Table 5.6 Prefixing verbs with lengthening in the non-singular forms

Singular	Paucal	Plural	Greater plural	
ɖamad	ɖama:d-j	ɖiɖma:d	ɖiɖma:d-j	'erase'
jibu	jibu:-j	jijbu:	jijbu:-j	'rush at'

Table 5.7 Prefixing verb with lengthening in the suffixed forms

Singular	Paucal	Plural	Greater plural	
jigyo	jigyo:-j	jijgyo	jijgyo:-j	'bite'

class, for example *dadgwank* 'many people beat up someone', while the bulk of them have the reverse linkage, *dadbi:lk* 'one person burns many things'. It is not clear what determines the difference (Watahomigie et al. 2001 do not discuss this). It is of course tempting to think this difference might be due to syntactic or semantic factors, but the data are unfortunately insufficient to judge. Transitivity does not appear to be a factor, because both types contain a mix of transitive (the majority) and intransitive verbs. And the examples of the first type are too few (only eight verbs) to make any kind of reliable semantic generalisation. In any case, for the present purposes it is enough that all these have the value *plural* in the proposed system.

The third class of verbs combines characteristics of the first two classes. It seems to be a small class (Watahomigie et al. 2001 list a dozen), and almost completely restricted to verbs with the causative prefix *s-*. Two examples are shown in Table 5.8. It looks as if these verbs have the causative prefix *d-*, but only with the higher number values. This is then subject to further prefixation (or reduplication) to add an increment of quantity. As a result, the same morphological opposition that contrasts a singular/paucal stem vs a plural/greater plural stem in the second verb class (e.g. *dalap-* ~ *dadlap-* in Table 5.4), here opposes plural vs greater plural forms (e.g. *dis'am* ~ *dids'am-j* in Table 5.8). Suffixation of *-j* follows patterns comparable to those already seen in the preceding classes. With the 'close' type, it is added to the unprefixed and to the prefixed stems to add an increment of quantity to each (redundantly in the latter case, because the greater plural also has a double prefix or reduplication). With the 'peel' type, suffixation follows the pattern found with some verbs of the first class, appearing in all non-singular forms. (Note also that the plural form here refers to plurality of the subject, just as with verbs of the first class.)

There is also a variant type with the same set of forms but with a set of functions quite different from that found elsewhere in the system. The two verbs in Table 5.9 are an example: 'pull by the hair' inflects like 'close' – also with lengthening in the prefixed forms – and 'erect a post' inflects like 'peel'. But this class of verbs appears to skip the paucal; thus *sijo-j* functions like a plural form, with a singular subject and plural object, *di-sjo:* functions like a greater plural ('many to erect many posts') and *did-sjo:-j* appears to add an increment of number to that, if I correctly interpret the contrasting glosses '(many) to erect many posts' vs '(many) to erect a lot of posts' provided by Watahomigie et al. (2001: 256). This type offers a particularly compelling demonstration of why treating this system in terms of two cross-cutting features

Table 5.8 Partially prefixing verbs

Singular	Paucal	Plural	Greater plural	
sa'am	sa'am-j	dis'am	dids'am-j	'close'[a]
sqwa:n	sqwa:n-j	disqwa:n-j	didsqwa:n-j	'peel'

[a] The deletion of the first stem vowel here and in some of the subsequent examples is phonologically conditioned by the addition of the prefix, which affects the prosodic structure.

Table 5.9 Verbs that skip the paucal

Singular	Paucal	Plural	Greater plural	Augmented plural(?)	
sijo	–	sijo-j	di-sjo:	did-sjo:-j	'pull by the hair'
sija	–	sija-j	di-sja-j	did-sja-j	'erect a post'

is inadequate: only through a single hierarchy of increasing number values can we relate these paradigms to the previous classes.

5.4 Reconciling Meaning and Form

The motivation for the present study is the observation that accounting for the distribution of the individual morphological markers that compose the Hualapai verb paradigm is a surprisingly unstraightforward affair. In §5.3 I stressed that the morphological markers followed an incremental principle, with the addition of markers corresponding to the addition of quantity in the system of morphosemantic number values. The obvious way to formalise this would be to associate the markers directly with values of the morphosemantic system, but I cannot see any clear way of doing that, because the distribution of markers according values is so variable across different verb paradigms. To see this, consider how a concrete representation of the feature values matches the morphological behaviour. Harbour (2014) offers a decomposition of number into binary features, which among other things accommodates the values paucal and greater plural that play a role in the current analysis. Two of the features he proposes will be relevant here: [±minimal] and [±additive]. They combine as in Table 5.10 to yield four number values.[6] The individual features are separated out in Table 5.11 according to their distribution in the paradigm. This illustrates clearly the quantitative hierarchy: [+minimal] covers the lowest value, [–additive] covers the lower three values, [–minimal] covers the higher three values, and [+additive] covers the highest two values.

Table 5.10 Decomposed number values in terms of Harbour (2014)

Singular	Paucal	Plural	Greater plural
+minimal	–minimal	–minimal	–minimal
–additive	–additive	–additive, +additive	+additive

Table 5.11 Values from Table 5.10 separated out

Singular	Paucal	Plural	Greater plural
+minimal			
–additive			
	–minimal		
		+additive	

Table 5.12 Paradigmatic distribution of -j suffixation (see Table 5.4)

	Singular	Paucal	Plural	Greater plural
'win' type		✓	✓	✓
'dig' type'			✓	✓
'tie something large' type	✓			✓

Table 5.13 Paradigmatic distribution of lengthening (see Tables 5.3 and 5.7)

	Singular	Paucal	Plural	Greater plural
'tie something large' type		✓	✓	✓
'dig' type			✓	✓
'bite' type		✓		✓

Table 5.14 Paradigmatic distribution of prefixation (reduplication) (see Tables 5.4 and 5.8)

	Singular	Paucal	Plural	Greater plural
'flatten' type			✓	✓
'close' type				✓

Now consider the paradigmatic distribution of the morphological markers in Tables 5.12–5.14, where each row corresponds to one of the patterns described in §5.3 (representative verb types are indicated here). While some of these configurations map onto the features, there is no consistency. For example, the distribution of suffixation or length sometimes corresponds to [−minimal] and sometimes to [+additive].[7] And the combination of paucal plus greater plural seen both in the distribution of suffixation and length finds no unified expression within this feature system.

The conclusion I draw from this is that while number values can be represented in terms of increasing quantities, this will not account for the behaviour of the morphological markers that realise them. In asserting that the markers follow a quantity-based incremental principle, I have been admittedly vague about how that is implemented, but now address the question explicitly. Since the morphosemantic paradigm – i.e. the content paradigm – does not contain the right terms, I will attempt simply to construct a morphological paradigm – i.e. the form paradigm – consisting of a list of forms in a fixed order that corresponds to the order of values reflected in the morphosemantic paradigm. The incremental principle will be modelled in the simplest fashion, by simply assigning each marker a number, then summing them for each form, which should yield a sequence from lower to higher for each paradigm. This number can be understood as the value of some feature, the nature of which I will return to in §5.5.

In order to assess the contribution each marker makes we must also recognise that they do not have equal worth, because forms within a paradigm still contrast even where they do not differ in the number of markers they bear. For example, paucal *gilgyo-j* with a suffix contrasts with plural *gilgyo:* with lengthening, even though each form contains just one marker. The morphological hierarchy in (5) results from assessing all such paradigmatic contrasts in the preceding sections.

(5) lesser quantity < greater quantity
     suffixation < length < prefixation (reduplication)

The first task is to ensure that the hierarchy in (5) is maintained, easily enough achieved by assigning the markers a value of '1', '2' and '3' respectively. The second task is to ensure that all combinations of markers that occur in a form yield a total value which yields the correct result. This is a problem in only one instance, the 'bite' type in Table 5.7, where the paucal form (*jigyo:-j*) and plural form (*jijgyo*) would have the same value on this scale: the paucal has a value of '3' (suffix = 1, length = 2), as does the plural (prefixation = 3). If instead we assign prefixation a value of '4', this ambiguity is resolved. The morphology of the paradigms discussed in §5.3 can now be represented as in Table 5.15. What matters is not the absolute numerical value ascribed to each form, but rather the ordering that results. Taken all together, the forms can be arranged in the quantificational hierarchy in Figure 5.1.

Table 5.15 Morphological paradigms generated through numerical values[a]

Forms	gilgyo	gilgyo-j	gilgyo:	gilgyo:-j
Value		1	2	2+1
Forms	hwal	hwa:l	hwa:l-j	
Value		2	2+1	
Forms	yom	yo:m-j		
Value		2 +1		
Forms	jigwan	jigwan-j	jijgwan	jijgwan-j
Value		1	4	4 + 1
Forms	jithul	jithul-j	jijthu:l	jijthu:l-j
Value		1	4 + 2	4+2+1
Forms	jigyo	jigyo:-j	jijgyo	jijgyo:-j
Value		2+1	4	4+2+1
Forms	sa'am	sa'am-j	dis'am	dids'am-j
Value		1	4	4+4 + 1
Forms	sqwa:n	sqwa:n-j	disqwa:n-j	didsqwa:n-j
Value		1	4 + 1	4+4 + 1

[a] One could assign a value to length or prefixation that was present in the entire paradigm (e.g. the causative prefixes), but of course that would not affect the relative value of the forms within the paradigm.

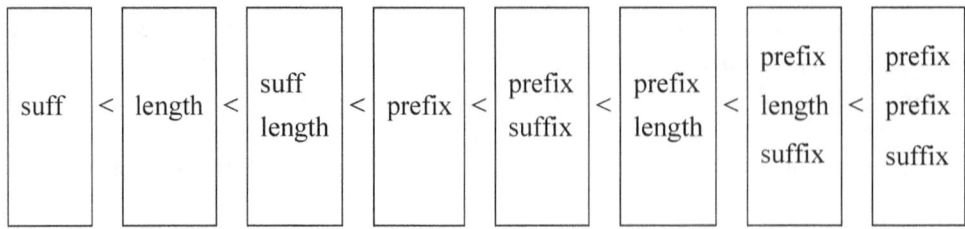

Figure 5.1 Morphological forms ranked by relative quantity that they express

The next task is to account for the relationship between the morphosemantic values and the morphological form. I represent this as the mapping between the two hierarchies, morphosemantic and morphological. In principle, any relationship is possible, so long as the lines of association do not cross. This then describes the shifting yet constrained nature of this relationship. The format of such a description is represented in Figure 5.2, on the basis of the non-singular forms of the verb *gilgyo* 'tie something large'. The complete set of verb types, as summarised in Table 5.15, is shown in Figure 5.3. While this might look complex, it is simply a by-product of

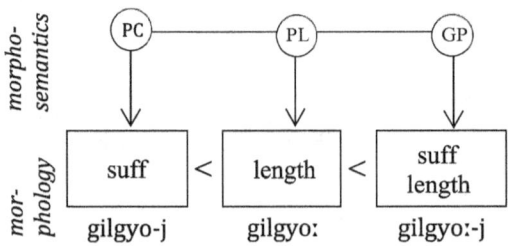

Figure 5.2 Morphosemantics–morphology mapping, illustrated by non-singular forms of *gilgyo*

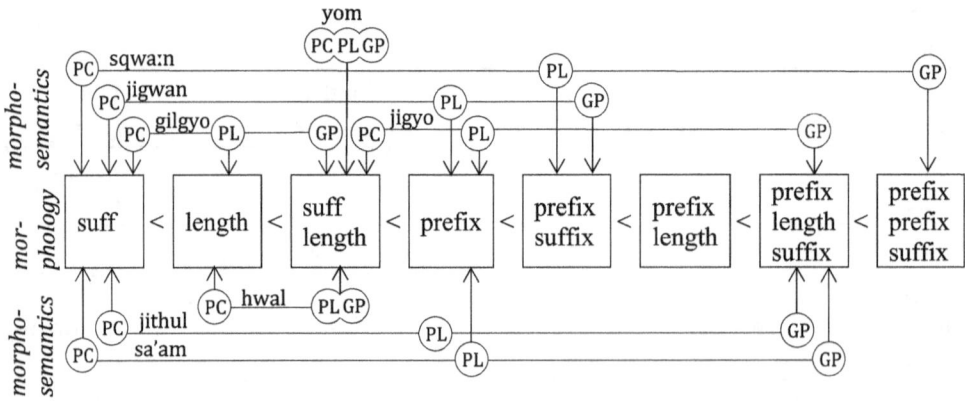

Figure 5.3 Morphosemantics–morphology mapping for the verbs in in Table 5.15

these two principles, namely maintenance of the dual hierarchies and non-crossing of association lines.

This restriction on crossing association lines has the effect of making the morphological paradigm iconic of the morphosemantic paradigm: given any pair of forms, it is always possible to say which one represents the higher number value, even without knowing anything about the rest of the paradigm or what particular values these forms denote in the context of an individual lexeme's paradigm.

5.5 Semi-autonomous Morphology

The idea that morphological paradigms do not necessarily have the same structure as the feature paradigms (morphosyntactic or morphosemantic) that they realise is hardly new. However, the way this has been understood (e.g. in Sadler and Spencer 2001 or Stump 2016) is still as an all-or-nothing affair, as evinced by the examples in (1): either there is a direct equivalence ('the opposition *ha*- vs *u*- in Chamorro maps onto the mood values realis vs irrealis') or there is not ('the opposition *-di* vs Ø in Gulmancema is simply a formal property that verbs may have, and maps onto various tense-aspect oppositions'). In Hualapai the two systems are not equivalent, but neither are they completely different. This is where FEATURE DUALITY comes in: similar but not identical notions of quantification are shared between the two otherwise distinct featural systems, morphological and morphosemantic. I have modelled this as paradigm linkage in the spirit of Stump (2016), but with an added constraint which imposes parallelism between the two systems. My purpose in doing so is not to hawk a new range of analytical devices, but merely to represent the curious relationship between form and function apparent in the Hualapai verbal paradigm. Whether this should be understood as a synchronically active system or the historical by-product of successive layers of otherwise banal paradigm configurations is not something I can say. If it does manifest a genuine system, I do not believe that current models of the form–function interface can do more than walk around it. This may be no great loss, as the problem does not come up that often (the situation in the roughly adjacent but unrelated Seri is similar; see Marlett 2016 and Baerman 2016), and could well be restricted to number systems, where the element of quantification perhaps lends itself more readily to an iconic morphological representation than would be the case with other features. But if we reject the formalisation of such configurations, then it seems that we are in effect declaring that where we think we see them, they are simply mirages. This could be the correct conclusion, in which case we should state up front that we believe that certain phenomena simply cannot exist, however much they may seem to.

Acknowledgements

The work reported here was funded by the Arts & Humanities Research Council (UK) under grant AH/P002471/1 ('Seri verbs'), whose support is gratefully acknowledged. I would also like to thank Oliver Bond and Andrew Hippisley for comments on earlier drafts of this paper.

Notes

1. Aspects worth clarifying here are that [j] represents a palatal affricate and [d̪] represents a voiceless dental stop, corresponding respectively to [č] and [t] in Redden (1966), and that ['] represents a glottal stop.
2. Watahomigie et al. (2001) do not provide a more detailed gloss for this two-word sequence.
3. The dictionary and reference grammar entries include the same subject suffix -k as part of the citation form. For the sake of clarity, this has been stripped from the tables that follow.
4. Some verbs lack lengthening, e.g. *mad ~ mad-j* 'win'.
5. A designation which is not always synchronically transparent, as some of the verbs are stative intransitives, such as 'be lopsided'. Not all the prefixed verbs in the dictionary (Watahomigie et al. 2003) have unprefixed counterparts, so it is possible that some of these stems are lexicalised and no longer transparent.
6. Note that this model allows for recursive specification of features, hence plural is specified as both [−additive] and [+additive].
7. One part of the variation in the distribution of the suffix *-j* could be accounted for by assuming that the different paradigm shapes in (4) correspond to different feature systems, i.e. that a three-cell paradigm was simply singular-paucal-plural, and a two-cell paradigm simply singular-plural. In that case, [−minimal +additive] would serve for plural in both these reduced paradigms, with the variation in marker distribution due to the presence or absence of a paucal value in the system. However, this would still not account for the paucal + greater plural distribution, nor for the pattern seen in Table 5.7, where all four values are distinguished. Nor would it account for the distribution of lengthening, which displays the same patterns as suffixation, but all within paradigms that maintain the four-value distinction. So this does not seem a profitable line of enquiry.

References

Baerman, Matthew (2016), 'Seri verb classes: Morphosyntactic motivation and morphological autonomy', *Language*, 92 (4), pp. 792–823.

Corbett, Greville G. (2000) *Number*, Cambridge: Cambridge University Press.

Corbett, Greville G., Sebastian Fedden and Raphael Finkel (2017), 'Single versus concurrent systems: Nominal classification in Mian', *Linguistic Typology*, 21 (2), pp. 209–60.

Harbour, Daniel (2014), 'Small pronoun systems and what they teach us', *Nordlyd*, 41, pp. 125–43.

Langdon, Margaret (1992), 'Yuman plurals: From derivation to inflection to noun agreement', *International Journal of American Linguistics*, 58 (4), pp. 405–24.

Marlett, Stephen A. (2016), 'Cmiique Iitom: The Seri Language', MS, University of North Dakota, <arts-sciences.und.edu/summer-institute-of-linguistics/faculty/marlett-steve/serigrammar.pdf> (last accessed 3 May 2018).

Naba, Jean-Claude (1994), *Le Gulmancema: essai de systèmatisation*, Cologne: Rüdiger Köppe.

Redden, James E. (1966), 'Walapai I: Phonology', *International Journal of American Linguistics*, 32, pp. 1–16.

Round, Erich R. and Greville G. Corbett (2017), 'The theory of feature systems: One feature versus two for Kayardild tense-aspect-mood', *Morphology*, 27 (1), pp. 21–75.

Sadler, Louisa and Andrew Spencer (2001), 'Syntax as an exponent of morphological features', in Geert Booij and Jaap van Marle (eds), *Yearbook of Morphology 2000*, Dordrecht: Kluwer, pp. 71–96.

Stolz, Thomas (2015), 'Chamorro inflection', in Matthew Baerman (ed.), *The Oxford Handbook of Inflection*, Oxford: Oxford University Press, pp. 465–90.

Stump, Gregory T. (2016), *Inflectional Paradigms: Content and Form at the Syntax–Morphology Interface*, Cambridge: Cambridge University Press.

Watahomigie, Lucille J., Jorigine Bender and Akira Y. Yamamoto (1982), *Hualapai Reference Grammar*, Los Angeles: American Indian Studies Center, UCLA.

Watahomigie, Lucille J., Jorigine Bender, Philbert Watahomigie Sr. and Akira Y. Yamamoto, with Elnor Mapatis, Malinda Powskey and Josie Steele (2001), *Hualapai Reference Grammar*, rev. and expanded edn, Endangered Languages of the Pacific Rim Project, A2-003, Osaka: ELPR Publications.

Watahomigie, Lucille J., Jorigine Bender, Malinda Powskey, Josie Steele, Philbert Watahomigie Sr. and Akira Y. Yamamoto (2003), *A Dictionary of the Hualapai Language*, Endangered Languages of the Pacific Rim Publications Series, A2-041, Osaka: ELPR Publications.

6

Canonical Syncretism and Chomsky's S

Mark Aronoff

6.1 Introduction

6.1.1 Canonical Non-canonicity

For over a decade, Greville Corbett and the members and affiliates of the Surrey Morphology Group have worked within a canonical approach to languages, or *Canonical Typology*[1] (Brown et al. 2013). A hallmark of this approach is to see all actual languages as departures from a (potentially) never-occurring canonical ideal. Within morphology, for example, a canonical system would be strictly agglutinative, with no homophonous affixes, and all structurally complex words would be semantically compositional. This view has produced remarkable empirical findings, notable among them databases on specific types of deviations from morphological canonicity: periphrasis, defectiveness, deponency, suppletion, and syncretism.[2] Positing a canonical ideal has inverted the focus of the field. Where once analysts had prized finding a hidden natural state in every language, we now delight in the structural intricacies of deviation from the norm. Tolstoy was right about languages too, though there are no happy languages. All languages are unnatural and every language is unnatural in its own way.

A good new perspective opens up new questions. In this paper, I will look at what we may think of as second-order canonicity. What is a canonical instance of non-canonicity? I will suggest that *polyvalent polymorphous* morphemes form a canonical variety of syncretism. In the light of this question I will discuss one of the most famous cases of apparent syncretism from this (non-)canonical perspective: the morpheme S in Chomsky's (1957) *Syntactic Structures*. The canonical approach reveals that this S is not a syncretic morpheme but rather not a morpheme at all. Our new understanding of S also clarifies the nature of another theoretical element: the morphome. The question also arises of why one would pursue an analysis that leads to such an unsatisfactory result. I couch my answer as a cautionary methodological tale.

Most work from the canonical point of view has been implicitly realist, equating descriptions and analyses of languages with the languages themselves. My approach here is nominalist: my object of study is not a language but instead a single well-known analysis of a small part of one very well-known language, written English.³ Here the (non-)canonical approach proves to be valuable in a way that has not previously been noticed, as a tool for identifying weaknesses in proposed analyses: an analysis that posits polyvalent monomorphous entities should raise a red flag and receive special scrutiny before we accept it. Non-canonicity thus becomes an evaluation metric of the sort that Chomsky sought after in his early work. *Syntactic Structures*, one of the most influential books of the last century, is the most famous piece in this canon.

6.1.2 Canonical Syncretism and Morphomes

Matthew Baerman, Dunstan Brown and Greville Corbett (2005) wrote the book on syncretism. The term's curious etymology bears repeating. The Classical Greek verb συγκρητίζειν, nominal συγκρητισμός 'of two parties, to conspire against a common enemy' (Plutarch), as defined by Liddell and Scott (1996), is formed by prefixation from the scurrilous verb κρητίζειν 'to speak like a Cretan; to lie', from κρης 'Cretan'. The noun became popular in the late Renaissance to denote 'Attempted union or reconciliation of diverse or opposite tenets or practices, esp. in philosophy or religion' (*OED* Online). The linguistic use is traced to Pott by Curtius (1863) (Baerman et al. 2005) and early uses of the term were all diachronic. The *OED* attributes the first use in English to Bloomfield (1933: 388): 'Homonymy and *syncretism*, the merging of inflectional categories, are normal results of sound-change.' The problem that has plagued the discussion of syncretism since is how to distinguish the two: accidental *homophony* (the more current term), where morphs just happen to be identical in form, and systematic syncretism, which is a 'failure to make a morphosyntactically relevant distinction' on the part of the morphology (Baerman et al. 2005: 2). Within the grammar, true syncretism is no accident.

Trommer (2016) classifies syncretisms in terms of their 'naturalness' or expectedness. Standard examples of natural or expected case syncretism are those in which cases that lie adjacent on the case hierarchy (Greenberg 1966; Malchukov 2017) are realised syncretically, for instance in Latin the dative and ablative, which are always identical in the plural and also in the singular in certain declensions; or again in Latin the always identical neuter nominative and accusative. Similarly, more marked cells are often syncretic with less marked cells. A well-known example is the Slovenian dual, whose genitive and locative cells are always syncretic with the plural (Corbett 2011). In short, we expect certain realisations to be syncretic, because the realised morphosyntactic elements are close to each other along some dimension. If syncretism is non-canonical, though, the most canonical type of syncretism should not be the most natural but rather the least natural. Nobody expects the Spanish Inquisition. Although I know of no way to measure degrees of unnaturalness, one species of unnatural syncretism has been much discussed since it was first discovered almost a quarter century ago: the morphome.⁴

Aronoff (2016: 24) defines morphomes as 'functions within an incremental-realizational theory of morphology that map morphosyntactic representations onto phonological realizations'. He identifies four types of morphomes, according to whether a given morphome realises one morphosyntactic feature array (making it *monovalent*) or a disjunction of feature arrays (making it *polyvalent*) and whether it has a single realisation (*monomorphous*) or a set of context-sensitive realisations (*polymorphous*). 'Since it was first introduced, however, the term morphome has come to be used especially for polyvalent polymorphous mappings' (Aronoff 2016: 25). Being polyvalent (analysable only in terms of disjunction), they must be unnatural, because they realise a disjunction of feature arrays, and being polymorphous, the distribution of forms should be arbitrary. Polyvalent monomorphous morphomes, by contrast, are always candidates for accidental homophony, and monovalent morphomes are morphomes in name only.

Trommer (2016) makes the important observation that (polyvalent) morphomes are always syncretic. He includes only such morphomes under his definition of the morphome as 'A systematic morphological syncretism which does not define a (syntactically or semantically) natural class' (Trommer 2016: 60). He calls morphomes parasitic, suggesting they are somehow unnatural, though the biological perspective should remind us that parasites are the most widespread and abundant species in nature and hence not unnatural at all. Setting aside the question of what a natural class is, which has troubled linguistics for the last half century, Trommer's concurring opinion allows us to conclude that the parasitic morphome is a canonical example of morphological non-canonicity.

6.2 Chomsky's Morpheme S

6.2.1 S in Syntactic Structures

We are now ready for Chomsky's S, a peculiar entity if there ever was one, and the question of whether it is a morphome rather than a morpheme. The answer is that it is neither, but rather an instance of accidental homophony. This leads us to ask next what would lead an analyst to posit such a strange creature. The answer is aesthetically driven methodology.

Chomsky introduced the morpheme S as part of his famous analysis of English verbs in *Syntactic Structures* (henceforth *SS*). I have discussed this analysis along with S in Aronoff (2018) against the backdrop of the school of linguistics in which Chomsky was raised, American Structuralism. A major goal of that article was to show that, while freeing himself from the strictures of having to follow 'a manual of useful procedures' (*SS* 55) of the sort that his mentor, Zellig Harris, had so zealously sought after in pursuit of scientific legitimacy, Chomsky did not find, in *SS* or any subsequent work, an adequate substitute for Harris's manual of procedures that would tell us whether we were on the right track, what he called an evaluation metric. As a consequence, since the success of *SS* and Chomskyan linguistics, the entire field has been flying without a net. We have no reliable way to begin to measure whether one analysis is better than another. All that we are left with are aesthetic criteria and the unmeasurable criterion of understanding. The aesthetic criterion that lies behind Chomsky's S is minimalism: less is more. In morphology especially, this criterion is powerful and dangerous.

6.2.2 Affix Hopping and the English Verb

Chomsky introduces S in a footnote on p. 29 to the passage where he shows that rewrite rules must be context sensitive. Here is the passage:

> We must be able to limit application of a rule to a certain context. Thus T [article] can be rewritten a if the following noun is singular, but not if it is plural; similarly, *Verb* can be rewritten 'hits' if the preceding noun is *man*, but not if it is *men*. In general, if we wish to limit the rewriting of X as Y to the context $Z - W$, we can state in the grammar the rule
> (16) $Z + X + W \rightarrow Z + Y + W$.
> For example, in the case of singular and plural verbs, instead of having *Verb* $\rightarrow$ *hits* as an additional rule of (13). we should have
> (17) $NP_{sing} + Verb \rightarrow NP_{sing} + hits$
> indicating that *Verb* is rewritten hits only in the context $NP_{sing}-$.
> Correspondingly, (13ii) will have to be restated to include NP_{sing} and NP_{pl}. This is a straightforward generalization of (13). (*SS* 28–9)

The footnote (fn.3) is appended to this last sentence:

> Thus in a more complete grammar, (13ii) might be replaced by a set of rules that includes the following:
> $NP \rightarrow \begin{Bmatrix} NPsing \\ NPpl \end{Bmatrix}$
> $NP_{sing} \rightarrow T + N + \emptyset$ (+ *Prepositional Phrase*)
> $NP_{pl} \rightarrow T + N + S$ (+ *Prepositional Phrase*)
> where S is the morpheme which is singular for verbs and plural for nouns ('comes,' 'boys'), and $\emptyset$ is the morpheme which is singular for nouns and plural for verbs ('boy,' 'come'). We shall omit all mention of first and second person throughout this discussion. Identification of the nominal and verbal number affix is actually of questionable validity. (*SS* 29)

The questionable validity of S and $\emptyset$ presumably arises from their peculiar crossing pattern. The two morphemes each have one form and share two contextually distributed meanings, singular and plural. They share these meanings in a crossing manner, as in Table 6.1. Nonetheless, Chomsky shrugs off any misgivings and, a few pages later, incorporates the two morphemes into the *pièce de résistance* of the book, his analysis of English finite verbs, whose most important ingredient is what came to be called *affix hopping*. The affixes that hop are *past*, S, $\emptyset$, *en*, and *ing*, and, again in a footnote, he remarks 'We assume here that (13ii) has been extended in the manner of fn. 3, above, p. 29, or something similar' (*SS* 39).

Table 6.1 The two morphemes S and Ø

Morpheme	Ø	S
Context	Meaning	
Noun	SINGULAR	PLURAL
Verb	PLURAL	SINGULAR

In what follows, I will set aside Ø (whose lack of concrete realisation makes it a slippery critter at best) and confine my attention to S. Both morphemes are suspect because they defy a major part of Bloomfield's definition of the morpheme in his *Language* (1933: 145), that 'each linguistic form has a constant and specific meaning'. Such morphemes became conceivable only with the abandonment of meaning in favour of distribution, championed most notably by Harris. A few years earlier, in his response to Hockett (1947) and Bloch (1947), Eugene Nida (1948), who was always wary of this turn on the part of the theoretical mainstream, had dismissed the exact same analysis that Chomsky proposed. He was ostracised as a consequence of this response.

> Hockett considers that complementary distribution is all that fundamentally counts. But the implications of this method seem to be greater than he may have anticipated. For example, consider what could be done on that basis with number distinctions in English. Not only would it be possible to combine all the plural affixes of nouns in one morpheme (a step which we should all agree to), but one could say that these are in complementary distribution with the partly homophonous third-singular suffix of verbs. A single morpheme could then be set up with the meaning 'number distinctiveness' and with the additional distributional characteristic that if an alternant occurs after the noun it does not occur after the verb, and vice versa, e.g. /ðə boyz rən/ the boys run vs /ðə boy rənz/ the boy runs. By slight extensions it might be possible to construct a descriptive system by which practically all the features of concord, government, and cross-reference could be treated on a submorphemic level. If this were done, we should only have succeeded in changing the meaning of the word 'morpheme' to apply it to certain distributionally related forms. (Nida 1948: 418)

Nothing at the core of Chomsky's analysis of English verbs depends on the identification of the nominal plural with the verbal third person singular that forms the problematic core of his S. Affix-hopping involves only the verbal suffix and is unharmed by separating the two. And there are good reasons not to equate nominal and verbal (orthographic) <-s>. Verbal S is always realised as orthographic <-s>. In contrast, if we combine all the plural affixes of nouns in one abstract noun-plural morpheme on the grounds of complementary distribution, 'a step which we should all agree to', in Nida's words, then nominal <-s> cannot be a morpheme on its own, but is rather merely the default among the numerous allomorphic realisations of the abstract noun-plural morpheme PLURAL, along with the *-en* of *oxen*, the ablaut of *geese*, the Ø of *deer*, and many others that are by and large lexically determined. If we gather this allomorphic <-s> together with the *S* of the third person singular, we are either comparing apples and oranges (the verbal *S* is an abstract morpheme realised as <-s>, while the plural <-s> is an allomorphic realisation of PLURAL, the output of morphophonemic rules in the framework of *SS*), or the two instance of <-s> (noun plural and verb singular) are each an allomorph of a different morpheme, in which case the identity of the two affixes is no more than a curiosity, a case of accidental homophony. As Nida so discreetly hints, the whole analysis is driven by accidental homophony, distributionalist zealotry, and deliberate disregard for meaning. It is as accidental as the overwhelming homophonic realisation of Chomsky's *past* and *-en* as <-ed>, which he makes no attempt to unify.

The suffix <-s> is ubiquitous in English. It is one of the allomorphs of PLURAL and the only allomorph of 3SG.PRES; it is the GENITIVE marker for all lexical items except the forms *my, mine, your, her,* and *their*; and it is the clitic form of *has, is,* and (in speech) *does*. The identity of all these forms is at the level of phonological form, the morph, not, as Chomsky had proposed, at the level of the morpheme.

6.2.3 Is S a Morphome?

S has been dubbed a morphome. Aronoff (2016) gives it as his example of a polyvalent monomorphous morpheme, without comment. More precisely, he lists a morphome Z whose morphosyntactic value is any one of the members of the set {PLURAL, 3SG.PRES, GENITIVE, and the clitic version of *is, has,* and *does*}, but whose realisation is always [-z]. Could Chomsky's S be subsumed under this morpheme? In the passage cited above, Nida says that any such homophony-driven entity is suspect. The problem, in more current terms, is that polyvalent monomorphous morphomes suffer from the general methodological weakness of being hard to distinguish from cases of accidental homophony. In this instance, there is a further problem: although -Z is the default realisation of all these morphosyntactic values, both PLURAL and GENITIVE have other realisations as well. In a realisational framework like Network Morphology (Brown and Hippisley 2012), the non-default realisations would be ordered before the defaults by general principles and then each morphosyntactic value would be realised as the default [-z]. But this means that there is no single rule or constraint that unites all four default [-z] values. Put another way, there is no morphomic function as there is with a polyvalent polymorphous morpheme like Chomsky's *-en*, where both PASSIVE and PERFECT always have the same value for each verb and this value depends on the individual verb (Aronoff 1994). The [-z] is instead the result of four distinct realisation rules or constraints that all coincide on the same phonological segment. This identity of form has no role in this theory or in any other morphological theory that I know of. It is an accident. In short, the morphome Z is the result of a faulty analysis, driven by the same minimalist desire to avoid homophony at all costs that undergirded Chomsky's S. We should not go so far as to conclude that there are no polyvalent monomorphous morphomes, but this example shows how difficult it is to sift such entities out from the predations of accidental homophony in actual naturally unnatural languages.

It is worth reminding ourselves frequently that morphomes are not affixes but morphosyntactic functions of a simple mathematical sort. A morphome with many inputs and a constant shape must always be viewed with suspicion. We can understand why Trommer included only polyvalent polymorphous morphomes in his definition, because only this type of morphome is always undeniably morphomic. It is a canonical variety of (morphologically non-canonical) syncretism, precisely because it is not syncretic in its form. The syncretism lies only on the morphosyntactic side.

6.3 Minimalism: Less Is More

What, besides the Harrisian distributionalist method, might have driven Chomsky to propose this S? And why have its faults been ignored for 60 years, despite Nida's earlier scepticism? The answer lies in the modernist scientistic aesthetic sensibility that pervaded linguistics at the time, and still does. The community of linguists, like most other academic communities outside the hard sciences, has tried since the nineteenth century to establish its scientific bona fides. Early on, it enjoyed some success by linking linguistic and biological evolution (Schleicher 1869) but this tie dissipated with the rise of synchronic linguistics early in the twentieth century (Aronoff 2018). Linguists persisted by trying to put their synchronic analytical practices on a firm empirical footing. Bloomfield (1926) published an article entitled 'A set of postulates for the science of language'. Sapir (1929: 207) proclaimed that 'For all of [the social sciences] linguistics is of basic importance: its data and methods show better than those of any other discipline dealing with socialized behaviour the possibility of a truly scientific study of society.' Tellingly, both articles appeared in early volumes of *Language*, the ideological organ of American linguistics. Both linguists were preaching to the choir and there is little evidence that these proclamations had much effect on anyone outside the small house of worship that was the Linguistic Society of America.

The greatest empirical successes of the first century of linguistic science were methodological: the comparative method that established historical relations among languages and the distributional method for establishing phonemic structure. Harris (1951) extended the distributional method to morphology and syntax, proclaiming that it constituted a procedure for analysing the structure of a language. His colleagues greeted his announcement with glee. Finally, he felt, linguistics could be a truly objective science.

The most lasting achievement of *Syntactic Structures* was to burst this bubble. Harris's greatest student had undermined Harris's greatest claim, a Shakespearean turn. What remained was the one most pervasive aesthetic pillar of scientism and of modern thought more generally: minimalism. Though the name did not become popular until the 1960s, and then in painting, the idea behind it, that less is more, had emerged first in nineteenth-century art, then in architecture and design along a path from Josef Hoffmann in Vienna to early Le Corbusier and the Bauhaus, culminating in the work of Mies van der Rohe, the most influential urban architect of the post-war period. Mies is the person most closely associated with the motto 'less is more', though its first occurrence was in the poem 'Andrea del Sarto', by Robert Browning in 1855, about a painter. Even Ludwig Wittgenstein dabbled in minimalist architecture in the interval at home in Vienna between his two encounters with philosophy. The door and window handles that he designed for his sister's house in 1927 bear his name and are manufactured to this day.

Linguists associate minimalism with the Minimalist Program, the name that Chomsky (1995) gave to his most recent theory of syntax. But Chomsky's minimalist sensibilities go much further back. Zellig Harris practised minimalist analysis, as did another of Chomsky's mentors, Bernard Bloch, of whom Martin Joos (1957: 254) wrote that 'In principle, Bloch's procedure is to adopt a set of axioms and then to develop the consequences of the set à outrance.' Minimalists are what biologists since Darwin have called lumpers (as opposed to splitters). They believe that it is always better to reduce the number of postulates, entities, and categories to a minimum. For linguistic lumpers, identical forms are the great temptation. Reductionism of identical forms is Harris's unspoken guiding principle and it lies behind Chomsky's S, at the cost of sense. Yes, Chomsky wrote in footnote 3 that S was 'of questionable validity', but in footnote 4 he adopted it anyway. The reductionist aesthetic was too strong.

6.4 Conclusion

I hope that I have convinced the reader of the value of extending Greville Corbett's general framework of canonical morphology to the detailed study of one of the general types of departure from canonicity: syncretism. Polyvalent polymorphous morphemes constitute a canonical variety of syncretism. Placing one famous example of syncretism, Chomsky's S, under the morphomic lens provides a cautionary tale: this S is not a morpheme or even a morphome, but the result of a reductionist methodological zeal that strives to lump homophones together. The polyvalent monomorphous morphome as an analytical category might tempt the lumper, but this example provides a cautionary tale to the overeager analyst. Whether all monomorphous morphomes should be discarded is a question for further research. One might ask further what the value is of this taxonomy. We might seek deeper explanation, a framework in which such sports as polyvalent monomorphous morphomes simply do not emerge. What a canonical framework does, regardless, is to help us to distinguish actual from spurious cases and we have Greville Corbett to thank for it.

On a more general plane, Chomsky's S provides yet another cautionary tale against over-dependence on analytical methods and principles in the search for truth. Returning to architecture, we may take a lesson from Le Corbusier. He began his career by formulating five points of architecture, meant to guide all building design. These dictated the form of most of his many buildings over a 40-year career and laid the foundation for institutional modern architecture. His acknowledged masterpiece, the chapel of Notre-Dame du Haut in Ronchamps, designed later in life, flouts all of them.

Notes

1. See <http://www.smg.surrey.ac.uk/approaches/canonical-typology/> (last accessed 18 September 2018).
2. See <http://www.smg.surrey.ac.uk/databases/> (last accessed 18 September 2018).
3. The nomenclature of morphemes in *Syntactic Structures* is orthographically inspired, which makes it easier to couch the discussion here in terms of these orthographic suffixes, among which <-s> is the most important. For discussion of English orthographic <-s> and other morphological spellings in written English, see Berg et al. (2014).
4. This paper excludes morphomic stems (Maiden 2005), which deserve their own treatment in terms of syncretism.

References

Aronoff, Mark (1994), *Morphology by Itself: Stems and Inflectional Classes*, Cambridge, MA: MIT Press.
Aronoff, Mark (2016), 'Unnatural kinds', in Ana R. Luís and Ricardo Bermúdez-Otero (eds), *The Morphome Debate*, Oxford: Oxford University Press, pp. 11–32.
Aronoff, Mark (2018), 'English verbs in syntactic structures', in Norbert Hornstein, Howard Lasnik, Pritty Patel-Grosz and Charles Yang (eds), *Syntactic Structures after 60 Years: The Impact of the Chomskyan Revolution in Linguistics*, Berlin: De Gruyter, pp. 381–402.
Baerman, Matthew, Dunstan Brown and Greville G. Corbett (2005), *The Syntax–Morphology Interface: A Study of Syncretism*, Cambridge: Cambridge University Press.
Berg, Kristian, Franziska Buchmann, Katharina Dybiec and Nanna Fuhrhop (2014), 'Morphological spellings in English', *Written Language and Literacy*, 17 (2), pp. 282–307.
Bloch, Bernard (1947), 'English verb inflection', *Language*, 23, pp. 399–418.
Bloomfield, Leonard (1926), 'A set of postulates for the science of language', *Language*, 2, pp. 153–64.
Bloomfield, Leonard (1933), *Language*, New York: Henry Holt.
Brown, Dunstan, Marina Chumakina and Greville G. Corbett (eds) (2015), *Canonical Morphology and Syntax*, Oxford: Oxford University Press.
Brown, Dunstan and Andrew Hippisley (2012), *Network Morphology*, Cambridge: Cambridge University Press.
Chomsky, Noam (1957), *Syntactic Structures*, The Hague: Mouton.
Chomsky, Noam (1995), *The Minimalist Program*, Cambridge, MA: MIT Press.
Corbett, Greville G. (2011), 'Higher order exceptionality in inflectional morphology', in Horst J. Simon and Heike Wiest (eds), *Expecting the Unexpected: Exceptions in Grammar*, Berlin: De Gruyter Mouton, pp. 107–26.
Greenberg, Joseph (1966), *Language Universals: With Special Reference to Feature Hierarchies*, The Hague: Mouton.
Harris, Zellig S. (1951), *Methods in Structural Linguistics*, Chicago: University of Chicago Press.
Hockett, Charles (1947), 'Problems of morphemic analysis', *Language*, 23, pp. 321–43.
Joos, Martin (1957), *Readings in Linguistics I*, 4th edn, Chicago: University of Chicago Press.
Liddell, H. G. and R. Scott (1996), *A Greek–English Lexicon*, 9th edn with revised supplement, Oxford: Oxford University Press.
Maiden, Martin (2005), 'Morphological autonomy and diachrony', in Geert Booij and Jaap van Marle (eds), *Yearbook of Morphology 2004*, Dordrecht: Springer, pp. 137–75.
Malchukov, Andrei (2017), 'Case', in *Oxford Research Encyclopedia of Linguistics*, <http://linguistics.oxfordre.com/view/10.1093/acrefore/9780199384655.001.0001/acrefore-9780199384655-e-247> (last accessed 21 November 2017).

Nida, Eugene A. (1948), 'The identification of morphemes', *Language*, 24, pp. 414–41.
Sapir, Edward (1929), 'The status of linguistics as a science', *Language*, 5, pp. 207–14.
Schleicher, August (1869), *Darwinism Tested by the Science of Language*, trans. Alexander V. W. Bikkers, London: J. C. Hotten.
Trommer, Jochen (2016), 'A postsyntactic morphome cookbook', in Daniel Siddiqi and Heidi Harley (eds), *Morphological Metatheory*, Amsterdam: John Benjamins, pp. 59–94.

7

Canonical Tough Cases

Johanna Nichols

7.1 Introduction

In a steady stream of influential work over the years, Grev Corbett has clarified and cleared up question after question in morphosyntactic description and comparison, Slavic and general. His path-breaking notion of canonicality and the theoretical work it has triggered (Corbett 2007, 2013, 2015; Corbett and Fedden 2016; and many other publications) has solved a number of thorny problems in descriptive and comparative morphosyntax, and it can force us to look closely at familiar but underexamined phenomena and in some cases can make it possible to ask entirely new questions. This paper gives some examples of what I consider familiar but underexamined phenomena and entirely new questions exposed by canonicality theory. It started when a survey of morphological complexity led me to an attempt to determine canonical values for some common kinds of morphemes that do not obviously add meaning or fulfil any function. A key idea behind canonicality is the ideal of one form, one function, and patterns such as syncretism, deponence and suppletion are non-canonical because they do not map a single form to a single function. Here I deal with some phenomena which seem not only to fail to meet the one-form-one-function ideal but also to lack any logical ideal extreme type and/or anything that fits at all easily under the term 'function'. At the very least they need more work. All of them cause dilemmas for linguists concerned with interlinears, historical comparison and complexity, but have not had the theoretical attention they deserve.

A nut case, or syntactic nut, in its technical sense in linguistics (Culicover 1999; Fodor 2001; Yang 2016: 8), is a phenomenon so problematic or difficult to accommodate in the Universal Grammar (UG) core that the author calls for it to be removed entirely from the core or radically reanalysed. For theoretical approaches such as canonicality and typology more generally, which lack anything like the UG core, the technical notion of syntactic nut does not apply, but there are phenomena that call for rethinking. The purpose of this paper is to call attention to some of these, show how they challenge identifying what is canonical, and (I hope) trigger some in-depth work on them.

7.2 Extensions

A good starting point is extensions, the meaningless morpheme-like sequences that accompany formation of different stems in some languages.[1] Occasional examples occur in many languages, e.g. the isolated *-r-* in English *children*, for which the root is the morpheme *child*, the plural stem is *child-r-* with idiosyncratic root ablaut plus the extension, and the inflectional ending is the rare variant *-en*. What then is the *-r-*? It is as neatly segmentable as any discrete morpheme, limited as to grammatical context (plural only), and accompanied by plural inflection which suffices to mark the category of number. It can arguably be said to have plural meaning or to have no meaning, and the fact that ascribing to it no meaning is arguable is what is of interest here.

A similar example from Russian is the *-j-* in the plural stem of *brat : brat'ja* 'brother', for which the root is *brat*, the ending *-a* (atypical for this declension class but productive for another), and the extension *-j-*.

In Nakh-Daghestanian languages (central to eastern Caucasus) noun extensions play a much more conspicuous role. Many or most nouns have an extension that forms the oblique stem and another that forms the plural stem. The various oblique case endings are then suffixed to the extension. In Karata (Andic branch), most nouns have no oblique extension; many have an extension in *-a*, *-o*, *-u* or *-i* (which is used on which noun is not predictable; any stem-final vowel is truncated before the extension); attributive words (adjectives, participles) and kin terms have *-ššu* (masculine gender) or *-łi* (other genders), and a few nouns with root-final vowels take *-la* or *-lo* (unpredictably) (Magomedova and Khalidova 2001: 452–4). Closely related Tindi (also Andic) has most of the same extensions but with a somewhat different distribution. In less closely related Avar, the ergative case suffix serves as extension for the other oblique cases. There are three allomorphs of the ergative case suffix, distributed according to the gender of the word (Saidov 1967: 733–4). In other Daghestanian languages (e.g. Kryz of the Lezgian branch) it is the genitive that serves as base for the other oblique cases. For a survey of the different extensions and declension patterns in the Daghestanian languages, see Kibrik (2003).

In theory there are two possible analyses of Avar: the ergative suffix switches its function to oblique stem extension in the other cases; or the nominative and ergative suffixes both have the same zero form, and the zero is added to the root or bare stem in the nominative but to the oblique extension in the ergative (and the other oblique cases have non-zero endings). Analogously for Kryz and others where the genitive serves as oblique base: on the analysis of the extension as pure extension, it is then the genitive that has a zero allomorph. (This is also true of the nouns with no oblique extension in Kryz: they have a zero nominative and genitive but an overt ending in the ergative; see Authier 2009: 29ff.) The practice in Russian field-based description is to interlinearise the oblique extension separately as OBL. The plural stems in these languages also usually involve a suffix, but since that suffix figures in the nominative (whose ending is -Ø) as well as the oblique cases, and since the singular and plural case endings are mostly identical, it can be analysed as a plural suffix rather than as a plural extension. In all these languages the oblique extension serves no purpose other than to form the oblique stem – clearly so in the languages where the oblique extension is not also a case suffix on its own, and arguably so in those where it is.

In the Daghestanian languages there is generally some correlation between the oblique extension allomorph and other properties of the word: sometimes the phonology of the final segment, more often the gender or the semantics, with high-animacy categories such as human nouns and kin terms taking distinctive oblique suffixes. Are the oblique suffixes then inflectional suffixes marking gender and/or semantic classes? Or derivational suffixes deriving human nouns or nouns of one or another gender? The best answer would appear to be No to both. The correlation with gender is not one-to-one, and gender in Nakh-Daghestanian (as for most languages) is marked by agreement on other words and not on the noun (though see §7.4 below on auto-gender). Semantic classes such as human nouns, kin terms, etc. are not inflectional categories in these languages. There may be strong, even perfect, correlations between semantic classes and genders: in Avar and the Andic languages the gender categories are masculine human, feminine human and neuter (= all other, whether animate or inanimate). But these again are not inflectional categories but simply lexical properties that predict gender. Nor are the oblique extensions derivational suffixes: they do not derive one word from another, forming a new word from the bare stem; and what they form is not words but stem allomorphs. The oblique extensions are then stem formatives with a form but no meaning or function, and the different oblique extensions of any one language are allomorphs. Their distribution can be described as *sensitive to* or *constrained by* gender, animacy, or other factors, but this does not mean that they are *markers* of those properties. Nor does it mean that those properties are grammatical categories: animacy is not; gender is, but because of agreement on other words and not because of the oblique stem form.

It is not obvious what, if anything, might be canonical here. It may be important that, though not canonical, the extensions of Nakh-Daghestanian are not mere glitches or hindrances; they are a system with structure and constraints and language-to-language differences showing that there are factors that push and pull evolution.

7.3 Other Stem-Forming Morphology

There are other examples of morphological formatives that are an integral part of stems but have little or no appreciable function. These are sometimes known as *thematic* or *stem-forming* affixes, and there are other terms. Table 7.1 gives examples of Old Church Slavic verbs in their two stem forms. There are root, or radical, verbs that have no suffix, and a number of suffixed types. Verbs have two stems, infinitive (a.k.a. aorist) and present, lexically specified. In some verb classes the infinitive and present stem suffixes are the same; in others they are different. There is fairly good predictability of one stem form from the other; what is generally not predictable is

Table 7.1 Old Church Slavic verb types. ъ, ь are schwa-like vowels (respectively back and front) that underwent phonologically predictable vowel-zero alternations

		Infinitive stem	Present stem		Productive?
Root 'athematic'[a]		ěd-	ěd-	'eat'	No
Root 'thematic'		nes-	nes-	'carry'	No
Suffixed	-nǫ/-n	sъx-nǫ-	sъx-n-	'get dry'	Yes
	a/-j-	pьs-a-	piš- < *pis-j-	'write'	No
	-a/-j-	cěl-ov-a	cěl-u-j-	'greet'	Yes
	-a/-aj-[b]	děl-a-	děl-aj-	'do'	Yes
	-ě/-ěj-	bel-ě-	běl-ěj-	'look white'	Yes
	-i-	nos-i	nos-i-	'carry' (iter.)	Yes
	-ě-/-i-	mьn-ě-	mьn-i-	'think'	No

[a] Traditional Slavistic use of the terms *thematic* and *athematic* follows traditional Indo-Europeanist usage. The terms refer not to stem-forming elements but to the presence or absence of the vowel *e/o in the ending. That is, they are terms for classes of inflectional endings, not classes of stems.
[b] The -*a/aj*- and -*e/ej*- classes are traditionally described as having distinct infinitive and present suffixes. In the one-stem system that dominated description in the late twentieth century they are treated as having the same suffix -*aj*- or -*ej*- in both stems, with phonological or morphophonological rules truncating the -*j*- in the infinitive stem.

which verb takes which suffix pair. In some verbs, like 'write' in Table 7.1, the two stems were also differentiated by vowel ablaut.

There are some semantic and grammatical correlations, however. Verbs with -*nǫ/-n*- are often inchoative ('become') intransitives, and the suffix is sometimes described as deriving inchoative verbs from adjective roots or stems. Verbs with -*i*- are generally factitive (denominal) or causative, and in a handful of verbs mostly having to do with motion they form iterative counterparts to verbs of other classes, as in *nes*- and *nos-i*- in Table 7.1.[2] For these two classes the suffixes are generally regarded as derivational, and the whole set is often considered derivational.

For those suffixes that have no clear function, the main grounds for considering them derivational is that they are not inflectional. They can better be classified as extensions, whose only function is to allow the verb to be conjugated. The root verb classes have been unproductive at least since early Proto-Slavic and probably since Proto-Balto-Slavic.[3] Therefore, any newly formed, borrowed or restructured verb, and any verb belonging to an open class, must have a suffix in order to function as a verb. Just as the Daghestanian oblique noun stem extensions allow nouns to decline in the oblique cases, the Slavic verb extensions allow verbs to conjugate. (There is no Slavic verbal analogue to the Daghestanian nominative singular, which always has a zero ending and lacks any extension. Imperatives sometimes have zero allomorphs but never lack extensions.)

Another similarity of Slavic verb extensions to Daghestanian noun extensions is that for both there is a sizable set of words without extensions. An alternative analysis might be that all words have extensions, one of which is a zero extension.

Since extensions are generally a partial phenomenon, and often a minority one, I will consider words with no overt extension to have no extension and not a zero extension.

Table 7.2 The Russian paradigm for *bel-* 'white'. Words are in the citation form (nominative singular masculine for adjectives, nominative singular for nouns, infinitive for verbs)

Word	POS	Meaning
bel-yj	Adjective	'white'
bel-et'	Verb	'turn white; be white, show white'
bel-it'	Verb	'bleach, whiten'
bel'	Noun	†'whiteness'; 'non-sturgeon fish'

	Morphology	
Root	Suffix	Ending (inflectional)
bel-		-yj
bel-	ej-	-t'
bel-	i-	-t'
bel-		-'Ø

† Indicates archaic meanings.

The correlations with semantics and grammar are more problematic, as they were for noun extensions. Consider the Russian words in Table 7.2.

The suffixes on the two verbs are the possibly extensional type at issue. The traditional analysis is that the *-i-* suffix forms denominal or deadjectival transitive verbs, and is therefore a derivational suffix, specifically a factitive; and that the *-ej-* suffix forms inchoative and stative verbs and is derivational. Neither the adjective nor the noun has an extension or derivational suffix. They differ in part of speech and consequently have different inflectional categories and different endings in modern Russian. They belong to different declension classes.[4] The noun had a non-zero nominative singular in Proto-Slavic, but that was the nominative ending of its declension class; it was not a derivational suffix. That is, as both noun and adjective *běl- was a basic or elementary word, not derived and without an extension. Its part of speech was therefore ambiguously, or flexibly, noun-adjective. Since the adjectival functions (attributive, predicate nominal, probably also P-compound for use as a resultative secondary predicate) are the more frequent, it might be argued that the word is a basic adjective and the unsuffixed noun is derived by conversion.[5] But frequency is shaky grounds for establishing part of speech, so the analysis as flexible is more sound.

On the traditional analysis the suffixes in Table 7.2 are derivational, *-i-* deriving factitive verbs and *-ěj-* deriving inchoative verbs from nominal and adjectival bases. Then the suffixes are both extension and derivation, or the verb has no extension but only a derivational suffix.

Consider now an analysis where the suffixes are extensions. Just as some

Daghestanian oblique extensions are associated with animacy or gender properties, these verb suffixes are associated with valence and aktionsart: -*i*- with transitivity and telicity (specifically, accomplishments) and -*ej*- with intransitivity and inchoative meaning. Word sets like these with *bel*- are fairly common in Russian, and they can be viewed as lexeme paradigms consisting of an adjective, sometimes an unsuffixed noun, and a pair of verbs, transitive and intransitive. Word formation creates such paradigms. The analysis can stop with the description of the paradigm, or we can go further and ask what the part of speech of the base *bel*- is. If the suffixes are extensions and not derivational, the answer can only be that it is a flexible noun/adjective/verb. I think this is ultimately the best answer, but the important point for typology is that it is an arguable answer. Based on preliminary work (Nichols 2016; Foley in preparation), this state of affairs is relatively common in Germanic and Slavic languages. It is very common in English and famously near-universal in Riau Indonesian (Gil 1994) and Kharia (Munda; Peterson 2010), all of which languages lack inflectional classes, extensions, etc. that make parts of speech visible in languages with more morphology. There are also languages in which extremely few words are flexible as to part of speech (e.g. Ingush, a Nakh-Daghestanian language of the Nakh branch; or Mongolian). These are languages with amounts of morphology more or less comparable to German or Russian, but great differences in the number of flexible words.

To summarise, an analysis where all the Slavic verb suffixes including the factitive -*i*- are extensions seems to be the most parsimonious. On any analysis we have a lexeme paradigm where noun and adjective are unsuffixed and verbs are suffixed (as verbs generally are in Russian). The base of the paradigm is *bel*- and on the analysis where suffixes are extensions that base is a flexible noun/adjective/verb.[6] The extensions are associated with aktionsart and valence types, but do not mark or derive those categories.

§7.2 and §7.3 have probably raised more questions than they have answered, but I hope they have at least laid bare the issues and can prompt theoretical work. A further question in need of work is whether derivation derives lexemes from lexemes or lexemes from stems (or even lexemes from roots). If derivation applies to stems (or roots) rather than lexemes, the analysis of the Slavic suffixes as derivational is more plausible.

The main conclusion is that extensions (whether they include all of the Slavic verb suffixes or only some of them, excluding the factitive and causative) have form but no meaning, are neither inflectional nor derivational, and raise questions for canonicality theory.

The next three sections deal with grammatical phenomena that are ordinarily (and canonically) marked on words other than the ones that control or govern them, but in these cases are marked on that word itself. Terminology in the literature varies (for those that have been discussed; most have not), so I use a single convention of terms beginning with *auto*- to capture the distinctive factor: *auto-gender, auto-person, auto-valence*.

7.4 Auto-gender

Gender, in those languages that have it, is a lexical property of nouns that is marked by agreement on other words (Corbett 1991; Corbett and Fedden 2016). In some languages, though, gender is marked on the nouns themselves. The clearest example is Bantu languages, in which all or nearly all nouns bear gender prefixes that mark the same gender as the nouns trigger on other words. Another is a number of northern Australian languages in which most nouns have gender markers (often called noun class markers in grammars) though some nouns lack them (e.g. Ngan'gityemerri; Reid 1997). In Nakh-Daghestanian languages, a minority (often a small minority) of nouns bear initial gender markers. Table 7.3 shows some examples, in which some cognates have initial /b/ or another labial consonant while others have no initial consonant or the corresponding dental. This gender class has a labial as its usual agreement marker (probably Proto-ND *b, with subsequent assimilation and analogical change).

A few sets differ in gender and consequently in auto-gender markers. Table 7.4 is an example. Languages in which 'dust' belongs to B gender are prone to have auto-gender; others are not, except that in the Nakh languages (here, Ingush) 'dust' belongs to a different gender and has auto-gender marking for that gender. A few words have apparent auto-gender initials that conflict with their actual gender, e.g. Ingush *jett* (B gender) 'cow'. That the initial *j* is segmentable is shown by the fact that this is one of a handful of nouns with initial *j-* in only the nominative case (oblique cases: genitive ʕatta, dative ʕattaa, etc.).[7] All other such words belong to J gender.

Nakh-Daghestanian auto-gender is what Fedden and Corbett (2016) call *head class marking* or *overt gender* and treat as gender marking or classifier marking where the noun is both controller and target. For them the question about auto-gender would be whether it is the same system as the agreement gender marking, and the answer in their terms is yes: it has the same forms and marks the same gender classes as agreement gender does, so it is a single system. Nakh-Daghestanian auto-gender differs from their examples, however, in some interesting respects. One is that their definition is phrased as 'same form and same **semantics**' because most of

Table 7.3 Nakh-Daghestanian cognate sets showing nouns of B gender with auto-gender (gender markers underlined)

Language	'sun'	'moon'	'tongue'	'eye'	'nettle'
Ingush	maalx	butt	mott	bʕar-jg[a]	nitt
Avar (Chadakolob dialect)	baq'	moc'	mac'	ber	mic'
Lak	bargh	barz	maz	–[b]	miʕč'
Dargwa	berhʕi	bac	mecc	hʕuli	niz
Lezgi (Axty dialect)	ragh	warz	mez	ul	–
Xinalug	ynq'	vac'	mic'	pil	myč'

[a] ʕ indicates pharyngealisation.
[b] – stands for no cognate attested.

Table 7.4 Selected Nakh-Daghestanian cognates for 'dust, sand', with their actual gender and auto-gender classes indicated. The marker for gender 3 is a labial, probably Proto-N-D *b

Language	Cognate	Actual gender	Auto-gender
Ingush	jost	J (5)	J (5)
Avar (Chadakolob dialect)	muceru	3	3
Andi	sur	4	–
Karata	soro	2	–
Hinuq	mese	3	3
Archi	sarsi	4	–

the languages they survey have a classifier system that is semantically based, while in most Nakh-Daghestanian languages the gender of non-human nouns is arbitrary. (In the Avar-Andic group gender assignment is semantic, with a single non-human gender as well as human male and human female.) Therefore, I have phrased it as 'same form and same gender'.

Another anomaly is that its distribution over targets is very different from that of agreement gender, a matter that does not come up for Fedden and Corbett. In most languages, agreement is determined by syntax and part of speech of targets, and is ordinarily exhaustive: if verbs are agreement targets, all verbs agree; if adjectives are agreement targets, all or most agree.[8] In Nakh-Daghestanian, agreement is lexically determined and highly non-exhaustive. Not all verbs take gender agreement; those that do are a minority in most of the languages. A smaller percentage of adjectives take agreement. In some languages the occasional adposition or numeral does. And so on; I am not aware of any Nakh-Daghestanian language in which a word class exhaustively admits agreement. That is, words lexically specify whether they can be agreement targets. For nouns, the percentage that have auto-gender is smaller than for the major lexical class agreement targets. Auto-gender is lexically specified, but what is it that is specified: ability to host agreement as target? Or whether or not the word has auto-gender at all? The fact that controller and target are the same word, and that auto-gender is almost always the same as agreement gender, makes it difficult to determine just what we are looking at.

A third anomaly is that auto-gender is not merely non-exhaustive but in fact a small minority phenomenon in all the languages (and note that cognate nouns often disagree as to whether they have auto-gender or not, as in Table 7.3). Traditional discussions usually regard it as frozen gender marking, though there is no productive gender marking pattern in any Nakh-Daghestanian of which auto-gender might represent a frozen example. Consider Ingush *jett* 'cow' discussed above, which belongs to B gender but has J auto-gender. Is this really J auto-gender, or is this a word without auto-gender with an initial consonant that just happens to be the same as a gender marker? In this case the etymological evidence suggests that the Ingush initial consonant is secondary, but that does not prove that it is specifically auto-gender.

And in fact the same can be said for the same-auto-gender words as well: can we be sure that this is auto-gender rather than that some words just happen to have an initial consonant that echoes their gender? I made a survey of nouns in several Nakh-Daghestanian languages and found that the frequency of /j/, /b/ and /d/ initials in nouns of J, B and D gender respectively was statistically highly significantly greater than that of non-matching initials (Nichols 2007, 2008), which shows that the phenomenon is non-random but does not prove that it is specifically gender marking rather than, say, a phonesthemic tendency. Nor does it tell us whether the gender-echoing initial of any particular word is auto-gender; it simply tells us that of the words with gender-echoing initials those that do have auto-gender are more numerous than expected.[9]

To summarise, though Nakh-Daghestanian auto-gender and gender qualify as a canonical single system in the terms of Fedden and Corbett (2016), auto-gender itself is highly non-canonical in its non-exhaustiveness, represents a low-frequency phenomenon cross-linguistically, and is anomalous in that its very existence is uncertain.

7.5 Auto-person

Analogously, person is usually controlled by arguments and possessors and marked by indexation on other words. In European languages person is a lexical category of pronouns and nouns (all nouns being third person) and an inflectional category elsewhere. Looking beyond Europe we find many languages in which, at least morphologically, pronouns have person as an inflectional category but not as a lexical category. Examples are numerous in North America and nearly ubiquitous among head-marking languages there. An example is Cree in Table 7.5, where the independent pronouns consist of a possessive prefix *ni:-* or *ki:-* plus a generic base that carries number marking but no person marking. (See Nichols 2013 for more on such pronouns.) Such pronouns have inflectional person but no lexical person.

Work on Canonical Typology generally assumes that person is a lexical category of pronouns and present in all languages, and in addition languages may or may not have bound person forms, i.e. person indexation (Chumakina et al. 2014, who speak of the (universal) cognitive category of person vs the (possible) morphosyntactic category; I read Siewierska 2004: xv, 13 as compatible with this claim). But in languages like Cree there is no morphological evidence, and to my knowledge no lexical evidence, for lexical pronouns or other lexemes having person as part of their meaning: person is added to personless word stems by inflection. The person prefixes in Table 7.5 are not agreement as they are located on the originating word itself. Now, canonical agreement should be syntactically simple, affixal and redundant rather than

Table 7.5 Independent pronouns in Cree (Algonquian; Wolfart 1996: 424, with colon for his raised dot)

1SG	2SG	INCL	1PL	2PL
ni:-ya	ki:-ya	ki:-ya:-naw	ni:-yanan	ki:-yawa:w

informative (Corbett 2007). Though in languages like Cree person is exclusively inflectional and not lexical, the fact that it is arguably agreement in some contexts (as argument indexation on verbs and possessor indexation on nouns) but clearly not agreement on independent pronouns makes it difficult to judge it by the criteria for canonical morphosyntactic features (Corbett 2013).

Auto-person on nouns is rare. One language with noun auto-person is Cherokee (Iroquoian; south-eastern US and Oklahoma), in which all human nouns obligatorily take person-number prefixes indexing the subject when the noun functions as predicate nominal, but otherwise simply index the person and number of the noun itself when the noun functions as argument.[10]

(1) Cherokee (Montgomery-Anderson 2015: 135)
a-sgaya
3SGA-man[11]
'man; He's a man.'

(2) Cherokee (Montgomery-Anderson 2015: 136)
iisdii-júúja   eesdiiyvvha
2DUA-boy   TOC-2DUA-enter-IMM
'You two boys come inside.'

The third person singular prefix is used in the citation form of nouns. The same prefixes function possessively in non-human nouns.

(3) Cherokee (Montgomery-Anderson 2015: 137)
hi-ʔlééni
2SG-ear
'your ear' (not 'You are an ear.')

That is ordinary possessive marking; only on human nouns (which are evidently non-possessible) are they auto-person.

7.6 Auto-valence

Kemmer (1993) describes a cross-linguistic category of middle voice as a distinctive form class of verbs centring on a prototype involving valence-related, aspect-related and pragmatic properties. Over time, the form class is likely to extend to other verbs, losing or at least diffusing whatever valence/aspect/pragmatic properties it once had.

The many lexicalised reflexive verbs in Balto-Slavic, Germanic and Romance languages have this history. Two examples from modern Russian are *smejat'-sja* 'laugh' (reflexive *-sja*), which was an unpaired reflexive in late Proto-Slavic and descends from Indo-European **smei-* 'laugh, smile' (Rix 2001: 72–3, 568–9), an underived intransitive; and *varit'-sja* 'boil, be boiling, cook', derived from transitive *varit'* 'boil, cook (something)'. By now, reflexivisation as derived intransitivity is quite common, and the set of lexicalised intransitives hardly bears any generalisation at all other than that they are intransitive.[12] Thus the *-sja* suffix or clitic marks valence and little else – not on the arguments, where cases mark the valence, but on the governing verb itself. Even the valence loses relevance on a closer look: many of these verbs govern oblique objects (e.g. *bojat'sja* 'fear' takes an accusative object), and oblique-object verbs are called intransitive in traditional grammar but usually not in modern linguistics; furthermore, a number of them are beginning to govern the accusative, i.e. direct objects (including *bojat'sja*). Thus, the reflexive element has a form but, increasingly, no function (other than the circular one of marking a verb as belonging to the formal class of the marker).

This kind of reflexivisation, and any kind of middle voice that carries some marker, might well be called auto-valence.

7.7 Toggles

I use this term for morphology that switches stems back and forth between two categories, or between a category and its absence. The clearest example is number marking in the Kiowa-Tanoan languages of North America (Watkins and McKenzie 1984: 78ff.; Wonderly et al. 1954; Merrifield 1959). Verbs distinguish the three number categories of singular, dual and plural, and agree with nouns in these categories. Nouns are inherently singular-dual or dual-plural, and an inverse number suffix changes inherent singular-dual nouns to plural but inherent dual-plural nouns to singular. Kiowa examples include: *báò* 'cat' (SG, DU), *báò-dɔ̀* (cat-INVERSE) 'cats' (PL); *a:-dɔ̀* (sticks-INVERSE) 'stick' (SG), *á:* 'sticks' (DU, PL) (Merrifield 1959: 269–70, from Wonderly et al. 1954).

Another example may be possessive marking in Tzotzil (Mayan; Laughlin 1975: 24), where a suffix -*Vl* (*V* = cover symbol for several vowels) is part of the possessive marking, animate and inanimate possession are grammatically distinct in various ways, and for one subclass of nouns -*Vl* toggles between animate and inanimate possession.

It is not difficult to describe the function of toggle morphemes, but it is difficult to ascribe a category meaning to them. They are reminiscent of the category mismatches such as gender in Romanian, where nouns distinguish only masculine vs feminine but a neuter category is identifiable as triggering masculine agreement in the singular and feminine in the plural. This is non-canonical in that it deviates from the principle that features and their values are clearly distinguished formally (Corbett 2013: 49–50). Toggle morphology adds the further complication of semantic non-uniqueness.

7.8 Registration

Here I follow the definitions of *indexation* and *registration* in Nichols (1992: 47–8): indexation is any form of morphological marking that copies or duplicates or otherwise takes on features or categories of one word or morpheme on another. The clearest example is agreement, but the term covers all kinds of marking on verbs of argument properties such as person, number and gender. It was intended as a term that would cover both agreement and what is variously known as cross-reference (of arguments on verbs) or pronominal arguments, without regard to theoretical frameworks. Since person, of all categories, is highly prone to be indexed on phrase heads, and since actually demonstrating whether a given verbal person-marking structure is agreement or a pronominal argument can be difficult (Hengeveld 2012), it is important to have a term that covers person indexation broadly and will be robust to discoveries about individual languages and to evolution of theory. In addition, person indexes may well always be referential (Kibrik 2011), making it difficult to argue conclusively for agreement vs pronominal arguments.

Registration is marking that reflects the presence of a word or morpheme in the phrase or clause, without including any of its features. Like indexation, it is frequently but not necessarily on the verb, and the examples discussed here are all verbal. Probably the clearest example is focus marking in Tagalog, where the verb takes an affix (usually called a voice affix) that registers an argument in a particular argument role: A in (4a), O in (4b), location in (4c). There is no agreement with person, number or any other property of the argument. The arguments themselves take case-marking prepositions, except that whichever is registered on the verb takes a focus preposition that neutralises all case distinctions and marks only focus.

(4) Agent, object, and local focus in Tagalog (Foley 2008: 23, 30)
    a. b-um-ili   ng   isda   sa   tindahan   **ang**   **lalake**
        vc-buy   CORE   fish   OBL   store   FOC   man
        '**The man** bought fish in the store.'
    b. bi-bilh-in   ng   lalake   sa   tindahan   **ang**   **isda**
        IRR-buy-VC   CORE   man   OBL   store   FOC   fish
        'The man will buy **the fish** in the store.'
    c. bi-bilh-an   ng   lalake   ng   isda   **ang**   **tindahan**
        IRR-buy-VC   CORE   man   CORE   fish   FOC   store
        'The man will buy **fish in the store**.'

Another example is verb object marking in Hungarian, which has two conjugation types for transitive verbs. In both of them the verb agrees in person and number with the subject and, in what is called the definite conjugation, it also registers the presence of an object without indexing its person or number.

(5) Hungarian
    a. látok / lát
       'I see.' / 'He sees.'
    b. állok / áll a sarokban
       'I stand / s/he stands in the corner.'
    c. Indefinte   d. Definite
       látok / lát   egy   házat   látom / látja   a   házat
       see.1SG / see.3SG   one   house.ACC   see.1SG / see.3SG   the house.ACC
       'I see / s/he sees a house.'   'I see / s/he sees the house.'

The indefinite conjugation is used when there is no object (5a,b), including with intransitive verbs (5b), or with an indefinite object (5c); the definite conjugation is used when there is a definite object (5d). Stated in terms of registering, the definite conjugation registers the presence of an object in the clause and in addition there is differential object marking, so that only if an object is definite is it registered on the verb.

An example of registration from a different domain is honorifics, respect forms and the like. In many European languages the relevant social parameter is marked by the number category of second person forms, and this is indexed on verbs. In Asian languages that lack verb agreement, verb morphology registers the presence, not in the clause but in the speech act, of a person with the relevant status. Japanese, for instance, has both addressee-controlled polite forms, which register the presence of an honorific addressee, and referent-controlled polite forms, which register the presence in the clause of a noun referring to an honorific individual (Shibatani 1990: 375–6).

Possible examples of registration come from the domain of number marking, where verbs of many languages have an affix indicating that there is a plural argument in the clause. In what seems to be the most common pattern, the plural affix is ambiguous as to argument role, indicating plural subject, object or both. Leer (1991) uses the term 'promiscuous number marking' for this kind of ambiguous number marking on verbs. Examples from Crow are given in (6).

(6) Crow (Siouan; Graczyk 2007: 122–3)
 dii-waa-lit-úu
 2-1-hit-PL
 'I hit you (PL).', 'We hit you (SG).', 'We hit you (PL).'

The person prefixes index the person, but not the number, of the O and A, and the plural marker registers the presence of a plural core argument in the clause but does not identify a particular argument as plural. Though deciding whether to call this registration (of a plural argument) or indexation (of the number of an argument, with syncretism) is difficult, there are two possible arguments in favour of calling it registration. One is that the bound pronominal arguments do not distinguish number (though the emphatic and contrastive pronouns that are the closest Crow approximation to independent pronouns do distinguish number, suffixing to the singular stem what may be an allomorph of the verb plural marker; Graczyk 2007: 60–1 describes the verb plural suffix as supplanting plural marking in the bound pronominals).[13] Another is the very ambiguity of the verb plural marker, which is to be expected if it simply reacts to the presence of a plural argument; if this were agreement, the ambiguity would be unexpected (though possible). (As an instance of neutralisation or syncretism, it would also be non-canonical.) The question needs deeper theoretical consideration, but at least a case can be made for saying that promiscuous number marking is registration and not indexation.

Promiscuous number marking occurs on nominals as well. In Turkic languages, the plural suffix for nouns and third person pronouns is *-lAr and the third person plural possessive suffix either is or contains *-lAr. Only one token of *-lAr occurs per word, so third person possessive forms with that suffix are ambiguous, e.g. Turkish /tašlary/ {taš-lar-y} or (stone-PL-3) 'his/her/its stones', 'their stone', 'their stones' (Csató and Johanson 1998: 209); Yakut *at-tar-a* (horse-PL-3) 'his/her horses', 'their horse', 'their horses' (Stachowski and Menz 1998: 422). This seems to be an instance of haplology, removing one token of {lAr} from {noun-lAr-lArI} (noun-PL-3PL}. First and second person plural pronouns and possessive suffixes have a different plural suffix and do not trigger haplology. Haplology presents no problems for canonicality, provided it can be assessed on the underlying forms, but a typologically related pattern in Erzya Mordvin suggests that there may be a deeper issue than the phonological duplication targeted by haplology. Erzya nouns have regular singular and plural forms but do not make this distinction when possessed, so that all possessed forms are ambiguous as to the number of the noun (but unambiguous as to the number of the possessor) (Zaicz 1998: 194–5). The noun plural suffix and the plural element of the plural possessive suffixes are formally different, so this is neutralisation and not haplology.

While in Tagalog argument roles are registered but not indexed on the verb, in most languages with head marking of argument roles they are indexed. In Mayan languages, A and S/O are indexed in the forms of person markers, e.g. Tzutujil (Dayley 1985: 62–4) singular forms, shown (in part) in (7) with an example in (8).

(7) Tzutujil singular person-number-role indexes
        S/O   A
1SG in-   nuu-/n-/in-
2SG at-   aa-/a-
3SG Ø-   ruu-/r-/uu-

(8) Tzutujil (Dayley 1985: 65)
x-in-aa-choy
TAM-1SGO-2SGA-hit
'You hit me.'

The relative positions of the prefixes also help identify the arguments, but the indexation of specific arguments is shown in the prefix forms.

This leaves the status of role indexation uncertain for languages of the West Caucasian family (Abkhaz, Abaza, Adyghe, Kabardian). Verbs in these languages have three different argument indexation slots, for A, G and S/O in that order, interspersed among other affixes, and the three sets of markers have almost entirely identical underlying forms. What identifies their function as A, G or S/O is partly their relative position, partly any intervening affixes, and partly sandhi effects triggered by some affixes.

Finally, there are languages like those of the Kartvelian family, where verbs index three arguments (A, O and G) in only one slot. This too is indexation of role, because there are some differences in the forms of A, O and G markers. Most remaining ambiguities are resolved by a person and role hierarchy that determines access to the slot (for a clear statement, see Öztürk and Pöchtrager 2011: 45–9 on Pazar Laz).

To summarise, in languages in which A and/or O, and S, are head-marked, there is usually argument role indexation, with different morphological forms marking different arguments. What they actually index is not just argument role but that plus valence. The most common pattern is for the A marker to index the person and number of the default form of A, and the O marker to index the default form of O (usually known as direct object). Oblique subjects and objects may take some other form of indexation, or may not trigger agreement at all, depending on the language. Kibrik (2012) regards the verb markers as indexing case, the same category that is marked directly on the nouns in dependent-marking patterns. Where there are two or more argument slots on the verb, the relative position of the arguments is an important part of the indexation (Kibrik 2012, who reports that position is almost always important), and in the West Caucasian languages it is virtually the only indication. If affix position can be regarded as a form, and the argument role/valence/case structure that it indexes is a function, then the West Caucasian system meets the one-form-one-function ideal and is canonical. However, I leave open the question of what is canonical for the effects of ordering, and likewise for hierarchically determined access to slots.

A well-known and uncontroversial example of registration is applicatives and similar valence-related derivations. Applicative is a derivation that adds a core argument, usually an object, which bears case and/or triggers indexation much like a non-derived argument. Applicative marking on the verb most often just registers the presence of the additional object, and differences of agreement show up in the regular agreement slots and not on the applicative morpheme.

Indexation and registration do not exhaust the possible kinds of head marking; there is also incorporation, not discussed here. I note, though, that incorporated nouns are generally reported to be non-referential, i.e. they lack the referential index that is essential to the definition of nouns (Baker 2003). Incorporation must then be non-canonical for the noun involved.

7.9 Conclusions

To summarise, several morphological phenomena reviewed here either require more work in canonicality theory or in some cases may be outright anomalies for the theory. A possible anomaly is extensions and thematic suffixes (which I have argued are the same kind of element as extensions and should fall under the same term), which have a clear form with clear segmentability but no function. They are much the same thing as conjugation or declension class markers, which are unnecessary and without meaning or function, therefore non-canonical in the broader scheme of things. Where they do exist, they should canonically all be different from each other, so such things as overlaps and syncretisms between them are non-canonical (these points from Corbett 2007, 2013, 2015). At least in languages with inherited Indo-European noun morphology, overlaps and syncretisms do abound in declension classes, making the systems quite non-canonical, while the Daghestanian extension systems are more canonical (or less non-canonical) in exhibiting very little syncretism. Inherited

Indo-European verb thematic suffixes, like those for Old Church Slavic shown in Table 7.1 above, also exhibit a number of instances of syncretism, where two classes share the same present stem or the same infinitive stem while the other stem differs. What makes extensions different from ordinary declension and conjugation classes is, first, their clear segmentability, which naturally leads linguists to interlinearise them as morphemes; and second, at least for the Indo-European examples, the fact that extensions are a form of stem flexivity (in the terms of Bickel and Nichols 2007) while what are usually called declension and conjugation classes in the literature are classes of ending flexivity.

Interestingly, the trend over the years in many Indo-European branches has been to decrease the non-canonicality in systems of extensions. The clearest case is languages that have abolished the declension system entirely by losing case inflection, but there are also languages like Ossetic which has replaced the inherited declension paradigms by a single paradigm without declension classes. Incidentally, but also intriguingly, over time Russian has decreased the non-canonicality of ending flexivity in its noun paradigms by increasing the extent to which declension class correlates with gender, to the point that in modern Russian there is very high predictability of gender from declension class (Corbett 1982). A possible example from verb extensions in Slavic is the extension *-nǫ of late Proto-Slavic (shown for Old Church Slavic in Table 7.1), an occasional inchoative formation in the protolanguage but extended in some languages (often in a more archaic form *-nū-) to become a more general marker of perfective verbs with an ingressive, inceptive or inchoative sense (see Andersen 1999).

Auto-gender, auto-person and auto-valence are problematic for canonicality analysis in that they mark on the originating word a category that is usually marked only on another word, as agreement or other controlled or governed morphology. They also raise hurdles for deciding what (if any) category they actually do represent. Nakh-Daghestanian languages present occasional examples of nouns with an auto-gender initial that differs from their agreement gender; sometimes the auto-gender points to an earlier gender in a noun that has changed its gender, but sometimes it does not. Also, at least for Nakh-Daghestanian, where auto-gender affects a small minority of nouns, it is difficult to argue for any given noun that its initial consonant is auto-gender rather than an actual coincidence of random initial consonant with a gender marker. Some Bantu languages or close sisters have lost their gender agreement entirely, while retaining the initial former gender markers, which thereby become number markers (since the original gender classes consist of a pair of singular and plural gender markers, with a variety of both singular and plural forms). The gender system has thereby evolved into a number system, with a variety of singular and plural markers whose distribution is largely predictable from semantics (as the gender classes of Bantu languages are) (see Maho 1999). This history suggests the hypothesis that auto-category markers can rather easily evolve into markers of an entirely different category, while ordinary agreement markers rarely come to mark an entirely different category.

We might also ask whether case (in its traditional sense of inflectional affixes marking argument role as mediated by valence) might not better be termed 'auto-case', reserving *case* for the argument-role marking performed by person-number markers on verbs. (See again Kibrik 2012 for the analysis of these verb affixes as marking case.) If (as hypothesised above) auto-category markers relatively easily change the category they mark, there is a possible supporting example for case from the Slavic languages. Modern Macedonian and Bulgarian have lost case entirely but retain what were formerly nominative case endings of different declension classes which correlated partly with gender. In the modern languages these former case suffixes have thereby evolved into gender markers (imperfect markers in that they correctly indicate gender often but not always, a situation inherited from the imperfect correlation of declension class and gender in earlier Slavic). This is much like the evolution of Latin case-gender endings into the auto-gender markers *-o, -a* in Spanish nouns.

Alternatively, perhaps it is the verbal phenomenon that should be termed 'auto-case' while traditional case continues to be called case. Verbs govern valence types, nouns bear the cases that mark valence types, but the specific case governed, say in an oblique object, by a specific verb is a matter of oblique argument marking as imposed by the case system of the language. The ways in which case is different from the other auto-categories, and the uncertainty as to which word, the governing verb or the case-inflected noun filling the valence position, carries the auto-category and which carries the plain category, are probably due to the difference between agreement (in gender, number or person, the clear auto-categories discussed here) and government (of case and/or valence).

Continuing with the summary, toggle morphemes probably do not present real obstacles to canonicality theory, but require some tweaking of the criterion of one form, one function. Registration is not an obstacle at all, but simply needs more investigation, theoretical and otherwise; it happens that most work on canonical morphosyntax has dealt with indexation or direct marking (i.e. of noun functions on nouns, as with case) but not registration. Recognition of registration simply requires some expansion of the notions of marking and function. The discussion of registration here did, however, raise the further questions of whether number marking on verbs is indexation or registration; whether the object conjugation of Hungarian is differential object marking (DOM) affecting registration or indexation of definiteness (the decision here was for DOM); and whether marking by pure ordering (as with the argument markers on West Caucasian verbs) is a kind of form and amenable to canonicality analysis.

Much of this concluding section has been speculative, even highly speculative. But that is just the point: to show that canonicality theory not only answers questions about morphology and morphosyntax but also makes it possible to ask questions that, to my knowledge, have not been and could not have been asked before.

Notes

1. For Bantu and other African language families the term 'extension' is used for meaningful derivational suffixes that derive verbs such as causative, applicative, passive, etc. from other verbs. Here I use it in the sense I am familiar with for Eurasian languages, though what is really needed is distinct terms for these two very different kinds of morphemes. 'Extension' is presumably old in Bantu work; I am not sure how old it is elsewhere, but the related term 'stem extender' goes back at least to mid-twentieth-century work on Romance linguistics by Yakov Malkiel.
2. Nichols (2010) argues that these and most of the putative causatives are denominal.
3. The 'athematic' type is a small set with four members in Late Proto-Slavic and has tended to shrink over time in most daughter languages. The 'thematic' root type is not particularly small; Townsend (1975: 98–9) lists 67 members for modern Russian.
4. In Proto-Slavic, adjective endings were identical to those of nouns in the default declension classes (the IE *o-stem for masculine and neuter nouns and *a-stem for feminines). The noun in Table 7.3 happens to belong to a non-default declension class.
5. For P-compounds, see Szajbel-Keck (2015); Szajbel-Keck et al. (2012). A modern Russian example of a resultative is *dobela* in, for example, *pomyt' dobela* 'wash clean', lit. 'wash white'.
6. The semantics of the adjective and verbs in these sets is predictable, but the meanings of the noun include both the expectable abstraction 'whiteness' and the one-off 'fish other than sturgeon'. This is probably evidence that the base is a flexible adjective-verb and the nouns are derived by conversion (or it is a flexible noun-adjective-verb and additional nouns are derived by conversion), but the point will not be pursued here.
7. The oblique case forms are written with an initial pharyngeal segment, but in fact it is pharyngealisation of the automatic initial glottal stop on vowel-initial words. Pharyngealisation in Ingush is a syllable feature which is phonetically attracted to glottals.
8. Non-agreeing adjectives exist in Old Church Slavic and the other older Indo-European languages I know of, but they are a small and closed class. For IE agreement in adjectives, see also Matasović (2014).
9. Etymological evidence strongly suggests that auto-gender descends from a formerly more widespread pattern that was connected to definiteness; but it is the synchronic analysis of the modern languages that is at issue here.
10. I am not sure myself whether I have used *index* felicitously in this sentence. There is no evidence of an independent nominal (zero in form in (1) and (2)) whose person and number are copied on the noun; the noun itself simply has that person and number (not inherently, as (3) shows, but in context). I assume the noun heads an NP in (1) and (2), so the person marker is on the head, as is all indexation in Cherokee.
11. There are two classes of person-number prefixes, A (in these examples, and as A of transitive verbs and S of active intransitives) and B (S of stative verbs; also for inverse possession, where the possessed noun is predicate noun and the possessor outranks it in the animacy hierarchy; see Montgomery-Anderson 2015: 144–6).
12. The inherited situation was the reverse: the intransitive was underived and the transitive derived (with causative/factitive morphology): 'boil' in late Proto-Slavic was intransitive *vьr-ě-ti* : transitive *var-i-ti*, in which the vowel grade and the *-i-* suffix were part of the factitive morphology.
13. Evidence – possibly counterevidence, but certainly bearing on the issue – comes from possessive constructions: *b-apé* (1-nose) 'my nose', *b-ap-úua* (1-nose-PL) 'our noses'; *bas-iilaalee* 'my car', *bas-iilaalee-o* 'our car(s)' (Graczyk 2007: 52, 53). Here too the person prefix (possessive) does not distinguish number and a plural marker on the noun

indicates plural possessor. Possessed nouns make no overt distinction of number of the noun itself, which is entirely ambiguous (*noses* in *our noses* has to be understood as plural because the noun is inalienable and each person has a nose). But in the examples with plural marking the possessor is unambiguously plural. If this were promiscuous number marking, readings 'my cars' and (nonsensical) 'my noses' should be possible.

References

Andersen, Henning (1999), 'The western South Slavic contrast Sn. *sah-ni-ti* // SC *sah-nu-ti*', *Slovenski jezik/Slovene Linguistic Studies*, 2, pp. 47–62.

Authier, Gilles (2009), *Grammaire kryz (Langue caucasique d'Azerbaïdjan, dialecte d'Alik)*, Collection linguistique de la Société de linguistique de Paris, 93, Leeuven and Paris: Peeters.

Baker, Mark C. (2003), *Lexical Categories: Verbs, Nouns, and Adjectives*, Cambridge: Cambridge University Press.

Bickel, Balthasar and Johanna Nichols (2007), 'Inflectional morphology', in Tim Shopen (ed.), *Language Typology and Syntactic Description, 3*, Cambridge: Cambridge University Press, pp. 169–240.

Chumakina, Marina, Anna Kibort and Greville G. Corbett (2014), 'Determining a Language's Feature Inventory in Archi', MS, University of Surrey, revised version of paper by same title in Peter K. Austin and Andrew Simpson (eds) (2007), *Endangered Languages*, special issue of *Linguistische Berichte*, 14, Hamburg: Helmut Buske, pp. 143–72, <http://epubs.surrey.ac.uk/1314/> (last accessed 18 September 2018).

Corbett, Greville (1982), 'Gender in Russian: An account of gender specification and its relation to declension', *Russian Linguistics*, 2, pp. 197–232.

Corbett, Greville G. (1991), *Gender*, Cambridge: Cambridge University Press.

Corbett, Greville G. (2007), 'Canonical typology, suppletion, and possible words', *Language*, 83 (1), pp. 8–42.

Corbett, Greville G. (2013), 'Canonical morphosyntactic features', in Dunstan Brown, Marina Chumakina and Greville Corbett (eds), *Canonical Morphology and Syntax*, Oxford: Oxford University Press, pp. 48–65.

Corbett, Greville G. (2015), 'Morphosyntactic complexity: A typology of lexical splits', *Language*, 91 (1), pp. 145–93.

Corbett, Greville G. and Sebastian Fedden (2016), 'Canonical gender', *Journal of Linguistics*, 52, pp. 495–531.

Csató, Éva Ágnes and Lars Johanson (1998), 'Turkish', in Lars Johanson and Éva Ágnes Csató (eds), *The Turkic Languages*, London: Routledge, pp. 203–35.

Culicover, Peter W. (1999), *Syntactic Nuts: Hardcases, Syntactic Theory, and Language Acquisition*, Oxford: Oxford University Press.

Dayley, Jon P. (1985), *Tzutujil Grammar*, Berkeley and Los Angeles: University of California Press.

Fedden, Sebastian and Greville G. Corbett (2016), 'Gender and Classifiers as Concurrent Systems: A First Typology', MS, University of Surrey.

Fodor, Janet Dean (2001), 'Parameters and the periphery: Reflections on syntactic nuts', *Journal of Linguistics*, 37 (2), pp. 367–92.

Foley, William A. (2008), 'The place of Philippine languages in a typology of voice systems', in Peter Austin and Simon Musgrave (eds), *Voice and Grammatical Relations in Austronesian Languages*, Stanford, CA: CSLI Publications, pp. 22–44.

Foley, William A. (in preparation) *The Epidemiology of Language: The Evolution of Word Class Categorialization in the Austronesian Languages*.

Gil, David (1994), 'The structure of Riau Indonesian', *Nordic Journal of Linguistics*, 17, pp. 179–200.
Graczyk, Randolph (2007), *A Grammar of Crow*, Lincoln, NE: University of Nebraska Press.
Hengeveld, Kees (2012), 'Referential markers and agreement marks in Functional Discourse Grammar', *Language Sciences*, 34 (4), pp. 468–79.
Kemmer, Suzanne (1993), *The Middle Voice*, Amsterdam and Philadelphia: Benjamins.
Kibrik, Aleksander E. (2003), 'Nominal inflection galore: Daghestanian, with side glances at Europe and the world', in Frans Plank (ed.), *Noun Phrase Structure in the Languages of Europe*, Empirical Approaches to Language Typology EUROTYP, 20-7, Berlin: Mouton de Gruyter, pp. 37–112.
Kibrik, Andrej A. (2011), *Reference in Discourse*, Oxford: Oxford University Press.
Kibrik, Andrej A. (2012), 'What's in the head of head-marking languages?', in Pirkko Suihkonen, Bernard Comrie and Valery Solovyev (eds), *Argument Structure and Grammatical Relations: A Crosslinguistic Typology*, Amsterdam: Benjamins, pp. 211–40.
Laughlin, Robert M. (1975), *The Great Tzotzil Dictionary of San Lorenzo Zinacantn*, Washington DC: Smithsonian Institution Press.
Leer, Jeff (1991), 'Evidence for a Northern Northwest Coast language area: Promiscuous number marking and periphrastic possessive constructions in Haida, Eyak, and Aleut', *IJAL*, 57 (2), pp. 158–93.
Magomedova, P. T. and R. Sh. Khalidova (2001), *Karatinsko-Russkij Slovar*, St Petersburg and Makhachkala: Scriptorium and Daghestan Scientific Center, RAN.
Maho, Jouni (1999), *A Comparative Study of Bantu Noun Classes*, Gothenburg: Acta Universitatis Gothoburgensis.
Matasović, Ranko (2014), 'Nominal agreement in PIE from the areal and typological point of view', in Sergio Neri and Roland Schuhmann (eds), *Studies on the Collective and Feminine in Indo-European from a Diachronic and Typological Perspective*, Leiden: Brill, pp. 233–55.
Merrifield, William R. (1959), 'Classification of Kiowa nouns', *IJAL*, 25, pp. 269–71.
Montgomery-Anderson, Brad (2015), *Cherokee Reference Grammar*, Norman: University of Oklahoma Press.
Nichols, Johanna (1992), *Linguistic Diversity in Space and Time*, Chicago: University of Chicago Press.
Nichols, Johanna (2007), 'Chechen morphology (with notes on Ingush)', in Alan S. Kaye (ed.), *Morphologies of Asia and Africa (including the Caucasus)*, Winona Lake, IN: Eisenbrauns, pp. 1161–80.
Nichols, Johanna (2008), 'Variation in the distribution of source gender in Nakh-Daghestanian', presented at International Morphology Meeting, Vienna.
Nichols, Johanna (2010), 'Slavic indeterminate motion verbs are denominal', in Renee Perelmutter and Viktoria Driagina-Hasko (eds), *New Approaches to Slavic Verbs of Motion*, Philadelphia: Benjamins, pp. 47–65.
Nichols, Johanna (2013), 'The origin and evolution of case-suppletive pronouns: Eurasian evidence', in Dik Bakker and Martin Haspelmath (eds), *Languages across Boundaries: Studies in Memory of Anna Siewierska*, Berlin: De Gruyter Mouton, pp. 313–45.
Öztürk, Balkiz and Markus A. Pöchtrager (eds) (2011), *Pazar Laz*, Munich: Lincom Europa.
Peterson, John (2010), *A Grammar of Kharia, a South Munda Language*, Leiden: Brill.
Reid, Nicholas (1997), 'Class and classifier in Ngan'gityemerri', in Mark Harvey and Nicholas Reid (eds), *Nominal Classification in Aboriginal Australia*, Amsterdam: John Benjamins, pp. 165–228.
Rix, Helmut (ed.) (2001), *Lexikon der Indogermanischen Verben: Die Wurzeln und ihre Primärstammbildungen*, Wiesbaden: Reichert.

Saidov, Magomedsajid (1967), *'Urus Mac'atlul Slovar'/Avarsko-Russkij Slovar'*, Moscow: Sovetskaja Ènciklopedija.

Shibatani, Masayoshi (1990), *The Languages of Japan*, Cambridge: Cambridge University Press.

Siewierska, Anna (2004), *Person*, Cambridge: Cambridge University Press.

Stachowski, Marek and Astrid Menz (1998), 'Yakut', in Lars Johanson and Éva Ágnes Csató (eds), *The Turkic Languages*, London: Routledge, pp. 417–33.

Szajbel-Keck, M. (2015), *Secondary Predication in Polish*, PhD dissertation, University of California, Berkeley.

Szajbel-Keck, Małgorzata, Cammeron Girvin, Johanna Nichols and Elizabeth J. Purdy (2012), 'Highly non-canonical adjectives in Slavic languages', presented at AATSEEL annual meeting, Bellevue, WA.

Townsend, Charles E. (1975), *Russian Word Formation*, Columbus: Slavica.

Watkins, Laurel J. and Parker McKenzie (1984), *A Grammar of Kiowa*, Lincoln, NE: University of Nebraska Press.

Wolfart, H. Christoph (1996), 'Sketch of Cree, an Algonquian language', in Ives Goddard (ed.), *Handbook of North American Indians. Volume 17: Languages*, Washington DC: Smithsonian Institution, pp. 390–439.

Wonderly, William, Lorna P. Gibson and Paul L. Kirk (1954), 'Number in Kiowa: Nouns, demonstratives, and adjectives', *IJAL*, 20, pp. 1–7.

Yang, Charles (2016), *The Price of Linguistic Productivity: How Children Learn to Break the Rules of Language*, Cambridge, MA: MIT Press.

Zaicz, Gábor (1998), 'Mordva', in Daniel Abondolo (ed.), *The Uralic Languages*, London and New York: Routledge, pp. 184–218.

PART II
WORDS AND PARADIGMS

8

Paradigm Uniformity and the French Gender System

Olivier Bonami and Gilles Boyé

8.1 Introduction

Corbett's view of canonical inflection (see, for example, Corbett 2009) holds that, in the canonical case, all lexemes belonging to the same part of speech should have the same paradigm structure. Obvious violations of the canon are defectivity (a lexeme missing a paradigm cell) and overdifferentiation (a lexeme with an extra paradigm cell). These are usually defined in terms of lexical exceptionalism: we have an expected paradigm shape, and a few irregular lexemes unexpectedly deviate from that paradigm shape. Another interesting family of deviations from paradigm uniformity involve situations where there is a systematic distinction of multiple paradigm shapes within a single part of speech. One obvious example comes from conjugation in languages exhibiting object agreement: clearly, in such languages, intransitive and transitive verbs have different paradigm shapes, and this is not a matter of lexical exceptionalism. In this paper we report on what we take to be another systematic case of paradigmatic non-uniformity resulting from the distribution of gender on personal nouns in contemporary French. Table 8.1 summarises the types of gender behaviour exhibited by French nouns, which we comment on in detail below.

In languages whose grammatical gender system opposes a masculine and a feminine, it is commonly the case that most nouns referring to males are masculine and most nouns referring to females are feminine. We refer to such nouns as gender-iconic nouns. Hence, French masculine *homme* 'man' and feminine *femme* 'woman' are gender-iconic nouns, but feminine *personne* '(male or female) person', *table* 'table' or *sentinelle* 'watchman' are not. It is also common, in such languages, for many gender-iconic nouns to come in pairs of morphologically related words; for instance, *instituteur* 'male schoolteacher' and *institutrice* 'female schoolteacher' belong to the same morphological family, as do *tigre* 'tiger' and *tigresse* 'tigress'. Such pairs of nouns we call gender-iconic pairs.

The main issue addressed in this paper is the morphological status of gender-iconic

Table 8.1 Attested gender assignment situations for French nouns

Type	Simplex	Derived
Personal nouns		
Single-gendered,		
non-iconic	personne$_F$ 'person'	mauvi-ette$_F$ 'wimp'
iconic	homme$_M$ 'man'	ménag-ère$_F$ 'housewife'
Common gender	enfant$_{M/F}$ 'child'	dent-iste$_{M/F}$ 'dentist'
Non-homophonous pairs	avocat$_M$/avocate$_F$ 'lawyer'	jou-eur$_M$/jou-euse$_F$ 'player'
Inanimate nouns	table$_F$ 'table'	lav-erie$_F$ 'laundry'
Single-gendered		
Common gender	clope$_{M/F}$ 'cigarette' (informal)	auto-route$_{M/F}$ 'highway'
Non-homophonous pairs	ravin$_M$/ravine$_F$ 'ravine'	photocopi-eur$_M$/ photocopi-euse$_F$ 'copy machine'

pairs. A century-old line of argumentation takes gender-iconic pairs to be pairs of derivationally related lexemes (e.g. Nyrop 1936; Zwanenburg 1988; Matthews 1991). A main motivation for this position seems to be the very definition of grammatical gender as a classification of nouns (see Corbett 1991 for detailed discussion): if gender classifies nouns, then every noun should have one and only one gender. This tradition, however, is in striking contrast with the practice of lexicographers and traditional grammarians, who uniformly list gender-iconic pairs under a single entry. This suggests a conception where gender-iconic pairs correspond to a single lexeme, with each gender-iconic noun constituting a slab of that lexeme's paradigm.

Closely related to that issue is the status of common gender nouns, i.e. situations where the exact same form can be used in the masculine or feminine, with the use of grammatical gender matching social gender; compare *le dentiste* 'the male dentist' with *la dentiste* 'the female dentist' (Corbett 1991: 67, 181–2).[1] There are two possible views of such nouns, which are linked with the two possible views of gender-iconic pairs as derivationally or inflectionally related: (i) a common gender noun could be taken to have just two paradigm cells, and be underspecified for gender; or (ii) a common gender noun could be taken to be a gender-iconic pair, i.e. a pair of a masculine and a feminine noun, where the masculine and feminine forms happen to be homophonous. Note that both views are compatible with both approaches to gender-iconic pairs as derivationally or inflectionally related, although, as we will see below, there is some degree of congruence between the two issues.

Whether gender-iconic pairs are inflectionally or derivationally related should be decided, we argue, on a language-by-language basis, by examining which means the morphology deploys to relate gender-iconic nouns. In §8.2, we collect relevant empirical evidence on the French situation. We first evaluate the prevalence of common gender nouns and gender-iconic pairs in the lexicon, showing that both are far too high to be considered lexically exceptional. We then examine how productive lexeme formation processes derive new personal nouns. We show that the formation of masculine and feminine personal nouns almost always goes in parallel, either through the formation of a common gender noun, or through parallel affixations.

In §8.3 we discuss the theoretical consequences of our findings, and argue that, for contemporary French, the traditional view of the lexicographers is the correct one: gender-iconic pairs correspond to a single inflectional paradigm. Our argument is twofold. First, we argue that the productive formation of common gender nouns cannot be reconciled with the view that normal nouns are gender specific: a vast, open and quickly growing family of French nouns are compatible with both genders. Second, we argue that parallel derivation of masculine and feminine forms for gender-iconic pairs can only be accommodated by postulating that gender-iconic pairs correspond to a single inflectional paradigm. We conclude that there cannot be paradigmatic uniformity of nouns in French: almost all inanimate nouns indisputably have only two paradigm cells, while thousands of personal nouns have four.

A study of the gender system of contemporary French cannot be undertaken without taking into account the rapid evolution of the system under social pressure, both in the form of language planning (see, for example, Bousquet and Abily 2015) and spontaneous evolution. As a striking piece of anecdotal evidence, the noun *médecin* 'physician' is traditionally masculine, and had no recognised feminine counterpart until the beginning of the twenty-first century, as evidenced by examination of both the Google Books and Frantext collections of texts. However, using *médecin* in the feminine when referring to a female, as in the following newspaper example, has become the de facto standard in recent years, despite much conservative prescriptive outrage. Note also the use of *gynécologue* as a common gender noun, and the explicitly feminine form of *obstétricienne*.[2]

(1)   Le tribunal dit que le décès de l'enfant est imputable à des fautes commises par la **médecin gynécologue obstétricienne**. (*Le Télégramme*, 31 July 2006, T. Charpentier)
'The court states that the death of the child is due to mistakes made by the$_F$ **medical_ doctor gynecologist obstetrician$_F$**.'

In this paper we do our best to document actual usage in a quickly evolving domain where conscious planning is frequent, while making abstraction both of political debate on the relationship between social and grammatical gender, and of the numerous fundamental sociolinguistic questions raised by the evolution of the system.

8.2 Empirical Evidence

In this section we assess empirically the status of common gender nouns and gender-iconic pairs in French. We first examine the prevalence of common gender nouns and gender-iconic pairs in the extant lexicon, as documented in dictionaries and other lexical resources. We then examine the organisation of lexeme formation processes producing nouns with respect to gender.

8.2.1 Gender in the Stable Lexicon

We begin by examining the distribution of common gender nouns and gender-iconic pairs in the French lexicon. The Morphalou lexicon (Romary et al. 2004) is a machine-readable French lexicon derived from information contained in the *Trésor de la langue française* dictionary. As such, it provides explicit information about pairs of morphologically related nouns differing only in gender, irrespective of whether the two forms are homophonous and of whether the noun refers to an animate entity. This gives us a quantitative basis to evaluate how prevalent these are. As Table 8.2 indicates, about 15 per cent of feminine nouns form a pair with a masculine, and, conversely, about 15 per cent of the masculines form a pair with a feminine.

These proportions are hard to interpret, however, because of the high prevalence of inanimate nouns. First, there exist some pairs of gender-differentiated synonymous inanimate nouns (e.g. *photocopieur*$_M$ vs *photocopieuse*$_F$ 'copy machine') or pairs of an animate and an inanimate noun (e.g. *perceur*$_M$ 'piercer' vs *perceuse*$_F$ 'drill'), so that it is not obvious what proportion of the 4,441 paired nouns actually are common gender nouns or gender-iconic pairs. Second, it would be more informative to know the relative type frequency of these types of nouns among nouns with human reference; however, Morphalou does not document any semantic information. To make up for that limitation, we rely on a handmade classification by a research assistant of all the nouns in the Flexique lexicon (Bonami et al. 2014),[3] indicating for each noun whether it has established uses referring to a human, animal, inanimate or abstract entity, as documented in lexicographic sources. There are 24,990 nouns in Morphalou that are also fully documented in Flexique; among these, 4,544 were validated as personal nouns. As Table 8.3 indicates, among the validated personal nouns, 78 per cent of feminine nouns and 51 per cent of masculine nouns are associated with a noun of contrasting gender.

We now turn to the distribution of common gender nouns. These are listed as paired nouns in Morphalou, and hence included in the counts in Table 8.3. To assess which pairs have homophonous masculine and feminine forms, we use transcriptions

Table 8.2 Types of M and F nouns in the overall Morphalou lexicon

	With associate	Without associate	Proportion
Feminine nouns	4,441	28,223	15%
Masculine nouns	4,441	28,276	15%

Table 8.3 Types of validated personal F and M nouns in the Morphalou lexicon

	With associate	Without associate	Proportion
Feminine nouns	2,021	575	78%
Masculine nouns	2,021	1,948	51%

Table 8.4 Homophonous and non-homophonous pairs of personal nouns in Morphalou

	M = F	M ≠ F	Prop. M = F
Validated personal nouns	846	1,175	42%

from Flexique (Bonami et al. 2014). As Table 8.4 indicates, it turns out to be the case for 42 per cent of our validated personal nouns.[4]

In the end then, we have established the existence of at least 846 common gender nouns and another 1,175 gender-iconic pairs with non-homophonous masculines and feminines in French. These correspond in turn to 33 per cent (homophonous) and 45 per cent (non-homophonous) of all validated feminine personal nouns, and respectively to 21 per cent (homophonous) and 30 per cent (non-homophonous) of all validated masculine personal nouns. These numbers should be taken to be low estimations, in terms of both absolute and relative frequency. In absolute terms, remember that Flexique is a relatively small lexicon; in particular, remember that Morphalou contained about two times more pairs of morphologically related nouns contrasting in gender. In relative terms, the proportion of common gender nouns and gender-iconic pairs is certain to be underestimated. As we said before, Morphalou derives from the *Trésor de la langue française*, a dictionary constructed between the late 1960s and the early 1990s, and intended to reflect usage from the late eighteenth century to 1960. Given social change in the last half century, and a strong push towards using gender-iconic nouns for professions and activities, we have a strong expectation that the prevalence of gender-iconic pairs in contemporary usage is significantly higher. A precise estimation will have to await future research,[5] but it is important for the arguments to follow to remember that, if anything, we are underestimating the prevalence of common gender nouns and gender-iconic pairs.

A final piece of evidence that can be derived from the present dataset is the distribution of morphophonological alternations within gender-iconic pairs. This is indicated in Table 8.5. It is striking that the alternation types are well-behaved, and

Table 8.5 Phonological alternation types among confirmed Morphalou gender-iconic pairs

		Example		
Alternation	Count	M	F	Translation
X ~ XC	445	avocat	avocate	'lawyer'
Xœʁ ~ Xøz	318	joueur	joueuse	'player'
XṼ ~ XVn	238	voisin	voisine	'neighbour'
Xœʁ ~ Xʁis	145	auditeur	auditrice	'listener'
Xf ~ Xv	11	veuf	veuve	'widow(er)'
X ~ Xɛs	10	traître	traîtresse	'traitor'
Xo ~ Xɛl	6	jumeau	jumelle	'twin'
XṼ ~ XVnœʁɛs	1	devin	devineresse	'soothsayer'
Xk ~ Xʃɛs	1	archiduc	archiduchesse	'archduke'

match almost exactly the types of alternations found between the masculine and feminine forms of adjectives (Bonami and Boyé 2005): loss of a final consonant in the masculine with possible nasalisation of the preceding vowel, devoicing of /v/ /o/ ~ /ɛl/ alternation, and the two suffix pairs *-eur/-euse* (attaching to the default stem) and *-eur/-rice* (attaching to a learned stem). The only exceptions are the last two types, each found in only one lexeme, and which exhibit a combination of the use of the feminine suffix *-esse* and some other morphological or phonological process.[6]

Another striking observation is that, overall, the language almost never uses an affix to derive a feminine personal noun from a masculine one or the other way around. Only *-esse* is used for that purpose, and this happens only 0.5 per cent of the time. This suggests that we should take a more thorough look at the place of gender in the lexeme formation system, which we turn to presently.

8.2.2 Gender in Lexeme Formation

In this section we examine how the French lexeme formation system constrains the gender of derived nouns.

8.2.2.1 Suffixation

Most processes forming nouns involve suffixes. French has plenty of independent gender-specific affixes forming nouns denoting inanimate entities, as illustrated in Table 8.6.

It is striking, however, that there barely is any suffixal process specifically devoted to forming feminine personal nouns. The only relevant suffix is *-esse*$_2$. However, this suffix is little used: we found only 46 relevant examples in the *Trésor de la langue française*, and 69 attested in the massive Google ngrams dataset (Michel et al. 2010). Moreover, the suffix has stopped being productive for a long time. The *Trésor de la langue française* documents only 8 coinings in the nineteenth century, and none after 1867. The Google ngrams dataset provides three relevant *-esse* nouns with a later first attestation date, the youngest being *emmerderesse* 'annoying woman (vulgar)' first seen in 1955, and clearly a play on words. In addition to not being productive, *-esse*$_2$

Table 8.6 French gender-specific suffixes

Masculine	-age	marier 'to marry'	mari-age 'wedding'
	-ment	sentir 'to feel'	senti-ment 'feeling'
	-at	assassin 'murderer'	assassin-at 'murder'
	-isme	race 'race'	rac-isme 'racism'
Feminine	-ion	presser 'to press'	press-ion 'pressure'
	-ité	digne 'dignified'	dign-ité 'dignity'
	-ure	blesser 'to wound'	bless-ure 'wound'
	-ance	confier 'to confide'	confi-ance 'confidence'
	-esse$_1$	rude 'rough'	rudesse 'roughness'
	-esse$_2$	traître 'male traitor'	traîtresse 'female traitor'

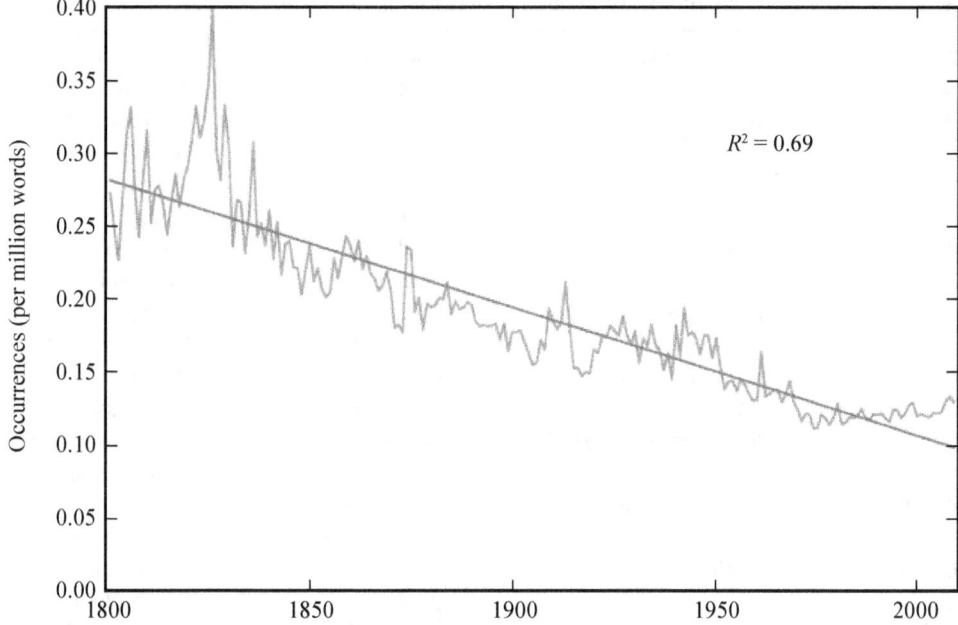

Figure 8.1 Cumulated relative frequency over time of feminine personal nouns in -*esse*. All nouns are taken from the *Trésor de la langue française* dictionary, frequency data from the Google ngrams dataset

nouns are progressively disfavoured by usage since the middle of the nineteenth century, as indicated by the decay of their use in the Google ngram dataset (Figure 8.1).

It is thus a very clear property of the contemporary French system that creation of new feminine personal nouns by suffixation to the corresponding masculine noun simply does not happen.

On the other hand, many affixes are compatible with both genders, as exemplified in Table 8.7. Most of these affixes can form personal nouns (the single exception is -*oir*/-*oire*), and hence affixes compatible with both genders are a major source of new common gender nouns.

Finally, many French affixes compatible with an animate denotation actually come in pairs of related affixes, combining a masculine and a feminine form in a clear

Table 8.7 French suffixes agnostic to gender

-able	contribuer 'contribute'	contribu-able$_{M/F}$ 'taxpayer'
-aire	révolution 'revolution'	révolutionn-aire$_{M/F}$ 'revolutionary'
-iste	journal 'newspaper'	journal-iste$_{M/F}$ 'reporter'
-ite	Jésus 'Jesus'	jésu-ite$_{M/F}$ 'Jesuit'
-oir(e)	raser 'to shave'	ras-oir$_{M}$ 'razor'
	baigner 'to bathe'	baign-oire$_{F}$ 'bathtub'

Table 8.8 Pairs of morphologically related suffixes with contrasting genders

-ain/aine	Tibet 'Tibet'	tibét-ain$_M$	'male Tibetan'
		tibét-aine$_F$	'female Tibetan'
-ien/ienne	Italie 'Italy'	ital-ien$_M$	'male Italian'
		ital-ienne$_F$	'female Italian'
-ais/aise	France 'France'	franç-ais$_M$	'Frenchman'
		franç-aise$_F$	'French woman'
-ant/ante	perdre 'to lose'	perd-ant$_M$	'male loser'
		perd-ante$_F$	'female loser'
-ier/ière	police 'police'	polic-ier$_M$	'policeman'
		polic-ière$_F$	'policewoman'
-eur/euse	chasser 'to hunt'	chass-eur$_M$	'hunter'
		chass-euse$_F$	'huntress'
-eur/rice	inspecter 'to inspect'	inspect-eur$_M$	'male inspector'
		inspect-rice$_F$	'female inspector'
-on/onne	sauvage 'savage'	sauvage-on$_M$	'wild boy'
		sauvage-onne$_F$	'wild girl'
-et/ette	poule 'hen'	poul-et$_M$	'cockerel'
		poul-ette$_F$	'young hen'
-in/ine	plaisanter 'to joke'	plaisant-in$_M$	'male joker'
		plaisant-ine$_F$	'female joker'

morphological relation. These pairs of affixes are a prolific source of gender-iconic pairs.[7] Table 8.8 provides relevant examples.

These observations on gender and French suffixes already provide motivation for most of the observations derivable from Table 8.5. There are few types of alternations in gender-iconic pairs because the grammar systematically proposes paired strategies for coining new personal nouns: either a single suffix used for both the masculine and the feminine, or two morphologically related suffixes for the masculine and feminine. It is no coincidence that the processes under examination can also be used to form adjectives, and hence need to provide parallel strategies for masculine and feminine forms.[8] Be that as it may, the end result is that gender-iconic pairs typically have the exact same structure as adjectival paradigms.[9]

8.2.2.2 Composition

Having considered suffixal lexeme formation, we turn to other processes, and establish a surprising generalisation: all non-suffixal processes that form new personal nouns form nouns of common gender. We start with different kinds of compounding and then move to non-concatenative processes.

French VN compounds (Villoing 2009) provide a striking example of the strong productivity of common gender personal nouns. It is a well-established generalisation that inanimate VN compounds are always masculine. This, however, is not true in contemporary French for those VN compounds that are personal nouns. Table 8.9 illustrates the general pattern, and (2) exhibits some attested examples.

Table 8.9 Examples of VN compounds

Inanimate	
ouvrir 'open', boîte$_F$ 'can'	ouvre-boîte$_M$ 'can-opener'
presser 'to press', papier$_M$ 'paper'	presse-papier$_M$ 'paper-weight'
tirer 'to pull', bouchon$_M$ 'cork'	tire-bouchon$_M$ 'cork-screw'
Personal nouns	
casser 'to break', pied$_M$ 'foot'	casse-pied$_{M/F}$ 'irritating person'
rabattre 'to lower', joie$_F$ 'joy'	rabat-joie$_{M/F}$ 'kill-joy'
porter 'to carry', parole$_F$ 'speech'	porte-parole$_{M/F}$ 'spokesperson'
lécher 'to lick', botte$_F$ 'boots'	lèche-botte$_{M/F}$ 'boot-licker'
piquer 'to steal', assiette$_F$ 'plate'	pique-assiette$_{M/F}$ 'freeloader'
pisser 'to piss', copie$_F$ 'copy'	pisse-copie$_{M/F}$ 'hack'
briser 'to break', coeur$_M$ 'heart'	brise-coeur$_{M/F}$ 'heart-breaker'

(2) a. Ce **casse-pied** de photographe nous aura fait gagner pas mal de temps. (*Terreur sur Saïgon*, 2014, Philippe Geluck, p. 29)
'This$_M$ **ball-breaker** of a photographer finally saved us quite some time.'
b. Ta mère est une belle **casse-pieds**, et ton mec réagit au quart de tour. (forum.aufeminin.com, 15 October 2012, adoravel)
'Your mother is a$_F$ perfect$_F$ **ball-breaker**, and your guy responds instantly.'

We observe the same general situation with other types of compounds, as illustrated in Table 8.10: while inanimates have a fixed gender, personal nouns have common gender, or at least readily acquire it if the social conditions are such that both male and female referents are available. The examples in (3) provide empirical support for these claims.

(3) a. « Bonjour, je suis le **sage-femme** qui va vous prendre en charge. ». (jactiv.ouest-france.fr, 8 March 2015, D. Le Normand)
'Hello, I am the$_M$ **midwife** who is going to take care of you.'

Table 8.10 Other examples of gender in compounds

Inanimate	
bloc$_M$ 'block', moteur$_M$ 'engine'	bloc-moteur$_M$ 'engine block'
chou$_M$ 'cabbage', fleur$_F$ 'flower'	chou-fleur$_M$ 'cauliflower'
pause$_F$ 'break', café$_M$ 'coffee'	pause-café$_F$ 'coffee break'
Personal nouns	
sage 'wise', femme$_F$ 'woman'	sage-femme$_{M/F}$ 'midwife'
sans 'without', papiers$_M$ 'papers'	sans-papiers$_{M/F}$ 'illegal immigrant'
sans 'without', abri$_M$ 'shelter'	sans-abri$_{M/F}$ 'homeless person'
faire 'to make', valoir 'to be worth'	faire-valoir$_{M/F}$ 'stooge'

Table 8.11 Examples of human-denoting neoclassical compounds

-logue	zoo- 'animal'	zoo-logue$_{M/F}$ 'zoologist'
-pathe	psycho- 'psyche'	psycho-pathe$_{M/F}$ 'psychopath'
-phile	haltéro- 'weight'	haltéro-phile$_{M/F}$ 'weight lifter'
-vore	herbi- 'grass'	herbi-vore$_{M/F}$ 'herbivore'
-mane	mytho- 'myth'	mytho-mane$_{M/F}$ 'mythomaniac'
-morphe	poly- 'several'	poly-morphe$_{M/F}$ 'polymorph'

b. Avec son film, Martin Provost voulait rendre hommage à sa manière à la **sage femme** qui lui sauvé la vie à la naissance. (www.allocine.fr, 8 March 2015, D. Le Normand)
'Through this movie, Martin Provost wished to pay a tribute of his own to the$_F$ **midwife** who saved his life at birth.'

We have again a very similar situation with neoclassical compounding. The gender of a neoclassical compound is determined by the head (second element), and it is obviously fixed for inanimates (e.g. *démocratie*$_F$ 'democracy', *théocratie*$_F$ 'theocracy', etc. vs *homicide*$_M$ 'homicide', *génocide*$_M$ 'genocide', etc.). However, animate neoclassicals are systematically of common gender, as illustrated in Table 8.11.

8.2.2.3 Truncation

We now turn to non-concatenative processes. French very commonly uses clipped nouns to form colloquial new nouns that may be more or less synonymous with their base (Kerleroux 2004).[10] Where the base form denotes an inanimate, the clipped form inherits the gender of its base (e.g. *manifestation*$_F$ 'demonstration' > *manif*$_F$, *vélocipède*$_M$ 'bicycle' > *vélo*$_M$). However, where the base form denotes a human, the clipped form normally has common gender. Table 8.12 illustrates the patterns, and (4) provides attestations.

(4) a. Ce n'est que le lendemain, lorsque vous vous rendrez compte que vous êtes en présence d'un authentique **beauf**, que vous réaliserez votre erreur. (www.demotivateur.fr, 6 September 2016, N. Weber)
'It is only on the following day, that you will realise that you are with an$_M$ authentic **dork**, and understand your mistake.'

b. Qu'est-ce qu'il insinuait? Qu'elle avait l'air d'une **beauf** qui avait gagné au loto? (*Ma vie, mon ex et autres calamités*, 2014, M. Vareille, p. 124)
'What was he hinting at? That she looked like a$_F$ **dork** who just won the lottery?'

(5) a. Ou, plus vraisemblablement, comme un **clando** se glisse jusqu'à un zodiac râpeux alors que des mouettes couinent dans le noir. (*Jours tranquilles d'un prof de banlieue*, 2011, M. Quenehen, p. 51)
'Or, more plausibly, like an$_M$ **illegal** floats towards an old dinghy while seagulls squeal in the night.'

Table 8.12 Examples of personal clipped nouns

Simple truncations	
beau-frère$_M$ 'brother-in-law'	beauf$_{M/F}$ 'dork'
chef-opérateur$_M$/-trice$_F$ 'chief cameraman'	chef-op$_{M/F}$ 'chief cameraperson'
documentaliste$_{M/F}$ 'school librarian'	doc$_{M/F}$ 'school librarian'
indicateur$_M$ 'personal informant'	indic$_{M/F}$ 'personal informant'
instituteur$_M$/-trice$_F$ 'teacher'	instit$_{M/F}$ 'teacher'
prématuré$_M$/-ée$_F$ 'premature baby'	préma$_{M/F}$ 'premature baby'
professeur$_M$ 'professor'	prof$_{M/F}$ 'professor'
sous-officier$_M$ 'non-commissioned officer'	sous-off$_{M/F}$ 'NCO'
quinquagénaire$_{M/F}$ 'fifty year old'	quinqua$_{M/F}$ 'fifty year old'
Affixed truncations	
clandestin$_M$/-ine$_F$ 'illegal immigrant'	clando$_{M/F}$ 'illegal immigrant'
propriétaire$_{M/F}$ 'owner'	proprio$_{M/F}$ 'owner'
anglais$_M$/-aise$_F$ 'English'	angliche$_{M/F}$ 'English'
bolchévique$_{M/F}$ 'bolchevik'	bolcho$_{M/F}$ 'bolchevik'

b. Elle, une bombasse mais elle parle comme une **clando**. Lui, il est dégueulasse mais il roule en lambo. (*On peut pas tout avoir*, 13 December 2010, Rohff) 'Her, a hottie but she speaks like a$_F$ **clandestine**. Him, he's disgusting but he drives a Lamborghini.'

Note that, interestingly, the gender status of clipped personal nouns does not have to match that of its base. *Instituteur/institutrice* or *indicateur/indicatrices* clearly are gender-iconic pairs with distinct masculine and feminine forms, but the clipped forms coincide, giving rise to a common gender noun. On the other hand, *beau-frère* is indisputably masculine because of its lexical meaning, but readily acquires common gender as a clipped noun with a shifted meaning. Of particular interest is the case of *professeur*, which, despite belonging to the family of agent nouns in -*eur* based on a Latinate stem, lacks a matching feminine, as do all similar nouns based on stems in -*s* (Bonami and Boyé 2006). Probably because of the prestige and conservatism associated with the professorial function, *professeur* resisted becoming a common gender noun for decades after female teachers had become frequent.[11] In the meantime, *prof* has been commonly used in both genders at least since the 1950s.[12]

8.2.2.4 Acronyms

We now turn to acronyms, which reveal a very similar picture. Nominal acronyms referring to inanimate entities have fixed gender, usually inherited from the head of the source phrase (e.g. *confédération$_F$ générale des travailleurs* 'general confederation of workers' > *CGT$_F$*, name of a trade union). However, when an acronym refers to a human, whether the source phrase already had human reference or the use of the acronym has somehow shifted from inanimate to human reference, the result is

Table 8.13 Gender of acronym personal nouns

Bon Chic Bon Genre 'posh' good chic, good style	$BCBG_{M/F}$ 'posh person'
X 'École Polytechnique'	$X_{M/F}$ 'an X graduate'
Sans Domicile Fixe 'homeless' without a fixed address	$SDF_{M/F}$ 'homeless person'
Compagnie Républicaine de Sécurité 'riot squad' national squad of security	$CRS_{M/F}$ 'member of the CRS'
Very Important Person 'V.I.P.'	$VIP_{M/F}$ 'V.I.P.'
Vice-Président 'vice-president'	$VP_{M/F}$ 'V.P.'
Directeur Général 'C.E.O.'	$DG_{M/F}$ 'C.E.O.'

readily of common gender. Table 8.13 provides a few examples, and some attestations are given in (6).

(6)   a. Le comédien est hilarant dans ce teen-movie potache, sorte de parcours initiatique à l'envers, où un **BCBG** coincé va progresser . . . en régressant. (*Côté Ciné*, 6 December 2013, T. Séguéla, p. 14)
'The actor is hilarious in this farcical teen-movie, kind of a reverse spiritual journey, where a_M rigid$_M$ **posh_guy** will evolve . . . by regressing.'

       b. Imposant régulièrement l'image d'une **BCBG** un peu coincée, sa popularité grandit à l'orée des années 1980 avec « Les hommes préfèrent les grosses » et « Y a-t-il un Français dans la salle ? ». (fr.wikipedia.org, 21 May 2008, Alexdarkchild)
'Promoting on a regular basis the image of a_F rather stiff$_F$ **posh_woman**, her fame started to grow in the 80s with « Les hommes préfèrent les grosses » and « Y a-t-il un Français dans la salle ? ».'

8.2.2.5 Borrowing

We end this discussion by considering gender assignment in borrowed nouns. While the situation is complex and many such nouns initially had a single gender, current usage readily uses them in both genders. Whether a gender distinction exists in the source language is mostly immaterial. Table 8.14 provides some examples, the use of which is documented in (7) and (8).

(7)   a. Lorsque j'ai empoigné les ciseaux et commencé à raccourcir les cheveux de mon **cobaye**, un attroupement s'est formé. (*Champion!*, 2015, R. Poulidor, p. 14)
'When I grabbed the scissors and started to shorten my$_M$ **guinea_pig**'s hair, a crowd gathered.'

       b. Tu as de la chance d'avoir trouvé une **cobaye** qui adore les maths! (*La vie commence demain*, 2017, C. Sébillon, p. 49)
'You are lucky to have found a_F **guinea_pig** with a taste for maths!'

(8)   a. Tu vois, finalement, je l'ai trouvé mon **baby-sitter** confident, sauf qu'on l'appelle un psy. (*L'irrésistible confident*, 2015, E. Peille, p. 90)

Table 8.14 Borrowed personal nouns

Example	Translation	Source language
cobaye$_{M/F}$	'guinea pig'	Portuguese
cosaque$_{M/F}$	'Cossack'	Russian
minus$_{M/F}$	'moron'	Latin
yankee$_{M/F}$	'American'	English
baby-sitter$_{M/F}$	'babysitter'	English
nabab$_{M/F}$	'nabob'	Urdu
clebs$_{M/F}$	'dog'	Arabic
toubib$_{M/F}$	'physician'	Arabic
soprano$_{M/F}$	'soprano'	Italian

'You see, in the end, I found him, my$_M$ **babysitter** and confidant, only he's called a shrink.'

b Je me rappelle qu'on m'avait confié quelques jours aux Fulconis, les parents de ma **baby-sitter**. (*Comment tu parles de ton père*, 2016, J. Sfar)
'I remember being left for a few days with the Fulconis, my$_F$ **babysitter**'s parents.'

8.2.3 Interim Conclusion

In this section we examined the place of common gender and gender-iconic pairs in the French nominal system, both from the point of view of their prevalence and classification in the extant lexicon, and from the point of view of the resources of the lexeme formation system. Three overall conclusions emerge from that exploration.

First, the prevalence of common gender nouns and gender-iconic pairs in the French system is high and on the rise. From dictionaries documenting conservative usage about 50 years ago, it can be ascertained beyond doubt that more than half of personal nouns either are common gender nouns or belong to a gender-iconic pair. All relevant evidence points to the conclusion that this proportion has risen starkly in the ensuing years.

Second, the common strategies for generating new personal nouns are either common gender (identical forms in the masculine and feminine) or paired gender-specific derivational affixes. The strategy of deriving a feminine personal noun from a masculine personal noun, common as it may be in other languages, basically died out in the middle of the nineteenth century.

Third and most importantly, common gender has the status of a default strategy. Wherever the lexeme formation system does not provide a systematic way of deriving parallel masculine and feminine forms through paired affixes (gender-ambiguous suffixes, compounding, clipping, acronyms, borrowing), newly coined personal nouns acquire common gender, and previously gender-specific nouns tend to shift in that same direction.

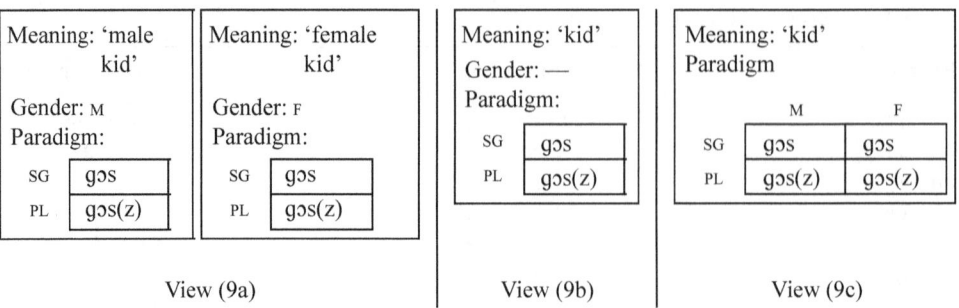

Figure 8.2 Schematic lexical entries for *gosse* 'kid' under three views of common gender nouns

In the next section we draw theoretical consequences of these observations for a proper analysis of the French gender system.

8.3 The Shape of French Nominal Paradigms

Let us now reflect on the consequences of our findings for the structure of French nominal paradigms. We start by examining the status of common gender nouns, and then move on to gender-iconic pairs.

8.3.1 Common Gender and Gender Specificity

There are three possible ways of conceiving of the status of common gender nouns in the lexicon. Figure 8.2 illustrates the status of the common gender noun *gosse* 'kid' under these three views.

(9) a. A maximally conservative view holds that all nouns have to be gender specific by definition, and hence that the intuition that a common gender noun is a single noun with two genders is illusory: we are really dealing with two homophonous nouns differing in grammatical gender.
   b. A first alternative maintains paradigm uniformity but abandons universal gender specificity. Under this view, a French common gender noun has only two paradigm cells, but is underspecified for gender.
   c. A second alternative assumes that common gender nouns have separate paradigm cells for masculine and feminine, but that the morphology happens to syncretise the realisation of masculine and feminine forms. This view abandons both paradigm uniformity and universal gender specificity.

The evidence presented in §8.2 provides a strong argument against view (9a). If homophonous masculine and feminine nouns correspond to different lexemes, given their high prevalence and the productive introduction of new such pairs in the lexicon, they have to be morphologically related. Thus, under this view one would have to posit a highly productive process of gender-changing conversion for personal nouns. The prediction is then that this conversion should be able to apply to any personal noun matching its input: in other words, there should be derivations such as *laveur*_M 'male washer' > *laveur*_F 'female washer', or, conversely, *laveuse*_F 'female washer' > *laveuse*_M 'male washer'. But such derivations are clearly unattested: wherever the grammar provides an alternate-gender strategy, the use of that strategy is mandatory – common gender noun formation only occurs when that is not possible. There is no way to capture this generalisation under view (9a), short of enumerating as exceptions to the application of gender conversion bases formed with exactly these affixes which happen to be paired with an alternate-gender affix.

It is clear then that universal gender specificity cannot be maintained in the context of productive common gender noun formation: one must admit that, while some nouns, including almost all inanimates, are gender specific, many nouns are compatible with both genders.[13] It is worth emphasising that, at least in French, these nouns are too numerous to be treated as individually listed lexical exceptions: while productive common gender nouns may be a sign of non-canonical gender (Corbett and Fedden 2016), they have to be taken at face value as a systematic pattern.

We are thus left with alternatives (9b) and (9c): either common gender nouns are simply underspecified for gender, or they have separate paradigm cells for masculine and feminine. Which of these two possibilities is preferable depends on the status of gender-iconic pairs in the language, to which we turn now.

8.3.2 Gender-Iconic Pairs and Paradigm Uniformity

As stated in the introduction, there are two ways one may see the relation between the masculine and feminine words in a gender-iconic pair. The status of the gender-iconic pair *avocat, avocate* under each view is outlined in Figure 8.3.

(10)   a. One may see the two nouns as being derivationally related: we are dealing with two lexemes belonging to the same derivational family. Under such a view, paradigm uniformity is maintained: each noun has a single gender and all nouns may have the same number of paradigm cells, whether or not they belong to a gender-iconic pair.

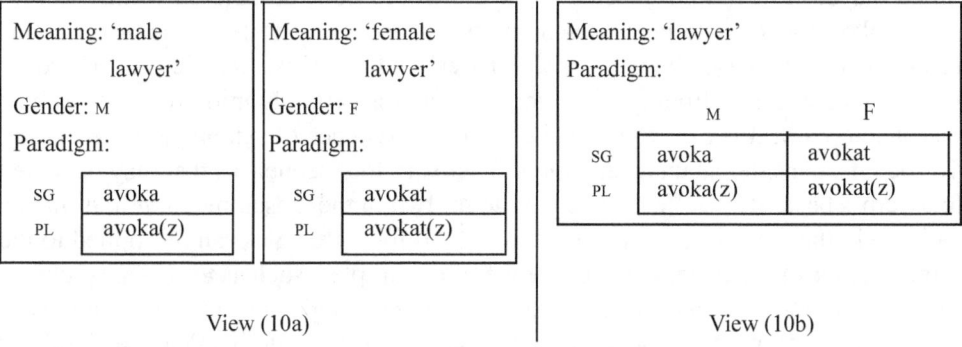

Figure 8.3 Schematic lexical entries for *avocat/avocate* 'lawyer' under two views of gender-iconic pairs

b. One may see the two nouns as inflectionally related. Gender-iconic pairs constitute a single lexeme, with separate paradigm cells for masculine and feminine. This view abandons paradigm uniformity.

Which view is correct clearly depends on the language.[14] In languages (or language states) where feminine personal nouns are productively derived from masculine personal nouns, (10a) is clearly warranted. As 8.2 showed in detail, this is not so at all in French.

8.3.2.1 Gender-iconic pairs as derivationally related

Let us consider the consequences of view (10a) for an analysis of the French system. As in the case of common gender nouns, if gender-iconic pairs are separate lexemes, then they must somehow be related by the lexeme formation system. There are two possibilities here: either the two gender-iconic nouns derive from one another, or they are both derived from other sources.

We start with the first possibility, and consider the consequences of taking the two purported lexemes in a gender-iconic pair to be derived from one another. A cursory look at Table 8.5 reminds us that the processes under consideration would include final consonant truncation, substitutions of suffixes, and various marginal operations. View (10a) then leads to three problems. First, one is forced to postulate highly non-canonical processes in what seems to be an otherwise very simple system. Second, it is a mystery why each process is restricted in the way it is; for instance, why can the process of final consonant truncation not apply to feminine nouns in *-rice*? Third and finally, one is left with no account for the observation that the set of derivational alternations found with gender-iconic pairs coincides with the set of inflectional alternations found with adjectives.

Having refuted the idea that gender-iconic pairs could be related directly by a lexeme formation process, we turn to the alternative possibility that they be pairs of lexemes both deriving from a third lexeme. The simplest instantiation of this idea assumes that they are derived in parallel from their immediate base: thus *joueur*$_M$ 'male player' and *joueuse*$_F$ 'female player' would both be derived from the verb *jouer* 'play' by separate processes outputting masculine and feminine agent nouns respectively. Likewise, *épicier*$_M$ 'male grocer' and *épicière*$_F$ 'female grocer' would be derived separately from *épice* 'spice'. While this certainly initially seems to be a reasonable view, it is hard to reconcile with the existence of synonymous processes. To see this, consider again agent nouns. There are four sequences that may be added to a verb's basic stem to form an agent noun: two in the masculine, *-eur* and *-ateur*, and two in the feminine, *-euse* and *-atrice*.[15] All four strategies can be applied to the same bases, as is attested by the existence of quadruplets such as *exporteur*$_M$, *exportateur*$_M$, *exporteuse*$_F$, *exportatrice*$_F$ 'exporter'. The strategies seem to be essentially in free variation. If masculine and feminine agent nouns were derived independently of each other, we would then expect to find situations where the lexicon contains an *-eur* noun and an *-atrice* noun but no *-ateur* or *-euse*, or, equivalently, where it contains an

-*ateur* noun and an -*euse* noun but no -*eur* or -*atrice*; i.e. any combination of a masculine and a feminine agent noun formed on the same base should be able to constitute a gender-iconic pair. But, strikingly, such a situation does not arise. In fact, the French version of Wiktionary, by far the largest and most permissive lexicographic source for French, documents no such case.[16]

It seems clear then that the idea that gender-iconic pairs are derived by parallel suffixal derivation processes is not defensible. However, this is not the only way that the masculine and feminine nouns could be related derivationally. In the context of an analysis of French adjectives in -*eur*, Bonami and Boyé (2005) present an alternative. Building on previous work by Corbin and Corbin (1991), we proposed that many French personal nouns are derived from adjectives by conversion: from the adjective *directeur* 'guiding' with feminine form *directrice*, we hypothesised two separate conversion operations leading to the two personal nouns *directeur*$_M$ 'male director' and *directrice*$_F$ 'female director'. Whatever the merits of such an analysis, it does not scale up to the full set of gender-iconic pairs, as there are whole classes of gender-iconic pairs whose morphological family does not contain a corresponding adjective. This is the case, for instance, for nouns denoting sport practitioners. These are productively formed by suffixing -*eur*$_M$ and -*euse*$_F$ to the name of the sport, e.g. *basket* 'basketball' > *basketteur*$_M$ 'male basketball player', *basketteuse*$_F$ 'female basketball player'.

8.3.2.2 Gender-iconic pairs as inflectionally related

To sum up, we have seen that there is no clear way of maintaining the idea that gender-iconic pairs consist of two lexemes related by lexeme formation, directly or indirectly. It thus becomes clear that view (10a) maintains paradigm uniformity at the expense of completely failing to capture the shape of the French morphological system. We thus propose to adopt the alternative view (10b), and take gender-iconic pairs in French to be inflectionally rather than derivationally related. Under such a view, lexeme formation processes outputting gender-iconic pairs provide strategies for the derivation of both a masculine and a feminine stem, used concurrently for the formation of masculine and feminine forms. Hence, we have one rule forming agent nouns with stems in -*œʁ* and -*œz* from a verb's main stem, and a separate rule forming agent nouns with stems in -*œʁ* and -*ʁis* from a verb's Latinate stem; a rule forming nouns with stems in -*je* and -*jeʁ* from a noun; etc.

Positing lexeme formation processes outputting multiple stems for the same lexeme is unusual, but, we argue, independently motivated. Bonami and Boyé (2005, 2006) show that such processes are necessary to account for productive stem allomorphy in the inflection of French adjectives – a situation where positing distinct lexemes is not an option. Hence, we can account directly both for the fact that masculine and feminine affixes come in pairs, and for the parallelism between the paradigms of gender-iconic pairs and those of adjectives.

Finally, let us return to the relationship between common gender nouns and gender-iconic pairs. At the end of §8.3.1 we left open whether it was more adequate for common gender nouns to have a smaller paradigm with gender underspecification or a larger paradigm with syncretism between masculine and feminine forms. Now that we have concluded that gender-iconic pairs are inflectionally related, and hence that paradigm uniformity across all French nouns is not attainable, we have good reasons to opt for option (9c), which amounts to saying that common gender nouns are a special case of gender-iconic pairs with heavy syncretism. There are two immediate motivations for this. First, this makes good sense of the fact that new personal nouns default to common gender. If, by hypothesis, new personal nouns are normally gender-iconic pairs, and non-syncretic gender-iconic pairs involve two stems standing in an allomorphic relation, we expect that the default situation for a new gender-iconic pair is to have no stem allomorphy – hence to use the same form in the masculine and the feminine. Thus, processes that do not provide explicit separate strategies to form two stem alternants will output a single stem and give rise to common gender nouns. Second, this allows for a single locus for iconic gender assignment, which applies to both common gender nouns and gender-iconic pairs: whereas single-gendered nouns may be gender-iconic or not, it is categorically true of both common gender nouns and gender-iconic pairs that their grammatical gender (as manifest in agreement) has to match their social gender.[17] If common gender nouns are a special case of gender-iconic pairs and both are characterised by an expanded paradigm, this paradigm can be stated to be the structure of which the constraint holds.

We thus conclude that common gender nouns are a special case of gender-iconic pairs, and that both instantiate a situation where masculine and feminine nouns form together a single inflectional paradigm. There are thus two types of nouns in French: some have a smaller paradigm and only one gender, while others have a larger paradigm providing distinct cells for both genders.

8.3.3 Variable Content Paradigms, Uniform Form Paradigms

Much work remains to be done before we fully understand the interplay of grammatical gender and semantic gender within the French system. One important concern that needs to be explored in future research is the relationship between derived adjectives and animate and inanimate nouns. It is a general observation that all three types of lexemes tend to rely on the same derivational suffixes, and that these suffixes come in gendered pairs. For instance, *-eur* and *-rice* form in parallel masculine and feminine forms of adjectives (e.g. *moteur/motrice* 'driving', *directeur/directrice* 'guiding'), gender-iconic pairs (e.g. *directeur*$_M$ 'male director', *directrice*$_F$ 'female director') and gender-specific inanimate nouns (e.g. *moteur*$_F$ 'motor', *motrice*$_F$ 'power car'). A promising strategy to capture this parallelism is to rely on the distinction between content and form paradigms (Stump 2006, 2015). The idea is that all French nouns and adjectives share the same basic bidimensional paradigm structure distinguishing two genders and two numbers; lexeme formation processes that output nouns or adjectives need to provide strategies to fill that enlarged paradigm, i.e. to generate paired masculine and feminine forms. The difference between gender-iconic pairs and other nouns would then stand at the interface between form and content paradigms: by virtue of being specified for gender lexically, non-gender-iconic pairs have a content paradigm that is smaller than their form paradigm by using only forms corresponding to one gender.

One attraction of this analytic scheme is that it is congruent with the current fluidity between gender-specific personal nouns and gender-iconic pairs: many nouns that were historically masculine are becoming gender-iconic pairs under the influence of social change. The system already predicts a feminine form for most of these nouns, by virtue of their morphological make-up. This is exactly what the notion of uniformly gender-variable form paradigms provides: even when a noun has a single gender by lexical stipulation, the forms corresponding to the other gender are readily available if that stipulation is dropped.

8.4 Conclusion

In this paper we have argued against paradigm uniformity across lexemes for French nouns. We started by observing that common gender nouns are too numerous to be treated as lexical exceptions; indeed, they form an open class, and common gender is the default situation for newly coined personal nouns. We then saw that pairs of distinct but morphologically related personal nouns were also very common, and were formed by parallel suffixation, rather than by derivation of one noun from the other. We accounted for both observations by proposing that, in addition to an unsurprising class of single-gendered nouns, French possesses a class of nouns with variable and semantically potent gender. These nouns have a larger paradigm by virtue of accommodating separate masculine and feminine cells.[18]

Although this proposal may go against analytic muscle memory, we submit that it solves more problems than it raises. Non-uniformity of paradigm shape is seldom discussed in the context of nouns, but is an unescapable reality in the conjugation of languages with object agreement; hence, there is no reason it would not also sometimes be found in the nominal domain. In the view we defend, gender is still inherent inflection on nouns, although, for some nouns, it is semantically potent, in the same way that number is. Be that as it may, it can still be defined as a morphosyntactic property of nouns manifest in agreement. Finally, single nominal lexical items with more than one gender value are generally recognised as an existing phenomenon in the case of common gender nouns (we purposefully paraphrase Corbett and Fedden 2016: 507); our contention is only that these are much more frequent than is usually recognised, and that the consequences of that fact for models of morphology should be taken at face value.

Acknowledgements

We thank Heather Burnett and Jean Lowenstamm for discussion of the data and analysis presented in this paper, as well as Sebastian Fedden, Anna M. Thornton and the editors of this volume for comments on a previous version. This work was partially supported by a public grant overseen by the French National Research

Agency (ANR) as part of the 'Investissements d'Avenir' programme (reference: ANR-10-LABX-0083).

Notes

1. Although there are also a few inanimate nouns of common gender, as exemplified in Table 8.1, these are not the focus of this paper. In the interest of readability, we take the liberty of referring to only personal nouns with the label 'common gender nouns'.
2. We decided not to provide full glosses of illustrative examples, as only gender marking in one NP is relevant. Rather, we indicate with a subscripted M or F in the translation which relevant words carry explicit gender marking. We also highlight in boldface nouns under consideration.
3. We thank Aurélie Chlebowki for her work on this project.
4. The proportion falls to 27 per cent if one looks at homography rather than homophony. This is due to the fact that French orthography quite often marks an overt gender difference by suffixing an <e> to the feminine that has no phonological reality. All classifications in this paper rely on phonology rather than orthography. An account based on written forms leads to different analyses in individual cases but does not alter the overall phenomenology.
5. As a first step in that direction, we examined whether nouns that are documented as single-gendered in Morphalou were found in co-occurrence with a determiner of the other gender in at least 1 per cent of their occurrences in the FrWac web corpus (Baroni et al. 2009). This was true for 435 purported masculines and 357 purported feminines. We refrain from drawing any strong conclusion from this observation in the absence of human validation.
6. There are other candidate pairs instantiating minor patterns that happen not to be part of the present dataset. One prominent example is the association between *serviteur* 'male servant' and *servante* 'female servant'. The main point holds that such unsystematic associations are strikingly rare.
7. Note that it is not possible, in Modern French, to segment sequences such as -*aine* into a derivational affix -*ain* and a gender suffix -*e*. Such a possibility is only suggested by the misleading orthographic conventions of French: the final orthographic -e does not indicate the realisation of a vowel, but the fact that the preceding orthographic consonant is realised phonetically. The pairs of words in Table 8.8 hence enter alternations that are morphologically principled but not phonologically predictable. See Bonami and Boyé (2005) for a relevant discussion of the parallel facts in adjectival paradigms.
8. At this point it is unclear whether homophonous nouns and adjectives such as *défenseur* 'defender/defending' should be said to be derived in parallel or in a conversion relation, or if that question even makes sense, *pace* Bonami and Boyé (2005).
9. Even the suffix -*esse* is marginally used in adjectival inflection: witness *le bras vengeur* 'the avenging arm' vs *la main vengeresse* 'the avenging hand'.
10. The length of the clipped form is variable, but most commonly two syllables. Sometimes clipping is accompanied by some sort of suffixation, mostly of -o: *propriétaire* 'owner' > *proprio*, *bolchévique* 'bolshevik' > *bolcho*, etc.
11. Such conservative usage is now quickly decaying, and *professeur* has common gender in the spontaneous speech of contemporary university students. In writing both *la professeur* and the homophonous *la professeure* are both commonly used, although the ultra-conservative *Madame le professeur* is still in usage in some circles. Conscious planning is too frequent in this area for one to be able to establish what spontaneous usage is.
12. The Frantext database provides attestations in correspondence between Jean-Paul Sartre and Simone de Beauvoir in 1937.

13. There are a few inanimate nouns found with both genders in the speech of the same speaker with no meaning difference, such as *autoroute* 'highway' and *après-midi* 'afternoon'. These, however, are not numerous enough to be of much consequence on the shape of the system.
14. It is actually quite conceivable that different gender-iconic pairs in the same language receive contrasting analyses. That was probably the case in French at some point, where productive *-esse* coexisted with paired suffixes. The existence of doublets such as *demandeuse* and *demanderesse* as the feminine counterpart of *demandeur* 'requester' testifies to such a state of the system.
15. In the terms used above, this is a consequence of *-eur/-rice* being suffixed to a Latinate stem, and the augment *-at* being used by default in the formation of Latinate stems (Bonami et al. 2009).
16. We established this by searching through the GLÀFF lexicon (Hathout et al. 2014), which compiles in tabular form information from the French Wiktionary.
17. We leave aside the proper treatment of hypernymic use of one of the two genders, as when *professeur* is used to refer to either male or female referents. Note that such uses are not limited to gender-iconic pairs (e.g. *homme* 'men' is sometimes used to refer to either men or women, despite being morphologically unrelated to *femme* 'woman'), and are clearly conventionalised (e.g. *garçon* can only refer to boys). Whatever the correct account of such uses, it remains that both common gender nouns and gender-iconic pairs exhibit systematic parallelism between grammatical gender and semantic properties of the referent, which may not exactly coincide with being male or female.
18. We make no claim that such an analysis generalises to other languages, or even to older varieties of French. See, for instance, Rainer (2012) for convincing evidence that German feminine agent nouns are derived from their masculine counterparts.

References

Baroni, Marco, Silvia Bernardini, Adriano Ferraresi and Eros Zanchetta (2009), 'The wacky wide web: A collection of very large linguistically processed web-crawled corpora', *Language Resources and Evaluation*, 43, pp. 209–26.

Bonami, Olivier and Gilles Boyé (2005), 'Construire le paradigme d'un adjective', *Recherches Linguistiques de Vincennes*, 34, pp. 77–98.

Bonami, Olivier and Gilles Boyé (2006), 'Deriving inflectional irregularity', in *Proceedings of the 13th International Conference on HPSG*, Stanford, CA: CSLI Publications, pp. 39–59.

Bonami, Olivier, Gilles Boyé and Françoise Kerleroux (2009), 'L'allomorphie radicale et la relation flexion-construction', in Bernard Fradin, Françoise Kerleroux and Marc Plénat (eds), *Aperçus de morphologie du français*, Saint-Denis: Presses de l'Université de Vincennes, pp. 103–25.

Bonami, Olivier, Gauthier Caron and Clément Plancq (2014), 'Construction d'un lexique flexionnel phonétisé libre du français', in Franck Neveu, Peter Blumenthal, Linda Hriba, Annette Gerstenberg, Judith Meinschaefer and Sophie Prévost (eds), *Actes du quatrième congrès mondial de linguistique française*, pp. 2583–96.

Bousquet, Danielle and Gaëlle Abily (2015), *Guide pratique pour une communication publique sans stéréotype de sexe*, Tech. rep. Haut Conseil à l'Égalité entre les femmes et les hommes.

Corbett, Greville G. (1991), *Gender*, Cambridge: Cambridge University Press.

Corbett, Greville G. (2009), 'Canonical inflectional classes', in Fabio Montermini, Gilles Boyé and Jesse Tseng (eds), *Selected Proceedings of the 6th Décembrettes: Morphology in Bordeaux*, Somerville, MA: Cascadilla Proceedings Project, pp. 1–11.

Corbett, Greville G. and Sebastian Fedden (2016), 'Canonical gender', *Journal of Linguistics*, 52, pp. 495–531.
Corbin, Danièle and Pierre Corbin (1991), 'Un traitement unifié du suffixe -ier(e)', *Lexique*, 10, pp. 61–145.
Hathout, Nabil, Franck Sajous and Basilio Calderone (2014), 'GLÀFF, a large versatile French lexicon', in Nicoletta Calzolari, Khalid Choukri, Thierry Declerck, Hrafn Loftsson, Bente Maegaard, Joseph Mariani, Asuncion Moreno, Jan Odijk and Stelios Piperidis (eds), *Proceedings of LREC 2014, Ninth International Conference on Language Resources and Evaluation*, European Language Resources Association, <http://www.lrec-conf.org/proceedings/lrec2014/index.html> (last accessed 26 September 2018).
Kerleroux, Françoise (2004), 'Sur quels objets portent les opérations morphologiques de construction?', *Lexique*, 16, pp. 85–123.
Matthews, P. H. (1991), *Morphology*, 2nd edn, Cambridge: Cambridge University Press.
Michel, Jean-Baptiste, Yuan Kui Shen, Aviva Presser Aiden, Adrian Veres, Matthew K. Gray, The Google Books Team, Joseph P. Pickett, Dale Hoiberg, Dan Clancy, Peter Norvig, Jon Orwant, Steven Pinker, Martin A. Nowak and Erez Lieberman Aiden (2010), 'Quantitative analysis of culture using millions of digitized books', *Science*, 14, pp. 176–82.
Nyrop, Kristoffer R. (1936), *Grammaire historique de la langue française, tome troisième formation des mots*, Copenhagen: Nordisk Forlag.
Rainer, Franz (2012), 'Morphological metaphysics: Virtual, potential, and actual words', *Word Structure*, 5 (2), pp. 165–82.
Romary, Laurent, Suzanne Salmont-Alt and Gil Francopoulo (2004), 'Standards going concrete: From LMF to Morphalou', in Michael Zock and Patrick Saint Dizier (eds), *ElectricDict '04 Proceedings of the Workshop on Enhancing and Using Electronic Dictionaries*, Stroudsburg, PA: Association for Computational Linguistics, pp. 22–8.
Stump, Gregory T. (2006), 'Heteroclisis and paradigm linkage', *Language*, 82, pp. 279–322.
Stump, Gregory T. (2015), *Inflectional Paradigms*, Cambridge: Cambridge University Press.
Villoing, Florence (2009), 'Les mots composés VN', in Bernard Fradin, Françoise Kerleroux and Marc Plénat (eds), *Aperçus de morphologie du français*, Saint-Denis: Presses Universitaires de Vincennes, pp. 175–98.
Zwanenburg, Wiecher (1988), 'Flexion et dérivation: le féminin en français', in Ronald Landheer (ed.), *Aspects de linguistique française, hommage à Q. I. M. Mok*, Amsterdam: Rodopi, pp. 191–208.

9

Case Loss in Pronominal Systems: Evidence from Bulgarian

Alexander Krasovitsky

9.1 Dialectal Variation in Case Marking on Personal Pronouns in Bulgarian

This paper investigates the loss of morphological case marking on personal pronouns using data from contemporary Bulgarian dialects. Bulgarian underwent massive loss of morphological case marking in the Middle Bulgarian period (twelfth to fifteenth centuries) when a rich system of case inflections inherited from Proto-Slavonic was largely lost (Mirčev 1963: 144–5; Pârvev 1975: 80–98).[1] As a result, Bulgarian lost morphological case on nouns (except for a restricted set of lexemes which preserve residual case forms in some of the dialectal systems; Stojkov 1954). Personal pronouns, however, preserve case distinction, although in a reduced form compared with the original Proto-Slavonic system. In different regional varieties of Bulgarian, we find either a three-case distinction, nominative, accusative and dative, or a two-case distinction, nominative and accusative. One striking instance of such cross-dialectal variation is attested in the dialects of North-West Bulgaria where personal pronouns vary with respect to the number of case distinctions they are able to show (Stojkov 1981). This variation is illustrated in (1) and (2) using as an example the third person singular masculine pronoun *toj* 'he'.

(1) Three-case distinction: nominative, accusative and dative
    a. **Toj**   idva.
       he(M.NOM) go[3.SG]
       'He goes.'
    b. Vižda-m   **nego**.
       see-1.SG   **him(M.ACC)**
       'I see him.'
    c. Dava-m   **nemu**.
       give-1.SG   **him(M.DAT)**
       'I give to him.'

(2) Two-case distinction: nominative and accusative
    a. **Toj**   idva.
       he(M.NOM) go[3.SG]
       'He goes.'
    b. Vižda-m   **nego**.
       see-1.SG   him(M.ACC)
       'I see him.'
    c. Dava-m   **na nego**.
       give-1.SG   on him(M.ACC)
       'I give to him.'

The sentences in (1) and (2) may be taken as a basic illustration of a diachronic process leading to the reduction of case paradigms in personal pronouns: in (1), we find a three-case system with distinct morphological (synthetic) forms for nominative, accusative and dative; examples in (2) illustrate a more advanced stage of case loss in the pronominal system: a two-way distinction (nominative/accusative) with dative functions assigned to analytical constructions which include a preposition and an accusative form of a pronoun.[2]

In-between these two clear-cut patterns of case marking currently observed in Bulgarian dialects, we find multiple intervening patterns where a three-case distinction is possible only with some PERSON/GENDER/NUMBER combinations, leaving the rest with two distinct case forms. From a diachronic perspective, this presents us with multiple outcomes of the historical process which results in case deterioration and loss. But what is the pattern of this process? Are some parts of the pronominal system more prone to this change than others? Variation outlined above enables us to investigate this historical problem by tackling the distribution of case-marking patterns and alternative means (such as the prepositional constructions) across various personal pronouns.

9.2 The Data

The data for this case study come from 418 locations in North-West Bulgaria, as presented in volume IV of the *Bulgarian Dialectological Atlas* (BDA IV) covering North-West Bulgaria (Stojkov 1981). The dialects in question are known for their relatively conservative inflectional morphology: unlike the majority of dialects further east, they preserve distinct nominative and accusative, and less frequently, dative case forms for a number of animate nouns, and three distinct case forms (nominative, accusative and dative) on personal pronouns.

The data showing the distribution of accusative and dative pronominal morphological forms and prepositional constructions were manually extracted from the individual maps in BDA IV and accumulated in a database, enabling analyses which will be presented in the subsequent sections.[3] For this study, data on the following personal pronouns were used:

Table 9.1 Inflection of personal pronouns in North-West Bulgarian dialects (based on BDA IV)[a]

	1PL 'we'	2PL 'you'	3SG.M 'he'	3SG.N 'it'	3SG.F 'she'	3PL 'they'
Nominative	nie/ni	vie/vi	on/toj	ono/to	ona/tja	oni/te
Accusative	nas/naze	vas/vaze	nego/nega	nego/nega	[no data]	nix/tjax
Dative	nam	vam	nemu	nemu	noj/nej	nim/tjam

[a] Note that there are no gender distinctions in plural.

- first person plural (Map 248 accusative; Map 249 dative)
- second person plural (Map 248 accusative; Map 249 dative)[4]
- third person singular masculine and neuter (Map 240 accusative; Map 241 dative)
- third person singular feminine (Map 244 dative)
- third person plural (Map 252 accusative; Map 253 dative).

A three-case paradigm for six personal pronouns based on BDA IV may be presented as shown in Table 9.1.[5]

Unfortunately, BDA IV does not include information on first and second person singular pronouns in the accusative and dative. However, compared with other BDA volumes, this volume provides the most detailed account on variation in case marking on personal pronouns for six PERSON/GENDER/NUMBER combinations (see above), which is why it was chosen for this case study.

9.3 Cross-Dialectal Variation

The conservative situation presented in Table 9.1, as well as the opposite situation, with just two distinct case forms for each pronoun, nominative and accusative, where the latter case took over all dative functions, are relatively infrequent. The overwhelming majority of dialectal pronominal systems may be considered as transitional between these two states. In these transitional systems different PERSON/GENDER/NUMBER combinations allow different numbers of case distinctions. The data from BDA IV reveal cross-dialectal variation with respect to (i) the number of case values available to a given personal pronoun in a dialect, and (ii) the inventory of grammatical means, i.e. synthetic case forms and analytical (prepositional) constructions assigned to a given case value.

In the subsequent sections, I will concentrate on the interplay between accusative and dative forms which is at the heart of the historical process leading to the transition from a three-case to a two-case pronominal system; I do not address nominative forms which are distinct from accusative and dative in all dialects and which do not interfere with the latter two cases in the historical change under investigation. The use of the term 'accusative' here is justified from a formal point of view; however, it should be borne in mind that we are speaking about a historical accusative form which in a three-case system has accumulated functions of genitive, instrumental and locative.[6] In this paper I adhere to a convention implicitly followed in a number

Table 9.2 Variation in case marking on personal pronouns (based on Stojkov 1981)

Type	Accusative function	Dative function
A	Accusative form	Dative form
B	Accusative form	Accusative form
C	Accusative form	Preposition + accusative form
D	Accusative form	Preposition + dative form
E	Dative form	Dative form
F	Dative form	Preposition + dative form

of studies including BDA. By 'accusative functions' in a three-case system I mean functions which are now fulfilled by historical accusative forms and which correspond to historical accusative, genitive, instrumental and locative. The term 'dative' with respect to such dialects is used in its original sense and denotes original dative functions, such as, for example, the recipient of a ditransitive verb. Chronologically, such pronominal systems represent the most archaic type of case distribution (type A in Table 9.2 illustrated by examples in (3)) currently available for observation in the dialects under investigation, with three distinct morphological case forms for three case values, nominative, accusative and dative. I take this type as a conventional starting point of the analysis and examine attested deviations from this type. These deviations result in a number of outcomes, illustrated by the other five types, from (B) to (F). Dialects which belong to these five types either generalise one of the case forms, accusative or dative, across the two case values, as in type B and type E, or develop analytical (prepositional) constructions to be used in the dative sense, as we see in types C, D and F.[7]

Cross-dialectal variation in the North-West dialects summarised in Table 9.2 is illustrated in (3) using examples with the first person plural pronoun *we*.

(3) Type A. Vižda-t **nas.** Dava-t **nam.**
 see-3.PL **we**(ACC) give-3.PL **we**(DAT)
 Type B. Vižda-t **nas.** Dava-t **nas.**
 see-3.PL **we**(ACC) give-3.PL **we**(ACC)
 Type C. Vižda-t **nas.** Dava-t **na nas.**
 see-3.PL **we**(ACC) give-3.PL **on we**(ACC)
 Type D. Vižda-t **nas.** Dava-t **na nam.**
 see-3.PL **we**(ACC) give-3.PL **on we**(DAT)
 Type E. Vižda-t **nam.** Dava-t **nam.**
 see-3.PL **we**(DAT) give-3.PL **we**(DAT)
 Type F. Vižda-t **nam.** Dava-t **na nam.**
 see-3.PL **we**(DAT) give-3.PL **on we**(DAT)
 'They see us.' 'They give to us.'

I will analyse rich synchronic variation with respect to case marking on personal pronouns in Bulgarian dialects and will argue that differences in the use of case marking and alternative strategies (i.e. analytical constructions) which are found across different personal pronouns, as well as different rates at which the loss of case proceeds within different classes are to a significant extent associated with the features PERSON and NUMBER. These features have an effect on synchronic variation and historical change under investigation.

This case study shows, in particular, that personal pronouns which are different only in NUMBER show a uniform pattern in the way they retain original case forms or lose them in the exchange of prepositional constructions (as illustrated by the examples in (3)). This uniformity does not hold for personal pronouns which are different in PERSON: the majority of the dialects included in this study reveal a split between first and second person on the one hand and third person on the other as these two groups of pronouns have different preferences when it comes to the expression of case. The data provided in BDA IV enable the comparison across SINGULAR and PLURAL only for third person pronouns. This comparison reveals the similarity of diachronic patterns across third person pronouns irrespective of NUMBER. If, however, we compare across PERSON, we can see that first and second person pronouns cluster together in terms of their diachronic behaviour, exhibiting strong preferences for a two-way case distinction. As for third person pronouns, they clearly stand out as a relatively conservative part of the pronominal system with stronger preferences for three-case marking.

9.4 Directions of Change

According to the data from BDA IV, the transition from a three-case to a two-case marking on personal pronouns leading to the loss of accusative–dative distinction manifests itself in two diachronic processes: first, in the spread of analytical (prepositional) constructions with the preposition *na* ('*na* + ACC' or '*na* + DAT') replacing original dative forms, as illustrated in (3c,d,f), and, second, in the generalisation of one morphological form, accusative or, less frequently, dative, across both paradigm cells, as exemplified in (3b,e).

The majority of dialectal pronominal systems in North-West Bulgaria are affected by the transition from synthetic to analytical case: only 72 dialects (out of 418) show no evidence of this process while in the remaining 346 dialectal systems, analytical (prepositional) constructions compete with or fully replace original dative forms for at least one PERSON/GENDER/NUMBER combination. At the same time, there are 49 dialects where the transition from morphologically expressed dative case to analytical constructions is completed, i.e. synthetic dative forms are ousted by prepositional constructions in all five PERSON/GENDER/NUMBER combinations presented in BDA IV (see §9.2 for the list of combinations). In a large proportion of the dialects, prepositional constructions replacing synthetic forms include a corresponding *accusative* form of a pronoun (as illustrated in (3c)); however, there is certain number of dialects where such constructions include *dative* forms (3d). The fact that the analytical constructions replacing synthetic dative forms may include either accusative or dative forms in Bulgarian dialects (not only in the North-West, but also in the South-West dialects for which we have comparable, though less comprehensive, data; see Stojkov 1975) has not received due attention in the literature. I revisit this below.

A second process leading to the loss of the accusative–dative distinction is the generalisation of one pronominal form across the two case values. As it is the case with prepositional constructions, this is a two-way road: while in most of the dialects accusative replaces dative, as illustrated in (3b), there is a significant number of systems where dative takes over accusative generalising across both paradigm cells, as we see in (3e).

The data from BDA show that while accusative clearly dominates as a preferred form in the historical competition between accusative and dative, the outcome of this competition is not uniform across all Bulgarian dialects. This fact has a theoretical significance which so far has been largely overlooked. As mentioned above, among 418 dialects presented in BDA IV, there is a significant number where dative pronouns act as so-called 'general oblique' forms replacing all cases apart from nominative (we have seen this in (3e)). From a typological perspective, a situation where dative wins over accusative which is higher in the hierarchy of cases (Blake 2001: 89–90) is not uncommon: consider, for example, Old English where dative took over accusative forms at a relatively early stage (e.g. Baugh 1971: 193). Bulgarian dialectal data reveal a highly complex diachronic process. Consider again a summary of the data from BDA IV presented in Table 9.2.

While there is a tendency observed in many dialects to generalise one form (either accusative or dative) over two cases, the surviving form may be *either* accusative *or* dative, which rules out insufficiency or phonological vagueness of a disappearing form as a reason for this historical change. Rather, we likely observe the effect of a systematic (paradigmatic) requirement which encourages speakers to generalise across paradigm cells. Equally, the penetration of prepositional constructions into syntactic slots which originally belonged to the dative is unlikely to be a result of a repair strategy intended to 'clarify' a relationship expressed by a dative form. Here, again, we are most likely dealing with the effects of a syntactic process which imposes its requirements on syntactic positions (namely, a requirement for a given relationship to be expressed by a given syntactic construction, i.e. the preposition *na* + an accusative form of a personal pronoun).[8] This results in the spread of analytical (prepositional) constructions either with accusative or with dative, where the actual grammatical content of a pronominal form and of the preposition is bleached. This is particularly clear as we observe combinations of the preposition *na* with dative forms which previously could not govern the dative.[9] The data from BDA IV demonstrate consecutive stages of the grammatical and semantic bleaching of case forms involved in analytical (prepositional) constructions. Thus, along with the 'pure' types listed in Table 9.2, there is a number of dialects which combine several different patterns, e.g. B and C or E and F. This results in the competition of case forms and analytical constructions, as illustrated in (4):

(4) Accusative function   Dative function
     Vižda-t **nas**.   Dava-t **nam**.   Dava-t   na   **nas**.
     see-3.PL we(ACC)   give-3.PL we(DAT)   give-3.PL on   we(ACC)
     'They see us.'   'They give to us.'

9.5 Patterns of Synchronic Variation: Quantitative Data

In this section, I present quantitative data which should elucidate variation in personal pronouns' case marking and explain differences in patterns of diachronic change observed across different classes of personal pronouns.[10] I start by calculating the number of dialects where a given form or construction may occur and do this for all five PERSON/GENDER/NUMBER combinations presented in BDA IV. The results are presented in Table 9.3 (for accusative) and in Table 9.4 (for dative). Figures in the tables show percentages of dialects where a given form or construction occurs with a given PERSON/GENDER/NUMBER combination. I took the total number of dialects presented in BDA IV as 100 per cent.[11]

Several important observations may be made on the basis of these data. First, as Table 9.3 shows, there is a number of dialects where original accusative forms (third person plural) are replaced by dative forms which fulfil accusative functions (29 dialects, 7 per cent). In all of these dialects original accusative forms are eliminated.

Table 9.3 The occurrence of forms/constructions in accordance with the original accusative forms in the North-West Bulgarian dialects

Form/construction	Dialects where a given form is attested (percentages and absolute numbers)			
	1&2 PL	3SG.M & N	3SG.F	3PL
Accusative form	100% (418)	100% (418)	N/A[a]	92% (383)
Dative form	1.4% (6)	–	N/A[a]	7% (29)[b]

[a] Data are not provided in BDA IV.
[b] For six locations data are not provided.

Table 9.4 The occurrence of forms/constructions in the North-West Bulgarian dialects in accordance with the original functions of dative forms

Form/construction	Dialects where a given form is attested (percentages and absolute numbers)			
	1&2 PL	3SG.M & N	3SG.F	3PL
Dative form	23% (95)	61% (255)	74% (309)	67% (278)
Preposition + dative form	2% (10)	15% (63)	6% (26)	11% (47)
Accusative form	47% (195)	–	0.2% (1)	0.7% (3)
Preposition + accusative form	41% (172)	24% (100)	30% (125)	28% (118)

Second, the data for dative (Table 9.4) reveal an important split between first and second person on the one hand, and third person on the other with respect to preferences for formal means. Thus, while the original first and second person plural dative forms are preserved in 23 per cent of the dialects, they are 2.5–3 times more frequent with the third person pronouns both in singular and in plural. Another striking difference is found in the use of prepositionless accusative forms used in a dative function: almost half of the dialects allow this form for first and second person plural but it is almost impossible in combination with the third person. Less striking but still significant differences isolating third person from first and second person pronouns are found in the preference for prepositional constructions with accusative and dative forms.

Further dissimilarity between different classes of personal pronouns with respect to their case marking strategies becomes clear if we consider the frequency of the types of pronominal case paradigms presented in Table 9.2. Tables 9.5, 9.6 and 9.7 show numbers of the dialects where a given type is attested and also include separate data for mixed types (i.e. dialects where several alternative strategies may be used with respect to one case function, for example an accusative form and a prepositional construction for dative, as in type AC in Tables 9.5 and 9.6).

These quantitative data reveal significant differences between first and second person pronouns on the one hand and third person pronouns on the other both with respect to their synchronic behaviour and to the extent they have advanced towards a two-way distinction in the case paradigm (i.e. nominative–accusative). While in the majority of the dialects presented in BDA IV third person pronouns retain the original accusative–dative opposition (255 dialects for third person singular and 226 for third person plural), thus preserving a three-case system, there is only a minority of dialects where this distinction holds for the first and second person pronouns: these include

Table 9.5 Case marking and alternative strategies for first and second person plural pronouns

Type	Accusative function	Dative function	Dialects where a given combination is attested (absolute numbers)
A	Accusative	Dative	89
B	Accusative	Accusative	142
C	Accusative	Preposition + accusative	94
D	Accusative	Preposition + dative	4
E	Dative	Dative	2
F	Dative	Preposition + dative	–
AC	Accusative	Dative; preposition + accusative	25
AD	Accusative	Dative; preposition + dative	3
BC	Accusative	Accusative; preposition + accusative	53
EF	Dative	Dative; preposition + dative	3

Table 9.6 Case marking and alternative strategies for third person singular pronouns (masculine and neuter)[a]

	Accusative function	Dative function	Dialects where a given combination is attested (absolute numbers)
A	Accusative	Dative	255
B	Accusative	Accusative	–
C	Accusative	Preposition + accusative	9
D	Accusative	Preposition + dative	63
E	Dative	Dative	–
F	Dative	Preposition + dative	–
AC	Accusative	Dative; preposition + accusative	15
AD	Accusative	Dative; preposition + dative	–
BC	Accusative	Accusative; preposition + accusative	75
EF	Dative	Dative; preposition + dative	–

[a] Third person singular masculine and neuter pronouns are syncretic in all cases apart from nominative. In BDA they are counted together.

Table 9.7 Case marking and alternative strategies for third person plural pronouns

Type	Accusative function	Dative function	Dialects where a given combination is attested (absolute numbers)
A	Accusative	Dative	226
B	Accusative	Accusative	1
C	Accusative	Preposition + accusative	81
D	Accusative	Preposition + dative	32
E	Dative	Dative	17
F	Dative	Preposition + dative	11
AC	Accusative	Dative; preposition + accusative	–
AD	Accusative	Dative; preposition + dative	25
BC	Accusative	Accusative; preposition + accusative	–
EF	Dative	Dative; preposition + dative	1

89 dialects with a 'pure' type A and 28 dialects with mixed types AC and AD as shown in Table 9.5; the latter two types show a tendency for a transition to analytical constructions. Further evidence, showing a strong tendency for the first and second person pronouns to progress to a two-case system, is the syncretism of accusative and dative which we find in more than a third of dialectal systems presented in BDA IV (142 dialects in Table 9.5). This is not the case for the third person pronouns: as Table 9.6 and Table 9.7 show, such syncretism per se is practically non-existent

in the dialects under investigation and occurs only in mixed systems in combination with prepositional constructions BC; however, significantly less frequently than with first and second person pronouns (75 occurrences with third person singular pronouns; Table 9.6). One more difference which the data in Tables 9.5, 9.6 and 9.7 reveal is in the preference for a particular type of analytical construction to replace original dative forms. Thus, first and second person pronouns from our sample show a relatively strong preference for constructions with accusative: type C – 94 dialects, and mixed types AC and BC – 78 dialects (see Table 9.5). At the same time, these pronouns seem to disfavour dative in prepositional constructions: there are only 10 dialects where such constructions occur either on their own or in competition with other strategies (types D, AD and EF). With the third person pronouns (both singular and plural) we find a significantly stronger tendency to retain original dative forms and to use them in analytical constructions: there are 63 dialects where such constructions are attested with the third person singular pronouns (Table 9.6) and 86 (including mixed types) with the third person plural pronouns (Table 9.7).

The data discussed above demonstrate significant differences between various classes of personal pronouns with respect to synchronic variation and with respect to their diachronic behaviour. The first and second person pronouns clearly stand out as propagators of change, leading to the reduction of case paradigms and to the transition from three-case to two-case systems. At the same time, the third person pronouns on the whole are more conservative and preserve original forms more frequently. The difference between the first and second person pronouns on the one hand, and the third person pronouns on the other has been widely discussed in the literature, in general terms (see Benveniste 1971) and with respect to particular languages (e.g. Haig 2008 for Iranian languages; Cappellaro 2016 for Italian). In Romance languages, for example, as in Bulgarian, case was lost in nominal declensions but pronouns (in particular, first and second person singular pronouns) preserve case distinctions (Sornicola 2011; Cappellaro 2016). While evidence from Bulgarian points to a different trajectory of change (third person pronouns are more likely to preserve case distinctions than first and second person plurals, although we do not have any data for first and second person singular to allow a correct comparison with Romance languages) we can see that pronouns which are different in PERSON show dramatically different diachronic patterns. At the same time, the data indicate that pronouns which differ only with respect to NUMBER (i.e. third person singular masculine/neuter and third person plural pronouns) follow similar patterns with respect to patterns of synchronic variation and diachronic change. In other words, the feature PERSON may account for asymmetries in case marking across different classes of personal pronouns, while the feature NUMBER does not account for any significant splits.

9.6 Conclusions

This study has shown that even within a relatively small dialectal area we can find multiple paths which the loss of case in pronominal systems may take. It is noteworthy that the variety of the diachronic patterns attested in the investigated dialects has typological parallels; for example, dative forms generalising over accusative, a phenomenon found in a few dozen out of 418 localities covered by BDA IV, was a mainstream process in the history of English. The nature of the data available for this study does not allow to take the next logical step and to investigate the role of different factors contributing to case loss and the rationale behind speakers' choices in situations of intra-dialectal variation when alternative means are available for the same case function. However, large quantitative data derived from the *Bulgarian Dialectological Atlas* reveal the complexity of change leading to the reduction and loss of case distinctions. The data presented here suggest that the outcome of this change is conditioned by an interaction of morphological and syntactic factors and thus contribute to a long-term debate on the nature of processes leading to case loss in a variety of languages.

Notes

1. The inherited Proto-Slavonic system included six cases (nominative, accusative, genitive, dative, instrumental and locative) and vocative forms (Schenker 2002).
2. From a historical perspective these two situations which are available for observation in contemporary Bulgarian dialects represent relatively late stages of case loss in pronominal systems: in both of them genitive, instrumental and locative functions have been generalised under one pronominal (accusative) form which is used with a variety of prepositions: *bez nego* 'without him' (genitive function); *s nego* 'with him' (instrumental function); *za nego* 'about him' (locative function).
3. I am grateful to Maria Petrunova and Nick Harff for their enormous help in extracting and processing the data from the BDA.
4. In the BDA first and second person plural pronouns are mapped together, which apparently suggests that they follow the same pattern.
5. The data in the BDA do not allow to deduce paradigms for other personal pronouns. Note that some pronouns have alternative forms. In Table 9.1 alternative forms are given in one cell and separated by a slash (e.g. *nas/naze* 'we' ACC). Usually, only one of the alternative third person pronouns is allowed in a given dialect; alternative first and second person forms frequently co-occur in one dialect, though no data on their possible distribution within a given dialect are available. From a historical point of view, the alternative forms represent different stages in development of the Bulgarian pronominal system. For further details on the origin of these forms and on the diachronic relationships between them, see Mirčev (1963: 168–73); Pârvev (1975: 124–33); Todorov (2002).
6. Bulgarian dialectologists sometimes use the term *glomerativen padež* to denote a case form which combines historical functions of genitive, instrumental and locative, and the term *aglomerativen padež* for case forms combining historical genitive, dative, instrumental and locative. These terms, however, are not generally accepted.
7. In many dialects synthetic and analytical means compete, for example *nas* 'we-ACC' and *na nas* 'on we-ACC' used in the dative sense, but BDA IV does not provide information on whether there are any morphosyntactic, semantic or pragmatic factors which condition their competition.
8. The use of analytical means (such as prepositional constructions) to express case relationships is frequently listed among prominent morphosyntactic effects of the Balkan Sprachbund (e.g. Mišeska Tomić 2006: 27). However, the question as to why this tendency manifests itself in so many different outcomes, not just across language or dialectal borders but also within a given variety (e.g. across lexical classes), calls for further

research (cf. Miloradović's 2003 survey of a group of East Serbian dialects affected by the loss of morphological case).
9. Government requirements of this preposition in such dialects change and become less specific. Further down this track, this preposition loses the ability to govern any specific form and is used as a marker of a syntactic function (as is the case in Standard Bulgarian and in the majority of regional dialects where nouns do not inflect for case).
10. Bulgarian dialects demonstrate significant variation in the form of personal pronouns for every class considered here. Thus, a second person plural pronoun *you* in the accusative has two forms, *nas* and *naze*, and the third person plural pronoun has different stems in different dialects, i.e. *nim* and *tjam* (3.PL.DAT). Further consideration of these differences is outside the scope of this paper. For a detailed historical analysis of personal pronouns in Bulgarian, see Todorov (2002).
11. It should be taken into account that in each dialect, there may be two or even more alternative means for expressing a given PERSON/GENDER/NUMBER combination, for example there may be an original case form and a prepositional construction, which is why a total for a column may exceed 100 per cent.

References

Baugh, Albert C. (1971), *A History of the English Language*, London: Routledge & Kegan Paul.
Benveniste, Émile (1971), 'Subjectivity in language', in Émile Benveniste, *Problems in General Linguistics*, Coral Gables, FL: University of Miami Press, pp. 223–30.
Blake, Barry J. (2001), *Case*, Cambridge and New York: Cambridge University Press.
Cappellaro, Chiara (2016), 'Tonic pronominal system: Morphophonology', in Adam Ledgeway and Martin Maiden (eds), *The Oxford Guide to the Romance Languages*, Oxford: Oxford University Press, pp. 722–41.
Haig, Geoffrey (2008), *Alignment Change in Iranian Languages: A Construction Grammar Approach*, Berlin and New York: Mouton de Gruyter.
Miloradović, Sofija (2003), *Upotreba padežnix oblika u govoru Paraćinskog Pomoravlja. Balkanistički i etnomigracioni aspekt*, Beograd: Etnografski institut SANU.
Mirčev, Kiril (1963), *Istoričeska gramatika na bâlgarskija ezik*, Sofia: Nauka i izkustvo.
Mišeska Tomić, Olga (2006), *Balkan Sprachbund Morpho-syntactic Features*, Dordrecht: Springer.
Pârvev, Xristo (1975), *Očerk po istorija na bâlgarskata gramatika*, Sofia: Nauka i izkustvo.
Schenker, Alexander M. (2002), 'Proto-Slavonic', in Bernard Comrie and Greville G. Corbett (eds), *The Slavonic Languages*, London: Routledge, pp. 60–121.
Sornicola, Rosanna (2011), 'Romance linguistics and historical linguistics: Reflections on synchrony and diachrony', in Martin Maiden, John Charles Smith and Adam Ledgeway (eds), *The Cambridge History of the Romance Languages. Volume I: Structures*, Cambridge: Cambridge University Press, pp. 1–49.
Stojkov, Stojko (1954), *Bâlgarskata dialektologija*, Sofia: Nauka i izkustvo.
Stojkov, Stojko (ed.) (1975), *Bâlgarski dialekten atlas. T. III. Jugozapadna Bâlgaria. Čast 1. Karti. Čast 2. Statii, komentari, pokazalci* [Bulgarian Dialectological Atlas. Volume III. South-West Bulgaria. Part 1. Maps. Part 2. Articles, Commentaries, Indices], Sofia: Bâlgarskata akademija na naukite.
Stojkov, Stojko (ed.) (1981), *Bâlgarski dialekten atlas. T. IV. Severozapadna Bâlgaria. Čast 1. Karti. Čast 2. Statii, komentari, pokazalci* [Bulgarian Dialectological Atlas. Volume IV. North-West Bulgaria. Part 1. Maps. Part 2. Articles, Commentaries, Indices], Sofia: Bâlgarskata akademija na naukite.
Todorov, Todor (2002), *Starobâlgarskoto anaforično mestoimenie i negovite novobâlgarski zastâpnici*, Sofia: Izdatelstvo 'Prof. Marin Drinov'.

10

Measuring the Complexity of the Stem Alternation Patterns of Spanish Verbs

Enrique L. Palancar

10.1 Introduction

Greville G. Corbett has taught us to look at the physics and topology of morphosyntax. From his work, we have learned how to deal with linguistic organisation by way of Network Morphology and of how to deal with linguistic diversity – internal or external – by way of Canonical Typology. Like many scholars that have crossed his path, I have learned many things from Grev. Four of them are relevant to this work. I learned to appreciate the wonder of morphological splits in paradigms. I learned that zero morphemes should not be dismissed, but they should not always be represented with mathematical zeros, because mathematical zeros give the wrong message about the morphosyntactic mapping between form and meaning, and they distract us from observing the different jobs bare stems can do by themselves. I also learned that being able to explain the distribution of a morphological phenomenon in phonological terms is often and unfairly misinterpreted as being explained by the phonology. And finally, I learned that regardless of where you may end up putting it in your explanation, all information that is required to account for a given morphological phenomenon needs to be stored somewhere in your representation of the lexeme, and it always counts.

This paper is about the inflection of Spanish verbs and it has two goals. On the one hand, I want to present a comprehensive overview of Spanish verbal inflection by means of a novel description which has the benefit of combining the strengths of two different approaches, the traditional approach in Alcoba (1999) and the more innovative stem-based approach in Boyé and Cabredo (2006), which is in turn based on Bonami and Boyé (2002, 2003). This is the purpose of §10.2. This description makes essential reference to the morphomic patterns involving stem alternations signalled in Maiden (1992, 2009, 2016). The different patterns are discussed in scattered ways in the morphological literature. This is because most authors assume that readers will or should know the essentials of Spanish verbal inflectional morphology, based on the fact that Spanish is one of the most widely spoken languages in the world. However, I think it is still convenient to have all patterns presented and discussed in only one place. This is attempted in §10.3. The specific way I deal with the structure of such patterns in this paper is based on the specific model I propose for regular inflection.

In this connection, stem alternation patterns are deviations from the inflection of regular verbs. The second goal of the paper proposes a way of measuring how lexemes compare with each other regarding their inflection,[1] and it aims to tackle how to deal with such inflectional deviations. This is achieved in §10.4. My proposal is grounded on a defaults-based framework like Network Morphology by Brown and Hippisley (2012), where deviations are seen as default overrides where each override adds an additional element to the set of rules, giving a concrete measure of irregularity. In this light, processing the inflection of a deviating verb is judged to be more costly for the system than processing a default pattern.[2] In the paper, I first use a model of complexity *à la* Kolmogorov, according to which a structure is more complex than another if it needs to be described with a longer description. I show that the application of such a model provides a straightforward, but simplistic account of the complexity of verbs with stem alternation patterns. To compensate for this, I propose a different alternative view of complexity that takes into account implicative relations (Ackerman et al. 2009; Ackerman and Malouf 2013; Bonami and Beniamine 2016, among others). Under such a view, some stem alternation patterns can be seen as defaults for certain verbs and are thus less costly for the overall complexity of the system. To be able to calculate the cost of each pattern, I establish notebooks of what counts as an inflectional default and what as a default override in the grammar of Spanish for the context of each specific deviation. I establish such notebooks based on token frequency of types in a corpus of 3,698 verbs. The results of such an alternative view are given in §10.5. §10.6 concludes the paper.

The traditional approach to Spanish verbal inflection departs from the idea that an ideal inflected form of a Spanish verb consists of the four main elements in (1). This is done in such a way that the forms for the imperfect indicative of the verb CANTAR 'sing' *cantabas* /kantábas/ and *cantaba* /kantába/ for the 3SG and the 2SG could be analysed as in (2).[3]

(1) Radical-Thematic Vowel (TV)-TAM-Subject's Person/Number

(2) a. cant-á-ba-s   b. cant-á-ba
        sing-TV-IMPF-2SG   sing-TV-IMPF[3SG]
        'You were singing.'   'S/he/it was singing.'

In contrast, following a stem-based approach Boyé and Cabredo (2006) propose the existence of 11 stem spaces in a paradigm of a Spanish verb. For the forms in (2), they propose the segmentation in (3) by appealing to the occurrence of a so-called Stem 7 (S7) of a verb, which is only used to build the imperfect tense. Note that the new suffix in (3) serves as a cumulative exponent for both imperfect and person/number of the subject.[4]

(3) a. cantáb-as　　　　　b. cantáb-a
　　　sing.s7-2SG.IMPF　　　　sing.s7-3SG.IMPF
　　　'You were singing.'　　　'S/he/it was singing.'

My description of Spanish verbal inflection is based on an analysis that tries to combine the best of both approaches. For example, I propose to segment the forms in (2) and (3) like in (4), where I minimise the allomorphy involving the exponence of person/number, and I propose a stem shape that feels more natural to Spanish word phonology.

(4) a. cantába-s　　　　　b. cantába
　　　sing.IMPF-2SG　　　　　sing.IMPF[3SG]
　　　'You were singing.'　　　'S/he/it was singing.'

Similarly, in the received view of Spanish verbal inflection verbs are conceived of as falling into three inflectional classes or conjugations. The infinitival form of a verb (the citation form) is most informative to signal membership of a verb in such classes. This is so to such an extent that in language pedagogy the conjugations are talked about as the *-ar*, the *-er* and the *-ir* classes. In the traditional view, the classes contrast both in the distribution of the thematic vowel and in the allomorphy of exponents. For example, a verb like CANTAR 'sing' is seen as belonging to the *-ar* class and TEMER 'fear' to the *-er* class because both classes contrast in the way they build the imperfect subparadigm, like in (5).

(5) a. cant-**á-ba**-s　　　　b. tem-**ía-Ø**-s
　　　sing-TV$_{ar}$-IMPF$_{ar}$-2SG　　fear-TV$_{er}$-IMPF$_{er}$-2SG
　　　'You were singing.'　　　'You were fearing.'

Boyé and Cabredo's (2006) analysis does away with inflectional classes. The authors base their analysis on stem classes, instead. This means that the information that makes (5a) and (5b) contrastive is instead encapsulated by way of two different stem building rules, like in (6), in such a way that the Stem 7 of CANTAR 'sing' is /kantáb-/, whereas the Stem 7 of TEMER 'fear' is /temí-/, and not /*kantí/ or /*temáb-/, for that matter.

(6) a. **cantáb**-as　　　　　b. **temí**-as
　　　CANTAR/sing.s7-2SG.IMPF　　TEMER/fear.s7-2SG.IMPF
　　　'You were singing.'　　　'You were fearing.'

In this paper, I follow the main guidelines in Boyé and Cabredo's (2006) proposal, and I also claim that verbs in Spanish fall into two large paradigm types depending on how they inflect. The membership of such types can be largely determined from the phonological shape of their lexical stem (see below for details). To achieve the right perspective of what is regular or irregular in the stem alternation patterns in Spanish verbal inflection, I depart here from the paradigms of regular verbs, which I treat as basic verbs. This is the subject of the next section.

10.2 Basics of Spanish Verbal Inflection: Inflectional Classes

In this section, I introduce the paradigm of verbs in Spanish that have the simplest inflectional apparatus because the apparatus requires the minimal amount of morphological information. In other words, in Kolmogorov's complexity terms they represent a paradigm type that requires the shortest description. I call such verbs 'basic' verbs. The inflection of basic verbs represents the most direct morphosyntactic mapping of form and grammatical meaning that is possible in Spanish verbal inflection. In other words, basic verbs represent the morphosyntactic mechanism that would operate as a general default in the elsewhere case.

In my description of Spanish verbs, I propose that verbs in Spanish fall into two main inflectional classes, whose membership is predictable from the phonological shape of their lexical stem. The first inflectional class (Class I) contains verbs whose lexical stem ends in /a/, like VENDAR 'bandage' or AMAR 'love' with lexical stems /benda/ and /ama/ respectively. The other inflectional class (Class II) is made up of verbs whose basic stem ends in either /e/ or /i/, like VENDER 'sell', PONER 'put', VIVIR 'live' or VENIR 'come', whose respective lexical stems are /bende/, /pone/, /bibi/ and /beni/. In Table 10.1, I give the population size of these two classes in a sample of 3,700 verbs from Mungía Zatarain et al. (1998).[5]

Table 10.1 shows that Class I is by far the one with the largest number of verbs in Spanish. It is also the only productive class. The two verbs characterised as 'other' are the verbs IR 'go' and SER 'be' which have stem suppletion patterns that are not attested in the inflection of any other verb and which make it difficult to characterise them as members of the two main classes.[6]

10.2.1 The Paradigm of Regular Verbs of Class I

Verbs in Standard Peninsular Spanish inflect in six person/number values, three moods (indicative, subjunctive and imperative) and various tense/aspects (present, imperfect, past, future and conditional). The regular or exemplary verb of Class I uses four stems. First, we have a basic stem that is the lexical representation of the lexeme (i.e. how it is stored phonologically in the lexicon). This stem consists of a bound root /bend-/ plus the final vowel /a#/, which in traditional approaches serves as a thematic vowel. This stem also has the broader distribution. The other three stems are 'inflectional': one of such stems is used to build the present subjunctive; a second one is used to build the imperfect indicative; and a third one to build the past participle.[7]

Table 10.1 Inflectional classes in the sample

Inflectional class	Total	%
I	3,104	84
II	594	16
Other	2	(0.05)
Total	3,700	100

All three such inflectional stems are built by means of simple phonological rules that involve replacing the final vowel of the basic stem with specific and invariant stem building material. The paradigm of a regular verb of Class I appears in Table 10.2, exemplified with the verb VENDAR 'bandage'.

Besides inflectional stems, some subparadigms still require further TAM affixation such as the future indicative, conditional indicative and imperfective subjunctive. In my analysis, the sets of suffixes to realise person/number of subject is reduced to two: a default one with the broader distribution and another one that is only used for the past indicative (shaded in grey in Table 10.2).

The only cell that involves a morphophonological adjustment is the 1SG present indicative, which in my analysis involves the suffix -o (homophonous with the -o that realises 3SG past indicative). A phonological rule avoiding diphthongisation in an unstressed syllable prompts the deletion of the stem's final vowel /a/ in contact with a vocalic suffix, i.e. *béndao→béndo. This takes us to stress patterns.

Stress patterns operate regularly and they apply to all verbs regardless of inflectional class. In my approach, there are three main patterns:[8] a rhizotonic pattern that I treat as 'pattern I' /(...)'CVCΣV(...)/; 'pattern II' that has stress over the syllable of the thematic vowel /(...)CV'CΣV(...)/; and 'pattern III' that has stress specified over the suffix /(...)CVCΣV-'Aff(...)/.[9] The distribution of stress patterns is commonly distributed by subparadigm, but there are two morphomic exceptions: one involves the split of 1PL and 2PL forms from the rest of the person values in the present tenses (O'Neill 2014); and another the split of 1SG and 3SG from the rest of the person values in the past indicative.[10]

10.2.2 The Paradigm of Regular Verbs of Class II

Regular verbs of Class II (those with stems in /e#/ and /i#/) differ from Class I verbs in two main ways: one way involves stem building; the other a difference in exponence. The stem building rules for inflectional stems are different than Class I verbs. This is shown in (a) in Table 10.3. Additionally, Class II verbs further require two more stems. This is shown in (b). The stem zone for these two extra stems is morphomic because one stem is used for the past indicative for all persons except the 3PL, and the other is used for the gerund, the imperfect subjunctive, and the 3PL of the past indicative. Nevertheless, the rules that apply to building such stems are simple and regular; the only twist being that the stem /XV_LEX→Xi/ for verbs of stem class /i#/ is homophonous with the lexical stem.

As for rules of exponence, Class I and Class II verbs contrast in only one cell: the 1SG past indicative. While verbs of Class I have the overt exponent -e for 1SG past (e.g. VENDAR 'bandage' has vendé /bend(a)-é/), verbs of Class II use a bare stem (e.g. VENDER 'sell' has vendí /bendí/ and VIVIR 'live' has viví /bibí/).11

Finally, verbs of Class II with stems in /i#/ display the rhizotonic forms in (b) in Table 10.4 (with a final /e/) instead of the expected forms in (a) (with a final /i/).

There are different ways in which the data in (b) in Table 10.4 can be accounted for. One possible interpretation is that the contrast is one involving a contrast in

Table 10.2 The paradigm of a basic verb of Class I (stem class /a#/): VENDAR 'bandage'

		Stem level		TAM/NF	PER/NUM	Stress pattern		Forms	
		benda	Xa^{LEX}	-r		(...)CV¹C$^\Sigma$V(...)	II	/bendár/	vendar
IMP	2SG	benda			—	(...)'CV¹C$^\Sigma$V(...)	I	/bénda/	venda
	2PL	benda			-d^a	(...)CV¹C$^\Sigma$V(...)	II	/bendád/	vendad
PRS.IND	1SG	bend(a)			-o	(...)'CV¹C$^\Sigma$V(...)	I	/béndo/	vendo
	2SG	benda			-s	(...)'CV¹C$^\Sigma$V(...)	I	/béndas/	vendas
	3SG	benda			—	(...)'CV¹C$^\Sigma$V(...)	I	/bénda/	venda
	1PL	benda			-mos	(...)CV¹C$^\Sigma$V(...)	II	/bendámos/	vendamos
	2PL	benda			-is	(...)CV¹C$^\Sigma$V(...)	II	/bendáis/	vendáis
	3PL	benda			-n	(...)'CV¹C$^\Sigma$V(...)	I	/béndan/	vendan
FUT.IND	1SG	benda		-re	—	(...)CV¹C$^\Sigma$V-¹Aff(...)	III	/bendaré/	vendaré
	2SG	benda		-ra	-s	(...)CV¹C$^\Sigma$V-¹Aff(...)	III	/bendarás/	vendarás
	3SG	benda		-ra	—	(...)CV¹C$^\Sigma$V-¹Aff(...)	III	/bendará/	vendará
	1PL	benda		-re	-mos	(...)CV¹C$^\Sigma$V-¹Aff(...)	III	/bendarémos/	vendaremos
	2PL	benda		-re	-is	(...)CV¹C$^\Sigma$V-¹Aff(...)	III	/bendaréis/	vendaréis
	3PL	benda		-ra	-n	(...)CV¹C$^\Sigma$V-¹Aff(...)	III	/bendarán/	vendarán
COND.IND	1SG	benda		-ria	—	(...)CV¹C$^\Sigma$V-¹Aff(...)	III	/bendaría/	vendaría
	2SG	benda		-ria	-s	(...)CV¹C$^\Sigma$V-¹Aff(...)	III	/bendarías/	vendarías
	3SG	benda		-ria	—	(...)CV¹C$^\Sigma$V-¹Aff(...)	III	/bendaría/	vendaría
	1PL	benda		-ria	-mos	(...)CV¹C$^\Sigma$V-¹Aff(...)	III	/bendaríamos/	vendaríamos
	2PL	benda		-ria	-is	(...)CV¹C$^\Sigma$V-¹Aff(...)	III	/bendaríais/	vendaríais
	3PL	benda		-ria	-n	(...)CV¹C$^\Sigma$V-¹Aff(...)	III	/bendarían/	vendarían
PST.IND	1SG	bend(a)			-e	(...)CV¹C$^\Sigma$V-¹Aff(...)	III	/bendé/	vendé
	2SG	benda			-ste	(...)'CV¹C$^\Sigma$V(...)	II	/bendáste/	vendáste
	3SG	bend(a)			-o	(...)CV¹C$^\Sigma$V-¹Aff(...)	III	/bendó/	vendó
	1PL	benda			-mos	(...)CV¹C$^\Sigma$V(...)	II	/bendámos/	vendamos

				-steis -ron				
IMPF.SUB	2PL	benda				(...)CV¹C²V(...)	II	/bendásteis/	vendasteis
	3PL	benda				(...)CV¹C²V(...)	II	/bendáron/	vendaron
	1SG	benda		-ra[b]	—	(...)CV¹C²V(...)	II	/bendára/	vendara
	2SG	benda		-ra	-s	(...)CV¹C²V(...)	II	/bendáras/	vendaras
	3SG	benda		-ra	—	(...)CV¹C²V(...)	II	/bendára/	vendara
	1PL	benda		-ra	-mos	(...)CV¹C²V(...)	II	/bendáramos/	vendaramos
	2PL	benda		-ra	-is	(...)CV¹C²V(...)	II	/bendárais/	vendarais
	3PL	benda		-ra	-n	(...)CV¹C²V(...)	II	/bendáran/	vendaran
GER		benda		-ndo		(...)CV¹C²V(...)	II	/bendándo/	vendando
PRS.SUB	1SG	bende	Xa^LEX→Xe		—	(...)CVC²V(...)	I	/bénde/	vende
	2SG	bende			-s	(...)CVC²V(...)	I	/béndes/	vendes
	3SG	bende			—	(...)CVC²V(...)	I	/bénde/	vende
	1PL	bende			-mos	(...)CV¹C²V(...)	II	/bendémos/	vendemos
	2PL	bende			-is	(...)CV¹C²V(...)	II	/bendéis/	vendeis
	3PL	bende			-n	(...)CVC²V(...)	I	/bénden/	venden
IMPF.IND	1SG	bendaba	Xa^LEX→Xaba		—	(...)CV¹C²V(...)	II	/bendába/	vendaba
	2SG	bendaba			-s	(...)CV¹C²V(...)	II	/bendábas/	vendabas
	3SG	bendaba			—	(...)CV¹C²V(...)	II	/bendába/	vendaba
	1PL	bendaba			-mos	(...)CV¹C²V(...)	II	/bendábamos/	vendábamos
	2PL	bendaba			-is	(...)CV¹C²V(...)	II	/bendábais/	vendabais
	3PL	bendaba			-n	(...)CV¹C²V(...)	II	/bendában/	vendaban
PST.PTCP		bendado	Xa^LEX→Xado[c]		—	(...)CV¹C²V(...)	II	/bendádo/	vendado

[a] For most speakers of Peninsular Spanish the realisation of this cell involves the suffix -r instead of -d (the resulting form is homophonous with the infinitive). For such speakers, the form with -d is a learned one.

[b] This subparadigm can also be realised by the suffix -se in a well-known case of overabundance treated in Thornton (2011a, 2011b) and pointed out in Stump (2016: 151).

[c] Speakers may also have participles ending in diphthongs /ao/ and /io/. This phenomenon is often talked about as 'the loss of intervocalic /d/', which has a complex distribution (for details, see Estrada Arráez 2012).

Table 10.3 Paradigm comparison between Class I and Class II

			Class I		Class II		
			VENDAR 'bandage'		VENDER 'sell'		VIVIR 'live'
(a)			Xa^LEX	benda	Xe^LEX/Xi^LEX	bende	bibi
	PRS.SUB		Xa^LEX→Xe	bende	Xe^LEX→Xa	benda	biba
	IMPF.IND		Xa^LEX→Xaba	bendaba	Xe^LEX→Xja	bendia	bibia
	PST.PTCP		Xa^LEX→Xado	bendado	Xe^LEX→Xido	bendido	bibido
(b)	PST.IND	1SG	Xa^LEX	benda	Xe^LEX→Xi	bendi	bibi
		2SG		benda		bendi	bibi
		3SG		benda		bendi	bibi
		1PL		benda		bendi	bibi
		2PL		benda		bendi	bibi
		3PL		benda	Xe^LEX→Xje	bendie	bibie
	IMPF.SUB	1SG		benda		bendie	bibie
		2SG		benda		bendie	bibie
		3SG		benda		bendie	bibie
		1PL		benda		bendie	bibie
		2PL		benda		bendie	bibie
		3PL		benda		bendie	bibie
	GER			benda		bendie	bibie

exponence. This would make verbs with a stem in /i#/ stand out as a different inflectional class from verbs with a stem in /e#/. In my analysis, however, I prefer to explain the contrast as resulting from the phonological rule in (7), which involves an adjustment in the phonotactic nature of the word form. The adjustment is prompted by a constraint that would disallow having an unstressed syllable with an /i/ in coda position in Spanish.

(7) (...)|CVCΣi(C)#→(...)|CVCΣe(C)#

The rule in (7) has generalised scope in Spanish phonology. Except for loanwords,[12] no word in Spanish has an unstressed /i/ or /iC/ in coda position.[13] In this light, forms such as *vive*, *vives* and *viven* could be explained as being surface realisations of underlying forms /bíbi/, /bíbis/ and /bíbin/.[14]

In this section, I have presented the paradigm types in the inflection of Spanish verbs that have the simplest array of inflectional rules. Other verbs have a different inflectional behaviour from the regular ones. I call such verbs 'deviating' verbs (OBS. I restrict the term 'irregular verb' to idiosyncratic verbs). I present such verbs in the following section.

Table 10.4 Stress rules for Class II

PRS.IND					(a)		(b)	
VENDER	1SG	bend(e)	-o	I	/béndo/		vendo	(...)'CVC$^\Sigma$V(...)
'sell'	2SG	bende	-s	I	/béndes/		vendes	(...)'CVC$^\Sigma$V(...)
	3SG	bende	–	I	/bénde/		vende	(...)'CVC$^\Sigma$V(...)
	1PL	bende	-mos	II	/bendémos/		vendemos	(...)CV'C$^\Sigma$V(...)
	2PL	bende	-is	II	/bendéis/		vendeis	(...)CV'C$^\Sigma$V(...)
	3PL	bende	-n	I	/bénden/		venden	(...)'CVC$^\Sigma$V(...)
VIVIR	1SG	bib(i)	-o	I	/bíbo/		vivo	(...)ICVCΣV(...)
'live'	2SG	bibi	-s	I	*/bíbis/	/bíbes/	vives	(...)ICVCΣi(...)→(...)ICVCΣe(...)
	3SG	bibi	–	I	*/bíbi/	/bíbe/	vive	(...)ICVCΣi(...)→(...)ICVCΣe(...)
	1PL	bibi	-mos	II	/bibímos/		vivimos	(...)CVICVΣV(...)
	2PL	bibi	-is	II	/bibís/		vivis	(...)CVICVΣV(...)
	3PL	bibi	-n	I	*/bíbin/	/bíben/	viven	(...)ICVCΣi(...)→(...)ICVCΣe(...)

10.3 Inflectional Deviations: Stem Classes and Stem Alternation Patterns

A considerable number of verbs in Spanish deviate in their inflection from the exemplary paradigms presented in the previous section. The greater type of inflectional deviation we observe is based on stem alternation patterns.[15] Stem alternation patterns are patterns that involve an alternating stem (different from the lexical and the inflectional stems that I have presented so far) that occurs in an array of cells in the paradigm. This array of cells is treated as a pattern. In the sense of Aronoff (1994), all patterns are morphomic because the array of cells where the alternating stem is found does not form a natural class, making the distribution of the alternating stem not accountable in either morphosyntactic or morphosemantic terms.[16] A great deal of the distribution of the patterns is more linked to the phonological aspects of the stems than to the inflectional class of verbs. This suggests that an account of the distribution of stem patterns that appeals to stem classes is more effective. In this light, and following a traditional account, I propose that there are three stems classes,[17] which I refer to as stem class /a#/, stem class /e#/ and stem class /i#/.[18] Table 10.5 shows the overall deviating behaviour of verbs involving stem alternation patterns.

Table 10.5 provides two views of inflectional deviation: (a) is a view across stem classes and (b) separates regular verbs from deviating verbs across the classes. The figures in (b) show that verbs of stem class /a#/ are very regular (i.e. 91 per cent of basic verbs are found in stem class /a#/), while 92 per cent of deviating verbs belong to stem classes /e#/ (58 per cent) and /i#/ (34 per cent). But verbs of stem class /e#/ are significantly more prone to deviation than verbs of stem class /i#/ even

Table 10.5 Basic and deviating verbs per stem class

Stem class	(a)		(b)			
			Regular		Deviating	
/a#/	3,104	84%	3,077	91%	27	8%
/e#/	271	7%	84	2.5%	187	58%
/i#/	323	9%	212	6.5%	111	34%
Total	3,698	100%	3,373	100%	325	100%

though, as indicated in (a), the sample has an almost equal share of verbs from both classes.[19]

In the remainder of this section, I introduce the five different stem alternation patterns that account for such deviations.

10.3.1 Stem Alternation Pattern 1

Some verbs in Spanish (165 in my sample) display a stem alternation pattern that in the literature has been referred to as the morphomic 'N-pattern' (Maiden 2005) and which I treat here as 'pattern 1' (P1). P1 involves an alternating stem in the present subparadigms (indicative and subjunctive) and the singular imperative (which is based on the indicative). The pattern feeds an alternating stem to the stem spaces already provided by the suprasegmental morphomic pattern based on rhizotonic cells (see last paragraph of §10.2.1). P1 is phonologically restricted to verbs with roots in /e/, /i/ and /o/. The alternating stem is produced by the apophony of the root vowel with predictable outcomes: /i→je/ (e.g. ADQUIRIR 'acquire' /adkiri, adkjeri/) and /o→we/ (e.g. MORIR 'die' /mori, mweri/).

However, verbs with roots in /e/ of stem class /i#/ split into two classes. This can be seen in the shape of the alternating stem: Class A involves the rule /e→je/ (e.g. MENTIR 'lie' /menti, mjenti/) and Class B has the rule /e→i/ (e.g. PEDIR 'ask for' /pedi, pidi/). The membership of these two classes is lexical.[20] Examples of both appear in Table 10.6, where cells affected by the pattern are given in grey.

10.3.2 Stem Alternation Pattern 2

In Table 10.6 in the previous section, we could already see that the forms for the 1PL and 2PL present subjunctive have a root in /i/ instead of the expected /e/. These forms instantiate a second stem alternation pattern that I treat as 'pattern 2' (P2). This new pattern is found in 92 verbs in my sample. It is illustrated in Table 10.7, where cells affected by the pattern are shaded in light grey (for convenience, the cells affected by P1 have been shaded in dark grey).[21] Like P1, P2 also has morphomic structure, but it is only attested in verbs of stem class /i#/ with root vowels in /e/ and /o/. The outcome of the alternating stem involves the root apophony rule /e→i/ and /o→u/. This means that for verbs of Class B, the alternating stem for P2 is incidentally homophonous with the alternating stem of P1. This homophony may give the impression that those

Table 10.6 Verbs with root in /e/ for P1: MENTIR 'lie' and PEDIR 'ask for'

PRS.SUB			
	1SG	miénta	pída
	2SG	miénta-s	pída-s
	3SG	miénta	pída
	1PL	mintá-mos	pidá-mos
	2PL	mintá-is	pidá-is
	3PL	miénta-n	pída-n

verbs instantiate yet a different, larger pattern. I have preferred to analyse the data as displaying two patterns.

10.3.3 Stem Alternation Pattern 3

Verbs in Spanish (182 in my sample) may display another stem alternation pattern that has been referred to in the literature as the 'L-pattern' (Maiden 2005; Bermúdez-Otero and Luís 2016), whose modern productivity is discussed in Nevins et al. (2015). I treat such a pattern as 'pattern 3' (P3). The pattern affects the cells of the present subjunctive and the cell for the 1SG present indicative. The shape of the alternating stem can be predicted if the basic stem involves a shape such as /XV(C$_{SONORANT}$)θV#/ or /XVnV#/, in which case it is /XV(C$_{SONORANT}$)θkV#/ and /XVnV#/ respectively, unless specified. In other cases, the outcome is listed. This alternation type is illustrated in Table 10.8, which shows cases where P3 (shaded light grey) operates alone or in overlap with P1 (shaded dark grey). In the latter case, P3 is superimposed on P1.

10.3.4 Stem Alternation Pattern 4

Another stem alternation pattern found in 66 verbs in my sample is 'pattern 4' (P4). This pattern involves an alternating stem in the past indicative and the imperfect subjunctive. Except for the gerund, the alternating stem operates in the stem zone where simple verbs of Class II have the two extra stems when compared with the verbs of Class I (see §10.2.2).[22] The lexical root of the alternating stem is not predictable by rule and needs to be listed. The pattern involves not only root suppletion, but also its own stress pattern set. More specifically, it cancels the requirement of stress pattern III (/(...)CVC^{Σ}V-$^|$Aff(...)/) for the cells of the 1SG and the 3SG of the past indicative. Instead, it requires rhizotonic pattern II (/(...)CV$^|$C^{Σ}V(...)/) (OBS. the form for 1SG further undergoes the phonological adjustment in (7) that involves i→e). The pattern is illustrated in Table 10.9 with cells shaded in light grey (for convenience, the cells affected by P4 have been shaded in dark grey). The occurrence of P4 is linked to P3; that is the reason why I have also included P3 in the table.

Table 10.7 P1 and P2

		MORIR 'die' P1+P2	MENTIR 'lie' P1.A+P2	PEDIR 'ask for' P1.B+P2
INF		morí-r	mentí-r	pedí-r
IMP	2SG	muére	miénte	píde
	2PL	morí-d	mentí-d	pedí-d
PRS.IND	1SG	muér-o	miént-o	píd-o
	2SG	muére-s	miénte-s	píde-s
	3SG	muére	miénte	píde
	1PL	morí-mos	mentí-mos	pedí-mos
	2PL	morí-(i)s	mentí-(i)s	pedí-(i)s
	3PL	muére-n	miénte-n	píde-n
PST.IND	1SG	morí	mentí	pedí
	2SG	morí-ste	mentí-ste	pedí-ste
	3SG	muri-ó	minti-ó	pidi-ó
	1PL	morí-mos	mentí-mos	pedí-mos
	2PL	morí-steis	mentí-steis	pedí-steis
	3PL	murié-ron	mintié-ron	pidié-ron
IMPF.SUB	1SG	murié-ra	mintié-ra	pidié-ra
	2SG	murié-ras	mintié-ras	pidié-ras
	3SG	murié-ra	mintié-ra	pidié-ra
	1PL	murié-ramos	mintié-ramos	pidié-ramos
	2PL	murié-rais	mintié-rais	pidié-rais
	3PL	murié-ran	mintié-ran	pidié-ran
GER		murié-ndo	mintié-ndo	pidié-ndo
PRS.SUB	1SG	muéra	miénta	pída
	2SG	muéra-s	miénta-s	pída-s
	3SG	muéra	miénta	pída
	1PL	murá-mos	mintá-mos	pidá-mos
	2PL	murá-is	mintá-is	pidá-is
	3PL	muéra-n	miénta-n	pída-n

Table 10.8 P3

		Stem class /e#/		Stem class /i#/
		PADECER 'suffer from'	TENER 'have'	DECIR 'say'
		P3	P1.A + P3	P1.B + P3
PRS.IND	1SG	padéθk-o	téng-o	díg-o
	2SG	padéθe-s	tiéne-s	díθe-s
	3SG	padéθe	tiéne	díθe
	1PL	padeθé-mos	tené-mos	deθí-mos
	2PL	padeθé-is	tené-is	deθí-(i)s
	3PL	padéθe-n	tiéne-n	díθe-n
PRS.SUB	1SG	padéθka	ténga	díga
	2SG	padéθka-s	ténga-s	díga-s
	3SG	padéθka	ténga	díga
	1PL	padeθká-mos	tengá-mos	digá-mos
	2PL	padeθká-is	tengá-is	digá-is
	3PL	padéθka-n	ténga-n	díga-n

10.3.5 Stem Alternation Pattern 5

Finally, pattern 5 (P5) is attested by the verb DECIR 'say'. It affects the stem used to build the future and the conditional: instead of lexical /deθi/, the verb has the suppletive stem /di/, i.e. 1SG future /di-ré/ instead of */deθi-ré/ (see Table 10.11 below for a detailed illustration).

10.3.6 A Typology of Deviations Involving Stem Alternation Patterns

In the previous sections, we have seen that verbs can have up to five different stem alternation patterns. We have also seen that some verbs may have more than one pattern. The way the patterns are instantiated results in nine types of possible combinations. The relevant data, based on the same figures as Table 10.5 above, are presented in Table 10.10. Here the letter phi (Φ) is used to indicate the occurrence of a given pattern. Letters A and B represent the two classes involved in P1. Verbs that lack a stem alternation pattern are treated as Type 0.

The nine different types of combinations in Table 10.10 give us an insight as to how inflectional deviations work in the inflectional system of Spanish:

Table 10.9 P3 and P4

		TRAER 'bring' P3 + P4			
PST.IND	1SG	*traxí	→ *tráxi	→ tráxe	traje
	2SG	traxí-ste			trajiste
	3SG	*trax-ó	→	tráx-o	trajo
	1PL	traxí-mos			trajimos
	2PL	traxí-steis			trajisteis
	3PL	*traxjé-ron	→	traxé-ron[a]	trajeron
IMPF.SUB	1SG	traxé-ra			trajera
	2SG	traxé-ras			trajeras
	3SG	traxé-ra			trajera
	1PL	traxé-ramos			trajeramos
	2PL	traxé-rais			trajerais
	3PL	traxé-ran			trajeran
PRS.IND	1SG	tráig-o			traigo
	2SG	tráe-s			traes
	3SG	tráe			trae
	1PL	traé-mos			traemos
	2PL	traé-is			traeis
	3PL	tráe-n			traen
PRS.SUBJ	1SG	tráiga			traiga
	2SG	tráiga-s			traigas
	3SG	tráiga			traiga
	1PL	traigá-mos			traigamos
	2PL	traigá-is			traigais
	3PL	tráiga-n			traigan

[a] The expected stem would be /traxje/ instead of /traxe/, but speakers of the Standard do not allow for the cluster [xje], while the stem /traxje/ is known to exist in substandard varieties.

Table 10.10 Combinations of stem alternation patterns in types

Sample							3,104	271	323	3,698
Type	P1		P2	P3	P4	P5	/a#/	/e#/	/i#/	Total
0	–		–	–	–	–	3,077	84	212	3,373
1	Φ(A)		–	–	–	–	24	35	2	61
2	–		–	Φ	–	–	0	115	6	121
3	–		–	–	Φ	–	3	0	0	3
4 i	Φ(A)		Φ	–	–	–	0	0	39	39
ii		Φ(B)	Φ	–	–	–	0	0	38	38
5	–		–	Φ	Φ	–	0	25	11	36
6	Φ(A)		–	–	Φ	–	0	2	0	2
7	Φ(A)		–	Φ	Φ	–	0	10	0	10
8	Φ(A)		Φ	Φ	Φ	–	0	0	11	11
9		Φ(B)	Φ	Φ	Φ	Φ	0	0	4	4
	120		45							
Total	165		92	182	66	4	27	187	111	325

- Types 1–3 involve verbs that display only one stem alternation pattern, i.e. verbs with such types have only one pattern of deviation. The rest of the types involve more than one pattern.
- The distribution of the patterns is not balanced across stem classes: 92 per cent of stem alternation patterns are found in stem classes /e#/ (187) and /i#/ (111).
- Also, the degree of expectation for the occurrence of a stem alternation pattern differs dramatically from verbs of stem class /a#/ to verbs of stem class /e#/: only 1 per cent of verbs of stem class /a#/ have a stem alternation pattern, while 70 per cent of stem class /e#/ have it. The expectation for verbs of stem class /i#/ is more balanced: 35 per cent of them have such patterns.
- Stem classes /e#/ and /i#/ have stem alternation patterns, but the expectation is very different as to the way they display such patterns: 80 per cent of deviating verbs of stem class /e#/ have only one pattern (Type 1 with P1.A and Type 2 with P3), while 93 per cent of deviating verbs of stem class /i#/ have more than one pattern (Types 4, 5, 8 and 9).

Type 9 represents a case of a paradigm which is rich in stem alternation patterns and it deserves our attention because it also shows a case of levelling that uncovers the subjacent presence of other patterns. The type is attested by the verb DECIR 'say', as illustrated in Table 10.11 below.

The verb DECIR 'say' forms part of a family of lexemes that share the same stem /(X)deθi#/: DES+DECIR=SE 'retract'; CONTRA+DECIR 'contradict'; (archaic) ENTRE+DECIR 'interdict'; BEN+DECIR 'bless'; MAL+DECIR 'curse/damn'; and PRE+DECIR 'foretell'.

Families like this are the outcome of historical word formation processes from Latin and further back in time, but for the most part the member lexemes are no longer semantically linked and are learned as independent words (see Spencer 2016). Despite being independent words, in the default case the lexemes in such families happen to share morphological properties associated to their old basic stem, and they show a remarkably consistent inflectional behaviour. Interestingly, the only exception is the /(X)deθi#/ family.

Three of the members of the /(X)deθi#/ family (i.e. ben+decir 'bless', mal+decir 'curse' and pre+decir 'predict') have undergone levelling in a portion of the paradigm. The levelling involves the past participle, the future and the conditional, which as a result are now built attending to the default paradigm. This is shown in Table 10.11. This in turn means they have done away with a suppletive stem and the morphomic P5.[23] The breaking of the inflectional link with DECIR 'say' is creating inflectional uncertainty for most speakers elsewhere in the paradigm. This is producing further levelling resulting in overabundance involving the cells of P4. The lifting of P4 reveals the occurrence of P2 over which it was superimposed, and which could only be observed in the gerund. The conservative forms are recommended by the standard and they are learned; the innovative ones are of common use, but are still judged negatively as improper and unrefined.

Having presented the main stem alternation patterns in Spanish and their overall distribution, an important question still remains: how can we tackle the weight such patterns have for the inflectional system of Spanish? In the following section, I attempt to provide an answer to this question.

10.4 Calculating the Inflectional Complexity of Spanish Verbs

In §10.2, I first introduced the two verbal paradigm types in Spanish that have the simplest array of inflectional rules. In the previous section, we have seen that other verbs have other arrays involving stem alternation patterns. I have considered such patterns as inflectional deviations. My approach to inflectional deviations is inspired by the defaults-based framework of Network Morphology in Brown and Hippisley (2012), where each override of a default adds an additional element to the set of rules, giving a concrete measure of irregularity.[24] In other words, an inflectional deviation counts as a default override. To deal with the deviations imposed by stem alternation patterns in a comprehensive way, it is not only desirable to be able to pinpoint where they happen (as in the previous section), but also to be able to say something about how lexemes relate to each other regarding degree of deviation, which in turn would render them in a scale of morphological complexity. But to do that, we first need a way to measure the internal complexity of a system.

In this paper, I propose a simple method to evaluate the inflectional complexity of a given verb with respect to other verbs.[25] For this we provide a score for each inflectional dimension that is susceptible of deviation. The basic scores I propose are spelled out in (8), where an increase in inflectional complexity is viewed as an increase in bits of information.[26]

Table 10.11 The verbs DECIR 'say' and BENDECIR 'bless' compared

		DECIR 'say' /deθi#/	Pattern		BENDECIR 'bless' /bendeθi#/	Pattern		Pattern
PST.PTCP		díčo	SCª		ben+díθie-ndo	–ᵇ		
FUT	1SG	di-ré	P5	≠	ben+deθi-ré	–		
	2SG	di-rás	P5	≠	ben+deθi-rás	–		
	3SG	di-rá	P5	≠	ben+deθi-rá	–		
	1PL	di-rémos	P5	≠	ben+deθi-rémos	–		
	2PL	di-réis	P5	≠	ben+deθi-réis	–		
	3PL	di-rán	P5	≠	ben+deθi-rán	–		
FUT	1SG	di-ría	P5	≠	ben+deθi-ría	–		
	2SG	di-rías	P5	≠	ben+deθi-rías	–		
	3SG	di-ría	P5	≠	ben+deθi-ría	–		
	1PL	di-ríamos	P5	≠	ben+deθi-ríamos	–		
	2PL	di-ríais	P5	≠	ben+deθi-ríais	–		
	3PL	di-rían	P5	≠	ben+deθi-rían	–		
IMP	2SG	di	SC	≠	ben+diθe	P1		
PRS.IND	1SG	dig(a)-o	P3	=	ben+dig(a)-o	P3		
	2SG	díθe-s	P1	=	ben+díθe-s	P1		
	3SG	díθe	P1	=	ben+díθe	P1		
	1PL	deθí-mos	–	=	ben+deθí-mos	–		
	2PL	deθí-(i)s	–	=	ben+deθí-(i)s	–		
	3PL	díθe-n	P1	=	ben+díθe-n	P1		
PRS.SUB	1SG	díga	P3	=	ben+díga	P3		
	2SG	díga-s	P3	=	ben+díga-s	P3		
	3SG	díga	P3	=	ben+díga	P3		
	1PL	digá-mos	P3	=	ben+digá-mos	P3		
	2PL	digá-is	P3	=	ben+digá-is	P3		
	3PL	díga-n	P3	=	ben+díga-n	P3		
PST.IND	1SG	díxe	P4	=	ben+díxe	P4	≠	ben+deθí	–
	2SG	dixí-ste	P4	=	ben+dixí-ste	P4	≠	ben+deθí-ste	–
	3SG	díx(i)-o	P4	=	ben+díx(i)-o	P4	≠	ben+diθi-ó	P2
	1PL	dixí-mos	P4	=	ben+dixí-mos	P4	≠	ben+deθí-mos	–
	2PL	dixí-steis	P4	=	ben+dixí-steis	P4	≠	ben+deθí-steis	–
	3PL	dixé-ran	P4	=	ben+dixé-ran	P4	≠	ben+diθíe-ron	P2
IMPF.SUB	1SG	dixé-ra	P4	=	ben+dixé-ra	P4	≠	ben+diθíe-ra	P2
	2SG	dixé-ras	P4	=	ben+dixé-ras	P4	≠	ben+diθíe-ras	P2
	3SG	dixé-ra	P4	=	ben+dixé-ra	P4	≠	ben+diθíe-ra	P2
	1PL	dixé-ramos	P4	=	ben+dixé-ramos	P4	≠	ben+diθíe-ramos	P2
	2PL	dixé-rais	P4	=	ben+dixé-rais	P4	≠	ben+diθíe-rais	P2
	3PL	dixé-ran	P4	=	ben+dixé-ran	P4	≠	ben+diθíe-ran	P2
GER		diθié-ndo	P2	=				ben+díθie-ndo	P2

ª SC stands for suppletive cells.
ᵇ – stands for default.

(8) a. A verb abiding by a default adds 0 bits of information to its inflectional complexity.
  b. A verb overriding a default (i.e. a deviating verb) adds:
  - 1 bit when the deviation involves a pattern that is different than the patterns described for the default
  - 1 bit when the deviation further involves a stem that needs to be listed in the lexicon and cannot be produced from regular morphophonological rules (i.e. it is a suppletive stem).

In a Kolmogorov-style view of complexity, stem alternation patterns are deviations that represent an increase in the overall morphological complexity of the system.[27] In such a view, every stem alternation pattern, whatever it is, represents an increase in the degree of complexity of a given verb. Such a view has the following consequences: (i) verbs of Types 1–3 would be equally complex because they would involve the same amount of description (i.e. verb X involves stem alternation pattern Y); (ii) among the deviating verbs, verbs of Types 1–3 would be less complex than verbs of other types because their description would be necessarily shorter (i.e. Types 4–9 involve more patterns, hence longer descriptions); a verb of Type 4 with two stem alternation patterns would necessarily be less complex than one of Type 9 with five patterns. Such a view of complexity would render things quite straightforward. The results are given in Table 10.12. Here the 325 verbs having a stem alternation pattern would be seen as deviating verbs. According to (8b), the increase in complexity they would display depends on how many patterns they require and whether the shape of the alternating stem in each of the patterns can or cannot be predicted.

However, under an alternative view of complexity, not all patterns added to a simple paradigm necessarily have to be seen as equally costly if their application can be predicted by the presence of other patterns. In other words, following the proposals of implicative morphology in Ackerman et al. (2009); Ackerman and Malouf (2013); Montermini and Bonami (2013); Sims (2010); and Bonami and Beniamine (2016), among others, we can also take the predictive power of implicative relations into account. For example, the occurrence of P2 and P5 is dependent on the occurrence of other patterns under specific circumstances (i.e. P2 only occurs in verbs of stem

Table 10.12 First scoring of the morphological complexity of Spanish verbs

	0	+1	+2	+3	+4	+5	+6	+7
/a#/	3,104	3,077	24	3	—	—	—	—
/e#/	271	84	146	4	17	20	11	4
/i#/	323	212	6	79	11	—	—	—
Total	3,698	3,373	176	86	28	20	11	4
Deviating			325					

class /i#/ and it is dependent on P1). In this way, it would not suffice to say that verbs having P2 are more complex than verbs having P1, when the presence of P2 is a given for certain verbs having P1. In this light, we can consider cases of minimal entropy according to the principle in (9).

(9) If all instances of pattern A are predicted from the presence of pattern B, and vice versa (i.e. with 0 entropy), the occurrence of one of the patterns does not add bits to the structural complexity of the lexeme that has both patterns.

This opens the possibility that some patterns are less costly than others. To be able to calculate the general cost to the system we need to establish a series of notebooks of what counts as an inflectional default and what as a default override in the grammar of Spanish for the context of each specific deviation.

10.4.1 Measuring the Deviation of P1 and P2

The distribution of P1 and P2 in the sample is given in Table 10.13.

Table 10.13 shows that the distribution of P2, which only occurs with verbs of stem class /i#/, is implicatively linked to the existence of P1. The correlation works both ways making the entropy level very low. I assume that the implication bears no impact on the structural complexity of the system, and hence the occurrence of P2 costs nothing for verbs of stem class /i#/. From the distributional properties of the patterns, I propose the defaults notebook in (10). In all such notebooks, defaults cost 0 bits.

(10) Defaults notebook for P1 and P2:

Verbs of stem class /a#/:
I. The default for a verb of stem class /a#/ is **not** to have P1. This default is based on the observation that P1 only occurs in less than 1 per cent of the sample.
   If this default is overridden, a verb of stem class /a#/ with P1 adds 1 bit to its complexity.

Verbs of stem class /e#/:
II. The default for a verb of stem class /e#/ is **not** to have P1. This default is based on

Table 10.13 Distribution of P1 and P2

	Stem class /a#/			Stem class /e#/			Stem class /i#/			
	P1	P2	None	P1	P2	None	P1		P2	None
							A	B		
Root in /e/	17	–	573	27	–	156	89	(44) (45)	89	5
Root in /i/	0	–	848	0	–	0	2		–	70
Root in /o/	7	–	507	20	–	38	3		3	1
Total	24	–	1,928	47	–	194	92		92	76

the observation that P1 only occurs in 20 per cent of verbs with stems in /eCe#/ and /oCe#/.

If this default is overridden, the verb adds 1 bit to its complexity.

Verbs of stem class /i#/:
III. The default for a verb with a root in /e/ (i.e. stem in /XeCi#/) **is** to have P1 and to be of Class B. P2 comes for free for such verbs. If this default does not apply, the expectation is that a verb in /XeCi#/ will have P1 and belong to Class A instead.

Default overrides add 1 bit to the complexity of the verb.

IV. The default for a verb with roots in /o/ or /i/ is **not** to have P1 (or P2).

If the default is overridden, the verb adds 1 bit to its complexity.

10.4.2 Measuring the Deviation of P3–P5

P3 is restricted to verbs of Class II, i.e. stem classes /e#/ and /i#/. The distribution of P3 is given in Table 10.14, where the verbs are organised according to stem shape (CSONORANT involves /l/, /n/, /r/ and more rarely /s/).

P3 is common in verbs of stem class /e#/, because half of them have it: 148 out of 271 verbs have it (54 per cent). But the pattern is **not** at all common in stem class /i#/, where only 10 per cent do (32 out of 323). In principle this uneven distribution could be taken to reveal something about the nature of P3, but in reality the pattern is linked to the phonological profile of the lexical stem. Because of this, I propose the defaults notebook for P3 in (11).

(11) Defaults notebook for P3:

For verbs of stem class /e#/:
V. The default for a verb whose lexical stem has one of the following shapes is to have P3:

/Xe(CSONORANT)θe#/→/Xe(CSONORANT)θka#/, e.g. ABORRECER 'dislike'
/Xo(CSONORANT)θe#/→/Xo(CSONORANT)θka#/, e.g. CONOCER 'know'

Table 10.14 Distribution of P3 for stem classes /e#/ and /i#/

	Stem class /e#/			Stem class /i#/		
	Total	+3	−3	Total	+3	−3
/Xe(C$_{\text{SONORANT}}$)θV#/	103	103	0	7	7	0
/Xo(C$_{\text{SONORANT}}$)θV#/	5	2	3	0	0	0
/Xa(C$_{\text{SONORANT}}$)θV#/	8	8	0	0	0	0
/XuθV#/	0	0	0	15	15	0
/XenV#/	10	10	0	0	8	1
/XonV#/	13	13	0	0	0	0
Other	132	12	120	301	2	290
Total	271	148	123	323	32	291

Table 10.15 Correlation between P3 and P4

	Total	P3	–P3	P4	–P4	No. of verbs with P4 that also have P3		No. of verbs with P3 that also have P4	
Class /a#/	3,104	0	3,104	3	3,101	0 out of 3	0%	0 out of 3	0%
Class /e#/	271	148	123	37	234	35 out of 37	95%	35 out of 148	24%
Class /i#/	323	32	291	26	297	26 out of 26	100%	26 out of 32	81%
Total	3,698	180	3,518	66	3,632				

/Xa(C$_{SONORANT}$)θe#→Xa(C$_{SONORANT}$)θka#/, e.g. NACER 'be born'
/Xene#→Xenga#/, e.g. TENER 'have'
/Xone#→Xonga#/, e.g. PONER 'put'

For verbs of stem class /i#/:

VI. The default for a verb whose lexical stem has one of the following shapes is to have P3:

/Xeni#→Xenga#/, e.g. VENIR 'come'
/Xu(C$_{SONORANT}$)θi#→Xu(C$_{SONORANT}$)θka#/, e.g. LUCIR 'be bright'

Other verbs with P3 add 1 bit extra to their complexity and 1 for the suppletive alternating stem.

The implicative relation between the occurrence of P3 and P4 is shown in Table 10.15. Here we can see that 95 per cent of the verbs of stem class /e#/ and 100 per cent of all verbs of stem class /i#/ that have P4 also have P3. However, the correlation does not work both ways, because not all verbs with P3 have P4.

This correlation helps lower the complexity level of the verbs that require P4. Attending to the distribution of P4 in the sample, I propose the defaults notebook in (12).

(12) Defaults notebook for P4:

For verbs of stem class /a#/:
VII. The default for a verb of stem class /a#/ is **not** to have P4.
   If this default is overridden, a verb of stem class /a#/ with P4 adds 1 bit to its complexity for the pattern and 1 bit for the suppletive alternating stem.

For verbs of stem class /e#/:
VIII. The default for a verb of stem class /e#/ is **not** to have P4.
   If this default is overridden, the verb adds 1 bit to its complexity for the pattern and 1 for the suppletive alternating stem.

For verbs of stem class /i#/:
IX. The default for a verb of stem class /e#/ **is** to have P4 if it has P3. For these verbs, P4 comes for free, but the verbs add 1 for the suppletive alternating stem.

Finally, P5 is only attested by the verb DECIR 'say' and other related verbs. Establishing the pattern for such verbs costs 1 bit to each verb, plus 1 bit extra for the suppletive stem they require.

10.5 Reducing the Inflectional Complexity of Spanish Verbs

In Table 10.12 above, I attempted a calculation of the morphological complexity of Spanish verbs based on a straightforward application of a Kolmogorov-style view of complexity. Under such a view, from a sample of 3,698 verbs belonging to stem classes /a#/, /e#/ and /i#/, 3,363 of them (90 per cent) are the only verbs with zero morphological complexity because they are the ones that do not have stem alternation patterns. The rest, which do, would be more complex depending on the number of stem alternation patterns they have and on how predictable the shape of their alternating stem is.

In contrast to this view, in a more balanced take on complexity based on implicative relations, I have proposed that for a number of deviating verbs, the stem alternation pattern adds 0 bits to their structural complexity under specific circumstances (i.e. under the dictates of default notebooks). The results of applying this alternative view are given in Table 10.16.

This alternative view has the advantage of reducing the overall complexity of the system using the same measures. The ratio of the verbs abiding by an inflectional default increases from 91 per cent to 95 per cent, but more significantly, 47 per cent of deviating verbs are no longer seen as irregular and those that are irregular are regarded as less so. On the other hand, the fact that we can reduce the overall complexity of the system does not necessarily mean that we have to reduce the descriptions, but that the descriptions become a description of another type of inflectional regularity.[28] Exemplar verbs for each possible type of deviation and complexity scores are given in Table 10.17 from the total of 325 verbs with stem alternations patterns.

Table 10.16 Second scoring of the morphological complexity of Spanish verbs

		Basic	Verbs with stem alternation patterns							
		0		+1	+2	+3	+4	+5	+6	+7
/a#/	3,104	3,077	–	24	3	–	–	–	–	–
/e#/	271	84	111	35	19	12	10	–	–	–
/i#/	323	212	42	55	10	4	–	–	–	–
Total	3,698	3,373	153	114	32	16	10			
Total of 0			3,526							
Total of deviating verbs				325						

Table 10.17 Examples of verbs for inflectional deviations

	Example		Stem alternation patterns					No.	Complexity scoring					
		Type	P1	P2	P3	P4	P5		P1	P2	P3	P4	P5	Total
/a#/	NEGAR 'deny'	1	Φ(A)	–	–	–	–	24	+1	–	–	–	–	+1
	ANDAR 'walk'	3	–	–	–	Φ	–	3	–	–	–	+2	–	+2
								27						
/e#/	MOVER 'move'	1	Φ(A)	–	–	–	–	50	+1	–	–	–	–	+1
	VENCER 'win'	2	–	–	Φ	–	–	111	–	–	0	–	–	0
	VALER 'cost'	2	–	–	Φ	–	–	4	–	–	+2	–	–	+2
	CABER 'fit in'	5	–	–	Φ	Φ	–	10	–	–	+2	+2	–	+4
	QUERER 'want'	6	Φ(A)	–	–	Φ	–	2	+1	–	–	+2	–	+3
	TENER 'have'	7	Φ(A)	–	Φ	Φ	–	10	+1	–	0	+2	–	+3
								187						
/i#/	ADQUIRIR 'adquire'	1	Φ(A)	–	–	–	–	2	+1	–	–	–	–	+1
	SALIR 'exit'	2	–	–	Φ	–	–	2	–	–	+2	–	–	+2
	LUCIR 'shine'	2	–	–	Φ	–	–	4	–	–	0	–	–	0
	HERIR 'wound'	4.i	Φ(A)	Φ	–	–	–	39	+1	0	–	–	–	+1
	ELEGIR 'chose'	4.ii	Φ(B)	Φ	–	–	–	38	0	0	–	–	–	0
	TRADUCIR 'translate'	5	–	–	Φ	Φ	–	11	–	–	0	+1	–	+1
	VENIR 'come'	8	Φ(A)	Φ	Φ	Φ	–	8	+1	0	0	+1	–	+2
	BENDECIR 'bless'	8	Φ(B)	Φ	Φ	Φ	–	3	0	0	0	+1	–	+1
	DECIR 'say'	9	Φ(B)	Φ	Φ	Φ	Φ	4	0	0	0	+1	+2	+3
								111						

10.6 Concluding Remarks

In this paper, I have studied the inflectional behaviour of 3,700 verbs in Spanish and have proposed a somewhat innovative description of the regular inflection of such verbs by combining a stem-based approach with a more traditional approach based on generalised affixation. In the description I propose, verbs in Spanish divide into two large inflectional classes whose membership is predictable from the shape of the lexical stem. Only one such class is productive. I then explored deviations from such basic inflection by way of stem alternation patterns, which are all morphomic in nature. To understand the distribution of the patterns, it is more convenient to see verbs in terms of stem classes. Once the descriptive apparatus had been presented, I then introduced the question as to how we can deal with inflectional deviations. I proposed two simple approaches to the phenomenon based on a straightforward comparison of two models of inflectional complexity. One is a Kolmogorov-style model, according to which a verb with a stem alternation pattern would be inflectionally more complex than a basic verb because it needs a longer description. The other is a model of complexity based on implicative relations. Under such a model, stem alternation patterns may differ in complexity weight under specific circumstances depending on how predictable they are. The second model, which is aimed to reduce the complexity of a system when implicative relations are found, involves a series of notebooks of information on which to base the implicative relations. I have proposed that the descriptions involved in the making of such notebooks is a type of information that should also be stored somewhere in the system, but probably at a less costly price.

Acknowledgements

This paper was written under the auspices of the 2105–17 CNRS research project *PICS* 'Mesoamerica and the syntax of the relative clause'. I want to thank Matthew Baerman, Oliver Bond and Andrew Hippisley for inviting me to participate in this special volume. I also want to thank the editors in their role as reviewers because their comments and constructive criticism helped enormously to improve the quality of the paper. I am very grateful to Anna Thornton for all her wise comments and suggestions.

Notes

1. The second goal is further inspired by the analyses on the verbal inflection of other Romance languages like Italian and French in terms of macro- and microclasses in Dressler and Thornton (1991) and Dressler et al. (2003).
2. This is in accordance with a model of complexity *à la* Kolmogorov, according to which a structure is less complex than another if it can be described with a shorter description.
3. A note on Spanish orthography: I render Spanish data in an orthography that is more transparent to the phonological reality of Standard Peninsular Spanish instead of in conventional orthography. I use the acute accent over a vowel to mark what syllable has the primary accent in an inflected form.
4. The forms themselves are also a case of extended exponence, because S7 is only used for the imperfect. I thank Anna Thornton for this observation.
5. Mungía Zatarain et al. (1998) include a total of 4,805 verbs. I decided, somewhat arbitrarily, to reduce the number of verbs by excluding 1,018 verbs of Class I that were obviously derived, because they all represented three specific types, i.e. verbs in /X(f)ika#/, e.g. DIVERSIFICAR 'diversify' /dibersifika/ (89); in /Xiθa#/, e.g. AROMATIZAR 'aromatize' / aromatiθa#/ (300); and /Xea#/, e.g. APALEAR 'club' /apalea#/ (629). This left us with a sample of 3,787 verbs, which I admit still includes non-basic verbs. To round it down to 3,700, I have cleansed the sample of another 87 verbs that either were defective (I pay no heed to defectiveness as a deviation in this paper) or were not part of my mental lexicon (at least at the time of cleaning the corpus . . .), i.e. *himpar* 'have hiccups' (a variant of *hipar*), *hirmar* 'set firmly', *hozar* 'for a pig to remove ground with the root', *vahar* 'give off fumes or steam' (a variant of *vahear*, itself not very frequent either), *hispir* 'bristle' (a synonym of *erizarse*, *esponjarse*), etc. I strongly believe that it will be the same for most readers. After rounding down the corpus to 3,700 verbs, I have to exclude the verbs IR 'go' and SER 'be' from this analysis, because they are very irregular. The sample thus consists of 3,698 verbs.
6. I have decided to leave them out of the analysis, because they stand out and by themselves

from all other verbs. All in all, besides a stem which could be treated as their basic one (i.e. the one used for the infinitive, imperative, future and conditional), these verbs could be said to have a variety of stem alternation patterns (P2, P3 and P4, treated in §10.3). Such patterns would account for at least three of their different stems. The verbs have one stem for the gerund; one for the present indicative; and another one for the imperfect indicative. In addition, IR 'go' has a suppletive stem for the imperative singular, while SER 'be' has two more extra stems: one for the 2SG and another for the 3SG of the present indicative. In total, SER 'be' has nine different stems, while IR 'go' has eight.

7. I use the term 'inflectional stem' for a stem that replaces the lexical base stem in specific portions or cells in the paradigm, regardless of whether the portion they occur in results in a motivated or a non-motivated split (i.e. morphomic) (Corbett 2015). In the regular case, an inflectional stem is derived from the lexical stem by a specific set of phonological rules; in other cases, it is listed.
8. For a more specialised account of stress, see Harris (1987).
9. The notation CVCΣV represents an idealisation of a stem shape, where ΣV corresponds to the thematic vowel and V to the root vowel. 'Aff' indicates suffixed material that is specified for stress; (...) refers to any phonological material inert to stress rules.
10. The two cells are also given the same realisation by means of a bare stem in many of the subparadigms.
11. Alternatively, Harris (1987) treats the difference of exponence as involving -e vs -i with a similar result. In my proposal, the distribution of the allomorphy is predicted from the phonological shape of the stem in question (i.e. the final /i/ of the special stem of classes /Xe#/ and /Xi#/ triggers zero, while the final /a/ of verbs of class /Xa#/ triggers the selection of -e).
12. Anna Thornton has called my attention to the loanword *kiwi* /kígwi/ as an exception to this rule. Another exception would be the loanword *mini* /míni/ designating a BMC economy car.
13. In contrast, apart from monosyllables such as *si* 'if', *sí* 'yes' or *ni* 'nor', which are out of the equation for being monosyllables, there is a sizable number of words in Spanish with stressed /i/ in coda, such as *alhelí* 'wallflower', *frenesí* 'frenzy', *jabalí* 'boar', etc. or adjectives such as *magrebí* 'Maghrebi', *israelí* 'Israeli', etc.
14. The same applies to the form for the 2SG imperative, which is homophonous to the 3SG present indicative.
15. Other deviations involve only one cell. The cells in questions may involve the form for the first person indicative present, the past participle and the imperative. Two verbs require a suppletive stem for the 1SG present indicative, i.e. SABER 'know' has *se* instead of *sépo */sép(a)-o/, which would be the expected form from P3; and HABER 'AUX' has *he* (instead of *hay-o). The latter verb also has *he-mos* for 1PL, instead of the expected *habe-mos. The form *habemos* exists in Latin American Spanish as an inflected form of the verb HABER but in its restricted use as an existential verb, like in *habemos muchos de nosotros que*... 'There are many of us who ...' (the paraphrase for such an expression in Peninsular Spanish would need an impersonal form, i.e. *hay muchos de nosotros que* ...). Verbs with a monosyllabic form for the 1SG present indicative have the exponent /-oj/ <oy> istead of /-o/; for example, DAR 'give' with basic stem /da#/ would have the form **d(a)-o*→*do, but instead we have *dói* <doy>. The alternant /-oj/ is provided by the morphology, but its distribution is phonologically conditioned. Furthermore, 30 verbs of Class II have a suppletive stem for the past participle (e.g. PONER 'put', PST.PTCP *ponido→*puesto*; MORIR 'die', PST.PTCP *morido→*muerto*); and 45 verbs of Class II have a shortened form for the imperative singular (e.g. PONER 'put', IMP *pone→*pon*). The verbs DECIR 'say' and IR 'go' have the suppletive forms *di* and *ve*.

16. In a more recent typology of morphemes in Round (2015), the structures would qualify as 'metamorphomes'.
17. These stem classes can already be seen at work in Class II. In the previous section, we have seen that verbs of Class II show a slightly different behaviour depending on what the shape of their lexical stem is. In other words, while the inflectional behaviour of all such verbs could be treated in a unified way as forming one inflectional class, verbs whose lexical stems end in /i#/ have different surface outcomes than those whose lexical stems end in /e#/.
18. In reality, the split into stem classes only really makes sense for verbs of Class II, because all verbs of Class I belong to stem class /a#/ and vice versa.
19. The sample is representative of the Spanish lexicon because the vast majority of existing verbs belonging to classes /e#/ and /i#/ are included in the sample.
20. However, the alternating stem with a mutated root in /je/ and /we/ is very informative as a cue for P1. There are only a few verbs that carry a root in /je/ and /we/ in their basic stem, and none belong to stem classes /e#/ or /i#/. This means that encountering these diphthongs in inflected forms of verbs of these stem classes indicates that the verb in question has P1.
21. Areas of the paradigm that remain untouched by P2 are the imperfective indicative, the future, the conditional, plus the past participle and the infinitive.
22. This can be taken as evidence that the gerund forms a stem zone by itself. Further evidence for this comes from the fact that irregular verbs SER 'be' and IR 'go' have an irregular gerund that is based on P1.A (*sie-ndo* and *ye-ndo*).
23. See Esher (2013, 2015) for the morphomic behaviour of this pattern in Occitan.
24. I do not use here the formal model proposed in Brown and Hippisley (2012).
25. The method is internal to Spanish and is not intended to provide comparable measures of complexity across different systems.
26. I adopt here a view on morphological complexity that is based on Baerman et al. (2009, 2015), where morphological complexity is seen as a relational concept involving the amounts of morphological information speakers need to deal with in order to be able to inflect a given lexeme.
27. My focus is on morphological complexity. I leave other processes out of the equation such as those that could be seen as operating at a more superficial level by virtue of phonological adjustments. One such adjustment operates in the future, where /Xn'rVX/ is phonotactically adjusted to /Xnd'rVX/, i.e. VENIR 'come' 1SG.FUT /bendɾé/ *vendré* instead of /benɾé/. A more complex adjustment affects forms of verbs of stem class /i#/ with a stem shape in /Xui#/, such as CONSTRUIR 'build' /konstrui#/. The adjustments involve the palatalisation of /i/ in contact with vocalic suffixes as a result of resyllabification: /úa/ and /úe/ are rendered as [úja] and [úje], (a); /úio/ as [újo], (b); /uió/ and /uié/ become [ujó] and [ujé], (c); and /uái/ develops an excrescent [j] in [ujái], (d). Similarly impossible diphthongs such as /aé/ and /oé/ are broken as [ajé] and [ojé], as shown in (e) with the verbs TRAER 'bring' and ROER 'gnaw'.

a.	1SG.PRS.SUB	*konstrúa		→ konstrúja	*construya*
	2SG.PRS.IND	*konstrúis	→ *konstrúes	→ konstrújes	*construyes*
b.	1SG.PRS.IND	*konstrúio		→ konstrújo	*construyo*
c.	3SG.PST.IND	*konstruió		→ konstrujó	*construyo*
	1SG.IMPF.SUB	*konstruiéra		→ konstrujéra	*construyera*
d.	2PL.PRS.SUB	*konstruáis		→ konstrujáis	*construyais*
e.	GER	*traéndo		→ trajéndo	*trayendo*
		*roéndo		→ rojéndo	*royendo*

28. The new descriptions in the default notebook still have to be stored somewhere, probably in the space where all morphophonological interface phenomena are stored, where they would burden that space with further complexity.

References

Ackerman, Farrell, James P. Blevins and Robert Malouf (2009), 'Parts and wholes: Implicative patterns in inflectional paradigms', in James P. Blevins and Juliette Blevins (eds), *Analogy in Grammar*, Oxford: Oxford University Press, pp. 54–82.

Ackerman, Farrell and Robert Malouf (2013), 'Morphological organization: The low conditional entropy conjecture', *Language*, 89, pp. 429–64.

Alcoba, Santiago (1999), 'La flexión verbal', in Ignacio Bosque and Violeta Demonte (eds), *Gramática Descriptiva de la Lengua Española*, Madrid: Espasa Calpe, pp. 4915–92.

Aronoff, Mark (1994), *Morphology by Itself*, Cambridge, MA: MIT Press.

Baerman, Matthew, Dunstan Brown and Greville G. Corbett (2009), 'Morphological complexity: A typological perspective', paper read at the conference 'How Do We Cite Words in Action: Interdisciplinary Approaches to Understanding Word Processing and Storage', Pisa, 11–14 October.

Baerman, Matthew, Dunstan Brown and Greville G. Corbett (eds) (2015), *Understanding and Measuring Morphological Complexity*, Oxford: Oxford University Press.

Bermúdez-Otero, Ricardo and Ana R. Luís (2016), 'A view of the morphome debate', in Ana R. Luís and Ricardo Bermúdez-Otero (eds), *The Morphome Debate*, Oxford: Oxford University Press, pp. 309–40.

Bonami, Olivier and Sacha Beniamine (2016), 'Joint predictiveness in inflectional paradigms', *Word Structure*, 9 (2), pp. 156–82.

Bonami, Olivier and Gilles Boyé (2002), 'Suppletion and dependency in inflectional morphology', in F. Van Eynde, L. Hellan and D. Beerman (eds), *Proceedings of the HPSG '01 Conference*, Stanford, CA: CSLI Publications, pp. 51–70.

Bonami, Olivier and Gilles Boyé (2003), 'Supplétion et classes flexionnelles dans la conjugaison du français', *Langages*, 152, pp. 102–26.

Boyé, Gilles and Patricia Cabredo (2006), 'The structure of allomorphy in Spanish verbal inflection', *Cuadernos de Lingüística del Instituto Universitario Ortega y Gasset*, 13, pp. 9–24.

Brown, Dunstan and Andrew Hippisley (2012), *Network Morphology: A Defaults-Based Theory of Word Structure*, Cambridge Studies in Linguistics, 133, Cambridge: Cambridge University Press.

Corbett, Greville G. (2015), 'Morphosyntactic complexity: A typology of lexical splits', *Language*, 91 (1), pp. 145–94.

Dressler, Wolfgang U., Marianne Kilani-Schoch, Rossella Spina and Anna M. Thornton (2003), 'Le classi di coniugazione in italiano e francese', in Mathée Giacomo-Marcellesi and Alvaro Rocchetti (eds), *Il verbo italiano. Studi diacronici, sincronici, contrastivi, didattici. Atti del XXXV Congresso della Società di Linguistica Italiana, Parigi, 20–22 settembre 2002*, Rome: Bulzoni, pp. 397–416.

Dressler, Wolfgang U. and Anna M. Thornton (1991), 'Doppie basi e binarismo nella morfologia italiana', *Rivista di Linguistica*, 3 (1), pp. 3–22.

Esher, Louise (2013), 'Future and conditional in Occitan: A non-canonical morpheme', in Silvio Cruschina, Martin Maiden and John Charles Smith (eds), *The Boundaries of Pure Morphology: Diachronic and Synchronic Perspectives*, Oxford: Oxford University Press, pp. 95–115.

Esher, Louise (2015), 'Formal asymmetries between the Romance synthetic future and conditional in the Occitan varieties of the Western Languedoc', *Transactions of the Philological Society*, 113 (2), pp. 249–70.

Estrada Arráez, Ana (2012), 'The loss of intervocalic and final /d/ in the Iberian Peninsula', special issue of *Dialectologia*, 3, pp. 7–22.

Harris, James W. (1987), 'The accentual patterns of verb paradigms in Spanish', *Natural Language and Linguistic Theory*, 5, pp. 61–90.

Maiden, Martin (1992), 'Irregularity as a determinant of morphological change', *Journal of Linguistics*, 28, pp. 285–312.

Maiden, Martin (2005), 'Morphological autonomy and diachrony', in Geert Booij and Jaap van Marle (eds), *Yearbook of Morphology 2004*, Dordrecht: Springer, pp. 137–75.

Maiden, Martin (2009), 'From pure phonology to pure morphology in the reshaping of Romance verbs', *Recherches linguistiques de Vincennes*, 38, pp. 45–82.

Maiden, Martin (2016), 'Morphomes', in Adam Ledgeway and Martin Maiden (eds), *The Oxford Guide to the Romance Languages*, Oxford: Oxford University Press, pp. 708–21.

Montermini, Fabio and Olivier Bonami (2013), 'Stem spaces and predictability in verbal inflection', *Lingue e linguaggio*, 12 (2), pp. 171–90.

Mungía Zatarain, Irma, Martha E. Mungía Zatarain and Gilda Rocha Romero (1998), *Larousse de la conjugación*, Mexico City: Larousse.

Nevins, Andrew, Cilene Rodrigues and Kevin Tang (2015), 'The rise and fall of the L-shaped morphome: Diachronic and experimental studies', *Probus*, 27 (1), pp. 101–55.

O'Neill, Paul (2014), 'Similar and differing patterns on allomorphy in the Spanish and Portuguese verbs', in Patrícia Amaral and Ana Maria Carvalho (eds), *Portuguese–Spanish Interfaces: Diachrony, Synchrony, and Contact*, Amsterdam: John Benjamins, pp. 175–202.

Round, Eric (2015), 'Rhizomorphomes, meromorphomes and metamorphomes', in Matthew Baerman, Dunstan Brown and Greville G. Corbett (eds), *Understanding and Measuring Morphological Complexity*, Oxford: Oxford University Press, pp. 29–52.

Sims, Andrea D. (2010), 'Probabilistic paradigmatics: Principal parts, predictability and (other) possible particular pieces of the puzzle', paper read at the Fourteenth International Morphology Meeting, Budapest.

Spencer, Andrew (2016), *Lexical Relatedness: A Paradigm-Based Model*, Oxford: Oxford University Press.

Stump, Gregory T. (2016), *Inflectional Paradigms: Content and Form at the Syntax–Morphology Interface*, Cambridge: Cambridge University Press.

Thornton, Anna M. (2011a), 'Overabundance (multiple forms realizing the same cell): A non-canonical phenomenon in Italian verb morphology', in Martin Maiden, John Charles Smith, Maria Goldbach and Marc-Olivier Hinzelin (eds), *Morphological Autonomy: Perspectives from Romance Inflectional Morphology*, Oxford: Oxford University Press, pp. 358–81.

Thornton, Anna M. (2011b), 'Overabundance: A Non-canonical Phenomenon in Morphology', MS, Università degli Studi dell'Aquila.

11

Verb Root Ellipsis

Bernard Comrie and Raoul Zamponi[1]

11.1 Introduction

Linguists, on the basis of their experience with languages and the analytical tools they have constructed to systematise that experience, often have clear intuitions about particular phenomena being expected or unexpected in human language. One such intuition, a constraint on the kinds of morphemes that can appear as zero morphemes, is formulated as follows by Trommer:

> It is a common intuition that Ø-morphemes are only possible for very specific types of morphemes. They are expected to occur as affixes, but not as roots. Moreover, Ø seems more likely with functional material (whether affixal or not) than with lexical morphemes. (Trommer 2012: 353)

Trommer carefully formulates this intuition in terms of probability ('more likely to occur'), and in this paper we wish to examine one set of counterexamples to the generalisation, namely Verb Root Ellipsis.

By Verb Root Ellipsis we understand a word whose root, while usually overt, can be absent, with the same array of other morphemes in the word, under certain, usually pragmatic circumstances. The mini-dialogue in (1) illustrates the phenomenon in Inuktitut – for further details on the language and its Verb Root Ellipsis possibilities, see §11.4.1.

(1) Inuktitut (Swift and Allen 2002: 147)
    a. *Traci   qaiju*
       Traci-Ø   qai-juq
       Tracy-ABS.SG come-PAR.3SGS
       'Tracy is coming.'
    b. *Quurmat*
       Ø-qquuq-mmat

LROOT-probably-CTG.3SGS
'She probably [is coming].'

In (1a), the first speaker informs the hearer that Tracy is coming. The hearer affirms the first speaker's observation with the elliptical construction in (1b) in which the root has been elipted, as recoverable from the immediately preceding context, leaving behind only the modal postbase -*qquuq* 'probably' and a subject person-number marker.

The phenomenon is surprising, in line with Trommer's stated intuition. Indeed, to the best of our knowledge only four independent cases have been argued for in the literature, these being in addition to Inuktitut: Kwaza, Akabea (and other related Great Andamanese languages) and Jingulu, to which we return in §11.4.4.

Our aim in this paper is to provide cogent evidence in favour of the phenomenon of Verb Root Ellipsis, however rare it may be cross-linguistically, and to extract what generalisations we can about the cross-linguistic behaviour of the phenomenon, though noting that our account can only be preliminary given the few languages known or believed to show the phenomenon.

More specifically, the paper is organised as follows. In §11.2, we discuss the formally related phenomenon of zero verb roots (including zero allomorphs of verb roots), noting carefully how the two phenomena are to be distinguished from one another in addition to pointing out similarities, since both go against the intuition formulated by Trommer. In §11.3, we examine a functional parallel found in many languages that does not, however, involve ellipsis of the root of a verb, but rather of the whole verb word, and thus does not go against Trommer's intuition; again, both similarities to and differences from Verb Root Ellipsis are noted. §11.4 is the core of the paper, presenting and analysing Verb Root Ellipsis in each of the four independent cases, concluding that Inuktitut, Kwaza and Akabea present clear cases, while Jingulu may be open to alternative analyses. §11.5 looks at possible problems posed by Verb Root Ellipsis for constraints on phonological words in the languages in which the phenomenon has been identified, while §11.6 notes comparisons, both functional-semantic and formal, between Verb Root Ellipsis and other phenomena, noting both similarities and differences, with a subsection devoted to ellipsis of affixes in the same set of languages. Finally, §11.7 draws conclusions.

11.2 Zero Verb Roots and Zero Allomorphs of Verb Roots

Another type of grammatical word that contains no root and occurs only with affixes can be observed in some, though not many, languages in which root ellipsis is not permitted. In these languages, one or more lexical meanings, rather than being expressed by a phonologically overt root, are indicated by a root that has no phonological expression. One such language is Bardi, a member of the Nyulnyulan family of northern Australia. The meaning expressed here by a phonologically null, or zero, root is 'give' (Bowern 2012: 549).

(2) Bardi (Bowern 2012: 579)
anyngarr   nga-Ø-na   goorlil   bardi   rooban   ginyinggi
in.vain   1S-give-REMPST   turtle   yesterday   in_return   3MIN
goorlil-nyarr   arra   oo-la-Ø-na=ngay
turtle-COM   NEG   3S-IRR-give-REMPST=1.MO
'I gave her turtle meat yesterday although she didn't give me any when she had turtle.'

Cross-linguistically, grammatical words with a zero lexical root are for the most part verbs, although the existence of zero-root pronouns (see Mel'čuk 2006: 472–3) and nouns (see Bloomfield 1939: 108 as regards Menomini) is also reported in the linguistic literature. Specifically, as in Bardi, in some languages, a verb may have no overt root in all its paradigmatic forms and be phonologically realised only by verb affixation. The empty root usually gets its necessary indexical support from its overtly expressed dependents and/or derivational affixes contained in the verb. In other languages, a verb may have a root that is overtly expressed in specific forms and is phonologically null in the rest of its paradigm, i.e. a root with a zero allomorph. This is the case, for example, in Siroi, a non-Austronesian language of the Rai Coast of Papua New Guinea (Nuclear Trans New Guinea family). In Siroi, when the verb 'give' is used with a singular recipient, it has an overt root. With a non-singular recipient, the verb has a zero root (Wells 1979: 34).

(3) Siroi (Wells 1979: 123)
    a. ... ye ne   ndametiŋ   ti-n-i
           I you   money   give-2SGO-1SGS.POT
       'I will give you the money.' (Wells 1979: 128)
    b. ... 5 dola   5 dola   Ø-sing-na
           5 dollar   5 dollar   give-1PLO-3SGS.PST
       'He paid (lit. "gave") us each five dollars.'

Nimboran is a language that has several verbs with a root that always has a zero realisation. There are somewhere between 10 and 20 such verbs in this non-Austronesian language of West Papua (Nimboranic family). Among the many positions that characterise the verb morphology in Nimboran, there is one position reserved for what Inkelas (1993: 574) calls 'particles'. And it is these 'particles', lacking a clear inherent meaning, that carry the burden of distinguishing among these zero root verbs in various cases (see Table 11.1).

As seen in Table 11.1, the zero root-'particle' pair (Ø-, -rár-) 'bring' occurs only when the action of the verb is directional, while the pair (Ø-, -tár-) 'make cat's cradles' occurs only when the action is non-directional. These semantic restrictions are of exactly the same type that characterise overt roots (see Table 11.2), and never apply to 'particles' directly.

Other verbs with a phonologically empty root in Nimboran are motion verbs that imply a voluntary movement on foot by the subject and existential verbs. In zero-root

Table 11.1 Some verbs with zero roots in Nimboran (based on Inkelas 1993: 611)[a]

Root	Particle	Gloss	Restrictions
Ø-	-ta[+A]-*[b]	'be present'	S = SG.3N; –iter
Ø-	-rár-	'bring'	+dir
Ø-	-rár-	'dream (of)'	–dir
Ø-	-tam[+A]-*	'kiss'	S = SG
Ø-	-rá-	'laugh'	+iter
Ø-	-tár-*	'make cat's cradles'	–dir
Ø-	[+A]	'say to'	S = PL; +iter

[a] [+A] stands for apophony.
[b] The asterisk indicates additional positional constraints.

Table 11.2 Two verbs with overt roots in Nimboran (based on Inkelas 1993: 612)

Root	Particle	Gloss	Restrictions
bekéi-	-dár-	'rise'	–dir
kéŋ-	-tár-	'dream (of)'	+dir

motion verbs there is a directional suffix that implies movement, so that even without an overt root the motion is fully specified (May 1997: 105–6).

(4) Nimboran (May 1997: 106)
Ø-ke-ban-t-e
move_on_foot-DUS-BELOW_TO_HERE-PRS-2S
'You came up here (just now).'

Zero-root existential verbs include a prefix, in initial position, chosen according to the kind of entity which is subject of the verb (May 1997: 107–8).

(5) Nimboran (May 1997: 109)
imeno ndie ho kasнem
imeno ndie ho ka-Ø-sa-um
Imeno there at PLACE-exist-OVER_THERE-3.nmS
'Imeno (a village) is over there.'

In various non-Austronesian languages spoken on the Huon Peninsula of Papua New Guinea (Nuclear Trans New Guinea family), one or more of the verb subclasses contain a verb root morpheme represented by zero and are distinguished from one another by the allomorphs of the object-marking suffixes (McElhanon 1973: 43). In Selepet, for example, the zero roots mean 'see' with subclass I object-marking allomorphs (6b), 'give' or 'bite' with subclass II object-marking allomorphs (7b) and 'hit, kill' with subclass III object-marking allomorphs (8b) (McElhanon 1972: 39).

(6) Selepet (McElhanon 1973: 43)
    a. gâi-nek-sap
       cut-1sGO-3sGS.IMMPST
       'He cut me.'
    b. Ø-nek-sap
       see-1sGO-3sGS.IMMPST
       'He saw me.'

(7) a. mabot-nihi-ap
       await-1sGO-3sGS.IMMPST
       'He awaited me.'
    b. Ø-nihi-ap
       give/bite-1sGO-3sGS.IMMPST
       'He gave it to me; it bit me.'

(8) a. tân-noho-ap
       help-1sGO-3sGS.IMMPST
       'He helped me.'
    b. Ø-noho-ap
       hit-1sGO-3sGS.IMMPST
       'He hit me.'

Yet another language with different zero-root verbs is Pawnee, a Caddoan language of Oklahoma. Specifically, Pawnee has a small number of (discontinuous) verb stems based on the combination of a preverb with a non-overt root: *-ut-...Ø* 'to be (in a condition)' or *-ir-...Ø* 'to be one's'. The preverb (*ut-* or *ir-*) in these stems behaves as in descriptive verbs in that in non-subordinate forms with singular or dual subjects the vowel of the preverb reduplicates as in verbs with overt roots. If a subject plural prefix follows the preverb, its vowel reduplicates following the same rule (Parks and Pratt 2008: 53).

Other languages, as far as we know, have just a single verb with a root that has a zero realisation. This verb, in various languages of New Guinea, is the verb 'give'. The languages in question belong to different branches and sub-branches of the Nuclear Trans New Guinea family, but the vast majority of them are spoken in a defined area facing Astrolabe Bay (Madang Province of Papua New Guinea).

MADANG
  CROISILLES
    MABUSO
      GUM: Amele (Roberts 1987: 313, 316, 390), Sihan, Gumalu, Isebe, Bau and Panim (Z'graggen 1980a: 130)[2]
      KOKON: Girawa (Z'graggen 1980a: 130)
  RAI COAST
    KABENAU: Arawum and Lemio (Z'graggen 1980b: 130)

NURU: Erima (Ogea) (Z'graggen 1980b: 130)
KAINANTU-GOROKA
  KAINANTU
    GAUWA
      AWA-OWEINA: Awa (Loving and McKaughan 1973: 45)

As these languages require indexing of person and number of the recipient, the recipient marker could be regarded as a surrogate root to which the other bound forms are attached.[3]

(9)   Amele (Roberts 1987: 316)
    ija   dana   leis   sab   Ø-al-ig-a
    I   man   two   food give-3R-1S-TODPST
    'I gave the two men food.'

(10) Awa (Loving and McKaughan 1973: 45)
    wegàh néne póédáhq món   aní   Ø-aw-í-d-e
    he   my   pig   another child give-3SGR-NEARPST-3SGS-AUG[4]
    'He gave my pig to another person.'

The verbal content 'give' is also expressed by a zero root in Bardi, as we saw above in §11.1, as well as in the closely related Yawuru (Hosokawa 1991: 165) and in Koasati (Kimball 1991: 102), a language of the Muskogean family spoken in Louisiana and Texas. In the Bardi example in (2) and in the following examples from Yawuru and Koasati in (11) and (12), the verb 'give' exhibits a recipient marker and other bound morphemes, but no root material, exactly like the verb forms in (9) and (10).

(11) Yawuru (Hosokawa 1991: 320)
    yangki-ni i-na-Ø-nda-ngayu   wanangarri
    who-ERG   3S-TR-give-PFV-1O money(ABS)
    'Who gave me the money.'

(12) Koasati (Kimball 1991: 199)
    tabakcampó:lin ą́hískamá:łon í:palǫ
    tabáhk-campó:li-n   ám-Ø-híska-má:l-on   í:pa-l-o-Y
    bread-sweet-ACC   1O-give-2SGS-MODAL-SW.FOC eat-1SGS-be-PTM
    'Were you to give me some cake, I'd eat it.'

In Chamorro, the Austronesian language indigenous to Guam and the Northern Mariana Islands (Micronesia), although the verb *na'i* 'give' must be recognised as a word in its own right, it can be decomposed etymologically into a sequence of two affixes: a causative prefix *na'-* and a suffix *-i*, the latter described as a referential focus marker or as the marker of 3–2 advancement (Newman 1996: 19).

This indicates that the cross-linguistic occurrence of 'give' zero verb roots, though limited quantitatively, is not so geographically.

Also in Gahuku (or Alekano), a Nuclear Trans New Guinea language of the Eastern Highlands of Papua New Guinea, there is a single verb with a phonologically null root. This verb expresses existence of human entities and is used also with certain adjuncts in constructions, like (13), which often have an idiomatic meaning (Deibler 1976: 15, 36, 38).

(13) Gahuku (Deibler 1976: 38)
mohona no-Ø-ive
stroll PROG-be-3SGS
'He is strolling around.'

The rootless verb of Bukiyip, a language of the Nuclear Torricelli family of the East Sepik Province of Papua New Guinea, covers the 'hit/kill' range (Conrad and Wogiga 1991: 16, 27).

(14) Bukiyip (Conrad and Wogiga 1991: 18)
nabotik ch-a-Ø-nú n-a-gak
yesterday 3PL.MIXS-R-hit-3SG.MO 3SG.MS-R-die
'Yesterday they hit him, and he died.'

In Anêm, an isolate of West New Britain Province in Papua New Guinea, it is the root of the verb 'eat' that has no phonological realisation (Thurston 1982: 48; 1987: 57).

(15) Anêm (Thurston 1982: 48)
eni de-Ø-nis
devil 3SG.FS-eat-1PLO
'The devil will eat us.'

In Menomini, a moribund language of the Algonquian branch of the Algic family originally spoken in northern Wisconsin and Michigan, there is no surface manifestation of the root of the verb 'use' (Bloomfield 1962: 62–63, 72).

In addition, we are aware of one Indo-European language of Europe where there is a verb with a stem that, segmentally, shows nothing that could be called a root, namely Russian. The zero-root verb is *vynut'* 'take out (PFV)', composed of a prefix *vy-* 'out', a perfective suffix *-nu* and an infinitive suffix *-t'*. A zero-root verb with a modal function is historically present also in Japanese: *e-ru*, i.e. *Ø-e-ru* 'get, be able to', which is formally the potential mood of the now lost basic verb *Ø-u* 'get'. This last belongs to a small group of verbs whose other members have a monoconsonantal root (the others being *k- 'come', *s- 'do' and *p- 'pass'). Unless the vowel anlaut is assumed to represent a hidden consonant segment (a glottal?), the verb *Ø-u* has to be analysed as having a zero root (Janhunen 2010: 178).[5]

We indicated above that a verb may have a root that is phonologically empty in certain contexts and full in others. Perhaps it is not surprising that in other languages of the Astrolabe Bay area in Papua New Guinea (all in the Rai Coast subdivision of the Madang branch of the Nuclear Trans New Guinea family), the verb root that exhibits this kind of suppletion is the verb 'give'. In all these languages, suppletion depends on the person and/or number of the recipient.[6]

> KABENAU: Siroi *s-* (to 1SG), *ti-* ~ *ta-* (to 2SG), *t-* (to 3SG), *Ø-* (to DUAL/PL) (Wells 1979: 34)
> MINDJIM: Bongu *u-* (to 3), *Ø-* (to 1/2) (Z'graggen 1980b: 130)
> NURU: Rerau *si-* (to 1SG/2SG), *ti-* (to 3SG), *Ø-* (to PL); Yangulam *s-* (to 1SG), *t-* (to 2SG), *to-* (to 3SG), *Ø-* (to PL) (Z'graggen 1980b: 130)
> PEKA: Danaru *is-* (to 1SG), *ta-* (to 2SG/3SG), *Ø-* (to PL) (Z'graggen 1980b: 130)
> YAGANON: Yabong *n-* (to SG), *Ø-* (to PL) (Z'graggen 1980b: 130)

Also in Warrwa, a sister language of Yawuru and Bardi, the verb root 'give' has both a zero alternant and an overt partner (*-wa*), according to McGregor (1994: 49) (who does not provide further details concerning this alternation).

In other languages, the verb whose root has a phonologically empty allomorph is the copula 'be'. In Wai Wai, a Cariban language spoken in Guyana and northern Brazil, the zero allomorph of the copula root (the root with most allomorphic variation) occurs in the presence of a stem formative suffix *-a* when there is an overt personal prefix (Hawkins 1998: 167–8).

(16) Wai Wai (Hawkins 1998: 168)
    w-Ø-a-s   1S-be-SF-INP   'I am/will be'
    n-Ø-a-y   3S-be-SF-UNP   'he is/will be'
    Ø-x-a-kñe   3S-be-SF-UP   'he was'

In Kulina, an Arawan language of Brazil and Peru, there is a zero-root alternant of the copula root when it is used with negation and there is no overt personal prefix (Dienst 2014: 233).

(17) Kulina (Dienst 2014: 233)
    a. hada-ni   o-ha-ni
        old-F   1SGS-COP-F
        'I (F) am old.' (Dienst 2014: 81)
    b. zodo   bami   Ø-Ø-hara-i
        opossum   game   3S-COP-NEG.M-DEC.M
        'Opossums aren't game.'

In the (Western) Itelmen language of the Kamchatka Peninsula (Siberia, Chukotko-Kamchatkan family), the root of the verb 'be' (*ł-* in the infinitive form *ł-ka-s*) has a zero form in all the six present indicative forms marked by suffixes (including *-s-* ~ *-sə-*, which expresses present tense) and partly also prefixes (see Table 11.3).

In Basque, the verb *izan* 'be' (which also functions as an intransitive auxiliary) has a zero root in the third person singular present indicative form and in the second person singular formal, third person singular and first person plural past indicative forms (see Table 11.4).

Table 11.3 The verb 'be' in Itelmen (Holst 2014: 39)

	SG	PL
1	t-Ø-s-kiçen	n-Ø-s-kiçen
2	Ø-sə-ç	Ø-sə-sx
3	Ø-sə-n	Ø-sə-'n

Table 11.4 The verb 'be' in Basque (Saltarelli 1988: 302)

	PRS	PST
1SG	n-a-iz	n-in-tz-en
2SG (INFORMAL)	h-a-iz	h-in-tz-en
2SG (FORMAL)	z-a-ra	z-in-Ø-en
3SG	d-a-Ø	z-Ø-Ø-en
1PL	g-a-ra	g-in-Ø-en
2PL	z-a-re-te	z-in-e-te-n
3PL	d-i-ra	z-i-r-en

In yet other languages, the verb root with a zero alternant is that of a motion verb. In Madi (Jarawara dialect), a sister language of Kulina spoken in Brazil, the root 'be in motion' has a null realisation when it is preceded by a personal prefix and is followed by a suffix -*ke* ~ -*ki* 'COMING'.

(18) Madi (Dixon 2009: 127)
  a. bati   ka-ke
     father be_in_motion-COMING
     'Father is coming.'
  b. o-Ø-ke
     1SGS-be_in_motion-COMING
     'I am coming.'

In Udi, a Nakh-Daghestanian language spoken in Azerbaijan, Russia and Georgia, the root that expresses an inherently directed motion, associated to locative preverbs to produce meanings such as 'come', 'go', 'go up' and 'go down', is zero in the present tense (Harris 2008: 220). In the isolate Burushaski of northern Pakistan, two verbs have a root with a zero alternant: 'come' and 'go'. In the converbal paradigm, these two verbs are distinguished only by different prefixes *d*- (a derivational prefix with an opaque meaning) for 'come' and *n*- (a primarily converbal prefix) for 'go', as in *d-áa-Ø-n* 'I having come' and *n-áa-Ø-n* 'I having gone' (Tikkanen 1999: 297).

In Kâte, a Nuclear Trans New Guinea language spoken on the tip of the Huon Peninsula in Papua New Guinea, the verb covering the range 'hit/kill' has a phonologically full root (*qa-*) only in the third person singular (see Table 11.5).

In the aforementioned Menomini, it is the root *ɛn-* 'say so to' that is replaced

Table 11.5 The verb 'hit/kill' in Kâte (Suter 2014: 19)

	SG	DU	PL
1	Ø-nu	Ø-nâfo	Ø-nâpo
2	Ø-gu	Ø-ŋofa	Ø-ŋopa
3	qa-Ø	Ø-jofa	Ø-jopa

Table 11.6 The French verb *avoir*

1SG	2SG	3SG	3PL		1PL	2PL
Ø-ai	Ø-as	Ø-a	Ø-ont	vs	av-ons	av-ez

by zero. This happens before the inflectional suffix -ək-: enēw 'he says so to him', ekwāh 'the other one says so to him', netēkwah 'he says so to me' (Bloomfield 1939: 108).

For the idiosyncratic forms of the verb 'have', a zero root suppletion has been assumed even for French and Italian (Hall 1983: 47; Gaeta 2009: 46; Thornton, this book); see the present indicative forms of the French verb *avoir* in Table 11.6.

In the dialect of the town of Macerata in central Italy, we may recognise a zero root in two (identical) present indicative forms of the verb 'have', but we may also observe that, when the same verb is used as an auxiliary, its root is phonologically empty in five of its six present indicative forms (see Table 11.7).

In several cases, the zero verb root or the zero alternant of a verb root results from phonological erosion of a phonologically full root morpheme and/or the assimilation of phonetic material of an overt root morpheme to adjacent sounds. The zero root 'give' of Bardi, for example, was historically *-wa-, but the glide *w* was lost through regular sound change and the vowel *a* never surfaces independently of the affixes which surround it (Bowern 2012: xliii). The zero root of the Koasati verb 'give' was originally *a, inflected by means of the auxiliary *ka*, with obligatory dative prefixes. In the language ancestral to Koasati and Alabama, the syllable canon changed so that monosyllabic verb roots were unacceptable. The auxiliary *ka fused with the root and prefixes, which then underwent syncope, and the auxiliary was reinterpreted as the classifying suffix -*ka* (Kimball 1991: 102). And if in any of the above-mentioned Itelmen forms of the verb 'be' the root *ɬ*- 'be' does not appear, this is due to its assimilation to the sibilant of the present tense suffix -*s* ~ -*sə* in present indicative

Table 11.7 Present indicative forms of the verb 'have' in the dialect of Macerata

		1SG	2SG	3SG	1PL	2PL	3PL
'have'	Main verb	[ˈaɟː-o]	[a-i]	Ø-[a]	[a-ˈimo]	[a-ˈete]	Ø-[a]
	Auxiliary	[ˈaɟː-o]	Ø-[i]	Ø-[a]	Ø-[ˈimo]	Ø-[ˈete]	Ø-[a]

forms of the copula (Holst 2014: 39). The zeroisation of the root 'come' and 'go' in Burushaski, on the other hand, may have been triggered by haplology in some forms (Janhunen 2010: 178).[7] Moreover, the zero allomorphs of the root 'have' in French and Italian are the result of phonological reduction in individual languages (and dialects) given that there is no Proto-Romance verb for whose root we need reconstruct a zero allomorph, as Hall (1983: 47) notes.

It will certainly have appeared to be evident that the roots subject to zeroisation or with a zero alternant have minimal linguistic form and are, usually, semantically light or basic – despite occasional exceptions like Nimboran 'make a cat's cradle'. The light or basic semantics of these morphemes could also have been a contributing factor in their complete phonological erosion or assimilation to adjacent sounds or, at least, it does not prevent these processes. This is particularly the case with the roots of the verbs 'give' and 'be'.

The cross-linguistic variation relating to zero roots can be viewed as the interplay between two conflicting principles. On the one hand, one expects morphemes, especially lexical root morphemes, to have overt expression, as in the quote from Trommer (2012) in §11.1. On the other hand, morphemes, even lexical root morphemes, tend to be shorter the lighter or more basic they are, with zero being simply the extreme case of shortening. The lexical root 'give', being a verb that profiles a transfer of a thing from agent to recipient without any further modification, has been claimed to be devoid of any semantics of its own, in that it merely 'lexicalizes the basic three-participant event, understood as a relation that involves an agent, a theme and a recipient' (Kittilä 2006: 600). Most languages nonetheless have an overt lexical root, following the first principle outlined in this paragraph. Exceptions to this, as in various languages of New Guinea, Yawuru and Bardi in Australia and Koasati in North America, might reflect the second principle, with conceptual basicness corresponding to a more basic kind of linguistic form (Newman 2002: 79).[8]

The copula 'be' is a verb that completely lacks referential meaning, but instead indicates a semantic relation between its two core arguments, subject and complement, and, often, performs the role of the carrier of a number of grammatical categories which have to be marked in the clause. Although in some languages (like Wai Wai, Kulina, Itelmen and Basque) the copula root has a zero alternant in certain forms, it must be kept in mind that in no language, as far as we are aware, is the copula root phonologically empty in every circumstance.[9]

Another factor that may be evoked to explain the presence of zero roots or of roots with zero allomorphs in verbs like 'give', 'hit', 'come', 'go' and 'be' is the recoverability of such roots based on the combined semantics of the categories with which they occur. When a human agent combines with a non-human patient and a human recipient, the most typical action is the transference of a thing from the control of one person to the control of another. When a human agent combines with an animate patient, the most typical action is probably hitting. When a human subject combines with a destination or provenance, the most typical action is motion-related. The copula is not in itself a requirement to establish a predication relation. In various languages, it is omitted whenever the nature of the semantic relation can be inferred from the referents of subject and complement (Dixon 2010: 180), while in some other languages (e.g. Cavineña), as we will see in §11.3, it is normally ellipted whenever the information encoded by its inflectional affixes is held to be not essential.

Limiting ourselves to the motion verbs with a zero root or with a root that is zero in certain contexts, we saw that in three languages (Nimboran, Madi and Udi) such verbs contain an affix that implies motion or specifies a directed motion which, per se, would be sufficient to fully describe a motion-related action.

11.3 Verb Ellipsis

Although verbs are, in a sense, the backbone of a verbal clause, since they determine what other elements can and must occur with them and impose restrictions on the semantic nature of their co-occurring elements, in very many languages there are specific configurations that permit their ellipsis.

A useful, though not entirely unproblematic, distinction concerning the phenomenon of ellipsis in general is made between intersentential and intrasentential contexts. Where the recoverable material that supports an ellipsis is to be found outside the sentence, the notion of intersentential ellipsis applies. Where the recoverable material that supports an ellipsis is to be found inside the sentence (whether or not across a clause boundary), the notion of intrasentential (or syntactic) ellipsis applies. With specific reference to verbs, three basic configurations that permit intrasentential ellipsis can be recognised: (i) interclausal parallelism (including gapping and stripping),[10] (ii) a lexical licenser (sluicing and verb phrase ellipsis),[11] and (iii) a combination of lexical categories in what McShane (2005: 154) calls 'Multilicensor Verbal Ellipsis'. In the last case, it is the combined semantics of the overt categories that both licenses the ellipsis and, sometimes with the help of the context, ensures recoverability of verb meaning.

In this short section, we will briefly pause to discuss the Multilicensor Verbal Ellipsis strategy of intersentential verb ellipsis, in search of possible analogues to the phenomenon of Verb Root Ellipsis, which, as we will see in §11.4, may be restricted to the presence of specific lexical categories within a single sentence. Our attention will focus on the semantics of the verbs involved in Multilicensor Verbal Ellipsis rather than on the syntactic structures in which Multilicensor Verbal Ellipsis is used and its licensers.

One salient aspect of Multilicensor Verbal Ellipsis is that often a whole semantic class of verbs is implied rather than one specific meaning associated with one specific verb. McShane observes that

> for example, when a verb of motion is elided, the motion might be on foot or in a vehicle, fast or slow; when a verb of speaking is elided, the speech might be storytelling, asking, lecturing, or blathering on; and when a verb of hitting is elided, the hitting might be punching, smacking, or walloping with a frying pan. (McShane 2005: 154)

Of the semantic classes of verbs that can be elided using the Multilicensor Verbal Ellipsis licensing strategy, verbs that express motion, speaking and hitting (illustrated by examples (19a–c), also showing the licensers involved) are privileged in Russian, at least in terms of frequency of use.

(19) Russian (McShane 2005: 158)
    a. Motion: MOVER + MOTION-GOAL
        Ja   v   kino
        I.NOM to movies.ACC
        'I [am going] to (or: I [am off] to, I [am heading] to) the movies.'
    b. Speech: SPEECH-CONTENT + SPEAKER
        O   čëm   on?
        about what he.NOM
        'What [is] he [talking] (or: [asking], [yelling] and so forth) about?'
    c. Hitting: HITTER + PATIENT + ADVERB$_{MANNER}$
        Ja   emu   ne   sil'no
        I.NOM he.DAT NEG hard
        'I [did] not [hit] (or: [punch], [smack] and so forth) him hard.'

In Polish and Czech, the most productive use of Multilicensor Verbal Ellipsis is for elided verbs of hitting.

(20) Polish (McShane 2005: 173)
    Hitting: HITTER + PATIENT + INSTRUMENT/SITE
    On   mnie z   byka, a   ja   go   w   szczękę
    he.NOM I.ACC with head[12] and I.NOM he.ACC in jaw.ACC
    'He [butted] me with his head and I [belted] him in the jaw.' (McShane 2005: 174)

(21) Czech (McShane 2005: 173)
    Hitting: HITTER + PATIENT + INSTRUMENT + SITE
    A   já   mu   pěstí   do   buku
    and I.NOM he.DAT fist.INS into side.GEN
    'And I [jammed] my fist into his side.' (McShane 2005: 173)

There are, however, also fixed patterns that convey a meaning straddling 'speak' and 'react' in the two languages.

(22) Polish (McShane 2005: 174–5)
    Speech: SPEAKER + SPEECH-CONTENT
    Ona   stawia   czajnik: "Zimno". Ja   nic.
    she.NOM put_on.3SGS kettle.ACC cold   I.NOM nothing.ACC
    'She puts on the kettle: "It's cold." I don't [respond].'

(23) Czech (McShane 2005: 174–5)
    Speech: SPEAKER + SPEECH-CONTENT
    A   on   pořad   jen   o   svých   problémech.

and he.NOM constantly only about own.PREP problem.PL.PREP
'And he's always [talking] about his own problems.'

In addition, there is one configuration in which a verb of motion can be elided, but it applies only to Polish, not to Czech.

(24) Polish (McShane 2005: 175)
Motion: MOVER + MOTION-GOAL
Pan   do   kogo?
you.M.NOM   to   who.GEN
'Who are you here for?'

Other languages, differently from Russian, Polish and Czech, employ Multilicensor Verbal Ellipsis with just one semantically defined verb class (or to privilege one preponderantly), which usually is that of verbs of motion or that of verbs of saying. Among the languages in which Multilicensor Verbal Ellipsis would seem used only for motion verbs we note here two Austronesian languages of Sumatra: Karo Batak (Woollam 1996: 289) and Gayo (Eades 2005: 140). Typical examples from the two languages are given below in (25) and (26), with MOTION-GOAL used here in the broader sense of 'destination or provenance'.

(25) Karo Batak (Woollam 1996: 289)
Motion: MOTION-GOAL + MOVER
ja   nari   kam   ndai
where   from   you   before
'Where [have] you [come] from?'

(26) Gayo (Eades 2005: 140)
Motion: MOVER + MOTION-GOAL
aku   ben   ari   kedé
I   just   from   market
'I have just [come] from the market.'

In Toqabaqita, an Austronesian language of the Solomon Islands, it is specifically the verb 'come' that may be elided in a clause with a MOVER and the ventive particle *mai*.

(27) Toqabaqita (Lichtenberk 2008: 945)
Motion: MOVER + PARTICLE$_{VENTIVE}$
kamuluqa   mai
you   VENT
'You, [come] here!'

It is a well-known fact that most of the Germanic languages can use modal verbs with non-verb complements (directionals) without the necessity of the motion verb 'go', as in the German example in (28) and in the Dutch one in (29).[13]

(28) German
    Ich   muss   nach   Leipzig   (geh-en)
    I.NOM   must.PRS.1SGS   to   Leipzig   go-INF
    'I must [go] to Leipzig.'

(29) Dutch (Barbiers 1995: 150)
    Jan   wil   weg   (gaa-n)
    John   want.PRS.3SGS   away   go-INF
    'John wants [to go] away.'

Two ways to analyse such constructions have been proposed. The majority view has been that the modal verbs in such examples are main verbs, i.e. fully lexical verbs, constructed directly with a directional. Another interpretation is that the modals are functional verbs, i.e. auxiliaries, and hence there is a silent motion verb present in the syntactic structure (Geerts et al. 1984: 558; Vanden Wyngaerd 1994: 65–8; van Riemsdijk 2002, 2012). In this respect, van Riemsdijk (2002) provides evidence for the following assumptions: (i) the presence of the empty verb is licensed by the presence of a modal verb and under adjacency to it, i.e. they have to occur within the same verb cluster; and (ii) directionals are not directly dependent on the modal verb: the invisible verb of motion mediates between the two. A further, alternative view would be to assume some kind of verb ellipsis: rather than a lexical insertion of a null form, a complete deletion of the verb 'go' would be involved. This option, however, is refuted with a range of arguments by Barbiers (1995: 150–4), who notes, among other things, that, whereas in (29) 'go' seemingly can be present or absent at the phonological level under identity of interpretation, in other cases, like (30) for example, the presence of overt 'go' leads to an entirely different interpretation: it forces the interpretation that the books go away by themselves. No such interpretations are available for the sentence in (31) without 'go'.

(30) Dutch (Barbiers 1995: 151)
    Die   boek-en   mog-en   weg   gaa-n
    those   book-PL   may-PRS.PLS   away   go-INF
    'Those books can go away.'

(31) Die   boek-en   mog-en   weg
    those   book-PL   may-PRS.PLS   away
    'Those books can [be thrown] away.'

Similarly, in Kayardild, a Tangkic language of northern Australia, the absence of the verb *warraja* 'go' changes the interpretation of a proposition like (32) significantly.

(32) Kayardild (Evans 1995: 318)
    nguku-ntha   karndi-ya   kunawun
    water-OBL   woman-NOM   child.NOM
    'The women and children [have to go] for water.'

With no verb, it outlines a general obligation of wives and children to fetch water; with the verb, it would describe a single concrete situation (Evans 1995: 318). Sentences like (31) (without *gaan*) and (32) are clearly cases that cannot be simply analysed as involving a missing verb constituent.

Among the languages in which Multilicensor Verbal Ellipsis would seem to be used only for verbs of saying, we mention here Ma'di (Blackings and Fabb 2003: 360), a Central Sudanic language spoken in South Sudan and Uganda, and Urubu-Kaapor (Kakumasu 1986: 338), a Tupian language spoken in north-eastern Brazil. In both languages, the SPEECH-CONTENT licenser is realised as a direct quote. Two examples of this are given in (33) and (34).

(33) Urubu-Kaapor (Kakumasu 1986: 338)
      Speech: SPEECH-CONTENT + CONNECTIVE
      anĩ   aja   riki
      no   thus   EMPH
      '"No," thus [he said].'

(34) Ma'di (Blackings and Fabb 2003: 360)
      Speech: SPEAKER + SPEECH-CONTENT
      mā   nɨ̄   ōgù   ōndʒɨ
      I   PR   theft bad
      'I then [told] her "theft is not good".'

Dixon (2004: 117–18) notes that in the Jarawara dialect of Madi, the verb *ati -na-* 'say', consisting of the invariable lexical word *ati* and the auxiliary *-na-*, loses the lexical component *ati* if and only if the auxiliary has a first person singular, second person singular or O-construction prefix. This, therefore, happens independently of the presence of a SPEECH-CONTENT constituent.

In many languages, the copula verb can or must be omitted under specific grammatical conditions. Most commonly, the copula is omitted, either obligatorily or optionally, in the less marked tense forms, such as the present tense or the aorist (Wetzer 1996: 134). There are also several languages, however, in which copula omission is restricted neither to particular grammatical conditions, apart from the presence in the clause of a subject constituent and a complement constituent, nor to prior linguistic context, and can be said to be properly optional (Pustet 2003: 34). Cantonese (Sino-Tibetan, Sinitic), Kam (Tai-Kadai, Kam-Tai) and Mohave (Yuman-Cochimí, Yuman) are examples of languages in which copula dropping is not limited to a particular context, but rather may apply in any context in which there is an overtly expressed subject and an overtly expressed complement.

(35) Cantonese (Matthews and Yip 2011: 145)
      gó   bun   syū   (haih) ngóh   ge
      that   CL   book   (COP)   I   LP
      'That book (is) mine.'

(36) Kam (Yang and Edmondson 2008: 532)
mau³³ (tɕaŋ³³) ŋən¹¹ hu¹³
he (COP) person big
'He (is) a poor man.'

(37) Mohave (Munro 1976: 50)
mahʷat-č (ido-pč-m)
bear-NOM COP-TNS-TNS
'It (is) a bear.'

Another such language is Cavineña, a member of the Tacanan family spoken in Bolivia. Given that the main function of the copula predicate is to carry verbal affixes in Cavineña, speakers very often leave out the copula predicate when they do not judge it necessary to express the verbal categories encoded by these affixes.

(38) Cavineña (Guillaume 2008: 97)
mu-da=tu matuja=kwana
scary-ASF=3sGS(-FM) caiman=PL
'The caimans [were] scary.'

Based on the literature consulted, we may tentatively conclude that verbs that express motion, verbs of speaking and the copula 'be' are the verbs most prone to Multilicensor Verbal Ellipsis cross-linguistically (without a change in the interpretation of the sentence). We hinted in §11.2 at the recoverability of the meaning of a zero-root verb expressing motion from the combined semantics of the overt categories of subject (MOVER) and destination or provenance (MOTION-GOAL). The recoverability of verbs of saying in the context indicated above is manifest. When a human subject (SPEAKER) combines with reported speech (SPEECH-CONTENT), as in (33) and (34), the action which takes place cannot but be speech-related.

Although economy is widely believed to be a major force in the design of natural languages, we should keep in mind that Multilicensor Verbal Ellipsis remains a relatively rare phenomenon from a global perspective.

11.4 Verb Root Ellipsis

Verb Root Ellipsis is a phenomenon considerably less common than verb ellipsis and even rarer than the rather uncommon phenomenon of zero verb roots (and zero allomorphs of verb roots). We are aware of very few languages where ellipsis of the root of a verb is permitted: two native American languages, Inuktitut (§11.4.1) and Kwaza (§11.4.2), Akabea and two other members of the Great Andamanese family (§11.4.3) and possibly – although we will present an alternative analysis – the Aboriginal Australian language Jingulu (§11.4.4).

11.4.1 Inuktitut

Verb Root Ellipsis in Inuktitut is discussed in Swift and Allen (2002), on which our discussion is based. Inuktitut is a language or group of languages of the Eskimo branch of the Eskimo-Aleut family spoken in northern Canada.[14] The variety discussed by Swift and Allen is the Tarramiut (Hudson Bay) dialect of Arctic Quebec, which forms part of Eastern Canadian Inuktitut. Interestingly, Verb Root Ellipis is apparently not found outside Inuktitut, in particular not in the closely related Greenlandic varieties nor in more distantly related Yupik varieties. It thus seems to be an innovation within Inuktitut.

In order to understand Verb Root Ellipsis in Inuktitut, it is necessary to understand the structure of an Inuktitut word (with the same principle applying to other Eskimo languages). This structure is shown in (39).

(39) BASE (+ POSTBASES) + ENDING (+ ENCLITICS)

The normally obligatory parts of a word are the base and the ending. The base includes the root, but may also include some derivational suffixes. Endings, in the case of verbs, are inflectional suffixes encoding mood and person-number, the latter of the subject in intransitive verb forms, of both subject and object in transitive verb forms. Postbases encode a wide range of phenomena, including some that change word class (like the verbaliser *-it-*) and others that express TAM. Enclitics play no significant role in what follows and will not be further discussed.

What is ellipted in Inuktitut is strictly speaking the base (and not just the root, where there are derivational suffixes), and along with the base some postbases can also be ellipted. Rather than glossing what is ellipted as LROOT, we therefore prefer the gloss LBASE. There is, however, ellipsis of the root, in the sense that the root is obligatorily ellipted as part of the ellipsis process, and we will continue to use the term Verb Root Ellipsis. Some postbases exclude the possibility of Verb Root Ellipsis, for example the verbaliser *-it-*.

Swift and Allen's (2002) illustration of Inuktitut Verb Root Ellipsis is based on a corpus originally collected as part of a project on Inuktitut child language acquisition, which includes in addition to children's speech a large set of utterances of adults speaking to children and speaking to other adults in the context of childcare activities. They note that Verb Root Ellipsis is not confined to such speech, however, but is a regular part of Inuktitut conversation between adults.

Assuming that all grammatical constraints on Verb Root Ellipsis are satisfied, under what circumstances is it actually permitted in Inuktitut discourse? Following Swift and Allen (2002), we note that in nearly all instances (with the possible exception of conventionalised expressions), the ellipted material must be recoverable from the context. In many cases, this is the immediately preceding conversational turn, as in (40). The first speaker introduces the notion of playing in (40a), the first word of the response in (40b) ellipts this content and consists overtly simply of an ending encoding dubitative mood (thus corresponding in translation to the indirect question in English) and a third person plural intransitive subject.

(40)   Inuktitut (Swift and Allen 2002: 150)
  a. *Aala atsakuttit pinnguatui maani*[15]
     aala   atsa-kkut-tit   pinnguaq-juq-it   ma-ani

listen aunt-ASPL-ABS.2SG>PL play-NMLS-ABS.PL here-LOC
'Listen, your aunt and her friends are playing out here.'
b. *Mangata takulaukkinai*
Ø-mmangata taku-lauq-kkit=ai
LBASE-DUB.3PLS see-POL-IMP.2SGS>3PLO=EMPH
'Please look to see if they are [playing].'

In other instances, the ellipted material is recoverable rather from the situation, as in (41). The background to this utterance is that Louisa has made it clear that she wants her pillow back. In her mother's utterance (41), the part of the word corresponding to the semantic content 'get back' is ellipted, so that the resulting word consists solely of a postbase (encoding tense) and an ending (encoding mood and the person-number of subject and object).

(41) Inuktitut (Swift and Allen 2002: 144)
(Mother to Louisa, who wants her pillow back)
Langagaviuk
Ø-langa-gaviuk
LBASE-NEARFUT-CTG.2SGS>3SGO
'You will soon [get] it [back].'

Example (42) might be similarly analysed: the context makes it clear what the speaker wants to do, and the actual word, consisting of a postbase, an ending and an enclitic, asks for permission to carry out this action. However, Swift and Allen note that this utterance seems to have been conventionalised as a translation equivalent of English '(It's) my turn'. This leaves open the possibility that while (42) has the morphological structure of an instance of Verb Root Ellipsis, it needs to be listed in the lexicon as an idiom.

(42) Inuktitut (Swift and Allen 2002: 136)
Laurlangali
Ø-lauq-langa=li
LBASE-POL-IMP.1SGS=and
'My turn.' (lit. 'Please let me.')

These Inuktitut examples, or at least the non-conventionalised ones in (40) and (41), illustrate what will be a recurrent theme in the treatment of Verb Root Ellipsis, namely that ellipsis of the verb is licensed primarily by pragmatic constraints, in particular: the content of the ellipted material must be retrievable from the context, whether this is linguistic context (e.g. a preceding conversation turn) or the non-linguistic situation.

11.4.2 Kwaza

Kwaza is an unclassified language spoken in the state of Rondônia in Brazilian Amazonia. Our understanding of Kwaza is based on van der Voort (2004), especially

§7.5.2 (pp. 578–90) on ellipsis of roots, supplemented by further discussion kindly provided by the author. To the best of our knowledge, which includes asking specialists on the languages of this area, Verb Root Ellipsis has not been attested in other languages of the area, although this is a region whose languages remain generally underdescribed, even if valiant efforts are being made to correct the situation.

The verb in Kwaza is always root-initial, and the root can be followed by a number of suffixes, of which the person and mood suffixes are obligatory. Van der Voort suggests that a number of Kwaza constructions might reflect grammaticalisation of Verb Root Ellipsis, but here we are concerned exclusively with instances of Verb Root Ellipsis that are productive. Verb Root Ellipsis involves, in formal terms, literally the ellipsis of the verb root, with retention of all suffixes, in particular the obligatory person and mood suffixes.

Van der Voort (2004: 578–9) notes that Verb Root Ellipsis is particularly frequent 'in dialogues, as a minimal response to questions, remarks or comments'. Mini-dialogues (43) and (44) illustrate just this situation. The root missing from (43b) is retrievable as *ku'ro-* 'close' from the immediately preceding question, likewise the root *o'ja-* 'leave' in (44b) as the response to (44a).

(43) Kwaza (van der Voort 2004: 579)
    a. ku'ro-xa-xa-re
       close-2S-AS-Q
       'Did you close the door?'
    b. Ø-'a-xa-ki
       LROOT-1PLS-AS-DEC
       'We did.'

(44) Kwaza (van der Voort 2004: 579)
    a. o'ja-xa-tsy-re
       leave-2S-POT-Q
       'Are you going?'
    b. Ø-'da-tsy-tse
       LROOT-1SGS-POT-DEC
       'I am.'

In (45) and (46), examples of full and ellipted responses are provided in parallel in the (b) and (c) sentences. Example (45b) is a possible non-ellipted response to (45a), while (45c) is its ellipted equivalent; in all cases the root is *ja-* 'eat'. Example (46b) is the attested ellipted response to the question in (46a), with the relevant root being *kui-* 'drink'. Example (46c) is a close formal parallel to (46b) without ellipsis of the verb root; the only difference is that (46c) also includes the suffix *-je?e* 'again'.

(45) Kwaza (van der Voort 2004: 579)
    a. ja-'e-da-mỹ
       eat-again-1SGS-VOL
       'I'm going to eat again.'

b. ja-e-'ra
   eat-again-IMP
   'Eat again!'
c. Ø-ca-'ra
   LROOT-EMPH-IMP
   'Do so!'

(46) Kwaza (van der Voort 2004: 580, 533)
   a. kui-'nã-xa-re
      drink-FUT-2S-Q
      'Are you going to drink?'
   b. Ø-'he-nã-da-ki
      LROOT-NEG-FUT-1sGS-DEC
      'I'm not.'
   c. kui-'he-je?e-nã-da-ki
      drink-NEG-again-FUT-1sGS-DEC
      'I'm not going to drink more/again.'

In addition, van der Voort (personal communication; see also 2004: 581) directs us to examples where the lexical content of the root is retrievable from the context of situation rather than from the linguistic context, as in (47) (which is the first part of conversational turn (64) in van der Voort 2004).

(47) Kwaza (van der Voort 2004: 763, 766)
   Ø-'da-ta'ra-tsɛ
   LROOT-1sGS-PROC-DEC
   'I'm [going].'

The context for this example is that the son has told his mother that the interview is over for today, and that there will be another session tomorrow. The mother then utters (47), and continues to say that it is now unbearably hot and that there will indeed be another opportunity tomorrow. Nothing in the linguistic context prompts identification of 'go' as the semantic context of the ellipted root.

Kwaza provides a classic illustration of Verb Root Ellipsis: it is precisely the verb root that is ellipted, and provided formal constraints are satisfied, such ellipsis is licensed by pragmatic conditions, whether from the linguistic or the extra-linguistic context.

11.4.3 Akabea and Other Great Andamanese Languages

Great Andamanese is a small group of genealogically related languages (with unknown external relations) that were once spoken in Great Andaman (the main archipelago of the Andaman Islands) and nearby islands. It is an effectively extinct family of which today there remain only five 'rusty' speakers (with varying degrees of competence) of an amalgam of dialects of North Andaman Island (Akajeru, Akabo, Akakhora and Akachari) called 'Present-day Great Andamanese' or, simply, 'Great Andamanese'.

Relatively well documented, Present-day Great Andamanese has been described in various works, including a reference grammar (Abbi 2013) and a dictionary (Abbi 2012). For the remaining (traditional) varieties of the family, which ceased to be spoken within the first half of the twentieth century, the following material, in large part by two British government servants, Maurice V. Portman and Edward H. Man, remains: a 'manual' of Akabea, Opuchikwar, Akakede and Akachari comprising a comparative vocabulary and a phrase-book (Portman 1887), grammar notes, lexical material and texts of Akabea, Akarbale, Opuchikwar, Okojuwoi and Okol (Portman 1898), a dictionary of Akabea (Man 1919–23), an incomplete, manuscript grammar of the same language (Man 1878) one section of which was published in a limited number of copies (Man and Temple 1878), and an important monograph on the Andamanese societies by Alfred R. Radcliffe-Brown, which includes, *passim*, words, phrases and sentences in various Andamanese languages (Radcliffe-Brown 1933).

The possibility of omitting the root of a verb is attested for three of the eleven Great Andamanese varieties, namely Akabea (Middle and South Andaman and islands that surround the latter), Opuchikwar (area between Middle Strait and Homfray Strait) and Okojuwoi (interior of the southern half of Middle Andaman). The available descriptions of Present-day Great Andamanese do not mention this phenomenon and neither is there any trace of it in the sparse documentation of Akachari, one of the heritage dialects of the last speakers (or rememberers) of Present-day Great Andamanese. This absence of evidence, of course, is not per se evidence of absence of the phenomenon in Present-day Great Andamanese and Akachari. The greatest variety of Verb Root Ellipsis possibilities is found in Akabea, the best-documented traditional Great Andamanese language. A typical verb structure in Akabea is the following.

(48)   CLITIC_PRONOUN + SOMATIC_PREFIX (+ NUMBER) + ROOT + TAM[16]

Three or, perhaps, four productive types of Verb Root Ellipsis are attested in Akabea (Zamponi and Comrie forthcoming: §3.3). Note that if Verb Root Ellipsis leaves behind only a suffix, Man and Portman write it as part of the preceding orthographic word; if, however, the result includes a prefix (with or without a suffix), then the result is written as a separate orthographic word; we return to this in §11.5.

(a) The root can be omitted if it is clear from the preceding conversational turn, for example where the verb occurs in a command and can therefore be presupposed in the response, as in (50) from Man.[17]

(49)   Akabea (Man 1878: ch. 34)
       Âchitik [sic] *reg dama màgke*
       aʧitek   reg   dama   mek-ke
       now   pig   flesh   eat-NPST
       '(You) will eat some pork now!'

(50)   Akabea (Man 1878: ch. 34)
       Yabada, wai dîlalen dôke

yaba=da	wai	dila=len	d-o	Ø-ke
NEG=COP	FOC	evening=LOC	1SG-S.SG	LROOT-nPST

'No (lit. "(It) is not"). I will in the evening.' (Man 1878: ch. 34)

(b) The root of the motion verb ɔn 'come, go' can be omitted if it is clear from the context, typically because an adverb or a postpositional phrase indicates the direction (MOTION-GOAL) and an animate subject (MOVER) is implied, as in (51)–(53), all from Portman, while Man gives example (54), without such an indication of direction.

(51) Akabea (Portman 1898: 158)
Israel *ér-len kátik-ké*

Israel	er=len	katik	Ø-ke
Israel	land=LOC	there.SPAT	LROOT-nPST

'In the land of Israel, (you) will [go] there!'

(52) Akabea (Portman 1898: 146)
Dó yát taijnga látké

d-o	yat	taidʒ-ŋa=lat	Ø-ke
1SG-S.SG	fish	shoot-NMLS=ALL	LROOT-nPST

'I [go] to shoot fish.'

(53) Akabea (Portman 1898: 134, 136)
... *á 'en-iji-múg-éni-nga l'át-ré*

Ø-a	en-idʒ-i-mug-eni-ŋa=lat	Ø-re
3-O	PREV-SP-REFL-forehead-catch-NMLS=ALL	LROOT-PRET

'(We) [are come] to worship him.'

(54) Akabea (Man 1878: ch. 9)
Ka wai dôke

ka	wai	d-o	Ø-ke
DEM.PROX	FOC	1SG-S.SG	LROOT-nPST

'I am off now!'

This type of Verb Root Ellipsis is also attested in Opuchikwar and Okojuwoi.

(55) Opuchikwar (Portman 1887: 146)
... *uk taiye péne láteke*

Ø-uk	taiye	pene=late	Ø-ke
3SG-S	fish	catch=ALL	LROOT-nPST

'He [goes] to catch fish.'

(56) Okojuwoi (Portman 1887: 151)
... *á Egypt láte-chíkan*

Ø-a	Egypt=late	Ø-kitʃikan
3SG-S.SG	Egypt=ALL	LROOT-PRET

'He (Joseph) [went] to Egypt.'

At least in Akabea, ellipsis of the root ɔn 'come, go' appears licensed and recoverable also based on the combination of the root with a comitative adverbial. We have one example of this in Man's dictionary, given in (57).

(57) Akabea (Man 1919–23: 21)
Dikke itikke dâke
d-ik   Ø-ke
1SG-COM   LROOT-nPST
Ø-it-ik   Ø-ke   dake
3-PL-COM   LROOT-nPST   NEG.DEB
'(You) will [come] with me! Don't [go] with them!'

(c) Man gives various examples of ellipsis of the verb root *perek* 'hit, strike (with a stick or weapon)'. All these examples, except the one in (61), include an overtly expressed human or inanimate agent (HITTER) and an overtly expressed human patient. The sentence in (61) only contains an overtly expressed patient. The sentences in (58a,b) show a minimal pair with and without the verb root. All examples with ellipsis show the retention of a somatic prefix that specifies the body part struck and a tense suffix despite the ellipsis of the verb root, while (60a) also includes a plural prefix before the somatic prefix. All examples also show an object pronoun procliticised to this rootless verb form.

(58) Akabea (Man 1878: ch. 34)
   a. *Dô ngôtpàreke*
      d-o   ŋ=ot-perek-ke
      1SG-S.SG   2O=SP-strike-nPST
      'I will strike you on the head.'
   b. ... *do ngôtke*
      d-o   ŋ=ot-Ø-ke
      1SG-S.SG   2O=SP-LROOT-nPST
      'I will [strike] you on the head.'

(59) Akabea (Man 1878: ch. 34)
   Kâto êla dôngre
   kato   ela   d=on-Ø-re
   DEM.DIST   pig-arrow   1SGO=SP-LROOT-PRET
   'That pig-arrow [struck] me in the hand/foot.'

(60) Akabea (Man 1878: ch. 35)
   a. *Michîba ngitigre?*
      miʧiba   ŋ=it-ig-Ø-re
      what   2O=PL-SP-LROOT-PRET
      'What [has struck] you (pl.) on the eyes?'
   b. *Michîba ngabre*
      miʧiba   ŋ=ab-Ø-re

        what   2O=SP-LROOT-PRET
        'What [has struck] you on the body?'
   c.   *Michîba ngâkâre*
        miʃiba   ŋ=aka-Ø-re
        what   2O=SP-LROOT-PRET
        'What [has struck] you on the mouth?'

(61) Akabea (Man 1878: ch. 34)
     Kichîkachâ ngôngre?
     kiʧikaʧa ŋ=on-Ø-re
     how   2O=SP-LROOT-PRET
     'How did (he) [hit] you on the hand/foot?'

(d) One Akabea sentence recorded by Portman might lead one to suppose a fourth type of Verb Root Ellipsis represented by an omission of the copula root *eda ~ =da* 'be' not linked to particular grammatical conditions. This sentence is a negated verbal clause and, given that negation of verbal clauses in Akabea is expressed by nominalising the affirmative clause and presenting it as the subject argument of a negated copular clause (Zamponi and Comrie forthcoming: §5.2), its expected form contains a full copula verb, like the negated copular clause in (63).

(62) Akabea (Portman 1887: 144)
     Éda [sic] *yádí dutnga yábairé* [sic]
     Ø-oda   yadi   dut-ŋa   yaba   Ø-re
     3-S   turtle_sp. harpoon-NMLS   NEG   LROOT-PRET

     'They have not harpooned any edible turtle.' (lit. 'There was not their harpooning of turtles.')

(63) Akabea (Portman 1887: 108)
     Kárin óda kóinga yábada
     karin   Ø-oda   koi-ŋa   yaba=da
     here   3-S   dance-NMLS   NEG=COP
     'They will not dance here.' (lit. 'There is not their dancing here.')

This possible type of Verb Root Ellipsis finds no further corroboration in the Akabea material at our disposal, apart from one sentence also recorded by Portman, in (64), that might also be analysed as lacking the copula root *eda ~ =da*.[18]

(64) Akabea (Portman 1887: 119)
     ... *béringa-ke*
     beriŋa   Ø-ke   (or beriŋa-ke)
     good   LROOT-nPST   be_good-nPST
     '(The pig) will be good.'

Yet a further type of Verb Root Ellipsis is attested by only one Opuchikwar complex sentence contained in Portman's 'manual', given in (65). The root of the verb in the second of two juxtaposed clauses can be omitted if the same root is overtly expressed in the preceding clause and the two parts are parallel. In the Opuchikwar sentence in question, clause juxtaposition serves to express interrogative disjunction.

(65) Opuchikwar (Portman 1887: 126)
Án ngóng chélewe [sic] *lír írtilu* [sic]*, án chélebírma kétewe* [sic] *líír?*

an	ŋ-oŋ	ʧelewa	l=ir-tilu
Y/N	2-S/A.SG	ship	DEF=SP-see
an	ʧele-birma	ketawa	l=ir-Ø
Y/N	ship-funnel	small	DEF=SP-LROOT

'Do you (SG) see the ship or the steam launch?' (lit. 'Do you (SG) see the ship? Do [you see] the small steamship?')

This last type of Verb Root Ellipsis recalls the gapping strategy of intrasentential verb ellipsis that, as indicated in note 10, applies to the verb (in its entirety) in the latter clause(s) of a coordinate or comparative structure.

11.4.4 Jingulu

Jingulu, also known as Djingili, is a member of the small Mirndi language family of Australia's Northern Territory. The discussion in this section is based primarily on Pensalfini (2003), but see also Chadwick (1975) and Pensalfini (2011, 2015). On the basis of our understanding of the Jingulu material, it is possible that the language has Verb Root Ellipsis, and indeed Pensalfini (2003) uses the terms 'root drop' and 'root ellipsis' on p. 84, although in quotes and without making it clear whether this is to be considered a distinct process or construction.

The basic structure of a Jingulu verb word (or verb complex) is presented in (66), using Pensalfini's terminology, which we retain. A verb forms a single grammatical word (there is no possibility of reordering the constituents or putting anything between them, for example) and a single phonological word (only one primary stress, for example).

(66) (COVERBAL_ROOT +) SUBJECT/OBJECT_INDEX(ES) + LIGHT_VERB

The coverbal root encodes the lexical meaning of the verb, and is followed in turn by the subject/object indexes and the light verb. The subject/object index(es) encode the person-number of the subject and, in transitive verbs, the object. If the subject is third person singular and there is no overt indexing of the object, then in the presence of a coverbal root the subject/object index is null. The index for a third person object is always null. There are three light verbs, which express basically motion towards the deictic centre (or 'come'), motion away from the deictic centre (or 'go') and everything else (or 'do', although often English 'be' will be a more plausible translation). The light verbs express tense suppletively – compare the forms for 'do' in (70)–(73) – which means that there is a large number of forms although only three light verbs are involved. In addition, some modal values, like irrealis (which is also used to express commands, in which case subject agreement can be dropped), are expressed by a distinct element in the light verb position, thus neutralising the three-way opposition found elsewhere. Relevant examples with an overt coverbal root are presented in (67)–(75).

(67) ngibi-wunyu-wardu
 have-3DUS-go.PRS
 'Those two are taking it.'
 (Pensalfini 2003: 39)

(68) ngibi-wunyi-jiyimi
 have-3DUS-come.PRS
 'Those two are bringing it.'
 (Pensalfini 2003: 39)

(69) wungkarra-jiyimi
 whistle-come.PRS
 'S/he comes whistling.'
 (Pensalfini 2003: 39)

(70) marliyi-ngirri-ju
 be_ill-1PL.EXCLS-do.PRS
 'We are ill.' (Pensalfini 2003: 45)

(71) imbiyi-mindi-ju
 speak-1DU.INCLS-do.PRS
 'We two are speaking.'
 (Pensalfini 2003: 209)

(72) yurriyi-ngurri-yi
 play-1PL.INCLS-do.FUT
 'Let's play.'
 (Pensalfini 2003: 210)

(73) miyi-wunya-ana-nu
 hit-3DUS-1O-do.PST
 'They two hit me.'
 (Pensalfini 2003: 216)

(74) kabija-anyu-mi
 smile-2DUS-IRR
 'You two smile!'
 (Pensalfini 2003: 231)

(75) ngaba-mi
 have-IRR
 'Bring it.'
 (Pensalfini 2003: 230)

The irrealis suffixes in (74) and (75) presumably replace, respectively, the light verbs 'do' and 'come', the latter judging from the translation.

Pensalfini (2003: 84–5) notes that verb complexes frequently appear without a coverbal root, describing this by saying that the coverbal root is 'entirely optional' and that the corresponding clause is 'root-less'.

Some examples, such as (76) and (77), do seem remarkably similar to instances of Verb Root Ellipsis in the other languages that we consider, in the sense that a specific interpretation is given by the context. Thus, in (76) 'do' is interpreted as 'drink', although there are at least some other things one can do with water/beer, while in (77) it is interpreted as 'cut through' – we are unsure what the culturally appropriate constraints might be on the range of things one can do to innards with a boomerang.

(76) ibilka-rni-mbili   wurru-wardi
     water-FOC-LOC   3PLS-do.HAB
     'They just do [drink] beer.'
     (Pensalfini 2003: 85)

(77) kurrubardi-rni   kurdkulyu-kaji   ngirri-marriyimi
     boomerang-FOC   mucus-through   1PL.EXCLS-do.DISTPST
     'We'd do [cut through] the innards with a boomerang.'
     (Pensalfini 2003: 85)

However, in other instances there seems to be no reason to appeal to the lexical content of a coverbal root that has been omitted. In (78), for instance, the two light verbs simply receive their literal meaning of motion away from the deictic centre and motion towards the deictic centre, while (79) receives the interpretation of a generic verb meaning that is not motion towards or away from the deictic centre and is compatible with the transitive clause structure. Adding a coverbal root to (78) or (79) would presumably change the meaning by rendering it more specific, as one would expect from the addition of an optional element.

(78) ya-ardu   kardarda   ya-jiyimi
     3SGS-go.PRS   always   3SGS-come.PRS
     'He's always coming and going.'
     (Pensalfini 2003: 84)

(79) nya-anu-ju
     2SGS-1O-do.PRS
     'You do (it) to me.'
     (Pensalfini 2003: 84)

In yet other instances a verb complex without a coverbal root appears in collocation with an independent word, as in (80) (lit. 'do tired') and (81) (lit. 'come close'). These independent words are clearly distinct from coverbal roots, both phonologically, in that they take their own primary stress, and grammatically, in that they can be separated from the verb complex by other words and can occur after the verb complex. It is not clear what, if any, coverbal root could be omitted in (80) and (81).

(80) wayabij   nya-ju
     tired   2SGS-do.PRS
     'You are tired.'
     (Pensalfini 2003: 59)

(81) lurdba   ya-jiyimi
     close   3SGS-come.PRS
     'It's approaching.'
     (Pensalfini 2003: 67)

One issue to be resolved is whether examples like (76)–(77) and (78)–(79) illustrate a uniform phenomenon – the fact that the coverbal root slot is optional – or whether one needs to distinguish two phenomena, ellipsis of the coverbal root under appropriate pragmatic conditions in (76)–(77) vs its mere absence in (78)–(81).[19] We know of no evidence in favour of such a dichotomy, and if there is indeed no such evidence, then considerations of parsimony would recommend a uniform analysis. One might think that valency might provide a possible criterion, given that the interpretation of a verb might be constrained by its valency, in addition to pragmatic factors involved in Verb Root Ellipsis. However, Pensalfini (2003: 63–4) is quite explicit that in principle any Jingulu verb complex can be used either transitively or intransitively, provided a plausible interpretation can be assigned. This suggests that valency cannot be used as a criterion to argue for two distinct constructions.

If there is only one construction, then the question remains as to exactly what it is. We see two possibilities. One would be to argue that instances where there is no coverbal root actually have a zero root in that position, interpreted as 'go', 'come' or 'do/be' according to the choice of light verb. One problem with this solution is that the proposed zero root would add nothing to the semantics already given by the light verb, i.e. this morpheme would have neither form nor meaning.

An alternative analysis would be to treat the combination of coverbal root and light verb as a discontinuous stem, with the coverbal root and light verb as morphologically distinct root elements. Most Jingulu verbs would thus have a discontinuous stem, with the coverbal root providing the bulk of the semantics, the light verb the three-way distinction that it expresses. A few verbs, namely 'go', 'come' and 'do/be', would have a non-discontinuous stem consisting solely of the light verb. This would parallel typologically, for instance, the analysis of the Ket verb stem proposed by Vajda (2015: 630–1; and elsewhere), whereby most verb stems are discontinuous, comprising a morpheme in position P7 that provides the bulk of the lexical meaning and a morpheme in position P0 that contributes less to the lexical meaning.[20] However, about 80 verbs lack a morpheme in position P7 and have only the one in P0. The statistics are somewhat different between Ket (with about 80 distinct morphemes in position P0) and Jingulu (with only 3 light verbs), but the basic principle is the same.[21] The reader may wonder why we have drawn the parallel to discontinuous stems in Ket rather than to the combination of 'uninflecting verbs' (also known as coverbs, preverbs and verbal particles) and 'inflecting verbs' that is an areal feature of languages of northern Australia, including Jingulu's distant relative Jaminjung (Schultze-Berndt 2015: 1119–20). However, there is a significant difference, presumably an innovation in Jingulu, that pushes that language in the direction of Ket, namely the fact that the combination constitutes a single word grammatically (fixed order, no possibility of inserting material other than the subject/object index(es)) and phonologically (a single primary stress).

To conclude our discussion of Jingulu, it is possible that the language has Verb Root Ellipsis, but our current bias is rather towards an analysis with discontinuous stems, in which case Jingulu would not illustrate the phenomenon that is at the centre of this paper. Since the obligatory light verb is root material, no Jingulu verb form would have no root.

11.5 Verb Root Ellipsis and Phonological Words

If speakers of a language decide that they are going to be able to ellipt verb roots, then they must have a way of pronouncing the result. The problem that might arise can be illustrated on the basis of English concatenative inflectional morphology, as illustrated by the third person singular present tense form *sing-s*. The root is pronounceable in isolation as an English word, and is indeed identical to the citation form *sing*, also used for the imperative and for other person-number combinations in the present tense. However, the affix is not so pronounceable, since it does not constitute a possible syllable in English, and an English word must consist of at least one syllable. But even a syllabic affix, as in the corresponding form *buzz-es* of the verb *buzz*, is not pronounceable in isolation, since its only vowel is unstressed, and English words require at least one stress. Thus, if English were to develop Verb Root Ellipsis, it would need to find some solution to the apparently unpronounceable result, either changing the rules on phonological word structure or establishing a rule to attach the orphaned affix to something else.

But it should be emphasised that not all languages are like English in this respect. Indeed, there are languages where roots are not pronounceable in isolation, like Italian, where most roots are consonant-final, as, for example, *gatt-* 'cat' (singular *gatt-o*, plural *gatt-i*), although phonological words must be vowel-final (with some exceptions restricted to non-pre-pausal position; Lepschy and Lepschy 1988: 94). And conversely, some affixes in some languages have a structure that would be possible as a phonological word, for example the Turkish plural suffix *-lar*; compare the lexical item *dar* 'narrow'. Moreover, in many languages at least some affixes bear stress in at least some words, as when in Russian the genitive singular of *stól* 'table' is *stol-á*, where stress (indicated here by means of an acute accent) falls on the inflection.

If we turn momentarily to the phenomenon of clitics, which like affixes must be integrated into the phonological word, then we find a similar phenomenon. In Polish, for instance, the negative particle *nie* is proclitic on a following verb form. Polish has penultimate stress on words of more than one syllable, so that if we mark stress by a straight apostrophe before the stressed syllable, we find forms like '*wiemy* 'we know' and *nie* '*wiemy* 'we do not know'. However, with a monosyllabic verb, the stress will fall on the negative proclitic, as in '*wiem* 'I know', '*nie wiem* 'I do not know'. In other words, stress can sometimes fall on a clitic and not on the word on which the clitic leans.

But languages can also have specific rules that produce pronounceable phonological words. We illustrate this with material from Bulgarian (Scatton 1984: 324, 376–7) involving the negative proclitic *ne=* and the enclitic forms of the present tense of the copula, illustrated here by first person singular *=səm*; such enclitic copular forms are used, for instance, to construct the perfect, in combination with the aorist active participle of the lexical verb. Under normal circumstances, the negative particle is proclitic on the following word, as in (82), where this word is as most often a verb, and in (83), which shows that the following word does not have to be a verb.

(82) Bulgarian (Scatton 1984)
    níkoj   ne=píše
    nobody   NEG=write.IPFV.PRS.3SGS
    'No one writes.'

(83) ne=pismó=li   píše?
    NEG=letter=Q   write.IPFV.PRS.3SGS
    'Doesn't s/he write *a letter*?'

The enclitic copula is illustrated in (84), where it is attached to the lexical verb with which it forms the periphrastic perfect, and in (85), to show that it can also follow other elements, in this case the subject pronoun – overt subject pronouns are used for emphasis.

(84) čél=səm
    read.IPFV.AOR.ACT.PTCP=be.PRS.1SGS
    'I have read.'

(85) áz=səm   čél
    'I=be.PRS.1SGS   read.IPFV.AOR.ACT.PTCP
    '*I* have read.'

What happens if one combines the negative particle and the copula as part of the periphrastic perfect, bearing in mind that Bulgarian here invokes an ordering constraint that the negative particle must precede the copula? The result is an apparent dilemma: the negative particle must be proclitic on what follows, namely the copula, but the copula must be enclitic on what precedes, namely the negative particle. Bulgarian solves the problem by fiat: in this combination, stress falls exceptionally on the copula, as in (86), which thus consists of the two phonological words *ne=sə́m* and *čél*.[22]

(86) ne=sə́m   čél
      NEG=be.PRS.1SGS   read.IPFV.AOR.ACT.PTCP
      'I have not read.'

With the foregoing as background, we can now investigate how instances of Verb Root Ellipsis are pronounced in the three clear cases and one questionable case of which we are aware.

In the case of Akabea, a language that died out without having been documented in audio recordings, the evidence is necessarily indirect, requiring as it does interpretation of the orthographic conventions of the non-native speakers who noted the language down. One point that does seem clear, though, is that in Akabea stress falls on the first syllable of the root, and never on a prefix or suffix (Zamponi and Comrie forthcoming: §2.4). For the phonological word, the best evidence we have is the division into orthographic words undertaken by the non-native recorders of the language, though we recognise that use of this evidence carries with it a number of obvious dangers. In general, though, word division is reasonably consistent in the attested material, and remarkably so in the case of Verb Root Ellipsis. When Verb Root Ellipsis in Akabea leaves behind only a suffix, as in (51)–(54) and (57), that suffix is always written as part of the preceding word, and we assume that it is phonologically attached to that preceding word. This is also the case in Opuchikwar example (55) and Okojuwoi example (56). When the result of Verb Root Ellipsis includes a prefix (and possibly suffixes and clitics), then this sequence is written consistently as a separate word, suggesting that it may have been pronounced as a separate phonological word, as in Akabea examples (58b)–(61). This applies also to Opuchikwar example (65), where what is left behind is a monosyllable consisting of the non-syllabic proclitic definite article and a VC somatic prefix; this is the only suffixless example in our Great Andamanese corpus. However, this leaves open the question of how such a phonological word would have been stressed if polysyllabic, since the general rule stressing the first syllable of the root is clearly inapplicable.

For Inuktitut, Swift and Allen (2002: 155) state that the language 'has relatively predictable prosodic word structure ...', though without going into further detail. Instances of Verb Root Ellipsis, which inevitably (given the root-initial word structure of Inuktitut) consist of a string of suffixes (and possibly clitics), are always written by Swift and Allen as single separate phonological words, and we assume from this that they probably follow the same relatively predictable prosodic structure of words that do not involve Verb Root Ellipsis, though it would be good to have a full analysis of this that would either confirm or disconfirm this supposition.

In Kwaza, a verb form that is a phonological word remains a phonological word under Verb Root Ellipsis. Since the verb root is always word-initial, Verb Root Ellipsis gives rise to a succession of suffixes, i.e. the phonological word is a sequence of suffixes. How does this affect stress? The stress system of Kwaza is relatively complex, but the following seem to be the main relevant principles as they apply to verb forms. First, a given word can take stress on different syllables depending on such factors as emphasis or focus; in particular, it is possible to stress an affix in order to emphasise or focus its content. In the absence of this factor, certain affixes attract stress, such as the imperative suffix *-ra*, which is why this suffix is stressed in (45b) (with an overt root) and (45c) (with Verb Root Ellipsis). Beyond this, stress is normally on the final syllable of the root, but this is of course not implementable in the case of Verb Root Ellipsis. At least in the case of elliptic responses to questions, words consisting of sequences of affixes none of which attracts stress are stressed on the first syllable (van der Voort 2004: 579), as in (43b) and (44b); this may have to be stipulated, though it could possibly fall out automatically since this syllable is closest to the one that would have been stressed in the absence of Verb Root Ellipsis. Note that initial stress on a verb form with Verb Root Ellipsis may reflect either the fact that its initial suffix attracts stress (as in the case of negative *-he* in (46b) – the same suffix is stressed in (46c), with an overt verb root), or the result of the last mentioned rule assigning stress to the initial syllable, as in (43b) and (44b). Kwaza syllable structure is relatively simple, maximally CGVG (where G = glide), and all lexical items and affixes are either a syllable or a sequence of syllables – see the Kwaza–English vocabulary and the indices of affixes in van der Voort (2004: 817–967, 1009–17) – so there are no phonotactic problems resulting from Verb Root Ellipsis. In sum, the structure of the phonological word in Kwaza makes Verb Root Ellipsis a relatively straightforward process phonologically, with the only additional stipulation being perhaps the word-initial stress assigned to a string of suffixes that is not assigned stress by any other rule.

We noted in §11.4.4 that Jingulu may well not have Verb Root Ellipsis, but either way the relevant forms in the language pose no problem for its phonology. Jingulu has a minimal phonological constraint whereby a phonological word must consist of at least two moras, where a long vowel or diphthong counts as two moras. Bi-moraic words take stress (marked here by means of an acute accent) on the penultimate mora, longer words on the penultimate or antepenultimate mora; no word has stress on the final mora. Secondary stress (marked here with a grave accent) appears on either the second or the third mora before the primary or other secondary-stressed mora. The choice between penultimate and antepenultimate stress is complex and partly lexicalised, though the details are not relevant to present concerns. For our purposes, the crucial point is that a phonological word must be at least two moras long. For further details, see Pensalfini (2003: 36–40).

Verb complexes, which constitute a single phonological word, usually satisfy the minimal bi-moraic constraint trivially, even in the absence of the coverbal root, since the subject/object index (or indexes) nearly always contains at least one mora, and the light verb always contains at least one mora. This is illustrated in (87)–(89).

(87) kùnyu-rrúku
    2DUS-go.PST
    'You two went.'
    (Pensalfini 2003: 39)

(88) ngá-rruku
   1sgS-go.PST
   'I went.'
   (Pensalfini 2003: 40)

(89) míndu-was
   1DU.INCLS-go.FUT
   'You and I will go.'
   (Pensalfini 2003: 40)

There is, however, one subject/object index that is zero, namely that for third person singular in the absence of overt object indexing, as illustrated in (90), which contains an overt coverbal root. Since the light verb consists of a single mora, the stress falls on the coverbal root.

(90) àmbayá-ju
   speak-do.PRS
   'S/he speaks.'
   (Pensalfini 2003: 39)

Under one and only one set of circumstances, however, there is an overt third person singular subject index in the verb, namely if there is no coverbal root. Here there is an overt subject prefix with allomorphs *ya-* and *ka-*. Thus, although (91) has no coverbal root, a third person singular subject and a mono-moraic light verb, the result satisfies the minimal bi-moraic constraint because of the overt subject index. It should be noted, incidentally, that the rule for the use of overt *ya-* ~ *ka-* is morphological rather than phonological. Although in (91) it saves the phonological word from violating the minimal bi-moraic constraint, it is equally required in (92), where the light verb already has three moras.[23]

(91) yá-ju
   3sgS-do.PST
   'S/he/it does.'
   (Pensalfini 2003: 210; stress added by B. C.)

(92) yà-jiyími
   3sgS-come.PRS
   'S/he comes.'
   (Pensalfini 2003: 40)

One might continue by speculating whether there are other phonological or morphological factors that facilitate the development of Verb Root Ellipsis in a language, although the small number of independent cases means that this is necessarily very speculative. With the exception of the Great Andamanese languages, the other cases all involve word-initial roots (or bases, in the case of Inuktitut), so that ellipsis of the root might arguably be facilitated by the clear bipartite Root +

Affixes structure. However, this is clearly not a necessary condition, since the Great Andamanese languages have ellipsis of word-medial roots. Most of the languages with Verb Root Ellipsis have little relevant morphophonological alternation at the boundary between root and affixes, an agglutinating structure which again might be seen as facilitating ellipsis of the root. Inuktitut is, however, an exception. Examples (1b) and (40b) show degemination of the suffix-initial consonant in word-initial position. Swift and Allen (2002: 145) allude to more complex cases, though without going into further detail or providing multiple examples; this is something that future work might develop further. Even if such structural properties facilitate the development of Verb Root Ellipsis, they are clearly not sufficient conditions, given the large number of root-initial agglutinative languages that lack Verb Root Ellipsis, such as Turkish.

11.6 Comparisons

11.6.1 Functional and Semantic Parallels

Most of the instances of Verb Root Ellipsis presented in §11.4 are based on the fact that the potential, complete form of a verb can be deduced from material to be found outside the sentence in which the verb occurs or within the current sentence.

What we could call Intersentential Verb Root Ellipsis is a type of Verb Root Ellipsis found in all languages with Verb Root Ellipsis, where it typically occurs in contextual rejoinders across speakers in dialogue or conversation. It concerns elements that would otherwise have been repeated from a previous turn, as in answers to questions and in responses to requests. Intersentential Verb Root Ellipsis is thus a functional analogue to the ellipsis of main verbs in English leaving behind an auxiliary, as in the English translations to (93b), (94b) and many other examples throughout this paper, but with the crucial difference that what is ellipted in English is a complete word, like *going* in (94b).

> *Inuktitut*: 'Elliptical constructions are often used in contiguous utterance pairs, such as a request and elliptical response or a question and elliptical answer.' (Swift and Allen 2002: 135)

(93) Inuktitut (Swift and Allen 2002: 136)
    a. *Anaana qajurturumajunga*
       anaana   qajuq-tuq-guma-junga
       mother   soup-consume-want-PAR.1SGS
       'Mother, I want to have a soup.'
    b. *Nialirqutit siaru*
       Ø-niaq-liq-vutit   siaru
       LBASE-TODAY-FUT-ING-IND.2SGS   later
       'You will [have soup] later today.'

> *Kwaza*: '... root ellipsis occurs frequently in dialogues, as a minimal response to questions, remarks or comments' (van der Voort 2004: 578–9). 'About elliptic

responses ..., one could say that the specific root is physically absent but that it is understood, and identifiable from the context' (van der Voort 2004: 588).

(94) Kwaza (van der Voort 2004: 579) (= (44))
  a. o'ja-xa-tsy-re
     leave-2S-POT-INT
     'Are you going?'
  b. Ø-'da-tsy-tse
     LROOT-1S-POT-DEC
     'I am.'

Akabea: 'In all cases of this kind [of elliptical use of verbs] the actual sense of these verbs is derived from the circumstances under which the sentences where they occur are spoken. ... The use of such elliptical sentences as these shows up the intensely colloquial character of the language in a strong light' (Man 1878: ch. 34). See examples (49) and (50) in §11.4.3.

Jingulu (if indeed it has Verb Root Ellipsis): 'Root-less clauses are primarily used to express coming and going ..., or in tandem with other words to create clauses with predictable meanings ..., but they can also be used when the root meaning is understood, in 'root ellipsis' constructions.' (Pensalfini 2003: 84)

What we could call Intrasentential Verb Root Ellipsis is attested only in Akabea and, fragmentarily, in Opuchikwar and Okojuwoi. Two subtypes can be recognised: one that applies across a clause boundary and another that does not. These two subtypes could therefore be called, respectively, Interclausal Verb Root Ellipsis and Intraclausal Verb Root Ellipsis.

Interclausal Verb Root Ellipsis is attested only for Opuchikwar and just by one sentence consisting of two juxtaposed clauses (64). In this sentence, we see a gap in place of a verb root that would be identical to the root of the first verb in the first clause. We indicated in §11.4.3 that this type of Verb Root Ellipsis appears parallel to the strategy of gapping, which is a special case of sentence-bound verb ellipsis.

Intraclausal Verb Root Ellipsis does not need an antecedent. It is just the semantics of some co-clausal overt lexical category that plays a role in licensing this type of Verb Root Ellipsis. Intraclausal Verb Root Ellipsis, therefore, recalls the strategy of intrasentential verb ellipsis mentioned in §11.3 (Multilicensor Verbal Ellipsis), although, in the latter case, it is the combined semantics of two or more overt categories that licenses the ellipsis and permits recoverability of the verbal meaning. The verbs implied in Intraclausal Verb Root Ellipsis in Akabea, as indicated in §11.4.3, include 'come, go' (but one might also argue that the whole semantic class of motion verbs is involved rather than one specific verb), some forms with the basic meaning 'hit, strike (with a stick or weapon)' including a somatic prefix that specifies the body part struck and, perhaps, the copula 'be'.

In the available Akabea material, the elision of the root ɔn 'come, go', semantically speaking, requires only overt specification of the destination of the motion,

Table 11.8 Meanings and realisations of MOTION-GOAL licensers in Akabea

Syntactic category	Semantic class	Examples
Adverb	Spatial related	(51)
Postpositional phrase = [NVC]$_{NP}$ + =*lat* 'allative'	Place (destination)	(52)–(53)

namely a MOTION-GOAL licenser, or the presence of a comitative adverbial. This may be deduced from examples (51), (53) and (57). In (52), there is one extra category that may or may not play a role in licensing the ellipsis: the subject *do* 'I', namely the MOVER. The MOVER cannot be considered a minimal licenser because (51), (53) and (57), which lack it, are grammatical. However, it is likely that the pronoun *do* in (52) somehow facilitates the ellipsis without being minimally required to license it. The means by which the MOTION-GOAL licenser can be realised, based on examples (51)–(53), are shown in Table 11.8. The comitative adverbial of example (57) consists of a personal pronoun.

In (54), the MOVER is overtly expressed, but there is no MOTION-GOAL licenser. This seems to indicate that not even the MOTION-GOAL is, really, a licenser of the root ɔn 'come, go'. Our feeling, however, is that the utterance in (54) is an idiomatic expression. What we are dealing with, in other words, is likely a case of conventionalised verb root deletion, in our opinion.

Eliding the root *perek* 'hit, strike (with a stick or weapon)' requires the PATIENT to be overt in (58b)–(61). The HITTER is not a licenser, given that it does not appear in (60). Probably, its presence in (58b) and (59) serves to facilitate the ellipsis. PATIENT and HITTER are realised by pronouns in (58b)–(60c), except in (59) in which the HITTER is realised by a full noun phrase. The HITTER may be either a human being (58b) or an instrument (59); the PATIENT is always a human being in (58b)–(61).

Ellipsis of the copula root *eda* ~ =*da*, if our interpretation of examples (62) and (64) as elliptical constructions is correct, requires only the overt expression of the copula subject in a copular existential clause (62) or of the complement in a nominal copular clause (64).

We saw, in §11.2, that in three languages (Nimboran, Udi and Madi [Jarawara dialect]) the root of a verb of motion that contains a morpheme that supplies indication of motion is phonologically null, at least in certain forms. We also saw, in §11.3, that, in some other languages (Russian, Polish, Karo Batak, Gayo and others), motion verbs are prone to be elided from sentences that overtly specify the person or thing moving and the destination or source of the motion. Ellipsis of the root ɔn 'come, go' in Akabea therefore aligns with a tendency of verb concepts of motion to produce a linguistic expression as reduced as possible in constructions with bound morphemes or lexical items that give a motion-related specification.

The verb 'hit' has a zero root in Selepet and in Bukiyip and a root that is usually zero in Kâte (§11.2). The verb in question, in addition, may be elided in Russian, Polish and Czech when the HITTER and the PATIENT are overtly expressed (§11.3).

Ellipsis of the root *perek* 'hit, strike (with a stick or weapon)' in Akabea is licensed by an overtly expressed PATIENT and facilitated by the presence of an overtly expressed HITTER. Verbs of hitting share with verbs of motion the nuances of speed and immediacy. Hitting is probably the simplest instance of a schema in which an agent affects a patient by means of an intentional action. The minimal or absent linguistic expression of this action, in our opinion, must therefore be linked to its cognitive basicness.

With regard to the copula verb 'be', which completely lacks referential meaning, the possible elision of its root in Akabea perfectly matches the ancillary character of the verb, as described in §11.3, and also justifies its possible elision in many languages of the world and the presence, in some other languages, of a copula root with a zero alternant (e.g. Wai Wai, Kulina, Itelmen and Basque).

Although verbs of speech tend to be elided when SPEAKER and SPEECH-CONTENT are overtly specified, there are neither examples nor indications of a possible ellipsis of the verb root *yab* 'speak, say, tell' in the available material of Akabea. Moreover, ellipsis of the verb root *man ~ a* 'give' is not attested in Akabea, and this contrasts with the expression of the verb concept of transfer by a null form root or a root that, in certain contexts, is phonologically silent that we observed in Yawuru, Bardi, Koasati and various non-Austronesian languages of New Guinea.

A third type of Verb Root Ellipsis can be observed in Inuktitut and Kwaza: the missing root (or base) is recoverable from the situation, the extralinguistic factors of the context, not from surrounding linguistic material. There is nothing of this in the Great Andamanese linguistic documentation at our disposal, though given the limited documentation this is absence of evidence, not necessarily evidence of absence. The following Kwaza utterance represents a response to the behaviour of the hearer. Also in this case there is no linguistic licenser that permits the ellipsis of the root in the first verb.

(95) Kwaza (van der Voort 2004: 581)
  Ø-xa-'he-tsy-tse   ɛ-'ra   mã   ca'ri-hata-'tsi
  LROOT-2S-NEG-POT-DEC go-IMP mother kill-3S.2O-MON
  'Don't you persist, go away!, lest your mother will kill you.' (van der Voort 2004: 581)

11.6.2 Formal Parallels

With the exception of instances of Verb Root Ellipsis in Akabea, which give rise to a suffix that must be attached to the preceding word (see examples (50)–(54) in §11.4.3), all instances of Verb Root Ellipsis give rise to a phonological word that lacks a root. In formal terms, this is an exact parallel to instances of zero roots: one has a sequence of affixes without a root, and as discussed for Verb Root Ellipsis in §11.5, the language must find some way of treating this as a phonological word. This is a close formal parallel between Verb Root Ellipsis and zero roots.

The treatment of suffix-only outputs of Verb Root Ellipsis in Akabea does, however, suggest another possible solution, namely the attachment of the result of Verb Root Ellipsis to an adjacent word. We are not aware of, and would be surprised to find, parallels in the case of zero roots, i.e. a verb form with a zero root that is attached to an adjacent word. This may be a significant formal distinction between the two phenomena, although the evidence to date is meagre, to say the least.

We assume that Verb Root Ellipsis arises in the same way as other kinds of ellipsis, through omission of predictable material. Zero roots seem, however, to have a completely different origin, although there are not too many cases where the historical development can be traced. Zero roots, as indicated in §11.2, seem to arise primarily through phonological changes that erode the material that originally constituted the root, as in the shift of Proto-Nyulnyulan *-wa- to the Bardi zero root 'give'. In addition, analogical changes can give rise to zero roots, as in the case of Russian *vy-nu-t'*, whose imperfective is *vy-nima-t'*. On the basis of other etymologically related verbs with different prefixes, such as the imperfective–perfective pairs *pri-nima-t'/pri-nja-t'* 'accept' and *s-nima-t'/s-nja-t'* 'take off', one would have expected the perfective of the verb 'take out' to be *vy-nja-t'*. However, -*nu* is a productive perfective suffix in Russian, and it seems that by analogy to perfective verbs with the suffix -*nu*, the root -*nja* in this form was replaced by the suffix -*nu*, thus giving rise to a form lacking a root.

The accidental production of zero roots through phonological change can be illustrated by the optional contraction of two auxiliary verbs in Japanese (Martin 1988: 514–15, 538–9). The auxiliary verbs in question are *i-ru* and *ik-u*, where -*(r)u* is the present tense suffix, the part preceding the hyphen the root. Both combine with the converb in -*te* of the lexical verb. As an auxiliary, *i-ru* expresses progressive or resultative aspect; the corresponding lexical verb *i-ru* means 'be located (of an animate entity)', although there is no animacy constraint on the auxiliary. The auxiliary *ik-u* covers a range of meanings, including gradual attainment of a result; as an independent verb, it means 'go'.

After the converb in -*te*, both auxiliary verbs can optionally lose their initial *i*, as illustrated in (96) and (97). In the case of *ik-u*, this simply leads to an overt allomorph of the root. In the case of *i-ru*, however, whose root consists solely of the vowel *i*, the root disappears altogether, giving rise to a zero root, more precisely a zero allomorph. This shows how the operation of the same phonological process can, accidentally, give rise to a zero morpheme/allomorph in one case, but not another.

(96) Japanese (Martin 1988)
    a. nat-te   ik-u
       nat-te   k-u
       become-CVB go-PRS
       'is gradually becoming more'
    b. ture-rare-te   it-ta
       ture-rare-te   t-ta
       take_away-PASS-CVB go-PST
       'was being taken away'

(97) Japanese (Martin 1988)
   a. si-te   i-ru
      si-te   Ø-ru
      do-CVB be-PRS
      'is doing'
   b. si-te   i-ta
      si-te   Ø-ta
      do-CVB be-PST
      'was doing'

The citation from Trommer (2012) with which we began this paper might suggest that if we find Verb Root Ellipsis, we might be even more likely to find Verb Affix Ellipsis, and indeed in all three languages that we have identified as clear instances of Verb Root Ellipsis this is the case. Tense markers can be ellipted in Akabea (Zamponi and Comrie forthcoming: §4.3.3.4). Van der Voort (2004: 576–8) notes ellipsis of the verbal inflectional affixes expressing subject person and mood in Kwaza, provided the information is retrievable from the linguistic context. Ellipsis of inflections in Inuktitut is noted by Swift and Allen (2002: 137–8), although they also observe that it is far more common in child speech than in caretaker speech. Jingulu does not permit affix ellipsis, i.e. ellipsis of the subject/object index(es) (or of the light verb), again setting it apart from the other languages.

11.7 Conclusions

In this paper, we hope to have shown that at least Inuktitut, Kwaza and Akabea (and at least two other Great Andamanese languages) have the phenomenon of Verb Root Ellipsis, whereby the root of a verb that is otherwise overt can be ellipted if it is retrievable from the context. This context may be either linguistic (such as a preceding conversational turn) or situational. It is possible that Jingulu may also evince the phenomenon, although our current assessment goes against this analysis.

The pragmatic condition of retrievability from context links Verb Root Ellipsis with word ellipsis, but differs in that the latter poses no challenges for the morphology – one simply omits a word – while the former challenges basic notions in proposing a word that consists of affixes without a root. The formal absence of an overt root links Verb Root Ellipsis with lexical zero roots (including zero allomorphs of roots that also have non-zero allomorphs), and gives rise to similar problems in principle of the phonological realisability of the output, but the two phenomena differ in that zero roots are lexically determined and are not dependent on pragmatic conditions of retrievability. Zero roots are also more widespread cross-linguistically than is Verb Root Ellipsis.

With only three or four known independent cases, Verb Root Ellipsis is a rare phenomenon indeed. While we would expect that more cases would be uncovered as more languages are investigated, it is significant that a large number of languages have been investigated to a degree where the occurrence of Verb Root Ellipsis would surely have been detected if present, strongly suggesting that only a minute fraction of the world's languages show this fascinating phenomenon. The rarity of the phenomenon can be viewed in terms of the canonical typological approach to the possible word, which operates in terms of form–meaning pairings as the ultimate canonical situation. Given that the root carries the basic lexical meaning of the word, the canonical expectation is that the overt meaning should be paired with an overt root. Zero roots and Verb Root Ellipsis both go against this expectation. Zero roots seem typically to be the result of the accidental, blind operation of phonological change. By contrast, Verb Root Ellipsis seems to be a wilful violation of the canonical form–meaning pairing, and is therefore predicted to be particularly rare, but not necessarily impossible. The kind of phenomenon of which one might say, 'I won't believe it until I see it' – but once one sees it, there is no excuse for not believing.

Acknowledgements

We thank all those who gave us comments on earlier versions of this paper, in particular Matthew Baerman, Andrew Hippisley and the audience at the 2016 Annual Meeting of the Linguistics Association of Great Britain. All remaining errors of fact and interpretation are our own.

Appendix: Languages Referred to and Their Language Family

Akabea	Great Andamanese
Akabo	Great Andamanese
Akachari	Great Andamanese
Akajeru	Great Andamanese
Akakhora	Great Andamanese
Akarbale	Great Andamanese
Alabama	Muskogean
Amele	Nuclear Trans New Guinea
Anêm	isolate
Arawun	Nuclear Trans New Guinea
Awa	Nuclear Trans New Guinea
Bardi	Nyulnyulan
Basque	isolate
Bau	Nuclear Trans New Guinea
Bongu	Nuclear Trans New Guinea
Bukiyip	Nuclear Torricelli
Bulgarian	Indo-European
Burushaski	isolate
Cantonese	Sino-Tibetan
Cavineña	Tacanan
Chamorro	Austronesian
Czech	Indo-European

Danaru	Nuclear Trans New Guinea
Dutch	Indo-European
English	Indo-European
Erima	Nuclear Trans New Guinea
French	Indo-European
Gahuku	Nuclear Trans New Guinea
Gayo	Austronesian
German	Indo-European
Girawa	Nuclear Trans New Guinea
Gumalu	Nuclear Trans New Guinea
Inuktitut	Eskimo-Aleut
Isebe	Nuclear Trans New Guinea
Italian	Indo-European
Itelmen	Chukotko-Kamchatkan
Jaminjung	Mirndi
Japanese	Japonic
Jingulu	Mirndi
Kam	Tai-Kadai
Karo Batak	Austronesian
Kâte	Nuclear Trans New Guinea
Kayardild	Tangkic
Ket	Yeniseian
Koasati	Muskogean
Kulina	Arawan
Kwaza	isolate
Lemio	Nuclear Trans New Guinea
Ma'di	Central Sudanic
Madi	Arawan
Menomini	Algic
Mian	Nuclear Trans New Guinea
Mohave	Yuman-Cochimí
Nimboran	Nimboranic
Okojuwoi	Great Andamanese
Okol	Great Andamanese
Opuchikwar	Great Andamanese
Panim	Nuclear Trans New Guinea
Pawnee	Caddoan
Polish	Indo-European
Rerau	Nuclear Trans New Guinea
Russian	Indo-European
Selepet	Nuclear Trans New Guinea
Sihan	Nuclear Trans New Guinea
Siroi	Nuclear Trans New Guinea

Toqabaqita	Austronesian
Tundra Nenets	Uralic
Turkish	Turkic
Udi	Nakh-Daghestanian
Urubu-Kaapor	Tupian
Wai Wai	Cariban
Warrwa	Nyulnyulan
Waskia	Nuclear Trans New Guinea
Yabong	Nuclear Trans New Guinea
Yangulam	Nuclear Trans New Guinea
Yawuru	Nyulnyulan
Yupik	Eskimo-Aleut

Notes

1. Although both authors bear responsibility for the paper as a whole, Comrie bears primary responsibility for §11.1, §11.3, §§11.4.1–11.4.2, §11.4.4 and §11.6.2, Zamponi for §11.2, §11.4.3, §11.6.1 and §11.7.
2. A zero root for 'give' is very likely a genealogical feature of this language group. Note that in Amele the transitive verb 'get, take' also has a phonologically null root when the object is singular: *Ø-* (SG) ~ *ced-* (PL) (Roberts 1987: 201, 272).
3. One could easily imagine such a system being reinterpreted as a richer suppletion system, and this seems to have happened with the verb 'give' in a language spoken a little north of Astrolabe Bay, Waskia, with distinctions according to person-number of the recipient: *tuiy-* ~ *tuw-* (to 3SG), *kisi-* (to 2SG), *asi-* (to 1SG), *idi-* (to PL) (Ross and Paol 1978: 43). These forms seem to include recipient markers etymologically, but not with sufficient transparency to permit precise reconstruction. Synchronically, there is no object agreement in the language (Comrie 2003: 279).
4. Loving and McKaughan gloss the last word as having a first person singular subject, but it is clear from their list of suffixes (1973: 41) and translation that this is an error for third person singular.
5. The element *-ru ~ -u* is, of course, a suffix, though it may diachronically have absorbed a trace of the stem-final vowel that may have been present in all the roots concerned at an earlier stage of the language.
6. Detailed analysis of the individual languages, excluding Siroi, is needed to identify the precise system in each case.
7. Note that in the Hunza dialect of Burushaski the roots *-t-* 'do', *-l-* 'sting' and *-l-* 'hit' also disappear by assimilation before the suffix for present tense (or aspect) *-ć*; for example, *é-t-ć-um*, surfaces as *ećum* 'doing, doing it' (Holst 2014: 38).
8. Compare also the segmentally null root denoting a general meaning 'transfer' in Mian (Fedden 2010: 469; 2011: 271), a language of the Nuclear Trans New Guinea family spoken in the Western Highlands of Papua New Guinea. The root in question is interpreted as 'give' when both theme and recipient are indexed (with a classificatory prefix and an object suffix respectively) and as 'take' when only the object is indexed (with a classificatory prefix). Although it contains neither consonants nor vowels, this root is not zero, however, in that it has a tone: all verb forms based on the root in question have an HLH tonal melody, represented by ˆ in example (i) from Mian.

(i) skemdâng=o   om-Ø^-n=e
    small_knife=N2   3SG.F_CL.O-give.PFV-1SG.R=HORT
    'Give me the small knife!' (Fedden 2011: 273)

9. In some works (e.g. Kibrik 1994; Janhunen 2010), reference is made to an enclitic zero-root/stem copula that consists of just inflectional morphemes in order to describe how copula complements are inflected in a way that is somewhat similar to that in which verbs are normally inflected, as in Tundra Nenets in example (ii).

(ii) (mən'°)   wæwa-dəm-c'°
     I   bad-1SGS-PST
     'I was bad.' (Nikolaeva 2014: 252)

We believe it unnecessary to introduce a hidden zero root/stem in such cases, preferring to analyse this as direct attachment of the inflections to the complement. Also note that the zero-root existential verbs of Nimboran and Gahuku we mentioned in this section should not be considered a type of copula. For a verb to be identified as a copula, it must occur with two core arguments, subject and complement, covering at least the identity relation and/or the attribution relation (Dixon 2010: 160). This is not the case with the existential verbs of Nimboran and Gahuku.

10. Gapping renders unexpressed the verb and, optionally, other elements of the verb phrase in the latter clause(s) of a coordinate or comparative structure (*The soprano sang the high notes and the tenor Ø the low notes*). Stripping is a special case of gapping that strips away all but one main constituent in the ellipsis clause under identity with the antecedent clause (*I like to read in the evening, and Priscilla Ø too*). Non-main constituents, like adverbs or negation, can be overt in the stripped clause as well (*Neighbours often come to visit her and sometimes relatives Ø*).

11. Sluicing describes sentences in which an interrogative clause is elided leaving only its wh-word (or phrase) overt (*We need to ask someone, but we don't know who Ø*). Verb phrase ellipsis is the omission of the verb and its objects or adjuncts licensed by an immediately preceding auxiliary (*Jack doesn't eat meat, but Victor does Ø*).

12. The idiom *z byka* (lit. *z byk-a* from bull-GEN), variant *bykiem* (lit. *byk-iem* bull-INS), in combination with an overt or, as in (20), covert verb of hitting means '[hit] with the head', 'butt'. The most neutral overt verb of hitting is *uderzyć* 'hit, strike', but other verbs whose interpretation incorporates a semantic element of hitting are also possible, such as *walnąć* 'knock down' (Dereń and Polański 2008: 87).

13. Even in English we sometimes find this use of modal verbs in older forms of the language. In two of Shakespeare's famous tragedies, for instance, the following lines occur: *I your Commission will forthwith dispatch, And he to England shall along you* (Hamlet III, iii, 3–4), *I will to morrow (And betimes I will) to the weyard Sisters* (Macbeth III, iv, 131–2) (Blake 2002: 221).

14. In Canada, the term 'Inuit' is preferred.

15. We follow Swift and Allen (2002) in giving a first line that represents standard orthography, followed by a second line that undoes some of the morphophonology in order to allow a clear division into morphemes.

16. The number (plural) marker precedes the somatic prefix when the latter is *ig-* ~ *idʒ-*.

17. We present Akabea (and other Great Andamanese) examples with a first line that reproduces exactly the spelling of the original, including diacritics and word divisions, and a second line that gives our semi-phonemic representation and shows morpheme and clitic boundaries.

18. In Akabea, several roots appear as multicategorial lexical bases. Some roots, specifically,

are able to function both adjectivally and verbally (Zamponi and Comrie forthcoming: §3.1). We cannot exclude that *beriŋa* is also such a root.
19. Pensalfini (2003: 84–5) actually distinguishes three subtypes: (a) clauses expressing coming and going; (b) clauses with predictable meanings; and (c) clauses where the root meaning is understood, with only the last called 'root ellipsis'; but it not clear whether this indicates an analysis with three different constructions, or whether these are just different interpretations of a single rootless construction.
20. The notation Pn indicates a prefix n positions away from P0 in the Ket verb structure template. Many Ket verb stems also have a third component, a thematic consonant in position P5, which finds no analogue in Jingulu.
21. It would remain to be worked out how morphemes like the irrealis fit into this analysis, given that they would occur in the second root position but do not convey lexical information.
22. See Baerman (2001) for more details, including comparison with differing resolutions in Bulgarian dialects, some of which have stress on the negative particle in combination with some following clitics. Baerman argues for an analysis for these dialects where *ne=* is inherently stressed and loses its stress under certain circumstances. In the standard language, however, in the absence of contrastive stress the negative particle is never stressed, and a clitic is stressed if and only if it immediately follows the negative particle.
23. Note that *iyi* is the orthographic representation of the long vowel [iː].

References

Abbi, Anvita (2012), *Dictionary of the Great Andamanese Language: English–Great Andamanese–Hindi*, Delhi: Ratna Sagar.
Abbi, Anvita (2013), *A Grammar of the Great Andamanese Language: An Ethnolinguistic Study*, Leiden and Boston: Brill.
Baerman, Matthew (2001), 'The prosodic properties of *ne* in Bulgarian', in Gerhild Zybatow, Uwe Junghanns, Grit Mehlhorn and Luka Szucsich (eds), *Current Issues in Formal Slavic Linguistics*, Frankfurt am Main: Peter Lang, pp. 59–68.
Barbiers, Sjef (1995), *The Syntax of Interpretations*, The Hague: Holland Academic Graphic.
Blackings, Mairi and Nigel Fabb (2003), *A Grammar of Ma'di*, Berlin: Mouton de Gruyter.
Blake, Norman F. (2002), *A Grammar of Shakespeare's Language*, Basingstoke and New York: Palgrave.
Bloomfield, Leonard (1939), 'Menomini morphophonemics', *Travaux du Cercle Linguistique de Prague*, 8, pp. 105–15.
Bloomfield, Leonard (1962), *The Menomini Language*, New Haven, CT and London: Yale University Press.
Bowern, Claire (2012), *A Grammar of Bardi*, Berlin and Boston: De Gruyter Mouton.
Chadwick, Neil (1975), *A Descriptive Study of the Djingili Language*, Canberra: Australian Institute of Aboriginal Studies.
Comrie, Bernard (2003), 'Recipient person suppletion in the verb "give"', in Mary Ruth Wise, Thomas N. Headland and Ruth M. Brend (eds), *Language and Life: Essays in Memory of Kenneth L. Pike*, Dallas: Summer Institute of Linguistics International and the University of Texas at Arlington, pp. 265–81.
Conrad, Robert J. and Kepas Wogiga (1991), *An Outline of Bukiyip Grammar*, Canberra: Pacific Linguistics.
Deibler, Ellis W. (1976), *Semantic Relationships of Gahuku Verbs*, Norman: Summer Institute of Linguistics of the University of Oklahoma.
Dereń, Ewa and Edward Polański (2008), *Wielki słownik języka polskiego*, Kraków: Krakowskie Wydawnictwo Naukowe.

Dienst, Stefan (2014), *A Grammar of Kulina*, Berlin and Boston: De Gruyter Mouton.
Dixon, R. M. W. (2004), *The Jarawara Language of Southern Amazonia*, Oxford: Oxford University Press.
Dixon, R. M. W. (2009), 'Zero and nothing in Jarawara', in Johannes Helmbrecht, Yoko Nishina, Yong-Min Shin, Stavros Skopeteas and Elisabeth Verhoeven (eds), *Form and Function in Language Research: Papers in Honour of Christian Lehmann*, Berlin: Mouton de Gruyter, pp. 125–37.
Dixon, R. M. W. (2010), *Basic Linguistic Theory*, vol. 2: *Grammatical Topics*, Oxford: Oxford University Press.
Eades, Domenyk (2005), *A Grammar of Gayo: A Language of Aceh, Sumatra*, Canberra: Pacific Linguistics.
Evans, Nicholas D. (1995), *A Grammar of Kayardild: With Historical-Comparative Notes on Tangkic*, Berlin and New York: Mouton de Gruyter.
Fedden, Sebastian (2010), 'Ditransitives in Mian', in Andrej Malchukov, Martin Haspelmath and Bernard Comrie (eds), *Studies in Ditransitive Constructions: A Comparative Handbook*, Berlin and New York: Mouton de Gruyter, pp. 456–85.
Fedden, Sebastian (2011), *A Grammar of Mian*, Berlin and Boston: De Gruyter Mouton.
Gaeta, Livio (2009), 'Inflectional morphology and productivity: Considering qualitative and quantitative approaches', in Patrick O. Steinkrüger and Manfred Krifka (eds), *On Inflection*, Berlin and New York: Mouton de Gruyter, pp. 45–68.
Geerts, G., W. Haeseryn, J. de Rooij and M. C. van den Toorn (1984), *Algemene Nederlandse spraakkunst*, Groningen: Wolters-Noordhoff.
Guillaume, Antoine (2008), *A Grammar of Cavineña*, Berlin and New York: Mouton de Gruyter.
Hall, Robert A. (1983), *Proto-Romance Morphology*, Amsterdam and Philadelphia: Benjamins.
Harris, Alice C. (2008), 'Light verbs as classifiers in Udi', *Diachronica*, 25, pp. 213–41.
Hawkins, Robert E. (1998), 'Wai Wai', in Desmond C. Derbyshire and Geoffrey K. Pullum (eds), *Handbook of Amazonian Languages*, vol. 4, Berlin and New York: Mouton de Gruyter, pp. 25–224.
Holst, Jan Henrik (2014), *Advances in Burushaski Linguistics*, Tübingen: Narr.
Hosokawa, Komei (1991), *The Yawuru Language of West Kimberley: A Meaning-Based Description*, PhD dissertation, Australian National University.
Inkelas, Sharon (1993), 'Nimboran position class morphology', *Natural Language and Linguistic Theory*, 11, pp. 559–624.
Janhunen, Juha (2010), 'Enclitic zero verbs in some Eurasian languages', in Lars Johanson and Martine Robbeets (eds), *Transeurasian Verbal Morphology in a Comparative Perspective: Genealogy, Contact, Chance*, Wiesbaden: Harrassowitz, pp. 165–80.
Kakumasu, James (1986), 'Urubu-Kaapor', in Desmond C. Derbyshire and Geoffrey K. Pullum (eds), *Handbook of Amazonian Languages*, vol. 1, Berlin, New York and Amsterdam: Mouton de Gruyter, pp. 326–406.
Kibrik, Aleksandr E. (1994), 'Khinalug', in Rieks Smeets (ed.), *The Indigenous Languages of the Caucasus*, vol. 4: *North East Caucasian Languages*, part 2, Delmar: Caravan Books, pp. 367–406.
Kimball, Geoffrey D. (1991), *Koasati Grammar*, Lincoln, NE and London: University of Nebraska Press.
Kittilä, Seppo (2006), 'The anomaly of the verb "give" explained by its high (formal and semantic) transitivity', *Linguistics*, 44, pp. 569–612.
Lepschy, Anna Laura and Giulio Lepschy (1988), *The Italian Language Today*, 2nd edn, London and New York: Routledge.

Lichtenberk, Frantisek (2008), *A Grammar of Toqabaqita*, vol. 2, Berlin and New York: Mouton de Gruyter.
Loving, Richard and Howard McKaughan (1973), 'Awa verbs part I: The internal structure of independent verbs', in Howard McKaughan (ed.), *The Languages of the Eastern Family of the East New Guinea Highland Stock*, Seattle and London: University of Washington Press, pp. 36–55.
McElhanon, Kenneth A. (1972), *Selepet Grammar. Part I: From Root to Phrase*, Canberra: Pacific Linguistics.
McElhanon, Kenneth A. (1973), *Towards a Typology of the Finisterre-Huon Languages, New Guinea*, Canberra: Pacific Linguistics.
McGregor, William (1994), *Warrwa*, Munich and Newcastle: Lincom Europa.
McShane, Marjorie J. (2005), *A Theory of Ellipsis*, Oxford: Oxford University Press
Man, Edward H. (1878), Andamanese grammar, annotated by Sir R. C. Temple, manuscript no. 111 in the Edward H. Man collection of the Royal Anthropological Institute of Great Britain and Ireland, London.
Man, Edward H. (1919–23), 'Dictionary of the South Andaman language'. Indian Antiquary 48 (1919) Supp., pp. 1–84, 49 (1920) Supp., pp. 85–136, 50 (1921) Supp., pp. 137–64, 51 (1922) Supp., pp. 165–88, 52 (1923) Supp., pp. 189–203.
Man, Edward H. and Richard T. Temple (1878), *A Grammar of the Bôjingîjîda or South Andaman Language*, Calcutta: Thacker, Spink.
Martin, Samuel E. (1988), *A Reference Grammar of Japanese*, 2nd edn, Rutland, VT and Tokyo: Charles E. Tuttle.
Matthews, Stephen and Virginia Yip (2011), *Cantonese: A Comprehensive Grammar*, 2nd edn, London and New York: Routledge.
May, Kevin (1997), *A Study of the Nimboran Language: Phonology, Morphology, and Phrase Structure*, MA thesis, La Trobe University.
Mel'čuk, Igor (2006), *Aspects of the Theory of Morphology*, ed. David Beck, Berlin: Mouton de Gruyter.
Munro, Pamela (1976), *Mojave Syntax*, New York and London: Garland
Newman, John (1996), *Give: A Cognitive Linguistic Study*, Berlin and New York: Mouton de Gruyter.
Newman, John (2002), 'Culture, cognition, and the grammar of "give" clauses', in N. J. Enfield (ed.), *Ethnosyntax: Explorations in Grammar and Culture*, Oxford: Oxford University Press, pp. 74–95.
Nikolaeva, Irina (2014), *A Grammar of Tundra Nenets*, Berlin and Boston: De Gruyter Mouton.
Parks, Douglas R. and Lula Nora Pratt (2008), *A Dictionary of Skiri Pawnee*, Lincoln, NE and London: University of Nebraska Press.
Pensalfini, Rob (2003), *A Grammar of Jingulu, an Aboriginal Language of the Northern Territory*, Canberra: Pacific Linguistics.
Pensalfini, Rob (2011), *Jingulu Texts and Dictionary*, Canberra: Pacific Linguistics.
Pensalfini, Rob (2015), 'Jingulu', in Nicola Grandi and Livia Körtvélyessy (eds), *Edinburgh Handbook of Evaluative Morphology*, Edinburgh: Edinburgh University Press, pp. 416–22.
Portman, Maurice V. (1887), *Manual of the Andamanese Languages*, London: W. H. Allen.
Portman, Maurice V. (1898), *Notes on the Languages of the South Andaman Group of Tribes*, Calcutta: Office of the Superintendent of Government Printing.
Pustet, Regina (2003), *Copulas: Universals in the Categorization of the Lexicon*, Oxford: Oxford University Press.

Radcliffe-Brown, Alfred R. (1933), *The Andaman Islanders*, 2nd edn, Cambridge: The University Press.
Roberts, John R. (1987), *Amele*, London, New York and Sydney: Croom Helm.
Ross, Malcolm with John Natu Paol (1978), *Waskia Grammar Sketch and Vocabulary*, Canberra: Pacific Linguistics.
Saltarelli, Mario (1988), *Basque*, London and New York: Routledge.
Scatton, Ernest A. (1984), *A Reference Grammar of Modern Bulgarian*, Columbus, OH: Slavica.
Schultze-Berndt, Eva (2015), 'Complex verbs, simple alternations, valency and verb classes in Jaminjung', in Andrej Malchukov and Bernard Comrie (eds), *Valency Classes in the World's Languages*, vol. 2, Berlin and Boston: De Gruyter Mouton, pp. 1117–62.
Suter, Edgar (2014), 'Kâte *he* 'hit' and *qa* 'hit': A study in lexicology', *Language and Linguistics in Melanesia*, 32, pp. 18–57.
Swift, Mary D. and Shanley E. M. Allen (2002), 'Verb base ellipsis in Inuktitut conversational discourse', *International Journal of American Linguistics*, 68, pp. 133–56.
Thurston, William (1982), *A Comparative Study in Anêm and Lusi*, Canberra: Pacific Linguistics.
Thurston, William (1987), *Processes of Change in the Languages of North-Western New Britain*, Canberra: Pacific Linguistics.
Tikkanen, Bertil (1999), 'Concerning the typology of Burushaski and the roots of its prefixes d- and n-', *Studia Orientalia*, 85, pp. 277–300.
Trommer, Jochen (2012), 'Ø-exponence', in Jochen Trommer (ed.), *The Morphology and Phonology of Exponence*, Oxford: Oxford University Press, pp. 326–54.
Vajda, Edward J. (2015), 'Valency properties of the Ket verb clause', in Andrej Malchukov and Bernard Comrie (eds), *Valency Classes in the World's Languages*, vol. 1, Berlin and Boston: De Gruyter Mouton, pp. 629–68.
Vanden Wyngaerd, Guido (1994), *PRO-legomena: Distribution and Reference of Infinitival Subjects*, Berlin and New York: Mouton de Gruyter.
van der Voort, Hein (2004), *A Grammar of Kwaza*, Berlin and New York: Mouton de Gruyter.
van Riemsdijk, Henk C. (2002), 'The unbearable lightness of GOing. The projection parameter as a pure parameter governing the distribution of elliptic motion verbs in Germanic', *Journal of Comparative Germanic Linguistics*, 5, pp. 143–96.
van Riemsdijk, Henk C. (2012), 'The absent, the silent, and the audible: Some thoughts on the morphology of silent verbs', in Esther Torrego (ed.), *Of Grammar, Words, and Verses: In Honor of Carlos Piera*, Amsterdam: John Benjamins, pp. 19–39.
Wells, Margaret A. (1979), *Siroi Grammar*, Canberra: Pacific Linguistics.
Wetzer, Harrie (1996), *The Typology of Adjectival Predication*, Berlin and New York: Mouton de Gruyter.
Woollam, Wilfred (1996), *A Grammar of Karo Batak, Sumatra*, Canberra: Pacific Linguistics.
Yang, Tongyin and Jerold A. Edmondson (2008), 'Kam', in Anthony V. N. Diller, Jerold A. Edmondson and Luo Yongxian (eds), *The Tai-Kadai Languages*, London and New York: Routledge, pp. 509–84.
Zamponi, Raoul and Bernard Comrie (forthcoming), 'A Grammar of Akabea', MS.
Z'graggen, Johannes A. (1980a), *A Comparative Word List of the Mabuso Languages, Madang Province, Papua New Guinea*, Canberra: Pacific Linguistics.
Z'graggen, Johannes A. (1980b), *A Comparative Word List of the Rai Coast Languages, Madang Province, Papua New Guinea*, Canberra: Pacific Linguistics.

12

Bound but Still Independent: Quotative and Verificative in Archi

Marina Chumakina

12.1 Introduction

The 'word', a basic concept used by all linguists independently of their area of interest and theoretical persuasion, is notoriously hard to define. The problems in delineating the notion of word are different for phonologists, morphologists, syntacticians, psycholinguists, etc. (Dixon and Aikhenvald 2002; Taylor 2015). The case I present in this paper concerns the basic, empirical issue of defining a word: how to treat instances of what seems to be one word phonologically, but is, syntactically and morphologically, clearly more than one word.

The two phenomena I discuss in this paper are found in a Nakh-Daghestanian language, Archi: the quotative marker *-(e)r* and a verificative marker *-k:us*. They both are phonologically bound elements and in many respects behave like typical clitics. However, unlike familiar instances of pronominal or auxiliary clitics, these two possess a large number of morphosyntactic properties of an independent word.

The paper is organised as follows: first, I give a short introduction to Archi morphosyntax. §12.3 and §12.4 discuss the quotative and verificative respectively. In each of these sections, I introduce the marker, its usage and meaning, then discuss its morphological and syntactic properties. Conclusions are presented in §12.5.

12.2 Archi Inflectional System at a Glance

Archi is a language belonging to the Lezgic group of the Nakh-Daghestanian family. It is spoken by about 1,200 people who live in several settlements situated within walking distance of each other in the highlands of Daghestan (Russian Federation). The whole group of settlements is perceived both by the Archi people and outsiders as one village. Despite such a small number of speakers, until the beginning of the twenty-first century, the language was vital, with all children monolingual in Archi well into their teens. Since the beginning of the twenty-first century, however, there has been a steady decline in the number of people living in the village and, consequently, of children speaking Archi as their first language.

This section provides information about those aspects of Archi grammar which are essential for understanding the examples in the main part of the paper.

Nouns in Archi are distributed across four genders: gender I comprises nouns referring to male humans; gender II, to female humans. The rest of the lexicon is distributed between genders III and IV with a tendency for animals and other live objects to be in gender III. Nouns are also inflected for case (see Chumakina et al. 2016 for details). The absolutive case form is typically used to express the only argument of an intransitive verb (S), and the patient-like argument of a transitive verb (P), such as *akɬ'* 'meat' in (1). The absolutive argument also controls agreement in gender and number (singular and plural) on its targets. Most verbs exhibit agreement; the ability to do so is part of the verb's lexical information (see Chumakina and Corbett 2015 for details). At least some members of all other parts of speech also agree with the absolutive argument of their clause (see Chumakina et al. 2016 for a detailed description and analysis of Archi agreement).

Ergative case forms are used to mark the agent-like argument of a transitive verb (A), as with *gatuli* 'cat' in (1). They can also be used to mark an instrument, such as *gullali* 'bullet' in (2).

(1) gatu-li   akɬ'   oχ:a-li   oqˤa
    cat(III)-SG.ERG   meat(IV)[SG.ABS]   [IV.SG]steal.PFV-CVB   [IV.SG]leave.PFV
    'The cat stole the meat.'

(2) wa-s   kɬ'an-kul   gulla-li   ača-s   kɬ'an
    2SG.OBL-DAT   love-NMLZ(IV)[SG.ABS]   bullet(III)-SG.ERG   [IV.SG]kill-FIN   want
    'You want to kill our love with a bullet.'
    (based on T1: 37)[1]

The dative case form is used to express a benefactive, recipient and other third arguments of three-placed verbs, and also the experiencer argument of the verbs of perception, emotion and cognition. Thus, in (2) the non-clausal argument of the verb *kɬ'an* 'want' is expressed by the dative *was* 'you'.

The extent of the verbal paradigm in Archi is considerable. The inflected word forms of a verbal lexeme are produced using several different verbal stems. The number of stems a lexeme has depends on the type of the verb that it is. Archi verbs can be divided into two major classes: dynamic and stative.[2] Orthogonal to this division is the division into simple and complex verbs. Simple verbs belong to a closed class of about 170 items. Complex verbs are composed of a simple verb and a non-inflecting element.

Dynamic verbs have four aspectual stems (perfective, imperfective, potential and finalis) and an imperative stem, which is often irregular. Stative verbs have only one stem. Tense forms are expressed by periphrasis (Chumakina 2013); periphrastic forms consist of (non-finite) converbs and a finite copula verb.

Table 12.1 Verbal stems, gender IV singular

	PFV	IPFV	POT	FIN	IMP
'get cold'	qa	qe⟨r⟩qi-r	qa-qi	qe-s	qeqi
'beat'	daχdi	da⟨r⟩χi-r	daχdi-qi	daχi-s	daχi

Table 12.1 shows an example of the aspectual stems and an imperative form of two dynamic verbs. The stems are shown in their gender IV singular form, which has no overt agreement exponent.

All verb stems can be used as independent fully inflected forms, or they can serve as a base for further morphology to form attributives, converbs and various mood forms. The perfective, imperfective and potential stems can be used as finite predicates (see Chumakina 2011 for examples and discussion of their semantics), the imperative heads an imperative clause, and the finalis is used very much like a Standard Average European infinitive.[3] In this paper, I discuss forms which have been considered by Kibrik (1977) to be part of the verbal paradigm: the quotative mood and the verificative converb. In §12.3 I argue that considering quotative a verbal mood is problematic since it attaches to any verbal form (including the modal ones), has no constraints on combining with any other verbal feature and is not an exclusively verbal marker.

Some details on the formation of non-finite verbal forms are required here, since the phenomena which are the focus of this paper interact with these forms in a non-trivial manner.

The non-finite verbal subparadigm is comprised of converbs, attributivised verbs (referred to here as 'attributives' for short) and masdars. Converbs head dependent clauses and serve as a component part of periphrastic verb forms; attributives head relative clauses; masdars head complement clauses of matrix verbs such as *sini* 'know', *bos* 'say' and others. It is important to note that, unlike many familiar non-finite forms, Archi converbs, attributives and masdars have the possibility to express agreement.

Different converbial suffixes select different verb stems. Thus, suffix *-li* gets selected by the perfective stem to form the consecutive converb, and denotes an action that has finished before the action of the main clause starts. It is also used for perfective periphrastic tenses. Converbial suffix *-ši* is selected by the imperfective stem to form the simultaneous converb, denoting an action that is going on at the same time as the action of the main clause, and it is also used for progressive periphrastic tenses. The same suffix gets selected by the potential stem to form a converb which denotes an action happening immediately after the action of the main clause. It is also used for the immediate future periphrastic tense. Archi also possesses an imperative converb, a unique feature among Nakh-Daghestanian languages (see Dobrushina 2008 for details), which is exemplified in (12) below.

Verbs are attributivised by the suffix *-t:u* which attaches to all aspectual stems. The resulting form agrees with its absolutive argument, just like a finite verb does, and also inflects for agreement with the head it modifies. As for the adverbial nouns, traditionally called masdars by the Caucasionists, it is sufficient to mention that in the clause headed by them, S and A can occur in the genitive case (see Chumakina et al. 2016 for details and examples).

12.3 Archi Quotative

In Archi, speech can be reported by the use of an independent matrix verb *bos* 'say' and by a morphologically bound element *=(e)r*. The latter is the focus of this section.

The Archi quotative is best defined as a clitic: although it has been demonstrated that this term does not describe a unified observable phenomenon, it nevertheless has its usages as a term applied language-specifically to describe elements which share traits with both word and affix (Spencer and Luís 2012a; Zwicky 1994; Haurholm-Larsen 2015, among others). Throughout this paper I will be using a clitic notation for the interlinear glossing, i.e. the quotative will be glossed with the = sign.

I will start with some general information on the Archi quotative (§12.3.1) where I will show that in many respects it combines properties of affix and word in the same way as more familiar clitic examples do. §12.3.2 and §12.3.3 describe its syntactic and inflectional properties, which show that the Archi quotative retains surprisingly more properties of a word than is usual for bound elements.

12.3.1 Archi Quotative: Introduction

Before turning to the morphologically bound quotative, I will discuss the usage of the independent speech verb *bos* 'say'. In (3), the past evidential form of this verb *boli* 'said' occurs with two arguments: the ergative subject *tuwmi* 'he' and the clause *teb abčas kʷabšuqi* 'they will have to be killed'.[4] Note that *boli* takes the final position in a sentence, which is a normal position for a matrix verb in Archi.

(3) ju-w-mi   te-b   a⟨b⟩ča-s
     this-I.SG-ERG.SG that.PL-I/II.PL[ABS] ⟨I/II.PL⟩kill-FIN
     kʷa⟨b⟩šu-qi   bo-li
     ⟨I/II.PL⟩must.PFV-POT say.PFV-EVID
     'He said: "They will have to be killed."'
     (T1: 27)[5]

A third argument, expressing the addressee of the speech, occurs in the contallative case, as in (4).

(4) zari   tu-w-mi-r-ši   salam   bo-li
     1.SG.ERG that-I.SG-OBL.SG-CONT-ALL   greeting say.PFV-EVID
     'I greeted him.' (lit. 'I said "Salam" to him.')

The verb *bos* can be used to report the speech of a third person (5), or for self-reporting (6). In these examples the speaker is not expressed by an overt argument. Since Archi verbs do not inflect for person, the identity of the speaker is typically understood only from the context of the utterance.

(5) ans   b-i   b-okło-qi   bo-li
    bull(III)[SG.ABS] III.SG-be.PRS   III.SG-give.PFV-POT   say.PFV-EVID
    'They said that there is a bull, and they would give it (away).'

(6) uc:i   bo
    I.SG.stand.IMP   say.PFV
    'I said (to a man): wait!'

Another way of indicating reported speech is by using the morphologically bound element =(e)r, exemplified in (7).

(7) a. ju-w-mi-r-ši   bo-li   un   daki   w-eːʕ-t'o=r
       that-I.SG-SG.OBL-CONT-ALL   say.PFV-EVID   2.SG.ABS   why   I.SG-come-POT.NEG=QUOT
       'They said to him: "Why wouldn't you come?"'
       (based on Mammadibir: 43)
    b. to-r   qiri-li-ł:u   d-aq:'qu-q=er
       that-II.SG[ABS]   old.woman(II)-OBL.SG-COMIT   II.SG-leave.PFV-POT=QUOT
       '(He$_i$) said that (he$_i$) will leave her with an old woman.'

In (7a), the quotative marker =r attaches to the verb weːʕt'u '(male) will not come' and introduces the complement of the verb boli 'said'. In (7b), however, the same marker (attached to the verb daq:'uqi 'will leave her') is used without the matrix verb. Example (7) demonstrates, therefore, that the =er can be used as a complementiser on the one hand and as an independent marker of reported speech on the other.

In contrast to the independent verb bos 'say', the quotative is used to report third person speech only, and cannot be used for self-reporting (8) or to report second person speech (9).

(8) *zari   to-r   qiri-li-ł:u   d-aq:'qu-q=er
     1SG.ERG   that-II.SG[ABS]   old.woman(II)-OBL.SG-COMIT   II.SG-leave.PFV-POT=QUOT
     Intended: 'I said that I will leave her with an old woman.'

(9) *un   to-r   qiri-li-ł:u   d-aq:'qu-q=er
     2SG.ERG   that-II.SG[ABS]   old.woman(II)-OBL.SG-COMIT   II.SG-leave.PFV-POT=QUOT
     Intended: 'You said that you will leave her with an old woman.'

Compare (8) and (9) with (10), where the source of the reported speech is third person (tuwmi) co-referential with the first person ergative argument of 'leave' (zari).

(10) tu-w-mi   zari   to-r   qiri-li-ł:u   old.woman(II)-OBL.SG-COMIT
     that-I.SG-SG.ERG   1SG.ERG   that-II.SG[ABS]
     d-aq:'qu-q=er
     II.SG-leave.PFV-POT=QUOT
     'He said: "I will leave her with an old woman."'

The quotative =(e)r originates from an imperfective form of the verb bos 'say'. This verb has the following stems: perfective bo, imperfective war, potential boqi, finalis *bos*, imperative *ba* and does not inflect for gender. The quotative represents a phonologically reduced form of *war* which cannot be used independently but must attach to another full word. It also gets stripped of its grammatical meaning: normally, the imperfective stem is used as a base for inflected forms denoting an ongoing action, whereas the quotative normally refers to the past completed action of speech.

The quotative attaches to different verbal forms. Thus, in (11) it attaches to the imperatives *ma* 'take', *bukne* 'eat', *bakłba* 'give' and to *ira*, the question form of the verb 'be'. Here, I translate the quotative as 'he would say' as it is clear from the context that it refers to habitual actions in the past. Each time the speaker's father went to the town, he would bring sweets for the kids and argue (contrary to what their mother would claim) that he had brought a nice, useful thing.

(11) χit:a   ma=r   bu-kne=r   b-akł-ba=r
     then   take.IMP=QUOT   III.SG-eat.IMP=QUOT   III.SG-give-IMP=QUOT
     jas:a   kʷa-t:u-t   hekł'ena   i-ra=r
     now   [IV.SG]need-ATTR-IV.SG thing(IV)[SG.ABS]   IV.SG.be.PRS-QUEST=QUOT
     dija-mu
     father(I)-SG.ERG
     'Then, "Take it!", he would say, "Eat!", he would say and "Give (to the kids)" he would say, "Is this a good thing (needed thing)?" – Father would say.'
     (Sisters: 47)

The quotative can also attach to a non-finite verbal forms such as a so-called imperative converb *bokłalli* 'sell' in (12). Besides verbs, the quotative can also attach to other parts of speech. Thus, (12) exemplifies its attachment to a noun *č'an* 'sheep'.

(12) k'an   jat:i-š   e⟨b⟩k'u-t:u-b=er   č'an=er
     most   top-EL   choose.⟨III.SG⟩PFV-ATTR-III.SG=QUOT   sheep(III)[SG.ABS]=QUOT
     b-okła-ll=er,   arso-wu   sa=r
     III.SG-sell.PFV-CVB.IMP=QUOT   money(IV)[SG.ABS]-and [IV.SG]take.IMP=QUOT
     'He said, choose the best sheep, sell it and take the money.'
     (T30: 38)

In (13) the quotative attaches to the question word *daki* 'why', an exclamative *helo* 'hey' as well as *q'ardili*, the past evidential form of the verb 'sit'.

(13) dak=er   heloww=er   eχ:ˤ-ut   gerk:e-r-ši
     why=QUOT   hey=QUOT   cheek(IV)-PL.ABS   hang.over-IPFV-CVB
     q'a⟨r⟩di-l=er
     ⟨II.SG⟩sit.PFV-EVID=QUOT
     'Why, (mother) says, you are sitting (here), she says, with cheeks hanging over (stuffed cheeks).'
     (Sisters: 71)

In (14) the quotative attaches to an exclamative *ja ja* 'well, well', to a periphrastic form *ark'uli erdi* 'has forced', to a pronoun *un* 'you', and to two finalis (infinitive) forms: *sark:es* 'to look' and *c'iχdi duχ:as* 'to steal'.

(14) ja   ja=r   ɬ:i   a⟨r⟩k'u-li   e⟨r⟩de=r
     well   well-QUOT   who.ERG   ⟨II.SG⟩drive.PFV-CVB   ⟨II.SG⟩be.PST=QUOT
     un=er   tus:əl-l-a-k   sa⟨r⟩k:e-s:=er
     2SG.ABS=QUOT   bag(IV)-SG.OBL-IN-LAT   ⟨II.SG⟩look-FIN-QUOT
     c'iχdi   du-χ:a-s:=er   buwa-mu
     steal   II.SG-steal-FIN-QUOT mother(II)-SG.ERG
     'Well, well (she) said, who made, (she) said, you, (she) said, look into the bag, (she) said, and steal, said mother.'
     (Sisters: 82)

Note here the ergative case form *buwamu* 'mother' which refers to the source of speech and appears at the end of the sentence; I will discuss such ergatives in the next section.

The quotative can be used together with the full verb of speech: in (15) the quotative is attached to *ʕummalla* 'never' (lit. 'in life'), a locative form of the noun *ʕummar* 'life' which directly follows the converbial form of the verb 'say' *warši* combined with a semi-auxiliary inchoative verb *ert:i* 'became'.

(15) χit:a   buwa   wa-r-ši   e⟨r⟩t:i
     then   mother(II)[SG.ABS] say-IPFV-CVB   ⟨II.SG⟩become.PFV
     ʕummal-l-a=r   hekʼen   š:ubu-s
     life(IV)-SG.OBL-IN=QUOT   thing(IV)[SG.ABS]   [IV.SG]buy-FIN
     i-t'o=r
     [IV.SG]be.PRS-NEG=QUOT
     'Then mother started saying: you never bought anything (useful) . . .'
     (Sisters: 36)[6]

Examples (10)–(15) show that the quotative attaches to (heads of) syntactic phrases rather than stems and displays 'promiscuous attachment', i.e. attaches to words of different word classes. As far as I could observe, the quotative never attaches to the elements inside the verb phrase – given that the verb phrase has the normal word order, i.e. OV. In this case, the quotative attaches to the (final) verb form. If, however, the object of the VP is moved to the right of the verb phrase for focusing purposes, as *č'an* 'sheep' in (12) and *un* 'you' in (14), the quotative attaches both to the verb and the object.

The statement that the quotative is not a phonologically independent word needs further elaboration: so far I have only demonstrated that one of the vowels gets deleted when the quotative attaches to a vowel-final host. However, all Archi auxiliary verbs also do this in normal-speed speech. Thus, *warši ert:i* 'started saying' from (15) is actually pronounced [waršert:i]. In the case of the auxiliaries, however, one can always pronounce them slowly with both vowels and other words can be put before the auxiliary for specific pragmatic purposes. Thus, the auxiliary construction in (15) can be modified as *warši buwa ert:i* 'mother started saying'. None of these can be done with the quotative: one cannot pronounce, say, *daq:'quqer* 'I will leave her' from (7) as *daq:'quqi er*, and nothing can be put between the quotative and its host. Moreover, besides vowel deletion, other morphophonological processes accompany the quotative attachment.

When attaching to a consonant-final host, the quotative is realised in its full form =*er*.

(16) dija-mu   ans   dołu-ma   b-e‹r›χ:a-r=er
     father(I)-SG.ERG bull(III)[SG.ABS] shed(III)-IN III.SG-‹IPFV›stay-IPFV=QUOT
     'Father says that the bull is staying in the shed.'

If the host form ends in a vowel, the vowel of the quotative gets deleted. Thus, in (17) where the host form ends with a question marker -*ra*, the quotative is realised as -*r*.

(17) bošor-mu   ł:onnol   a‹r›χu-ra=r
     man(I)-SG.ERG woman(II)[SG.ABS] ‹II.SG›sleep.PFV-QUEST=QUOT
     'The husband asked if (his) wife is asleep.'

If the host ends in either [i] or [u], the vowel of the quotative gets deleted and the word-final high vowel is lowered to [e] or [o] respectively. Thus, in (18) the host form used independently is *iwχ:uli* 'stayed'; in the quotative form it gets realised as *iwχ:ule* and the quotative as =*r*.

(18) buwa-mu   dija   nokł'a   i‹w›χ:u-le=r
     mother(II)-SG.ERG father(I)[SG.ABS] house(IV).IN ‹I.SG›stay.PFV-EVID=QUOT
     'Mother said that father stayed at home.'

In (19), the host form *eku* 'fell' is realised as *ekor* with the quotative.

(19) lo   eko=r
     child(VI)[SG.ABS] [IV.SG]fall.over.PFV=QUOT
     'Somebody said that the child fell over.'

Similarly, in (20) the host's independent form *darc'art'u* 'is not filled' ends in the negative marker -*t'u* which is lowered to -*t'o* in the presence of the quotative.

(20) buwa-mu   inž   d-a‹r›c'a-r-t'o=r
     mother(II)-SG.ERG LOGOPH.SG.ABS II.SG-‹IPFV›fill-IPFV-NEG=QUOT
     'Mother says she's not full (i.e. she is still hungry).'

All of the above show that the bound quotative has undergone the following processes of grammaticalisation: phonological reduction; loss of phonological independence; and loss of grammatical meaning (ongoing action normally referred to by the imperfective). Besides, the Archi quotative can be used several times in a sentence and can co-occur with full verbs of speech; all these point to a typologically familiar grammaticalisation path for quotatives (Deutscher 2011); compare Akkadian quotatives (Hopper and Traugott 2012: 194–6), quotative particles in Russian (Grenoble 1998: 134–7) and the quotative in Natchez (Kimball 2015: 410) to name just a few.

12.3.2 Syntactic Properties of the Quotative

Clitics often represent a phonologically reduced form of an auxiliary verb, a pronoun or a matrix verb. Simple clitics (following Zwicky 1985) are used in the same syntactic position in the clause as their non-reduced counterparts; special clitics have specific positioning rules; in either case there is no expectation of changes in the clause syntactic structure due to the presence of a clitic. So it is not surprising that Archi complement clauses headed by a full speech verb look exactly the same as the clauses where the quotative marks the reported speech: the arguments retain the case marking (such as the ergative of the agent), and the verb retains its original form as it would do in the case of direct speech (such as the imperative or the prohibitive; see example (11)).

The construction with full speech verb, however, is a biclausal one, so the presence of, say, two ergatives will be no surprise: one ergative is licensed by the verb of speech, another is licensed by the verb in the complement clause. When the quotative is used, however, the sentence contains only one verb and yet it can have two agentive ergatives and also a contallative licensed by the quotative.

(21) zumzum-li za-r-ši bošor-mi χʕon χir
 Zumzum(II)-SG.ERG 1SG-CONT-ALL husband(I)-SG.ERG cow(III)[SG.ABS] behind
 a⟨b⟩u-le=r
 ⟨III.SG⟩drive.PFV-EVID=QUOT
 'Zumzum told me that (her) husband brought the cow (with him).'

One can argue that in this respect the quotative behaves like a valency changing affix; after all, causatives and applicatives can also increase the number of arguments in one clause. But unlike the causatives, the Archi quotative does not modify the semantics of the verb it attaches to; and the next two properties of the quotative I discuss indicate that the sentence which contains the quotative should be interpreted as biclausal.

Another syntactic property that the quotative shares with the independent speech verb is the usage of the logophoric pronoun, namely in the instances where the quoted speaker is co-referential with the agent of the 'content' verb of the quoted speech, the latter is expressed by a special pronoun. Example (22) shows the usage of the logophoric pronoun (22a) as opposed to a third person pronoun (22b) in a sentence with the full verb of speech.

(22) a. buwa-mu to-r d-a⟨r⟩c'a-r-t'u bo
 mother(II)-SG.ERG that.SG.ABS II.SG-⟨IPFV⟩fill-IPFV-NEG say.PFV
 'Mother$_i$ said she$_j$ is not full (i.e. still hungry).'
 b. buwa-mu inž d-a⟨r⟩c'a-r-t'u bo

    mother(II)-SG.ERG   LOGOPH.SG.ABS   II.SG-⟨IPFV⟩fill-IPFV-NEG   say.PFV
    'Mother$_i$ said she$_i$ is not full (i.e. still hungry).'

If the quotative form is used instead of the full verb of speech, the logophoric pronoun is used also.

(23)   buwa-mu   inž   d-a⟨r⟩c'a-r-t'o=r
        mother(II)-SG.ERG   LOGOPH.SG.ABS   II.SG-⟨IPFV⟩fill-IPFV-NEG=QUOT
        'Mother$_i$ said she$_i$ is not full (i.e. still hungry).'

The logophoric pronoun *inž* indicates biclausality: it cannot be used in a single independent clause without the quotative.

Finally, there is some indication that the interpretation of adverbs can point towards the biclausal interpretation of the structure containing the quotative. Consider the sentence in (24).

(24)   Rasul-li   jasqy   w-eqʕe=r
        Rasul(I)-SG.ERG   today   I.SG-come.POT=QUOT
        'Rasul said that he will come today.'

Normally, the interpretation would be: Rasul will come today; but it is also understood by my Archi interpreters that he said it today. In certain contexts, however, it is possible to get the interpretation where the adverb modifies the quotative, as in (25).

(25)   Rasul-li   q'ʕot:ij⟨t⟩u   is
        Rasul(I)-SG.ERG   in.winter.EMPH⟨IV.SG⟩   [IV.SG]1SG.GEN
        oq-li-t:i-k   w-eqʕe=r
        wedding(IV)-OBL.SG-SUP-LAT   I.SG-come.POT=QUOT
        'Already in winter Rasul said that he will come to my wedding.' [Given context: the wedding happens in summer.]

The syntactic behaviour of the Archi quotative demonstrates that despite being a morphologically bound element, it retains most of the syntactic properties of the independent matrix verb, such as the ability to take a clausal complement while having all its own overt arguments and the ability to be modified by an adverb. This last property seems rather unusual for a clitic.

12.3.3 Inflectional Properties of the Quotative

Normally, the quotative markers originating from a speech verb lose the ability to inflect: thus, Russian quotative *mol*, originating from a verb of speech *molviti*, lost the ability to express any verbal features such as tense, person, number and gender. Such a situation is common for quotative markers (Deutscher 2011), although they sometimes retain the ability to inflect for person and number: this is the situation in the Arawak language Garifuna where a quotative clitic inflects for person and number (Haurholm-Larsen 2015).

The Archi quotative, however, retains all the inflectional possibilities of its origin, the imperfective stem. First of all it can form a progressive converb. Consider the example in (26).

(26) iqna   q'ot   χir   at:i-na
     day(IV).LOC book(IV).PL.ABS   behind   [IV.PL]drive.PVF-CVB
     w-a⟨r⟩kɬi-r=er-ši   e⟨r⟩t:i
     I.SG-come⟨IPFV⟩-IPFV=QUOT-CVB   ⟨II.SG⟩become.PFV
     'You always come back dragging some books behind, mother started saying (to father).'
     (Sisters: 45)

Here, the converbial affix -*ši* attaches to the quotative marker =*er* which in turn is attached to *warkɬir*, an imperfective form of the verb *akɬis* 'come'. The converbial form of the quotative combines with the semi-auxiliary *ert:i* 'became' in the same way as the independent verb does. The resulting form is repeated in (27).

(27) w-a⟨r⟩kɬi-r=er-ši   e⟨r⟩t:i
     I.SG-come⟨IPFV⟩-IPFV=QUOT-CVB   ⟨II.SG⟩become.PFV
     '"You (always) come back ...", – she started saying (to father).'

Note first of all, that the main verb *warkɬir* agrees with its subject (father, the hearer) by the gender I singular prefix *w-*, whereas the form *ert:i* agrees with a gender II singular argument (mother, the speaker) by the infix ⟨r⟩. The easiest way to disentangle this agreement is to present the corresponding full verb construction.

(28) w-a⟨r⟩kɬi-r   war-ši   e⟨r⟩t:i
     I.SG-come⟨IPFV⟩-IPFV   say-CVB   ⟨II.SG⟩become.PFV
     '"You (always) come back ...", – she started saying (to a male).'

In (28), the complement clause is headed by a predicate *warkɬir* 'come', in a present habitual tense agreeing with its non-overt argument (father) in gender I singular. The matrix clause is headed by a periphrastic predicate *warši ert:i*, a progressive inchoative realised by a progressive converb and an auxiliary verb 'become'. It agrees with its non-overt argument (mother) in gender II singular.

In the sentence where the quotative is used, all that is left of the form *warši ert:i* is =*erši ert:i* which now has to attach to something. It is a very interesting question (to which I have no answer) whether the whole periphrastic form (i.e. the converbial affix plus an auxiliary) is based on the quotative or whether the periphrastic form *warši ert:i* gets reduced to =*erši ert:i*.

Example (29) shows the usage of the quotative converb with an auxiliary *edi* 'was'.

(29) jamu   k'ʷa-le:=r-ši   abaj   e⟨b⟩di-li
     that(I)[SG.ABS]   die.I.SG.PFV-EVID=QUOT-CVB   parents.PL.ABS   ⟨I/II.PL⟩be.PFV-EVID
     'Parents were saying that he had died.'
     (T22: 37)

Here, again, the quotative selects for the converbial suffix -*ši* which then combines with the auxiliary *ebdili*. If the full verb of speech had been used, the periphrastic form would have been (*abaj*) *warši ebdili* '(parents) were saying' where the progressive aspect of the periphrastic form allows the agent to be in the absolutive (so-called biabsolutive construction; see Chumakina and Bond 2016 for further details). The absolutive case form *abaj* in (29) controls the I/II plural agreement in the auxiliary *ebdili*, whereas the verb *k'ʷale:rši* 'die' agrees prefixally with the absolutive *jamu* 'he' in gender I singular.

But agreement is not the only thing which makes these constructions difficult. In (29) the quotative is attached to the past evidential form *k'ʷali* 'he died' based on the perfective stem *k'ʷa-*. The quotative *-er* selects the suffix of the progressive converb *-ši*. This suffix attaches to the imperfective or potential stem only, and can never be selected by the perfective stem. The form *k'ʷale:rši* contains, therefore, two incompatible grammatical elements: the perfective stem of the verb 'die' and the suffix of the progressive converb. The only way to resolve this conflict is to suggest that the quotative makes the perfective stem of 'die' invisible for the progressive converb suffix. This is very much the behaviour of an independent word. On the other hand, despite losing its original imperfective grammatical meaning (ongoing action), the quotative retained the morphological ability of selecting for the affixes associated with the imperfective stem, i.e. the progressive converb suffix.

The attachment of the converbial suffix -*ši* to the quotative is not just an accident or an instance of some idiosyncratic behaviour of this suffix; the quotative can also select for the attributive suffix *-t:u* as shown in (30).

(30) to-w   za-r-ši   ar-ge=r-t:u   bošor
that-I.SG.ABS   1SG-CONT-ALL   [IV.SG]do-PROH=QUOT-ATTR.I.SG   man(I)[SG.ABS]
I.SG-see-w-ak:u
I.SG-see.PFV
'I saw that man who says "Do not work!" to me.'

The main clause here is 'I saw that man who said "Do not work!" to me' with the experiencer omitted (it would have been in the dative case form). The main verb *wak:u* 'saw' agrees with the head of the absolutive argument *bošor* 'man'. The embedded clause is *zarši argert:u* 'who is saying "Do not work" to me'. To make the comparison clearer, I will first show how it would have looked had there been the independent verb of speech rather than the quotative, and had there been no relativisation. Such a clause would look as in (31).

(31) za-r-ši   ar-gi   war
1SG-CONT-ALL   [IV.SG]do-PROH   say.IPFV
'(That man) tells me "Do not work!".'

The agent of speech is omitted here, and the addressee of the quoted speech is marked by a contallative case. The verb marking the content of speech is in the form of the prohibitive, which prompted the direct speech translation. Relativised, this clause would have looked as in (32).

(32) za-r-ši   ar-gi   war-t:u   bošor
     1SG-CONT-ALL [IV.SG]do-PROH say.IPFV-ATTR.I.SG man(I)[SG.ABS]
     'the man who tells me "Do not work!"'

The attributive suffix -*t:u* attaches to the imperfective form of the verb and agrees in gender (I) and number (singular) with the head that this relative clause modifies, i.e. *bošor* 'man'. What is important for us now is the fact that the quotative can form attributives exactly in the same way as the independent verb does (or, indeed, as a word belonging to any part of speech as long as it is an independent word).

The form of the prohibitive cannot attach the attributive suffix, a form **argit:u* is ungrammatical, so the quotative in *ar-ge-r-t:u* from (30) serves as the barrier which makes the prohibitive 'invisible' for the attributive suffix, just as it would be invisible if it was a separate word in the sentence.

If we follow Kibrik (1977) in analysing the quotative as a mood form of the verb it attaches to, we would have to postulate a very odd mood category (or at least odd for the Archi mood system): the mood which has its own argument structure, attaches to other mood forms (such as imperative and prohibitive), to past evidential forms, to other parts of speech and finally, the mood which has its own progressive converb and the attributive form. None of other Archi moods behave like this (see Chumakina 2018 for details).

12.3.4 Quotative: Conclusion

Archi quotative displays many of the familiar characteristics of a clitic: it is a morphologically bound form which has a distribution of an independent (although partly grammaticalised) word: in Spencer and Luís's (2012b) terms, it is an affix by form and a functional word by distribution. At the same time, it retains morphosyntactic properties of the full independent verb it originates from. This sets the Archi quotative apart from familiar examples of cliticised quotatives: the clause with the quotative =*er* can have all the arguments of the speech verb overt, =*er* can be modified by an adverb, and it can form converbs, attributives and periphrastic forms.

12.4 Archi Verificative

There is another morphologically bound element in Archi which behaves rather similarly to the quotative in that it originates from a matrix verb, and retains its argument structure and inflection. It is called the verificative. But unlike the quotative, the verificative in Archi is rather marginal phenomenon: its frequency in recorded texts is far lower than that of the quotative, and when I was discussing it with Archi speakers, they were less confident in judging the grammaticality of the examples.

There are two other Nakh-Daghestanian languages which also have the verificative, Lezgian and Agul (Lezgic). The Agul verificative is described in detail in Maisak (2016). The parallels between Archi, Agul and Lezgian verificatives are established in Daniel and Maisak (2014). Here I will only give a brief outline of the Archi verificative and concentrate on its inflection. The data were obtained during my fieldwork in Archi in 2006. As this phenomenon is rather marginal, I had to rely mostly on elicitation, although some examples will be from the spontaneous texts I recorded in Archi.

12.4.1 Archi Verificative: Origin

Consider the example in (33) from a recorded text.

(33) to-r-mi   kło-t'u-r-k:us   sak:a-r,
that-II.SG-SG.ERG   [IV.SG]give.PFV-NEG-QUEST-VERIF   [1PL]watch-IPFV
'We were looking at her, wondering whether she would not give us something.'

The meaning 'whether (she) would not give us something' is conveyed by the form *kłot'urk:us* which consists of the following elements: *kło*, a perfective stem of the verb 'give', negation suffix *-t'u-* and question marker *-r*. The morphologically bound element *-k:us* which introduces the complement of the verb *sak:ar* 'look at' is the focus of this section, the verificative.

Just like the quotative, the verificative can be used as a complementiser with a matrix verb (33) or independently (34).

(34) ja-t   wirχʷin-k:u-s
this-IV.SG[ABS]   [IV.SG]work.IPFV-VERIF-FIN
'(I will) find out whether this one works.'

There are two verbs in Archi which can be the origin of this marker, the verb *ak:us* 'see' and the verb *irk:us* 'search, check'. They have very similar morphology in terms of both stem formation and agreement marking. Table 12.2 shows the main stems of each verb and agreement forms for gender III singular and gender IV singular controller.

Although very similar morphologically, these verbs have different argument structures: the experiencer argument (A) of the verb *ak:us* 'see' occurs in the dative and the stimulus argument (P) occurs in the absolutive, as shown in (35), whereas *irk:us* 'search, look for, check out' takes an agent (A) in the ergative and a patient-like argument (P) in the absolutive, as shown in (36).

Table 12.2 Archi verbs *ak:us* and *irk:us*: stem formation and placement of agreement

	ak:us 'see'		irk:us 'search, check'	
	IV.SG	III.SG	IV.SG	III.SG
PFV	ak:u	b-ak:u	irk:u	b-irk:u
IPFV	ak:ur	b-ak:u-r	irk:u-r	b-irk:u-r
FIN	ak:us	b-ak:u-s	irk:u-s	b-irk:u-s
IMP	ak:ʷa	b-ak:ʷa	irk:ʷa	b-i-rk:ʷa

(35) Rasul-li-s   Ajša   d-ak:u
    Rasul(I)-OBL.SG-DAT Aisha(II) [SG.ABS]II.SG-see.PFV
    'Rasul has seen Aisha.'

(36) zari   b-is   dogi   b-irk:u
    1.SG.ERG   III.SG-SG.GEN donkey(III)[SG.ABS]   III.SG-look.for.PFV
    'I was looking for my donkey.'

It is most likely that the Archi verificative is a cliticised form of the verb *ak:us* 'see' which attaches to the question marker *-r-*. If we accept this, the verb *irk:us* itself is a verificative form of the verb *i* 'be', so literally it should be translated as 'to check whether X is there'. With time this verificative form gets lexicalised and is now perceived as an independent lexical item with a full morphological paradigm: all Archi speakers agree that *irk:us* is a separate verb, whereas forms like *kłot'urk:us* are perceived by the speakers as some modification of the main verb (in this example, the verb *kłos* 'give').

Another option is to consider the verificative to be the cliticised version of the verb *irk:us*, although this is less likely: the element which attaches to the host seems to be *-k:us* rather than *-rk:us*. This can only be seen when the verificative attaches to the evidential forms, however: in the evidential, the question marker *-r-* goes before the evidential marker *-li* (and assimilates with it), so the combination with the evidential host is the only instance when the verificative has the form *-k:us* and not *-rk:us*. To take the verb *kłos* 'give': it can have two verificative forms, *kło-r-k:us* give.PFV-QUEST-VERIF 'I will find out what (she) gave' and *kło-l-li-k:us* give.PFV-QUEST-EVID-VERIF 'I will find out what (she) apparently had given'.

Like the quotative, the verificative in Archi is a morphologically bound form which needs a host to attach to. Unlike the quotative, however, the verificative attaches to verbal forms only, as the examples below demonstrate: in (37) it attaches to the imperfective *war* 'say'; in (38), to the negated potential *gʷabq:'o:t'u*; in (39), to the evidential past *asuli* 'put'; and in (40), to the periphrastic form *asuli edili* 'had put on'.

(37) ašba   bo   buwa-r-ši   han   war-k:u-s
    wait.IMP   say.PFV   mother(II)-CONT-ALL   what(IV)[SG.ABS]   say.IPFV-VERIF-FIN
    'You wait, I said, and see what I say to mother.'
    (Sisters: 61)

(38) ha   kło-qi   zari   ja-t:-u
    ha   [IV.SG]give-POT   1SG.ERG   this-IV.SG-and
    gʷa⟨b⟩q:'o:t'u-rk:u-s   šʕortal
    ⟨III.SG⟩gather.POT.NEG-VERIF-FIN   together
    'Okay, I will give her that too, to find out whether she will tidy up with me.'
    (Sisters: 49)

(39) to-r-mi   han   asu-l-li-kːu-s
    that-II.SG-SG.ERG   what(IV)[SG.ABS]   put.on.PFV[IV.SG]-QUEST-EVID-VERIF-FIN
    '(I will) find out what she wears (lit. "what she has put on").'

(40) to-r-mi   han   asu-li
    that-II.SG-SG.ERG   what(IV)[SG.ABS]   [IV.SG]put.on.PFV-CVB
    edi-l-li-kːu-s
    [IV.SG]be.PST-QUEST-EVID-VERIF-FIN
    '(I will) find out what she wore then (lit. "had put on").'

12.4.2 Verificative: Inflectional Possibilities and Syntax

So far, we have only seen one form of the verificative, the finalis form of the original verb; it is indeed the only form accounted for in Archi texts. That is what prompted the interpretation in Kibrik (1977) where the form in *kːus* was defined as 'verificative converb'. However, all Archi speakers with whom I discussed the verificative agreed that it can have several forms: finalis, imperative and potential. Example (41) shows the verificative in the imperative form attached to the potential *weqʕi* and (42) shows the imperative form of the verificative attached to the perfective *uqʕa* of the verb 'go'.

(41) tu-w   ɬaɬu   w-eqʕi-rkːʷa
    that-I.SG[ABS] who-COMIT   I.SG-got.POT-VERIF.IMP
    'Find out who he will come with.'

(42) tu-w   daši   uqʕa-l-li-kːʷa
    that-I.SG[ABS] where   [I.SG]go.PFV-QUEST-EVID-VERIF.IMP
    'Find out where he went.'

The potential form of the verificative is shown in (43).

(43) zari   to-r-mi   gat'
    1SG.ERG   that-II.SG-SG.ERG   scarf(III)[SG.ABS]
    b-a⟨r⟩ča-r-kːu-qi
    III.SG-⟨IPFV⟩put.on-IPFV.QUEST-VERIF-POT
    'I will check whether she puts on a head scarf.'

In (41)–(43) the forms with the verificative, perceived by the speakers as one word, contain incompatible inflections: potential and imperative in (41), past evidential and imperative in (42), and imperfective and potential in (43). Just as was the case with the quotative, the presence of the verificative makes the verbal form 'invisible' for the inflections of the verificative. Here again we see a phonologically bound element retaining the inflectional possibilities of an independent word.

Example (43) shows another property of the Archi verificative: just as was the case with the quotative, it retains the argument structure of a regular finite verb, taking its A argument in the ergative case *zari* 'I'. Recall that this is different from the verb *akːus* 'see' which takes its A and P arguments in the dative and the absolutive respectively. The verb *irk:us* 'search', however, does take ergative and absolutive arguments.

12.4.3 Verificative: Conclusion

The Archi verificative is very similar in behaviour to the quotative: it is a phonetically dependent element which attaches to a fully inflected form and creates a biclausal construction without any syntactic fusion. As with the quotative, it also retains some inflectional possibilities of its origin and represents, therefore, another instance of an inflected clitic. However, it is more selective of the forms it attaches to, which potentially makes it one step closer to the affix.

12.5 Conclusion

Archi presents an interesting case of cliticised verbs that retain much more of their morphosyntactic independence than can be expected of a bound element. This includes the ability to retain the full argument structure, the ability to be modified by an adverb, and the ability to inflect for tense, mood and non-finite forms. As such, Archi cliticised verbs expand the limits of cross-linguistic variation for clitics on the one hand, and the notion or word on the other. The presence of these elements makes it possible to combine in one phonological word (also undoubtedly perceived by the speakers as one word) the elements which are normally incompatible according to the rules of Archi grammar: thus, perfective stem and progressive converb marker can be found in one Archi word as long as that word contains the quotative. The verificative presents the second bound element which allows different and normally incompatible inflections to be found in one word.

Notes

1. The text numbers refer to the online collection of Archi texts (Kibrik et al. 2007); the text titles refer to the texts collected during my fieldwork in 2004–12. If there is no reference after the example, it comes from my own field notes.
2. I follow Kibrik's (1977) terminology in calling these verbs dynamic and stative. Largely, membership of one or other of these groups is semantically predictable: stative verbs mostly denote states such as 'be big', 'be green', etc., whereas dynamic verbs mostly denote actions. However, the reason for the division is morphological: it is the number of stems associated with the lexeme which determines whether the verb is referred to as dynamic or stative.
3. The fact that this stem realises agreement makes labelling it as an infinitive potentially confusing. I follow Kibrik's (1977) solution to this problem by calling it the finalis stem.
4. I follow Kibrik (1977) in labelling these forms as 'evidential', but the extent to which they are really evidential needs further research. It is probably more instructive to treat the verbal forms in *-li* as finite synthetic forms of past tense.
5. In Archi, it is very hard to distinguish between direct and indirect speech, so this example sentence can be translated either as 'He said: "They will have to be killed"' or 'He said that they would have to be killed'. This holds for all other example sentences.
6. Note that the speaker argument, *buwa* 'mother' is not in the ergative case here but in the absolutive. This is due to the fact that some progressive forms in Archi allow variation in argument marking: the agent can be marked either by the ergative or by the absolutive

case, giving rise to a so-called biabsolutive construction which Nakh-Daghestanian languages are famous for. For details, see Chumakina and Bond (2016), among others.

References

Chumakina, Marina (2011), 'Morphological complexity of Archi verbs', in Gilles Authier and Timur Maisak (eds), *Tense, Aspect, Modality and Finiteness in East Caucasian Languages*, Diversitas Linguarum, 30, Bochum: Brockmeyer, pp. 1–24.

Chumakina, Marina (2013), 'Periphrasis in Archi', in Marina Chumakina and Greville G. Corbett (eds), *Periphrasis: The Role of Syntax and Morphology in Paradigms*, Proceedings of the British Academy, 180, Oxford: Oxford University Press and British Academy, pp. 27–52.

Chumakina, Marina (2018), 'Mood in Archi: Realization and semantics', in Diana Forker and Timur Maisak (eds), *The Semantics of Verbal Categories in Nakh-Daghestanian Languages: Tense, Aspect, Evidentiality, Mood and Modality*, Brill's Studies in Language, Cognition and Culture, Leiden and Boston: Brill, pp. 215–46.

Chumakina, Marina and Oliver Bond (2016), 'Competing controllers and agreement potential', in Oliver Bond, Greville G. Corbett, Marina Chumakina and Dunstan Brown (eds), *Archi: Complexities of Agreement in Cross-Theoretical Perspective*, Oxford: Oxford University Press, pp. 77–117.

Chumakina, Marina, Oliver Bond and Greville G. Corbett. (2016), 'Essentials of Archi grammar', in Oliver Bond, Greville G. Corbett, Marina Chumakina and Dunstan Brown (eds), *Archi: Complexities of Agreement in Cross-Theoretical Perspective*, Oxford: Oxford University Press, pp. 17–42.

Chumakina, Marina and Greville G. Corbett (2015), 'Gender–number marking in Archi: Small is complex', in Matthew Baerman, Dunstan Brown and Greville G. Corbett (eds), *Understanding and Measuring Morphological Complexity*, Oxford: Oxford University Press, pp. 93–116.

Daniel, Mikhail A. and Timur A. Maisak (2014), 'Grammatikalizacija verifikativa: ob odnoj agul′sko-arčinskoj paralleli' [The Grammaticalization of the Verificative: On an Agul-Archi Parallel], in Mikhail A. Daniėl′, Ekaterina A. Ljutikova, Vladimir A. Plungjan, Sergej G. Tatevosov and Ol′ga V. Fedorova (eds), *Jazyk. Konstanty. Peremennye: Pamjati Aleksandra Evgen′eviča Kibrika* [Language. Constants. Variables: In Memory of Alexandr Evgen′evič Kibrik], St Petersburg: Aletejja, pp. 377–406.

Deutscher, Guy (2011), 'The grammaticalization of quotatives', in Bernd Heine and Heiko Narrog (eds), *The Oxford Handbook of Grammaticalization*, Oxford: Oxford University Press, pp. 646–50.

Dixon, R. M. W. and Alexandra Y. Aikhenvald (eds) (2002), *Word: A Cross-Linguistic Typology*, Cambridge: Cambridge University Press.

Dobrushina, Nina (2008), 'Imperativnyj converb v arčinskom jazyke' [Imperative converb in Archi], in A. V. Arxipov, L. M. Zaxarov, A. A. Kibrik, A. E. Kibrik, I. M. Kobozeva, O. F. Krivnova, E. A. Ljutikova and O. V. Fĕdorova (eds), *Fonetika i nefonetika: K 70-letiju Sandro V. Kodzasova* [Phonetics and Non-phonetics: A Festschrift on the 70th Birthday of Sandro V. Kodzasov], Moscow: Jazyki slavjanskix kul′tur, pp. 195–206.

Grenoble, Lenore A. (1998), *Deixis and Information Packaging in Russian Discourse*, Amsterdam and Philadelphia: John Benjamins.

Haurholm-Larsen, Steffen (2015), 'Clitics, affixes, and wordhood in Garifuna (Arawak): A multidimensional continuum of morphosyntactic boundness', *Acta Linguistica Hafniensia*, 47 (2), pp. 81–100.

Hopper, Paul J. and Elizabeth Closs Traugott (2012), *Grammaticalization*, 2nd edn, Cambridge: Cambridge University Press.

Kibrik, A. E. (1977), *Opyt strukturnogo opisanija arčinskogo jazyka, 2 Taksonomičeskaja grammatika*, Moscow: Izdatel'stvo Moskovskogo Universiteta.

Kibrik, A. E., A. Arkhipov, M. Daniel and S. Kodzasov (2007), *Archi Texts Online*, <http://www.philol.msu.ru/~languedoc/eng/archi/corpus.php> (last accessed 14 February 2018).

Kimball, Geoffrey (2015), 'Natchez', in Heather K. Hardy and Janine Scancarelli (eds), *Native Languages of the Southeastern United States*, Lincoln, NE and London: University of Nebraska Press.

Maisak, Timur (2016), 'Morphological fusion without syntactic fusion: The case of the "verificative" in Agul', *Linguistics*, 54 (4), pp. 815–70.

Spencer, Andrew and Ana R. Luís (2012a), *Clitics: An Introduction*, Cambridge: Cambridge University Press.

Spencer, Andrew and Ana R. Luís (2012b), 'The canonical clitic', in Dunstan Brown, Marina Chumakina and Greville G. Corbett (eds), *Canonical Morphology and Syntax*, Oxford: Oxford University Press, pp. 123–50.

Taylor, John R. (2015), *The Oxford Handbook of the Word*, Oxford: Oxford University Press.

Zwicky, Arnold M. (1985) 'Clitics and particles', *Language*, 61 (2), pp. 283–305.

Zwicky, Arnold M. (1994), 'What is a clitic?', in Joel A. Nevis, Brian D. Joseph, Dieter Wanner and Arnold M. Zwicky (eds), *Clitics: A Comprehensive Bibliography, 1892–1991*, Amsterdam: Benjamins.

PART III
SYNTACTIC DEPENDENCIES

13

To Agree or Not to Agree?
A Typology of Sporadic Agreement

Sebastian Fedden

13.1 Introduction

Canonical agreement is productively marked on all agreement targets of a given type. Corbett (2006: 17) calls the specific non-canonical deviation from this, in which agreement is restricted to a subset of items in a word class, sporadic agreement.

I define sporadic agreement in (1).

(1) Definition of sporadic agreement: Two items belonging to the same word class in a language display different behaviour with respect to agreement. In the same syntactic context, one item agrees, whereas the other one does not.[1]

A simple example of sporadic agreement comes from Italian. Most Italian adjectives agree in gender and number with the noun they modify. Consider examples (2) and (3).

(2) Italian
 ciel-o azzurr-o
 sky(M)-SG azure-M.SG
 'azure sky'

(3) Italian
 ciel-i azzurr-i
 sky(M)-PL azure-M.PL
 'azure skies'

In (2), the colour adjective *azzurro* 'azure' ends in -*o*, thus showing agreement in number (singular) and gender (masculine) with the noun *cielo* 'sky', whereas in (3) *azzurri* ends in -*i*, agreeing in number (plural) and gender (masculine) with the noun *cieli* 'skies'. However, there are some adjectives, such as *blu* 'blue', which do not agree, hence *cielo blu* 'blue sky' and *cieli blu* 'blue skies', where *cielo* is singular and masculine and *cieli* is plural and masculine, but there is nothing on *blu* which indicates this.

This is not to say that invariable adjectives like *blu* are exempt from the agreement rule in Italian that obtains between heads and modifiers. Invariable adjectives are part of a larger system in which the majority of items agree, with which they form a syntactically homogenous word class. But invariable adjectives are exceptions in that their morphology fails to respond to the agreement rule because of certain properties of the lexeme; in the case of *blu* these are phonological properties (ending in a stressed vowel) and (possibly) etymological properties (being a loan from French), which will be discussed further in §13.3.2 and §13.3.5 respectively. Sporadic agreement is a morphological rather than a syntactic phenomenon. In the lexemes which make up the set of non-agreeing items in a word class which otherwise shows agreement, it is the morphology that fails to respond to the agreement rule, rather than the agreement rule itself not applying. However, there are interesting borderline cases which will be taken up in §13.4, especially modal verbs in English.

It is important to stress that the notion 'sporadic' is viewed across the lexicon. In order for agreement to be sporadic, it has to be confined to a subset of items in a word class. This is what we find in Italian: *azzurro* belongs to a set of adjectives which always agree, *blu* belongs to a set of adjectives which never agree. This situation needs to be distinguished from optional agreement, another type of non-canonical agreement (Corbett 2006: 14), where any given item can agree or not agree, e.g. the German colour adjective *lila* 'purple'.

(4) German
     eine lila   Jacke
     a   purple   jacket(F)[SG]
     'a purple jacket'

(5) German
     eine lila-ne   Jacke
     a   purple-SG.F jacket(F)[SG]
     'a purple jacket'

According to the author's native judgement, either (4) or (5) is possible. Optional agreement, and how it differs from sporadic agreement, will be taken up in §13.4.2.

Unlike Italian where sporadic agreement is confined to a tiny corner of the lexicon, namely a small set of adjectives, it is pervasive in Nakh-Daghestanian languages, such as Archi (Kibrik 1977a, 1977b; Chumakina et al. 2007), Ingush and Chechen (Nichols 1989) and Tsez (Polinsky and Comrie 1999; Polinsky and Potsdam 2001; Polinsky 2015). In these languages, sporadic agreement plays a role in various word classes. In terms of range of sporadic agreement, i.e. the proportion of affected lexemes, we find widely different scenarios.[2] It can be extreme as in Italian where more than 98 per cent of adjectives agree – either in gender and number (about 65 per cent) or only in number (about 33 per cent) (Thornton et al. 1997) – or minimal as in

Tsez where only 4 per cent of adjectives agree (Gagliardi 2012; Gagliardi and Lidz 2014). Tsez adjectives clearly show sporadic agreement, whereas for Italian, where almost all adjectives do agree, we might rather speak of sporadic non-agreement.

What all situations of sporadic agreement have in common is that we need additional information about the target in order to know whether a feature will be overtly realised. In other words, there are lexical prerequisites for agreement (Corbett 2006: 81–4). This research is the first step towards a typological investigation of sporadic agreement. I have surveyed a sample of 23 languages to find an answer to the question of whether, in a particular language with sporadic agreement, we can predict whether an item agrees or not, and what the factors are which allow us to make such a prediction. I will show that sporadic agreement in the sample is far from random, yet that there is rarely a factor that allows us to exhaustively predict the agreement potential of a word.

Given that sporadic agreement raises interesting questions about the persistence of morphological peculiarities, it is remarkable that the phenomenon itself has never been systematically investigated. On one view, sporadic agreement should not exist or should at least be ironed out over time. Since a subset of the word class in question does not agree, the system seems to work unproblematically without the agreement. It seems a plausible assumption that sporadic agreement should disappear over time by regularising all items as either agreeing or non-agreeing, particularly in skewed situations like Tsez adjectives, where the number of agreeing items is very small (4 per cent), or Italian adjectives, where the number of agreeing items is very large (98 per cent). However, far from a collection of random gaps, sporadic agreement in most cases follows recognisable patterns (phonotactic, phonological, morphological, semantic or etymological) which together with frequency effects might facilitate its persistence.

This chapter is structured as follows. In §13.2, I introduce the sample. In §13.3, I present the results in the form of the different factors that let us predict whether an item in a sporadic agreement system agrees. I will discuss the following factors: phonotactic (§13.3.1), phonological (§13.3.2), morphological (§13.3.3), semantic (§13.3.4) and etymological (§13.3.5). In §13.4, I present a range of interesting borderline cases which share (sometimes superficial) properties with sporadic agreement, but which I believe are ultimately different phenomena. §13.5 brings up the role of frequency in the persistence of morphological systems. Finally, in §13.6 I offer my conclusions.

13.2 The Sample

Sporadic agreement has been noted in a range of unrelated languages, such as Italian and Nakh-Daghestanian languages (Nichols 1989; Chumakina and Corbett 2008; Chumakina and Corbett 2015), but also in Papuan languages, such as Mian (Fedden 2010, 2011, in press; Corbett et al. 2017) and other Mountain Ok languages (Healey 1964; Fedden in press) and Teiwa (Klamer 2010; Fedden et al. 2013).

This pilot study is based on a (convenience) sample of 23 languages. I have tried to introduce some geographical spread, but languages from areas where sporadic agreement is known to be common like the Caucasus are overrepresented. The full list of languages can be found in the Appendix. While this sample is appropriate for identifying types of sporadic agreement, it will not tell us much about the distribution of the phenomenon. Hence, a word of caution. The results, which I will present in the following section, are based on qualitative observations from the sample. I will not make any claims about the quantitative significance of the identified types.

13.3 Predictors of Sporadic Agreement

Based on the sample we can identify the following predictors of sporadic agreement: phonotactic predictors in Tsez and Ingush, phonological predictors in Italian, morphological predictors in Archi, semantic predictors in Mian and Teiwa, and etymological predictors in (western varieties of) Basque. I will discuss these cases in more detail in this section. Borderline cases have been found in Hausa, Ngan'gityemerri, English and Russian (see §13.4).[3]

13.3.1 Phonotactic Predictors

The Nakh-Daghestanian language Tsez shows agreement in gender and number. Four genders are distinguished in the singular (I–IV), which are collapsed to two in the plural. Gender assignment uses a combination of semantic and formal criteria: male humans are gender I, female humans and some inanimates are gender II, animals and some inanimates are gender III, and the rest of the inanimates are gender IV. Tsez is morphologically ergative, i.e. the verb agrees with the absolutive argument. This is illustrated for an intransitive verb in (6) and for a transitive verb in (7).

(6) Tsez (Polinsky and Comrie 1999: 112)
 bikori b-exu-s
 snake(III)[SG.ABS] III.SG-die-PST.EVID
 'The snake died.'

(7) Tsez (Polinsky and Comrie 1999: 110)
 žek'-ā γutku r-oy-xo
 man(I)[SG]-ERG house(IV)[SG.ABS] IV.SG-make-PRS
 'The man is building a/the house.'

The agreement forms of Tsez are given in Table 13.1.

Table 13.1 Tsez agreement prefixes (Polinsky and Comrie 1999: 111)

Gender	Number	
	SG	PL
I	Ø-	b-
II	y-	
III	b-	r-
IV	r-	

The agreement system of Tsez is sporadic in the sense that only 27 per cent of verbs and 4 per cent of adjectives listed in the dictionary agree (Gagliardi 2012; Gagliardi and Lidz 2014: 68). No consonant-initial verb agrees, while almost all vowel-initial verbs agree. This is illustrated with the agreeing verb -ˤaq'il- 'increase, grow' in (8), and the non-agreeing verb k'oλi- 'run' in (9). These examples were provided by Maria Polinsky (personal communication).

(8) Tsez
    a. uži   ˤaq'il-si
       boy(I)[SG.ABS]   [I.SG]grow-PST.EVID
       'The boy grew up.'
    b. kid   y-ˤaq'il-si
       girl(II)[SG.ABS]   II.SG-grow-PST.EVID
       'The girl grew up.'
    c. meši   b-ˤaq'il-si
       calf(III)[SG.ABS] III.SG-grow-PST.EVID
       'The calf grew up.'
    d. łu   r-ˤaq'il-si
       water(IV)[SG.ABS] IV.SG-grow-PST.EVID
       'Water increased.'

(9) Tsez
    a. uži   k'oλi-s
       boy(I)[SG.ABS]   run-PST.EVID
       'The boy ran.'
    b. kid   k'oλi-s
       girl(II)[SG.ABS]   run-PST.EVID
       'The girl ran.'
    c. meši   k'oλi-s
       calf(III)[SG.ABS] run-PST.EVID
       'The calf ran.'
    d, łu   k'oλi-s
       water(IV)[SG.ABS] run-PST.EVID
       'Water ran.'

In order for a Tsez verb to agree with the absolutive argument, it is a prerequisite to be vowel-initial: while consonant-initial verbs never agree, there are a few vowel-initial verbs – Polinsky and Comrie (1999: 111) list ten – for which one assumes the presence of an underlying laryngeal which blocks agreement prefixes, just like any other consonant (Maria Polinsky, personal communication). Besides verbs, agreement prefixes can be found on some vowel-initial adjectives, some vowel-initial adverbs and several particles.

Tsez is a case where sporadic agreement is subject to phonotactic constraints (Polinsky and Comrie 1999: 111). Since the agreement prefixes (given in Table 13.1) are mainly single consonants, their affixation to consonant-initial stems would lead to illicit word-initial consonant clusters. In Tsez, the morphology fails to respond in lexemes displaying a phonotactic structure which prevents agreement prefixes from being realised. A similar situation can be found in the related Nakh-Daghestanian language Ingush, where about 30 per cent of verbs agree (Bickel and Nichols 2007: 172). Ingush examples can be found in Corbett (2006: 82). As in Tsez, being vowel-initial is a prerequisite for agreement.

13.3.2 Phonological Predictors

Unlike Tsez and Ingush where sporadic agreement is tied to phonotactic constraints, the relevant factors in Italian are phonological. Italian has three main types of adjective: (i) those that agree in gender (masculine vs feminine) and number (singular vs plural), e.g. *azzurro* 'azure', which has four forms *azzurro/azzurra/azzurri/azzurre*; (ii) those that agree only in number (singular vs plural), e.g. *veloce* 'fast', which has two forms *veloce/veloci*; and (iii) those which are invariable, e.g. *blu* 'blue'. According to Thornton et al. (1997: 68, 74), out of a total of 1,129 adjectives in the Italian Basic Vocabulary 1.9 per cent are of the invariable type. On (non-)canonicity in the inflection of Italian adjectives, see Thornton (this volume).

However, the factors underlying sporadic agreement in Italian are phonological rather than phonotactic. There is nothing in Italian phonotactics which would prohibit the sequences /uo, ua, ui, ue/. The adjective *blu* fits into a larger phonological pattern in Italian, according to which nouns and adjectives ending in a stressed vowel remain uninflected; compare to the invariable nouns *città* 'city', *virtù* 'virtue'. The other relevant phonological pattern is that all adjectives that end in /i/ are invariable, e.g. *pari* 'even', *dispari* 'odd'.[4] Again, there are no phonotactic constraints against agreement in these words, and as for *blu*, the pattern is operational in the language more widely, as can be seen from the following non-inflecting nouns, *ipotesi* 'hypothesis', *estasi* 'ecstasy', ending in /i/ (D'Achille and Thornton 2003: 225). The fact that *blu* is also a loanword (from French *bleu*) might have an effect as well, as there are cases of sporadic agreement which are sensitive to the etymological status of a word (see §13.3.5). In fact, there is another set of invariable adjectives in Italian, all ending in a consonant, e.g. *chic* 'chic' (D'Achille and Thornton 2003: 225). Their phonology does not prevent them from agreeing, so they do not fit into the patterns discussed here. These adjectives are non-agreeing because they are loanwords (see §13.3.5).

In Italian, sporadic agreement affects so few items that it would be more felicitous to speak of sporadic non-agreement, but for adjectives which end either in a stressed vowel or in /i/, this peculiar behaviour is predictable from their phonology.

13.3.3 Morphological Predictors

For Archi, the morphological build of a verb, i.e. the number of stems a verb has, is the best predictor of whether it agrees. The overwhelming majority of verbs with five stems agrees, while almost no verb with one stem agrees. The situation is less clear for the other word classes which show sporadic agreement.

Table 13.2 Lexical items and their agreement potential (reported in Chumakina and Bond 2016: 111, based on the Archi dictionary [Chumakina et al. 2007])

Word class	Total	Agreeing	Percentage agreeing
Verbs	1,248	399	32.0
Adverbs	383	13	3.6
Postpositions	34	1	2.9
Discourse clitics/particles	4	1	(25.0)[a]

[a] This figure appears in brackets to reflect the small numbers that this percentage is based on.

The Archi system is complex, therefore I will discuss it in some detail. In Archi, items from a wide range of word classes can realise agreement (Chumakina and Corbett 2008; Bond et al. 2016). However, at the level of the lexicon, the extent of agreement is much more limited, with most major word classes containing both agreeing and non-agreeing items. Proportions of agreeing items for the major word classes in Archi are given in Table 13.2, based on data from the Archi dictionary.

Table 13.2 shows that there are clear differences in coverage. Around a third of verbs (32 per cent), about a dozen adverbs, a single postposition, and the emphatic enclitic agree in Archi. Some personal pronouns also agree, but there are no figures (see Chumakina and Corbett 2015: 95). The rest are non-agreeing.

Archi has four genders (I–IV) and two number values (singular and plural). In terms of gender assignment, males are gender I, females gender II, and the rest of the noun vocabulary is divided between genders III and IV (Chumakina and Corbett 2015: 96). Relevant agreement domains are the NP where modifiers agree with the head noun in number and gender, and the clause where a range of targets agrees with the absolutive argument.

The ensuing discussion of sporadic agreement in Archi will be confined to the verbs.[5] Table 13.3 is a representation of the gender and number agreement system of Archi verbs (*x*- is the prefixal form, and <*x*> the infixal form) (Kibrik et al. 1977: 55–66).[6] The paradigms for other targets look slightly different.

Unlike Tsez and Ingush, where the phonological form of the verb stem is a very solid predictor (no consonant-initial verb agrees, whereas almost all vowel-initial verbs agree), the situation in Archi is more complex and phonology is a less useful

Table 13.3 Gender and number in Archi (verbal agreement)

Gender	Number	
	SG	PL
I	w-/‹w›	b-/‹b›
II	d-/‹r›	
III	b-/‹b›	Ø-/‹Ø›
IV	Ø-/‹Ø›	

predictor of sporadic agreement. Both vowel-initial and consonant-initial verbs can be either agreeing or non-agreeing. Examples of agreeing verbs are *acu* 'milk' and *qˤa* 'come'; examples of non-agreeing verbs are *abc'u* 'hew' and *barhu* 'look after'. The Archi agreement markers are single consonants like in Tsez and Ingush, but Archi allows vowel epenthesis between the prefix and the consonant-initial stem, pronounced as [ə], spelled the same as the stem vowel (Chumakina and Corbett 2015: 108), so that word-initial consonant clusters do not arise. An example is (10).

(10) Archi (Chumakina and Bond 2016: 112)
 ajša   da-qˤa
 PN(II)[SG]   II.SG-come.PFV
 'Aisha came.'

The best predictor of agreement potential is the morphological build of an Archi verb (Chumakina and Corbett 2015; Chumakina and Bond 2016: 112). 'Morphological build' refers to whether a verb has five stems, namely perfective, imperfective, finalis, potential and imperative, or only one stem, which is used in all word forms in the paradigm (Chumakina et al. 2016: 36). Five-stem verbs can be further divided into simple verbs and complex verbs, the latter consisting of an uninflected first part followed by a simple verb. There is a high correlation between the morphological build and the semantics of a verb: 1-stem verbs typically refer to states (Chumakina et al. 2016: 36 n.7), e.g. *aˤnt* 'be strong' or *č'iq'ʷˤ* 'have protruding teeth', while 5-stem verbs typically refer to processes, e.g. *c'ar* 'melt', or actions, e.g. *árt'ur* 'cut'.[7]

Looking at sporadic agreement in Archi verbs from the perspective of their morphology a clear picture emerges. Chumakina and Corbett (2015: 104, 115) report conspicuous correlations based on verbs listed in Kibrik (1977b). Within the set of simple 5-stem verbs the proportion of agreeing items is 87 per cent (rounded to full numbers), i.e. 142 of 163 verbs. Hence, it is the default expectation for a simple 5-stem verb to agree. We find the converse situation for 1-stem verbs: only 7 of 190 stative verbs agree, i.e. 4 per cent (rounded to full numbers), the default expectation being that stative verbs do not agree.[8]

Given the high correlation between morphological build (5-stem vs 1-stem verbs) and lexical semantics (dynamic vs stative meaning), the question remains as to whether a verb's morphology is really better than its semantics in predicting agreement potential. For by far the most Archi verbs, the morphology and the semantics are either both correct in their prediction or they are both wrong. We can distinguish four cases, given in (11).

(11) a. Morphology (5-stem) and semantics (dynamic) both correctly predict agreement, e.g. *áˤršur* 'deforest' (which agrees and should agree according to both criteria).
 b. Morphology (1-stem) and semantics (stative) both correctly predict non-agreement, e.g. *aˤnt* 'be strong' (which does not agree and should not agree according to both criteria).

c. Morphology (5-stem) and semantics (dynamic) both get it wrong, e.g. *abc'u* 'hew' (which does not agree, but should agree according to both criteria).
d. Morphology (1-stem) and semantics (stative) both get it wrong, e.g. *á:č'at'i* 'be empty' (which agrees, but should not agree according to both criteria).

This would not give us any reason to say that the morphology is any better than the semantics in its predictive power: they are either both correct or both wrong. However, in total there are more cases where the morphology is right and the semantics is not than vice versa. For example, *ák:ur* 'see' and *kor* 'hear' (5-stem verbs, stative semantics) agree, whereas *χ:ánk'bos* 'snore' and *batár* 'become impudent' (1-stem verbs, dynamic semantics) do not agree. In these cases, the agreement potential is correctly predicted by the morphological build, but not by the semantics. There are hardly any examples in the opposite direction, a possible one being *órł:ur* 'be silent', a 5-stem verb with stative semantics which does not agree.

Of course, an exact characterisation of Archi lexical verb semantics is difficult and for any given verb it can be hard to tell whether it has dynamic or stative semantics: does *lak:á* mean 'limp (slightly)' or 'be lame'; does *órł:ur* mean 'be silent' or 'shut up'? This makes the morphology more reliable than the semantics (it is easy to distinguish 1-stem verbs from 5-stem verbs, while it can be less straightforward to tell stative from dynamic meanings); another reason to privilege the morphology over the semantics for Archi.

13.3.4 Semantic Predictors

Semantic factors are relevant in the systems of the Papuan languages Mian and Teiwa. In Mian, verbal semantics allow us to identify several classes of agreeing verbs, at least to some extent, while it is the default for a verb not to agree.

All finite verbs in Mian agree with their subject in person (1, 2, 3), number (singular or plural) and gender (masculine, feminine, neuter 1 or neuter 2). Object agreement in transitive verbs, however, is sporadic. There are transitive verbs that agree in person, number and gender, such as *nâ'* 'hit, kill' in (12); verbs that agree only in number, such as *walò* 'cut off, split' in (13); and verbs that never agree with their object, such as *bou* 'hit with the palm, swat' in (14). Note that verbs that fail to agree with their object are not invariable, as they still agree with their subject.

(12) Mian (Fedden, field notes)
 máam=e a-nâ'-n-ebo=be
 mosquito(M)=SG.M 3SG.M.OBJ-hit.PFV-REALIS-2SG.SBJ=DECL
 'You hit the mosquito.'

(13) Mian (Fedden 2011: 268)
 dāb=e wa-lò-n-i=be
 seed(N1)=SG.N1 cut.off.SG.OBJ-hit.PFV-REALIS-1SG.SBJ=DECL
 'I cut off a seed.'

(14) Mian (Fedden, field notes)
máam=e   bou-n-ebo=be
mosquito(M)=SG.M   swat-REALIS-2SG.SBJ=DECL
'You swatted the mosquito.'

The verb *nâ'* 'hit, kill' in (12) agrees with its object *máam* 'mosquito' in person, number and gender through a prefix, whereas the verb *bou* 'hit with the palm, swat' in (14) does not agree. The verb *walò* 'cut off, split' in (13) agrees only in number with the object, but not in person or gender. For this verb class number is always marked through apophony (/a/ for singular and /ɛ/ for plural). If the object were plural, the verb form would have to be *welò*.[9]

In addition, Mian has a set of verbs which obligatorily take a classificatory prefix for their object.[10] This system is called a system of 'verbal classifiers' in Fedden (2011: ch. 5), mainly in order to differentiate it terminologically from the Mian gender system. The classifiers are in many respects gender-like in terms of assignment and agreement-like expression. Moreover, recent work has shown that a strict gender-classifier opposition should be abandoned (Fedden and Corbett 2017; Corbett et al. 2017). Therefore I include the classificatory prefixes here.

An example of the M-classifier *dob-* is given in (15), which is used for males and some inanimates, like *báangkli* 'stone adze (axe-like tool for cutting and digging)'.

(15) Mian (Fedden 2011: 185)
báangkli=e   dob-ò-n-o=a
stone.adze(N1)=SG.N1   3SG.M_CL.OBJ-take.PFV-SEQ-3SG.F.SBJ=MED
'She took the *báangkli* adze and then . . .'

There is also an F-classifier, which is used for females and many inanimates, and there are classifiers for long objects (e.g. arrow), covering objects (e.g. blanket), bundles (e.g. stringbag) and a residue classifier for the rest. For details on Mian nominal classification, see Fedden (2011: chs 4, 5); Corbett et al. (2017).

In terms of proportions of these four types of transitive verb in comparison with a total of 302 transitive verbs (31 of which are ambitransitive, i.e. they can be used either transitively or intransitively), we find the distribution given in Table 13.4.

Each Mian verb belongs to one and only one of these types. There is a substantial correlation between membership in the class of verbs that obligatorily take classifiers and lexical verb semantics of handling or movement. Some examples are given in Table 13.5.

However, there is leakage either way. On the one hand, this class contains some verbs without handling semantics, notably *halin* 'worry' and *suan* 'hate'; on the other hand, there are handling verbs which do not take a classifier, e.g. *mengge* 'pull'.

Next are transitive verbs that only agree in number with their object. This class is very small and only contains 'cut-and-break' verbs. All forms attested in the Mian corpus are given in Table 13.6.

Table 13.4 Proportion of Mian transitive verb types

Transitive verb type	Count	Percentage
Verbs that take a classifier	40[a]	13.2
Verbs that agree only in number	7	2.3
Verbs that agree in person, number and gender	7	2.3
Verbs that never agree	248	82.1

[a] Corbett et al. (2017) give the number of Mian verbs which obligatorily occur with the prefixal classifier as 37. This figure is based on a slightly different counting procedure.

Table 13.5 Examples of Mian transitive verbs that take a classifier

Verb	Meaning
atou	'put into the fire'
bià	'throw'
êb	'take (in order to carry)'
fâ	'put'
klafâ	'put on back (piggy-back style)'
meki	'hang up'
mikì	'take (child) into arms to lull to sleep'
môu	'put (pig or child) on shoulder'
ò	'take'
ski	'turn'
tangâa'	'hang up (item of clothing) to dry'
waa	'hide (tr.)'

Despite the neat 'cut-and-break' meanings of verbs in this class, semantics is of limited use in its definition since Mian has at least as many 'cut-and-break' verbs that are non-agreeing and therefore do not belong to this class. Superficially, we find formal factors at work in this verb class. Prima facie, members look as if they could be compounds consisting of one of a set of specific 'cut-and-break' verbs and a semantically more general verb, namely *lò* 'hit' or *tlâa'* 'remove', which would give this verb class a morphological definition. However, while these putative first elements exist as independent words, i.e. *bà* 'cut across', *dà* 'break off', *hà* 'cut alongside', *tà* 'cut off', or *wà* 'cut', these do not follow the ablaut pattern found in verbs which agree in number only. Thus, *hà* 'cut alongside' is *hà* regardless of object number; there is no form **hè* for a plural object.

Finally, there are transitive verbs that agree in person, number and gender with their object. Again, this class is extremely small, only consisting of seven items, which are given in Table 13.7. Their inherent aspect value is noted in brackets.

All of these transitive verbs – with the exception of *têm'* 'see' and *temê'* 'look at' – are high on the transitivity scale (Hopper and Thompson 1980), in that they implicate or entail a change of state in the object, which makes the object rank high in

Table 13.6 Mian verbs that only agree in number

Meaning	SG object	PL object
'cut, split'	balò	belò
'break off'	dalò	delò
'cut, break (wood)'	halò	helò
'cut off'	talò	telò
'cut off, split'	walò	welò
'break, tear apart'	batlâa'	betlâa'
'pry out'	datlâa'	detlâa'

Table 13.7 Mian transitive verbs that agree in person, number and gender

Verb	Meaning
e	'hit, kill (IPFV)'
fû'	'grab (PFV)'
lò	'hit, kill (PFV)'
nâ'	'hit, kill (PFV)'
ntamâ'	'bite (PFV)'
têm'	'see (PFV)'
temê'	'look at (IPFV)'

affectedness (Tsunoda 1985; Beavers 2011). On the other hand, there are many other transitive verbs, e.g. *klutaka* 'smash', which have a highly affected object, but which do not agree.

For Mian, we can say that semantics is helpful to some extent. This is particularly the case for the verbs which take a classifier, which mostly have meanings involving handling an object or movement. Semantics works less well for the other classes because of the higher degree of leakage.

Now we turn to semantic factors in Teiwa sporadic agreement, which work along the lines of animacy of the object. In Teiwa, and in Alor-Pantar languages more generally (Klamer 2017), verbs do not agree with their subject, shown in (16), while a proper subset of transitive verbs agrees with their object, shown in (17). The object of an agreeing verb is typically animate.

(16) Teiwa (Klamer 2010: 169)
    a   her
    3SG climb
    'He climbs up.'

(17) Teiwa (Klamer 2010: 159)
    name, ha'an n-oqai   g-unba'?
    sir   2SG   1SG.POSS-child 3SG-meet
    'Sir, did you see (lit. "meet") my child?'

Example (18) illustrates the use of a transitive verb *kiri* 'pull', which does not agree with its (inanimate) object.

(18) Teiwa (Fedden et al. 2013: 35)
 bif   eqar   kopang nuk tei   baq kiri
 child female small   one tree log pull
 'A little girl is pulling a log.'

In Teiwa, 22 per cent of transitive verbs agree with their object. In contemporary Teiwa, the two verb classes are not semantically fully transparent. Almost all transitive verbs belong either to the agreeing class or to the non-agreeing class and they allow objects of any animacy value as long as the lexical semantics of the verb permits this. For example, the verb *kiri* 'pull' (see example (18)) could be used to describe a situation in which a person is pulling another person and *kiri* would not suddenly agree with the object. So while arbitrary verb classes have formed in Teiwa, they are probably a development from a semantically transparent earlier stage of differential object marking (DOM), in which animate objects required the verb to agree, whereas there was no agreement with inanimate objects.[11] The formation of the present-day verb classes is likely related to the animacy value of the objects a verb typically occurs with (Fedden et al. 2013, 2014; Fedden and Brown 2017).

While sporadic agreement in Teiwa is not transparently related to object animacy any more, semantics remains a powerful predictor in Teiwa of whether a verb agrees with its object. In Teiwa, as in Mian, agreeing and non-agreeing verbs are essentially verb classes whose membership a verb has to be lexically specified for. Semantics is of limited use in predicting class membership.

13.3.5 Etymological Predictors

Loanwords can be a source of sporadic agreement. This is not unexpected given that loanwords often behave differently from native words as far as their phonology and morphology are concerned. An example can be found in western varieties of Basque (Trask 2003: 137), where a number of adjectives, mostly borrowed from Spanish, exceptionally mark gender, whereas Basque normally does not have gender. Examples are given in (19).

(19) Basque (Trask 2003: 137)
 a. *majo/maja* 'nice'
 b. *tonto/tonta* 'foolish'
 c. *katoliko/katolika* 'Catholic'

These adjectives show gender agreement even though native Basque adjectives are invariable. All of these adjectives are Romance loanwords, i.e. they come from languages in which adjectives usually agree in gender. But unlike the Romance languages which rely on a combination of semantic and formal gender assignment, Basque uses these borrowed adjectives in a semantically transparent fashion, employing the feminine form for female humans and the masculine form for everything else. According to Trask (2003: 137), Bizkaian Basque has hundreds of these agreeing adjectives, whereas the eastern varieties only borrowed the masculine form of Romance adjectives, which would then be as invariable as native Basque adjectives. A similar case is the Austronesian language Chamorro (Stolz 2012), which also borrowed a gender distinction together with Spanish adjectives.

The special status of loanwords can be found in other languages of the sample as well. In §13.3.2, we saw that the Italian adjective *blu* 'blue' not only belongs to a set of invariable items which can be defined by their phonology, but that it is also a French loan. Being a loanword can supersede the phonology. In Italian, adjectives ending in a stressed vowel or in /i/ do not agree. Consonant-final adjectives, such as *chic* 'chic' and *super* 'super', do not meet this phonological description. They do not agree because they are loans. Similarly, in Macedonian, vowel-final adjectives are invariable – the ones which were typically borrowed from Turkish, e.g. *taze* 'fresh' (Friedman 1993: 266–7); but Macedonian has a small number of consonant-final adjective loans that do not agree, e.g. *super* 'super', which is invariable though it does not meet the phonological structure of invariable adjectives in the language (Friedman 1993: 266–7; Corbett 2006: 81).

13.4 Borderline Cases

The sample contains examples which prima facie might look like sporadic agreement but which on reflection should be excluded from it. These are cases in which phonological processes make morphological ones invisible, for example like-segment coalescence in Hausa adjectives (§13.4.1), optional agreement in Ngan'gityemerri (§13.4.2), separate word classes illustrated by English modal auxiliaries (§13.4.3), and word class continua as exemplified by cardinal numerals in Russian and Italian (§13.4.4). In this section, I will briefly discuss each of these phenomena and provide reasons for excluding them.

13.4.1 Phonology Obscuring Morphology: Like-Segment Coalescence in Hausa Adjectives

Sometimes phonological processes can render morphological processes invisible. In Hausa, like-segment coalescence after inflection can lead to homophony and thus give the impression of invariability. Hausa adjectives agree in gender and number. The feminine form is built by adding a suffix -$\bar{a}$ to the masculine form. If the masculine form ends in a short or a long /a/, both forms are identical, e.g. *jā* 'red (M)' and *jā* 'red (F)' (Newman 2000: 23). Only looking at the singular (Hausa adjectives do agree in number), we might get the impression that the adjective *jā* 'red' does not agree in gender, when what actually happens is that the feminine suffix is invisible on the surface due to like-segment coalescence.

In such cases, there is no reason to say that the target does not agree. Rather, it does agree, but the morphological process is obscured by the phonology.

13.4.2 Optional Agreement: Modifiers in Ngan'gityemerri

In contrast to canonical agreement, which is obligatory, there are cases of optional agreement (Corbett 2006: 14) and it is important to keep it apart from sporadic agreement. Optional agreement can be found in modifiers in Ngan'gityemerri, a Daly language from north Australia. Ngan'gityemerri has 15 genders. An example of the animate gender is given in (20).

(20) Ngan'gityemerri (Reid 1997: 181)
 a-syensyerrgimi (a=)tyentyenmuy
 ANIM-white.rock.wallaby (ANIM=)tame
 'a tame white rock wallaby'

Phonological processes account for the analysis of the marker on the noun as a prefix and the marker on the agreement target as a proclitic (Reid 1997: 212–15). All of these agreement-marking proclitics on modifiers in Ngan'gityemerri are optional (Reid 1997: 168).

Optional agreement is a different phenomenon from sporadic agreement. While both are non-canonical, the former presupposes that agreement is possible and the question is whether it is obligatory, whereas for the latter we have to compare items across the lexicon, the question being whether any given item can agree at all (Corbett 2006: 17).

13.4.3 Different Word Class: Modal Auxiliaries in English

Sometimes a case can be made for treating agreeing and non-agreeing items as belonging to separate word classes subject to different syntactic rules or sets of syntactic rules, rather than treating them as lexemes of the same word class that show different agreement behaviour. Contrary to English full verbs, modal verbs do not show any agreement in the third person singular present tense (cf. *John sings often* vs *John must sing all night*).

Is this a case of sporadic agreement, or rather, non-agreement (agreeing verbs being much more numerous than non-agreeing, i.e. modal, verbs in English)? While it might be possible to analyse English modals as verbs which lack agreement in the third person singular present tense, it seems more promising to me to say that English modals are actually their own word class, which lacks subject agreement altogether. The reason for this lies in the fact that modals differ substantially from full verbs in their syntactic behaviour with respect to complementation, negation and question formation (among others). For all criteria and examples, see Quirk et al. (1985: 121–8). Full verbs take infinitival complements with 'to', modal auxiliaries take bare infinitives as complements; full verbs need do-support under negation, modals simply take *not* (or =*n't*); finally, full verbs require do-support in questions, while modals require inversion.

The syntactic peculiarities of English modal auxiliaries prompt me to treat them as a word class of their own rather than as an instance of sporadic non-agreement in verbs.

13.4.4 Word Class Continua: Cardinal Numerals in Russian and Italian

Corbett (1978) proposes a typological universal: if there is a syntactic difference between lower and higher numerals, the former behave like adjectives, while the latter behave like nouns. Corbett uses Russian as a particularly clear instance of this universal. The Russian numerals from 'one' to 'four' display adjective-like morphology and syntax to varying degrees. The numeral *odin/odna/odno* 'one' agrees in case and gender with the noun. It also agrees in (syntactic) number, as can be seen with pluralia tantum nouns, e.g. *odni sani* [one.PL sled(PL)] 'one sled' (Corbett 1978: 356). From here, numerals start to lose adjectival properties. The numeral *dva* 'two' agrees in gender in the nominative, but not in the oblique cases where it agrees in case. The numerals *odin* 'one', *dva* 'two', *tri* 'three' and *četyre* 'four' mark animacy of the noun (in the sense that they take the animate accusative). Numerals from *pjat'* 'five' onwards do not agree at all. Larger numerals – *sto* 'hundred' (only to a very limited extent), *tysjača* 'thousand' and *million* 'million' – start to display noun properties. They can (or must) take agreeing determiners, have their own inflectional paradigms, and/or take the noun in the genitive plural throughout. The distribution of adjective-like and noun-like properties in Russian cardinal numerals is given in Table 13.8, brackets indicating a limited extent, ± indicating an alternative.

Italian also fits the universal, and its system is simpler: the numeral 'one' agrees in gender with the noun (*uno/una*) and numerals from *due* 'two' onwards are invariable.[12] *Milione* 'million' displays noun syntax in that it takes a determiner and is followed by the preposition *di* 'of'.

As Russian cardinal numerals from *pjat'* 'five' onwards and Italian cardinal numerals from *due* 'two' onwards do not agree, one might treat this as a case of

Table 13.8 Adjectival properties of Russian cardinal numerals (from Corbett 1978: 359)

	odin	dva	tri	pjat'	sto	tysjača	million
	'one'	'two'	'three'	'five'	'hundred'	'thousand'	'million'
1. Agrees with noun in syntactic number	+	–	–	–	–	–	–
2. Agrees in case throughout	+	–	–	–	–	–	–
3. Agrees in gender	+	(+)	–	–	–	–	–
4. Marks animacy	+	+	+	–	–	–	–
5. Does not have own plural	+	+	+	+	(–)	–	–
6. Does not take agreeing determiner	+	+	+	+	+	–	–
7. Does not take the noun in the genitive plural throughout	+	+	+	+	+	±	–

Table 13.9 Proportions of agreeing and non-agreeing verbs and adjectives in a Tsez corpus of child-directed speech (Gagliardi 2012: 50)

	Agreeing verbs	Agreeing adjectives
Dictionary	27%	4%
Corpus types	60%	35%
Corpus tokens	84%	77%

sporadic agreement. However, here we do not have one word class which contains agreeing and non-agreeing items, but rather a word class continuum which stretches from items which are mostly like adjectives to items which are mostly like nouns (Corbett 1978: 355). Higher numerals are less like adjectives (and more like nouns), and a symptom of this is that they lose their ability to agree.

13.5 Frequency

Frequency of usage is often implicated in the stability of irregularities in language, for instance in the persistence of irregular verbs in the Germanic languages (Booij 2005: 240). We also have some enlightening frequency figures for Tsez. In this language, only 27 per cent of verbs and 4 per cent of adjectives (dictionary entries) agree. Such low proportions of agreeing items raise the question of how children can learn the gender of nouns and how the system can persist.

Gagliardi (2012) shows in a study of a Tsez corpus of child-directed speech that the corpus frequency of agreeing verbs and adjectives is actually much higher than a count of dictionary entries would suggest. The results of this study are set out in Table 13.9.

In the Tsez corpus, agreeing types (i.e. agreeing lexemes in the corpus) are more frequent with 60 per cent and 35 per cent for verbs and adjectives respectively, while corpus tokens (i.e. individual agreeing word forms in the corpus) are more frequent still, with 84 per cent and 77 per cent for verbs and adjectives respectively. While the number of types showing agreement may be comparatively low in the dictionary, the number of corpus types and corpus tokens is much higher as highly frequent adjectives and verbs show agreement. This frequency effect contributes to the learnability and the stability of the Tsez agreement system.

Whether what has been shown for Tsez is the case for other systems of sporadic agreement is an empirical question, but the Tsez case is a plausible scenario.

13.6 Conclusions

Sporadic agreement is a type of non-canonical agreement where two items belonging to the same word class in a language display different agreement behaviour: in the same syntactic context, one item shows agreement, whereas the other one does not. All situations of sporadic agreement have in common that we require additional information about a potential agreement target. Just to know its word class is not sufficient. In this sense, the phenomenon of sporadic agreement (or sporadic non-agreement) can be treated as an extreme case of inflectional classes where one class marks nothing.

In this typological study, I have tried to show that sporadic agreement is not random but follows recognisable patterns: phonotactic, phonological, morphological, semantic or etymological. Phonotactic patterns account for the fact that in Tsez and Ingush, agreement prefixes can only attach to vowel-initial stems. Phonological patterns in Italian define a very small subset of adjectives as invariable. The phonological patterns of ending in a stressed vowel or ending in /i/ are operational outside the word class of adjectives; they are also relevant for nouns. In Archi, the best predictor of whether a verb agrees is its morphological build, i.e. whether a verb has a single stem or five stems. In many cases, the morphology and the semantics make the same prediction as to whether a verb agrees, but the former is ultimately the better predictor for Archi. Semantic factors are at work in Mian and Teiwa, if to a limited extent. In Mian, not to agree with the object is the default for transitive verbs. It is possible to pick out one verb class relatively reliably by appealing to lexical semantics. It is expected that verbs with a meaning of handling or movement take a classifier. In Teiwa, verb classes presumably have formed according to the animacy value of objects that a verb typically occurs with. Finally, we have seen in Basque that loan adjectives can be agreeing while the native members of the same word class are invariable, or the opposite situation in Macedonian, where loan adjectives do not agree, whereas native adjectives do. Four borderline cases were discussed and distinguished from sporadic agreement: phonological processes rendering morphological ones invisible (Hausa), optional agreement (Ngan'gityemerri), word class differences (English) and word class continua (Russian).

Despite the existing phonotactic, phonological, morphological, semantic and etymological patterns in sporadic agreement, there is rarely a factor which would allow us to predict in all cases whether an item agrees or not. It seems that most inflectional systems involving sporadic agreement show leaks which ultimately have to be stopped by lexical specification. But the salient nature of the underlying patterns might actually contribute to the persistence of sporadic agreement. In addition, it has been found in the Nakh-Daghestanian language Tsez that agreeing verbs and adjectives – although the minority in the dictionary – are very frequent in discourse, both in term of types and in terms of tokens, and thus are highly visible to the child learner.

Further research on sporadic agreement will have two main tasks: (i) to study a larger and more balanced sample of languages, which would enable us to be more confident about the statistical distribution of the phenomenon in the languages of the world; and (ii) to engage in corpus studies of languages with sporadic agreement to either substantiate or disprove the frequency effects that have been found for Tsez, which apparently greatly contribute to the learnability and survivability of sporadic agreement.

Acknowledgements

I am grateful to Matthew Baerman and Oliver Bond for very helpful editorial comments. The support of the University of Sydney ('Research Incubator Grant') is gratefully acknowledged. I also thank Siva Kalyan (Australian National University) for participating in this project as a research assistant. I am grateful to the following colleagues for discussion of language data: Matthew Baerman (English), Marina Chumakina (Archi), Sasha Krasovitsky (Russian), Tania Paciaroni (Italian), Masha Polinsky (Tsez) and Anna Thornton (Italian). Special thanks to Marina Chumakina for making Archi verb lists available to me. I would like to thank Anna Thornton for reading and commenting on a previous version of this paper. All remaining errors are mine. Versions of this paper were presented at the Workshop 'Typologie et modélisation des systèmes morphologiques' at Université Paris Diderot – Paris 7 in January 2017, the 'Vielfaltslinguistik-Konferenz' at the University of Leipzig in March 2017 and the Workshop 'Niches in Morphology' at the 50th Annual Meeting of the Societas Linguistica Europaea in Zurich in September 2017. I thank the respective audiences for helpful comments and discussion, in particular Farrell Ackerman, Olivier Bonami, Gilles Authier, Tom Güldemann, Björn Wiemer, Peter Arkadiev, Pier Marco Bertinetto and Grev Corbett.

Appendix: Languages in the sample

Language	Genealogical affiliation	ISO 396-3 code	Glottolog code	Sources
Abkhaz	Northwest Caucasian	abk	abkh1244	Hewitt 1979
Archi	Northeast Caucasian, Lezgic	aqc	arch1244	Kibrik 1977a, 1977b; Chumakina et al. 2007; Bond et al. 2016
Ingush	Northeast Caucasian, Nakh	inh	ingu1245	Nichols 1989; Bickel and Nichols 2007
Tsez	Northeast Caucasian, Tsezic	ddo	dido1241	Polinsky and Comrie 1999; Polinsky and Potsdam 2001; Polinsky 2015; Maria Polinsky, personal communication
Apurinã	Arawakan, Southern Arawakan	apu	apur1254	da Silva Facundes 2000
Barasano	Tucanoan, Eastern Tucanoan	bsn	bara1380	García and Sánchez 1975; Jones and Jones 1991

Guarani	Tupi-Guarani	gug	para1311	Guasch 1996; Ayala 2000
Hixkaryána	Carib	hix	hix1239	Derbyshire 1985
Plains Cree	Algonquian	crk	plai1258	Dahlstrom 1991
Chamorro	Austronesian, Nuclear Malayo-Polynesian	cha	cham1312	Topping 1973; Stolz 2012
Fijian	Austronesian, Oceanic	fij	fiji1243	Dixon 1988
Egyptian Arabic	Afro-Asiatic, Semitic	arz	egyp1253	Aboul-Fetouh 1969; Gairdner 1926
Hausa	Afro-Asiatic, Chadic	hau	haus1257	Newman 2000
English	Indo-European, Germanic	eng	stan1293	Quirk et al. 1985
Italian	Indo-European, Romance	ita	ital1282	Thornton et al. 1997; Anna Thornton, personal communication
Russian	Indo-European, Slavonic	rus	russ1263	Timberlake 1993; Corbett 1978; Alexander Krasovitsky, personal communication
Finnish	Uralic, Finnic	fin	finn1318	Niemi 1945
Ngan'gityemerri	Non-Pama-Nyungan, Daly	nam	nang1295	Reid 1997
Mian	Trans New Guinea, Ok	mpt	mian1256	Fedden 2010, 2011, in press; field notes
Teiwa	Alor-Pantar	twe	teiw1235	Klamer 2010; Fedden et al. 2013
Basque	Isolate	eus	basq1248	Trask 2003
Burushaski	Isolate	bsk	buru1296	Yoshioka 2012

Notes

1. Sporadic agreement is a subtype of what one could call 'sporadic inflection' (Matthew Baerman, personal communication), pertinent examples of which are English count nouns that do not distinguish overtly between singular and plural, such as *sheep* or *-craft* compounds, e.g. *hovercraft*. All instances of sporadic inflection are violations of Criterion 4 for canonical morphosyntactic features and their values: 'Canonical features and their values are distinguished consistently across lexemes within relevant parts of speech' (Corbett 2012: 163).

2. On the notion of 'range' as a measure of the number of lexemes displaying non-canonical behaviour, see Corbett (2012: 163).
3. For the following languages the sources as specified in the Appendix do not provide any evidence of sporadic agreement: Abkhaz, Apurinã, Barasano, Guarani, Hixkaryána, Plains Cree, Fijian, Egyptian Arabic, Finnish and Burushaski.
4. Further, we find the invariable conversions *rosa* 'pink' and *viola* 'purple', from the nouns *rosa* 'rose' and *viola* 'violet' respectively. However, being a conversion is not a sufficient condition for an adjective to be invariable, as can be seen from *marrone* 'brown' (< *marrone* 'type of chestnut'), which can (but does not have to) agree in number (Thornton 2004: 530).
5. For the other word classes which display sporadic agreement, both Chumakina and Corbett (2015) and Chumakina and Bond (2016) are more pessimistic when trying to find factors which allow us to predict agreement potential. On the agreeing postposition *eq'en* 'up to', which is derived from an irregular converb of the verb *eq'is* 'reach', see Chumakina and Brown (2015).
6. Archi verbs use prefixes and infixes to show agreement. Once determined whether a verb agrees at all, there are further complications related to the realisation of the agreement: some verbs take a prefix, some take an infix, and some take either a prefix or an infix depending on the stem. For details, see Chumakina and Corbett (2015: 105–15).
7. Kibrik (1977a) uses the terms 'stative' and 'dynamic'. Stative verbs have a single stem, whereas dynamic verbs have five stems. Kibrik's choice of terminology is due to the very high correlation between morphological build and semantics. Since I am evaluating the predictive power of a verb's morphology as opposed to its semantics with respect to agreement potential, I will keep these notions terminologically apart, using 'stative' and 'dynamic' only for the semantics and resorting to the terms '5-stem verb' and '1-stem verb' to refer to the morphological build.
8. As these figures are based on Kibrik (1977b), rather than the Archi dictionary, the proportion of agreeing verbs is not entirely parallel to the one given in Table 13.2.
9. This is an ambitransitive verb that works on an absolutive basis, i.e. it agrees in number with the object if used transitively, or with the subject if used intransitively (with the sense 'split', cf. *the wood split*). In the latter case the verb agrees doubly with the subject. Number is indicated by apophony, and person, number and gender are indicated through the subject suffix.
10. Like the verbs which only agree in number, classifiers work on an absolutive basis. In transitive verbs that obligatorily take a classifier, classification extends to the object; for the single intransitive verb *mêin* 'fall', classification extends to the subject.
11. For differential object marking and relevant factors like animacy, volitionality and affectedness, see Hopper and Thompson (1980); Tsunoda (1985); Croft (1988); Bossong (1991); Aissen (2003); von Heusinger and Kaiser (2011); Fedden et al. (2013); Fedden et al. (2014), and references there.
12. Even *duecento* 'two hundred' is invariable in Italian, in contrast to Latin and Spanish, where it is in fact declinable (Corbett 1978: 364).

References

Aboul-Fetouh, Hilmi M. (1969), *A Morphological Study of Egyptian Colloquial Arabic*, The Hague: Mouton.
Aissen, Judith (2003), 'Differential object marking: Iconicity vs economy', *Natural Language and Linguistic Theory*, 21 (3), pp. 435–83.
Ayala, Valentín (2000), *Gramática Guaraní*, Asunción: Centro Editorial Paraguayo.

Beavers, John (2011), 'On affectedness', *Natural Language and Linguistic Theory*, 29 (2), pp. 335–70.
Bickel, Balthasar and Johanna Nichols (2007), 'Inflectional morphology', in Timothy Shopen (ed.), *Language Typology and Syntactic Description*, 2nd edn, Cambridge: Cambridge University Press, pp. 169–240.
Bond, Oliver, Greville G. Corbett, Marina Chumakina and Dunstan Brown (eds) (2016), *Archi: Complexities of Agreement in Cross-Theoretical Perspective*, Oxford: Oxford University Press.
Booij, Geert (2005), *The Grammar of Words: An Introduction to Linguistic Morphology*, Oxford: Oxford University Press.
Bossong, Georg (1991), 'Differential object marking in Romance and beyond', in Dieter Wanner and Douglas A. Kibbee (eds), *New Analyses in Romance Linguistics: Selected Papers from the XVIII Linguistic Symposium on Romance Languages 1988*, Amsterdam: Benjamins, pp. 143–70.
Chumakina, Marina and Oliver Bond (2016), 'Competing controllers and agreement potential', in Oliver Bond, Greville G. Corbett, Marina Chumakina and Dunstan Brown (eds), *Archi: Complexities of Agreement in Cross-Theoretical Perspective*, Oxford: Oxford University Press, pp. 77–117.
Chumakina, Marina, Oliver Bond and Greville G. Corbett (2016), 'Essentials of Archi grammar', in Oliver Bond, Greville G. Corbett, Marina Chumakina and Dunstan Brown (eds), *Archi: Complexities of Agreement in Cross-Theoretical Perspective*, Oxford: Oxford University Press, pp. 17–42.
Chumakina, Marina and Dunstan P. Brown (2015), 'Charting Adposition Agreement', MS, University of Surrey and University of York.
Chumakina, Marina, Dunstan Brown, Greville G. Corbett and Harley Quilliam (2007), *A Dictionary of Archi: Archi–Russian–English*, online edn, University of Surrey, <http://dx.doi.org/10.15126/SMG.16/2> (last accessed 21 September 2018).
Chumakina, Marina and Greville G. Corbett (2008), 'Archi: The challenge of an extreme agreement system', in A. V. Arxipov, L. M. Zaxarov, A. A. Kibrik, A. E. Kibrik, I. M. Kobozeva, O. F. Krivnova, E. A. Ljutikova and O. V. Fëdorova (eds), *Fonetika i nefonetika: K 70-letiju Sandro V. Kodzasova* [Phonetics and non-phonetics: a festschrift on the 70th birthday of Sandro V. Kodzasov], Moscow: Jazyki slavjanskix kul´tur, pp. 184–94.
Chumakina, Marina and Greville G. Corbett (2015), 'Gender–number marking in Archi: Small is complex', in Matthew Baerman, Dunstan P. Brown and Greville G. Corbett (eds), *Understanding and Measuring Morphological Complexity*, Oxford: Oxford University Press, pp. 93–116.
Corbett, Greville G. (1978), 'Universals in the syntax of cardinal numerals', *Lingua*, 46, pp. 355–68.
Corbett, Greville G. (2006), *Agreement*, Cambridge: Cambridge University Press.
Corbett, Greville G., Sebastian Fedden and Raphael Finkel (2017), 'Single versus concurrent feature systems: Nominal classification in Mian', *Linguistic Typology*, 21 (2), pp. 209–60.
Croft, William (1988), 'Agreement vs case marking and direct objects', in Michael Barlow and Charles A. Fergusson (eds), *Agreement in Natural Language: Approaches, Theories, Descriptions*, Stanford, CA: CSLI Publications, pp. 159–79.
D'Achille, Paolo and Anna M. Thornton (2003), 'La flessione del nome dall'italiano antico all'italiano contemporaneo', in Nicoletta Maraschio and Teresa Poggi Salani (eds), *Italia linguistica anno Mille – Italia linguistica anno Duemila. Atti del XXXIV Congresso della Società di Linguistica Italiana*, Rome: Bulzoni, pp. 211–30.
Dahlstrom, Amy (1991), *Plains Cree Morphosyntax*, New York: Garland.

da Silva Facundes, Sidney (2000), *The Language of the Apurinã People of Brazil*, doctoral dissertation, State University of New York.

Derbyshire, Desmond C. (1985), *Hixkaryana and Linguistic Typology*, Dallas: Summer Institute of Linguistics.

Dixon, R. M. W. (1988), *A Grammar of Boumaa Fijian*, Chicago: University of Chicago Press.

Fedden, Sebastian (2010), 'Ditransitives in Mian', in Andrej Malchukov, Martin Haspelmath and Bernard Comrie (eds), *Studies in Ditransitive Constructions: A Comparative Handbook*, Berlin: De Gruyter Mouton, pp. 456–85.

Fedden, Sebastian (2011), *A Grammar of Mian*, Mouton Grammar Library, 55, Berlin: De Gruyter Mouton.

Fedden, Sebastian (in press), 'Grammaticalization in Mountain Ok', in Walter Bisang and Andrej Malchukov (eds), *Comparative Handbook of Grammaticalization Scenarios*, Berlin: Mouton.

Fedden, Sebastian and Dunstan P. Brown (2017), 'Participant marking: Corpus study and video elicitation', in Marian Klamer (ed.), *The Alor-Pantar Languages: History and Typology*, 2nd edn, Berlin: Language Science Press, pp. 403–47.

Fedden, Sebastian, Dunstan P. Brown, Greville G. Corbett, Marian Klamer, Gary Holton, Laura C. Robinson and Antoinette Schapper (2013), 'Conditions on pronominal marking in the Alor-Pantar languages', *Linguistics*, 51 (1), pp. 33–74.

Fedden, Sebastian, Dunstan P. Brown, František Kratochvíl, Laura C. Robinson and Antoinette Schapper (2014), 'Variation in pronominal indexing: Lexical stipulation vs referential properties in the Alor-Pantar languages', *Studies in Language*, 38 (1), pp. 44–79.

Fedden, Sebastian and Greville G. Corbett (2017), 'Gender and classifiers in concurrent systems: Refining the typology of nominal classification', *Glossa: A Journal of General Linguistics*, 2 (1), 34, pp. 1–47.

Friedman, Viktor A. (1993), 'Macedonian', in Bernard Comrie and Greville G. Corbett (eds), *The Slavonic Languages*, London: Routledge, pp. 249–305.

Gagliardi, Ann C. (2012), *Input and Intake in Language Acquisition*, doctoral dissertation, University of Maryland, <http://drum.lib.umd.edu/bitstream/1903/13173/1/Gagliardi_umd_0117E_13440.pdf> (last accessed 21 September 2018).

Gagliardi, Ann C. and Jeffrey Lidz (2014), 'Statistical insensitivity in the acquisition of Tsez noun classes', *Language*, 90 (1), pp. 58–89.

Gairdner, W. H. T. (1926), *Egyptian Colloquial Arabic: A Conversation Grammar*, 2nd edn, London: Oxford University Press.

García, Germán Franco and José Raúl Monguí Sánchez (1975), *Gramática yebámasá: Lingüística aplicada*, Bogotá: Universidad Social Católica de 'La Salle'.

Guasch, P. Antonio (1996), *El idioma guaraní: Gramática y antología de prosa y verso*, 7th edn, Asunción, Paraguay: CEPAG.

Healey, Alan (1964), *A Survey of the Ok Family of Languages, Reconstructing Proto-Ok*, PhD dissertation, Australian National University.

Hewitt, B. George (1979), *Abkhaz*, Lingua Descriptive Studies, vol. 2, Amsterdam: North-Holland.

Hopper, Paul J. and Sandra A. Thompson (1980), 'Transitivity in grammar and discourse', *Language*, 56 (2), pp. 251–99.

Jones, Wendell and Paula Jones (1991), *Barasano Syntax*, Studies in the Languages of Colombia, 2, Dallas: Summer Institute of Linguistics and the University of Texas at Arlington.

Kibrik, Aleksandr E. (1977a), *Opyt strukturnogo opisanija arčinskogo jazyka II: Taksonomičeskaja grammatika* [A Structural Description of Archi II: Taxonomic Grammar], Moscow: Izdatel'stvo Moskovskogo Universiteta.

Kibrik, Aleksandr E. (1977b), *Opyt strukturnogo opisanija arčinskogo jazyka III: Dinamičeskaja grammatika* [A Structural Description of Archi III: Dynamic Grammar], Moscow: Izdatel´stvo Moskovskogo Universiteta.

Kibrik, A. E., S. V. Kodzasov, I. P. Olovjannikova and D. S. Samedov (1977), *Opyt strukturnogo opisanija arčinskogo jazyka: I: Leksika, fonetika* [A Structural Description of Archi: I: Lexis, Phonetics], Publikacii otdelenija strukturnoj i prikladnoj lingvistiki, 11, Moscow: Izdatel´stvo Moskovskogo Universiteta.

Klamer, Marian (2010), *A Grammar of Teiwa*, Mouton Grammar Library, 49, Berlin: De Gruyter Mouton.

Klamer, Marian (ed.) (2017), *The Alor-Pantar Languages: History and Typology*, 2nd edn, Berlin: Language Science Press.

Newman, Paul (2000), *The Hausa Language: An Encyclopedic Reference Grammar*, New Haven, CT: Yale University Press.

Nichols, Johanna (1989), 'The Nakh evidence for the history of gender in Nakh-Daghestanian', in Howard I. Aronson (ed.), *The Non-Slavic Languages of the USSR: Linguistic Studies*, Chicago: Chicago Linguistic Society, pp. 158–75.

Niemi, Clemens (1945), *Finnish Grammar*, 3rd edn, Duluth, MN: C. H. Salminen.

Polinsky, Maria (2015), 'Tsez Syntax: A Description', online draft, <lingbuzz/002315> (last accessed 21 September 2018).

Polinsky, Maria and Bernard Comrie (1999), 'Agreement in Tsez', in Greville G. Corbett (ed.), *Agreement*, special issue of *Folia Linguistica*, 33 (2), pp. 109–30.

Polinsky, Maria and Eric Potsdam (2001), 'Long-distance agreement and topic in Tsez', *Natural Language and Linguistic Theory*, 19 (3), pp. 583–646.

Quirk, Randolph, Sidney Greenbaum, Geoffrey Leech and Jan Svartvik (1985), *A Comprehensive Grammar of the English Language*, London: Longman.

Reid, Nicholas (1997), 'Class and classifiers in Ngan'gityemerri', in Mark Harvey and Nicholas Reid (eds), *Nominal Classification in Aboriginal Australia*, Amsterdam: John Benjamins, pp. 165–228.

Stolz, Thomas (2012), 'Survival in a niche. On gender-copy in Chamorro (and sundry languages)', in Marine Vanhove, Thomas Stolz, Aina Urdze and Hitomi Otsuka (eds), *Morphologies in Contact*, Berlin: Akademie, pp. 93–140.

Thornton, Anna M. (2004), 'Conversione in aggettivi', in Maria Grossmann and Franz Rainer (eds), *La formazione delle parole in Italiano*, Berlin: Mouton de Gruyter, pp. 526–33.

Thornton, Anna M., Claudio Iacobini and Cristina Burani (1997), *BDVDB: Una base di dati per il vocabolario di base della lingua italiana*, 2nd edn, Rome: Bulzoni.

Timberlake, Alan (1993), 'Russian', in Bernard Comrie and Greville G. Corbett (eds), *The Slavonic Languages*, London: Routledge, pp. 827–86.

Topping, Donald M. (1973), *Chamorro Reference Grammar*, Honolulu: University of Hawaii Press.

Trask, R. L. (2003), 'The Noun Phrase: Nouns, determiners and modifiers; pronouns and names', in José Ignacio Hualde and Jon Ortiz de Urbina (eds), *A Grammar of Basque*, Berlin: Mouton de Gruyter, pp. 113–70.

Tsunoda, Tasaku (1985), 'Remarks on transitivity', *Journal of Linguistics*, 21 (2), pp. 385–96.

von Heusinger, Klaus and Georg Kaiser (2011), 'Affectedness and differential object marking in Spanish', *Morphology*, 21 (1), pp. 1–25.

Yoshioka, Noboru (2012), *A Reference Grammar of Eastern Burushaski*, doctoral dissertation, Tokyo University of Foreign Studies.

14

Where Are Gender Values and How Do I Get to Them?

Oliver Bond

14.1 Introduction

It is generally assumed that the features of the head of a phrase (and not its dependents) are the most important ones for determining clause-level morphosyntactic processes like predicate agreement. For instance, in English, the number value of a subject noun phrase controlling agreement is determined by the feature specification of the head of that phrase – as in (1a,b) – not the number value of a subconstituent (in this case a possessor), as shown by the ungrammaticality of (1c,d).[1]

(1)   a. [The child's mother]$_{SG}$ was happy.
          b. [The child's parents]$_{PL}$ were happy.
          c. *[The children's mother]$_{SG}$ were happy.
          d. *[The child's parents]$_{PL}$ was happy.

Similar patterns are observed for other morphosyntactic features. This is particularly clear where there is a contrast between the feature values associated with the head, and those associated with a dependent of that head. For instance, in (2) from French, the head of a subject noun phrase is responsible for determining the correct gender and number form of the predicative adjective, and number agreement on the copula *être* 'be'.[2]

(2)   [Les   gants   neufs/*neuves   de   la
           DET.PL   glove.PL(M)   new.M.PL/*new.F.PL   of   DET.F.SG
           femme]$_{M.PL}$ sont/*est   blancs/*blanches
           woman(F)[SG]   be.3PL.PRS/be.3SG.PRS   white.M.PL/white.F.PL
           'The woman's brand-new gloves are white.'

Formal models of syntax have naturally been designed – and adapted – to cope with a wide range of agreement phenomena, but two syntactic notions related to headedness prevail in some form in the prominent theories of syntax.

First, there is a (set of) principle(s) governing 'feature percolation' or 'feature inheritance', a notion that ensures that the featural properties of a phrase that are relevant for morphosyntactic processes such as agreement are determined by their head and not some other dependent element within that phrase (Moravcsik 1978; Lieber 1980; Bresnan 1982; Gazdar et al. 1985; Pollard and Sag 1987).

Second, there are locality constraints on agreement; the relation between controllers and targets of agreement must be within a well-defined syntactic domain (Mahajan 1990; Koopman and Sportiche 1991; Chomsky and Lasnik 1993; and many others). Agreement domains set limits on the permissible structural distance between the controller and target, with close proximity, or locality, being canonical (Corbett 2006). While the exact definition of locality differs across frameworks and authors (compare, for example, Chomsky 2000; Koopman 2003; Sag 2012), a local domain can be informally defined as the relation between a head and those elements with which it bears a grammatical relation (subject of, complement of, etc.). For verbal heads, this is the minimal clause, for nouns it is the NP/DP and for adpositions it is the PP. Agreement is non-local (and, hence, unexpected in the strictest of approaches) when the controller is at a different level of structural selection than the target. Either the controller is outside the local domain (i.e. the controller is outside the minimal clause of the target), or it is within another domain embedded within the local domain (i.e. the controller is within the complement clause of the target or the controller is some other dependent, internal to an argument of the target). For a general typology of non-local agreement, see Polinsky and Potsdam (1999) and Polinsky 2003; for a typology of internal possessors controlling agreement, see Nikolaeva et al. (2019).

These two notions put the phrasal head at the centre of explanations of agreement. A pattern in which the feature profile of the head of a phrase is the source of the morphosyntactic features of its phrase is generally adhered to across linguistic systems and can be considered to be an attribute of canonical syntactic heads or perhaps 'canonical syntactic phrases', though a wide range of alternative patterns are attested (Nichols 1986; Corbett 2016; Bond and Corbett 2017). In some languages, however, there is more to say about the constraints on this process, which raises questions about restrictions on locality and the means by which the features of controllers and targets come to unify (in monostratal models such as HPSG and LFG, e.g. Borsley 2016; Sadler 2016), get valued (Chomsky 2000, 2001) or form 'feature bundles' (in recent accounts of agreement in the Minimalist Program, e.g. Polinsky 2016). Under certain conditions, verbal agreement targets can be controlled by terms which are not arguments of the agreeing predicate, thereby defying expected syntactic restrictions on locality (see Polinsky and Potsdam 2001; Comrie 2003; and papers in Bárány et al. 2019, in particular Nikolaeva et al. 2019). The mechanism by which these non-canonical agreement patterns are achieved consequently requires a modified or alternative explanation of the way in which target and controller features are 'matched' in syntax.

I illustrate this point through data from Kulina (ISO 639-3: cul), an Arawan language spoken in Brazil and Peru. Kulina is known to exhibit two orthogonal systems of gender agreement. A language can be said to exhibit orthogonal gender systems when each noun can be observed to have more than one inherent gender value; crucially, these values do not belong to the same feature, rather each value is associated with a distinct, cross-cutting gender feature (Fedden and Corbett 2017). For instance, in Kulina, there is a sex-based gender system (with feminine and masculine values) and a second class-based system with a morphologically unmarked general gender contrasting with a morphologically marked gender, with the agreement exponent *ka-* (Chapman and Derbyshire 1991; Aikhenvald 2010; Dienst 2014).[3] Each noun has both a sex-based gender value and a class-based gender value, resulting in nouns with four possible combinations of values:

(i) masculine; general gender
(ii) masculine; *ka*-gender
(iii) feminine; general gender
(iv) feminine; *ka*-gender.

I use the term 'class-based gender' to refer to this second system of agreement to capture the fact that it is difficult to identify the semantic core of these gender values (see §14.3.1). The mutually exclusive values in the class-based gender system will be referred to as the general gender and the *ka*-gender. Agreement with *ka*-gender controllers will be referred to as *ka*-agreement.

The set of examples in (3) show the basic pattern of exponence: sex-based gender (F and M) is indicated by a series of suffixes that also mark TAM or negation. Class-based gender is realised by a prefix, *ka-* (glossed with K), which alternates with the default general gender (indicated in glosses with G). The general gender is signalled by the absence of class-based gender agreement morphology on targets.

(3) a. makhidehe zokhe-i
       man(M,G)   [3.G]die.SG-DECL.M
       'The man died.'
    b. amonehe   zokhe-ni
       woman(F,G) [3.G]die.SG-DECL.F
       'The woman died.'
    c. makaari   ka-zokhe-i
       squirrel(M,K) K-[3]die.SG-DECL.M
       'The squirrel died.'
       (Dienst 2014: 108, 90)

The Kulina gender systems are particularly interesting from the perspective of agreement modelling, because their analysis presents a set of challenges that is difficult to explain using frameworks that treat agreement as strictly syntactic. Data from inalienable possessive constructions within the language provide evidence that general syntactic constraints on either feature percolation or locality can be overridden under certain semantic and/or information-structural conditions. While verbs in

Kulina agree in sex-based gender with their A or P argument (§14.2.5), class-based gender can additionally be controlled by noun phrases that are not core arguments (§14.3.4), namely possessors internal to a possessive phrase.

The crucial evidence is presented in (4). In (4a), the P argument *zomahi nokho* 'jaguar's eye' controls agreement in sex-based gender on the auxiliary verb. Neither the head *nokho* 'eye' nor the dependent possessor *zomahi* 'jaguar' belongs to the *ka*-gender, and there is no class-based gender agreement on the verb. In (4b), the sex-based gender agreement on the auxiliary is masculine again, but this time it also agrees in class-based gender, as indicated by the verbal prefix *ka*-.

(4) a. [zomahi   nokho]$_{M,G}$ saka   o-za-i (< o-na-za-i)
        jaguar(M,G)   eye[3.M.POSS](G)   gouge   1SG-[G]AUX.IN-DECL.M
        'I gouged the jaguar's eye.'
    b. [anobeze   nokho]$_{M,K}$ saka   o-ka-na-za-i
        collared.peccary(M,K) eye[3.M.POSS](G)   gouge   1SG-K-AUX-IN-DECL.M
        'I gouged the collared peccary's eye.'
        (Dienst 2014: 91)

The important issue about (4b) is that the head of the P argument, *nokho* 'eye', does not belong to the *ka*-gender – as supported by the absence of class-based gender agreement in (5) – and therefore could not provide the feature value necessary to control class-based gender agreement on the auxiliary if a strict view of feature percolation is adhered to (e.g. Lieber 1980).

(5)   makhidehe   nokho   ohari-i
        man(M,G)   eye[3.M.POSS](G)   [3.G]be.one-DECL.M
        'The man has only one eye.' (lit. 'The man's eye is one.')
        (Dienst 2014: 137)

Assuming that the possessor and possessed entity are part of a syntactically coherent noun phrase (see §14.3.4.3 for details), it appears that the verb in (4b) is agreeing in class-based gender with an embedded dependent of the P noun phrase. This is striking, because agreement with possessors is unexpected in theoretical models of language in which locality restrictions of agreement domains prohibit this.

Using terminology coined by Nikolaeva (2014), I will refer to this as an instance of POSSESSOR PROMINENCE – the phenomenon in which a free or bound possessor internal to a syntactically coherent possessor phrase appears to control syntactic processes such as agreement or switch-reference (see Nikolaeva et al. 2019 for a more precise definition).

I argue that patterns like this contribute to a growing body of evidence that suggests an adequate theory of agreement must be sensitive to semantics and/or information structure, in addition to syntactic information (cf. Barlow 1999; Polinsky and Comrie 1999; Polinsky and Potsdam 2001; Corbett 2006; Miyagawa 2010; Dalrymple and Nikolaeva 2011; É. Kiss 2017; Nikolaeva et al. 2019).

The objective of this paper is to set out some observations about where gender values are in the architecture of grammar and what types of interfaces might be required to account for phenomena (such as possessor prominence or referential agreement) that present a challenge for approaches to agreement that cast it as an entirely syntactic notion. I conclude that even within a single language, a range of agreement mechanisms may be at work, namely syntactic, semantic and referential agreement.

The discussion presented here is based on a substantial reanalysis of agreement data from the Purus dialect of Kulina described by Dienst (2008a, 2008b, 2014), with supplementary evidence from Adams and Marlett (1987); Adams Liclan and Marlett (1990); Wright (1995); and Tiss (2004). Due to the complexity of the system, I make a series of stepwise observations, first picking out the relevant properties of the sex-based gender system, before exploring the properties of the class-based gender system in §14.3. The consequences for the analysis presented are discussed in §14.4, together with general conclusions.

14.2 Sex-Based Gender in Kulina

The sex-based gender system in Kulina has two values: feminine and masculine. It is noteworthy for being among a minority set of languages in which feminine is the default (sex-based) gender value (Corbett 1991; Aikhenvald 2016).

14.2.1 Distribution of Sex-Based Gender Values

Nearly all Kulina nouns have an inherent sex-based gender value (i.e. an invariable grammatical gender value). The basic division is between a feminine gender (with human females at the semantic core) and a masculine gender (with human males at the semantic core). Non-human animates and inanimates are distributed across the two genders, but when the biological sex of an animal is of particular relevance, masculine agreement is used for male animals and feminine for females (Dienst 2014: 71).

The sex-based gender system operates in the clausal domain and in the nominal domain. Agreement targets in the nominal domain are demonstratives and attributive adjectives. Relativised forms of verbs in clauses that modify a noun or pronoun also agree in gender with the noun that is being modified (for examples, see Dienst 2014: 72–3, 247–8).[4]

In the clausal domain, sex-based gender is marked by suffixes and clitics on inflecting dynamic and stative verbs, auxiliaries and predicative adjectives.[5] Agreement is also indicated on the topic marker *=pa/=pi* and the additive particle *noko/naki* 'also' (Dienst 2014: 80). Tiss (2004) provides evidence for an even more diverse set of agreement targets in the Juruá dialect of Kulina.

In morphologically unmarked transitive clauses with two third person arguments, agreement follows a nominative–accusative alignment pattern. However, if there is only one third person argument – whether the A or P – this will be the controller of sex-based gender agreement (see §14.2.5 for discussion). This indicates that sex-based gender agreement in Kulina is subject to co-argument sensitivity (Witzlack-Makarevich 2011; Witzlack-Makarevich et al. 2016).

Given the complexity of the Kulina agreement system and the lack of an in-depth investigation into the behavioural properties of grammatical functions in the language, I will refer to gender agreement in transitive clauses as A-agreement and P-agreement; the association between these macro-roles and the noun phrases controlling gender agreement allows a more agnostic approach than positing subject and object agreement. In what follows, the term 'subject' will only be used to refer to intransitive subjects (i.e. S) or when reporting the analyses of others.

Sex-based gender agreement on the predicate is realised by a series of verbal suffixes that also indicate TAM or negation. This is shown in (6a) and (6b) where the subject noun phrases are feminine and masculine respectively. Around half of the TAM suffixes distinguish sex-based gender, while the rest are invariant in form.

(6) a. amonehe   zokhe-hera-ni
       woman(F,G) [3.G]die.SG-NEG.F-DECL.F
       'The woman didn't die.'
    b. makhidehe   zokhe-hara-i
       man(M,G)   [3.G]die.SG-NEG.M-DECL.M
       'The man didn't die.'
       (Dienst 2014: 73)

Inflectional forms of some verbs are formed periphrastically through the use of auxiliaries. In such cases, most inflectional and derivation morphology – including sex-based gender – is marked on the auxiliary, as in (7). In the absence of a nominal subject, gender marking may be the only indication of the properties of a verb's arguments in a clause, as in (8) and (9). In (9), the differences in gender marking on the predicates of the first and second clauses indicate that the protagonists of the events are different referents, with different sex-based gender values. Masculine topic agreement in the second clause, which has a feminine subject, suggests that grammatical function and discourse function are logically independent parameters (see §14.2.5 for further discussion of agreeing topic markers).

(7)   tokozo   bohe ni-ma-i [< na-ma-i]
       black.caiman(M,G)   dive [3.G]AUX-UP-DECL.M
       'The black caiman is surfacing.'
       (Dienst 2014: 129)

(8)   hapi na-i
       bath [3.G]AUX-DECL.M
       'He is bathing.'
       (Dienst 2014: 142)

(9) "epehi-na" na-hari. naza=pa
    [3.G]suffice-IFUT [3.G]say-NAR.M then=TOP.M
    kha-rona-ni.
    [3.G]move-DOWN-DECL.F
    '"That'll be enough" he said. Then, she climbed down.'
    (Dienst 2014: 205)

The same pattern is observed with third person non-singular pronominal subjects, as in (10) and (11).[6] In (10), the number of the subject is indicated by the non-singular prefix *ke-*, while in (11), subject plurality (greater than two) is indicated on the lexical verb *hawi* 'move' and the plural prefix on the auxiliary is not permitted.[7]

(10) hidapana bakho ke-na-rana
     now arrive NSG-[3.G]AUX-NFRST.M
     'They've just arrived (I am told).'
     (Dienst 2014: 115)

(11) naza=pi hawi ni-haro=pi [< ha-ni-haro=pi]
     then=TOP.F move.PL [3.G]AUX.BACK-NAR.F=TOP.F
     'Then they returned.'
     (Dienst 2014: 233)

Kulina's sex-based gender system is unusual from a typological perspective in that feminine (not masculine) is the default value employed in agreement when a gender value is unspecified. Consequently, a dynamic verb agreeing with a first or second person subject is always feminine, regardless of the sex (or number) of the referent of the pronoun (Dienst 2014: 76), as in (12)–(15).

(12) hapi o-na-ni
     bath 1SG-[G]AUX-DECL.F
     'I'm bathing.' (male or female speaker)
     (Dienst 2014: 142)

(13) o-kha-ni-hera-ni towi
     1SG-[G]move.SG-BACK-NEG.F-DECL.F FUT
     'I will not return.' (male or female speaker)
     (Dienst 2014: 114)

(14) bazima ha i-ke-he-ra-haro
     all be.tired 1NSG-NSG-[G]AUX-NSG-NAR.F
     'We are all tired.' (male or female speaker)
     (Dienst 2014: 104)

(15) ti-didi-mana-hi!
     2-[G]be.silent-NSG-IMP.F
     'Be silent!' (male or female addressees)
     (Dienst 2014: 102)

It is of course possible to claim that first and second person pronouns have a feminine gender value as part of their featural specification. Indeed, this analysis is adopted for Kulina by Dienst (2014) and is also proposed for Jarawara by Dixon (2000, 2004). However, providing a defaults-based approach to morphology is adopted, there is no clear reason to posit this (as opposed to the absence of a grammatical gender feature).[8] Predicates exhibit masculine agreement when there is a masculine controller, and feminine forms are used elsewhere.

In a similar vein, Baerman and Corbett (2013) discuss a number of languages where it superficially appears as though first and second person pronouns control neuter agreement (in three-gender systems). In their examples, it is even more convincing that this occurs by default, rather than inherent specification. Whichever analysis is adopted, the gender specification of first and second person arguments differs from that of third person ones, whose gender is determined through reference to the biological or grammatical gender of their antecedents.

My first analytical claim about sex-based gender values that will become relevant to an analysis of feature percolation is as follows:

> **Observation 1:** First and second person pronouns in Kulina do not have a grammatical gender value.

Contra the analysis presented by Dienst (2014), I propose that first person and second person pronominals do not have a grammatical gender value, therefore there is no grammatical gender value to 'percolate up' to the phrase level. These pronouns appear to control feminine gender agreement only because this is the default agreement form in Kulina. This is an instance of what Corbett (1991) calls neutral agreement. In §14.2.5, I propose that the absence of inherent gender values in the featural specification of first and second person pronouns also accounts for the distribution of sex-based gender agreement in transitive clauses with one or more first or second person arguments.

14.2.2 Nouns with Variable Sex-Based Gender Agreements

A handful of nouns that can be used to refer to referents of either sex may control feminine or masculine agreement. These include *ehedeni* 'child' and *madiha* 'person, Kulina' (Dienst 2008a). For instance, in (16), masculine agreement on the verb indicates that the referent of the (head of the) subject is male (i.e. male offspring), while feminine agreement in (17) indicates that the referent of the (head of the) subject is female, thus a daughter.

(16) o-kha   ehedeni   shiri-i
      1SG-ASS child[M,G]   [3.G]be.cold-DECL.M
      'My son is (feeling) cold.'
      (Dienst 2014: 158)

(17) o-kha   ehedeni   wada-ni
    1SG-ASS   child[F,G]   [3.G]sleep-DECL.F
    'My daughter is sleeping.'
    (Dienst 2014: 145)

Dienst (2014: 71, 84) observes that when nouns of this type are used to refer to groups that comprise members of both sexes, the masculine form of agreement targets is used, as in (18).

(18) o-kh-ehedeni   [< o-kha ehedeni]   pama-i
    1SG-ASS-child[NSG]   [3.G]be.two-DECL.M
    'I have two children.' (lit. 'My children are two.')
    (Dienst 2014: 137)

This indicates that while the feminine agreement is the default when there is no gender specified by a controller, masculine gender is the gender used in resolution.[9] This suggests that agreement with these nouns always depends on the 'real-life' properties of the referent of the noun, rather than some inherent semantic property (see Bond 2017, in preparation, for a similar, but more grammaticalised use of gender for number agreement in related Jarawara).

Agreement driven by the desire to explicitly reflect the biological sex of a referent is not restricted to S arguments, as demonstrated by agreement with the P argument in (19).[10] Here, gender agreement reflects the biological sex of an animal.[11] When the gender of the animal is unimportant, the grammatical (i.e. inherent) gender of the noun is used, so (19a) can be understood to refer to a male dog or a dog of unspecified biological sex (because it is an inherently masculine noun), while (19b) can only be used to refer to a female dog.

(19) a. ethe   khi   o-na-hara-pa
       dog[M](G)   see   1SG-[G]AUX-NEG.M-HPST
       'I didn't see the (male) dog.'
    b. ethe   khi   o-ne-hera-pa
       dog[F](G)   see   1SG-[G]AUX-NEG.F-HPST
       'I didn't see the female dog.'
    (Dienst 2014: 83)

I call this REFERENTIAL GENDER (and contrast it with INHERENT GENDER) because the relevant property is only available by virtue of the relationship between a formal (i.e. syntactic) representation of an entity and a more abstract yet accessible referential description of that entity's properties. This leads me to a second observation, based on arguments made by Dienst (2014):

Observation 2: Some nouns, which refer to animates that could have either biological sex, allow for referential agreement in sex-based gender. Masculine gender is used in non-singular gender resolution: when a noun that can control agreement in either gender value in the singular is used to refer to a group of individuals with mixed biological genders, masculine gender agreements occur.

There are various ways that this sort of data could be dealt with in models of the lexicon so as to ensure that the phrase controlling agreement has the same features as its target; homophonous items could be listed twice in the lexicon, for instance (see Corbett 2006 for a critique of this argumentation). But it is also possible – and more likely – that referential agreement is an interface phenomenon, whereby the 'percolation' of grammatical features is overridden (i.e. interrupted and replaced), or the process of matching the features of the target against those of the controller is intercepted or blocked by referential ones because of their informational relevance or semantic prominence.

14.2.3 Sex-Based Referential Agreement with Pronominal Controllers

While I have proposed that first and second person pronouns do not have an inherent gender value (see §14.2.1), there are certain circumstances where the gender of their referent is important in determining predicate agreement. Inflecting stative verbs in Kulina are unlike inflecting dynamic verbs in that they can agree with the (biological) gender of the referent of a pronominal subject, and thus do not take the default feminine form. This is an instance of referential agreement. For instance, the gender agreement on the stative verb *makho* 'be red' indicates that the speaker is a male (i.e. there is referential agreement with a property of the pronoun's referent), as in (20); however, the additive particle cannot participate in semantic agreement. It occurs in the feminine because the subject pronoun itself does not have an inherent grammatical gender value, resulting in the use of the feminine agreement by default.

(20) owa   naki   makho-w-i
     1SG   also.F   be.red-EPEN-M
     'I'm also (painted) red.' (male speaker)
     (Dienst 2014: 145)

Predicative adjectives behave in the same way as stative verbs in that they reflect the real-world biological gender of the entity referred to by the subject pronoun. This is shown by the contrast between (21a) and (21b). However, note that the copula inflects in the same way as a regular verb (i.e. it has the default feminine agreement pattern) as does the topic marker =*pi*.

(21) a. owa=pi   hada-i   o-ha-ni
        1SG=TOP.F   old-M   1SG-[G]COP-DECL.F
        'I'm old.' (male speaker)
     b. owa=pi   hada-ni   o-ha-ni
        1SG=TOP.F   old-F   1SG-[G]COP-DECL.F
        'I'm old.' (female speaker)
        (Dienst 2014: 169)

This pattern could have originated as attributive agreement with an elided noun phrase (i.e. 'I am an old man'), but there is insufficient evidence to argue this conclusively. This leads to the following observation:

Observation 3: Instances of agreement with the biological sex of the referents of first and second person pronouns is observed with stative verbs and predicative adjectives, but not other targets.

This shows that features of a distinct mental representation of an entity referred to by a controller are relevant for agreement on some types of target. Given that different targets have different agreement behaviours and, in the context of my proposal, that these pronouns do not have a grammatical gender value (§14.2.1), an account in which the default pattern of 'feature percolation' can be overridden would still only be a partial account, because it does not make reference to domains in which it is possible or the types of target involved. Further evidence to support this claim can be seen from agreement with inalienably possessed entities.

14.2.4 Agreement with Possessor Phrases

Kulina syntax distinguishes between two main types of possession, alienable and inalienable. These can be distinguished from one another based on their syntactic and morphological behaviour. Broadly speaking, inalienable possession constructions are found with body parts and certain culturally salient items closely associated with a single individual.

Alienable possession constructions are formed syntactically: both the possessor and possessed are free-standing words. I assume that phrases of this type are NPs, and the possessor is the specifier of the possessed nominal. When an inflecting stative verb occurs with an alienable possession phrase as its subject and the possessor is first or second person, the possessed entity determines the relevant value for gender agreement as in (22) and (23). In these examples the clause final clitic agrees with the gender value of the head of the subject.[12]

(22) ti-kha   amonehe   hia=ki?
     2-ASS   woman(F,G)   [3.G]be.pregnant=Q.F
     'Is your wife pregnant?'
     (Dienst 2014: 133)

(23) ti-kha   ato   ani=ko?
     2-ASS   older.brother(M,G)   [3.G]exist=Q.M
     'Do you have an older brother?'
     (Dienst 2014: 133)

Inalienable possession is expressed morphologically. Independent pronominal possessors are not usually attested alongside inalienable possessed nouns. However, third person nominal possessors can form a syntactic phrase with inalienable possessed entity. Nouns falling into this class have a possessive paradigm in which the person, number and grammatical gender (of third person) possessors determine their possible word forms. The (morpho)phonological rules determining the form of inalienable nouns are numerous, and discussed at length in Adams Liclan and Marlett (1990). A straightforward example is presented in Table 14.1.

Table 14.1 Possessive paradigm for the noun *zepe* 'hand' (Dienst 2014: 218)

zepe 'hand'		SG	NSG
1		o-zepe	i-zepe
2		ti-zepe	ti-zepe-deni
3	M	zepe	zepe-deni
	F	zapa-ni	zapa-ni-deni

In this paradigm, the possessed forms are built from the root *zepe*, through stem modification (gender), prefixation (person and number), suffixation (person, gender and number). This demonstrates that, in terms of their location in the grammatical system, sex-based gender values are important to the rules that generate word forms. The fact that all forms except the feminine ones share the same stem indicates that within the morphological system, masculine is the default value.

Inalienably possessed third person forms are specified for the gender of their possessor. I argue that this is not an inherent gender value of the possessed noun, but rather it is a contextual one that arises through agreement with a possessor controller, as shown by the contrast between (24a) and (24b).

(24) a. [makhidehe   shipori]   koma   ta-i [<to-na-i]
        man(M,G)   throat[3.M.POSS](G) ache   3.[G]AUX-DECL.M
        'The man's throat is aching.'
    b. [amonehe   shipori-ni]   koma   ta-ni [< to-na-ni]
        woman(F,G) throat-3.F.POSS(G)   ache   3.[G]AUX-DECL.F
        'The woman's throat is aching.'
        (Dienst 2014: 74)

Although the possessor and possessed often co-occur, the possessor is also frequently omitted, as in (25) and (26). In (25), the auxiliary appears in its masculine form because the possessor (the snake) of the head of the P argument, *tati* 'head', has masculine gender.

(25) tati   ka   o-na-maro-hari
     head[3.M.POSS](G)   cut 1SG-[G]AUX-UP-NAR.M
     'I cut off its head [a snake's head], moving up (from the body).'
     (Dienst 2014: 296)

In (26), the gender value of the possessor can be identified by the (default) masculine form of the possessed noun; compare the feminine *zotoni* 'her anus' (Dienst 2014: 64), which would control feminine agreement. While feminine is the default form of other agreement targets, masculine stems are the default forms in the possessive paradigm.

(26) zoto oki ta-i [< to-na-i]
    anus[3.M.POSS](G) greasy 3.[G]AUX-DECL.M
    'He is scared.' (lit. 'His anus is greasy.')
    (Dienst 2014: 277)

To summarise, when an adnominal possessor is overtly expressed by a full NP, it acts as a local antecedent for the inalienably possessed noun. When there is no possessor NP, the gender of the inalienably possessed noun is determined by the possessor, whether it is local or not. Consequently, I analyse inalienably possessed nouns as projecting a DP, which maps a single word form to two distinct nodes (D and N) through lexical sharing (Lowe 2016; Bond 2017). When present, the nominal possessor occupies the optional specifier of that DP, but it is not the head of the maximal projection. One consequence of this analysis is that inalienable possession phrases are DPs, while alienable possession phrases are NPs.

If the possessor of an inalienable noun is first or second person, then it is expressed morphologically, through affixation to a nominal stem, as in Table 14.1, with no other external representation of the possessor. Note that these forms are built from a stem, which, when bare, is used as the masculine singular stem. However, this does not mean that the first or second person forms have a masculine feature value. I propose that sex-based gender values are not part of the feature specification of these forms. Therefore, in the examples presented here, such as (27), no gender value is specified in the gloss of an inalienably possessed noun unless it is third person.

(27) o-zepe ime-ni
    1SG-hand[POSS](G) [3.G]be.big-DECL.F
    'My hand is big.' (male or female speaker)
    (Dienst 2014: 82)

When there is a first or second person possessor, agreement on the predicate is always feminine because this is the default gender for inflecting predicates.

While periphrastic stative verbs usually agree with the referential properties of a pronominal subject, this is not the case where the subject is an inalienably possessed noun with a first or second person possessor; the agreement must be feminine. This is seen in (28) where the semantics of the predicate indicate that the referent of the subject must be male, the auxiliary bears feminine agreement (i.e. default agreement).[13]

(28) o-doro pasho ta-ni [< to-na-ni]
    1SG-groin(G) hungry.for.flesh 3[G]AUX-DECL.F
    'I feel like having sex.' (male speaker, predicate restricted in use to males)
    (Dienst 2014: 277)

On the basis of data of this kind, I propose that inalienably possessed nouns do not have an inherent gender in Kulina. In this sense, they are unlike regular alienable nouns in the language. Since neither first and second person pronouns nor first and second person forms of inalienably possessed nouns have an inherent gender specification, neither can trigger syntactic agreement. This leads us to the next important observation relevant for a model of feature percolation:

> **Observation 4:** All alienable nouns in Kulina have an inherent grammatical gender. However, inalienably possessed nouns in Kulina do not. If third person, their sex-based gender value is determined by that of the antecedent of their possessor.

Data like these raise questions about whether contextual, sex-based gender values on a possessed head noun are sufficiently visible to phrase external processes to be responsible for controlling agreement. Do the contextual values of an inalienably possessed noun percolate up to the phrase level, or does the predicate agree with a dependent possessor, regardless of whether its antecedent is local or not? I will return to these questions in §14.4. First, I set out the distribution of agreement with respect to transitive predicates.

14.2.5 Constraints on Agreement in Transitive Predicates

Here I propose that transitive verbs in Kulina agree in sex-based gender with their A or P depending on the person, number and topicality of their arguments. While the arguments presented here build on the analyses presented in Dienst (2014: 76–80), they are substantially different. The objective of this reanalysis is to provide a much more straightforward explanation for the facts than the one provided by the complex set of constraints on agreement he proposes. Here I distinguish between direct predicates (§14.2.5.1) and inverse predicates (§14.2.5.2) in which an agreement alternation is observed.

14.2.5.1 Direct predicates

In transitive clauses with two third person nominal arguments, the morphologically unmarked (although not the most frequent) agreement pattern is one in which the verb agrees in person, number and gender with the A argument. Third person singular arguments are morphologically unmarked, unless the verb is stative, as illustrated by the contrast between the dynamic verb in (29) and stative verb in (30).[14]

(29) o-kha   amonehe   bani   hipa-ni
     1SG-ASS   woman(F,G)   meat(M,G) [3.G]eat-DECL.F
     'My wife ate meat.'
     (Dienst 2014: 78)

(30) zowato   poo   pha-de   to-ha-ni
     girl(F,G) manioc(M,G) plant-INF 3-[G]AUX-DECL.F
     'The girl is planting sweet manioc.'
     (Dienst 2014: 251)

If the A argument is third person, and there is a first or second person P argument, as in (31) and (32), the predicate also agrees in person and gender with the A argument.

(31) ethe   ia   ta-kha-i
     dog(M,G)   1NSG   PL.O-[3.G]bite-DECL.M
     'The dog has bitten us.
     (Dienst 2014: 77)

(32) osonaa   tia   shite   na-i
     Kashinawa(M,G)   2   shoot.with.arrow   [3.G]AUX-DECL.M
     'The Kashinawa has shot you with an arrow.'
     (Dienst 2014: 77)

Adams and Marlett (1987) propose that agreement in Kulina has an absolutive controller and that examples like (29)–(32) are antipassive constructions in which the verb agrees in gender with the (intransitive) subject in the absence of an object argument. Like Dienst (2008a, 2014), I do not find this analysis convincing. I am not aware of any independent syntactic evidence to suggest these predicates lack an object argument. Rather, agreement is sensitive to the featural properties of the co-arguments. If the A argument is first or second person and the P is third person, then P-agreement is observed, as in (33)–(35).[15]

In (33) the verb agrees with the masculine third person P argument. The additive focus particle also agrees with the P argument, demonstrating that this argument functions as the only controller in this clause with respect to sex-based gender. In (34) the verb agrees with the sex-based gender value of the head of the P argument. In (35), the verb agrees in gender with an understood patient, *aba* 'fish', which has masculine gender.

(33) owa   nako   bani   o-hipa-i
     1SG   too.M   meat(M,G)   1SG-[G]eat-DECL.M
     'I, too, ate meat.'
     (Dienst 2014: 78)

(34) o-kha   takara   o-tapa-bakhi-i
     1SG-ASS   chicken(M,G)   1SG-[G]feed-NSG.P-DECL.M
     'I'm going to feed my chickens.'
     (Dienst 2014: 105)

(35) koro   ti-ke-na-ho!
     hook   2-NSG.A-[G]AUX-IMP.M
     'Hook (NSG) (fish)!'
     (Dienst 2014: 101)

The pattern observed in (33)–(35) could be seen as a natural consequence of the claim made in §14.2.1. Since first and second person pronouns do not have a gender value, they are rather poor potential controllers of gender agreement.[16]

Based on this evidence, agreement in sex-based gender on direct transitive predicates is controlled by the highest ranking third person nominal candidate in terms of topicality. If both arguments are first or second pronouns (and therefore only have referential gender, but not a grammatical gender value), then the feminine agreement form occurs by default, as in (36).

(36) "kobeta=za   owa   hore   ta-khi-mana-hi [< ti-na-khi-mana-hi]"
blanket=INS   1SG   wrap   2.[G]AUX-ITER-NSG.A-IMP.F
o-na-za
1SG-say-TC
'When I said "Wrap me in a blanket!" . . .'
(Dienst 2014: 264)

The same pattern of agreement is typically observed with the topic marker, =pa/=pi and the additive focus marker nako/naki. In most cases, if the S or A of the clause is third person, the topic marker agrees with it in gender. This is shown in (37), where the feminine A argument of the clause – not the masculine P argument – controls agreement.

(37) i-kha   amonehe=pi   shabira
1NSG-ASS   woman(F,G)=TOP.F   giant.otter(M,G)
naha-de
[3.G]CAUS.penetrate-PST
'Our wives slept with giant otters.'
(Dienst 2014: 200)

When the A of a transitive clause is first or second person, and thus has no gender value, the topic marker agrees in gender with the next highest candidate on the hierarchy – a third person P, as in (38). A similar example with the additive focus marker agreeing with the P can be seen in (33) above.

(38) owa=pa   tapa   pha   o-na-i
1SG=TOP.M   maize(M,G)   plant   1SG-[G]AUX-DECL.M
'I'm planting maize.'
(Dienst 2014: 200)

In (39), repeated from (9), the topic marker is analysed as belonging structurally to the second clause, but it 'agrees' in sex-based gender with a masculine discourse topic.

(39) "epehi-na"   na-hari.   naza=pa
[3.G]suffice-IFUT   [3.G]say-NAR.M   then=TOP.M
kha-rona-ni.
[3.G]move-DOWN-DECL.F
'"That'll be enough" he said. Then, she climbed down.'
(Dienst 2014: 205)

These examples show that the controller of agreement for topic markers is not necessarily the host constituent, or even the only argument of an intransitive predicate, but a representation of a non-local referent that functions as a grammatical pivot of the clause. This type of agreement is referential (rather than syntactic or semantic) in nature, leading us to the following observation:

> **Observation 5:** Direct predicates agree in sex-based gender with the highest ranking grammatical relation that has a sex-based gender value: A-argument > P-argument. Topic markers agree with the topical grammatical pivot, not their host constituent.

These examples seem to indicate that some apparent targets of agreement (e.g. the topic marker) have an antecedent outside the local domain, while others must agree with a suitable local target.

14.2.5.2 Inverse predicates

An inverse pattern of agreement is observed when transitive verbs with a third person A agree in gender with a third person P. In such cases, third person verbs are prefixed with *i-*, as in (40). The majority of transitive clauses in Dienst (2014) are of this type, and therefore inverse predicates are frequent and less restricted in their distribution than direct predicates.[17]

(40) amonehe   wapima bani   bedi   ethe
     woman(F,G) all   animal(M,G)   small[M]   raise
     i-ha-mana-i
     INV-[G]AUX-NSG.A-DECL.M
     'All the women are raising pets.'
     (Dienst 2014: 104)

In such cases, the agreement controller is always one that would not be expected based on argument co-sensitivity constraints in direct predicates (i.e. the inverse of the direct pattern is observed). Recall that in direct predicates with third person arguments, the A controls agreement, as in (41).

(41) o-kha amonehe   mahi   hia   na-ni
     1SG   woman(F,G) sun(M,G)   make.warm   AUX-DECL.F
     'My wife is warming herself in the sun.'
     (Dienst 2014: 104)

When inverse marking is present, as in (42), (40) and (43), the inflecting verb or auxiliary agrees in sex-based gender with the P.

(42) amonehe   bazima poo   i-kaari-mana-i
     woman(F,G) all   manioc(M,G)   INV-[3.G]cook-NSG.A-DECL.M
     'All the women are cooking manioc.'
     (Dienst 2014: 102)

(43) makhidehe a-haro   zowato   i-kahi-ni
     man(M,G)   DEM-F   girl(F,G) INV-[3.G]marry-DECL.F
     'The man married that girl.'
     (Dienst 2014: 224)

The presence of *i-* is logically independent of gender marking, because some verb forms do not show any sex-based gender agreement, as in (44), yet *i-* is still marked.

(44) bowi   etero   wazi   i-rana (< i-na-rana)
     cow(M,G)   clothes(F,G)   chew   INV-[3.G]AUX.ADMON
     'The cow is going to chew the clothes.'
     (Dienst 2014: 115)

The inverse marker is also present when there is a deviation from the agreement pattern observed with direct predicates that have third person As and first or second person P arguments. In direct predicates, with this argument configuration, the target agrees in sex-based gender with the A, as in (45).

(45) ethe   bazima   ia   ta-kha-i
     dog(M,G)   many   1NSG   PL.O-[3.G]bite-DECL.M
     'Many dogs have bitten us.'

However, the inverse marker is required when there is agreement with the P, as in (46) and (47), where default feminine agreement is observed.

(46) awani   ia   kha   i-na-bakhi-mana-ni
     wasp(M,G)   1NSG   sting   INV-[3.G]AUX-NSG.P-NSG.A-DECL.F
     'The wasps stung us.'
     (Dienst 2014: 78)

(47) kobeta=za   owa   hore   i-na-khi-mana-haro
     blanket=INS   1SG   wrap   INV-[3.G]AUX-ITER-NSG.A-NAR.F
     'They wrapped me in a blanket.'
     (Dienst 2014: 264)

Based on their distribution in texts (for examples, see Dienst 2014: 287–97), inverse agreement constructions occur when there is continuity in reference to an agent across consecutive independent clauses, i.e. in inverse clauses the agent has a high degree of topicality. In these texts, the patient also has a high degree of topicality, and these clauses potentially have both a primary and a secondary topic (in the sense of Nikolaeva 2001; Dalrymple and Nikolaeva 2011).

I am not aware of any examples provided in Dienst (2014) in which inverse agreement is observed in a predicate with a first person or second person A (although see §14.3.4.3 for a possible example). However, Wright (1995) provides examples with first person and second person As in which the verb agrees in sex-based gender with the P (48a) or the A (48b), demonstrating that the inverse agreement pattern is possible regardless of the presence of the *i-* prefix. This leads to a situation where it is not always possible to determine which noun phrase is controlling agreement, as in (48c), where both potential controllers would trigger feminine agreement.

(48) a. Kodzo   tsʰite   o-na-hari
 lizard(M,G)   shoot   1SG-[G]AUX-DECL.M
 'I shot the lizard.'
 b. Kodzo   tsʰite   o-na-haro
 lizard(M,G)   shoot   1SG-[G]AUX-DECL.F
 'I shot the lizard.'
 c. Aoi   tsʰite   o-na-haro
 tapir(F,G)   shoot   1SG-[G]AUX-DECL.F
 'I shot the tapir.'
 (Wright 1995: 112)

Dienst (2014) analyses the *i-* prefix as marking a third person subject. There are a number of reasons why such an analysis might be seen as attractive:

(i) It only occurs with third person A arguments (although not all third person As and never with a third person S).
(ii) *i-* occurs in the same position as other person/number prefixes that index S/A arguments (and is thus incompatible with them).
(iii) *i-* has the same form as another person marking form, the 1NSG prefix (although this is probably only a homophonous pattern).
(iv) The same form is used on some 'inflecting postpositions' when used in reference to third person masculine (but not feminine) participants (for discussion, see Dienst 2014: 180–2).

In the Purus dialect of Kulina described by Dienst (2014), the prefix *i-* is incompatible with other prefixes that index features of the S/A arguments.[18] While it is likely that the origin of the prefix is as an agreement marker, any synchronic description of this as an agreement affix must minimally acknowledge that this prefix is only attested when the P argument is more topical than in direct predicates, and that the controller of agreement is not constant, but rather conditioned by co-argument sensitivity. However, a number of pieces of evidence support the inverse analysis proposed here:

(i) *i-* always occurs with third person singular As when sex-based gender agreement is with another controller; it alternates with zero marking of third person As, and does not occur in intransitives. Therefore, its occurrence is conditioned by more than having a third person 'subject'.
(ii) *i-* is found with transitive and ditransitive verbs only. It only occurs in constructions when an agreement alternation is possible.
(iii) Inverse agreement constructions occur in texts when (a) there is continuity in reference to an agent across consecutive independent clauses, and (b) the P argument is an established 'aboutness' topic.
(iv) Direct transitive constructions are used for a shift in protagonist (to establish the role of a new agent or introduce a generic or indefinite patient).

(v) Similar patterns of verbal morphology are found in Jarawara (Dixon 2004), where the prefix *hi-* alternates with person marking, and indicates that a topical object is the grammatical pivot of the clause.

While this construction may appear passive-like in that the P argument of the clause is promoted in terms of its discourse function, it does not appear to be like a passive in many other respects (based on the characterisation of passives in Siewierska 2013):

(i) Inverse predicates in Kulina are not pragmatically restricted relative to 'active' counterparts, and they have a much wider distribution than comparable direct predicates.
(ii) Other than the gender agreement alternation, there is no apparent structural asymmetry between the A and P arguments of direct and inverse predicates in terms of their formal coding, nor is there any word order alternation.
(iii) A arguments in inverse clauses control number agreement on the predicate in the same way that they do in direct clauses. This would not be expected in a passive: the inability of a 'demoted' A argument to control agreement is taken by Siewierska (2013) to be an important property for distinguishing passives from inverses.
(iv) There is no clear derivational relationship between inverse and direct predicates. While I describe *i-* as an inverse prefix, this is part of the inflectional morphology of the verb, and it is licensed in certain co-argument configurations. There is no special morphological marking on the verb characterising all inverse clauses of this type.

This leads us to the final observation about the sex-based gender system in Kulina:

Observation 6: Kulina exhibits a mixed alignment system in which topicality and co-argument sensitivity determine the agreement pattern. Inverse agreement is observed when an *i-* marked verb agrees in sex-based gender with a topical P argument.

Understanding this property of the Kulina sex-based gender agreement system will prove important in understanding how it differs from class-based gender agreement (§14.3) and what type of framework might be needed to model gender agreement in Kulina (§14.4).

14.2.6 Summary of Sex-Based Gender in Kulina

Kulina's sex-based gender agreement system is subject to a number of constraints at the morphological, syntactic, semantic and referential level. As in other Arawan languages, feminine is the default sex-based gender value in Kulina. Most nouns are either inherently masculine or feminine. However, some nouns, which refer to animates that could have either biological sex, allow for referential agreement in sex-based gender. This points to a theoretical analysis in which referential gender values are available under certain conditions. Masculine gender is used as the default value for gender resolution when a noun with variable gender agreements is used to denote a plural referent. This demonstrates that the absence of an inherent sex-based gender value and the resolution of gender agreement when more than one value is possible are different.

First and second person pronouns do not have an inherent grammatical gender value and therefore take feminine agreement by default. Instances of referential agreement with the biological gender of the referents of first and second person pronouns are observed with stative verbs and predicative adjectives, but not with other targets. Here, referential agreement overrides default agreement.

While most nouns have an inherent sex-based gender value, inalienably possessed nouns do not. Their sex-based gender value is determined by that of their (non-local) possessor.

Clause-level nominal controllers of sex-based gender agreement are in a hierarchical relationship with one another: A-argument > P-argument, most probably reflecting the propensity for agents to be more topical than patients. Direct predicates agree in gender with the most agentive grammatical relation that has a gender feature. Topic markers agree with the topical grammatical pivot, not the host constituent within their scope. Kulina exhibits systems of direct and inverse agreement. The inverse agreement pattern is observed when an *i-* marked verb agrees in sex-based gender with a topical P argument.

14.3 Class-Based Gender in Kulina

The two-value class-based gender system in Kulina (consisting of the *ka*-gender and the general gender) is orthogonal to the sex-based gender system. All nouns – including inalienably possessed nouns – are categorised within this gender system, with the majority of nouns falling into the general gender. Agreement with *ka*-gender items is found on verbal predicates, including relative clauses modifying nominals, and is realised by a *ka-* prefix on inflecting verbs and auxiliaries. Items in the general gender do not trigger any morphological exponence on agreement targets.

Class-based gender agreement in Kulina differs from sex-based gender agreement in a number of other important ways:

(i) The *ka*-gender in Kulina does not have a well-defined semantic core, but covers a disparate set of non-human entities, including some borrowings (§14.3.1).
(ii) *ka*-agreement is restricted to fewer targets than sex-based gender (§14.3.2).
(iii) *ka*-agreement is conditional on individuation (§14.3.3), and some other less well-defined parameters.
(iv) *ka*-agreement may be triggered by a wider range of controllers than sex-based gender agreement (§14.3.4).
(v) Sex-based and class-based gender agreement may be controlled by different controllers in the same clause simultaneously (§14.3.4).

We now look at these differences in turn, starting with the distribution of class-based gender values.

14.3.1 Distribution of Class-Based Gender Values

Dienst (2014: 86–7) explicitly identifies 47 items within the *ka*-gender (although examples throughout the work indicate that there are a number of additional members). Of these, 22 are inherently feminine and 18 are inherently masculine. Dienst subcategorises the members of the *ka*-gender into different semantic groups. Some examples of inherently masculine and feminine nouns are provided for each subgroup, where attested, in Table 14.2. The remaining 7 items refer to inalienably possessed body parts, all but one of which have both feminine and masculine forms (depending on the gender of the possessor).[19] These are listed in Table 14.3.

Many of the terms are for culturally significant animals and artefacts. Some of the items in the *ka*-gender are borrowings, such as *haizo* 'radio' from Portuguese *rádio*, *koshiro* 'knife' from Spanish *cuchillo* and *weni* 'river' from neighbouring Arawakan languages (Dienst 2014: 20, 278–9).

To exemplify the basic difference between the two class-based genders, a set of examples is provided in (49). In (49a) the *ka*-gender subject *makaari* 'squirrel' triggers class-based gender agreement on the verb, while the subject in (49), *makhidehe* 'man', which belongs to the general gender (indicated by the absence of agreement morphology), does not.

Table 14.2 Alienable nouns in the *ka*-gender

Semantic group	Example
Running waters	weni (M) 'river' bihitati (M) 'small stream'
Thin, straight objects	boba (M) 'arrow' dodo (F) 'pestle'
Objects which shine in the dark	amowa (M) 'star, firefly sp.', shishiede (F) 'lightning, firefly sp.'
Artefacts (except those made of clay)	phowi (M) 'hammock' wiwithari (F) 'bench'
Mammals	anobeze (M) 'collared-peccary' warikoze (F) 'great long-nosed armadillo'
Birds	onowana (M) 'king vulture' waba (F) 'pooto'
Fish	akomi (F) 'pirahna' bama (F) 'paca'

Table 14.3 Inalienable nouns in the *ka*-gender

Body part	M	F
ear	waribo	wariboni
tooth	ino	inoni
arm	bihi	bihini
leg	isho	ishoni
thigh	panakho	panakhoni
foot	amori	amorini
testicles	denephe	

(49) a. makaari   ka-zokhe-i
       squirrel(M,K) K-[3]die.SG-DECL.M
       'The squirrel died.'
    b. makhidehe   zokhe-i
       man(M,G)   [3.G]die.SG-DECL.M
       'The man died.'
       (Dienst 2014: 90, 108)

Note that in both examples the subject belongs to the masculine gender, as indicated by the verbal suffix. A minimal pair with feminine gender is found in §14.3.4.1.

14.3.2 Targets of Class-Based Gender

Contextual class-based gender values are limited to synthetic and periphrastic verb forms. When the predicate consists of an uninflecting verb and an auxiliary, *ka-* occurs on the auxiliary just like other inflection. In (50), *ka-* occurs between the directional prefix *to-* and the auxiliary stem of a dynamic periphrastic verb. An example with the auxiliary *hira* is provided in (51). In each of these examples, the verb agrees in sex-based and class-based gender with the subject NP.

(50) anobeze   bihini   hiphe   wahi   kona
     collared.peccary(M,K) stream   opposite.bank DIST.LOC swim
     to-ka-na-i
     [3]AWAY-K-AUX-DECL.M
     'The collared peccary is swimming to the opposite bank of the stream.'
     (Dienst 2014: 123)

(51) panera   phoko ka-hira-ni
     cooking.pot(F,K) hot   K-[3]AUX-DECL.F
     'The cooking pot is hot.'
     (Dienst 2014: 149)

Class-based gender agreement is also observed in relative clauses formed from quantifying verbs, as in (52) and (53). In (52) the *ka*-gender noun is the head of the subject of the main clause predicate, while in (53) it is the P argument. In both cases *ka*-agreement is evident in the relative clause and the main clause.

(52) moto   ka-pamee   keeeda-hona-ni [< ka-weda-hona-ni]
      boat(F,K)   K-[3]be.two.REL.F K.[3]move.DU-HITHER-DECL.F
      'Two boats are coming.'
      (Dienst 2014: 139)

(53) tahapa   ka-hari-e   mitha o-ka-na-na
      casting.net(F,K)   K-[3]be.one.RELF   buy   1SG-K-AUX-IFUT
      'I am going to buy one casting-net.'
      (Dienst 2014: 139)

Based on these data, the following observation can be made:

Observation 7: Class-based gender agreement is restricted to a subset of the targets of sex-based gender agreement, namely it is found only on verbs and auxiliaries in main clauses. Within the nominal domain, it is found on relative clauses only.

Further differences between the two types of gender marking can be seen by looking at semantic conditions on agreement.

14.3.3 Conditions on Class-Based Agreement

A number of important semantic conditions on class-based gender agreement are observed by Dienst (2014: 85–8). Verbs do not usually agree in class-based gender if the would-be controller has plural reference (§14.3.3.1), if the entity is in an 'altered' state (§14.3.3.2) or if a part, rather than the whole of the entity, is referred to (§14.3.3.3).

14.3.3.1 Individuation

Dienst (2014: 85) proposes that class-based gender agreement marking is conditional on number.[20] While *ka*-agreement is observed with controllers that are referentially singular or dual, general gender agreement is observed when a would-be *ka*-gender controller is used with plural (greater than two) reference. For instance, *mowi* 'night monkey' in (54a) has singular reference and the auxiliary verb agrees with the P argument in sex-based gender and class-based gender. In (54b), which has a plural P argument as indicated by the prefix *ta-*, the verb form is simplex, and *ka-* is omitted.[21]

(54) a. ahi=za   mowi   khi   o-ka-na-ni
          DEM.F=LOC   night.monkey(F,K)   see   1SG-K-AUX-DECL.F
          'Here I saw a night monkey.'
      b. ahi=za   mowi   o-ta-khi-ni
          DEM.F=LOC   night.monkey(F,K)   1SG-PL.O-see-DECL.F
          'Here I saw night monkeys.
          (Dienst 2014: 85)

An example of *ka*-agreement with a dual P argument can be seen in (55).

(55) poroko   pama-a   wa-k-ida-bakhi-na [< o-ka-k-ida-bakhi-na]
     pig(M,K) [3.G]be.two-REL.M 1SG.K-EPEN-beat-NSG.P-IFUT
     'I'm going to kill two pigs (beating them dead).'
     (Dienst 2014: 107)

The same pattern is found with intransitives. Predicates that morphologically express the number of the subject, as in (56) and (57), or encode quantities lexically, as in (58), do not agree with the *ka*-class controller.

(56) makaari   to-hika-i
     squirrel(M,K) 3-[G]die.PL-DECL.M
     'Many/Several squirrels died.'
     (Dienst 2014: 131)

(57) anobeze   wapima kahadiha-i
     collared.peccary(M,K) all   [3.G]sleep.NSG-DECL.M
     'All the collared peccaries are sleeping.'
     (Dienst 2014: 197)

(58) aha=za   anobeze   kahi   ta-de [< to-na-de]
     DEIC.M=PROX.LOC collared.peccary(M,K) numerous 3[G]AUX-PST
     'There used to be a lot of collared peccaries here.'
     (Dienst 2014: 188)

Since this is a tendency rather than an absolute condition, this appears to be a semantic or referential, rather than syntactic in nature. The available data suggest that agreement is favoured when the controller refers to individuated participants. This idea is explored further in §14.4.

14.3.3.2 Altered state

Nouns in the *ka*-gender trigger class-based gender agreement when referring to an item in a 'natural' state but do not when in an 'altered' state:

(i) Names for tree species trigger *ka*-agreement when referred to in a standing state, whereas felled trees referred to by the same name do not control *ka*-agreement.
(ii) Names for fruits trigger *ka*-agreement when in a hanging state, whereas picked or fallen fruit referred to by the same name does not control *ka*-agreement.
(iii) Names for bottles and containers trigger *ka*-agreement when in a full state, whereas empty containers referred to by the same term do not control *ka*-agreement.

Given the generality of this pattern, it is tempting to analyse this as a semantic condition on agreement for certain classes of nouns, rather than positing that each pair is represented by two related lexemes in the lexicon; however, more detailed information on agreement possibilities would be needed to confirm the most suitable analysis.

14.3.3.3 Part–whole relations

Finally, *ka*-agreement is also used to distinguish between part–whole relations (see Dienst 2014: 89 for discussion). For instance, in (59), the presence of *ka*-agreement indicates that a manioc plant is being referred to (and not a manioc tuber).

(59) poo   owa=za   ka-hari-a   da   ti-ka-na-ho
     manioc(M)[K] 1SG=IO   K-[3]be.one-REL.M   give   2-K-AUX-IMP.M
     'Give me a manioc plant!'
     (Dienst 2014: 176)

A handful of homophonous lexical items are distinguished by their class-based gender, but these distinctions are not in a part–whole relation with each other, as illustrated by the contrast in (60).

(60) a. zazio   zapori   wishi   o-ka-hiza-na [< o-ka-na-hiza-na]
        howler.monkey(M,G)   penis(M,K)   cut   1SG-K-AUX.THROUGH-IFUT
        'I am going to cut the howler monkey's penis off.'
     b. zazio   zapori   wishi   o-hiza-na [< o-na-hiza-na]
        howler.monkey(M,G)   tail(M,G)   cut   1SG-[G]AUX.THROUGH-IFUT
        'I am going to cut the howler monkey's tail off.'
        (Dienst 2014: 89)

In (60a) there is *ka*-agreement with the P argument *zazio zapori* 'howler money's penis' because the possessed entity belongs to the *ka*-gender. However, in (60a) there is no *ka*-agreement with the P argument because neither the possessor nor the possessed belongs to the *ka*-gender. Note that this is slightly different from the analysis presented in Dienst (2014: 89). These conditions on agreement are summarised in the following observation:

> **Observation 8:** Most nouns are exhaustively classified into the two class-based genders, including inalienable nouns (cf. inalienable nouns that do not have an inherent sex-based gender). However, there are also conditions on agreement. There is a tendency for controllers denoting individuated referents to trigger *ka*-agreement and a dispreference for agreement with plural controllers. Some nouns only trigger *ka*-agreement if their referent is in an unaltered state or considered to be whole (rather than a constituent part of a whole).

Just as class-based gender is more variable in terms of the conditions that exist on agreement, so are the grammatical functions of the possible agreement controller.

14.3.4 Controllers of Class-Based Gender Agreement

While sex-based gender agreement can be controlled by an S, A or P argument, class-based gender agreement can be controlled by intransitive subjects (§14.3.4.1), P arguments (§14.3.4.2), and possessors of S and A (§14.3.4.3). The fact that class-based gender agreement follows an ergative–absolutive alignment pattern, while sex-based gender agreement is sensitive to the featural specification of a verb's co-arguments, means that the different agreement systems can be controlled by different arguments within the same clause.

14.3.4.1 Agreement with an S argument

Intransitive verbs agree with their single argument in class-based gender agreement, as shown by the contrast between (61a) and (61b).

(61) a. noparina   ka-wi-ni
       oil.lamp(F,K) K-[3]go.out-DECL.F
       'The oil-lamp went out.'
    b. zipho   owi-ni
       fire(F,G)   [3.G]go.out-DECL.F
       'The fire went out.'
       (Dienst 2014: 40)

When the subject is a possessor phrase with an alienably possessed *ka*-gender noun as the head, as in (62), this feature of the head also percolates up to the phrasal level, as expected.

(62) o-kha   oza   oba   to-ka-na-ni
     1SG-ASS   house(F,K)   dirty 3-K-AUX-DECL.F
     'My house is dirty.'
     (Dienst 2014: 141)

Here, there is a simple 'percolation' of class-based feature values from the head to the phrase (but see §14.3.4.3 for some more challenging examples).

Examples with *ka*-gender As in transitive constructions are not explicitly discussed by Dienst (2014), and there are no examples of direct or inverse transitive predicates with inanimate As in either Dienst (2014) or Wright (1995). The example in (63), in which the main clause has a third person singular A in the *ka*-gender, suggests that class-based gender agreement is not available for all A arguments. Here the verb has an individuated singular feminine A, *akomi* 'piranha', but no class-based gender agreement is triggered.

(63) naza=pi   [aba   koro-koro   o-zi-phe-raa
     then=TOP.F   fish(M,G)   hook-REDUP   1SG-[G]AUX.IN-WATER-AVRS
     ata   haroro-ni=za]   akomi   owa   kha   to-za-haro
     mud(F,G)   muddy-F=LOC piranha(F,K)   1SG   bite 3-[G]AUX.IN-NAR.F
     'Then, when I was standing in the water hooking fish in the mud, a piranha bit me.'
     (Dienst 2014: 262)

The subject marking on the verb suggests that this could be an example of what Wright (1995: 122–9) calls an impersonal transitive, in which the specificity of the A is downplayed. However, the distribution of *to-* is complex and further analysis awaits a full investigation of the behavioural syntax of different grammatical functions.

14.3.4.2 Agreement with a P argument

Verbs agree in class-based gender with the P argument of transitive constructions. In (64), the verb agrees with *panera* 'metal cooking pot'.

(64) panera   nami=za   o-kaatha-na [< o-ka-watha-na]
     metal.cooking.pot(F,K)   ground=LOC   1SG-K.put-IFUT
     'I'm going to put the cooking pot on the ground.'
     (Dienst 2014: 136)

In (65a), the inverse-marked verb agrees in sex-based gender and class-based gender with the P argument *tahapa* 'casting net'. This contrasts with the example in (65b) where the P does not belong to the *ka*-gender and therefore only sex-based gender agreement is triggered.

(65) a. makhidehe   tahapa   e-kathema-ni [< i-ka-kathema-ni]
        man(M,G)   casting.net(F,K)   INV.K-[3]mend-DECL.F
        'The man mended the casting-net.'
     b. amonehe   etero   i-kathema-ni
        woman(F,G)   clothes(F,G)   INV-[3.G]mend-DECL.F
        'The woman mended the clothes.'
        (Dienst 2014: 43)

The fact that class-based gender agreement is only ever attested with S or P controllers, while the controller of sex-based gender agreement in transitive clauses varies according to the co-arguments and the presence of inverse marking, means that the different systems can be controlled by different arguments. For instance, in (66) the A of the direct clause controls masculine agreement on the auxiliary, while the theme 'his bracelet' (lit. 'his arm's (thing)') controls class-based gender agreement.

(66) makhidehe powa bihi-kha amonehe=za da
 man(M,G) 3.M arm[3.M.POSS](K)-ASS woman(F,G)=IO give
 to-ka-na-i
 [3]AWAY-K-AUX-DECL.M
 'The man is giving his bracelet to the woman.'
 (Dienst 2014: 129)

As with S arguments, when a possessive phrase functioning as a P argument has an alienably possessed *ka*-gender noun as the head, as in (67), this controls *ka*-agreement on the verb (note that the agreement prefix is realised as *wa-* in this example).

(67) naza=na o-kha oza owa o-wa-kathema-ni hini
 then=NFOC 1SG-ASS house(F,K) 1SG 1SG-K-repair-DECL.F NFUT
 'Then I'll repair my house.'
 (Dienst 2014: 114)

In some instances of class-based gender agreement, the controller is not expressed overtly in the clause, but is retrievable from a preceding clause. For instance, the presence of the *ka-* prefix on the auxiliary verb in in (68) indicates that the place that will be swept is in the *ka*-gender (in this case *oza* 'house').

(68) Hidapa=na howe o-ka-na-na
 now=NFOC sweep 1SG-K-AUX-IFUT
 'Now I'm going to sweep (the house).'
 (Dienst 2014: 89)

In the first clause of (69), the *ka*-gender possessed entity *mashi* 'vulva' controls *ka*-agreement on the verb on the auxiliary in each of the clauses.

(69) o-kha mashi moda o-ka-na-na khi
 1SG-ASS vulva(M,K) cover 1SG-K-AUX-IFUT see
 i-ka-na-mane-rana
 NV-K-[3]AUX-NSG.A-ADMON
 'I am going to cover my vulva, lest they see it.'
 (Dienst 2014: 103)

Similar examples of possessive phrases functioning as P arguments can be seen with *boba* 'arrow' (Dienst 2014: 32) and *phowi* 'hammock' (Dienst 2014: 191).

Dienst (2014: 92) explicitly states that verbs can also agree in class-based gender with indirect objects; however, no example is provided to support this statement. Adjuncts formed from *ka*-gender nouns do not control class-based gender agreement, as shown by (70) and (71).[22]

(70) siba koro o-zi-pha-na weni=za
 stone(F,G) throw 1SG-[G]AUX.IN-WATER-IFUT river(M,K)=LOC
 'I'm going to throw a stone into the river.'
 (Dienst 2014: 120)

(71) [Kanaú]ₛ [o-towi]_ADJ [moto bede-ni=za]_ADJ
 Kanaú 1SG-GOAL boat(F,K) small-F=INS
 kha-ni-poma-hari
 [3.G]move.SG-BACK-AGAIN-NAR.M
 'Kanaú returned again in a small boat to (meet) me.'
 (Dienst 2014: 240)

Based on the evidence presented here, and in §14.3.4.1, class-based gender agreement follows an ergative–absolutive pattern whereby S and P arguments control agreement.

Another substantive way in which class-based gender agreement and sex-based gender agreement differ is their behaviour with a class of stative verbs that take a nominal complement such as *kahi* 'have' in (72). Complement-taking verbs never agree with the verbal complement in sex-based gender, even when the subject of the clause is first or second person (Dienst 2014: 222–3).

(72) makhidehe oza ime-ni ka-kahi-i
 man(M,G) house(F,K) big-F [3]K-have-DECL.M
 'The man has a big house.'
 (Dienst 2014: 90)

Here, the subject is the controller of sex-based gender agreement, as would be expected of an intransitive. However, class-based gender does not pattern in the same way: if a *ka*-gender noun heads the complement phrase, as in (72), it can control agreement on the verb.[23] This shows that the verb can simultaneously agree in different genders with different controllers (i.e. intransitive subject and complement) and also suggests that controllers of class-based agreement cannot be defined solely by making reference to core grammatical functions such as subject and object.

14.3.4.3 Agreement with phrases headed by an inalienably possessed noun

When an inalienably possessed noun is possessed by a first or second person possessor, it triggers feminine agreement on the verb by default. This results in a pattern of agreement in which it superficially appears as though a possessor determines sex-based gender agreement (as proposed by Dienst 2014). As argued in §14.2.4, these nouns do not have an inherent sex-based gender value. When possessed by third person possessors, their gender value comes from their possessor. However, inalienably possessed nouns do have class-based gender. If the inalienable possessed entity belongs to the *ka*-gender, it controls *ka*-agreement on the verb. This is demonstrated in (73) and (74), where the first person possessed nouns *owamori* 'my foot' and *opanakho* 'my thigh' each belong to the *ka*-gender.

(73) o-w-amori tiro to-ka-na-ni
 1SG-EPEN-foot(K) break 3-K-AUX-DECL.F
 'I broke my foot.' (lit. 'My foot broke.')
 (Dienst 2014: 91)

(74) o-panakho   tiro   to-ka-na-ni
    1SG-thigh(K) hurt   3-K-AUX-DECL.F
    'My thigh is hurting.'
    (Dienst 2014: 90)

Compare these with the intransitive construction in (75), in which the inalienably possessed noun does not belong to the *ka*-gender and therefore does not trigger *ka*-agreement.

(75) o-wapi   phoko   ra-ni [< hira-ni]
    1SG-skin(G) hot   [3.G]AUX-DECL.F
    'I'm hot.' (lit. 'My skin is hot.')
    (Dienst 2014: 158)

In (76) and (77), repeated from (4a) and (60b) respectively, neither the nominal possessor nor the inalienably possessed noun belongs to the *ka*-gender.

(76) [zomahi   nokho]_{M,G}   saka   o-za-i [< o-na-za-i]
    jaguar(M,G)   eye[3.M.POSS](G)   gouge   1SG-[G]AUX.IN-DECL.M
    'I gouged the jaguar's eye.'
    (Dienst 2014: 91)

(77) zazio   zapori   wishi   o-hiza-na (< o-na-hiza-na)
    howler.monkey(M,G)   tail(M,G)   cut   1SG-[G]AUX.THROUGH-IFUT
    'I am going to cut the howler monkey's tail off.'
    (Dienst 2014: 89)

The form of an inalienable noun possessed by a third person possessor is determined by the gender of its antecedent. The verb agrees with the sex-based gender of the head of the P. If neither possessor nor possessed belongs to the *ka*-gender, then class-based gender agreement is not triggered.

For a theory of percolation, the data here are straightforward: the featural properties of the head percolate to the phrasal level to participate in clause-level morphosyntactic processes. However, if the nominal possessor internal to an P argument belongs to the *ka*-gender but the possessed item does not, then the NP will also control *ka*-agreement, as in (78) and (79), repeated from (4b) and (60a) respectively.

(78) [anobeze   nokho]_{M,K}   saka   o-ka-na-za-i
    collared.peccary(M,K) eye[3.M.POSS](G)   gouge   1SG-K-AUX-IN-DECL.M
    'I gouged the collared peccary's eye.'
    (Dienst 2014: 91)

(79) zazio   zapori   wishi   o-ka-hiza-na [< o-ka-na-hiza-na]
    howler.monkey(M,G)   penis(M,K)   cut   1SG-K-AUX.THROUGH-IFUT
    'I am going to cut the howler monkey's penis off.'
    (Dienst 2014: 89)

This appears to be a potential example of possessor prominence in the class-based gender agreement system. What remains unclear is whether *ka*-agreement is obligatory in (78). It is also unclear whether the part–whole relation between possessor and possessed is necessary for this pattern to be possible.

If we consider whether the same is possible in the sex-based gender system, we reach a theoretical impasse because inalienably possessed nouns always have the same gender specification as their possessor. Consequently, there is no principled empirical way of deciding whether the head or the dependent possessor directly (or indirectly) provides the feature. The only possible example I am aware of that could be an exception to this rule, in which there is a possible mismatch between the sex-based gender values of the possessor and possessed, is given in (80).

(80) madiha   athi   i-atha-ni
      Kulina(M/F,G) language[3.M.POSS](G)   1NSG-[G]learn-DECL.F
      'We are learning the Kulina language.'
      (Dienst 2014: 35)

Here the possessor *madiha* 'people, Kulina' belongs to the class of nouns which may control either masculine or feminine agreement (Dienst 2014: 71). Given the form of the inalienably possessed noun *athi* 'language', it appears as though the possessed entity in the P argument of the clause is masculine (the feminine form would be *athini*; Dienst 2014: 62) yet there is feminine agreement on the verb.

There are of course different options for analysing this sentence (notwithstanding a production/translation error). The simplest explanation is that the verb does not agree with the P argument at all. This would be inverse agreement with a first person A, parallel to the examples provided by Wright (1995: 112) in §14.2.5. Alternatively, there could be a genuine mismatch between the sex-based genders of the possessor and possessed and the verb agrees with the possessor. This would be a further example of possessor prominence and would parallel the example with class-based gender in (78). A further possibility is that *athi* is in the process of losing a formal distinction between masculine and feminine possessive marking (i.e. this phrase is feminine in terms of its features, but appears to be masculine in terms of its form). Levelling of this kind is commonplace in related Jarawara (Dixon 2004) and therefore not unexpected. A number of other analytical possibilities exist, but without further evidence, this patterns remains unresolved. Such configurations of person and gender require further investigation.

Returning to less controversial candidates for a prominent possessor analysis, a key question from the perspective of syntactic theory is whether the possessor is a dependent of the head when it controls agreement or whether it has an external representation. The purely syntactic evidence for determining the constituency of this phrase is scant, because negative evidence is not deployed in the references consulted. This is exacerbated by the fact that the possessor and the possessed do not need to form a unit (inalienably possessed items may occur without a local antecedent) and the semantically possessed noun frequently occurs independently of the possessor. However, there are a number of reasons to believe that the possessor is not an independent clause-level participant, i.e. they are not external possessors in the sense of Payne and Barshi (1999):

(i) *Valence:* There is no independent evidence to suggest that the valence of the clause increases when a possessor is present (i.e. that the possessors function as external arguments). There is no change in the form of the verb or the formal marking of dependents.
(ii) *Adjacency:* No material ever occurs between a possessor and an inalienably possessed noun, suggesting these elements form a syntactic unit as well as being part of the same referential description.
(iii) *Recursion:* Evidence from recursion suggests that possessor phrases are syntactic units that can be embedded within other possessive structures.

In terms of both constituency and functional structure, these possessors are internal to the noun phrase of the possessed entity. This apparent predicate–possessor agreement does not fit the standard theoretical view of agreement because an agreeing verb can look 'inside' its syntactic complement. It is therefore non-canonical in the sense of Corbett (2003, 2006), and poses a challenge to theories that assume both a strict view of percolation and local indexing.

14.3.5 Summary of Class-Based Gender in Kulina

The distribution of class-based gender marking differs from sex-based gender marking in several important ways. Class-based gender agreement is restricted to a subset of the targets of sex-based gender agreement, namely it is found only on verbs and auxiliaries in main clauses. Within the nominal domain, it is found on relative (i.e. dependent verbal) clauses only. Most nouns are exhaustively classified into the two class-based genders, including inalienable nouns (cf. inalienable nouns that do not have an inherent sex-based gender). However, there are also conditions on agreement. There is a tendency for singular and dual nouns to trigger *ka*-agreement and a dispreference for agreement with plural controllers. Some nouns only trigger *ka*-agreement if their referent is in an unaltered state or considered to be whole (rather than a constituent part of a whole). While sex-based gender agreement is always controlled by the (alienable) head of an S, A or P, class-based gender agreement can be controlled by S, P or possessors.

14.4 Discussion

The analysis of the Kulina gender systems presented here raises a number of issues that are challenging for theories of agreement. Specifically, where are feature values located in a formal model of language? And should all types of 'agreement' be modelled with the same infrastructure? Here, I discuss these in turn, highlighting some consequences and proposals for theory building, concluding that there is a module of grammatical structure responsible for the relative accessibility of referents (i.e. a module of grammar specialised for this purpose) that is distinct from syntax.

14.4.1 Modelling Non-syntactic Agreement

In the models of agreement generally assumed in the major syntactic frameworks, agreement is a syntactic relation. The feature values of the head of a phrase are the same as the feature values of the phrase as a whole, and the process of accessing agreement features is a syntactic one (whether your approach is monostratal or involves successive derivations). Some of the agreement operations in Kulina are clearly well-behaved syntactic ones (see, for instance, §14.1, §14.2.1). However, it is clear that this is not always the case. Under certain circumstances, agreement targets may by-pass the grammatical feature values of a would-be syntactic controller and instead have access to other properties of a referent that are not the same as the features expected to be involved in syntactic agreement (as with predicative adjectives in §14.2.3 that exhibit referential agreement with first person subjects based on the biological sex of their controller). In other cases, targets appear to agree with a non-local controller, meaning that the controller of agreement is not within the domain (i.e. the syntactically defined configuration) predicted to be relevant for this syntactic process. This is the case with 'prominent internal possessors' that trigger class-based gender agreement on the verb (§14.3.4.3). Targets may also be sensitive to the person properties of their arguments: given certain co-argument configurations, agreement may be controlled by the A or the P (§14.2.5). Assuming these differences do not reflect a difference in constituent structure, there are two potential approaches to modelling these sorts of agreement alternations.

I begin with the first approach, which I shall dub 'the semantic model'. For any given gender feature, two types of values associated with an agreement controller are available to participate in agreement: the grammatical (i.e. the inherent) gender value of the controller (which is part of the lexical description of a noun or pronoun) and its semantic gender (which is determined by the semantics of the expression). Under this approach, the featural description of a controller in syntax contains both sets of features as standard. No additional modules of grammar necessarily need to be posited, but the conditions determining deviations from agreement with grammatical agreement features must be explicit. In this scenario, all gender feature values relevant for agreement are inserted into syntactic structures at the same time as the lexical content of the terminal nodes themselves. This sort of model could be applicable to most instances of what Corbett (1979, 2006) calls semantic agreement, providing the relevant semantic features are predictable based on the lexical semantics of the controller. In sum, in the 'semantic model', non-syntactic agreement is modelled by positing that lexical semantic features of a controller that are always present in syntax but usually not visible to morphosyntactic processes become interpretable/unifiable under certain conditions, and in doing so, outrank the syntactic features usually involved in canonical agreement.

While appealing in its simplicity, it is unlikely that this model could be successfully adapted to account for the type of non-canonical agreement phenomena in Kulina because the relevant values are not properties of fixed semantic descriptions, but real-life properties of entities referred to by NPs or by indexation that become prominent because of their relative salience in discourse (hence the term referential gender). Two of the agreement patterns discussed above are particularly relevant here: (i) agreement in gender based on biological sex of the referent of a first or second person pronoun; and (ii) agreement in gender based on the biological sex of animals.

Recall that in §14.2.1, I proposed that first person and second person pronouns in Kulina do not have a grammatical gender value, and therefore, contra the analysis in Dienst (2014), they do not control syntactic agreement at all. Rather, as a default form in the morphological paradigm of verbs, the 'feminine' form is used precisely when there is not a viable controller with a masculine feature value, including when there is no specification of a gender feature value. However, certain targets – namely those which predicate properties (rather than events) – can access the referential gender value of a subject pronoun. Similar possibilities are available for nouns that have an inherent gender that does not necessarily align with the biological sex of a referent, as with certain animates (§14.2.2).

A second set of agreement operations found in Kulina indicates that elements within the clause can agree with feature values of a referent that does not have an argument function in the clause. This is seen in agreement with some internal possessors (§14.2.4, §14.3.4.3) but also where topic markers and adverbials agree with referents that are not represented clause internally (§14.2.5.1). These phenomena indicate that purely syntactic accounts of agreement modified to cope with semantic agreement phenomena might only be partially adequate in accounting for the empirical facts.

In the second model, grammatical agreement values are inherent properties of lexical descriptions, and grammatical agreement is a strictly syntactic phenomenon, but in what I refer to as REFERENTIAL AGREEMENT, targets are 'controlled by' and/or 'probe' featural information accessible from a different tier of representation. That is, there is a module of grammar that is responsible for managing descriptions of discourse active referents that is distinct from syntactic structure. Evidence presented in §14.2.5 above suggests that the module responsible for this process may have to do with the speaker's pragmatic construal of the situation, namely information structure (see, among many others, Mycock 2006; Dalrymple and Nikolaeva 2011). The important difference between this model and the semantic model is that (i) it necessarily requires a tier of representation beyond syntactic structure, and (ii) it need not assume the same constraints that syntactic agreement does. In particular, because agreement is with properties of referential entities that need not have representation as a predicate argument, an apparent relaxation of locality constraints appears to be possible.

The central observation about models of language that I wish to make is that whatever kind of language is being analysed, beyond the surface-level forms, there is a system of organisation responsible for monitoring the accessibility of referents within and across clauses. Unlike morphology (which is word-internal), constituent structure and grammatical relations (which are sentence/clause linkage-internal), information structure is not a property of a word or clause, but of relations between clauses and their propositional content. The extent to which indexing of these relationships is constrained by syntax varies from language to language.

14.4.2 Where Are Gender Values?

To be able to further assess the models discussed in §14.4.1, it is first pertinent to review where gender values are located in the grammatical architecture. For Kulina, we can answer this in the following way:

1. Sex-based and class-based gender values are part of the inherent lexical specification of all alienable nouns. This must be the case since the gender of most nouns cannot be predicted independently. Inalienable nouns only have an inherent class-based gender value (§14.3.1) because their sex-based gender value is contextual (§14.2.4).
2. Gender values are clearly present in the component of grammar responsible for forming inflected words. Rules of word formation referencing a feminine value are evident in the paradigms of inalienably possessed nouns (§14.2.4). Sex-based gender values are also crucial in the formation of the paradigms of demonstratives, adjectives, dynamic and stative verbs, and auxiliaries. Sex-based gender is also among the features of the topic marker and the additive particle (§14.2.1). Class-based gender values are only realised as exponents in paradigms of inflecting verbs and auxiliaries (§14.3.2). The differences in the distribution of these values simply reflects a difference in the historical development of the two gender systems.
3. Sometimes gender values are not there at all. Instead, the absence of a gender value leads to the presence of default agreement forms, as argued for sex-based gender values for first and second person pronouns (§14.2.1), and sex-based gender for inalienably possessed nouns with first or second person possessors (§14.2.4).
4. In addition to the inherent gender(s) of a noun specified in the lexicon, some nouns are associated with mental representations which have different, competing sets of values (§14.2.2). Pronouns are also linked to such representations with real-world gender values (§14.2.3), even when they do not have a grammatical gender value (as argued in §14.2.1). In §14.4.3, I argue that these values are available from an active catalogue of the properties of referents that is constantly updated as discourse progresses. I refer to these as information structure descriptions, and assume that they map to grammatical functions in a similar way to the analyses in Dalrymple and Nikolaeva (2011), I but leave open the question of whether it is possible to identify primitives of information structure (see Matić and Wedgwood 2013).

14.4.3 How Do I Get to Them?

Having established where gender values are in a speaker's grammar, we can turn to the mechanisms that are sensitive to their presence. Here, I set aside discussion of morphology internal inflectional processes (although these are of course fascinating in their own right) and focus on the grammatical processes that unify these feature values, namely 'agreement' in its broadest sense.[24] For Kulina, the following observations can be made:

1. Frequently, gender values, like other agreement values, unify in a way that would be expected in purely syntactic models of agreement. In these instances of syntactic agreement, inherent grammatical feature values of the controller are 'matched' with corresponding values on the target, within a local domain. The controller is predictable and does not vary in grammatical function. This is clearest with gender agreement in intransitive clauses. Such cases are the closest Kulina gets to exhibiting canonical agreement (Corbett 2006).
2. However, the fact that the person and relative topicality of a referent are better predictors of being a controller of agreement than grammatical function in transitive clauses demonstrates that syntax only partially restricts what is possible in terms of indexation of discourse participants. Consequently, sex-based gender agreement is not functionally redundant – it helps to track a topical referent across clauses independently of grammatical function. In languages that behave in this way, unification of agreement features must be mediated by corresponding information structure descriptions (see point 5 below for more on this).
3. Not all 'agreement' involves matching of values in a strict sense. In Kulina, the default forms of the verb, which can be controlled by a feminine trigger, also permit the absence of a sex-based gender value on a would-be-controller. However, they cannot tolerate a mismatch of features; masculine controllers cannot occur with feminine targets and vice versa. Neutral forms are widespread in syntactic agreement systems (Corbett 1991), and the most tempting analysis is one at the level of feature value types.
4. While the default form of targets in the sex-based gender system does not tolerate the presence of a conflicting inherent gender value on their controller, a different principle holds for the class-based system. The default general form can tolerate a *ka*-class controller (and, thus, is even 'sloppier' than the feminine contextual feature) in most contexts, except where the absence of agreement signals a semantically meaningful contrast (i.e. the entity is in an 'altered' state (§14.3.3.2) or if a part, rather than the whole of the entity, is referred to (§14.3.3.3). This is probably an effect of the attrition of a more robust class-based gender system, which is assumed to date back to Proto-Arawan (Dienst 2014: 85). Since membership of the *ka*-class gender is defined by an ability to control *ka*-agreement, would-be general class controllers are, naturally, ungrammatical with *ka*-class targets. This shows that in languages with more than one gender feature (see Fedden and

5. When *ka*-agreement is conditional, it has an individuating or differentiating function (§14.3.3.1). Based on the available evidence, I hypothesise that the ability to individuate participants (rather than knowing the grammatical number of a controller) is an important condition for triggering class-based gender agreement (i.e. it is a condition on differential argument marking). Individuation is known to be an important factor in definiteness (Polinsky 1992; Kibort 2010), which in turn is an indicator of topic-worthiness (Comrie 2003). If this is true, then *ka*-agreement is also functionally non-redundant since it either indicates a meaningful semantic contrast or helps track topical referents.
6. Sometimes agreement controllers are not syntactic arguments in a strict sense. They are accessible information structure descriptions that either do not have a formal expression in syntax (cf. allocutives; Antonov 2015), or map to a non-argument expression through sloppy identity. This is the case with prominent internal possessors in Kulina (§14.3.4.3). When the information structure descriptions of possessors are sufficiently accessible, they appear to control agreement, but only because of lax identity restrictions between a grammatical function and a discourse function. When a possessed entity controls agreement it is more or equally accessible in information structure than the possessor in terms of topicality, and it has its own representation in syntax and information structure. But when a possessor controls agreement, its discourse prominence means that sloppier identity restrictions are permitted (e.g. the part–whole relation observed in Kulina), and features of the information structure description of the possessor unify with features of the target. In some languages at least (e.g. languages discussed by Dalrymple and Nikolaeva 2011; Nikolaeva et al. 2019), feature unification in indexation is sensitive to properties of the information descriptions of referents.

Acknowledgements

This research was carried out as part of the project 'Prominent possessors' (AH/M010708/1). The AHRC's support is gratefully acknowledged. I am especially indebted to Matthew Baerman, András Bárány, Andrew Hippisley and Irina Nikolaeva for their insightful comments on a draft of this paper, and to Aicha Belkadi, Matthew Carroll, (an unwitting) Grev Corbett, Anja Hasse and Helen Sims-Williams for helpful discussion of its content.

Notes

1. Assuming, of course, that the possessed noun is the head in English possessive constructions. See Lowe (2016) for recent discussion of the structure of English possessive phrases in relation to the DP hypothesis.
2. In this paper, the grammatical genders of a noun are indicated in parentheses in the interlinear gloss. The exponence of gender on targets or as part on the morphology of the controller is indicated like other grammatical categories. Where the absence of marking

of a grammatical category is important for the interpretation of a default value, this is marked in brackets, e.g. [SG].
3. Kulina agreement is described as belonging to Type C in Fedden and Corbett's (2017: 27) typology of concurrent gender and classifier systems. This is because there is evidence for two independent systems of grammatical meaning.
4. Dienst (2014: 73) also describes the topic marker as belonging to the nominal agreement domain, but since the topic marker frequently agrees with clause-level arguments to which it is not attached, I treat it as a part of the clausal domain.
5. The labels 'dynamic' and 'stative' follow Dienst (2014). He is careful to note that these are merely helpful mnemonics for two distinct classes of verbs which are distinguished by morphological and syntactic criteria (Dienst 2014: 74).
6. No example sentences with independent third person pronominal subjects are provided in Dienst (2014).
7. Dienst (2014: 233) proposes that the root of the auxiliary *ha* is deleted here in the absence of prefixal morphology. A possible alternative analysis is that there is a zero stem in this part of the paradigm. See Comrie and Zamponi (this volume) for discussion of similar issues.
8. Bond (2017, in preparation) argues that adopting a defaults-based view of sex-based gender in Jarawara provides a natural explanation of possessive noun phrases that are troublesome in an analysis in which all pronouns and nouns have a gender value.
9. It is unclear whether feminine agreement could be used with an indefinite and non-specific use of *ehedeni* 'child' where the biological gender of the referent was irrelevant to the discourse.
10. I am not aware of any examples in Dienst (2014) in which there is semantic agreement with an A argument, but suspect this is a data gap rather than a grammaticalised distinction.
11. Agreement properties of transitive predicates are discussed in more detail in §14.2.5.
12. The existential verb *ani* is only attested with third person subjects and does not show agreement in person (Dienst 2014: 243).
13. Note that periphrastic statives – unlike simplex forms – agree in person with third person subjects with the prefix *to-*.
14. Dienst (2014: 251–2) explicitly notes that progressive constructions are monoclausal. In (30), *poo* is said to be the object of a complex predicate, not an embedded infinitive. Recall that the contrast between the so-called stative and dynamic ones is morphological and distributional rather than semantic (Dienst 2014: 74).
15. The only example I am aware of that could stand as an exception to this rule is discussed in §14.4.
16. One possible structural interpretation of this is that, in these examples, covert arguments are in a distinct structural position outside the clause and therefore unable to control agreement in gender. Instead, the next best candidate is selected, but this would not explain why number agreement is still possible, for instance. I propose that these pronominals simply do not have grammatical gender values so cannot control syntactic gender agreement.
17. The description preceding example (41) in Dienst (2014: 104) and the form of the auxiliary final suffix *-i* indicates that this agrees with the P, and that the feminine gloss used in the source is a typo.
18. In the Juruá dialect described by Tiss (2004), *i-* is compatible with *ke-*, a prefix found on auxiliaries that agrees with non-singular subjects (for examples, see Dienst 2014: 104) but not other prefixes indexing S/A arguments. In the Purus dialect, *i-* is not compatible with *ke-*, but an inverse agreement pattern is nevertheless possible in clauses with a third person P and a non-singular third person A (see Dienst 2014: 75, 104, 115).

19. *mashi* 'vagina, vulva' is one of only two body part nouns (the other being *ehebeko* 'fontanelle') that can be used as free nouns in Kulina (see Dienst 2014: 65–6). When it is a free noun, it has masculine gender. However, there are also derived inalienable forms, and therefore it is treated like other body parts here.
20. Number of a noun phrase can be indicated though the non-singular clitic *=deni* (see Adams Liclan and Marlett 1990: 107–9) or through the use of a quantifier. However, this is not obligatory and is usually only found with high animates.
21. The plural prefix *ta-* derives an inflectable verb from an otherwise uninflecting stem. Therefore, the contrast between (54a) and (54b) does not reflect an inflection number contrast but a derivational one.
22. Dienst (2014: 42) discusses an example in which the verb appears to agree in *ka*-gender with a covert adjunct. However, comparison with other examples of the same type (e.g. Dienst 2014: 264, example 664) which are glossed differently demonstrates that this is most likely the homophonous causative prefix.
23. It remains unclear what would happen if the subject of *kahi* 'have' belonged to the *ka*-gender.
24. In Chomskyan frameworks, this process involves probing, and the interpretation of features, or the creation of feature bundles.

References

Adams, Patsy and Stephen A. Marlett (1987), 'Gender agreement in Madija', in Paul D. Kroeber and Robert E. Moore (eds), *Native American Languages and Grammatical Typology: Papers from a Conference at the University of Chicago*, Bloomington: Indiana University Linguistics Club, pp. 1–18.

Adams Liclan, Patsy and Stephen A. Marlett (1990), 'Madija noun morphology', *International Journal of American Linguistics*, 56 (1), pp. 102–20.

Aikhenvald, Alexandra Y. (2010), *Language Contact in Amazonia*, Oxford: Oxford University Press.

Aikhenvald, Alexandra Y. (2016), *How Gender Shapes the World*, Oxford: Oxford University Press.

Antonov, Anton (2015), 'Verbal allocutivity in a crosslinguistic perspective', *Linguistic Typology*, 19 (1), pp. 55–85.

Baerman Matthew and Greville G. Corbett (2013), 'Person by other means', in Dik Bakker and Martin Haspelmath (eds), *Languages across Boundaries: Studies in Memory of Anna Siewierska*, Berlin: De Gruyter Mouton, pp. 13–26.

Bárány, András, Oliver Bond and Irina Nikolaeva (eds) (2019), *Prominent Internal Possessors*, Oxford: Oxford University Press.

Barlow, Michael (1999), 'Agreement as a discourse phenomenon', *Folia Linguistica*, 33 (1–2), pp. 187–210.

Bond, Oliver (2017), 'Possessor controllers of agreement', presented at the Annual Meeting of the Linguistic Association of Great Britain 2017, University of Kent, Canterbury, 6 September 2017.

Bond, Oliver (in preparation), 'When Possessors Do (Not) Control Agreement', MS, University of Surrey.

Bond, Oliver and Greville G. Corbett (2017), 'Heads and dependents: A canonical approach', presented at the 11th Biennial Meeting of the Association for Linguistic Typology, ANU, Canberra, 12 December 2017.

Borsley, Robert D. (2016), 'HPSG and the nature of agreement in Archi', in Oliver Bond, Greville G. Corbett, Marina Chumakina and Dunstan Brown (eds), *Archi: Complexities of Agreement in Cross-Theoretical Perspective*, Oxford: Oxford University Press, pp. 118–49.

Bresnan, Joan (1982), 'Control and complementation', *Linguistic Inquiry*, 13 (3), pp. 343–434.

Chapman, Shirley and Desmond C. Derbyshire (1991), 'Paumari', in Desmond C. Derbyshire and Geoffrey K. Pullum (eds), *Handbook of Amazonian Languages*, vol. 3, Berlin: Mouton de Gruyter, pp. 161–352.

Chomsky, Noam (2000), 'Minimalist inquiries: The framework', in R. Martin, D. Michaels and J. Uriagereka (eds), *Step by Step: Essays on Minimalist Syntax in Honor of Howard Lasnik*, Cambridge, MA: MIT Press, pp. 89–155.

Chomsky, Noam (2001), 'Derivation by phase', in M. Kenstowicz (ed.), *Ken Hale: A Life in Language*, Cambridge, MA: MIT Press, pp. 1–52.

Chomsky, Noam and Howard Lasnik (1993), 'The theory of principles and parameters', in Joachim Jacobs, Arnim von Stechow, Wolfgang Sternefeld and Theo Vennemann (eds), *Syntax: An International Handbook of Contemporary Research*, vol. 1, Berlin: Walter de Gruyter, pp. 506–69. [Reprinted in Noam Chomsky (1995), *The Minimalist Program*, Cambridge MA: MIT Press.]

Comrie, Bernard (2003), 'When agreement gets trigger-happy', *Transactions of the Philological Society*, 101 (2), pp. 313–37.

Corbett, Greville G. (1979), 'The Agreement Hierarchy', *Journal of Linguistics*, 15 (2), pp. 203–24.

Corbett, Greville G. (1991), *Gender*, Cambridge: Cambridge University Press.

Corbett, Greville G. (2003), 'Agreement: The range of the phenomenon and the principles of the Surrey Database of Agreement', *Transactions of the Philological Society*, 101 (2), pp. 155–202.

Corbett, Greville G. (2006), *Agreement*, Cambridge: Cambridge University Press.

Corbett, Greville G. (2016), 'Heads – a canonical approach', presented at the Workshop on Prominent Internal Possessor, SOAS, University of London, 23 September 2016.

Dalrymple, Mary and Irina Nikolaeva (2011), *Objects and Information Structure*, Cambridge: Cambridge University Press.

Dienst, Stefan (2008a), 'Why Kulina doesn't have an antipassive', *Amerindia*, 32, pp. 27–36.

Dienst, Stefan (2008b), 'The internal classification of the Arawan languages', *LIAMES Línguas Indígenas das Américas*, 8, pp. 61–7.

Dienst, Stefan (2014), *A Grammar of Kulina*, Berlin: De Gruyter.

Dixon, R. M. W. (2000), 'Categories of the Noun Phrase in Jarawara', *Journal of Linguistics*, 36 (3), pp. 487–510.

Dixon, R. M. W. (2004), *The Jarawara Language of Southern Amazonia*, Oxford: Oxford University Press.

É. Kiss, Katalin (2017), 'The Person-Case Constraint and the Inverse Agreement Constraint are manifestations of the same Inverse Topicality Constraint', *The Linguistic Review*, 34 (2), pp. 365–95.

Fedden, Sebastian and Greville G. Corbett (2017), 'Gender and classifiers in concurrent systems: Refining the typology of nominal classification', *Glossa*, 2 (1), 34, pp. 1–47.

Gazdar, Gerald, Ewan H. Klein, Geoffrey K. Pullum and Ivan A. Sag (1985), *Generalized Phrase Structure Grammar*, Oxford: Blackwell.

Kibort, Anna (2010), *Grammatical Features Inventory: Definiteness*, University of Surrey, <http://dx.doi.org/10.15126/SMG.18/1.06> (last accessed 24 September 2018).

Koopman, Hilda (2003), 'The locality of agreement and the structure of the DP in Maasai', in William E. Griffin (ed.), *The Role of Agreement in Natural Language: Proceedings of the Fifth Annual Texas Linguistics Society Conference*, Austin, TX: Texas Linguistic Forum, pp. 207–27.

Koopman, Hilda and Dominique Sportiche (1991), 'The position of subjects', *Lingua*, 85 (2–3), pp. 211–58.
Lieber, Rochelle (1980), *On the Organization of the Lexicon*, PhD dissertation, University of New Hampshire.
Lowe, John J. (2016), 'English possessive 's: Clitic and affix', *Natural Language and Linguistic Theory*, 34 (1), pp. 157–95.
Mahajan, A. K. (1990), *The A/A-bar Distinction and Movement Theory*, PhD dissertation, MIT.
Matić, Dejan and Daniel Wedgwood (2013) 'The meanings of focus: The significance of an interpretation-based category in cross-linguistic analysis', *Journal of Linguistics*, 49 (1), pp. 127–63.
Miyagawa, Shigeru (2010), *Why Agree? Why Move?*, Cambridge, MA: MIT Press.
Moravcsik, Edith A. (1978), 'Agreement', in Joseph H. Greenberg, Charles A. Ferguson and Edith A. Moravcsik (eds), *Universals of Human Language. Volume 4: Syntax*, Stanford, CA: Stanford University Press, pp. 331–74.
Mycock, Louise (2006), *The Typology of Constituent Questions: A Lexical Functional Grammar Analysis of 'wh'-questions*, PhD dissertation, University of Manchester.
Nichols, Johanna (1986), 'Head-marking and dependent-marking grammar', *Language*, 62 (1), pp. 56–119.
Nikolaeva, Irina (2001), 'Secondary topic as a relation in information structure', *Linguistics*, 39 (1), pp. 1–49.
Nikolaeva, Irina (2014), *A Grammar of Tundra Nenets*, Berlin: De Gruyter.
Nikolaeva, Irina, András Bárány and Oliver Bond (2019), 'Towards a typology of prominent internal possessors', in András Bárány, Oliver Bond and Irina Nikolaeva (eds), *Prominent Internal Possessors*, Oxford: Oxford University Press, pp. 1–38.
Payne, Doris L. and Immanuel Barshi (eds) (1999), *External Possession*, Amsterdam: John Benjamins.
Polinsky, Maria (1992), 'Maori *he* revisited', *Oceanic Linguistics*, 31 (2), pp. 229–50.
Polinsky, Maria (2003), 'Non-canonical agreement is canonical', *Transactions of the Philological Society*, 101 (2), pp. 279–312.
Polinksy, Maria (2016), 'Agreement in Archi from a minimalist perspective', in Oliver Bond, Greville G. Corbett, Marina Chumakina and Dunstan Brown (eds), *Archi: Complexities of Agreement in Cross-Theoretical Perspective*, Oxford: Oxford University Press, pp. 184–232.
Polinsky, Maria and Bernard Comrie (1999), 'Agreement in Tsez', in Greville G. Corbett (ed.), *Agreement*, special issue of *Folia Linguistica*, 33 (2), pp. 109–30
Polinsky, Maria and Eric Potsdam (1999), 'Cross-linguistic view of long-distance agreement', presented at the Third International Conference of the Association for Linguistic Typology, University of Amsterdam, August 1999.
Polinsky, Maria and Eric Potsdam (2001), 'Long-distance agreement and topic in Tsez', *Natural Language and Linguistic Theory*, 19 (3), pp. 583–646.
Pollard, Carl and Ivan Sag (1987), *Information-Based Syntax and Semantics*, vol. 1, Stanford, CA: CSLI Publications.
Sadler, Louisa (2016), 'Agreement in Archi: An LFG perspective', in Oliver Bond, Greville G. Corbett, Marina Chumakina and Dunstan Brown (eds), *Archi: Complexities of Agreement in Cross-Theoretical Perspective*, Oxford: Oxford University Press, pp. 150–83.
Sag, Ivan A. (2012), 'Sign-based construction grammar', in H. C. Boas and Ivan A. Sag (eds), *Sign-Based Construction Grammar*, Stanford, CA: CSLI Publications, pp. 69–202.
Siewierska, Anna (2013), 'Passive constructions', in Matthew S. Dryer and Martin Haspelmath (eds), *The World Atlas of Language Structures Online*, Leipzig: Max Planck Institute for

Evolutionary Anthropology, <http://wals.info/chapter/107> (last accessed 12 October 2018).
Tiss, Frank (2004), *Gramática da língua Madiha (Kulina)*, São Leopoldo: Oikos.
Witzlack-Makarevich, Alena (2011), *Typological Variation in Grammatical Relations*, PhD dissertation, University of Leipzig.
Witzlack-Makarevich, Alena, Taras Zakharko, Lennart Bierkandt, Fernando Zúñiga and Balthasar Bickel (2016), 'Decomposing hierarchical alignment: Co-arguments as conditions on alignment and the limits of referential hierarchies as explanations in verb agreement', *Linguistics*, 54 (3), pp. 531–61.
Wright, Pamela Sue (1995), 'Madija predicates', *Working Papers of the Summer Institute of Linguistics*, 39, pp. 93–140.

15

Focus as a Morphosyntactic and Morphosemantic Feature

Irina Nikolaeva

15.1 The Focus Feature

Grammatical features have long been known to provide a convenient tool for the expression of linguistic generalisations and have also been claimed to have a certain level of psychological reality. A useful typology of features was offered in Kibort and Corbett (2008, 2010) and Corbett (2012). One parameter of classification concerns the component of grammar in which the feature operates, i.e. phonology, morphology, syntax or semantics. For instance, a morphological feature only has a role within morphology and cannot be accessed by syntactic and/or semantic rules. A typical example is inflectional class.

We also find interface features which operate across components. Here a crucial distinction is made between morphosemantic features, on the one hand, and morphosyntactic features, on the other hand. Morphosemantic features are reflected in morphology and are semantically charged but are not relevant to syntax, while morphosyntactic features are semantically charged and relevant to both morphology and syntax. What counts as syntactic relevance, strictly speaking, depends on the particular view of syntax, but in neutral terms, for a feature to be relevant to syntax means that at least some of its values come from another syntactic entity, not the word the feature is marked on. In other words, a syntactically relevant feature is involved in the relation of agreement or government. With this definition, a typical example of a morphosemantic feature is tense: canonical tense is characterised as inherent inflection, which means that its value is not dictated by syntax. Number occurring only on nouns is morphosemantic too. The common morphosyntactic features are person, number, gender and case when involved in agreement, i.e. on attributive adjectives, but case is also assigned to nouns through government. This means that the role of the same feature may differ across languages and even across constructions within the same language (Corbett 2012: 49). It is also worth noting that morphosyntactic features are typically associated with unique morphological material, but Corbett

(2012: 239–51) shows that in some situations they can be justified even though they are not expressed by a dedicated morphological form.

Turning now to focus, although Kibort and Corbett (2008) list it as a possible candidate for a grammatical feature, its status within the typology outlined above remained unspecified. Focus is usually understood as a semantic or pragmatic property that plays a role in syntactic processes. There have been suggestions to integrate it into core syntax by postulating a relevant functional head which carries the semantic content of focusing, or as a syntactic feature assigned to a particular node in the phrase-structure representation (for an overview, see Aboh 2016; Surányi 2016). Syntactic focus is often responsible for movement. In focus-prominent languages, such as Hungarian, a focused item has to move to a designated position because a strong focus feature has to be overtly checked (Brody 1995; É. Kiss 1998, among others). Languages like German have no obligatory focus movement, but a (weak) focus feature has been postulated for such languages too (e.g. Jacobs 1993; Rosengren 1993).

The syntactic focus feature carries an instruction to phonology and semantics (Rooth 1992; Selkirk 1996; Krifka 2006, among others), and in this sense it can be viewed as a kind of interface feature, but it is generally assumed to be purely abstract and therefore irrelevant for morphology. Yet in some languages it may be overtly expressed; so the question is then whether there is evidence for a focus feature in morphology too. Consider, for instance, the so-called term focus, i.e. the focus that scopes over a non-verbal element. It may be expressed:

(i) by a morphological marker, including free-standing particles or case markers, which flag a non-verbal element as being focused, e.g. in Chickasaw (Munro and Willmond 1994), or a special form of the verb, e.g. conjoint forms in Makhuwa (van der Wal 2011); or
(ii) by interaction with other features relevant for morphology indicated either on a non-verbal element itself, e.g. interaction with noun classes in Aghem (Watters 1979, and others), or on the verb, e.g. interaction with agreement features in Khanty (Nikolaeva 1999) or with TAM in Noon (Soukka 2000).

In the former case, we are dealing with a dedicated focus form clearly realised by morphology, but typically there is no evidence that the focus feature is relevant for agreement or government, so at best we can view focus as morphosemantic. In the latter case, focus may be more appropriately characterised as a condition on the use of other morphosyntactic features, i.e. an independent factor which affects the values of other features but is not a feature itself (Corbett 2006: 116–22). For instance, in Khanty the availability of object agreement in number depends on whether the object is focused or not, but focus is not actually expressed in the agreement paradigm.

Convincing examples of double focus marking conveying the same semantic content are more difficult to find, because some instances of term focus marked both on the term and the verb have been analysed as biclausal, as, for example, in Byali (Reineke 2007). If monoclausal examples existed, it would perhaps be natural to treat them as a kind of agreement. This, in turn, will require a morphosyntactic focus feature. However, we may also ask whether we are dealing with some kind of multiple representation that does not result from the syntactic process of agreement but rather reflects the speaker's pragmatic decision to represent the same information several times independently of other instances.

The present paper aims to contribute to this discussion by analysing how the focus feature works in Tundra Nenets.[1] I will argue that this language comes as close as possible to a language in which postulating a residual morphosyntactic focus feature may be justifiable. §15.2 shows that Tundra Nenets has a morphological marker of exclusive focus and describes its basic semantics, syntactic distribution and morphological properties. The morphological behaviour of the focus marker appears to be unique for Tundra Nenets grammar. In the following two sections I show that it has a number of interesting syntactic properties too. In this paper I will only discuss the behaviour of focus in the nominal domain and take it to correspond to a DP phrase. §15.3 addresses the multiple representation of focus within this phrase, while §15.4 argues that focus is also involved in an agreement-like process which I refer to as FOCUS SPREADING. In §15.5 I will speculate on the typological status of the Tundra Nenets focus feature.

15.2 The Focus Marker

As is well known, the notion of focus is subject to multiple understandings, but in this paper I will be assuming the basic idea of the influential Alternative Semantics approach (Rooth 1992; Krifka 2007; Krifka and Musan 2012, among others). In the words of Krifka and Musan (2012: 7), '[f]ocus indicates the presence of alternatives that are relevant for the interpretation of linguistic expressions'. This general definition highlights the fact that the main function of focus consists in triggering a Common Ground update via invocation of relevant alternatives.

The focus semantic value is a set of propositions that differ from each other in that the denotatum of the focused expression is replaced by another object of the same type. These alternative propositions are evaluated as not true, so the role of focus is to exclude alternatives, either partially or fully. The so-called 'strong exclusive focus' indicates that all relevant alternatives are excluded; in contrast, 'weak exclusive focus' indicates that there is at least one excluded alternative, possibly more (cf. van der Wal 2011). Exclusive particles of the *only* type correspond to a universal quantifier which scopes over all alternatives generated by focus (König 1991; Horn 1996; Krifka 1998); they are therefore associated with strong exclusive focus. However, I will assume following the literature mentioned above that the distinction between 'strong' and 'weak' focus is a matter of degree and depends on other factors such as the size of the alternative set and its explicit mention vs implicit presupposition (see Repp 2010 for an extensive discussion). The semantically weakest type of focus is simply associated with the function of introducing new information into a discourse and is only related to the presence of alternatives in a rather indirect sense: the set of alternatives is entirely open.

Tundra Nenets has a focus marker *-r'i/-l'i*. It is fully integrated into a word's phonology and triggers the same phonological processes as regular suffixes in the language. The alternation *-r'i ~ -l'i* is phonologically conditioned by the quality of the preceding segment. The variant *-r'i* is used after a vowel, e.g. *xasawa-r'i* (man-FOC). The change *r' > l'* is parallel to *r > l* and regularly takes place after a consonant; compare the change in the second person singular possessive inflection *-r°* as in *n'um-l° < n'um-r°* (name-2SG) and in the focus marker as in *n'um-l'i < n'um-r'i* (name-FOC).

The *-r'i/-l'i* marking is not obligatory on a focused constituent. It presupposes a somewhat 'stronger' reading than the unmarked focus, so that *-r'i/-l'i* is termed 'limitative' in Salminen (1993–2012) and Nikolaeva (2014) and is often translated as 'only; nothing else than', suggesting a strong exclusive interpretation. In this paper it will be glossed as FOC, and its scope will be shown with square brackets as below: in (1a) it scopes over the subject and in (1b) over the predicate alone.

(1) a. sekunda-r'i wəyarə°
second-FOC pass.3SG
'Only [a second]F passed.'
b. ya-m p'ir'e-mpa-r'i-d°m
soup-ACC cook-DUR-FOC-1SG
'I only [cook]F the soup (I don't eat it).'

It is not true, however, that *-r'i/-l'i* must always generate a strong exclusive reading. In (2), where the focus scopes over an adverbial, the 'only' interpretation is hardly possible. Rather, the function of *-r'i-* appears to consist in some kind of emphasis, expressing counter-expectation and filling in the informational gap.

(2) n'is'a-w° m'er°-r'i-h yəŋkuma
father-1SG quick-FOC-GEN die.3SG
'My father died [quickly]F.'

Example (3) demonstrates that the focus marker is compatible with the free-standing strong exclusive focus particle *walakəda* 'only'. The meaning of *walakəda* is essentially the same as 'only' in English; thus, it excludes all other alternatives.

(3) t'on'a xaleq s'ump°-r'i walakəda ŋəworŋa
fox fish.GEN.PL back-FOC[ACC.PL] only eat.3SG
'The fox only eats [the backs of the fish]F.'

For the purpose of this paper I take these facts to mean that the actual contribution of *-r'i/-l'i* is simply to indicate exclusive focus that evokes a set of alternatives against which the focus constituent is evaluated, but its strongest reading is either generated through implicatures or requires additional expression. Obviously, the semantics of *-r'i/-l'i* needs further investigation, but nothing in the following discussion crucially depends on it. In most cases I will continue translating the focus marker as 'only' for convenience.

The focus forms are fully productive; the distribution of the focus marker is not subject to any accidental gaps. The narrow focus takes a scope over any non-verbal constituent (1a) or the verb alone to the exclusion of all other material (1b); such focus is morphologically marked on the respective constituent (subject to conditions discussed below).

Thus, the focus marker is not limited to one grammatical class but can occur on virtually all parts of speech without changing word class membership. As far as its morphological status is concerned, it is therefore not an instance of derivation, if canonical derivation is taken to be category-changing (Spencer 2013: 58–63). In some sense the focus marker is not dissimilar to evaluative morphology, which is known to have properties of both inflection and derivation (Stump 1993, and references therein). Although not without exception, canonical evaluative morphology tends to be external with respect to derivation and internal with respect to inflection in terms of morphotactics. This is what is generally observed for Tundra Nenets focus. For instance, the noun *xan'e-ləwa* 'hunting place' is derived from the verb *xan'e-* 'to hunt' by means of the suffix *-ləwa*, which forms locational nouns from verbs in a rather productive manner. Just as for non-derived nouns, the focus on such nouns must precede any inflectional morphology, i.e. case, number and possessive agreement,[2] but it follows the derivational suffix, e.g. *xan'e-ləwa-r'i-xən-ta* (hunt-N-FOC-DAT-3SG) 'only to his/her hunting place', *xan'e-ləwa-r'i-q* (hunt-N-FOC-PL) 'only the hunting places'. Adverbs and postpositions historically based on nouns exhibit the same distribution.

However, the morphotactic behaviour of the focus marker is in fact more complex, as we can see on other parts of speech. Just as on nouns, the focus on verbs precedes unambiguous inflectional categories such as agreement and tense, as well as certain moods, as shown in (4).[3]

(4)   *xæ-r'i-ŋku-waq*   leave-FOC-FUT-1PL
        ńaqm°-r'i-ś°ti-da   catch-FOC-HAB-3SG>SG.OBJ
        wad'eq-l'i-w°na-waq   tell-FOC-REP-1PL

Most verbs also have an oblique stem called 'the general finite stem' (initially by Salminen 1997). The oblique stem serves as the base of further inflection in the indicative present and past (except for the forms that express agreement with the plural object), as well as in the jussive mood. It is formed by adding either *ə* or *ŋa* to the primary stem, largely depending on phonology. For instance, the verb *meq-* 'to hold' derives the following forms from its primary stem: *meq-y°-da* (hold-PL.OBJ-3SG), *meq-mi°* (hold-PF.PTCP), *met°* < *meqt°* (hold-IMP.2SG>SG.OBJ), *meq-la°* (hold-INCH.3SG), and so on. Examples of forms derived from the oblique stem *meq-ŋa-* are *meq-ŋa-xəh-s'°* (hold-OBL-3DU-PST), *meq-ŋa-r°* (hold-OBL-2SG), *meq-ŋa-da* (hold-OBL-3SG>SG.OBJ) and *meq-ŋa-xəyu-da* (hold-OBL-DU.OBJ-3SG). The focus marker can either precede or follow *ŋa*; compare *me-l'i-ŋa-da* < *meq-r'i-ŋa-da* (hold-FOC-OBL-3SG>SG.OBJ) and *meq-ŋa-r'i-da* (hold-OBL-FOC-3SG>SG.OBJ). These forms are in free variation, although the former appears to be more frequent.

Note that intransitive verbs fall into two inflectional classes, traditionally called the 'subjective' and the 'reflexive' class. Class membership is a lexical feature of the verb, which is only made obvious in finite inflection (Nikolaeva 2014: 224–6). Only the 'subjective' intransitive verbs have the oblique stem. The reflexive verbs only have one stem, and the position of the focus marker is invariant on such verbs: it always follows the stem and precedes agreement. Thus, the position of the focus marker is sensitive to the inflectional class of the verb in the sense that variability is only observed in the subjective class.

Non-finite verb forms also demonstrate variable placement of the focus marker. In Tundra Nenets non-finites head dependent clauses and include participles (used in relative clauses), clausal nominalisations/action nominals (used primarily in complement clauses), and converbs (used primarily in adverbial clauses). All these forms are productively derived by suffixation.

The focus marker precedes the suffixes which derive converbs, e.g. *yab'erilə-r'i-b°q* (sparkle-FOC-COND.CVB) 'only if it sparkles', but must follow the suffixes of action nominals. Action nominals take agreement that cross-references the dependent subject and is formally identical to possessive agreement. The focus marker is internal to such agreement, e.g. *yeqy°tə-qma-r'i-da* (have.share-PF.AN-FOC-3SG) 'only him having his share'. The relative order of the focus marker and the participial suffixes is not fixed, e.g. *mənc°ra-na-r'i* (work-IPF.PTCP-FOC) ~ *mənc°ra-r'i-na* (work-FOC-IPF.PTCP) 'only working'. Consequently, we also find variation in the finite moods historically based on participles. For instance, the inferential, termed 'narrative' in Salminen (1997), is part of the modal paradigm. It is based on the grammaticalised perfective participles in *-wi°/-mi°/-me-/-we-* used as finite predicates, when the participial suffix was reanalysed as the inferential mood. Example (5) shows that the focus can be placed either before the inferential or after it, immediately before any agreement morphology.

(5) a. wərk°-h ŋæwa ŋæ-r'i-wi°
bear-GEN head be-FOC-INFR
'It turned out that it [was (indeed)]F a bear head.'
b. xasawa kniga-m tola-we-r'i-da
man book-ACC read-INFR-FOC-3SG>SG.OBJ
'The man only [read]F the book (he didn't write it).'

Even more interestingly, the focus marker can be infixed morpheme-internally. The Tundra Nenets locative case in *-xəna/-x°na* and the ablative in *-xəd°/-x°də* are historically complex and go back to locational cases usually reconstructed for Northern Samoyedic as *-kə̂-nå/*-kə̂-nä and *-kə̂-tə̂-* respectively (Mikola 2004: 98). According to the widely held view, the actual case markers here were *-nå/-nä and *-tə̂, whereas the element *-kə̂- is usually analysed as an old derivational affix with the locational meaning (Künnap 1971: 125), a postposition which in its turn could take case inflections (Mikola 1975) or an old lative/dative case (Mikola 2004: 101). The Tundra Nenets reflexes behave like morphologically simplex suffixes in the modern language, except that the nominal plural -q is inserted between -xə/-x° (< *-kə̂-), on the one hand, and -d°/-də (< *-tə̂) or -na (< *-nå/-nä), on the other hand. The focus in the singular precedes a local case, whereas in the plural it follows the number marker but precedes the actual complex case. This ensures that the element -xə/-x°- appears twice in the word form. In (6), infixation is shown using angle brackets.

(6) ŋəno   boat   'boat'
     ŋəno-xəna   boat-LOC   'in the boat'
     ŋəno-r'i-xəna   boat-FOC-LOC   'only in the boat'
     ŋəno-q   boat-PL   'the boats'
     ŋəno-r'i-q   boat-FOC-PL   'only the boats'
     ŋəno-xə<q>na   boat-LOC<PL>   'in the boats'
     ŋəno-xə<q><r'i>xəna   boat-LOC<PL><FOC>   'only in the boats'

There are also instances where the focus breaks a locational case even in the absence of the plural. Perfective action nominals in the ablative in -xəd°/-x°də head adverbial temporal clauses which express temporal anteriority with respect to the main clause, as shown in (7).

(7) xon'o-qma-x°də-n'i   sæwən°   wirmabərŋa-q
     sleep-PF.AN-ABL-1SG   eye.PL.1SG   hardly.open-3PL
     'After I have slept, my eyes can hardly open.'

In such forms the focus marker renders a meaning close to 'as soon as' and varies in position. It can precede the ablative -xəd°/-x°də, but it is also possible for it to 'break' the case suffix, as in (8).

(8) to-qma-r'i-x°də-n'i   ~   to-qma-xə<r'i>də-n'i
     come-PF.AN-FOC-ABL-1SG   come-PF.AN-ABL<FOC>-1SG
     'as soon as I came'

In the latter instance the position of the focus marker is the same as the position of the plural in the ablative.

Some kind of infixation is also observed on personal pronouns. They have a peculiar morphological structure and are historically based on pronominal stems augmented by what can be considered a (genitive or nominative) possessive affix in the respective person and number, i.e. mə-n'° 1SG, pidə-r° 2SG, pi-da 3SG, etc. Here -n'°, -r° and -da are regular possessive affixes for 1SG, 2SG and 3SG respectively, but they have been reanalysed as part of the pronominal stem. When these pronouns host the focus marker, it generally follows the residual possessive affix and may be followed by an additional possessive marker doubling the first one. This triggers some idiosyncratic phonological changes: mə-n'° > mə-n'°<r'i>n° (I-GEN.1SG<FOC>) 'only me', pidə-r° > pid°-r'i-r° (thou-FOC-2SG) 'only thou', pi-da > pi-d°<r'i>da (he/her-3SG<FOC>) 'only him/her'. Non-nominative cases are derived from suppletive pronominal stems. There is no doubling but the focus precedes the possessive marker; compare for the accusative *s'iq-l'i-m'i* (I.OBL-FOC-ACC.1SG) 'only me (ACC)' and *s'iq-l'i-mt°* (thou.OBL-FOC-ACC.2SG) 'only thou (ACC)'.

What this discussion appears to demonstrate is that the morphological status of the focus marker is somewhat more complicated than the status of regular suffixes, which never show variable placement in Tundra Nenets. If we apply Spencer and Luís's (2012) criteria, we can say that it exhibits some of the canonical properties of clitics. In particular, it is associated with a 'discourse function' and these do not tend to be expressed by either canonical inflection or canonical derivation. It also shows no or low selectivity towards its host.[4] However, given the word-based view of morphology which I am assuming here, the focus marker does not correspond to an independent syntactic terminal since it appears word-internally and is fully integrated into the phonology of the host word. I therefore conclude that *-r'i/-l'i* is an affix with a number of clitic-like properties.

I will take *-r'i/-l'i* to be a morphological expression of the focus feature [F]. For the present purpose its value can loosely be defined as some semantic expression that introduces a set of alternatives from which the focused element is drawn (see Rooth 1992 for standard formalisation). Admittedly, it is a non-canonical privative feature in the Jakobsonian sense, because no alternative values can be postulated and there is no active [–F]. While focus may be understood as a kind of semantic operator, no-focus is just a name for whatever is obtained without applying this operator, and the absence of focus is not associated with any special marking leaving the unfocused element underspecified. However, the realisation of [F] is sensitive to the morphological context (i.e. inflectional class) and conditions variation in form, at least with respect to morphotactics, therefore [F] appears to have some status in morphology.

15.3 Multiple Representation of Focus

This section deals with focus which scopes over the whole DP.[5] As expected, the exponent of focus is formally associated with the phrasal head, but it can also be hosted by a non-head daughter, without apparent difference in scope or meaning. The adnominal dependents that can host additional focus marking include simple adjectival modifiers and attributive participles. Participles define a clausal domain where the pronominal dependent subject triggers person/number agreement on the clause-external head noun.[6] Modification by adjectives and participles is shown in (9).

(9) a. pæw°d'a(-r'i)   pedara-r'i-x°na
 dark-FOC   forest-FOC-LOC
 'only [in the dark forest]F'

 b. [mən'°   s'erta-wi° / s'erta-we-r'i]   m'aq-l'i-m'i
 1SG   make-PF.PTCP / make-PF.PTCP-FOC   tent-FOC-1SG
 'only [the tent I made]F'

In (9) the focus marker on the modifier is optional and redundant from the semantic point of view. The demand comes from elsewhere: its presence is fully determined by the syntactic environment in which it occurs, namely the head-modifier configuration. So at the first glance it appears to qualify as an instance of attributive agreement.

Tundra Nenets does indeed exhibit optional attributive agreement on simple adjectives and participles, although it is rather infrequent and typically restricted to specific registers. Modifiers agree with the head noun in number (singular, dual or plural) and – more rarely – in grammatical case and person/number which cross-reference the possessor in possessive constructions. The rules regulating how these features interact are quite complex (see Nikolaeva 2014 for more discussion) and will not play a role here. Some combinations are illustrated below; (10c) shows that focus doubling is fully compatible with attributive agreement in person/number and case.

(10) a. serako-x°tət°   te-x°tət°
        white-PL.ABL.2SG reindeer-PL.ABL.2SG
        'from your white reindeer (PL)'
    b. wol°tampə-we-mt°   xoba-mt°
        dislike-PF.PTCP-ACC.2SG skin-ACC.2SG
        'the skin (ACC) that you disliked'
    c. serako-r'i-mta   te-r'i-mta
        white-FOC-ACC.3SG   reindeer-FOC-ACC.3SG
        'only [his/her white reindeer]F (ACC)'

Given these patterns, one may wonder whether focus doubling on the modifier should be analysed as an instance of attributive agreement on a par with agreement in case, number and possessive person/number. However, there are strong arguments against such an analysis. The patterns of agreement appear rather different from the rules that govern the occurrence of focus on the modifier.

First, as I argued in detail in Nikolaeva (2005), number, case and possessive person/number are encoded as part of the noun's CONCORD specification and therefore are (optionally) copied on the modifier via modifier–head agreement.[7] They must originate on the head noun, as indicated by the fact that these features cannot be expressed on the modifier alone when the head noun is not overtly specified for them. This can be seen from the following set of data. Possessive agreement on the head is optional when the possessor is lexical. Possessive affixes on the adjective/participle are only possible in the presence of possessive agreement on the head. When the adjective/participle bears no possessive marking, the head noun either takes the third person possessive affix or not (11a). However, when the adjective/participle is marked for person/number, the possessive affix is obligatorily present on the head (11b).

(11) a. Wəta-h   serako   ti / te-da
        Wata-GEN   white   reindeer / reindeer-3SG
        'Wata's white reindeer'
    b. Wəta-h   serako-da   te-da / *ti
        Wata-GEN   white-3SG   reindeer-3SG / reindeer
        'Wata's white reindeer'

The same is true for case and non-possessive number: these features are only available on the modifiers in the presence of overt markers of the same feature on the head, so (12) contrasts with (10a) above.

(12)   *serako-x°tət°   ti
       white-PL.ABL.2SG   reindeer
       'from your white reindeer (PL)'

This confirms that agreement in case, number and possessive person/number is an instance of true attributive agreement between the head and the modifier. In contrast, the focus marker is allowed to appear on the modifier alone in the absence of focus marking on the head, without any change of meaning; compare (9) and (13).

(13)   a. pæw°d'a-r'i   pedara-x°na
           dark-FOC   forest-LOC
           'only [in the dark forest]F'
       b. [mən'°   s'erta-we-r'i]   m'aq-m'i
           1SG   make-PF.PTCP-FOC   tent-1SG
           'only [the tent I made]F'

This is impossible as far as attributive agreement is concerned.

Second, attributive agreement is restricted to the dependents that participate in the modifier–head relation (adjectives and participles) and never occurs on non-modifiers. However, the 'doubling' focus marker is available on non-modifier sub-constituents, i.e. possessors. In this instance, too, the focus may be marked on the head alone, the possessor alone, or both the head and the possessor, without any effect on its semantic scope.

(14)   mən'° m'aq-l'i-m'i   1SG tent-FOC-1SG
       mən'°<r'i>n° m'aq-m'i   1SG<FOC> tent-1SG
       mən'°<r'i>-n° m'aq-l'i-m'i   1SG<FOC> tent-FOC-1SG
       'only [my tent]F'

The possessor never exhibits agreement with the head in number and/or case; a lexical possessor always stands in the genitive and a pronominal possessor is nominative. Therefore, the behaviour of CONCORD features contrasts with the behaviour of focus.

Third and perhaps most importantly, double representation of focus occurs in syntactic phrases other than DPs. In PPs the object of the postposition stands in the genitive case and can host the focus marker in the absence of focus marking on the postposition itself. Alternatively, the focus can be located on the postposition only or on both the genitive object and the postposition.

(15)   yes'a-r'i-h jeqm°n'a   money-FOC-GEN for
       yes'a-h yeq<l'i>w°na   money-GEN for<FOC>
       yes'a-r'i-h yeq<l'i>w°na   money-FOC-GEN for<FOC>
       'only [for money]F'

In (16) I show a construction with the content verb in the form of a non-changeable same-subject converb and an auxiliary-like verb; the latter has the properties of the syntactic head in terms of its position and inflectional behaviour. Such constructions are monoclausal and differ from regular complement clauses in that they are transparent for the purpose of object agreement (Nikolaeva 2014: 348–51). They also allow variation in the position of focus: if the scope of focus is the whole phrase, the exponence of focus may be hosted by the auxiliary verb, the non-head subconstituent or both.

(16) a. [ya-m   p′ir′empa-r′i-°]   p′irŋa-w°
         soup-ACC   cook-FOC-SS   can-1SG>SG.OBJ
    b. [ya-m   p′ir′empa-°]   p′ir-l′i-ŋa-w°
         soup-ACC   cook-SS   can-FOC-OBL-1SG>SG.OBJ
    c. [ya-m   p′ir′empa-r′i-°]   p′ir-l′i-ŋa-w°
         soup-ACC   cook-FOC-SS   can-FOC-OBL-1SG>SG.OBJ
         'I only [can cook soup]F (and don't do anything else).'

No other types of syntactic phrase smaller than clause can reliably be identified for Tundra Nenets, since the existence of VP is questionable (see Nikolaeva 2014 for some discussion). The variation in focus marking may then be taken as one of the tests for syntactic constituency.

The same pattern is observed in some biclausal structures, namely non-finite adverbial clauses headed by action nominals in the genitive case. They are introduced by postpositions which specify the type of semantic relation between the dependent and main clause; for example, the postposition *s′er°h* indicates a general temporal relation. The three alternative options for the position of the focus marker which takes scope over the whole adverbial clause are illustrated in (17).

(17) a. mən′°   to-wa-r′i-n′i   s′er°h
         1SG   come-IPF.AN-FOC-GEN.1SG   when
    b. mən′°   to-wa-n′i   s′er°r′i
         1SG   come-IPF.AN-GEN.1SG   when.FOC
    c. mən′°   to-wa-r′i-n′i   s′er°r′i
         1SG   come-IPF.AN-FOC-GEN.1SG   when.FOC
         'only [when I come]F'

The adverbial and complement clauses not based on postpositional constructions do not exhibit multiple marking of focus. It remains to be seen what synchronic properties of syntactic structure make it available in (17), but (17) is clearly parallel to (15) and perhaps it goes back historically to non-clausal postpositional constructions. The general point is this: the exclusive focus marker is located relatively freely within DPs, PPs, auxiliary verbal complexes and some dependent clauses, being able to attach to either the phrasal head or its immediate phrasal subconstituent. It can also be expressed more than once without producing any meaning-related effects.

To conclude this section, I have argued that multiple representation of focus does not fall under attributive (or indeed any other kind of) agreement, and is therefore better analysed as a piece of information that can be expressed simultaneously in more than one place in the appropriate syntactic domain due to structure-sharing and an independent requirement that it should be allowed to appear on all immediate sub-phrasal elements over which it has semantic scope (but not on more deeply embedded elements). Such repetition of information is known from other languages, and Corbett (2006: 29) suggests that it would be appropriate to term it 'concord'. Korean honorification is perhaps the best-studied example. Kim and Sells (2007) argued that multiple expression of honorific marking within the same clause has an incremental cumulative effect and progressively elevates the social status of the relevant referent. The multiple phrase-internal expression of focus in Tundra Nenets does not signify independent degrees of focusness as focus only gets interpreted once, but it appears to contribute some expressive information, being primarily restricted to the expressive language of folklore.

15.4 Focus Spreading

In this section I discuss the focus that only takes scope over a non-head daughter of a DP, in particular an attributive modifier or possessor. The interpretation goes as follows: 'only in a [dark]F forest (as opposed to a light forest)' or 'only [my]F tent (as opposed to yours)'. Unsurprisingly, the focus marker is hosted by the element within its scope, as in (18).

(18) a. pæw°d'a-r'i   pedara-x°na
       dark-FOC   forest-LOC
       'only in a [dark]F forest'
   b. mən'°<r'i>n°   m'aq-m'i
       1SG<FOC>   tent-1SG
       'only [my]F tent'

Crucially, focus must be a featural property of the head of the relevant phrase, even though it needs no morphological expression and semantically the head is excluded from its scope. The syntactic evidence for this claim comes from the distribution of object agreement.

As described in more detail in Dalrymple and Nikolaeva (2011) and Nikolaeva (2014), object agreement in Tundra Nenets is largely determined by information structure. Agreement is in number only; the marker of dual objects on the verb is -xəyu-/-x°yu-, and the marker of plural objects is -yə-/-iə-. The marker for singular objects is always phonologically null, so in this case the verb takes a cumulative agreement affix referring both to the person/number of the subject and to the singular object. Object agreement is optional in the sense that only a subset of objects agree. Agreeing and non-agreeing objects do not differ in their positional and/or behavioural properties, but are associated with different semantic properties and information-structure roles. The basic distribution is as follows. Only third person objects agree;

first and second person objects never trigger agreement. Third person objects must agree if they are either topical (typically, secondary topics as defined in Dalrymple and Nikolaeva 2011), or part of the wide focus domain and specific. A third person object in the scope of narrow focus never triggers agreement, regardless of specificity. Consider (19).

(19)   ti-m   xada° / xadaə-da
       reindeer-ACC   kill.3SG / kill-3SG>SG.OBJ
       'He killed a/the reindeer.'

In (19) the object-agreeing form of the verb *xadaəda* would be appropriate either in the answer to the question 'What did John do with the reindeer?', which establishes the secondary topic role for 'reindeer', or in the answer to 'What did John do?' when the object 'reindeer' is part of the focus domain and the speaker means a specific reindeer.[8] In contrast, the non-agreeing form *xada°* must be used in the answer to the question 'What did John kill?', which establishes a narrow focus role for the object, or in the answer to 'What did John do?' if the object is understood as non-specific.

So there is no actual agreement in focus/topic/specificity; instead these are agreement conditions in the sense of Corbett (2006). The important point for the present discussion is that agreement on the verb with the focused object is strictly ungrammatical; compare (19) and (20).

(20)   a. ti-m   xada° / *xadaə-da
          reindeer-ACC   kill.3SG / kill-3SG>SG.OBJ
          'He killed [a/the reindeer]F.'
       b. te-r'i-m   xada° / *xadaə-da
          reindeer-FOC-ACC   kill.3SG / kill-3SG>SG.OBJ
          'He only killed [a/the reindeer]F.'

The focused object in (20) cannot trigger agreement, whether it is associated with exclusive focus morphologically marked by *-r'i-* or is operationally defined as information focus and a target of a wh-question. Both types of focus show identical behaviour in the relevant respect.

Agreement is equally impossible when narrow focus is semantically associated with a subconstituent of the object DP instead of the object phrase as a whole. This is shown below for the possessor (21) and an adjectival modifier (22), either marked by *-r'i-* or not, but the same holds true for the nominal complements of the head noun.

(21)   *Whose reindeer did he kill?*
       a. [Wera-h   ti-m]   xada° / *xadaə-da
          Wera-GEN   reindeer-ACC   kill.3SG / kill-3SG>SG.OBJ
          'He killed [Wera's]F reindeer.'
       b. [Wera-r'i-h   ti-m]   xada° / *xadaə-da
          Wera-FOC-GEN   reindeer-ACC   kill.3SG / kill-3SG>SG.OBJ
          'He only killed [Wera's]F reindeer.'

(22) *What kind of reindeer did he kill?*
    a. [serako   ti-m]   xada° / *xadaə-da
       white   reindeer-ACC kill.3SG / kill-3SG>SG.OBJ
       'He killed a [white]F reindeer.'
    b. [serako-r'i   ti-m]   xada° / *xadaə-da
       white-FOC   reindeer-ACC kill.3SG / kill-3SG>SG.OBJ
       'He only killed a [white]F reindeer.'

In all these cases both the head of the DP and its dependent have to be specified as focus. That the dependent bears the focus feature is primarily evident from its semantics: it is in fact the only element that falls within the scope of narrow focus here. This may be additionally indicated by the overt focus marker -*r'i/-l'i*. That the head must be specified as [F] in syntax follows from the pattern of object agreement: the verbal form has access to information provided by the head of the object phrase. Morphosyntactic facts therefore make it clear that both the subconstituent and the head carry the same value for the focus feature [F], despite the head being semantically unfocused.

In the examples above the head noun does not carry focus marking, but the marking may actually be overt. An alternative way of expressing the same meaning is seen when one compares (18) above with (23). In (23) the morphological focus -*r'i-/-l'i-* is hosted by the head noun itself in the absence of focus marking on the semantically focused dependent element. These two options have fully identical readings.

(23) a. pæw°d'a   peda-r'i-x°na
           dark   forest-FOC-LOC
           'only in a [dark]F forest'
      b. mən'°   m'aq-l'i-m'i
           1SG   tent-FOC-1SG
           'only [my]F tent'

Example (23) demonstrates a mismatch between the morphological location of focus and its semantic scope. We can see that focus is not necessarily interpreted on each element where it appears and it is not necessarily marked on every element over which it scopes. This creates a certain level of ambiguity. When the focus is expressed once, either on the dependent or the head, it can take scope over either this dependent or the whole phrase.

(24) a. pæw°d'a-r'i   pedara-x°na
           dark-FOC   forest-LOC
      b. pæw°d'a   peda-r'i-x°na
           dark   forest-FOC-LOC
          (i) 'only [in a dark forest]F (not in the tundra)'
          (ii) 'only in a [dark]F forest (not in a light forest)'

However, when focus is overtly expressed both on the head and on its dependent, only one interpretation appears possible: the focus takes scope over the whole phrase, as demonstrated by a number of examples in §15.3.

In Matić and Nikolaeva (2014) we also showed that relative clauses behave identically to simple DPs with respect to focus-sensitive object agreement. If a subconstituent of a relative clause is focused and the relative clause modifies the object of the main verb, this verb cannot be marked for object agreement. There are no apparent syntactic restrictions on the type of the element which is immediately embedded within a relative clause and exhibits this kind of behaviour. Since the maximal projection also carries the focus feature as evidenced by the lack of agreement, we proposed that some kind of mechanism that passes the [F] feature to the head from where it can enter the syntactic relationship with the verb must be in place here.

Such mechanisms have been explored elsewhere, in particular for languages with the transmission of one element's focus to another known as 'focus pied-piping'. Examples include Hausa (Hartmann and Zimmermann 2007) and Hungarian (Horváth 2007), where only part of the syntactically moved material is pragmatically understood as focused (cf. Krifka 2006; Wagner 2006), as well as languages with covert focus movement that show violations of island effects (Ortiz de Urbina 1993; Nishigauchi 1990, 1999, among others).

Focus pied-piping is usually understood as resulting from the percolation of the abstract focus feature to a higher phrasal node.[9] The peculiarity of Tundra Nenets is that, unlike in most languages for which focus percolation has been postulated, exclusive focus is not abstract: it is associated with a dedicated morphological marker. The marker is associated with a semantically focused element, but the focus feature is passed to the phrasal head. It may receive overt expression on the head alone. These facts appear to indicate that both the head and its dependent are specified as [F], but [F] may not be phonologically realised more than once in the phrase, if the focus falls on the dependent.

This situation is not dissimilar to the phenomenon known as 'definiteness spreading', i.e. the multiple representation of definiteness. In Hebrew Construct State the head noun never carries the definite article, but at least for a certain class of Construct States the definiteness value of the entire phrase is determined by the definiteness of the embedded genitive. A number of analyses of definiteness spreading have been proposed in the literature; for an overview, see Danon (2008). Without going into details, most of them accept the idea that definiteness spreading is an instance of agreement; compare 'the definiteness agreement equation' in Welsh (Sadler 2000) or phrase-internal feature-sharing (Danon 2001, 2008).

If Tundra Nenets is to be analysed along the same lines, we can think of focus spreading from the element where it is interpreted to the higher node as some kind of agreement. The focused subconstituent acts as agreement controller and the head is the target. Although the expression of focus is optional on either constituent, focus spreading shows a number of canonical agreement properties as defined by Corbett (2006): it is realised in a local domain and has affixal marking; it is semantically redundant since the feature is realised twice but interpreted once;[10] it is syntactically simple and asymmetric; the controller must be present and its part of speech is irrelevant (given the domain); the target always agrees and has no choice of controller; there is no choice of feature value and no conditions. The question that is central for the present paper is what this means for the typological status of the focus feature.

15.5 The Status of the Focus Feature in Tundra Nenets

This paper has touched upon two issues that prove relevant for the typology of feature systems: the inventory of morphosyntactic features available in human language, and the relation between the features which operate in syntax, morphology and semantics.

Given how often we find focus effects in the languages of the world, there is rather limited evidence for a non-abstract focus feature, and if it is found, it is hardly ever morphosyntactic. Most commonly, focus is just a piece of semantic information imposed over the non-verbal phrase that can be marked either on this phrase itself or on the associated verb. I have shown that Tundra Nenets has a dedicated marker of (exclusive) focus which is fully morphologically and phonologically integrated into the inflected word form. Crucially, unlike in a number of other languages, focus-related information gets transmitted between distinct elements within a DP. Its behaviour within the DP domain was accounted for by two different mechanisms.

First, if focus semantically originates on the whole phrase or on its head alone, it is passed down from the head to the immediate subconstituents of the phrase and can have single or multiple representation. I have argued that multiple representation does not involve agreement. Focus is not assigned by government either, therefore for Tundra Nenets it should perhaps be qualified as an inherent morphosemantic feature whose value is determined semantically.

However, the situation is different when focus semantically originates on a non-head daughter of the phrase. In this instance it must be overtly realised once, either on the focused subconstituent itself or on the head of the phrase. I have proposed that this relationship can best be described in terms of an operation with the focus feature [F]. Independently of the location of the morphological focus marker, the head must be specified as [F] as is evident from its behaviour within the larger syntactic domain. I have referred to the mechanism that ensures that the head of the phrase and its subconstituent must share the same focus specification as 'focus spreading', by analogy to 'definiteness spreading'. Focus spreading has some properties of agreement, albeit not fully canonical, which makes [F] relevant for syntax and, consequently, a good candidate for a marginal morphosyntactic feature. This implies that the Tundra Nenets -r'i/-l'i should be viewed as a morphological exponent of two non-equivalent and not necessarily overlapping features: the morphosemantic focus and morphosyntactic focus. The former operates at the interface of morphology and semantics, and the latter is relevant for morphology, syntax and semantics, similar to the feature of definiteness in a number of languages.

In sum, the morphological expression of focus, semantic focusness and the syntactic role of focus do not always correlate. There is a fair amount of mismatch between the three components, but there is also (admittedly, rather limited) evidence for the focus feature in the morphological interfaces.

Notes

1. Tundra Nenets is a Uralic language spoken in the Arctic part of European Russia and north-western Siberia by about 20,000 people. Fieldwork on Tundra Nenets was conducted in 2003–16 and supported by an ELDP grant awarded to Tapani Salminen in 2003, a grant from the Academy of Finland awarded to Larisa Leisiö in 2009 (project number 125225), and an AHRC grant awarded to Irina Nikolaeva in 2015 (Ref. AN/M010708/1). The transcription is based on Nikolaeva (2014), where more information on Tundra Nenets grammar can be found. The sign ′ indicates palatalisation, while ° stands for an extra-short reduced vowel. The nominative case and singular number on nouns, as well as the present tense on verbs are formally unmarked and therefore I do not indicate them in glosses.
2. These often cumulate and therefore are not always separated in glosses.
3. Some (intransitive) verbs do not appear to have focus forms; instead a periphrastic strategy is employed in which the lexical verb takes the form of the accusative action nominal, hosts the focus marker and is followed by the finite auxiliary *meq-* 'to hold' or *pæ̃ər-* 'to do'. This strategy needs more investigation, but it shows similarity to other languages where a formal separation of the lexical content of the predicate from its morphosyntactic content is required for the purpose of focusing, as, for example, the English *do*-support structures (Birner and Ward 1998).
4. The property of 'promiscuous attachment' is shared by a number of other discourse markers in Tundra Nenets. These were referred to as 'multi-based affixes' in Nikolaeva (2014), but could perhaps be more appropriately characterised as mesoclitics. However, none of them shows variable placement nor can break up a morpheme like the focus marker.
5. Exactly the same patterns are observed in the (rare) situation when focus scopes over the head noun alone to the exclusion of dependent elements; I will not show these examples here for lack of space.
6. See Ackerman and Nikolaeva (2013) for a detailed discussion of this relative clause pattern.
7. In Nikolaeva (2005) I followed the basic insights of Wechsler and Zlatić (2003): CONCORD was understood as a sharing of morphosyntactic features between certain designated elements.
8. My assumption here is that information structure roles can be unambiguously established through question–answer pairs. This is fairly standard but a gross oversimplification; see, for example, Matić and Wedgwood (2013) in relation to problems with this approach.
9. For an alternative approach see Cable (2010) and Heck (2008, 2009), who argue that feature percolation has no place in syntactic theory.
10. At least in some relative clauses focus percolation has an additional semantic effect: it results in the formation of a pairwise list in which the head denotes a set of entities defined in terms of the properties specified in the focus phrase, so both the head of the phrase and its subconstituent are focused (Matić and Nikolaeva 2014). An agreement analysis would be less appropriate for such structures because focus percolation is semantically informative.

References

Aboh, Enoch O. (2016), 'Information structure: A cartographic perspective', in Caroline Féry and Shinichiro Ishahara (eds), *The Oxford Handbook of Information Structure*, Oxford: Oxford University Press, pp. 147–64.

Ackerman, Farrell and Irina Nikolaeva (2013), *Descriptive Typology and Linguistics Theory: A Study in the Morphosyntax of Relative Clauses*, Stanford, CA: CSLI Publications and Chicago University Press.

Birner, Betty and Gregory Ward (1998), *Information Status and Noncanonical Word Order in English*, Amsterdam: John Benjamins.

Brody, Michael (1995), 'Focus and checking theory', in István Kenesei (ed.), *Levels and Structures: Approaches to Hungarian, 5*, Szeged: JATE, pp. 31–43.

Cable, Seth (2010), *The Grammar of Q: Q-Particles, Wh-Movement, and Pied-Piping*, Oxford: Oxford University Press.

Corbett, Greville G. (2006), *Agreement*, Cambridge: Cambridge University Press.

Corbett, Greville G. (2012), *Features*, Cambridge: Cambridge University Press.

Dalrymple, Mary and Irina Nikolaeva (2011), *Objects and Information Structure*, Cambridge: Cambridge University Press.

Danon, Gabi (2001), 'Syntactic definiteness in the grammar of Modern Hebrew', *Linguistics*, 39, pp. 1071–116.

Danon, Gabi (2008), 'Definiteness spreading in the Hebrew construct state', *Lingua*, 118, pp. 872–906.

É. Kiss, Katalin (1998), 'Identificational focus versus information focus', *Language*, 74, pp. 245–73.

Hartmann, Katharina and Malte Zimmermann (2007), 'In place – out of place. Focus in Hausa', in Kerstin Schwabe and Susanne Winkler (eds), *On Information Structure, Meaning and Form*, Amsterdam: John Benjamins, pp. 365–403.

Heck, Fabian (2008), *On Pied-Piping: Wh-Movement and Beyond*, Berlin: Mouton de Gruyter.

Heck, Fabian (2009), 'On certain properties of pied-piping', *Linguistic Inquiry*, 40, pp. 75–111.

Horn, Larry (1996), 'Exclusive company: *Only* and the dynamics of vertical inference', *Journal of Semantics*, 13, pp. 11–40.

Horváth, Judith (2007), 'Separating "focus movement" from focus', in Simin Karimi, Vida Samiian and Wendy Wilkins (eds), *Phrasal and Clausal Architecture*, Amsterdam: John Benjamins, pp. 145–66.

Jacobs, Joachim (1993), 'Integration', in Marga Reis (ed.), *Wortstellung und Informationsstruktur*, Linguistische Arbeiten, 306, Tübingen: Niemeyer, pp. 63–116.

Kibort, Anna and Greville G. Corbett (2008), *Grammatical Features Inventory*, University of Surrey, <http://dx.doi.org/10.15126/SMG.18/1> (last accessed 24 September 2018).

Kibort, Anna and Greville G. Corbett (eds) (2010), *Features: Perspectives on a Key Notion in Linguistics*, Oxford: Oxford University Press.

Kim, Jong-Bok and Peter Sells (2007), 'Korean honorification: A kind of expressive meaning', *Journal of East Asian Linguistics*, 16, pp. 303–36.

König, Ekkehardt (1991), *The Meaning of Focus Particles*, London: Routledge.

Krifka, Manfred (1998), 'Additive particles under stress', in *Proceedings from SALT VIII*, Ithaca, NY: CLC, pp. 111–28.

Krifka, Manfred (2006), 'Association with focus phrases', in Valéria Molnár and Susanne Winkler (eds), *The Architecture of Focus*, Berlin and New York: Mouton de Gruyter, pp. 105–36.

Krifka, Manfred (2007), 'Basic notions of information structure', in Caroline Féry and

Manfred Krifka (eds), *Interdisciplinary Studies on Information Structure 6*, Potsdam: Potsdam University, pp. 13–55.

Krifka, Manfred and Renate Musan (2012), 'Information structure: Overview and linguistic issues', in Manfred Krifka and Renate Musan (eds), *The Expression of Information Structure*, Berlin: Mouton de Gruyter, pp. 1–47.

Künnap, Ago (1971), *System und Ursprung der kamassischen Flexionssuffixe*. Vol. 1. *Numeruszeichen und Nominalflexion*, Suomalais-Ugrilaisen Seuran toimituksia, 147, Helsinki: Suomalais-Ugrilainen Seura.

Matić, Dejan and Irina Nikolaeva (2014), 'Focus feature percolation: Evidence from Tundra Nenets and Tundra Yukaghir', in Stefan Müller (ed.), *Proceedings of the 21st International Conference on Head-Driven Phrase Structure Grammar (HPSG 2014)*, Stanford, CA: CSLI Publications, pp. 299–317.

Matić, Dejan and Daniel Wedgwood (2013), 'The meanings of focus: The significance of an interpretation-based category in cross-linguistic analysis', *Journal of Linguistics*, 49 (1), pp. 127–63.

Mikola, Tibor (1975), *Die Alten Postpositionen des Nenzischen (Juraksamojedischen)*, Budapest: Akadémiai kiadó.

Mikola, Tibor (2004), *Studien zur Geschichte der samojedischen Sprachen*, Szeged: SzTE Finnisch-Ugrisches Institut.

Munro, Pamela and Catherine Willmond (1994), *Chickasaw: An Analytical Dictionary*, Norman and London: University of Oklahoma Press.

Nikolaeva, Irina (1999), 'Object agreement, grammatical relations, and information structure', *Studies in Language*, 23, pp. 331–76.

Nikolaeva, Irina (2005), 'Modifier–head person concord', in G. E. Booij, Guevara A. Ralli, S. Sgroi and Sergio Scalise (eds), *Morphology and Linguistic Typology. Proceedings of the Fourth Mediterranean Morphology Meeting (MMM4) Catania, 21–23 September 2003*, Bologna: Università degli Studi di Bologna, pp. 221–34.

Nikolaeva, Irina (2014), *A Grammar of Tundra Nenets*, Berlin: De Gruyter.

Nishigauchi, Taisuke (1990), *Quantification in the Theory of Grammar*, Dordrecht: Kluwer.

Nishigauchi, Taisuke (1999), 'Quantification and wh-constructions', in Natsuko Tsujimura (ed.), *The Handbook of Japanese Linguistics*, Malden, MA and Oxford: Blackwell, pp. 269–96.

Ortiz de Urbina, Juan (1993), 'Feature percolation and clausal pied-piping', in José Ignacio Hualde and Juan Ortiz de Urbina (eds), *Generative Studies in Basque Linguistics*, 105, Amsterdam: John Benjamins, pp. 189–219.

Reineke, Brigitte (2007), 'Identificational operation as a focus strategy in Byali', in Enoch Oladé Aboh, Katharina Hartmann and Malte Zimmermann (eds), *Focus Strategies in Niger-Congo and Afro-Asiatic: On the Interaction of Focus and Grammar in Some African Languages*, Berlin: De Gruyter, pp. 223–40.

Repp, Sophie (2010), 'Defining "contrast" as an information-structural notion in grammar', Editorial, *Lingua*, 120, pp. 1333–45.

Rooth, Math (1992), 'A theory of focus interpretation', *Natural Language Semantics*, 1, pp. 75–116.

Rosengren, Inge (1993), 'Wahlfreiheit mit Konsequenzen – Scrambling, Topikalisierung und FHG im Dienste der Informationsstrukturierung', in Marga Reis (ed.), *Wortstellung und Informationsstruktur*, Linguistische Arbeiten, 306, Tübingen: Niemeyer, pp. 251–312.

Sadler, Louisa (2000), 'Noun phrase structure in Welsh', in Miriam Butt and Tracy Holloway King (eds), *Argument Realization*, Stanford, CA: CSLI Publications, pp. 73–110.

Salminen, Tapani (1993–2012), 'Tundra Nenets', <http://www.helsinki.fi/~tasalmin/sketch.html> (last accessed 25 September 2018).

Salminen, Tapani (1997), *Tundra Nenets Inflection*, Mémoires de la Société Finno-Ougrienne, 227, Helsinki: Finno-Ugric Society.

Selkirk, Elizabeth (1996), 'Sentence prosody: Intonation, stress and phrasing', in John A. Goldsmith (ed.), *The Handbook of Phonological Theory*, Cambridge, MA and Oxford: Blackwell, pp. 550–69.

Soukka, Maria (2000), *A Descriptive Grammar of Noon*, Munich: LINCOM Europa.

Spencer, Andrew (2013), *Lexical Relatedness: A Paradigm-Based Model*, Oxford: Oxford University Press.

Spencer, Andrew and Ana Luís (2012), *Clitics*, Cambridge: Cambridge University Press.

Stump, Gregory (1993), 'How peculiar is evaluative morphology?', *Journal of Linguistics*, 29, pp. 1–36.

Surányi, Balázs (2016), 'Discourse-configurationality', in Caroline Féry and Shinichiro Ishahara (eds), *The Oxford Handbook of Information Structure*, Oxford: Oxford University Press, pp. 422–40.

van der Wal, Jennike (2011), 'Focus excluding alternatives: Conjoint/disjoint marking in Makhuwa', *Lingua*, 121, pp. 1734–50.

Wagner, Michael (2006), 'Association by movement: Evidence from DPI-licensing', *Natural Language Semantics*, 14, pp. 297–324.

Watters, John R. (1979), 'Focus in Aghem: A study of its formal correlates and typology', in Larry M. Hyman (ed.), *Aghem Grammatical Structure*, Southern California Occasional Papers in Linguistics, 7, Los Angeles: University of Southern California, pp. 137–97.

Wechsler, Stephen and Larisa Zlatić (2003), *The Many Faces of Agreement*, Stanford, CA: CSLI Publications.

16

When Agreement and Binding Go Their Separate Ways: Generic Second Person Pronoun in Russian

Maria Polinsky

16.1 Introduction

The German *Mädchen* 'girl', a neuter noun denoting a female referent, is a commonplace example of a linguistic item whose formal and semantic features are at odds with each other. Another example is the French *sentinelle* 'watchman', a feminine noun denoting a (traditionally) male referent. Such gender dissociations are common and well known (Corbett 1991: 225–60), and they shed light on possible mismatches between syntax and morphology, an area that has received quite a bit of coverage in linguistic research. But the dissociation between formal and semantic features is not limited to gender, nor is it limited to the syntax–morphology interface. This paper probes into an underexplored type of feature dissociation, this time between person agreement on the one hand and binding properties as well as agreement features other than person on the other. The case in point is the Russian second person singular (2SG) pronoun used as an arbitrary pronoun. When it occurs in the nominative-subject position (i.e. the only constituent that triggers verbal agreement in Russian), this pronoun determines regular verb agreement in second person singular, but its other properties are different from those of a regular 2SG pronoun. The resulting mismatch informs our understanding of the ways syntax and semantics interface, in particular with respect to binding.

To make the data below slightly more user-friendly, let me start with the basics of Russian agreement. Russian verbs agree with their nominative subjects in number and person in the non-past tenses and in number and gender, with no person distinctions, in the past tense. A partial paradigm for the verb *igrat'* 'to play (imperfective)' is shown in Table 16.1 and Table 16.2.

Russian is not a pro-drop language; its limited inventory of null pronouns includes the 3SG expletive, which appears in weather expressions and some other typical expletive contexts, as in (1), and a 3PL null pronominal with the generalised meaning 'people', shown in the impersonal constructions in (3) (see Mel'čuk 1974; McShane 2005). In both cases, the null pronominal cannot alternate with an overt one.

Table 16.1 Russian agreement: non-past tense, stem *igraj-*

	SG	PL
1	igraj-u	igraj-em
2	igraj-eš'	igraj-ete
3	igraj-et	igraj-ut

Table 16.2 Russian agreement: past tense, stem *igra-*, tense suffix: *-l-*

	SG	PL
M	igra-l-∅	igra-l-i
F	igra-l-a	
N	igra-l-o	

(1) a. *expl/*ono stanovitsja xolodno.*
       it   become.3SG.PRS.REFL cold.NEUTER
   'It is getting cold.'
   b. *expl/*ono bylo pora exat'.*
       it   be.PST.NEUTER time go.INF
   'It was time to go.'

(2) a. *pro/*oni cypljat po oseni sčitajut.*
       they   chickens.ACC on autumn count.3PL.PRS
   'Don't count your chickens before they hatch.' (lit. 'They count chickens ...')
   b. *pro/*oni s det'mi tak ne razgovarivajut.*
       they   with children so not speak.3PL.PRS
   'One doesn't speak to children like that.'

In addition to the two types of non-alternating null pronominals, a null second person subject is optional in the imperative; null subjects in all three persons are also optionally available in certain types of embedded clauses, the majority of them subjunctive (Avrtuin and Babyonyshev 1997; Livitz 2014). Finally, the overt and null variants of the 2SG pronoun (*ty/pro*) alternate in the subject position; this pronoun, which I will be referring to as 'arbitrary 2SG', is the focus of this paper.

The structure of the paper is as follows. In §16.2, I introduce clauses with arbitrary 2SG and show how this type of pronoun differs from the impersonal 3PL and the addressee 2SG. Differences between the two types of 2SG pronouns will be discussed in §16.3, which concludes with a summary of the puzzle that needs to be accounted for, namely the disconnect between the second person singular agreement with the arbitrary 2SG and all other properties of that pronoun, including binding. §16.3 presents arguments in support of a generic interpretation of clauses with the arbitrary 2SG. Based on the generic properties of these clauses, I propose an account of the structural properties of arbitrary 2SG subjects in §16.4.

16.2 Structural Properties of Sentences with Arbitrary 2SG

16.2.1 The Pattern

The most common function of the second person pronoun is to indicate the addressee of the clause in question. The addressee pronoun in Russian can be null in imperatives (3), in some embedded clauses, such as the finite complement clauses shown in (3), and in root questions in the spoken language, where its distribution is reminiscent of the English subject drop observed with topic subjects (Haegeman 1990; Haegeman and Ihsane 1999), as in (3).[1]

(3) a. pro$_{addr}$ sygraj! Ty že obeščal [čto (ty)
         play.PFV.2SG.IMP 2SG.NOM EMPH promised.M that 2SG.NOM
     sygraješ'].
     play.2SG.FUT
     'Please play! You did promise that you were going to play.'
  b. pro$_{addr}$ xočeš' est'?
         want.2SG.PRS eat.IPFV.INF
     'Are you hungry?' (lit. 'Do you want to eat?')

In these contexts, a null second person pronoun is equally possible for the singular *ty* and for the plural *vy*. The latter can be used either for a plurality of addressees or as a polite form for a single person; compare (3) and the example in (4) used as a polite address.

(4) a. pro$_{addr}$ sygrajte! Vy že obeščali [čto (vy)
         play.PFV.2PL.IMP 2PL.NOM EMPH promised.PL that 2PL.NOM
     sygrajete].
     play.2SG.FUT
     'Please play! You did promise that you were going to play.'

The other use of the second person pronoun – the one that is at stake here – is to indicate an arbitrary referent, with a meaning close to English *you* and *one*, German *man*, or French *on*. Used with this arbitrary reading, the 2SG pronoun does not alternate with the 2PL pronoun. Moreover, the arbitrary 2SG pronoun can be easily omitted – much more easily than the addressee pronoun.

Arbitrary 2SG is common in proverbs and sayings, as shown in examples (5)–(7) (I will return to the common use of arbitrary 2SG in proverbs in the discussion of negation in §16.3.1 below).

(5) pro$_{arb}$ pospešiš', pro$_{arb}$ ljudej nasmešiš'. [2SG-ARB]
         hurry.2SG.FUT   people.ACC make.laugh.2SG.FUT
     'Haste makes waste.' (lit. 'If you hurry you will make people laugh.')

(6) Ljubov'   zla,   *pro*ₐᵣᵦ poljubiš'   i   kozla.   [2SG-ARB]
    love.NOM bitter   fall.in.love.2SG.FUT ADDITIVE billy.goat.ACC
    'Love is blind.' (lit. 'Love is unfair; you will fall in love even with a billy goat.')

(7) Kašu   maslom   *pro*ₐᵣᵦ ne   isportiš'.   [2SG-ARB]
    gruel.ACC butter.INSTR   not spoil.2SG.FUT
    'You can never have too much of a good thing.' (lit. 'You will not ruin porridge with butter.')

All such statements have a generic interpretation, the details of which I will examine in §16.3 below. Before I do so, let me discuss how such sentences differ from those with null 3PL subjects and those with a (non-arbitrary) 2SG addressee.

16.2.2 *2SG-ARB vs 3PL*

Clauses with arbitrary 2SG and impersonal 3PL subjects both involve a null subject pronoun, but there are several differences. First, as I have already stated, arbitrary 2SG can alternate with an overt pronoun, while impersonal 3PL cannot (see also §16.1), as shown in (8) and (9).

(8) Kogda *pro*ₐᵣᵦ/ty   idjoš'   po   nočnoj   Moskve...   [2SG-ARB]
    when   2SG.NOM go.2SG.PRS over nightly   Moscow
    'When one walks around Moscow at night...'

(9) Kogda *pro*/*oni   idut   po   nočnoj   Moskve...   [3PL]
    when   3PL.NOM   go.3PL.PRS over nightly   Moscow
    'When one walks around Moscow at night...'

Second, the two types of null subjects differ in their interpretation: arbitrary 2SG has to be interpreted as speaker-oriented, whereas impersonal 3PL excludes the speaker, and its use often implies a contrast (almost a face-off) between the speaker and the rest of the world (Peškovskij 1956: 330–4; Bulygina and Shmelev 1997: 347–51, and references therein). Compare the minimal pairs in (10) and (11).[2]

(10) a. V   ètom   dome   *pro*ₐᵣᵦ kuriš'   ne   perestavaja. [2SG-ARB]
        in   this   home   smoke.2SG.PRS   not stopping
        'At this house, you smoke nonstop.' (speaker included)
     b. V   ètom   dome   *pro*   kurjat   ne   perestavaja. [3PL]
        in   this   home   smoke.3PL.PRS   not stopping
        'At this house, they smoke nonstop.' (distancing the speaker from everyone else)
     (Bulygina and Shmelev 1997: 348)

(11) V   každom   igrajuščem   detstve... četyre   rojalja.   Vo-pervyx,   tot,
     in   each   performing   childhood   four   grand-pianos firstly   that
     za   kotorym   *pro*ₐᵣᵦ   sidiš'.   Vo-vtoryx,   tot,   za   kotorym
     behind which   sit.2SG.PRS secondly   that   behind   which
     pro   sidjat...

sit.3PL.PRS

'In every childhood that had musical instruments in it, there are four grand pianos. First, the piano that one likes to play (lit.: the one that you sit behind). Second, the piano that people have to play (lit.: the one that they sit behind).'
(Marina Tsvetayeva, cited in Bulygina and Shmelev 1997: 349)

Although clauses with the arbitrary 2SG subject are generally speaker-oriented, these clauses can also include constituents expressed by a 1SG pronoun, indexing the speaker. For example, in (12a) the object is expressed by a 1SG pronoun, and in (12b) that pronoun occurs in a prepositional phrase.

(12) a. pro_arb menja tak legko ne ubediš'. [2SG-ARB]
     1SG.ACC so easily not convince.2SG.FUT
     'There is no convincing me so easily.'
 b. pro_arb pogovoriš' so mnoj o global'nom poteplenii, [2SG-ARB]
    speak.2SG.PRS with 1SG about global warming
    pro_arb srazu vsjo uznaješ'.
    right.away all find.out.2SG.FUT
    'Let anyone talk to me about global warming, I will set them straight.' (ironic, meant to express empathy with someone else)

In such instances, the pragmatic conditions call for the exclusion of the speaker (despite the general speaker-orientation of the arbitrary 2SG). The result is an impression that the focus of empathy is removed from the speaker (Bulygina and Shmelev 1997: 349–51), as in (13). However, this seems to be a mere pragmatic implicature, which is cancellable.

(13) pro_arb menja tak legko ne ubediš'. Ja i
     1SG.ACC so easily not convince.2SG.FUT 1SG.NOM additive
     sama ne vsegda soglašajus' so svoimi dokazatel'svami.
     by.self.F not always agree.1SG.PRS with self's arguments
     'There is no convincing me so easily. I myself don't always agree with my own arguments.'

In sum, the meaning of the arbitrary 2SG presupposes speaker-orientation, whereas the meaning of the 3PL impersonal excludes the speaker.

Sentences with arbitrary 2SG also differ from sentences with impersonal 3PL in their modal flavour. Arbitrary 2SG clauses express general statements concerning (im)possibility or the fact that something is being done (or not done) in a certain way; impersonal 3PL clauses, by contrast, have a strong deontic interpretation. Such modal differences are particularly apparent under negation. In (14), the sentence with arbitrary 2SG has a habitual reading, indicating general impossibility, while the sentence with the impersonal 3PL subject has a deontic reading.

(14) a. Zdes' pro_arb ne pokuriš', #no Maša vsjo vremja [2SG-ARB]
     here   not smoke.PFV.2SG.PRS but Masha all time

narušaet.
break.rule.3SG.PRS
'There are obstacles to smoking here, #but Masha is constantly breaking the rule.'
b. Zdes'   pro   ne   kurjat,   no   Maša   vsjo   vremja.   [3PL]
   here   not smoke.IMPFV.3PL.PRS but Masha all   time
   narušaet.
   break.rule.3SG.PRS
   'It is not allowed to smoke here, but Masha is constantly breaking the rule.'

Assuming that the arbitrary 2SG subject imparts a generic interpretation, it is not surprising that clauses with this pronoun resist the deontic reading. Generics and the deontic interpretation are compatible only under a circumscribed, specific set of conditions (Krifka et al. 1995; Moltmann 2010; Zobel 2014). In (14b), the conditions are such that the place is designated as non-smoking, and the continuation refers to a violation of the rule imposed by someone.

16.2.3 2SG-ARB vs 2SG-ADDR: Distributional Differences

As mentioned above, the arbitrary 2SG pronoun differs from the addressee 2SG pronoun in that the former cannot alternate with the 2PL form. In addition, the addressee 2SG pronoun and the arbitrary 2SG pronoun can also *co-occur in the same clause* (see Bulygina and Shmelev 1997: 348ff. for similar observations and further examples). This co-occurrence is illustrated in (15a); note, however, that a co-referential use of the addressee 2SG within the same clause is impossible (15b), an issue that I will return to in the discussion of binding below.[3]

(15) a. *pro*_{arb}   tebja   tak   prosto   ne   ubediš'.   [2SG-ARB]
                             2SG.ACC   so   simply   not   convince.2SG.FUT
          'There is no convincing you (addressee) so easily.'
      b. *Ty_i   tebja_i   tak   prosto   ne   ubediš'.
          2SG.NOM   2SG.ACC   so   simply   not convince.2SG.FUT
          ('You won't convince yourself so easily.')

Crucially, for the two 2SG pronouns to co-occur, the arbitrary 2SG must be in the subject position, as in (15a); the opposite relationship between the two 2SG pronouns, where the subject denotes the addressee and the pronominal in the object position, be it overt or null, is interpreted arbitrarily, is impossible.

(16) a. *Ty_{addr-i}   tebja_{arb-j}   tak   prosto   ne   ubediš'.
          2SG.NOM   2SG.ACC   so   simply   not   convince.2SG.FUT
          ('You (= addressee) won't convince one so easily.')
      b. *pro_{addr}   tebja_{arb-j}   tak   prosto   ne   ubediš'.
                                    2SG.ACC   so   simply   not   convince.2SG.FUT
          ('You (= addressee) won't convince one so easily.')
      c. *Ty_{addr-i}   pro_{arb-j}   tak   prosto   ne   ubediš'.
          2SG.NOM   so   simply   not   convince.2SG.FUT

('You (= addressee) won't convince one so easily.')

d. *pro$_{addr}$ pro$_{arb-j}$ tak prosto ne ubediš'.[4]
                       so   simply not convince.2SG.FUT

('You (= addressee) won't convince one so easily.')

The co-occurrence data indicate that the addressee 2SG and arbitrary 2SG have very different properties. Clauses with the addressee 2SG differ from those with the arbitrary 2SG in other respects. The differences include binding, number specification, gender specification and animacy of the subject. I will discuss these in turn.

16.2.3.1 Binding properties

The addressee 2SG and arbitrary 2SG differ in their binding properties. In order to examine these properties, we need to consider the binding of non-possessive forms (i.e. the accusative reflexive form *sebja*), possessive binding forms (i.e. the possessive reflexive *svoj*) and reciprocal binding forms.

Both addressee and arbitrary 2SG pronouns occurring in the subject position can bind a clause-mate reflexive, either in the position of a noun phrase or in the position of a prepositional phrase. Compare (15) and the pair of sentences in (17), in which the anaphor appears in the object position.

(17) a. pro$_{arb-i}$ sebja$_i$ tak legko ne ubediš'. [2SG-ARB]
                 self.ACC so easily not convince.2SG.FUT
   'There is no convincing oneself so easily.'

b. Ty$_i$ sebja$_i$ tak legko ne ubediš'. [2SG-ARB/2SG-ADDR]
   2SG.NOM self.ACC so easily not convince.2SG.FUT
   'There is no convincing oneself so easily.'
   'You (= addressee) won't convince yourself so easily.'

In the pair of examples in (18), the 2SG pronoun in the subject position binds a prepositional phrase.

(18) a. pro$_{arb-i}$ v sebe$_i$ vsegda somnevaješ'sja. [2SG-ARB]
               in self always doubt.2SG.PRS
   'One always has doubts about oneself.'

b. Ty$_i$ v sebe$_i$ vsegda somnevaješ'sja. [2SG-ARB/2SG-ADDR]
   2SG.NOM in self always doubt.2SG.PRS
   'One always has doubts about oneself.'
   'You (= addressee) always have doubts about yourself.'

When the 2SG pronoun in the subject position binds a possessive reflexive, there is a clear contrast between the arbitrary type and the addressee type. The arbitrary 2SG can only bind a reflexive possessive, whereas the addressee 2SG can bind either a reflexive or a pronominal possessive, as shown in (19).

(19) a. Čego tol'ko pro$_{arb-i}$ ne sdelaeš' dlja svoix$_i$/*tvoix$_i$ druzej! [2SG-ARB]
   what.PART only   not do.2SG.PRS for self's/2SG.POSS friends

'The things one does for one's friends!' (lit. 'What wouldn't you do for self's friends!')

b. Čego   tol'ko ty$_i$ ne sdelaeš'   dlja   svoix$_i$/tvoix$_i$ [2SG-ADDR]
what.PART only   2SG.NOM   not do.2SG.PRS   for   self's/2SG.POSS
druzej
friends
'The things you (= addressee) do for your friends!' (lit. 'What wouldn't you do for self's/your friends!')

Turning to reciprocal binding, the addressee 2SG cannot bind a reciprocal, but the arbitrary 2SG can (Knyazev 2015), as shown in (20).

(20) a. Esli pro$_{arb-i}$ ljubiš'   drug druga$_i$,   vsjo   legko.   [2SG-ARB]
if   love.2SG.PRS   each other.ACC   all   easy
'If people love each other everything is easy.'

b. *Esli ty$_i$ ljubiš'   drug druga$_i$...   [2SG-ADDR]
if   2SG.NOM   love.2SG.PRS   each other.ACC
'If you are in love with one another...'

To summarise, the binding properties of the addressee 2SG and arbitrary 2SG pronoun in the subject position are shown in Table 16.3.

These results suggest that the arbitrary 2SG pronoun is not specified for the property [+participant] or at least does not have to be specified for it exclusively. In particular, this pronoun cannot bind a possessive pronoun specifically marked as [+participant] (cf. (19)). Furthermore, it is not semantically singular, as we can see from its ability to bind reciprocal anaphors.

16.2.3.2 Number specification

The addressee 2SG and arbitrary 2SG differ in their number specification. If the arbitrary 2SG pronoun is not semantically specified as [+singular], we predict that it should be compatible with other contexts where the singular interpretation is not required. This prediction is confirmed: arbitrary 2SG pronouns can occur with collective or distributive predicates, i.e. predicates that range over a plurality of individuals in the subject position. The same use is absolutely unacceptable for addressee 2SG pronouns. Consider the symmetrical predicate *deržat'sja za ruki*, which entails a

Table 16.3 Binding properties

	2SG addressee	2SG arbitrary
Binds reflexive in an argument position	✓	✓
Binds reciprocal in an argument position	X	✓
Binds possessive reflexive	✓	✓
Binds possessive 2SG pronoun	✓	X

plural subject, as shown independently by (21). This predicate can co-occur with the arbitrary 2SG subject.

(21) a. Deti   deržalis'   za   ruki.
        children.NOM hold.PL.PST   at   hands
        'The children held hands.'
    b. *Rebenok   deržalsja   za   ruki.[5]
        child.NOM hold.PST.M   at   hands
        ('The child held hands with others.')

(22) a. V   ètom tance   ty/pro_{arb} deržiš'sja   za   ruki.   [2SG-ARB]
        in this dance2SG.NOM   hold.2SG.PRS   at   hands
        'In this dance, dancers hold hands.'
    b. *V   ètom tance ty   deržiš'sja   za   ruki.   [2SG-ADDR]
        in this dance 2SG.NOM   hold.2SG.PRS at   hands
        ('In this dance, you (= addressee) hold at other's hands.')

Example (23) illustrates a symmetrical predicate with a reciprocal anaphor bound by the arbitrary 2SG subject (as in (20) above).

(23) a. pro_{arb-i} nagovoriš'   drug $drugu_i$ obidnogo,   a   potom   [2SG-ARB]
                       say.2SG.PRS   each   other   hurtful.GEN and   then
        rassaživaeš'sja   po   svoim   uglam   i   molčiš'
        spread.out.in.sitting.2SG.PRS over self's   corners   and   keep.silent.2SG.PRS
        po   očeredi.
        in   turn
        'First, people say hurtful things to each other, and then they spread out in their own spaces and take turns not saying anything.'
    b. *Ty_i nagovoriš'   drug $drugu_i$ obidnogo,   a   potom   [2SG-ADDR]
         2SG.NOM   say.2SG.PRS   each   other   hurtful.GEN and   then
        rassaživaeš'sja   po   svoim   uglam   i   molčiš'
        spread.out.in.sitting.2SG.PRS over   self's   corners and   keep.silent.2SG.PRS
        po   očeredi.
        in   turn
        ('First, people say hurtful things to each other . . .')

Turning now to collective predicates, their meaning presupposes a plurality of subjects and is incompatible with a singular subject: the English *collide* or *disperse* are good examples. The [+participant/+singular] *ty* is impossible with such predicates, but the arbitrary 2SG subject is fully acceptable, as in (24).

(24) a. Esli   ty/pro_{arb} prevosxodiš'   po   čislennosti   sosednie   [2SG-ARB]
        if   2SG.NOM   surpass.2SG.PRS over   number   neighbouring
        narody,   vsjo ravno   ne   stoit   ix   obižat'.
        peoples   nevertheless   not   necessary   them   hurt.INF
        'If you outnumber your neighbour nations there is no need to insult them.'

b. *Esli ty   prevosxodiš'   po   čislennosti sosednie   [2SG-ADDR]
   if   2SG.NOM   surpass.2SG.PRS over number   neighbouring
   narody, ...
   peoples
   ('If you (= addressee) outnumber your neighbour nations ...')

The resulting picture is that the arbitrary 2SG is not specified as semantically singular but all the while the morphological agreement with this pronoun must be in second singular.

16.2.3.3 Gender specification

The addressee 2SG and arbitrary 2SG differ in their gender specification. If the arbitrary 2SG is not semantically specified for singular, what about its gender? So far all the examples have been in the present tense, where morphological agreement is in person and number. Gender agreement in Russian verbs appears in the past tense, as was shown in Table 16.2, and in the subjunctive (whose forms are homophonous with past tense forms). Outside verb forms, gender agreement is visible on adjectival/participial secondary predicates.

In all these contexts, the gender of the addressee 2SG is determined by the natural gender of the speech participant. This is easy to show using predicates whose denotation specifies a particular gender; the Russian equivalents for 'get married' are a well-known example of this, with *ženit'sja* applying to males and *vyxodit' zamuž* to females, as shown in (25).

(25) a. V   Japonii ty   by   zamuž   ne   vyšla.   [2SG-ADDR]
        in   Japan   2SG.NOM   SBJV married not go.F
        'In Japan you would not have got married.' (speaking to a woman)
     b. V   Japonii ty   by   ne   ženilsja.   [2SG-ADDR]
        in   Japan   2SG.NOM   SBJV   not married.M
        'In Japan you would not have got married.' (speaking to a man)

The gender on secondary predicates (depictives) and resultatives must also match the natural gender of the addressee. Thus, (26a) has to be used when addressing a male hearer, and (26b) when addressing a female.[6]

(26) a. Ty   vsegda prixodiš'   ustalyj/ustalym.   [2SG-ADDR]
        2SG.NOM   always come.back.2SG.PRS tired.NOM.M/tired.INS.M
     b. Ty   vsegda prixodiš'   ustalaja/ustaloj.
        2SG.NOM   always come.back.2SG.PRS tired.NOM.F/tired.INS.F
        'You always come back tired.'

With that in mind, let us now turn to the arbitrary 2SG. It appears that the gender of this pronoun is set as masculine, as shown in (27) for verbal predicates and in (28) for depictives.

(27) V   srednie   veka   esli   ty   rodilsja   rabom,   [2SG-ARB]
     in   middle   ages   if   2SG.NOM   was.born.M   slave.INS
     to   rabom   i   umiral.
     then   slave.INS and   died.M
     'In the Middle Ages, if one was born a slave, one died a slave.'

(28) S   raboty   pro_{arb}   vsegda   prixodiš'   [2SG-ARB]
     from   work   always   come.back.2SG.PRS
     ustalyj/ustalym.
     tired.NOM.M/tired.INS.M
     'One always comes back tired after work.'

With human referents, the masculine is the default gender in Russian; if a noun phrase is not specified as [+FEMININE], then it should be treated as masculine (Corbett and Fraser 2000: 83; Corbett 2007: 266–8; Doleschal and Schmid 2001: 264). This requirement overrides world knowledge. For example, all the native speakers I consulted accept examples such as (29a) or (30a) where the referent clearly has to be female, and only a subset of speakers also allowed agreement in the feminine in (29b) and (30b).

(29) a. V   srednie   veka   esli   ty   zaboleval   sepsisom   [2SG-ARB]
         in   middle   ages   if   2SG.NOM   got.sick.M   sepsis.INS
         posle rodov,   to   ty   navernjaka   umiral.
         after childbirth then   2SG.NOM   for.sure   died.M
     b. %V   srednie   veka   esli   ty   zabolevala   sepsisom   [2SG-ARB]
         in   middle   ages   if   2SG.NOM   got.sick.F   sepsis.INS
         posle rodov,   to   ty   navernjaka   umirala.
         after childbirth then   2SG.NOM   for.sure   died.F
         'In the Middle Ages, if one developed sepsis after childbirth, one was doomed to die.'

(30) a. V   starye   vremena esli   ty   rožal   rebenka   [2SG-ARB]
         in   old   times   if   2SG.NOM   gave.birth.M   child.ACC
         bez   muža,   ty   podvergalsja   ostrakizmu.
         without husband 2SG.NOM   underwent.M   ostracism.DAT
     b. %V   starye   vremena esli   ty   rožala   rebenka   [2SG-ARB]
         in   old   times   if   2SG.NOM   gave.birth.F   child.ACC
         bez   muža,   ty   podvergalas'   ostrakizmu.
         without husband 2SG.NOM   underwent.F   ostracism.DAT
         'In the old days, if one had a child out of wedlock, one was ostracised.'

With secondary predicates, however, the masculine agreement is overridden in contexts where the generic statement specifically targets female participants, as in (31).

(31) Poka   ty/*pro*_{arb}   xodiš'   beremennaja/*beremennyj,   [2SG-ARB]
     want.2SG.PRS 2SG.NOM   go.2SG.PRS   pregnant.F/pregnant.M
     ty/*pro*_{arb}   vsjo   vremja   xočeš'   est'.
     2SG.NOM   all   time   want.2SG.PRS   eat.INF
     'While pregnant, one is always hungry.'

Crucially, such semantic overrides are only possible with the gender feature, not the number feature. Compare (28), and the ungrammatical plural depictive in (32).[7]

(32) *S   raboty   *pro*_{arb}   vsegda   prixodiš'   ustalymi.   [2SG-ARB]
     from   work   always   come.back.2SG.PRS   tired.INS.PL
     ('One always comes back tired after work.')

The semantic agreement in gender presents an interesting challenge to the well-known hierarchy of agreement targets (Corbett 1979, 1983). Following Corbett, there is a hierarchy of agreement targets (probes) with respect to whether they can show semantically motivated agreement, as opposed to solely formal (syntactic, in Corbett's terms) agreement. For targets on the scale in (33), if some element is able to show semantic agreement, then all positions to the right on the scale will also be able to show semantic agreement. Conversely, if a position can show formal agreement, then all positions to the left will also be able to show morphological agreement.

(33) attributive > predicate > relative pronoun > personal pronoun
     ← formal agreement   semantic agreement →

If we now compare the formal agreement in (29) with the semantic agreement in (31), we find that these data do not follow the predictions of the Agreement Hierarchy. I leave the question of how to reconcile the hierarchy in (33) with these particular results for future research.

Leaving the borderline examples aside, we can conclude that the arbitrary 2SG is not semantically specified for number or gender. Its morphological number is set as singular, and its morphological gender is set as masculine; both these feature specifications constitute the morphological defaults in Russian. This morphological default for gender (but not for number) can be 'overridden' by semantic information, as shown in (31).

16.2.3.4 Animacy requirements

The addressee 2SG and arbitrary 2SG differ in the animacy requirements on the subject. The 2SG addressee pronoun can index personified inanimate or non-human participants, as in (34).

(34) Kogda   že   ty   zakolosiš'sja,   pšenica?   [2SG-ADDR]
     when   indeed   2SG.NOM   become.eared.2SG.FUT   wheat
     'Oh wheat, when will you finally plump up (lit. "form ears")?'

No such interpretation is ever available for the arbitrary reading; the verb *kolosit'sja* 'form ears, spire', whose subject must be inanimate, is impossible with the arbitrary pronoun.[8]

(35) *V xolodnoe leto pro_arb ne zakolosiš'sja. [2SG-ARB]
     in cold   summer   not become.eared.2SG.FUT
     'Ears won't form on wheat when the summer is cold.'

The arbitrary 2SG is conceptualised as indexing a human, sentient referent, which explains the ungrammaticality of (28). In this property, the Russian arbitrary 2SG resembles English *one* and *you*, German *man* and French *on*, which also require a [+human] denotation (Wiltschko 2016).

Two additional observations provide further support for the generalisation that the arbitrary 2SG requires a [+human] referent. First, if the participant indexed by the arbitrary 2SG must be interpreted as sentient via coercion, then the use of the arbitrary form becomes acceptable. Such coercion can be provided by the set phrase *xočeš' ne xočeš'* 'whether you like it or not; willy-nilly', which presupposes a sentient referent.[9] The expression itself is the frozen form of the verb 'want' in 2SG, but it is currently used more broadly and is not limited to second persons. Compare the ungrammatical (35) with the felicitous sentence in (36).

(36) Xočeš' ne   xočeš', a   pro_arb zakolosiš'sja. [2SG-ARB]
     like   not like   but   become.eared.2SG.FUT
     'Whether you like it or not you will have to form ears.'

Likewise, in the sentence in (37), the referent is a personified animal, whose sentience is established via pragmatic coercion.

(37) Xočeš' ne   xočeš', a   pro_arb staneš'   lajat'   [2SG-ARB]
     like   not like   but   get.2SG.FUT   bark.INF
     za   ugoščenie.
     for treat
     'Whether you like it or not you will bark to get a treat.'

The second observation supporting the [+sentient] or [+human] feature of the arbitrary 2SG comes from verbs whose meaning varies depending on the humanness or animacy of the subject. For example, the verb *ržat'* has the meaning 'neigh' but can also be used figuratively in the meaning 'snicker', with a human subject. Only this latter meaning is possible with the arbitrary 2SG. Compare the literal meaning of (38), where the addressee is a horse, and the figurative meaning (the only one available) in (39).

(38) Čto   ty   ržoš',   moj kon'   retivyj? [2SG-ADDR]
     what 2SG.NOM neigh.2SG.PRS   my   steed proud
     'Why are you neighing, oh my proud steed?'
     (Pushkin)

Table 16.4 Addressee 2SG subject vs arbitrary 2SG subject

	2SG addressee	2SG arbitrary
Determines obligatory 2SG agreement on verbs in non-past tense (nominative subjects)	✓	✓
Binds 2SG possessive pronouns	✓	X
Is semantically specified as singular (cf. binding of reciprocals, occurrence with collective/distributive predicates)	✓	X
Is specified as morphologically masculine	X	✓
Must be interpreted as [+HUMAN]	X	✓

(39) Ot takim krikov byvalo ty/pro_{arb} tol'ko ržoš'. [2SG-ARB]
 from such yells usually 2SG.NOM only snicker.2SG.PRS
 'One would only snicker/*neigh upon hearing such yells.'

Table 16.4 summarises the differences between the arbitrary and addressee 2SG pronouns.

Throughout this section, I have concentrated on arbitrary 2SG in the nominative subject position. However, similar properties also hold of arbitrary 2SG in non-nominative forms when such forms encode an external argument (dative or accusative experiencer subjects; PP possessive subjects). Such external arguments do not determine verbal agreement, so it is harder to tell if the overt form of the pronoun can alternate with the null form, but the overt form has the same binding properties as the arbitrary 2SG in the nominative. Contrast the sentences in (19) with the pair in (40), where the arbitrary 2SG in the experiencer subject position can bind only the possessive reflexive.

(40) a. V xorošej kompanii tebe/?pro_{arb} veselo daže [2SG-ARB]
  in good company 2SG.DAT merry even
  ot svoix/*tvoix durackix šutok.
  from self's/2SG.POSS silly jokes
  'In good company, one gets merry even from one's own silly jokes.'
 b. V xorošej kompanii tebe veselo daže [2SG-ADDR]
  in good company 2SG.DAT merry even
  ot svoix/tvoix šutok.
  from self's/2SG.POSS jokes
  'In good company, you get merry even from your own jokes.'

Likewise, the arbitrary 2SG in the locative-possessor position (u-XP) can serve as the antecedent of a reciprocal; compare the minimal pair in (20) with the pair in (41).

(41) a. Kogda u   tebja/pro_arb voznikaet obida   drug na druga ...   [2SG-ARB]
        when by   2SG   occurs   grievance on.each.other
        'When people are upset with each other ...'
    b. *Kogda u   tebja   voznikaet obida   drug na druga ...   [2SG-ADDR]
        when by 2SG   occurs   grievance on.each.other
        'When you are upset with each other ...'

Thus, the arbitrary 2SG in the external argument position is not limited to the nominative.

In the next section, I will consider the semantic import of sentences with the arbitrary 2SG subject. Strictly speaking, the [+HUMAN] requirement and [+MASCULINE] preference should also be counted among the interpretive properties of the arbitrary 2SG subject, but since they have an effect on morphosyntactic agreement, I have included them in the tally of their structural properties.

16.3 Interpretive Properties of Sentences with Arbitrary 2SG

16.3.1 2SG-ARB Sentences vs 2SG-ADDR Sentences: Differences in Interpretation

Sentences with arbitrary 2SG have a number of interpretive restrictions, some of which are particularly vivid when compared with the use of addressee-2SG sentences. Addressee-2SG sentences can be episodic, express isolated facts, or denote repeated habitual events. They are also contextually free, in that they can occur in isolation and do not require special anchoring in terms of time or location. Meanwhile, as will be elaborated upon below, arbitrary-2SG sentences cannot have episodic readings and must be anchored in time or space (a typical property of generic sentences generally). I have already noted their generic flavour in the discussion above. The generic interpretation was particularly apparent in the comparison between (14a) and (14b), partially repeated in (42), where the former had the reading of impossibility, and the latter, a deontic interpretation.

(42) a. Zdes' pro_arb ne   pokuriš'.   [2SG-ARB]
        here   not smoke.PFV.2SG.PRS
        'It is impossible to smoke here.' (= (14a))
    b. Zdes' pro   ne   kurjat.   [3PL]
        here   not smoke.IMPFV.3PL.PRS
        'It is not allowed to smoke here.' (= (14b))

As I already mentioned, deontic readings are not easily compatible with genericity, so this contrast is understandable.

Following up on the generic interpretation, the distribution of individual-level predicates differs with addressee 2SG vs arbitrary 2SG. When the sentence in (43) is uttered out of the blue, the subject can only be interpreted as an addressee.

(43) Ty   prinadležiš'   k   izbrannomu obščestvu.   [2SG-ADDR]
     2SG.NOM   belong.2SG.PRS   to   select   society
     'You (= addressee) belong to an elite circle.'

In order for the subject of this sentence to be interpreted as arbitrary, it needs to be explicitly anchored to a set of events or locations, as in (44); again, this is a typical condition on the felicity of individual-level predicates in generic contexts (Krifka et al. 1995; Chierchia 1995).

(44) V   takix   universitetax *pro$_{arb}$/ty*   neredko   prinadležiš'   [2SG-ARB]
     in   such   universities   2SG.NOM   frequently   belong.2SG.PRS
     k   izbrannomu obščestvu.
     to   select   society
     'In such universities, one often belongs to an elite circle.'

The anchoring of clauses with arbitrary 2SG can be achieved in two major ways. First, two (or more) clauses, all under the scope of a generic quantifier, may co-occur in an utterance, with one clause serving as the conditional antecedent for the other. In such utterances, the arbitrary 2SG can appear in either of the clauses (or both). Crucial for their interpretation, the two clauses must be interpreted as forming a contrast. Example (45) illustrates the patterns. In (45a), the arbitrary 2SG appears in the first coordinate clause; in (45b), it occurs in both clauses; in (45c), it occurs in the second coordinate.

(45) a. Ty/*pro$_{arb}$*   prixodiš'   domoj,   a   tam   nikogo   net.   [2SG-ARB]
        2SG.NOM   come.2SG.PRS   home   but   there nobody   be.NEG
        'One comes home to find nobody there.'
     b. Ty/*pro$_{arb}$*   prixodiš'   domoj   i   nikogo tam   ne   naxodiš'
        2SG.NOM   come.2SG.PRS   home   and   nobody there   not   find.2SG.PRS
        'One comes home but does not find anybody there.'
     c. Doma   nikogo   net,   a   ty/*pro$_{arb}$*   vsjo ravno   ždjoš'   kogo-to.
        home   nobody   be.NEG   but   2SG.NOM   still   wait.2SG.PRS   someone
        'There is nobody home, but one still waits for someone.'

Although I have used coordinate clauses here for illustrative purposes, the same anchoring effect can be achieved if one of the clauses occurs as an adjunct or if (all) the clauses appear as root clauses.

We have seen above several other examples in which two or more clauses occur in the utterance and an arbitrary-2SG clause served as the antecedent: see (5), (6), (12) and (20). The antecedent clauses in these sentences often co-occur with the adverbial *byvalo* 'habitually, occasionally' (a fossilised habitual form of the verb 'be'); for instance, (46).

(46) a. Byvalo   na   nedelju   ujedeš',   i
        habitually   on   week   go.away.PFV.2SG.FUT   and

to zvoniš'.
still call.IMPFV.2SG.PRS
(Russian National Corpus)

b. Byvalo na nedelju ujezžaješ', i to pozvoniš'.
  habitually on week go.away.IMPFV.2SG.PRS and still call.2PFV.2SG.FUT
  'One would go away for just a week but would still call.'

In all these cases, there are no aspectual restrictions on the predicate of the 2SG-ARB sentence; the sentence can appear in the perfective or imperfective, as shown by the examples in (46).

The second way of anchoring clauses with the arbitrary 2SG involves the use of a temporary or locative adjunct, as already shown in (43) above. Such anchoring can also be implicit. Implicit anchoring is particularly common if the clause with the arbitrary 2SG is under the scope of negation; compare (7), (12), (14), (15), or the example in (47).[10]

(47) Vyše golovy pro$_{arb}$ ne prygneš'. [2SG-ARB]
  higher head.GEN not jump.2SG.PRS
  'A man can do no more than he can.' (lit. 'You can't jump higher than your head.')

Informally, it appears that negation may be one of the ways of marking focus; the presupposed contrast is between p and $\neg p$, and negation serves to exclude a range of possibilities. The association between focus and the matrix material in generic sentences is well established (Krifka 1995; Rooth 1995). Assuming that the generic interpretation of sentences with the arbitrary 2SG subject is on the right track, negation can serve as a formal means of identifying the matrix material in arbitrary 2SG clauses.

This hypothesis leads us to expect that other means of identifying focus should also play a role in arbitrary 2SG clauses. At least two observations confirm this expectation. First, I have already mentioned a number of examples where two clauses with the arbitrary 2SG subject are juxtaposed, and the propositions in these clauses are interpreted contrastively: one of the clauses serves as the presupposition against which the material in the other clause is asserted. Second, generic sentences with the arbitrary 2SG subject often occur with the additive particle *i* 'also; even' (see Gast and van der Auwera 2011 for the functions of this particle; a saying with this particle appeared in (6) above in a set expression). Outside set expressions, a constituent with the additive particle *i* precedes the verb and bears a clear focus intonation, with the high–low boundary tone (HL*). Compare (48).

(48) I ljagušek^{HL*} ty/pro$_{arb}$ budeš' est'. [2SG-ARB]
  ADDITIVE frogs.ACC 2SG.NOM AUX.2SG eat.INF
  'One would even eat frogs.'

These observations on focus associations in generic clauses are preliminary. The overall picture is complicated by the rampant scrambling that seems to be a hallmark of Russian syntax; the interaction between the prosodic, information-structural and propositional-semantic effects of scrambling is not fully understood, and more work needs to be done in this area.

To conclude, this section has suggested that the interpretive properties of clauses with the arbitrary 2SG subject follow from the generic interpretation of these clauses; focusing on the generic interpretation allows us to account for the differences between arbitrary 2SG subjects and addressee 2SG subjects.

16.3.2 *Null vs Overt* ty *in 2*SG*-ARB Sentences: Differences in Interpretation*

One of the issues that I have not yet addressed has to do with interpretive differences between overt and null arbitrary 2SG subjects. As shown by examples throughout this paper, both the overt and covert variants of this pronoun are generally possible, with the exception of sentences where the addressee 2SG also appears, such as (15). In set expressions, the null form predominates. Likewise, in sentences with the nominative form of the arbitrary 2SG subject, there is a preference for the null form appearing in that position; in 300 sentences with such subjects culled from the Russian National Corpus, 210 (about 70 per cent) had the null form. By contrast, when arbitrary 2SG is used in non-nominative position (as an experiencer dative, as a PP, etc.), there seems to be a preference for the overt form.

Null forms are independently known in the literature to correspond to bound forms (Landau 2004, 2015), and this expectation is confirmed by the null arbitrary 2SG data. The examples in (49) show the contrast between overt vs silent 2SG in an embedded *whether*-clause ((49a) vs (49b) respectively). In (49b), the only available reading for *pro* is that of a bound variable. The interpretation of the overt form of arbitrary 2SG in the minimal pair, (49a), is less clear; some speakers allow both readings, while others insist on the strict reading only.[11]

(49) a. Tol′ko   ty$_i$ odin   znaeš′,   smožeš′   li   ty$_{i/\%}$
       only   2SG.NOM   alone.M   know.2SG.PRS be.able.2SG.FUT COMP 2SG.NOM
       preodolet′   takoe   prepjatstvie.
       overcome.INF   [such   obstacle].ACC
       'Only the person himself$_i$ knows whether he$_{i/k}$ can overcome such an obstacle.'
   b. Tol′ko   ty$_i$ odin   znaeš′,   smožeš′   li   *pro*$_{i/*k}$
       only   2SG.NOM   alone.M   know.2SG.PRS be.able.2SG.FUT COMP
       preodolet′   takoe   prepjatstvie.
       overcome.INF   [such   obstacle].ACC
       'Only the person himself knows whether he/*one can overcome such an obstacle.'

The contrast between the overt and null arbitrary 2SG pronouns needs to be explored further, but since these differences do not play a critical role in the present discussion, I leave them for further research.

16.4 Putting It All Together

Now that we have observed structural and interpretive differences between clauses with the arbitrary 2SG subject and clauses with the addressee 2SG subject, it is time to

Table 16.5 Addressee 2SG subject vs arbitrary 2SG subject/highest external argument

	2SG addressee	2SG arbitrary
Determines obligatory 2SG agreement on verbs in non-past tense (nominative subjects)	✓	✓
Binds 2SG possessive pronouns	✓	X
Is semantically specified as singular (cf. binding of reciprocals, occurrence with collective/distributive predicates)	✓	X
Is specified as morphologically masculine	X	✓
Must be interpreted as [+HUMAN]	X	✓

examine where these differences come from. In a nutshell, clauses with the arbitrary 2SG subject are unusual in that their subject shares its agreement pattern with the addressee 2SG subject, but differs in its binding properties, plural interpretation, depictive/resultative agreement and obligatory human interpretation. The relevant properties are repeated in Table 16.5.

In §16.3, I showed that sentences with arbitrary 2SG have a generic interpretation. The literature on the semantics of generics is enormous, and I will not be able to do it justice here. For my purposes, the crucial ingredients of the analysis of generics are shown in (50): a covert quantifier, possibly adverbial in nature (Lewis 1975; Krifka et al. 1995), a restrictor and the matrix material (whose association with focus further supports the tripartite generic structure).

(50) **GEN** [x; y] (**Restrictor** [x]; ∃y **Matrix** [x y])

In the sentences considered in this paper, arbitrary 2SG is always in the subject position (or in some external argument position; for example, when it corresponds to the experiencer subject or to an external argument in the form of a PP, as in (40) and (41)). Assuming that universal (generic) quantification targets the highest structural position (Diesing 1992), the generic quantifier has scope over this arbitrary 2SG. The generalised form of arbitrary 2SG sentences is therefore as shown in (51).

(51) **GEN** [x; y; s] (x is in s & x is 2SG; ∃y & x V y)

Scoping over the arbitrary 2SG, GEN unselectively binds this pronoun, causing it to acquire all the indices associated with the situation variable s.[12] The arbitrary 2SG is no longer interpreted as uniquely associated with the addressee (although this association is still available, if only as an implicature). Example (52) repeated from (15a) shows that such an implicature can be cancelled: the sentence contains the overt addressee pronoun in the object position and the null arbitrary 2SG pronoun is interpreted as excluding the addressee.

(52) pro^{arb} tebja   tak   prosto   ne   ubediš'.
           2SG.ACC so   simply   not   convince.2SG.FUT
    'There is no convincing you (addressee) so easily.' (= (15a))

The binding and argument structure properties of the arbitrary 2SG subject follow from its being in the scope of GEN; the indices are passed down to the pronoun from all the possible situations *s* where the proposition denoted in the sentence holds true. The semantic representation is in (53). (The syntactic representation, where the generic quantifier is base-generated as an adjoined adverbial in the TP domain, is shown in Figure 16.1 below.)

(53) **GEN** $[s_1, s_2, \ldots s_n] (x_1, x_2, \ldots x_n) \ldots$

Binding by the generic quantifier forces a non-singular semantic interpretation on arbitrary 2SG as well as a gender-neutral interpretation, realised as the masculine. As a result, this pronoun in the subject/external argument position can fill the subject position of collective or distributive predicates and can bind reciprocal anaphors; in both of these contexts, the set of referents is two or more. Furthermore, the arbitrary 2SG *cannot* bind a 2SG possessive: to do so would require exclusion of all the other indices inherited from the quantifier above, leading to an interpretive clash.

We can now approach the mechanism of agreement in generic clauses with an arbitrary 2SG nominative in the subject position. In such clauses, the probing T head reaches the 2SG pronoun and values its phi-features [PERSON] and [NUMBER] in a straightforward way. In the past tense/conditional, agreement is in the masculine, as the default morphosyntactic feature. The structure illustrated in Figure 16.1 reflects a regular clause with a nominative subject and transitive verb in non-past tenses (irrelevant details are not shown).

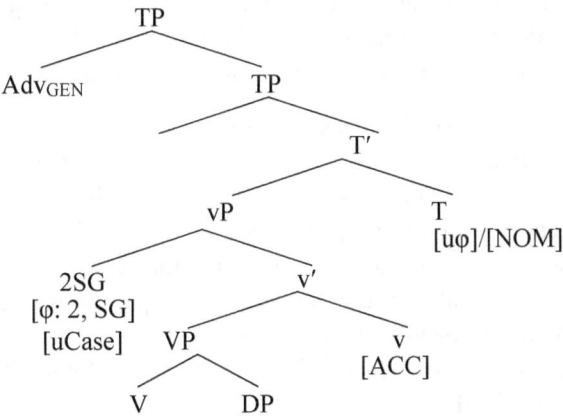

Figure 16.1 Structure of regular clause with a nominative subject and transitive verb in non-past tenses

Agreement is not sensitive to variable binding, so the end result of this derivation is that agreement in finite clauses with the arbitrary 2SG is the same as in clauses with the addressee 2SG. The presence of the generic quantifier is responsible for the binding properties and plural/masculine interpretation of the arbitrary 2SG subject, while agreement is established in the standard way without influence from the generic quantifier, which is adjoined to the T as shown in Figure 16.1.

The analysis presented here accounts for the bulk of the properties of generic sentences with an arbitrary 2SG subject listed in Table 16.5. However, the obligatory [+human] interpretation of the arbitrary 2SG subject remains unexplained. I do not have a solid account of this property at this time, but I expect that the connection between the clear speaker-orientation of generic sentences with the arbitrary 2SG and humanness is not accidental.

16.5 Conclusions

In this paper I have examined the dissociation between person agreement and binding properties of the Russian second person singular (2SG) pronoun *ty*, in those contexts where it has an arbitrary interpretation (ty_{arb}/pro_{arb}). Regardless of the interpretation, this pronoun controls regular verb agreement appropriate for the second singular, but its binding properties and its semantic properties (number, gender) are different from those of a regular 2SG pronoun. I proposed that the binding and number/gender properties of the arbitrary 2SG follow from its being in the scope of a generic operator; this is where these properties are no longer synchronised with agreement, thus offering a tantalising example of Janus-like behaviour so familiar from work on gender but explored much less in other domains of grammar.

In clauses without arbitrary interpretation, no generic operator is observed, and the binding properties of the pronoun are not dissociated from its agreement properties; it is well behaved and does everything that is expected of it. Of course, my main point in this paper was to illustrate the divergence between binding and agreement using empirical data from just one language, but the facts concerning the arbitrary 2SG in Russian can also inform our understanding of binding as a diagnostic of properties outside of narrow syntax. This result reiterates the proposal by Eric Reuland:

> [T]he conditions on anaphoric dependencies are the result of the interaction of many factors, some independent of language . . ., others irreducibly linguistic. Small differences in structure, entirely independent of binding, may give rise to what appear to be major differences in the way anaphoric dependencies manifest themselves. The following conclusion is unavoidable: . . . the superficial constraints on anaphoric dependencies tell us very little in isolation of other properties of a language. This means that in order to understand patterns of anaphora in one language – or language in general – one has to take into account a great many factors from different parts of the grammar. (Reuland 2011: xv)

Some of the properties of the arbitrary 2SG remain unaccounted for. In particular, why does it have to be animate? This puzzle leads us to a larger outstanding question of why it is the second person singular that is selected for using generic statements. How do the semantics of person, number and gender get co-opted for the generic reading: is there wholesale overriding of the normal semantics, or should we assume that Russian has two separate pronouns *ty*, each with its own set of properties? Nothing in the material presented here allows me to answer this question definitively; both options (overrides on a single lexical item and two lexical items) are available. Furthermore, the choice between these two options is not unique to the pronoun *ty* discussed here; it arises with respect to other lexical items, for instance control verbs (Perlmutter 1970; Polinsky 2000) or the English *climb* (Jackendoff 1985). In other words, the dilemma concerning the representations for the Russian *ty* goes well beyond that particular lexical item, but that does not make the problem go away.

Acknowledgements

I am grateful to Oliver Bond, Lena Borise, Leston Buell, Valentine Hacquard, Daniel Harbour, Andrew Hippisley, Norbert Hornstein, Tania Ionin and Eric Potsdam for helpful discussions of this project. I would also like to thank Lena Borise, Irina Dubinina, Elena Muravenko, Sol Polinsky, Ekaterina Rakhilina, Sergey Tatevosov, Igor Yanovich and Alex Yanovsky for help with the Russian data. I am solely responsible for any errors.

Notes

1. The comparison is not quite as exact. English diary drop is most commonly found in root declaratives; in Russian, similar pronoun drop is most common in questions, as in (3b).
2. In (11), the contrastive forms of the verb 'sit' occur in the same utterance.
3. The grammatical and ungrammatical versions with the overt pronoun are string-identical and differ only in their indices/interpretation. Therefore, the difference between (15a) and (15b) cannot be reduced to the difference between null and overt pronouns, consider example (i).

    (i) ?Ty_i $tebja_k$ tak prosto ne ubediš'.
    2SG.NOM 2SG.ACC so simply not convince.2SG.FUT
    'There is no convincing you so easily.'

4. This last sentence is acceptable on a different reading, where both null pronominals are interpreted anaphorically ('You (= addressee) won't be able to convince him/her/them so easily').
5. This sentence is acceptable on the irrelevant meaning 'The child supported himself/ herself by grabbing several hands at the same time.'
6. The case of the secondary predicate may vary (Nichols 1981), but this variation is irrelevant for the discussion here.
7. If a verbal predicate and a depictive co-occur in those contexts that force the feminine gender reading, the results are disastrous. Most speakers find such sentences unacceptable no matter what, as in example (ii), and look for paraphrases. Some speakers, however, accept the feminine both on the verb in the past tense and on the depictive, as in example (iii).

    (ii) *V starye vremena esli ty rožal
    in old times if 2SG.NOM gave.birth.M

nezamužnim/nezamužnej . . .
unmarried.INS.M/F
('In the old days, if one gave birth unmarried . . .')

(iii) %V starye vremena esli ty rožala nezamužnej . . .
in old times if 2SG.NOM gave.birth.F unmarried.INS.F
'In the old days, if one gave birth unmarried . . .'

8. The translation is rather figurative here, designed to render the general intended meaning.
9. I am grateful to Lena Borise for suggesting this set of examples.
10. This is probably the most common use of the arbitrary 2SG in proverbs and sayings.
11. The readings for (49) are less crisp than the corresponding readings for 'fake indexicals' reported for English or German (Partee 1989; Kratzer 2009). This may well be due to the availability of the null pronominal in Russian, as in (49b), an option unattested in English or German. If the null pronominal is used exclusively to mark bound variable readings, such readings may in turn be less available (or outright impossible) with the null pronominal's overt counterpart.
12. According to some analyses, GEN is an unselective binder; according to other approaches, it binds only the situation variable s, while all other apparent binding is indirect, derived from the binding of that s. Here, I will adopt the direct unselective-binding approach just for simplicity's sake – but both approaches, with their associated virtues and warts, are going to yield similar results for the purposes of the current discussion.

References

Avrtuin, Sergey and Maria Babyonyshev (1997), 'Obviation in subjunctive clauses and Agr: Evidence from Russian', *Natural Language and Linguistic Theory*, 15, pp. 229–62.

Bulygina, Tatiana V. and Alexey D. Shmelev (1997), *Jazykovaja konceptualizacija mira (na material russkoj grammatiki)*, Moscow: Jazyki russkoj kul′tury.

Chierchia, Gennaro (1995), 'Individual-level predicates as inherent generics', in Gregory N. Carlson and Francis Jeffry Pelletier (eds), *The Generic Book*, Chicago: University of Chicago Press, pp. 176–223.

Corbett, Greville G. (1979), 'The Agreement Hierarchy', *Journal of Linguistics*, 15 (2), pp. 203–24.

Corbett, Greville G. (1983), *Hierarchies, Targets and Controllers: Agreement Patterns in Slavic*, London: Croom Helm.

Corbett, Greville G. (1991), *Gender*, Cambridge: Cambridge University Press.

Corbett, Greville G. (2007), 'Gender and noun classes', in Timothy Shopen (ed.), *Language Typology and Syntactic Description. Vol. III: Grammatical Categories and the Lexicon*, 2nd edn, Cambridge: Cambridge University Press, pp. 241–79.

Corbett, Greville G. and Norman Fraser (2000), 'Default genders', in Barbara Unterbeck, Matti Rissanen, Terttu Nevalainen and Mirja Saari (eds), *Gender in Grammar and Cognition*, Berlin: Mouton de Gruyter, pp. 55–97. [Reprinted 2002 in the Mouton Jubilee Collection *Mouton Classics: From Syntax to Cognition: From Phonology to Text*, vol. 1, pp. 297–339.]

Diesing, Molly (1992), *Indefinites*, Cambridge, MA: MIT Press.

Doleschal, Ursula and Sonja Schmid (2001), 'Doing gender in Russian: Structure and perspective', in Hadumod Bussmann and Marlis Hellinger (eds), *Gender across Languages: The Linguistic Representation of Women And Men*, Amsterdam: John Benjamins, pp. 253–82.

Gast, Volker and Johan van der Auwera (2011), 'Scalar additive operators in the languages of Europe', *Language*, 87, pp. 2–54.

Haegeman, Liliane (1990), 'Understood subjects in English diaries', *Multilingua*, 9, pp. 157–99.
Haegeman, Liliane and Tabea Ihsane (1999), 'Subject ellipsis in embedded clauses in English', *English Language and Linguistics*, 3, pp. 117–45.
Jackendoff, Ray (1985), 'Multiple subcategorization and the θ-criterion: The case of *climb*', *Natural Language and Linguistic Theory*, 3, pp. 271–95.
Knyazev, Yuri (2015), 'Obobščenno-ličnye predloženija', MS, Moscow University.
Kratzer, Angelika (2009), 'Making a pronoun: Fake indexicals as windows into the properties of pronouns', *Linguistic Inquiry*, 40, pp. 187–237.
Krifka, Manfred (1995), 'Focus and the interpretation of generic sentences', in Gregory N. Carlson and Francis Jeffry Pelletier (eds), *The Generic Book*, Chicago: University of Chicago Press, pp. 238–64.
Krifka, Manfred, Francis Jeffry Pelletier, Gregory N. Carlson, Alice ter Meulen, Gennaro Chierchia and Godehard Link (1995), 'Genericity: An introduction', in Gregory N. Carlson and Francis Jeffry Pelletier (eds), *The Generic Book*, Chicago: University of Chicago Press, pp. 1–124.
Landau, Idan (2004), 'The scale of finiteness and the calculus of control', *Natural Language and Linguistic Theory*, 22, pp. 811–77.
Landau, Idan (2015), *A Two-Tiered Theory of Control*, Cambridge, MA: MIT Press.
Lewis, David (1975), 'Adverbs of quantification', in Edward L. Keenan (ed.), *Formal Semantics of Natural Languages*, Cambridge: Cambridge University Press, pp. 3–15.
Livitz, Inna (2014), *Deriving Silence and Dependent Reference: Focus on Pronouns*, PhD dissertation, New York University.
McShane, Marjorie J. (2005), *A Theory of Ellipsis*, Oxford: Oxford University Press.
Mel'čuk, Igor (1974), 'O sintaksičeskom nule', in Aleksandr Xoldovič (ed.), *Tipologija passivnyx konstrukcij. Diatezy i zalogi*, Leningrad: Nauka, pp. 343–61.
Moltmann, Friederike (2010), 'Generalizing detached self-reference and the semantics of generic', *One Mind & Language*, 25, pp. 440–73.
Nichols, Johanna (1981), *Predicate Nominals: A Partial Surface Syntax of Russian*, University of California Publications in Linguistics, 97, Berkeley, Los Angeles and London: University of California.
Partee, Barbara (1989), 'Binding implicit variables in quantified contexts', in Caroline Wiltshire, Randolph Graczyk and Bradley Music (eds), *Papers from the 25th Regional Meeting of the Chicago Linguistic Society. Part One, The General Session*, Chicago: Chicago Linguistic Society, pp. 342–65.
Perlmutter, David M. (1970), 'The two verbs begin', in Roderick A. Jacobs and Peter S. Rosenbaum (eds), *Readings in English Transformational Grammar*, Waltham, MA: Blaisdell, pp. 107–19.
Peškovskij, Alexander M. (1956), *Russkij sintaksis v naučnom osveščenii*, Moscow: Učpedgiz.
Polinsky, Maria (2000), 'Tsez beginnings', in *Proceedings of the 25th Annual Meeting of the Berkeley Linguistics Society: Special Session on Caucasian, Dravidian, and Turkic Linguistics*, Berkeley, CA: Berkeley Linguistics Society, pp. 14–29.
Reuland, Eric (2011), *Anaphora and Language Design*, Cambridge, MA: MIT Press.
Rooth, Mats (1995), 'Indefinites, adverbs of quantification, and focus semantics', in Gregory N. Carlson and Francis Jeffry Pelletier (eds), *The Generic Book*, Chicago: University of Chicago Press, pp. 265–99.
Wiltschko, Martina (2016), 'Fake form', in Patrick Grosz and Pritty Patel-Grosz (eds), *The Impact of Pronominal Form on Interpretation*, Berlin: De Gruyter, pp. 13–52.
Zobel, Sarah (2014), *Impersonally Interpreted Personal Pronouns*, PhD dissertation, University of Göttingen.

17

Rara and Theory Testing in Typology: The Natural Evolution of Non-canonical Agreement

Erich Round

17.1 Generalisation, Theory and *Rara*

Typological research seeks to make valid generalisations about the diversity of human language. It proceeds from observed linguistic traits, their distributions across geography and genealogy, and their relationships to other traits. Typological theories generate hypotheses, whose testing can prompt us to make more precise and systematic observations. Theories also propose explanations for observations. Corbett (2012), for example, generalises over extensive typological evidence to propose a theory of features, according to which, inflectional features are limited to only a handful of kinds. As in all sciences, theories in typology have apparent counter-examples. Rare linguistic traits, or *rara* (Plank 2000; Cysouw and Wohlgemuth 2010), often present such instances. If so, they challenge the theory, and warrant closer examination. Here I present an instance in which Corbett's theory prompted the re-examination of a *rarum*, namely the inflectional marking of complementised clauses in Kayardild. This led to a revised understanding of the phenomenon, and to support for the theory. Moreover, the re-examination presents the opportunity to compare three analyses of the same facts. The comparison highlights the methodological value for typology of attending to diachrony when evaluating *rara*. The argument has been made before that *rara* often arise through normal processes of historical change, only that because they require unlikely combinations of multiple changes, or rare preconditions, they are less likely to arise than common traits (Harris 2008, 2010; Grossman 2016). Here I emphasise two corollaries of the nature and scientific value of *rara*. Because *rara* are particularly useful for hypothesis testing and attendant theoretical progress, and since our understanding of *rara* often requires reference to diachrony, it follows that methodologically, typology should ideally include as much about diachrony as it can in its evidentiary base; and epistemologically, it would be mistaken to characterise typology as an ahistorical discipline (e.g. Daniel 2011), since diachrony is particularly important for understanding some of the best evidence for testing typological theories.

The *rarum* at the centre of the discussion will be 'subordinate clause complementisation marking', or SCCM, in Kayardild. In Kayardild, certain subordinate clauses (SCs) are morphologically marked as complementised (Evans 1995a; Round 2013). The complementised–uncomplementised opposition conveys information about co-reference between arguments of main and subordinate clauses, and about topic continuity in discourse (Evans 1995a). As it happens, in Kayardild there are two ways to mark a SC as complementised, by using two different inflectional markers. Both of the markers descend historically from exponents of CASE, and when they are used to mark complementisation they attach to every word, or nearly every word, in the complementised SC (in the case of subject pronouns, the pronoun is selected from an appropriate series; see the Appendix for conditions under which words escape marking for SCCM). The choice between these two types of SCCM is decided by the PERSON value (including clusivity) of the SC subject, and, if the subject is second person, according to whether 'the speaker wants to group him/herself with the addressee' (Evans 1995a: 494), a factor which I will refer to as SOLIDARITY. The first type of marking is illustrated for a first exclusive subject in (1), third person subject in (2), and second person subject (non-solidarity) in (3). The second type is illustrated for a second person subject (solidarity) in (4). For the moment, the markers of complementisation are glossed COMP1 and COMP2. (Examples are given as: practical orthography on line one; underlying phonological forms on line two; then comparative morphological categories, discussed further in §17.3; and the function of morphs on the final line.)[1]

(1) Kayardild [R2005-jul14a]
Thardabadija   wuranki,   [ngarrwaa   ngakathurrk].
ṯaṯa-patic-a   wuɻan-ki   ŋa-r-wa-a   ŋakaṯ-kurka
shoulder-carry-UNM food-XERGLOC   1-DU-XOBL-T   catch-XERGLOC:XDAT
shoulder-carry-UNM food-TrO   1-DU-COMP1[SBJ]   catch-PRES:COMP1
'We're carrying the food on our shoulders, that we're catching.'

(2) Kayardild [W1960]
Balmbu   nyingka   kurriju,   [ngaakantha   dangkantha
palmpu   ɲiŋ-ka   kuric+ku   ŋaːka-n̪ta   taŋka-n̪ta
tomorrow.XPROP   2SG-T   see-XPROP   which-XDAT   man-XDAT
tomorrow.FUT   2SG.SBJ   see-FUT   which-COMP1[SBJ] man-COMP1[SBJ]
ngijinjinaantha   wangalwujarranth.]
ŋiciɲ+kinaː-n̪ta   waŋalk-wuc-ŋara-n̪ta
1SG.XOBL-XABL-XDAT   boomerang-DON-XPST-XDAT
1SG-PST-COMP1[TrO]   boomerang-DON-PST-COMP1
'Tomorrow I will show you the man who gave me this boomerang.'

(3) Kayardild [E493.ex.12–13b]
Jinaa   bijarrb,   [ngumbaa   kurulutharranth]?
cina-a   picarpa   ŋuŋ+pa-a   kuɻuluṯ+ŋara-in̪ta

	where-T	dugong	2SG-XOBL-T	kill-XPST-XDAT
	where	dugong	2SG-COMP1	kill-PST-COMP1

'Where is the dugong which you killed?'

(4) Kayardild [E493.ex.12–13a]

	Jinaa	*bijarrb,*	[*nyingka*	*kurulutharray*]?
	cina-a	picarpa	ɲiŋ+ka	kuɻuluʈ+ŋara+ki-a
	where-T	dugong	2SG-T	kill-XPST-XERGLOC-T
	where	dugong	2SG[COMP2]	kill-PST-COMP2

'Where is the dugong which you killed?'

The correlation between PERSON and SOLIDARITY values, and the two SCCM types is summarised in Table 17.1

This chapter will be the fourth work to consider the analysis of SCCM in Kayardild. The proposal here is that SCCM is PERSON agreement, with some conditioning by SOLIDARITY. Supposing we accept this analysis, it can be noted that PERSON agreement in Kayardild is distinctly non-canonical, in the sense of Canonical Typology (Corbett 2005; Brown et al. 2013). It marks PERSON in a non-canonical location (across the whole clause, and only in complementised SCs), with a curious marker (etymological CASE) and with a non-canonical set of syncretisms that results in only a binary surface opposition (type 1 vs 2) for an underlying, four-valued distinction (1INCL, 1EXCL, 2, 3). Much of the chapter will be concerned with explaining how, just as for many *rara*, this non-canonical outcome arose out of natural historical changes. Interestingly, this is also the first occasion on which it is proposed that SCCM in Kayardild is PERSON agreement. In previous analyses, Evans (1995a, 2003) analyses SCCM as CASE agreement, where the choice between the two CASE values (corresponding to SCCM types 1 and 2) is conditioned by PERSON and SOLIDARITY, though Evans (2003) points out that it is unclear what the controller of agreement would be, or alternatively if SCCM is a matter of government, what the governor would be. Round (2013) accounts for SCCM with two inflectional features, COMPLEMENTISATION and SEJUNCT, the former associated syntactico-semantically with all complementised SCs and the latter with first exclusive, second (non-solidarity) and third person subjects. These analyses are compared towards the end of the chapter.

The chapter is arranged as follows. §17.2 sets out a framework to be used in later sections for discussing the historical emergence of non-canonical linguistic patterns through natural diachronic changes. §17.3 introduces the Tangkic language family and §17.4 its main inflectional traits. §17.5 reconstructs the historical development of SCCM. §17.6 considers the emergence of SCCM in terms of its shifting synchronic

Table 17.1 Choice of complementisation marking type in Kayardild

PERSON/SOLIDARITY	1EXCL	1INCL	2(SOL.)	2(NON-SOL.)	3
SCCM type	1	2	2	1	1

Figure 17.1 Change in causal links

systems of agreement. §17.7 reviews earlier analyses formulated in the absence of the historical backstory, and §17.8 concludes.

17.2 Non-canonical Outcomes of Natural Historical Changes

It has long been observed that unremarkable historical changes will at times give rise to synchronic rules, or patterns of alternation, that are typologically odd (Wang 1968; Bach and Harms 1972; Givón 1979; Anderson 1981, 1988). A common form that these changes take involves the loss of a mediating node in a causal chain. For example, prior to the change, an opposition between meanings A and A' is correlated with, or causes, an alternation between structures X and X', and moreover the alternation between X and X' causes a secondary alternation between structures Y and Y'. This is shown schematically in Figure 17.1a.

For instance, in the pre-Old English nominative of *fōt-* 'foot', a semantic alternation in NUMBER between SINGULAR (A) and PLURAL (A') was correlated with, or caused, an alternation in overt inflection between no suffix (X) and a suffix *-i* (X') which in turn caused a phonological alternation between a root vowel *ō* (Y) and *ø̄* (Y'). At this point, the causal link between {SG~PL} and {-Ø ~ -*i*} was one of relatively canonical inflection (Corbett 2007) and the causal link between suffixal {Ø ~ -*i*} and root vowel {*ō* ~ *ø̄*} was a matter of common vowel assimilation. Each of the causal links in Figure 17.1a is typologically unremarkable.

From this initial state, a change occurs. If that change obliterates the opposition between X and X', such as when the pre-Old English PLURAL suffix *-i* was lost, then the causally mediating node {X~X'} is removed from the network. A possible response by subsequent generations is to create a new causal link directly from {A~A'} to {Y~Y'}, as in Figure 17.1b. For Old English *fōt-* 'foot', this meant that the {SG~PL} alternation now directly caused root vowel apophony {*ō* ~ *ø̄*}. The new causal link was non-canonical: inflection was now realised in a non-canonical location (root medially) and by non-canonical means (apophony rather than affixation). A cognitive constraint upon this historical outcome is that speakers must be able to draw a new causal link from {A~A'} directly to {Y~Y'}.

Variants on the basic motif are imaginable. The initial situation may involve a more complex cause which gets simplified, as in Figure 17.2a,b; or the co-opting and establishment of a new cause (Figure 17.2c,d); or a partial mix of these (Figure 17.2e,f). In all cases, the constraining factor will be whether a new generation of speakers is able to infer a new causal network (Figure 17.2b,d,f), given only the evidence handed to it by history.

Non-canonicity can also arise through restructuring of fine-grained mapping

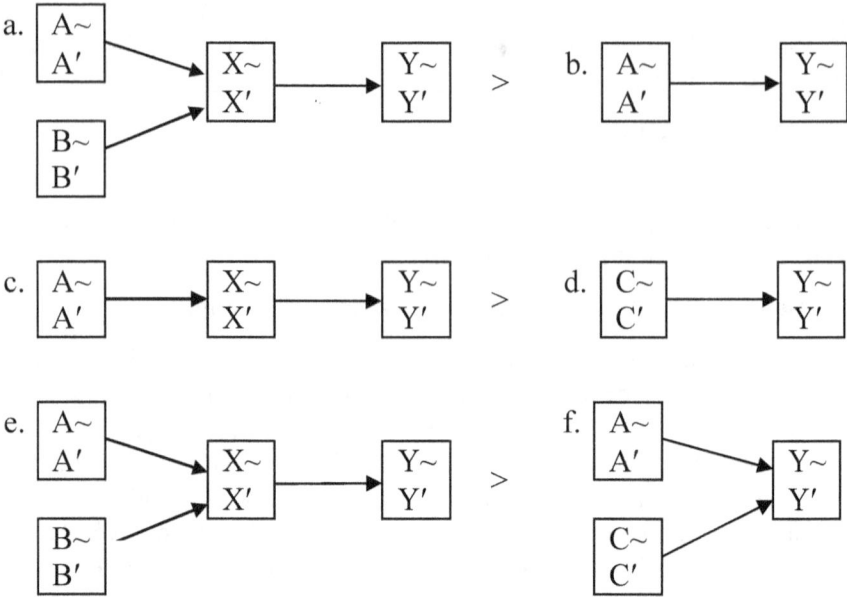

Figure 17.2 More complex changes in causal links

relationships within a single causal link. For example, suppose that prior to a change, the alternation in meaning is between four values {A~A′~A″~A‴} and the original mediating node likewise has four alternants {X~X′~X″~X‴}. The link from A values to X alternants is canonical, one-to-one. Suppose also that the secondary alternation was one of assimilation between two vowel heights, and so involved just two alternants {Y~Y′}. All of the causal links and mappings in this pre-change system are canonical. However, if the mediating node is lost and the four values {A~A′~A″~A‴} are then mapped directly onto just two alternants {Y~Y′}, the mapping now has a less canonical, many-to-one geometry.

In grammars causal links take many forms: the assignment of grammatical roles based on (i.e. caused by) semantic roles; morphological case based on grammatical roles; inflectional features of an agreement target based on features of an agreement controller; phonological exponence based on an inflectional feature structure; or the surface form of a phonological target based on its phonological environment. Important here is that first, any of these causal relationships may fill the role of 'causal link' in the schemata above, and second, that the process of historical restructuring may involve older causal links of one type being supplanted by new links of a qualitatively different type (Anderson 1992). Some types of qualitative shifts have established labels such as 'phonologisation', or 'morphologisation', but the range of conceivable types extends beyond those with established linguistic terminology.

In the following sections we will see in the prehistory of Kayardild the loss of a mediating causal node and the restructuring of the causal links in the SCCM system.

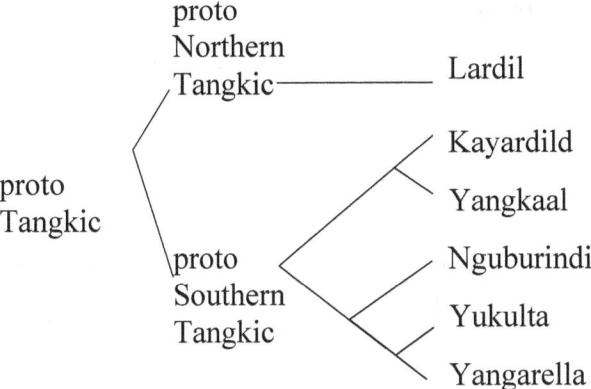

Figure 17.3 Tangkic family tree after Evans (2005)

17.3 Tangkic

The Tangkic family of languages traditionally was spoken in the southern Gulf of Carpentaria in northern Australia, on the small Wellesley Island group and the adjacent, low-lying mainland. The description in this section is based closely on Round (2017).

The customary family tree for Tangkic (Evans 2005) is in Figure 17.3. Relatively well described are Lardil (Hale 1973; Klokeid 1976; Ngakulmungan Kangka Leman 1996), Kayardild (Evans 1992, 1995a; Round 2009, 2013; Evans and Round 2017) and Yukulta (a.k.a. Gangalidda; Keen 1983; Nancarrow 2014; Round 2014). Less well studied are Yangkaal (a.k.a. Yangkaralda), for which some documentation exists (Cook 2017; Cook and Round 2017), and Yangarella and Nguburindi, for which only early colonial wordlists are available. Round (2017) is a comparative overview of Tangkic phonology, morphology and morphosyntax.

Historical relationships among the Tangkic languages are a matter of ongoing research. While the tree in Figure 17.3 is a reasonable representation of relatedness among the Tangkic languages in terms of lexicon, the history of Tangkic morphosyntax is complex. Round (2017) highlights strong resemblances between Kayardild (and Yangkaal) and Lardil in distinction from Yukulta, contradicting the relationships implied by Figure 17.3. Memmott et al. (2016) suggest, based also on phylogenetic analysis of vocabulary, that Tangkic may possess an 'Eastern' clade that resulted from a significant prehistoric contact event, resulting in a phylogenetic network as in Figure 17.4. Kayardild may well have inherited its vocabulary via the lower dashed arrow in Figure 17.4, but much of its morphosyntax via the upper dashed arrow.

Returning to the synchronic plane, as in many of Australia's languages (Nordlinger 2014), much of the syntactic structure in Tangkic sentences is reflected not in word order, but in inflectional morphology. Notably, inflectional features often take scope over a syntactic constituent such as DP, VP or even a whole clause, within which

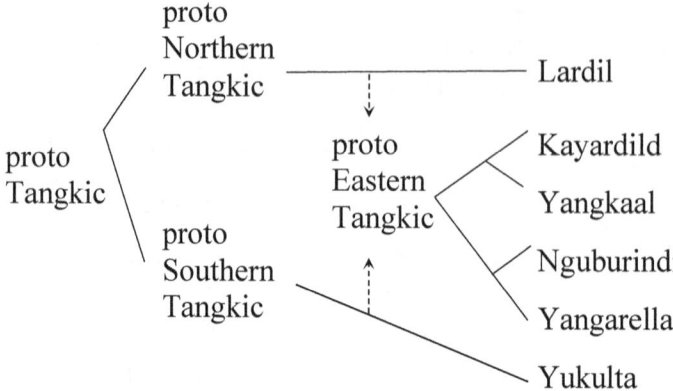

Figure 17.4 Tangkic family tree after Memmott et al. (2016)

all words inflect overtly for that feature. For example, in (5) the final two words represent one DP embedded in another.

(5) Lardil (Richards 2013: ex.3)
    Ngada   latha   karnjini   [[marunnganku]   maarnku]
    ŋata   ɻat̪-a   kaɲcin-iṉt̪a   maɻun-ŋan+kuɻu   maːɲ+kuɻu
    1SG   spear-UNM   wallaby-XDAT   boy-XGEN-XPROP   spear-XPROP
    1SG.SBJ spear-UNM   wallaby-TrO   boy-GEN-INS   spear-INS
    'I speared the wallaby with the boy's spear.'

The word *marunnganku* in the lower DP inflects for GENITIVE CASE (glossed on the lowest line as GEN). All words in the matrix DP, including *marunnganku* in the lower DP, inflect for INSTRUMENTAL CASE (glossed on the lowest line as INS). Consequently, the Tangkic languages are well known for their *Suffixaufnahme* (Evans 1995b; Richards 2013; Round 2013), the ability of a single word to accrue inflectional markings for multiple features, associated with multiple syntactic nodes that dominate it.

All Tangkic languages allow words in DPs to inflect for CASE. Core argument alignment is nominative–accusative in Lardil, Kayardild and Yangkaal. The more complex, mixed system of Yukulta is discussed in §17.4.4. A system of complementisation marking in subordinate clauses (SCs) functions to signal co-reference relationships between SCs and their main clauses (MCs). In Kayardild, SC complementisation also serves discourse functions; possible discourse functions of complementisation in other Tangkic languages are poorly understood, and in this paper I focus primarily on the syntactic use of complementisation, to signal co-reference in MCs and SCs. In all Tangkic languages, TENSE in SCs is marked not only on the verb but on the majority of non-subject DPs. In Lardil, Kayardild and Yangkaal, this is also true for TENSE in MCs (Klokeid 1976; Evans 1995a; Nordlinger and Sadler 2004; Round 2013; Round and Corbett 2017).

Tangkic word forms can be complex. Fully inflected words consist of a lexical stem followed by zero or more inflectional suffixes, and potentially end with a meaningless, monosyllabic 'termination' element (Round 2013, 2017). Because Tangkic words often contain multiple layers of inflection, it is useful to distinguish morphologically between lexical stems (prior to any inflection) and inflected stems, which themselves may serve as bases for more inflection. All Tangkic stems, whether lexical or inflected, can be classed either as thematic or as athematic. Inflectional allomorphy is often sensitive to the distinction. In (6), for example, a Yukulta SC (shown in square brackets) is inflected for PAST TENSE. The exponent of PAST TENSE is /+ŋarpa/ on the thematic stem /kurka̱t-/ but /+kinapa/ on the athematic stem /mija̱l/.

(6) Yukulta [K05-001917A]
    Gurrija=nganda   [*miyarlinaba*   *gurrgatharrba*].
    kuric-a=ŋa-nta   mija̱l+kinapa   kurka̱t+ŋarpa
    see-UNM   spear-XABL   take-XPST
    see-UNM=1SG.TRS>2SG.TRO-PST   spear-PST   take-PST
    'I saw you take the spear.'

The inflectional systems of Tangkic languages are striking for their use and re-use of the same suffixal forms, and sets of form alternants, for multiple functions. Round (2011, 2013, 2015, 2016) argues, based on Kayardild, that this systematic tethering of sets of forms to entire sets of functions is 'morphomic' in the sense of Aronoff (1994).[2] For expository purposes here, it will be useful to refer to what Hartwig (2014) has called 'comparative morphomic categories' in Tangkic. Each category comprises a set of forms. Those sets can be identified as cognate across the Tangkic family, and each set will have some number of functions in each modern language. Following Hartwig, I assign these form-set categories a label beginning with x, for example XDAT for the set of forms in Table 17.2.

Comparative morphomic categories have multiple forms and multiple functions in each language, so it is impossible for labels like 'XDAT' to convey an exhaustive characterisation of the categories' functions. Nevertheless, a basic mnemonic system is used, so that, for example, 'XDAT' is the label for the form-set, one of whose functions in proto Tangkic was to mark DATIVE CASE. Similarly, 'XERGLOC' labels the form-set, one of whose functions in proto Tangkic was to mark the homophonous ERGATIVE and LOCATIVE CASE. Even in proto Tangkic, though, the form-sets would have had multiple functions, often including the marking of CASE, SC TENSE and SC

Table 17.2 Sets of forms and functions of the comparative category XDAT

		Underlying allomorph, after		
	Inflectional functions	C	Front V	Back V
Lardil	ACC case, COMP	-in̪ta	-in̪ta	-in̪ta
Kayardild	OBL case, several tenses, COMP	-iɲca	-ɲca	-n̪ta
Yukulta	DAT case, COMP	-iɲca	-ɲca	-n̪ta

complementisation. Comparative morphomic categories appear in the third line of example sentence glosses.

17.4 Clausal Morphosyntax in Tangkic

17.4.1 Overview

The aim of §17.4 is to acquaint the readers with the major aspects of inflectional morphology in Tangkic main and subordinate, declarative clauses (see Round 2017 for a more comprehensive overview). The focus is on aspects of inflection which will be instrumental for reconstructing the history of subordinate clause complementisation marking, SCCM. Though there are many details to introduce here, I place special emphasis on those facts that are most relevant to the historical reconstruction; they are the main points to absorb from each subsection.

Any successful analysis of Tangkic clauses needs to distinguish carefully between CASE categories (such as ERGATIVE), versus the marking of such categories (such as by XERGLOC), versus the more underlying grammatical roles which map onto such categories (such as the 'transitive subject' role). In the analyses presented below, I assume that semantic predicates have semantic arguments, such as the more actor-like and less actor-like arguments of the two-place predicate 'hit'. These semantic arguments map onto certain grammatical roles. In Yukulta, a key distinction is between the Transitive Subject role, abbreviated and glossed as TRS; the Transitive Object role (TRO); and the Non-transitive Subject role (NTRS). Lardil and Kayardild typically treat TRS and NTRS equivalently, as a unitary Subject role SBJ. In addition, goal-like and recipient-like arguments of three-place predicates typically map to a grammatical Goal role (GOAL). Grammatical roles are posited because they interact with morphology and syntax in distinctive ways. The mapping from grammatical roles to morphological CASE categories can be affected by clause-level factors such as mood and polarity, and DP-level factors such as the distinction between pronominals and full nominal DPs. To facilitate comparison between the individual languages, the terminology I use is comparative. I will refer to the grammatical roles just introduced, and the comparative morphomic categories such as XDAT, rather than referring to the various language-specific labels that have been employed in the literature on individual languages.

The remainder of §17.4 provides a gradual introduction to the morphosyntax of the language family. §17.4.2 begins with the shared core of subordinate clause morphosyntax; §17.4.3 moves to the etymologically related main clauses of Lardil and Kayardild; §17.4.4 shifts to the historically more conservative and more complex main clauses of Yukulta.

17.4.2 Subordinate Clauses with No SCCM

Subordinate clauses (SCs) are similar across the Tangkic language family. All languages distinguish complementised SCs, with SCCM, from uncomplementised SCs, without SCCM. We return to complementised SCs in §17.5.

In all Tangkic SCs, including those without SCCM, subjects are morphologically unmarked for CASE (if pronominal, they are selected from the basic-stem series of pronouns) and objects are inflected not for CASE but for TENSE. The three main TENSE categories, typically interpreted relative to the tense of the main clause (MC), are SIMULTANEOUS, PAST and FUTURE.³ Subordinate SIMULTANEOUS TENSE is marked by XLOC; FUTURE by XPROP; and PAST by XPST in Lardil, or in Yukulta and Kayardild by XPST on thematic stems and XABL on athematics. Examples below illustrate the SIMULTANEOUS in Yukulta (7), PAST in Lardil (8) (see also (6), above, in Yukulta) and the FUTURE in Kayardild (9).⁴

(7) Yukulta [K5-001918A]
Ngada=nganbungarri,   gurri   [gamburiji.]
ŋat̪-ta=ŋanpuŋa-ri   kuri   kampuɻic+ki
1SG-T   watch   talk-XLOC
1SG[TRS]=1SG.TRS>3PL.TRO-TR.PRES watch[UNM] talk-SIMUL
'I'm watching them talking.'

(8) Lardil (Klokeid 1976: 142)
Mangarda   yuurr-denja   [wangalkarr   wungitharr.]
maŋ-ka=taŋka   jur-t̪æɲcac   waɲalk+ŋarpa   wuɲic+ŋarpa
{child-T=person} PRF-run   boomerang-XPST   steal-XPST
{child}[SBJ]   PRF-run[UNM]   boomerang-PST[TRO] steal-PST
'The child who stole a boomerang has run off.'

(9) Kayardild (Evans 1995: 523)
Nyingka karrngija, [marndiinangku,]
ɲiŋ-ka karŋic-a   manti<i>c-ŋaŋ+ku:
2SG-T   hold-UNM   deprive<PASS>-XNEG-XPROP
2SG.SBJ hold-IMP   deprive-PASS-NEG-FUT
'You look after (your country), so you won't be robbed of it.'

17.4.3 Main Clauses in Lardil and Kayardild

Lardil and Kayardild also have TENSE-marked objects in MCs. Evans (1995) argues that these TENSE-marked MCs emerged historically through the grammaticalisation of erstwhile uncomplementised SCs (§17.4.2), which increasingly took on 'insubordinated' MC functions. MCs inflected for FUTURE and PAST TENSE are shown in (10) and (11).

(10) Lardil (Hale 1996: 23)
Ngada   werethu   wangalku.
ŋata   wæɻæc+kuɻu   waɲalk+kuɻu
1SG   throw-XPROP   boomerang-XPROP
1SG.SBJ throw-FUT   boomerang-FUT[TRO]
'I will throw the boomerang.'

(11) Kayardild (Wurm 1960)
    Bilda   kabatharra   wurankina   kuruna?
    pi-l-ta   kapaṯ+ŋara   wuɻan+kina   kuɻu+kina
    3-PL-T   find-XPST   food-XABL   egg-XABL
    3-PL.SBJ   find-PST   food-PST[TRO]   egg-PST[TRO]
    'Have they found any eggs?'

Historically speaking, the FUTURE and PAST TENSE MCs of Lardil and Kayardild are direct inflectional continuations of old SCs. The same cannot be said of PRESENT TENSE MCs. In Lardil, PRESENT TENSE[5] MCs have objects inflected with XDAT, and verbs with an 'unmarked' suffix as in (12).

(12) Lardil [NKL 1996: 212]
    Diin   ngawa   betha=ku   ngithan   thakin   jayin.
    ṯi:n   ŋawu   bæc-a =kun   ŋiṯa-inṯa   ṯak-inṯa   ca-inṯa
    this   dog   bite-UNM =ACT   {1SG.XOBL}-XDAT   left-XDAT   foot-XDAT
    this[SBJ]   dog[SBJ]   bite-UNM =ACT   {1SG}-TRO   left-TRO   foot-TRO
    'This dog bit my left foot.'

As we will see in §17.4.4 next, this set of inflections (XDAT on objects, and 'unmarked' verbs) is the last remaining hold-over in Lardil of a much older MC inflectional system, one which remains intact in its more conservative cousin, Yukulta.

PRESENT TENSE MCs in Kayardild are mixed. Objects are inflected with XERGLOC, cognate with SC SIMULTANEOUS TENSE marking in Yukulta. Curiously enough, though, Kayardild's PRESENT TENSE verbs, like those in Lardil, are 'unmarked', as in (13).[6]

(13) Kayardild [W1960]
    Dathina   dangkaa   makuya   thardaya   buruth.
    ṯaṯina   ṯaŋka-a   maku+ki-a   ṯaṯa+ki-a   puɻuṯ-a
    that   man-T   woman-XLOC-T   shoulder-XLOC-T   grab-UNM
    that[SBJ]   man[SBJ]   woman-PRS[TRO]   shoulder-PRS[TRO]   grab-UNM
    'That man is grabbing the woman by the shoulder.'

At this stage our picture of Tangkic morphosyntax is already accruing a number of idiosyncrasies. The primary point to take away from §17.4.2 and §17.4.3 is that all Tangkic SCs have objects inflected for TENSE; Lardil and Kayardild now also use these inflectional patterns in MCs, at least in the non-present tenses.

17.4.4 Main Clauses in Yukulta

MCs in Yukulta are quite different to those of Lardil and Kayardild. TENSE is not marked on objects, and not even on verbs, but on a second-position clitic; and a major division separates transitive MCs (TRMCs) from 'non-transitives' (NTRMCs). The NTRMCs in turn can be divided into 'regular' NTRMCs and 'inverse' NTRMCs. For expository reasons, it is simplest to begin with the regular NTRMCs. As it happens, these are the etymological source of Lardil's PRESENT TENSE marking (with XDAT on objects and unmarked verbs) which we saw in §17.4.3.

Yukulta's regular 'non-transitive' MCs (Round 2014) include monovalent intransitives as well as bivalent MCs under specific, classically low-transitivity semantic conditions (Hopper and Thompson 1980): in irrealis mood, in the context of certain negative verbal inflections, as a strategy for formulating polite desideratives, and in clauses whose verbal predicate is drawn from the small class meaning 'wait for', 'fear', 'talk to', 'be sorry for' and 'dream or think of' (Keen 1983).

Subjects of NtrMCs have a NtrS grammatical role. NtrS full DPs have no overt CASE inflection (and pronouns take the basic-stem form). Example (14) shows an apposed, basic-stem pronoun *ngagulda* and full DP *burldamurra* in the NtrS role.

(14) Yukulta [K3-001789B]
Ngagulda=gula   *burldamurra* *warraja.*
ŋa-ku-l-ta=kul-a   puḻṭamur-a   warac-a
1-INCL-PL-T   three-T   go-UNM
1-INCL-PL[NtrS]=1INCL.PL.TrS-PRS.NTR three[NtrS] go-UNM
'We three can go.'

Objects of regular NtrMCs are in the GOAL grammatical role, and are assigned DATIVE CASE, marked by XDAT on full DPs and by a dative series of pronouns. In (15) non-transitivity is due to the presence of the lexical predicate *bulwij-* 'fear', and in (16) is triggered by negative inflection on the verb. The non-transitive status of Yukulta's NtrMCs is also marked on the second-position clitic.

(15) Yukulta [K3-001789B]
Bulwija=rnala   *gunawuna*   *dathininja.*
pulwic-a=ŋa-l-a   kunawuna   ṯaṯin-iɲca
fear-UNM   child   that-XDAT
fear-UNM=3SG.GOAL-3PL.NtrS-PRS.NTR   child[NtrS] that-GOAL
'The children are scared of that (man).'

(16) Yukulta [K5-001917B]
Warlirra=ngga   *dalmatharri*   *ngijinja.*
waḻira=ŋka   ṯalmaṯ+wari   ɲic-iɲca
NEG   chop-XPRIV   wood-XDAT
NEG=3SG.NtrS.PRES[3SG.GOAL] chop-NEG   wood-GOAL
'He's not chopping wood.'

In addition to its 'regular' NtrSCs, Yukulta has a second kind of non-transitive MC, whose use is required in bivalent clauses with 'inverse' combinations of subject and object PERSON values. The general triggering condition for inverse NtrSCs is that the object is higher than the subject on Yukulta's person hierarchy 1 > 2 > 3. Inverse objects are assigned an Inverse Object (InvO) grammatical role, and because of the way the inverse is triggered, an inverse object will necessarily be either FIRST or SECOND PERSON.

Cross-linguistic evidence shows that inverse systems are often partly idiosyncratic

(Jacques and Antonov 2014; Gildea and Zúñiga 2016; Witzlack-Makarevich et al. 2016), and Yukulta is no exception. In Yukulta, SECOND PERSON subjects acting specifically upon FIRST PERSON *singular* objects do not trigger the inverse.

In terms of inflectional marking, subjects in inverse NTRMCs appear as in any other NTRMC, while the marking of objects is what makes the inverse inflectionally distinctive. Inverse objects are realised morphologically by a pronominal stem inflected with the XERGLOC marker. Any apposed, full-DP objects are also marked with XERGLOC, as in (17), where the inverse object is 'us three'. Like other NTRMCs, inverse NTRMCs are marked as non-transitive in the second-position clitic.

(17)   Yukulta [K9-001841B]
       Jinkaja=guluwaninggi   ngaguluwanji   burldamurri.
       cinkac-a=kuluwa-ni-ŋki   ŋa-ku-lu+paɲ+ki   puʈamur+ki
       follow-UNM   1-INCL-PL-XOBL-XERGLOC three-XERGLOC
       follow-UNM=CLITIC   1-INCL-PL-OBL-InvO   three-InvO
       (CLITIC: 1INCL.PL.GOAL-3S.NTRS-FUT.NTR)
       'He will follow us three.'

Overall then, the inverse is distinguished by the marking of MC objects with XERGLOC instead of the usual NTRMC object marker, XDAT, and it is largely triggered by PERSON values (with only a minor role for NUMBER due to the second-on-first-singular idiosyncrasy). In sections below, the inverse system in MCs will turn out to play a crucial role in reconstructing the history of SCCM in SCs, so it is worthwhile making a mental note that it involves objects being marked by XERGLOC instead of XDAT, and is largely triggered by PERSON values.

Finally for this section, Yukulta also has transitive MCs. TRMCs are characterised by a typologically unremarkable, split-ergative system (Silverstein 1976; Dixon 1979; Goddard 1982). Full DPs are marked by XERGLOC in the TRS role, and in the TRO role they have no overt inflectional marking. Pronouns in both roles are realised by just one, basic-stem form. Example (18) shows an apposed, basic-stem pronoun *gilda* and full DP *burldamurri* in the TRS role. In the TRO role, (19) contains a full DP and (19) a basic-stem pronoun.

(18)   Yukulta [K5-001917B]
       Gilda   burldamurri=wurrgarri   marrija   dathinkiyarrngga?
       ki-l-ta   puʈamur+ki=wur-kari   maric-a   ʈaʈin+kijarŋ-ka
       3-PL-T   three-XLOC   listen-UNM   that-DU-T
       3-PL[TRS]   three-TRS=CLITIC   listen-UNM   that-DU[TRO]
       (CLITIC: 2PL.TRS>3NONSG.TRO-PRS.TR)
       'Are you three listening to them two?'

(19)   Yukulta [K6-001701A]
       Gurrija=ngarrngugarri   girra.
       kuric-a=ŋa-rŋu-kari   ki-r-a
       watch-UNM   2-DU-T

watch-UNM=1SG.TrS-2DU.TrO-PRS.TR 2-DU[TrO]
'I'm looking at you two'

A summary of core argument marking in Yukulta, for TrMCs and NtrMCs, is given in Table 17.3, where 'XDAT' indicates XDAT marking on full DPs and use of the dative form of pronouns, 'Ø' indicates absence of overt marking on full DPs, and for pronouns the use of the basic-stem form.

17.5 SCCM and Its Evolution

17.5.1 SCCM in Australian Languages

In §17.5 we turn to SCCM as we find it in the modern Tangkic languages and as it evolved from an earlier state. It will be useful first to set the broader typological scene.

In Australian languages, it is not uncommon for SCs to be CASE-marked, a function of CASE which Dench and Evans (1988) have referred to as 'complementizing CASE'. In some languages, complementising CASE may be marked on every word of the SC. One common use of complementising CASE marking is to signal which one, of several possible MC arguments, is co-referential with some argument in the SC; the SC then agrees in CASE with that MC argument. For example, in (20) from the Panyjima language of Western Australia, the SC subject is co-referential with the MC object; the MC object has accusative CASE, which the entire SC then agrees with.

(20) Panyjima (Dench and Evans 1988: 28–9)
Ngatha   wiya-rna   ngunha-yu   marlpa-yu
1SG.NOM   see-PST   that-ACC   man-ACC
paka-lalha-ku   nharniwali-ku   warrungkamu-la-ku.
come-PERF-ACC   here.ALL-ACC   morning-LOC-ACC
'I saw that man who came this way this morning.'

SCCM in the modern Tangkic languages is never entirely like complementising CASE agreement in this sense, though it bears some striking similarities.

17.5.2 SCCM in Yukulta

In Yukulta, SCCM signals co-reference relationships between a SC subject and certain MC arguments. We saw in §17.4.4 that the marking of MC arguments in Yukulta is sensitive to MC transitivity. SCCM in Yukulta is also sensitive to transitivity in the

Table 17.3 Case marking of core arguments in (non-)transitive clauses

Clause type	Subject marking	Object marking
TrMC	XERGLOC (full DP) ~ Ø (pro)	Ø
NtrMC (regular)	Ø	XDAT
NtrMC (inverse)	Ø	XERGLOC

matrix MC. When the matrix MC is transitive, overt SCCM is used when there is co-reference between the SC subject and the MC subject; the SCCM marker is XERGLOC, and it appears on every word of the SC. An example is shown in (21).

(21) Yukulta [K5-1918A]
Dangkaya=ganda balatha jardabu,
ṯaŋka+ki-a=kanta palaṯ-a caṯapu
person-XERGLOC-T kill-UNM emu
person-ERG[TrS]=TR.PST[3SGS>3SGO] kill-UNM emu[TrO]
[wurlankinabaya diyajarrbaya.]
wulan+kinapa+ki-a ṯiac+kinapa+ki-a
food-XABL-XERGLOC-T eat-XPST-XERGLOC-T
food-PST-COMP[TrO] eat-PST-COMP
'The man_i killed the emu after he_i'd eaten the food'.

When the matrix MC is non-transitive, overt SCCM is used when there is co-reference between the SC subject and the MC object.[7] The SCCM marker now is XDAT, which appears on every word of the SC. An example is in (22).

(22) Yukulta [K5-1917A]
Lardija=ngga dathina maku
laṯic-a=ŋka ṯaṯin-a maku
wait_for-UNM that-T woman
wait_for-UNM=3SG.NTRS.PRES[3SG.GOAL] that[NTRS] woman[NTRS]
dathininja dangkantha, [warrajurluntha.]
ṯaṯin-iṇca ṯaŋka-ṉta warac+kuḻu-ṉta
that-XDAT man-XDAT go-XPROP-XDAT
that-GOAL man-GOAL go-FUT-COMP
'That woman is waiting for the man_i to Ø_i leave.'

Figure 17.5 shows these facts schematically, indicating the markers that appear on subjects and objects in both the MC and SC, as well as the SCCM marker on the subordinate clause. The co-reference conditions which require the use of SCCM are indicated by a double-headed arrow. (To avoid unnecessary complexity, the MC CASE markers shown are for full NP arguments only; as discussed in §17.4.4, TrMC subject pronouns differ.)

In complex sentences with TrMCs, the co-referential MC subject argument is inflected with XERGLOC and the same marker used for SCCM. Similarly, for NTRMCs the co-referential MC object argument is inflected with XDAT, which is the same marker used for SCCM, all of which leads SCCM to look rather like complemen-tising CASE agreement. However, notwithstanding the broad-brush appearance, a CASE-agreement analysis would not work entirely for the facts of Yukulta. SCCM employs XERGLOC and XDAT markers, even when the MC co-referent is a pronoun which is marked otherwise; and SCCM is blind to the distinction in NTRMCs between inverse and non-inverse objects. For example, in (23) co-reference is between the SC

RARA AND THEORY TESTING IN TYPOLOGY | 429

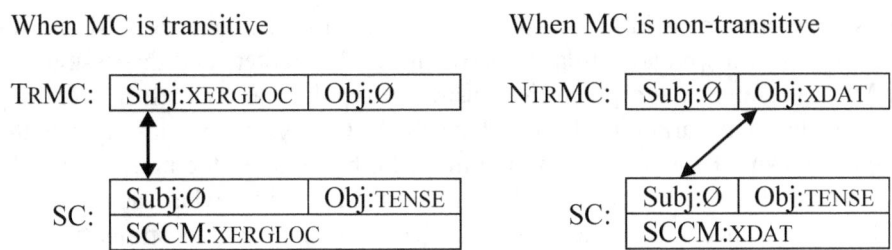

Figure 17.5 SCCM and associated co-reference in complex sentences (Yukulta)

subject and a NTRMC inverse object. Although the inverse object is now marked with XERGLOC, the SCCM marker is still XDAT, just as in (22) where co-reference was with a regular, XDAT-marked NTRMC object.

(23) Yukulta [K3-1790B]
  Warlirra=ngarrawa-nyi-nggi   ngarrawanji
  waḷira=ŋarawa-ɲi-ŋki   ŋa-ra-waɲ+ki
  NEG   1EXCL-DU-XOBL-XERGLOC
  NEG=1EXCL.DU.GOAL-2SG.NTRS-PST.IRR   1EXCL-DU-OBL-InvO
  gurri,   [ngaagawatharrbantha wirdijarrbantha.]
  kuri   ŋa:kawat̪+ŋarpa-ṉta   wit̪ic+ŋarpa-ṉta
  see   do_what-XPST-XDAT   stay-XPST-XDAT
  see[UMN]   do_what-PST-COMP   stay-PST-COMP
  'You haven't seen what we've been doing.' (lit. 'You haven't seen us, Ø,
  what-doing.')

To emphasise the point, Figure 17.6 shows the marking and co-reference relationships in complex sentences whose MC is non-transitive, for both regular and inverse NTRMCs.

Given these facts, a reasonable analysis of SCCM in Yukulta is that it hinges not upon the inflectional CASE category of the MC co-referent – it is not simple complementising CASE agreement – but on the co-referent's grammatical role: co-reference with a TRMC argument in the TRS role triggers XERGLOC SCCM, while co-reference

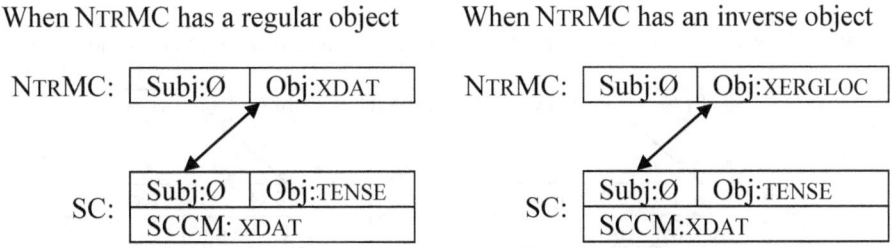

Figure 17.6 SCCM and associated co-reference in complex sentences with non-transitive main clauses (Yukulta)

with a NTRMC argument in the GOAL or INVO roles triggers XDAT SCCM. By the same token, given the broad similarity between SCCM markers and the CASE marking of MC co-referents, and given the Australian typological context, it is entirely conceivable that at an earlier diachronic stage, the SCCM system was a simple matter of complementising CASE agreement, and hinged directly upon the main-clause co-referents' CASE. In fact, let us now take a detour and consider what such a system would be like: a conceivable historical antecedent to Yukulta, with a straightforward complementising CASE agreement system. The focus will be on how this would operate in complex clauses with non-transitive MCs.

17.5.3 SCCM in a Plausible Ancestral State

If SCCM operated as simple complementising CASE agreement, at least in sentences with NTRMCs, then the diagram of marking and co-reference relationships for those sentences would appear as in Figure 17.7, i.e. in sentences with NTRMCs, SCCM would be marked under some circumstances by XDAT, and under other circumstances by XERGLOC. The assumption will be that the triggers of the inverse are the same here as in Yukulta (§17.4.4). Let us examine more carefully, then, what these 'some' and 'other' circumstances are, that govern the XDAT~XERGLOC SCCM alternation.

In what follows I will step through a chain of reasoning, to bring to the fore an interesting and rather non-obvious curiosity of this system, namely that the contrast between XDAT and XERGLOC SCCM is largely, though not entirely, predictable from the PERSON values of the subject of the *subordinate* clause. It will be worth the reader's while to double check each step in the logical chain, to be satisfied that it is valid. The end-point in the chain is an association between SC subject PERSON and SCCM which turns out to be very similar to what we find in modern Kayardild.

To begin the chain of reasoning: in Figure 17.7 we see that the use of XDAT vs XERGLOC SCCM is triggered by the contrast that exists between regular and inverse NTRMCs. Accordingly, one could equally say that the factors that directly trigger the regular/inverse contrast now also indirectly trigger the SCCM contrast. The factors triggering the regular/inverse contrast are predominantly the PERSON values of the MC subject and MC object, with a minor role for object NUMBER (due to the second-on-first-singular idiosyncrasy). Therefore, we can also say that the SCCM contrast

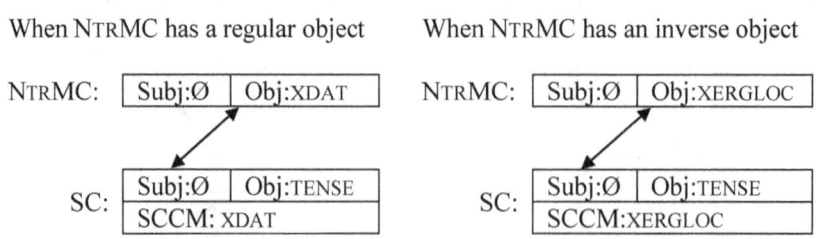

Figure 17.7 Marking and co-reference in complex sentences with non-transitive main clauses

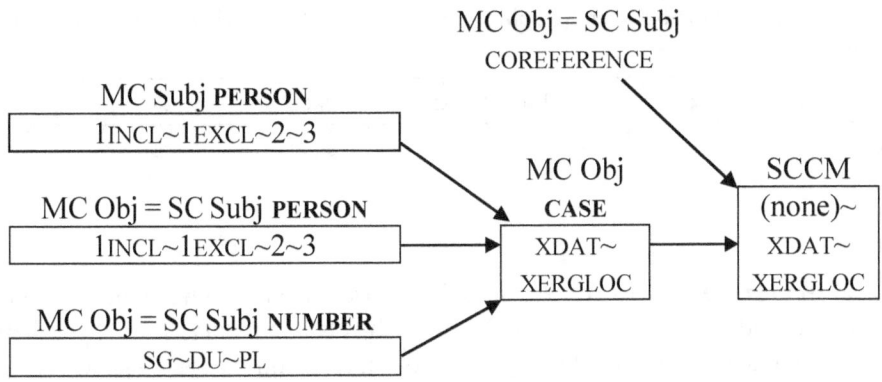

Figure 17.8 Causal links governing SCCM (hypothesised ancestor of Yukulta)

is ultimately triggered by MC subject PERSON and MC object PERSON and NUMBER values. Next, however, consider that SCCM in these sentences is used when there is co-reference between the MC object and the SC subject, in which case the PERSON and NUMBER values of the MC object and the SC subject will be identical to one another. Consequently, we could equally say – as odd as it might seem to do so – that the SCCM contrast is ultimately triggered by MC subject PERSON and *SC subject* PERSON and NUMBER.

This network of relationships can be set out in the manner of §17.2, as in Figure 17.8, where arrows show causal relationships and boxes contain sets of values that various parameters (or features) can take.

Figure 17.8 shows SCCM being ultimately determined by several factors. Working from the top, the question of whether the MC object and SC subject are co-referential determines whether there is any SCCM marker at all; then, all other factors 'flow through' the mediating causal node of MC object CASE. Those other factors are MC subject PERSON, and the PERSON and NUMBER values of the co-referential MC object/SC subject.

The next question I wish to examine is this: assuming that the MC object and SC subject are co-referential, how much can we predict about SCCM from SC subject properties alone? To begin answering this, Table 17.4 shows the combinations of

Table 17.4 Marking of objects in Yukulta non-transitive main clauses, according to subject and object properties; also, choice of SCCM marker according to the same factors in the hypothesised ancestor of Yukulta

		MC Object (= SC Subject)				
		1SG	1NONSG.EXCL	1INCL	2	3
MC Subject	1	<reflexive, or very rare in discourse>			XDAT	XDAT
	2	XDAT	XERGLOC	XERGLOC	<reflexive>	XDAT
	3	XERGLOC	XERGLOC	XERGLOC	XERGLOC	XDAT

Table 17.5 Correlation between SC subject properties and SCCM (hypothetical ancestor of Yukulta)

SC subject:	1SG	1NONSG.EXCL	1INCL	2	3
SCCM	XDAT~ XERGLOC	XERGLOC	XERGLOC	XDAT~ XERGLOC	XDAT

MC subject PERSON and MC object/SC subject PERSON and NUMBER which trigger the use of XDAT and XERGLOC marking on NTRMC objects in Yukulta. In our hypothetical ancestral language with complementising CASE agreement, these are also the triggers for the two SCCM markers.

Now, how much can be predicted purely from the SC subject? If the SC subject is THIRD PERSON, then the SCCM marker is entirely predictable; it is XDAT, irrespective of the MC subject (this is gleaned from Table 17.4 by looking vertically, down the rightmost column, corresponding to THIRD PERSON SC subject). Likewise, if the SC subject is FIRST PERSON INCLUSIVE, then the SCCM marker is entirely predictable; it is XERGLOC, irrespective of the MC subject. Continuing further, when the SC subject is FIRST PERSON SINGULAR, then the SCCM marker can be either XDAT or XERGLOC. When it is FIRST PERSON EXCLUSIVE NON-SINGULAR, then the SCCM is always XERGLOC, and when it is SECOND PERSON, then the SCCM marker can be either XDAT or XERGLOC. The correlations are summarised in Table 17.5.

Putting this together, first of all, Figure 17.8 highlighted the fact that this is a system where, if the SC subject and MC object are co-referential, then SCCM is ultimately predictable from MC subject PERSON and the MC object/SC subject PERSON and NUMBER. MC object CASE plays a mediating role in the causal network. Second, we established just above, that even if we ignore information about the MC subject, it is still possible to predict rather a lot about SCCM just from the properties of the SC subject. Keeping this in mind, in the next section we will examine the SCCM system of Kayardild. Kayardild lacks a MC inverse alternation. Consider, then, what would happen if we took the hypothetical system we have been discussing in this section and removed the MC inverse system. The initial effect on the causal network would be to remove the mediating node at its centre, leaving Figure 17.9.

Figure 17.9 represents something like what history would hand to learners of a language which previously had been as in Figure 17.8 but had just lost its main clause inverse system. We can note several things. First, the use vs non-use of SCCM is still transparently related to co-reference between SC subject and MC object: it is used only when they are co-referential. This would be a correlation that learners would apprehend with ease. Second, we established above that a large amount of the variation between the use of XDAT and XERGLOC as the SCCM marker is correlated with properties of the SC subject. It is highly likely that learners would also apprehend these correlations, between SC subject properties and SCCM marking, since they are all properties of the SC. The next question is,

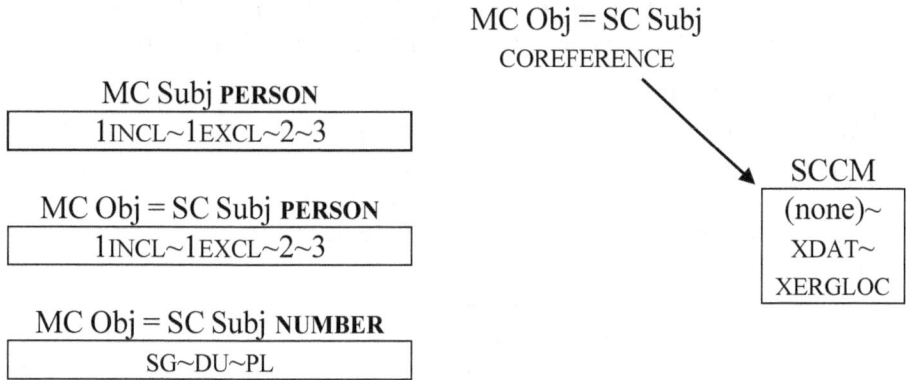

Figure 17.9 Causal network of Figure 17.8, but with the mediating node removed

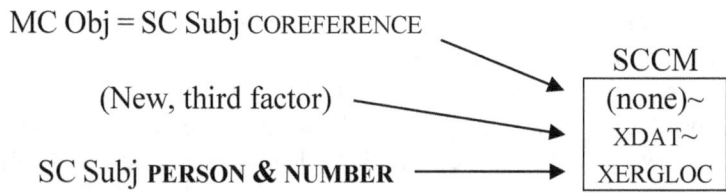

Figure 17.10 Causal network of Figure 17.9, relinked and simplified

would learners also detect the complex causal link between MC subject properties and SCCM? Perhaps so, but even if that link were acquired, it would come under strong pressure to be simplified, and either be eliminated from the system, or replaced by something else, by some third factor. Supposing it were replaced by a third factor, what remains is Figure 17.10.

Let us now turn to Kayardild.

17.5.4 SCCM in Kayardild

In Kayardild, there are two SCCM markers, XDAT and XERGLOC (cf. examples in §17.1). The use vs non-use of SCCM is related to co-reference between arguments in the SC and MC. The choice between XDAT and XERGLOC as the SCCM marker is primarily determined by SC subject PERSON, though there is a third factor, namely SOLIDARITY: whether 'the speaker wants to group him/herself with the addressee'. That is, Kayardild conforms very closely to what we predicted, just above, would result if a language with a Yukulta-like MC inverse system and complementising CASE agreement were to lose its MC inverse system. Kayardild, as mentioned earlier, lacks a MC inverse system.

There are some differences between Kayardild and the exact system we considered at the end of §17.5.3. First, Kayardild's SCCM is triggered by co-reference not only between SC subject and MC object, but between any combination of SC and MC subject and object other than subject–subject (Evans 1995a: 489–90).[8] For example, (24) shows the use of SCCM due to co-reference between SC and MC objects.

(24) Kayardild [W1960]
Nyingka   kurrijarr   ngijinjina   banganaa,
ɲiŋ-ka   kuric-ŋara   ŋiciɲ+kina: paŋa+kina:
2SG-T   see-XPST   1SG.XOBL-XABL   turtle-XABL
2SG.SBJ   see-PST   1SG.POSS-PST[TRO]   turtle-PST[TRO]
[ngijuwa   warijarrmatharranth?]
ŋicu-wa   waṭicarmaṯ-ŋara-ṉta
1SG.XOBL-T   bring_ashore-XPST-XDAT
1SG.COMP1[SBJ]   bring_ashore-PST-COMP1[9]
'Did you see my turtle$_i$, that I caught Ø$_i$?'

Second, the match between SC subject properties and the use of XDAT vs XERGLOC is not precisely the same as in §17.5.3, although most idiosyncrasies do match exactly: the only differences are in the FIRST EXCLUSIVE. In Kayardild, when the SC subject is FIRST PERSON SINGULAR, then the SCCM marker is XDAT only. In Table 17.4, it was XDAT or XERGLOC. And in Kayardild, when the SC subject is FIRST PERSON EXCLUSIVE NON-SINGULAR, then the SCCM is always XDAT; in Table 17.4, it is XERGLOC.

My conclusion from this is as follows. It is very likely that Yukulta and Kayardild share a common ancestor which had a MC inverse system and complementising CASE agreement. On the Yukulta branch of the family tree, complementising CASE agreement was restructured, resulting (in complex sentences with a NTRMC) in the loss of the earlier alternation between XDAT and XERGLOC SCCM and retention of the regular (non-inverse) XDAT alternant, which would have been more common in discourse. The inherited MC inverse system was retained, though. On the Kayardild branch of the tree, the MC inverse system was lost, and the SCCM causal network restructured. The restructuring involved the co-opting of SOLIDARITY to predict a residual, inherited alternation between XDAT and XERGLOC SCCM in SCs with SECOND PERSON subjects. In addition, the SCCM marker for all FIRST EXCLUSIVE SC subjects was regularised to just one form, XDAT. This may have occurred through a generalisation of the XDAT marker, which was already associated with FIRST SINGULAR, the most frequent FIRST EXCLUSIVE category in discourse. The causal network for modern Kayardild is shown in Figure 17.11.

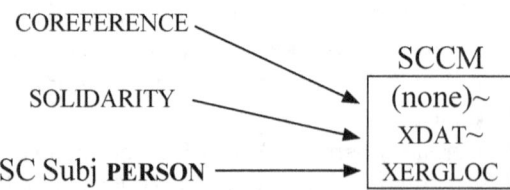

Figure 17.11 Causal network of SCCM in Kayardild

There is one outstanding question. In Yukulta, there is one kind of SCCM marking used in sentences with TRMCs, and another kind used in sentences with NTRMCs. Since §17.5.3, the discussion has only been about the latter, in terms of which we can account neatly for the modern Kayardild system. But why does Kayardild SCCM relate only to Yukulta's NTRMCs system, and not its TRMC system? Is there any evidence, other than in its SCCM XDAT~XERGLOC alternation, that pre-Kayardild lost the system of SCCM associated with TRMCs? The answer is yes, and there is both language-internal and comparative evidence.

The comparative evidence will come from Lardil, which we consider next. The language-internal evidence relates to co-reference. In Yukulta sentences with TRMCs, SCCM is triggered by co-reference between the subjects of the SC and MC. If pre-Kayardild retained some vestige of this system, we might expect it to continue this criterion of subject–subject co-reference. However, as mentioned earlier in this section, that is the one condition under which SCCM is *not* triggered in Kayardild. Thus, in Kayardild, the idiosyncrasies of the SCCM XDAT~XERGLOC alternation, and the criteria on co-reference point in the same direction, suggesting that pre-Kayardild entirely lost the equivalent of Yukulta's SCCM system associated with TRMCs.

In this section I have argued that Kayardild is one short historical step away from an ancestral language which possessed a MC inverse system and complementising CASE agreement – a language which is also one short historical step away from Yukulta, and which I reconstruct as ancestral to both.

17.5.5 SCCM in Lardil

In Lardil, there is just one SCCM marker, XDAT. Its use is triggered by co-reference between SC subject and MC object as in (25) or, in subordinate topicalised-object constructions (Klokeid 1976; Round 2017), between SC topicalised-object and MC object, as in (26).

(25) Lardil (Klokeid 1976: 461)

Ngada	rathur	kiinkur	ngawur,
ŋata	ɻac+kuɻu	ki:n+kuɻu	ŋawu+kuɻu
1SG	spear-XPROP	that-XPROP	dog-XPROP
1SG.SBJ	spear-FUT	that-FUT[TRO]	dog-FUT[TRO]

[*ngithunarrba betharrbanu.*]

ŋiṯun+ŋarpa-iṉṯa	peṯ+ŋarpa-iṉṯa=u
1SG-XPST-XDAT	bite-XPST-XDAT=ACT
1SG-PST-COMP[TRO]	bite-PST-COMP=ACT

'I'm going to spear the dog$_i$, which Ø$_i$ bit me.'

(26) Lardil (Klokeid 1976: 385)

Ngada	warnawuthur	kiinkur	wurdaljiwur
ŋata	waṉawuc+kuɻu	ki:n+kuɻu	wuṯalci+kuɻu
1SG	cook-XPROP	that-XPROP	meat-XPROP
1SG.SBJ	cook-FUT	that-FUT[TRO]	meat-FUT[TRO]

[*ngimbenin   wirimatharrba.*]
ŋiŋ+pæn-iṉta   wiṯimaṯ+ŋarpa-iṉta
2SG-XOBL-XDAT   bring-XPST-XDAT
2SG-SBJ-COMP   bring-PST-COMP
'I'll cook that food$_i$, that you brought [Ø$_i$]$_{\text{Topic}}$.'

In this sense, the co-reference triggers in Lardil sit part way between those of Kayardild and those of Yukulta's sentences with NTRMCs, as summarised in Table 17.6.

Like Kayardild, Lardil's co-reference triggers of SCCM correspond only to those of Yukulta's NTRMC sentences, not its TrMC sentences. Likewise, its SCCM marker XDAT corresponds only to SCCM in Yukulta's NTRMC sentences, not its TrMC sentences. And finally, it will be recalled from §17.4.3 that the inflectional properties of Lardil's present tense MCs also correspond to Yukulta's NTRMCs but not its TrMCs. Thus, while Lardil and Kayardild retain multiple points of morphosyntactic cognacy with Yukulta's NTRMC, they both appear to have undergone the wholesale loss of morphosyntax that is cognate with Yukulta's TrMCs.

17.5.6 Whence Kayardild's Syntax?

The lexicon of Kayardild is very similar to that of Yukulta, rather than Lardil. Even its inflectional forms and their allomorphy are more like those of Yukulta. Yet the functions that are served by its inflectional forms, and the syntax of its sentences are closer to those of Lardil. Explaining precisely how this came to be is a complex task, and beyond the remit of this chapter; however, I wish to make one observation that stems from the discussion above.[10]

Suppose, rather simplistically, that a language with a MC inverse system and complementising CASE agreement, as discussed in §17.5.3, co-opted the main clause syntax of Lardil, while largely keeping its own lexicon and morphological forms. The result would be the loss of the old TRMC system and loss of the MC inverse system. The alternating XDAT~XERGLOC SCCM with a causal network as in Figure 17.8 would lose its mediating node. Restructuring could ensue, and the result could quite plausibly be something like Kayardild. In the MC, objects would become TENSE-marked, largely mirroring TENSE marking in SCs; perhaps there would even be over-generalisation, resulting in TENSE-marked PRESENT TENSE MC objects (found in Kayardild

Table 17.6 Co-reference triggers of SCCM

Co-reference	Yukulta (TrMC)	Yukulta (NtrMC)	Lardil	Kayardild
SC Subj & MC Subj	✓			
SC Subj & MC Obj		✓	✓	✓
SC Obj & MC Obj			✓	✓
SC Obj & MC Subj				✓

but not Lardil). Clearly, this is far from a full reconstruction, but it illustrates, I hope, that if a recent ancestor of Lardil came into heavy contact with a language like that of §17.5.3, then an outcome like Kayardild has prima facie plausibility. By the same token, however, another route could deliver us to the same destination.

Suppose instead that Lardil itself traces back to a language as in §17.5.3, with a MC inverse system and complementising CASE agreement. Suppose then that its own internal changes led to the generalisation of old NTRMC morphosyntax at the expense of TRMCs, leading to the loss of the latter; and that it lost the old MC inverse system. This too could remove the mediating node from a causal network like Figure 17.8 and lead to the emergence, in pre-Lardil, of alternating XDAT~XERGLOC SCCM. Now, if this system came into heavy contact with a Yukulta-like language and was extensively re-lexified, the result would resemble Kayardild. Meanwhile, if the same system, in another dialect, lost its XDAT~XERGLOC SCCM alternation by generalising the XDAT marker, it would resemble Lardil.

The point here seems to be, first, that some kind of intense language contact event is likely to have been involved, but second, that it may have involved the borrowing of Lardil-like syntax into a language like in §17.5.3, or the borrowing of Yukulta-like lexicon into a language whose syntax resembled Lardil but with an XDAT~XERGLOC SCCM alternation. Finding evidence which distinguishes between these two scenarios is likely to be challenging, but there may be a lead here worth following up in future research, namely, (i) if we assume that proto Tangkic had a basic contrast between TRMCs and NTRMCs largely like in Yukulta, then logically, Lardil must have lost the old TRMC syntax at some point in its past; however, (ii) if proto Tangkic had a MC inverse system, then Lardil must have lost that too, and as I argued just above in my second scenario, loss of TRMCs and the MC inverse system is enough to trigger the creation of a Kayardild-like XDAT~XERGLOC SCCM alternation as an internal change in pre-Lardil, historically prior to the contact event that gave rise to the lexical–syntactic mix of pre-Kayardild. On the other hand, if proto Tangkic did not have a MC inverse system, and it was innovated in a shared ancestor of Yukulta and Kayardild, then the XDAT~XERGLOC SCCM alternation cannot have arisen internally in pre-Lardil since its preconditions would not have existed there; it must have arisen in pre-Kayardild, and quite possibly, then, as a consequence of the contact event. Interestingly, the fact that modern Lardil lacks an XDAT~XERGLOC SCCM alternation is not diagnostic, since it could easily have lost it (and note that in both scenarios above, such an alternation must have been lost in pre-Yukulta). Consequently, a key question for Tangkic historical research is, what evidence is there that the MC inverse system was present in proto Tangkic? This is work for the future.

17.6 Shifts in the Systems of Agreement

We turn now from the mechanics of Tangkic reconstruction, to its theoretical implications. Irrespective of whether it occurred in pre-Lardil or solely in pre-Kayardild, I have argued that the XDAT~XERGLOC SCCM alternation found today only in Kayardild resulted from the restructuring of a causal network whose mediating node was removed by the loss of a MC inverse system of a kind attested directly in modern Yukulta. One assumption made was that in the antecedent system there was complementising CASE agreement, so that the XDAT~XERGLOC marking on SCs was a matter of agreement in CASE between the subordinate clause, which in Corbett's (2006) terms was the agreement target, and a co-referential MC object, which was the agreement controller. The notion that the antecedent system could have possessed this kind of complementising CASE agreement draws its plausibility from three sources. First, although modern Yukulta does not have complementising CASE agreement system, for 'one' to refer back to. Second, only by assuming that the ancestral system was like this can we explain in considerable detail the empirical idiosyncrasies of Kayardild's XDAT~XERGLOC marking and their correlation with PERSON values. Third, complementising CASE agreement of this kind is typologically unremarkable in the Australian context.

In the antecedent system, therefore, the XDAT~XERGLOC marking on SCs was an exponent of CASE, but the modern Kayardild system is quite different. The choice of SCCM marker in Kayardild is determined primarily by subject PERSON with slight conditioning by SOLIDARITY, and the choice of whether any SCCM is used is determined by co-reference. In Corbett's (2006) terms, this too is agreement. The subordinate subject is the controller, all of the words of the subordinate clause are targets, the feature agreed for is PERSON, and there are two conditions on that agreement, the factors of co-reference and SOLIDARITY. Because of its historical source, though, this PERSON-agreement system is highly non-canonical. Its marker is etymologically CASE, the location where it is marked is the entire subordinate clause, and it contrasts only two surface categories despite having four underlying values. All of these non-canonical traits are due to its immediate history, as a system of complementising CASE marking in subordinate clauses, in agreement with main-clause objects that took two different CASE values.

17.7 Typology with and without Diachrony

The reconstruction in §17.5 is a novel contribution to Tangkic diachronic morphosyntax. Previous synchronic analyses of Kayardild SCCM did not have the benefit of it, and consequently they provide a retrospective case study in how challenging the typology of *rara* can be in the absence of a diachronic backstory.

Evans (1995a) analyses modern Kayardild SCCM as complementising CASE marking. As a starting point this is not unreasonable. Due to its recent history, SCCM in Kayardild has many traits in common with true complementising CASE systems. However, as Evans (2003) observes, it is unclear how one should account theoretically for such complementising CASE inflection, since if it is a matter of CASE agreement, then the agreement controller appears to be missing; and if it is a matter of CASE government, then the governor appears to be missing. Given the diachronic context, we can see why this is so. The causal network of true complementising CASE in the antecedent language system (Figure 17.8) was first impoverished when the MC inverse system was lost (Figure 17.9), removing the erstwhile controller of agreement, and then significantly rewired in the change to Kayardild (Figures 17.10 and 17.11). The modern system is no longer a system of complementising CASE, notwithstanding its superficial resemblances. In the absence of that diachronic context, Evans (2003) concludes that Kayardild poses problems for theories of agreement.

Round (2013) approaches Kayardild SCCM from another angle. Whereas Evans's analysis is in terms of a typologically not-uncommon feature (complementising CASE), and leads to problems accounting for the inflectional mechanism, Round (2013) provides a straightforward inflectional mechanism (feature percolation) but arrives at an analysis with two typologically unusual features. The first, COMPLEMENTISATION, corresponds in causal terms to the node 'COREFERENCE' in Figure 17.11: it is a feature that is introduced into the clause under the same conditions that trigger SCCM. The second feature is SEJUNCT, a purposefully unusual name for what Round (2013) argues is an unusual feature: one associated directly with first person exclusive, second person (non-solidarity) and third person. In causal terms, SEJUNCT corresponds to the merger of the two nodes 'SOLIDARITY' and 'SC Subj PERSON' in Figure 17.11. Round (2013) compares Kayardild SCCM to the typology of PERSON marking, but having observed that SCCM has just two surface oppositions, is marked across a whole clause, and intersects with the pragmatics of SOLIDARITY, the conclusion is that SEJUNCT is so unlike other synchronic PERSON systems, that to call it PERSON would be to mischaracterise it. Again, the diachronic context clarifies how the analyst reached this point. PERSON agreement in Kayardild is indeed very different to other PERSON agreement systems, because it has just evolved by a highly infrequent route, from a complementising CASE system fed by an inverse system.

Neither Evans (1995a, 2003) nor Round (2013) can be faulted for poor argumentation or poor typologising. Evans compared Kayardild SCCM to typological systems that resembled it in terms of morphological forms and their distributions (complementising CASE), and then noted that the mechanism was odd. Round compared SCCM to typological systems that resembled its function (PERSON agreement) and got the mechanism to work, but noted that the morphological forms were odd (in terms of syncretism and location). Both clearly signalled what was unusual. And this is the point at which observations about *rara* often stop (Cysouw and Wohlgemuth 2010); however, with the diachronic analysis in hand these issues can be resolved. Not only can we now explain the particulars of Kayardild SCCM and its apparent typological mismatches, but we can also characterise the system as PERSON agreement with conditioning by solidarity and co-reference, in the knowledge that there is good reason why a PERSON system might look like this. In the absence of the diachronic analysis, the act of declaring Kayardild SCCM to be PERSON marking may have resembled hammering a square peg into a round hole, but with it we have both resolved a quandary that Kayardild had posed, and extended our understanding of the typology of PERSON systems.

17.8 The Scientific Response to *Rara*: Examine Diachrony

Evans and Round both observed that the marking of complementised clauses in Kayardild constitutes a *rarum*, and identified where it clashed with our current understanding of empirical synchronic typological facts and our theories for explaining them. At face value, the *rarum* presented a challenge to theories such as Corbett's theories of agreement (Corbett 2006) and features (Corbett 2012), which propose that the variety of inflectional mechanisms and features available to human languages is circumscribed: Evans's analysis challenged the former, and Round's the latter. There are two broad responses to a state of affairs such as this, and the debate between them is ongoing. One is to doubt whether it is possible to circumscribe the variety of human language (Evans and Levinson 2009). The other is to persist with the task of composing empirical insights into circumscribed theories of language, embracing apparent counter-examples as a prompt both to revise those theories, and to seek avenues that bring improved insights into the empirical facts. Here I have sought to demonstrate that diachrony is one such avenue.

There are well-worn arguments that we should not underestimate the utility of diachrony for synchronic typologising (Greenberg 1966, 1978; Bybee 1988; Blevins 2004, among others). To take a whimsical example, if the world contained 100,000 languages, I would confidently predict that we would encounter a rare but recurring pattern of (i) subject PERSON agreement, (ii) found in subordinate but not main clauses, (iii) marked by etymological CASE markers with (iv) only two formal distinctions, in which (v) the most common pattern is that third person differs from first person, and second person is syncretic with either first or third person or both, and is conditioned (vi) by co-reference, and perhaps (vii) by some other factor in the second person. That is a terribly specific synchronic typological claim to make, and the fact I have any confidence in it is by virtue of diachrony. Of course, there are not 100,000 languages and so this generalisation is highly unlikely to emerge from synchronic observations alone. And that is the problem of *rara*: given our necessarily limited sample from the vast number of possible human languages, there very likely are many correct, synchronic typological generalisations which typologists will be capable of discovering only through diachrony.

Acknowledgements

A version of this paper was presented at the *New Fields for Morphology Workshop*, Melbourne 2016. My thanks to the audience there and to Nick Evans and two anonymous reviewers for discussion that has improved the paper. All shortcomings are my own. This research was supported by Australian Research Council grant DE150101024 to Erich Round.

Appendix: Kayardild Topic and Focus Constructions

Kayardild has two complementised clause constructions in which the marker of complementisation does not appear on every word of the clause (Round 2013). Example

(27) illustrates a Topic construction. The clause is complementised and words carry PERSON agreement with the first person exclusive subject (glossed 1SBJ); however, the Topic DP escapes PERSON agreement.

(27) Kayardild [W1960]
    Ngijuwa   *kuluujuuntha*   *birr.*
    ŋicu-wa   kulu:c+ku:-n̪ṯa   pi-r-a
    1SG.XOBL-T   scratch-XPROP-XDAT   3-PL-T
    1SG.1SBJ[SBJ]   scratch-FUT-1SBJ   3-PL[TOPIC.TRO]
    'I'll scratch them.'

In Kayardild, all inflectional features have a syntactic domain within which they appear. The Topic construction can be accounted for by assuming that the Topic DP is outside the domain of SCCM PERSON agreement (Round 2013).

More complicated is the Focus construction, as in (28). Here, the clause is complementised and words carry PERSON agreement with the third person subject (glossed 3SBJ). The Focus DP, however, lacks this XDAT inflection and is marked with XERGLOC.

(28) Kayardild [R2005-jul21]
    Dangkawalathiya   *dalinkiya*
    ṯaŋka+palaṯ+ki   ṯalic-n+ki
    person-PL-XERGLOC   come-XNOMZ-XERGLOC
    person-PL-LOC[FOCUS.SBJ]   come-NOMZ-LOC[FOCUS.SBJ]
    warrajuuntha   *wurankiiwathuunth.*
    wara-c+ku:-n̪ṯa   wuɻan+ki:waṯ+ku:-n̪ṯa
    go-XPROP-XDAT   food-COLL-XPROP-XDAT
    go-FUT-3SBJ   food-COLL-FUT-3SBJ
    'The people coming are going for food.'

In Kayardild, there are several feature values realised by XERGLOC, and we can ask which one it is that is being realised on Focus DPs. Round (2013: 95–6) presents diagnostic evidence suggesting that the XERGLOC on Focus DPs is neither TENSE nor CASE. The argument regarding TENSE is secure, but the argument regarding CASE hinges on one example, for which another analysis is possible.[11] I propose here, then, that Focus DPs are inflected with LOCATIVE CASE, bringing my analysis back closer to Evans's (1995a: 141–2) analysis of bare Focus DPs, which occupy a clause all on their own. It also simplifies the analysis of Focus constructions relative to the analysis in Round (2013), which used two features associated with complementisation. The analysis here is that there is only the one feature associated with complementisation, namely PERSON agreement. Focus DPs, like Topic DPs, are outside of the syntactic domain associated with that feature, and do not inflect for it; however, in contrast to Topic DPs which are not inflected at all, Focus DPs are inflected for LOCATIVE CASE.

Notes

1. Notes regarding interlinear glossing: (i) The phonological line distinguishes two types of morpho-phonological boundary, written '–' and '+'. Different phonological processes apply depending on the boundary type (Round 2009; 2013: 12–14). (ii) Not all functions have corresponding overt morphological exponents (cf. SINGULAR NUMBER in English nouns). Such functions are placed in square brackets on the fourth line. (iii) Some functions correspond to multiple pieces of morphology. These one-to-many relationships are glossed in braces on the third and fourth lines. (iv) The 'termination' element, glossed T on the third line of examples, is a piece of morphology with no meaning, and so is not glossed on line four. (v) Example sources are abbreviated as: [W1960] for Wurm's (1960) Kayardild recordings, [E+*page; example*] for Evans's (1995a) Kayardild material, [R+*tape date & number*] for Round's (2005, 2007) Kayardild recordings, [K+*tape number*] for Keen's (1970) Yukulta recordings, my transcriptions.
2. More narrowly, they are 'meromophomes': morphomic morphological pieces from which word forms are constructed, in contrast to 'rhizomorphomes' which are morphomic classes of roots, and 'metamorphomes' which are morphomic sets of cells within a paradigm (Round 2015).
3. Other subordinate clauses include apprehensives, which express events to be feared or avoided (cf. Dixon 1980: 380; Blake 1981: 136); desideratives; and in the Southern Tangkic languages, purpose-of-movement clauses. The basic tenses are used also with certain extended senses, such as PAST for conditional protases, and FUTURE for desires, potentials and commands.
4. In Lardil and Kayardild, the SIMULTANEOUS SCs differ from those in Yukulta, sharing their inflectional properties with MC PRESENT TENSE clauses, described in §17.4.3.
5. I use the term 'present tense' for comparative purposes. In modern Lardil, this clause type is a default non-future.
6. An inflectional equivalent of Yukulta's SC SIMULTANEOUS does occur rarely in Kayardild MCs, denoting events happening right at the point of utterance.
7. There is also a default case, which is not directly relevant to the present discussion: if the SC subject is co-referential with neither the MC subject nor the MC object, then the SC is complementised by default and the SCCM marker is XDAT. This is true irrespective of MC transitivity.
8. One exception appears to be sentences whose matrix clause is a 1INCL imperative, in which case SCCM may be used even when the only co-reference is between SC and MC subject; see Round (2017) regarding imperatives in Tangkic, and Evans (1995a: 508–14) for other idiosyncrasies in Kayardild's triggers of SCCM.
9. I use 'COMP1' in the gloss here for comparability with examples (23)–(26). A more informative gloss, consistent with the analysis developed above, would be '1EXCL.SUBJ'.
10. Many thanks to Nick Evans for discussion of these thorny questions.
11. In a two-word example *Ngada rarungki!* 'I'm in the south!', Round (2013: 96) observes that the pronoun *ngada* 'I' has no overt inflection while the word *rarungki* 'in the south' has XERGLOC inflection. Both are taken to be Focus DPs. Now, in complementised clauses with XERGLOC SCCM, pronouns are uninflected (like *ngada* is), whereas pronouns inflected with LOCATIVE CASE have overt inflection (unlike *ngada*). So, Round (2013) concludes, the lack of inflection on the Focus DP *ngada* can be explained in terms of the usual SCCM feature and not CASE, and this suggests that the XERGLOC marker on all Focus DPs is a realisation of the SCCM feature, not CASE. However, this misses another possible analysis of the key example. Directional stems like *rarung-* do not inflect for LOCATIVE CASE or for the 'ACTUAL' present TENSE (both marked by XERGLOC); at least, they

do not do so if they are the head of the NP. But they can inflect if they are modifiers in a NP, and it is possible that *rarungki* here is a modifier of a headless NP, which is not uncommon in Kayardild (Round 2013: 158–67). In that case, neither *ngada* nor *rarungki* needs to be analysed as a Focus DP. *Ngada* is a normal subject DP and *rarungki* is a modifier in a headless predicate DP which is inflected for either CASE or TENSE. The literal meaning of the utterance would be 'I'm in the south(ern land)', i.e. on Bentinck Island.

References

Anderson, Stephen R. (1981), 'Why phonology isn't "natural"', *Linguistic Inquiry*, 12, pp. 493–539.
Anderson, Stephen R. (1988), 'Morphological change', in David Sankoff and Frederick J. Newmeyer (eds), *Linguistics: The Cambridge Survey*, Cambridge: Cambridge University Press, pp. 324–62.
Anderson, Stephen R. (1992), *A-morphous Morphology*, Cambridge: Cambridge University Press.
Aronoff, M. (1994), *Morphology by Itself: Stems and Inflectional Classes*, Cambridge, MA: MIT Press.
Bach, Emmon and R. T. Harms (1972), 'How do languages get crazy rules?', in R. P. Stockwell and R. K. S. Macaulay (eds), *Linguistic Change and Generative Theory*, Bloomington: Indiana University Press, pp. 1–21.
Blake, Barry J. (1981), *Australian Aboriginal Languages*, Sydney: Angus & Robertson.
Blevins, Juliette (2004), *Evolutionary Phonology: The Emergence of Sound Patterns*, Cambridge: Cambridge University Press.
Brown, Dunstan, Marina Chumakina and Greville G. Corbett (2013), *Canonical Morphology and Syntax*, Oxford: Oxford University Press.
Bybee, Joan L. (1988), 'The diachronic dimension in explanation', in John A Hawkins (ed.), *Explaining Language Universals*, Oxford: Basil Blackwell, pp. 350–79.
Cook, Jacqueline (2017), *A Sketch Grammar of Yangkaal*, Honours thesis, University of Queensland.
Cook, Jacqueline and Erich R. Round (2017), 'Draft Yangkaal Dictionary', MS, University of Queensland.
Corbett, Greville G. (2005), 'The canonical approach in typology', in Zygmunt Frajzyngier, Adam Hodges and David S. Rood (eds), *Linguistic Diversity and Language Theories*, Amsterdam: John Benjamins, pp. 25–49.
Corbett, Greville G. (2006), *Agreement*, Cambridge: Cambridge University Press.
Corbett, Greville G. (2007), 'Deponency, syncretism, and what lies between', in Matthew Baerman, Greville G. Corbett, Dunstan Brown and Andrew Hippisley (eds), *Deponency and Morphological Mismatches*, Proceedings of the British Academy, 145, London: British Academy and Oxford University Press, pp. 21–43.
Corbett, Greville G. (2012), *Features*, Cambridge: Cambridge University Press.
Cysouw, Michael and Jan Wohlgemuth (2010), 'The other end of universals: Theory and typology of rara', in Jan Wohlgemuth and Michael Cysouw (eds), *Rethinking Universals: How Rarities Affect Linguistic Theory*, Berlin: Walter de Gruyter, pp. 1–10.
Daniel, Michael (2011), 'Linguistic typology and the study of language', in Jae Jung Song (ed.), *The Oxford Handbook of Linguistic Typology*, Oxford: Oxford University Press, pp. 43–68.
Dench, Alan and Nicholas Evans (1988), 'Multiple case-marking in Australian languages', *Australian Journal of Linguistics*, 8, pp. 1–47.
Dixon, R. M. W. (1979), 'Ergativity', *Language*, 55, pp. 59–138.

Dixon, R. M. W. (1980), *The Languages of Australia*, Cambridge: Cambridge University Press.
Evans, Nicholas (1992), *Kayardild Dictionary and Thesaurus*, Parkville: Department of Linguistics and Language Studies, University of Melbourne.
Evans, Nicholas (1995a), *A Grammar of Kayardild, with Historical-Comparative Notes on Tangkic*, Berlin: Walter de Gruyter.
Evans, Nicholas (1995b), 'Multiple case in Kayardild: Anti-iconic suffix ordering and the diachronic filter', in Frans Plank (ed.), *Double Case: Agreement by Suffixaufnahme*, Oxford: Oxford University Press, pp. 396–428.
Evans, Nicholas (2003), 'Typologies of agreement: Some problems from Kayardild', *Transactions of the Philological Society*, 101, pp. 203–34.
Evans, Nicholas (2005), 'East across a narrow sea: Micro-colonization and synthetic prehistory in the Wellesley Islands, Northern Australia', in Toshiki Osada (ed.), *Linguistics, Archaeology and the Human Past*, Kyoto: Research Institute for Humanity and Nature, pp. 9–39.
Evans, Nicholas and Steven Levinson (2009), 'The myth of language universals: Language diversity and its importance for cognitive science', *Behavioral & Brain Sciences*, 32 (5), pp. 429–48, 472–92.
Evans, Nicholas and Erich R. Round (2017), *Kaiadilt: Kayardild Dictionary App*, Canberra: Centre of Excellence for the Dynamics of Language.
Gildea, Spike and Fernando Zúñiga (2016), 'Referential hierarchies: A new look at some historical and typological patterns', *Linguistics*, 54, pp. 483–529.
Givón, Talmy (1979), *On Understanding Grammar*, Orlando: Academic Press.
Goddard, Cliff (1982), 'Case systems and case marking in Australian languages: A new interpretation', *Australian Journal of Linguistics*, 2, pp. 167–96.
Greenberg, Joseph H. (1966), 'Synchronic and diachronic universals in phonology', *Language*, 42, pp. 508–17.
Greenberg, Joseph H. (1978), 'Diachrony, synchrony, and language universals', in Joseph H. Greenberg, Charles A. Ferguson and Edith A. Moravcsik (eds), *Universals of Human Language. Volume 1: Method and Theory*, Stanford, CA: Stanford University Press, pp. 61–91.
Grossman, Eitan (2016), 'From rarum to rarissimum: An unexpected zero person marker', *Linguistic Typology*, 20, pp. 1–23.
Hale, Kenneth L. (1973), 'Deep-surface canonical disparities in relation to analysis and change: An Australian example', in T. A. Sebeok (ed.), *Current Trends in Linguistics 8: Linguistics in Oceania*, The Hague: Mouton de Gruyter, pp. 401–58.
Harris, Alice C. (2008), 'On the explanation of typologically unusual structures', in Jeff Good (ed.), *Linguistic Universals and Language Change*, Oxford: Oxford University Press, pp. 54–76.
Harris, Alice C. (2010), 'Explaining typologically unusual structures: The role of probability', in Jan Wohlgemuth and Michael Cysouw (eds), *Rethinking Universals: How Rarities Affect Linguistic Theory*, Berlin: Walter de Gruyter, pp. 91–103.
Hartwig, Luke (2014), *Case Marking and Clause Function in Tangkic Languages: A Comparative Morphological Study*, Honours thesis, University of Queensland.
Hopper, Paul J. and Sandra A. Thompson (1980), 'Transitivity in grammar and discourse', *Language*, 56 (2), pp. 251–99.
Jacques, Guillaume and Anton Antonov (2014), 'Direct/inverse systems', *Language and Linguistics Compass*, 8, pp. 301–18.
Keen, Sandra (1970), Materials in the Yukulta language, 1968–1970, Items KEEN_S01,3,5,6,9; PMS907–9,911, Australian Institute of Aboriginal and Torres Strait Islander Studies.

Keen, Sandra L. (1983), 'Yukulta', in R. M. W. Dixon and B. J. Blake (eds), *Handbook of Australian Languages, Volume 3*, Canberra: ANU Press, pp. 190–304.

Klokeid, Terry J. (1976), *Topics in Lardil Grammar*, PhD dissertation, Massachusetts Institute of Technology.

Memmott, Paul, Erich Round, Daniel Rosendahl and Sean Ulm (2016), 'Fission, fusion and syncretism: Linguistic and environmental changes amongst the Tangkic people of the southern Gulf of Carpentaria, northern Australia', in Jean-Christophe Verstraete and Diane Hafner (eds), *Land and Language in Cape York Peninsula and the Gulf Country: Culture and Language Use*, Amsterdam and Philadelphia: John Benjamins, pp. 105–36.

Nancarrow, Cassy (ed.) (2014), *Ganggalida Dictionary and Thesaurus: A Vocabulary of the Yugulda Language of the Ganggalida People, North-West Queensland*, Cairns: Carpentaria Land Council Aboriginal Corporation.

Ngakulmungan Kangka Leman (1996), *Lardil Dictionary: A Vocabulary of the Language of the Lardil People, Mornington Island, Gulf of Carpentaria, Queensland; with English–Lardil Finder List*, Gununa: Mornington Shire Council.

Nordlinger, Rachel (2014), 'Constituency and grammatical relations in Australian languages', in Harold J. Koch and Rachel Nordlinger (eds), *The Languages and Linguistics of Australia: A Comprehensive Guide*, Berlin: De Gruyter, pp. 215–62.

Nordlinger, Rachel and Louisa Sadler (2004), 'Nominal tense in crosslinguistic perspective', *Language*, 80, pp. 776–806.

Plank, Frans (2000), *Das grammatische Raritätenkabinett: A Leisurely Collection to Entertain and Instruct*, <http://typo.uni-konstanz.de/rara/intro/index.php> (last accessed 26 September 2018).

Richards, Norvin (2013), 'Lardil "case stacking" and the timing of case assignment', *Syntax*, 16, pp. 42–76.

Round, Erich R. (2005), *A First Kayardild Audiovisual Text Corpus, with Prosodic Annotations: End of Award Report (FTG0025)*, New Haven, CT: Yale University Press.

Round, Erich R. (2007), *Linguistic and Ethnographic Documentation of Kayardild: End of Award Report (IGS0039)*, New Haven, CT: Yale University Press.

Round, Erich R. (2009), *Kayardild Phonology, Morphology, and Morphosyntax*, PhD dissertation, Yale University.

Round, Erich R. (2011), 'Morphomes as a level of representation capture unity of exponence across the inflection–derivation divide', *Linguistica*, 51, pp. 217–30.

Round, Erich R. (2013), *Kayardild Morphology and Syntax*, Oxford: Oxford University Press.

Round, Erich R. (2014), 'A description of Ganggalida grammar', in Cassy Nancarrow (ed.), *Ganggalida Dictionary and Thesaurus: A Vocabulary of the Yugulda Language of the Ganggalida People, North-West Queensland*, Cairns: Carpentaria Land Council Aboriginal Corporation, pp. 173–205.

Round, Erich R. (2015), 'Rhizomorphomes, meromorphomes, and metamorphomes', in Greville G. Corbett, Dunstan Brown and Matthew Baerman (eds), *Understanding and Measuring Morphological Complexity*, Oxford: Oxford University Press, pp. 29–52.

Round, Erich R. (2016), 'Kayardild inflectional morphotactics is morphomic', in Ana R. Luís and Ricardo Bermúdez-Otero (eds), *The Morphome Debate*, Oxford: Oxford University Press, pp. 228–47.

Round, Erich R. (2017), 'The Tangkic languages of Australia: Phonology and morphosyntax of Lardil, Kayardild and Yukulta', in Mark Aronoff (ed.), *Oxford Research Encyclopedia of Linguistics*, <http://linguistics.oxfordre.com/view/10.1093/acrefore/9780199384655.001.0001/acrefore-9780199384655-e-159> (last accessed 26 September 2018).

Round, Erich R. and Greville G. Corbett (2017), 'The theory of feature systems: One feature versus two for Kayardild tense-aspect-mood', *Morphology*, 27, pp. 21–75.

Silverstein, Michael (1976), 'Hierarchy of features and ergativity', in R. M. W. Dixon (ed.), *Grammatical Categories in Australian Languages*, Canberra: Australian Institute of Aboriginal Studies, pp. 112–71.

Wang, William S. Y. (1968), 'Vowel features, paired variables, and the English vowel shift', *Language*, pp. 695–708.

Witzlack-Makarevich, Alena, Taras Zakharko, Lennart Bierkandt, Fernando Zúñiga and Balthasar Bickel (2016), 'Decomposing hierarchical alignment: Co-arguments as conditions on alignment and the limits of referential hierarchies as explanations in verb agreement', *Linguistics*, 54 (3), pp. 531–61.

Wurm, Stephen A. (1960), Recordings made in the Gayadilt language of Bentinck Island, Items WURM_S01;2173-2174, Australian Institute of Aboriginal and Torres Strait Islander Studies.

Language Index

Abaza (West Caucasian), 161
Abkhaz (Northwest Caucasian), 161, 321
Adyghe (Northwest Caucasian), 161
Aghem (Bantu), 371
Agul (Nakh-Daghestanian), 293
Akabea (Great Andamanese), 234, 249, 254–7, 264, 268–71
Akabo (Great Andamanese), 253
Akachari (Great Andamanese), 253, 254
Akajeru (Great Andamanese), 253
Akakede (Great Andamanese), 254
Akakhora (Great Andamanese), 253
Akarbale (Great Andamanese), 254
Akkadian (Afro-Asiatic), 289
Alabama (Muskogean), 242
Amele (Trans New Guinea), 237, 238, 275
Andi (Nakh-Daghestanian), 155
Anêm (Isolate), 239
Apurinã (Arawakan), 321
Arawun (Trans New Guinea), 237
Archi (Nakh-Daghestanian), 5, 155, 281–99, 304, 306, 308–11, 320, 321, 323
Avar (Nakh-Daghestanian), 149, 150, 154, 155
Awa (Trans New Guinea), 238

Barasano (Tucanoan), 321
Bardi (Nyulnyulan), 234, 235, 238, 242, 243, 270, 271
Basque (Isolate), 240, 241, 243, 270, 306, 315, 316, 320, 322
Bau (Trans New Guinea), 237
Bininj Gun-wok (Gunwinyguan), 12

Bongu (Trans New Guinea), 240
Bukiyip (Torricelli), 239, 269
Bulgarian (Indo-European), 22, 164, 193–204, 263, 277
Burushaski (Isolate), 241, 243, 275, 322
Byali (Niger-Congo), 372

Cantonese (Sino-Tibetan), 58, 248
Cavineña (Tacanan), 244, 249
Chamorro (Austronesian), 124, 135, 238, 316, 322
Chechen (Nakh-Daghestanian), 304
Cherokee (Iroquoian), 157, 165
Chickasaw (Muskogean), 371
Chinese *see* Cantonese
Chukchi (Chukotko-Kamchatkan), 41, 45, 46, 54, 55, 61
Cree (Algonquian), 156–7
Crow (Siouan), 160
Czech (Indo-European), 245–6

Dagaare (Niger-Congo), 58
Danaru (Trans New Guinea), 240
Dargwa (Nakh-Daghestanian), 154
DhoLuo (Nilo-Saharan), 48, 50
Dutch (Indo-European), 38, 246, 247

Egyptian Arabic (Afro-Asiatic), 322
English (Indo-European), 4, 16, 36, 41, 45–7, 50–56, 61, 139, 140, 142, 143, 149, 153, 198, 262, 306, 316, 317, 320, 322, 327, 392, 402, 412, 417, 442

Erima (Trans New Guinea), 238
Erzya (Uralic), 161

Fijian (Austronesian), 322
Finnish (Uralic), 47, 60, 322
French (Indo-European), 17, 22, 36, 46, 51, 171–92, 228, 242, 243, 304, 308, 390, 392, 402

Gahuku (Trans New Guinea), 239, 276
Garifuna (Arawak), 290
Gayo (Austronesian), 246, 269
German (Indo-European), 3, 38, 42, 43, 44, 45, 54, 61, 153, 246, 247, 304, 371, 390, 392, 402, 412
Girawa (Trans New Guinea), 237
Greek (Indo-European), 85, 139
Guarani (Tupi-Guarani), 322, 323
Gulmancema (Niger-Congo), 124, 135
Gumalu (Trans New Guinea), 237

Hausa (Afro-Asiatic), 49, 306, 316, 320, 322, 384
Hebrew (Afro-Asiatic), 384
Hinuq (Nakh-Daghestanian), 155
Hixkaryána (Carib), 322
Hualapai (Cochimi-Yuman), 125–35
Hungarian (Uralic), 38, 49, 54, 159, 371, 384

Ingush (Nakh-Daghestanian), 153–5, 165, 304, 306, 308, 320, 321
Inuktitut (Eskimo-Aleut), 22, 233, 234, 249, 251, 264, 267, 270, 272
Iranian (Indo-European), 202
Isebe (Trans New Guinea), 237
Italian (Indo-European), 21, 34, 65–99, 228, 242, 243, 262, 303, 304, 305, 306, 308, 316, 318, 320, 322
Itelmen (Chukotko-Kamchatkan), 240, 241, 243, 270

Jaminjung (Mirndi), 262
Japanese (Japonic), 46, 55, 56, 57, 60, 160, 239, 271–2
Jarawara (Arawan), 248, 334, 346, 365
Jingulu (Mirndi), 14, 15, 234, 249, 258–62, 265–7, 268, 272

Kabardian (Northwest Caucasian), 161
Kam (Tai-Kadai), 248, 249

Karata (Nakh-Daghestanian), 149, 155
Karo Batak (Austronesian), 246, 269
Kâte (Trans New Guinea), 241, 242, 269
Kayardild (Tangkic), 5, 23, 247, 414–42
Ket (Yeniseian), 261, 262, 277
Khanty (Uralic), 371
Kharia (Munda), 153
Kiowa (Kiowa-Tanoan), 158
Koasati (Muskogean), 238, 242, 243, 270
Kolami (Dravidian), 67, 68
Komnzo (Yam), 120
Korean (Koreanic), 381
Kryz (Nakh-Daghestanian), 149
Kulina (Arawan), 5, 12, 23, 240, 241, 243, 270, 328–64
Kurdish (Indo-European), 48
Kwaza (Isolate), 22, 234, 249, 251, 253, 264, 265, 267, 268, 270, 272

Lak (Nakh-Daghestanian), 154
Lardil (Tangkic), 419–42
Latin (Indo-European), 6, 7, 8, 9, 11, 12, 13, 101, 139, 164, 220
Latvian (Indo-European), 51
Lemio (Trans New Guinea), 237
Lezgi, Lezgian (Nakh-Daghestanian), 154, 293
Lithuanian (Indo-European), 61
Lower Sorbian (Indo-European), 10, 11
Luo *see* DhoLuo

Ma'di (Central Sudanic), 244, 248
Macedonian (Indo-European), 90, 164, 316, 320
Macerata (Indo-European), 242
Madi (Arawan), 241, 269
Makhuwa (Bantu), 371
Menomini (Algic), 239, 241
Mian (Trans New Guinea), 275, 305, 306, 311–15, 320, 322
Mohave (Cochimi-Yuman), 248, 249
Mongolian (Mongolic), 153

Nama (Yam), 115
Natchez (Isolate), 289
Nêlêma (Austronesian), 58
Nen (Nambu branch, Yam family), 100–23
Ngan'gityemerri (Southern Daly), 154, 306, 316, 317, 320, 322
Ngkolmpu (Yam), 120
Nguburindi (Tangkic), 419

LANGUAGE INDEX | 449

Nimboran (Nimboranic), 235, 236, 243, 244, 269, 276
Noon (Niger-Congo), 371

Okojuwoi (Great Andamanese), 254, 255, 264, 268
Okol (Great Andamanese), 254
Old Church Slavic (Indo-Euopean), 150, 151, 163, 165
Opuchikwar (Great Andamanese), 254, 255, 258, 264, 268
Ossetic (Indo-Euopean), 163

Panim (Trans New Guinea), 237
Panyjima (Pama-Nyungan), 427
Pawnee (Caddoan), 237
Pazar Laz (Kartvelian), 161
Persian (Indo-European), 61
Plains Cree (Algonquian), 322
Polish (Indo-European), 245, 246, 262, 269
Proto Eastern Tangkic (Tangkic), 419–42
Proto Northern Tangkic, 419–42
Proto Southern Tangkic, 419–42
Proto Tangkic, 419–42
Proto-Balto-Slavic, 151

Rerau (Trans New Guinea), 240
Riau Indonesian (Austronesian), 153
Romanian (Indo-European), 67, 158
Russian (Indo-European), 3, 6, 7, 8, 10, 11, 12, 23, 91, 96, 149, 152, 153, 157, 163, 165, 239, 245, 246, 262, 269, 271, 306, 316, 318, 320, 322, 390–413

Selepet (Trans New Guinea), 236, 237, 269
Semitic family (Afro-Asiatic), 47, 48, 322
Seri (Isolate), 135
Sihan (Trans New Guinea), 237
Siroi (Trans New Guinea), 235, 240, 275

Slovene (Indo-European), 10, 18, 139
Spanish (Indo-European), 22, 91, 164, 205–32
Swahili (Niger-Congo, 100

Tagalog (Austronesian), 159
Teiwa (Timor-Alor-Pantar), 305, 306, 311, 314, 315, 320, 322
Tindi (Nakh-Daghestanian), 149
Tok Pisin (Indo-European), 121
Toqabaqita (Austronesian), 246
Tsez (Nakh-Daghestanian), 304–8, 319, 320, 21
Tucano (Tucanoan), 5
Tundra Nenets (Uralic), 23, 276, 372–86
Turkish (Turkic), 49, 50, 51, 54, 61, 100, 161, 262, 316
Tzotzil (Mayan), 158
Tzutujil (Mayan), 161

Udi (Nakh-Daghestanian), 241, 244, 269
Urubu-Kaapor (Tupian), 246

Wai Wai (Cariban), 240, 243, 270
Warlpiri (Pama-Nyungan), 100
Warrwa (Nyulnyulan), 240
Waskia (Trans New Guinea), 275
Welsh (Indo-European), 384
West Greenlandic (Eskimo-Aleut), 55

Xinalug (Nakh-Daghestanian), 154

Yabong (Trans New Guinea), 240
Yakut (Turkic), 161
Yangarella (Tangkic), 419
Yangkaal (Tangkic), 419, 420
Yangulam (Trans New Guinea), 240
Yawuru (Nyulnyulan), 238, 243, 270
Yukulta (Tangkic), 419–42
Yupik (Eskimo-Aleut), 250

Zuni (Isolate), 54

Author Index

Abbi, Anvita, 254
Abily, Gaëlle, 173
Aboh, Enoch, 371
Aboul-Fetouh, Hilmi M., 322
Ackerman, Farrell, 38, 206, 222, 386
Acquaviva, Paolo, 85, 86
Adams, Patsy, 331, 341
Adams Liclan, Patsy, 331, 366
Aikhenvald, Alexandra Y., 281, 329, 331
Aissen, Judith, 323
Alcoba, Santiago, 205
Allen, Shanley E. M., 233, 249–51, 264, 267, 272
Andersen, Henning, 163
Anderson, Stephen R., 100, 417, 418
Antonov, Anton, 364, 426
Arka, Wayan, 101, 102,
Arkhipov, A., 297
Arnold, Doug, 46, 52
Aronoff, Mark, 3, 108, 140, 143, 144, 213, 421
Auderset, Sandra, 41, 59, 61
Audring, Jenny, 19
Authier, Gilles, 149
Avrtuin, Sergey, 391
Ayala, Valentin, 322

Babyonyshev, Maria, 391
Bach, Emmon, 417
Baerman, Matthew, 3, 4, 5, 10, 11, 13, 14, 100, 101, 120, 135, 139, 230, 277, 334
Baker, Mark C., 53, 61, 62, 162
Bárány, András, 328, 330, 364
Barbiers, Sjef, 247

Barlow, Michael, 330
Baroni, Marco, 190
Barshi, Immanuel, 358
Basciano, Bianca, 46
Battista, Marco, 71, 74
Bauer, Laurie, 60
Baugh, Albert C., 198
Beavers, John, 314
Bender, Jorigine, 125–30, 136
Beniamine, Sacha, 206, 222
Benveniste, Émile, 202
Berg, Kristian, 146
Bermúdez-Otero, Ricardo, 215
Bernardini, Silvia, 190
Bickel, Balthasar, 21, 41, 59, 61, 122, 162, 308, 321, 332, 426
Bierkandt, Lennart, 332, 426
Birner, Betty, 386
Bisetto, Antonietta, 32–5, 60
Blackings, Mairi, 248
Blake, Barry J., 198, 442
Blevins, James P., 206, 222, 440
Bloch, Bernard, 142, 145
Bloomfield, Leonard, 142, 144, 235, 239, 242
Bonami, Olivier, 5, 22, 95, 174, 175, 176, 181, 187, 190, 191, 205, 206, 222
Bond, Oliver, 19, 32, 90, 91, 94, 282, 284, 292, 298, 304, 309, 310, 321, 328, 335, 339, 365
Booij, Geert, 89, 319
Borsley, Robert, 328
Bossong, Georg, 323
Bousquet, Danielle, 173

Bowern, Claire, 234, 235, 242
Boyé, Gilles, 5, 22, 95, 176, 181, 187, 190, 205, 206, 207
Bresnan, Joan, 328
Brody, Michael, 371
Brown, Dunstan, 3, 11, 12, 13, 19, 23, 31, 32, 96, 100, 101, 120, 138, 139, 143, 206, 220, 230, 305, 309, 315, 323, 416
Buchmann, Franziska, 146
Bulygina, Tatiana V., 393, 394, 395
Burani, Cristina, 72, 80, 304, 308, 322
Bybee, Joan L., 440

Cable, Seth, 386
Cabredo Hofherr, Patricia, 205, 206, 207
Calderone, Basilio, 191
Camilli, Amerindo, 71
Cappellaro, Chiara, 202
Carlson, Gregory N., 395, 405, 408
Caron, Gauthier, 174, 175
Carroll, Matthew, 3, 101, 102, 120
Casillas Martínez, 23
Ceccagno, Antonella, 46
Chadwick, Neil, 258
Chapman, Shirley, 329
Chiari, Isabella, 79
Chierchia, Gennaro, 395, 405, 408
Choi, Yun Jung, 101, 102
Chomsky, Noam, 138–47, 328
Chumakina, Marina, 5, 14, 19, 31, 32, 96, 138, 156, 282, 283, 284, 292, 293, 298, 304, 305, 309, 310, 321, 323, 416
Clark, Eve V., 46
Comrie, Bernard, 4, 14, 254, 257, 264, 272, 275, 277, 304, 306, 321, 328, 330, 364
Conrad, Robert J., 238
Cook, Jacqueline, 419
Corbett, Greville G., 1, 2, 3, 4, 5, 6, 7, 8, 10, 11, 12, 13, 14, 15, 16, 17, 18, 19, 20, 21, 22, 31, 32, 65, 66, 67, 68, 69, 72, 73, 76, 79, 80, 83, 86, 88, 90, 95, 96, 100, 101, 119, 120, 126, 127, 138, 139, 148, 154, 155, 156, 157, 158, 162, 163, 171, 172, 185, 187, 205, 230, 282, 284, 303, 304, 305, 308, 310, 312, 315, 316, 317, 318, 319, 321, 322, 323, 328, 329, 330, 331, 334, 336, 359, 360, 363, 370, 371, 381, 384, 395, 400, 414, 416, 417, 420, 438, 440
Corbin, Danièle, 187
Corbin, Pierre, 187
Creissels, Denis, 47, 49

Croft, William, 323
Csató, Éva Ágnes, 161
Culicover, Peter W., 148
Cysouw, Michael, 414, 439

D'Achille, Paolo, 72, 79, 86, 87, 308
Dahlstrom, Amy, 322
Dalrymple, Mary, 330, 344, 361, 362, 381, 382
Daniel, Michael, 414
Daniel, Mikhail A., 293
Danon, Gabi, 384
da Silva Facundes, Sidney, 321
Dayley, Jon P., 161
Deibler, Ellis W., 239
De Mauro, Tullio, 79, 95
Dench, Alan, 427
Derbyshire, Desmond C., 322, 329
Dereń, Ewa, 276
Deutscher, Guy, 289
Di Domenico, Elisa, 77
Dienst, Stefan, 240, 329, 331–64, 365, 366
Diesing, Molly, 408
Dixon, R. M. W., 241, 244, 248, 276, 281, 322, 334, 346, 358, 426, 442
Dobrushina, Nina, 283
Döhler, Christian, 101, 102, 120
Doleschal, Ursula, 400
Dressler, Wolfgang U., 79, 83, 96, 228
Dunn, Michael J., 55
Dybiec, Katharina, 146

Eades, Domenyk, 246
Edmondson, Jerold A., 249
É. Kiss, Katalin, 330, 371
Esher, Louise, 230
Estrada Arráez, Ana, 211
Evans, Nicholas, 3, 12, 21, 87, 101, 102, 104, 112, 117, 121, 247, 248, 415, 419, 420, 423, 427, 434, 438, 439, 440, 442

Fabb, Nigel, 248
Fedden, Sebastian, 14, 16, 19, 72, 148, 154, 155, 156, 185, 189, 275–6, 305, 311, 312, 315, 322, 323, 363, 365
Ferraresi, Adriano, 190
Finkel, Raphael, 310
Fitch, W. Tecumseh, 41
Fodor, Janet Dean, 148
Foley, William A., 58, 153, 159
Forker, Diana, 23

Fraser, Norman, 6, 7, 8, 10, 11, 12, 13, 23, 400
Francopoulo, Gil, 174
Friedman, Viktor A., 316
Fuhrhop, Nanna, 146

Gaeta, Livio, 94, 242
Gagliardi, Ann C., 305, 307, 319
Gairdner, W. H. T., 322
Garcia, Germán Franco, 321
Gast, Volker, 101, 102, 406
Gazdar, Gerald, 6, 23, 328
Geerts, G., 247
Gerdts, Donna B., 55
Gibson, Lorna P., 158
Gil, David, 153
Gildea, Spike, 426
Girvin, Cammeron, 165
Gisborne, Nikolas, 23
Givón, Talmy, 417
Goddard, Cliff, 426
Göksel, Aslı, 49
Graczyk, Randolph, 160, 165
Gray, Matthew K., 176
Greenbaum, Sidney, 317, 322
Greenberg, Joseph, 139, 440
Grenoble, Lenore A., 289
Grossman, Eitan, 414
Guasch, P. Antonio, 322
Guevara, Emiliano, 60
Guillaume, Antoine, 249

Haegeman, Liliane, 392
Haeseryn, W., 247
Haig, Geoffrey, 202
Hale, Kenneth L., 419, 423
Hall, Robert A., 242
Harbour, Daniel, 131
Harms, R. T., 417
Harris, Alice C., 241, 414
Harris, James W., 229
Harris, Zellig, 142, 144, 145
Hartmann, Katharina, 384
Hartwig, Luke, 421
Haspelmath, Martin, 3, 21, 57, 58, 94
Hathout, Nabil, 191
Haurholm-Larsen, Steffen, 284, 289
Hawkins, Robert E., 240
Healey, Alan, 305
Hecht, Barbara Frant, 46
Hek, Fabian, 386

Hengeveld, Kees, 159
Hewitt, B. George, 321
Hippisley, Andrew, 11, 13, 23, 100, 101, 120, 143, 206, 220, 230
Hjelmslev, Louis, 2
Hockett, Charles F., 119, 122, 142
Holst, Jan Henrik, 241, 243, 275
Holton, Gary, 305, 315, 323
Hopper, Paul J., 289, 313, 323
Horn, Larry, 372
Horváth, Judith, 384
Hosakawa, Komei, 238
Huddleston, Rodney, 46, 52, 61
Hulk, Aalfe, 17, 23
Hyman, Larry M., 21

Iacobini, Claudio, 69, 71, 72, 77, 80, 304, 308, 322
Iggesen, Oliver A., 14
Ihsane, Tabea, 392
Inkelas, Sharon, 235–6

Jackendoff, Ray, 7, 411
Jacobs, Joachim, 371
Jacques, Guillaume, 426
Jakobson, Roman O., 2
Janhunen, Juha, 239, 243, 276
Johanson, Lars, 161
Jones, Paula, 321
Jones, Wendell, 321
Joos, Martin, 145

Kageyama, Taro, 46, 55, 56, 57
Kaiser, Georg, 323
Kakumasu, James, 248
Kalnača, Andra, 51
Karlsson, Fred, 47
Kashima, Eri, 101, 102
Keen, Sandra, 419, 425
Kemmer, Suzanne, 157
Kenesei, Istvan, 38, 61
Kerleroux, Françoise, 180, 191
Kerslake, Celia, 49
Khalidova, R. Sh., 149
Kibort, Anna, 5, 14, 156, 364, 370, 371
Kibrik, Aleksander E., 149, 283, 293, 296, 297, 304, 309, 310, 321, 323
Kibrik, Andrej A., 159, 162, 164
Kilani-Schoch, Marianne, 97, 228
Kim, Jong-Bok, 381

Kimball, Geoffrey D., 238, 242, 289
Kirk, Paul L., 158
Kittilä, Seppo, 243
Klamer, Marian, 305, 314, 315, 322, 323
Klein, Ewan H., 328
Klokeid, Terry J., 419, 420, 423, 435
Knyazev, Yuri, 397
Kodzasov, Sandro, 297, 309
König, Ekkehard, 372
Koopman, Hilda, 328
Koptjevskaja-Tamm, Maria, 61
Krasovitsky, Alexander, 14, 96, 322
Kratochvil, František, 323
Kratzer, Angelika, 412
Krifka, Manfred, 371, 372, 384, 395, 405, 406, 408
Künnap, Ago, 375
Kürschner, Sebastian, 42

Lambton, Ann K. S., 48
Landau, Idan, 407
Langdon, Margaret, 127
Lasnik, Howard, 328
Laughlin, Robert M., 158
Lee, Jenny S., 120
Leech, Geoffrey, 317, 322
Leer, Jeff, 160
Lepschy, Anna Laura, 262
Lepschy, Giulio, 262
LeSourd, Philip, 38
Levinson, Steven, 440
Lewis, David, 408
Lewis, Geoffrey L., 49, 51, 61
Lichtenberk, Frantisek, 246
Liddell, Henry G., 139
Lidz, Jeffrey, 305, 307
Lieber, Rochelle, 328
Link, Godehard, 395, 405, 408
Livitz, Inna, 391
Lokmane, Ilze, 51
Loving, Richard, 238, 275
Lowe, John J., 339, 364
Luís, Ana R., 32, 215, 284, 293, 377

McElhanon, Kenneth A., 236–7
McGregor, William, 240
McKaughan, Howard, 238, 275
McKenzie, Parker, 158
McShane, Marjorie J., 244–6, 390
Magomedova, P. T., 149

Mahajan, Anoop Kumar, 328
Maho, Jouni, 163
Maiden, Martin, 205, 214, 215
Maisak, Timur, 293
Malchukov, Andrei, 139
Malouf, Robert, 206, 222
Man, Edward H., 254–7, 268
Mancini, Federico, 97
Marlett, Stephen A., 135, 331, 341, 366
Martin, Samuel E., 271
Matasović, Ranko, 165
Matić, Dejan, 362, 384, 386
Matthews, P. H., 73, 77, 95, 101, 172, 248
May, Kevin, 236
Mel'čuk, Igor, 235, 390
Melloni, Chiara, 60
Memmott, Paul, 420
Menz, Astrid, 161
Merrifield, William R., 158
Michel, Jean-Baptiste, 176
Mikola, Tibor, 375, 376
Miller, Julia Colleen, 102
Miloradović, Sofija, 204
Miner, Kenneth L., 54
Mirčev, Kiril, 193, 203
Mišeska Tomić, Olga, 203
Mithun, Marianne, 53
Mittag, Emil, 101, 102
Miyagawa, Shigeru, 330
Moltmann, Friederike, 395
Montermini, Fabio, 222
Montgomery-Anderson, Brad, 157, 165
Moravcsik, Edith, 328
Mungía Zatarain, Irma, 208, 228
Mungía Zatarain, Martha E., 208, 228
Munro, Pamela, 249, 371
Musan, Renate, 372
Mycock, Louise, 361

Naba, Jean-Claude, 124
Nancarrow, Cassy, 419
Napoli, Donna Jo, 79
Nevins, Andrew, 215
Newman, John, 238, 243, 316, 322
Ngakulmungan Kangka Leman, 419
Nichols, Johanna, 3, 41, 59, 61, 122, 153, 156, 158, 163, 165, 304, 308, 321, 328, 411
Nida, Eugene A., 142, 144
Niemi, Clemens, 322

Nikolaeva, Irina, 14, 23, 46, 59, 276, 328, 330, 344, 361, 362, 364, 371, 373, 375, 378, 380, 381, 382, 384, 386
Nishigauchi, Taisuke, 384
Nordlinger, Rachel, 420
Nyrop, Kristoffer R., 172

Olovjannikova, I. P., 309
Olsen, Susan, 59
Olsson, Bruno, 101, 102
Ortiz de Urbana, Juan, 384
Öztürk, Balkiz, 161

Palancar, Enrique L., 3, 80, 81, 84, 87, 93, 96
Paol, John Natu, 275
Partee, Barbara, 412
Pârvev, Xristo, 193, 203
Payne, Doris L., 358
Pelletier, Francis Jeffrey, 395, 405, 408
Pensalfini, Robert J., 15, 258–62, 265–7, 277
Perlmutter, David M., 411
Peškovskij, Alexander M., 393
Peterson, John, 153
Pirelli, Vito, 71, 74
Plancq, Clément, 174, 174
Plank, Frans, 414
Pöchtrager, Marcus A., 1612
Polański, Edward, 276
Polinsky, Maria, 14, 16, 304, 306, 321, 328, 330, 364, 411
Pollard, Carl, 328
Popova, Gergana D., 32
Portman, Maurice V., 254–8
Potsdam, Eric, 304, 328, 330
Powskey, Malinda, 125–30, 136
Presser Aiden, Aviva, 176
Priestly, T. M. S., 10, 18
Pullum, Geoffrey K., 46, 52, 61, 328
Purdy, Elizabeth J., 165
Pustet, Regina, 248

Quilliam, Harvey, 309
Quinn, Kyla, 101, 102
Quirk, Randolph, 317, 322

Radcliffe-Brown, Alfred R., 254
Rainier, Franz, 191
Redden, James E., 128, 136
Reid, Nicholas, 154, 317, 322
Reineke, Brigitte, 372

Repp, Sophie, 372
Reuland, Eric, 410
Ricca, Davide, 88
Richards, Norvin, 420
Rix, Helmut, 157
Roberts, John R., 237, 238, 275
Robinson, Laura C., 305, 315, 323
Rocha Romero, Gilda, 208, 228
Rodrigues, Cilene, 215
Romary, Laurent, 174
de Rooij, J., 247
Rooth, Math, 371, 372, 377, 406
Rosen, Sara, 53
Rosendahl, Daniel, 420
Rosengren, Inge, 371
Ross, Malcolm, 275
Round, Erich, 5, 108, 126, 230, 415, 416, 419, 420, 421, 422, 424, 435, 439, 440, 441, 442, 443
Russi, Cincia, 87

Sadler, Louisa, 46, 52, 135, 328, 384, 420
Sadock, Jerrold M., 53
Sag, Ivan A., 328
Saidov, Magomedsajid, 149
Sajous, Franck, 191
Salminen, Tapani, 373, 374, 375
Salmont-Alt, Suzanne, 174
Saltarelli, Mario, 241
Samedov, D. S., 309
Sánchez, José Raúl Monguí, 321
Santilli, Enzo, 88
Sapir, Edward, 144
Scalise, Sergio, 32–5, 60
Scatton, Ernest A., 263
Schapper, Antoinette, 305, 315, 323
Schenker, Alexander M., 203
Schleicher, August, 144
Schmid, Sonja, 400
Schokkin, Dineke, 101, 102
Schultze-Berndt, Eva, 262
Scott, Robert, 139
Selkirk, Elizabeth, 371
Sells, Peter, 381
Serianni, Luca, 71, 88, 89
Shen, Yuan Kui, 176
Shibatani, Masayoshi, 160
Shmelev, Alexey D., 393, 395, 396
Siegel, Jeff, 101, 102, 115
Siewierska, Anna, 156, 346

Silverstein, Michael, 426
Sims, Andrea D., 222
Sornicola, Rosanna, 202
Soukka, Maria, 371
Spencer, Andrew, 19, 32, 34, 39, 41, 45, 46, 49, 55, 59, 135, 220, 284, 293, 374, 377
Spina, Rossella, 95, 228
Sportiche, Dominique, 328
Stachowski, Marek, 161
Starosta, Manfred, 11, 23
Steele, Josie, 125–30, 136
Stojkov, Stojko, 193, 194
Stolz, Thomas, 124, 316, 322
Stone, Gerald, 23
Stump, Gregory T., 9, 66, 67, 94, 135, 188, 211, 374
Surányi, Balázs, 371
Suter, Edgar, 242
Svartvik, Jan, 317, 322
Swift, Mary D., 233, 249–51, 264, 267, 272
Szajbel-Keck, Malgorzata, 165
Szczepaniak, Renata, 42

Tama, Philip, 101, 102
Tang, Kevin, 215
Taylor, John R., 281
Tellier, Christine, 17, 23
Temple, Richard T., 254
ter Meulen, Alice, 395, 405, 408
Thompson, Sandra A., 313, 323
Thornton, Anna, 20, 66, 68, 69, 71, 72, 76, 77, 79, 80, 83, 85, 86, 87, 90, 95, 96, 211, 228, 304, 308, 322, 323
Thurston, William, 239
Tiberius, Carol, 11, 96
Tikkanen, Bertil, 241
Timberlake, Alan, 13, 322
Tiss, Frank, 331, 365
Todorov, Todor, 203, 204
Topping, Donald M., 322
Townsend, Charles E., 165
Trask, R. L., 315, 316, 322
Traugott, Elizabeth Closs, 289
Trommer, Jochen, 139, 140, 233, 234, 243, 272
Tsunoda, Tasaku, 314, 323
Tucker, A. N., 48

Ulm, Sean, 420

Vajda, Edward J., 261
van den Toorn, M. C., 247
Vanden Wyngaerd, Guido, 247
van der Auwera, Johan, 406
van der Voort, Hein, 251–3, 265, 267–8, 270, 272
van der Wal, Jennike, 371, 372
van Geenhoven, Veerle, 55, 62
van Riemsdijk, Henk C., 247
van Tongeren, Charlotte, 101, 102
Vedovelli, Massimo, 95
Veres, Adrian, 176
Villoing, Florence, 178
Vincent, Nigel, 69
Vogel, Irene, 79
Voghera, Miriam, 95
von Heusinger, Klaus, 323

Wagner, Michael, 384
Wang, William S. Y., 417
Ward, Gregory, 386
Watahomigie, Lucille J., 125–30, 136
Watahomigie, Philbert Sr., 125–30, 136
Watkins, Laurel, 158
Watters, John R., 371
Wechsler, Stephen, 18, 386
Wedgwood, Daniel, 362, 386
Welch, Betty, 5
West, Birdie, 5
Wetzer, Harrie, 248
Widmer, Manuel, 41, 59, 61
Widmer, Paul, 41, 59, 61
Wilkins, David, 117
Willmond, Catherine, 371
Witzlack-Makarevich, Alena, 332, 426
Wogiga, Kepas, 238
Wohlgemuth, Jan, 414, 439
Wolfart, H. Christoph, 156
Wonderly, William, 158
Woollam, Wilfred, 246
Wright, Pamela Sue, 331, 344, 345, 353, 354, 358
Wurm, Stephen A., 424
Wurzel, Wolfgang U., 94

Yamamoto, Akira Y., 125–30, 136
Yang, Charles, 148,
Yang, Tongyin, 248
Yip, Virginia, 248
Yoshioka, Nobura, 322

Zaicz, Gábor, 161
Zakharko, Taras, 332, 426
Zamponi, Raoul, 4, 254, 257, 264, 272, 275, 277
Zanchetta, Eros, 190
Z'graggen, Johannes A., 237, 238, 240
Zimmerman, Malte, 384
Zlatić, Larisa, 18, 386
Zobel, Sarah, 395
Zúñiga, Fernando, 332, 426
Zwanenburg, Wiecher, 172
Zwicky, Arnold, 9, 284, 289

Subject Index

adposition, 33, 35, 47, 51, 155, 328
agreement, 49151, 67, 72, 76, 78–9, 91, 96,
    101–2, 110, 120–1, 127, 150, 154–65, 171,
    188–9, 258, 275, 282–4, 291–2, 294, 297,
    303–23, 327–66, 390–412
  absolutive agreement, 306–7, 341, 353–6
  agreement conditions, 16, 22–3, 328–30,
    350–2, 359–60, 382–5, 438
  agreement controller, 15, 16, 18–19, 22,
    79, 154–5, 328–9, 334–8, 384–5, 416,
    438
  agreement potential, 305, 309–10, 323
  agreement target, 15–17, 19, 22–3, 39, 67,
    154–5, 303, 305, 309, 319–20, 328–9,
    335–9, 349–50, 360–1, 363–4, 384–5, 401,
    418, 438
  attributive agreement, 16–17, 34, 331, 336,
    370, 377–81, 401
  canonical agreement, 19, 22–3, 36, 55, 72,
    303–4, 317, 360, 363
  object agreement, 78, 101, 104–5, 108, 111,
    126, 129, 332, 371, 380–4
  possessive agreement, 47–8, 50, 70, 156,
    330–1, 337–40, 352–3, 356–9, 364
  referential agreement, 159, 335–6, 342–3,
    346–7, 350–1, 360–1
  semantic agreement, 5, 12–13, 16–19, 78, 336,
    401
  sporadic agreement, 22–3, 303–23
  syntactic agreement, 15–19, 360–1, 363
Agreement Hierarchy, 16–18, 165, 401
anaphora, 17, 56–7, 396–9, 408–11

antiperiphrasis, 65, 69, 88, 93
argument sensitivity, 331–2, 343–6

binding, 16, 23, 390–412

canonical inflection, 2, 19, 21, 65–70, 72, 74, 76,
    79, 81–6, 89, 91–6, 138, 171, 377
Canonical Typology, 2, 19, 21, 23, 31–5, 54,
    59–61, 65, 87, 90, 92, 148–64, 205, 273, 416
  exploratory, 32, 60
  retrospective, 32, 35, 60
case, 10–11, 14–15, 22, 46–9, 60, 66, 70, 102–3,
    113, 139, 193–203, 415–16, 420–1, 423–43
case agreement, 318, 370, 378–9
causal links, causal network, 417–18, 430–9
clitic, 32, 70, 78–9, 87, 94, 143, 157–8, 250–1,
    256, 262–4, 276, 277
clause complementation, 415–16, 422–43
complexity, 22
  Kolmogorov complexity, 206, 208, 222,
    226–7
  morphological, 148, 206, 220–8
composite nominal, 45, 52–3, 60–1
  appositional, 34, 39
  attributive, 34, 37, 45–6, 48, 52, 59
  coordinative, 58–9
  copulative, 58–9, 63
  endocentric, 33–4, 40, 49, 60
  exocentric, 33–4, 40, 58–61
  subordinative, 34–5
  synthetic, 34, 41, 54
  verb-verb, 45, 55, 58, 63

compound, 19, 21, 31–61, 178–80, 313
    P-compound, 152, 165
    see also composite nominal
construct state, 48, 50, 323, 375, 380
converb, 241, 271

DATR, 9, 10, 12, 23, 333–42, 361–3, 365, 400–2, 442
defaults, 1, 2, 5, 6, 8–9, 11–13, 15, 143, 162, 183, 188, 206, 208–9, 220, 223–6, 384–5
deponency, 13–14, 21, 6, 65, 67, 69, 79, 87, 93, 100–3, 110, 117, 119–21, 138, 148, 374–5
derivation, 13, 19, 38, 39, 40, 55, 59, 61, 71, 88, 94, 121, 150, 151–3
    personal nouns, 172, 185–7, 345, 365
diachrony, 23, 65, 70, 87, 102, 139, 194, 197–8, 202–3, 340–7
dialect variation, 22, 193–203, 414–22, 427–40
direct predicates, 340–7, 353–4
distributed deponency, 21, 100–2, 119, 121
distributed exponence, 3, 100, 101, 120
double articulation, 119, 350–1, 359, 378, 381

ellipsis, 9
    root, 22, 249–67, 374
    verb, 22, 244–9, 267–70
ezafe, 48–9, 51, 61

featural inconsistency, 4, 65, 68–9, 72–3, 78, 88–93
feature, 1, 3, 4, 6, 10–16, 18–19, 21–3, 35, 55, 68–70, 72–3, 77, 79, 82, 90–5, 100–1, 103, 105, 118, 124, 126–7, 130–2, 135–6, 140, 142, 322, 327–66, 370–86, 390–403, 409, 419, 427
    feature decomposition, 131–2
    morphological (purely/strictly), 4, 13, 133–5, 370
    morphosemantic, 14, 17, 125, 127, 131–2, 134–5, 371–2, 385
    morphosyntactic, 5, 11, 14, 17–19, 21, 101, 127, 156–7, 164, 189, 322, 327–8, 370–2, 385–6
focus, 14, 23, 46, 341–2, 370–86, 406–8, 441–3
    additive focus, 341–2
    exclusive focus, 372–3, 382–3, 385
    focus doubling, 377–9
    focus feature, 371–2, 377, 383–6
    focus spreading, 384–5
    narrow focus, 374, 382–3

Fugenelement, 42, 45
fused exponence, 65, 68, 73, 76, 92

gender, 1, 3, 5, 6, 10–15, 17–19, 22–3, 48–9, 69, 70, 72, 77–8, 86, 88, 90–1, 94–6, 149, 150, 154–6, 303–19, 328–66, 390–1, 399–401
    class-based gender, 12, 95, 329–31, 347–59
    common gender, 22, 171–89
    gender resolution, 17, 18, 335, 347
grammaticalisation, 46, 55, 102, 119, 252, 423–4

haplology, 161, 243
heteroclisis, 3, 8, 65, 67, 69, 72, 75–6, 79, 87, 93, 120
hierarchy, 7, 12, 16–18, 24, 127, 131, 133, 139, 343, 347, 401, 425
    morphological, 12, 133–4
honorific, 57, 381

iconicity (morphological), 127, 135
indexation, 13, 104, 110–11, 121, 156–62, 158–62, 360–1, 363–4
inflection class, 3, 4, 6–9, 11–14, 23, 25, 65, 67, 69, 72, 76, 79, 80–2, 84–7, 90, 91, 93–8, 120, 146, 153, 127–31, 150–2, 162–4, 207–28, 236–7, 319–20, 375, 377, 421
information structure, 23, 81, 361–4, 370–86
inheritance, 7–9, 11–12, 328
inverse predicates, 343–7, 354, 358, 365, 425–39
irregularity, 5, 6, 8, 76, 120, 206, 319
izafet, 49–51

juxtaposition, 21, 35, 258

light verb, 57, 258–61
locality, 328–30, 339–43, 347, 358–63, 384

markedness, 3
masdar, 283–4
mismatches, 2, 5, 13, 15–17, 21, 101, 120, 158, 358, 363, 390
    form–feature (meaning), 2, 21
    morphological, 13, 15, 101, 120
    paradigmatic, 2
modifier, 17, 23, 34–5, 37–8, 45–8, 50, 52–3, 55, 59
MorboCompo, 33–5, 60, 63
morpheme, 4, 39, 100, 108, 110, 112, 118, 122, 138, 140–3, 145–9, 158, 159, 162–5

SUBJECT INDEX | 459

morphological autonomy, 1–3, 135
morphome, 100, 101, 108, 110, 117–19, 138–40, 205, 209, 213–14, 227, 421–2, 442
multi-variate typology, 23, 24

Network Morphology, 6, 8, 12, 23, 121, 143, 205, 206, 220
noncanonical, 1, 19, 21–2, 23, 31, 32, 36–8, 40, 41, 45–7, 162, 53–4, 56, 58, 60–1, 68, 70, 72, 74–6, 80, 82–3, 86, 89, 92, 95–6, 100, 138–40, 144, 148, 156, 158–60, 162–3, 168, 185–6, 303–4, 319, 323, 328, 359–60, 377, 416–17, 438
noun incorporation, 34, 41, 45, 53–5, 61, 162
number, 1, 3, 5, 10, 13–14, 16, 18–19, 22, 48, 50, 66, 69, 70, 72, 77–8, 83–4, 87–8, 90, 91, 94–6, 101–3, 105–6, 108, 110–22, 125–33, 135, 141–2, 145, 148–9, 313–14, 318, 366, 378–9, 397–9, 409–11, 430–3
  greater plural (number) 101, 103, 110–22, 125, 127–32, 131–2, 136
  nominal 125–6
  verbal, 101, 141, 127

overdifferentiation, 67, 69, 89–90, 93, 171

paradigm, 1, 2–5, 10, 11, 19–23, 65, 66–73, 75–81, 83, 84–91, 94, 100–2, 105, 115, 117, 120–2, 124–5, 127–8, 131–3, 135–7
  paradigm linkage, 135, 135
  paradigm shape, 5, 22, 23, 136, 171, 184, 187, 189, 191
  paradigm structure, 67, 122, 125–7, 135
  paradigm uniformity, 94, 184–9
part of speech (cf. word class), 5, 7, 67, 79, 81, 91, 152–3, 303–5, 309, 316–20
percolation, 328–9, 330, 334, 336–7, 340, 553, 357, 359, 384, 386, 439
periphrasis, 4, 32, 65, 67, 68, 69, 70, 76–9, 88, 92, 138, 263
person, 5, 14, 22, 50, 68, 70, 78, 89, 94, 96, 103–7, 108, 110, 112–14, 116, 118, 141–4, 156–8, 313–14, 333–4, 336–7, 339–47, 360–1, 390–411, 415–16, 425–6, 430–4, 438–41
pied-piping, 384
polyvalent, 138–40, 143–5
positional verb, 107, 112, 114, 116–19, 121, 122

possession, 50, 158, 165, 354–5, 358–9, 364–5, 374–9, 396–7, 403, 408–9
  alienable possession, 158, 160–1, 165, 329–30, 337–40, 348, 352, 362
  inalienable possession, 329–30, 337–40, 349, 356–9, 362, 366
possessor prominence, 330–1, 357–8, 360–1, 364
productive, productivity, 33, 35, 40–1, 45–6, 48, 51, 55–7, 60, 86, 95, 149, 151, 173, 178, 184–7, 208, 215, 227, 303, 374–5
pronouns, 10, 16, 17, 22, 48, 69, 70, 87, 96, 103, 121, 193–203, 390–412
  addressee pronoun, 78, 392–411
  arbitrary pronouns, pro*arb*, 390–411
  null pronouns, 390–6, 403, 407–12
  reciprocal pronouns, 396–8, 408–9
  reflexive pronouns, 396–7, 403

quotative, 22, 281–93

reconstruction, 122, 427–37
recursive function, 41, 44
registration, 158–62
relational adjective, 52–3

scope, semantic, 52, 371–4, 377, 379–84, 386, 405–10
semi-regularity, 8
serial verb construction, 57, 59, 103
small construction, 46
solidarity, 415–16, 433–4, 438–9
stem, 2, 3, 8–13, 22, 37, 39, 42–3, 45–7, 53–7, 66–71, 73–6, 83, 85–6, 92–5, 98, 101, 106, 107, 116, 118, 127–30, 136, 146
  alternations, 3, 65, 68, 70, 71, 83, 92, 94, 175–6, 187–8, 205–28
  discontinuous, 237, 261–2
  extensions, 149–50
  stem-forming affixes, 150–3
superclassing/superclassed gender, 15, 23
suppletion, 3, 10, 32, 65, 67–8, 70, 71, 75, 83, 92, 110, 112–13, 116, 118, 138, 148, 208, 215, 217, 220, 222, 225–6, 229, 240, 242, 258
suspended affixation, 61
syncretism, 2–4, 6, 9–11, 20, 65, 67–8, 71, 72, 90–3, 116, 118, 120, 138–41, 143–8, 160, 162–3, 184, 188, 201–2, 416
syntactic structures, 138–40, 144, 146

toggles, 158
topic, topicalisation, 332–3, 336, 340–7, 362–5, 382, 392, 435–6, 441
transparency, phrasal, 38, 40, 56
triple articulation, 119
truncation, 180–1

unification, 101, 103–4, 117, 118, 360, 363–4

valence, 106, 153, 157–8, 261, 359
Venus effect, 45
verificative, 293–7

word,
   phonological, 234, 258, 262–6
   syntactic, 35–8, 40–3, 262–6

zero, 4, 73, 74, 75, 76, 105, 149, 151, 205, 365
   root, 4, 22, 234–44, 270–2, 365

EU representative:
Easy Access System Europe
Mustamäe tee 50, 10621 Tallinn, Estonia
Gpsr.requests@easproject.com

www.ingramcontent.com/pod-product-compliance
Lightning Source LLC
Chambersburg PA
CBHW082019300426
44117CB00015B/2281